THE INDIAN

ANNUAL REGISTER

January—June 1941

VOL. I

THE INDIAN
ANNUAL REGISTER

An Annual Digest of Public Affairs of India

Recording the Nation's Activities each year in matters Political, Economic, Industrial, Educational, Social Etc.

1919–1947

(In 58 Volumes)

Volume I 1941

(Volume 44)

By

H.N. Mitra
N.N. Mitra

Introduction by

Bipan Chandra

GYAN

THE INDIAN
ANNUAL REGISTER
JANUARY—JUNE 1941

TABLE OF CONTENTS

TRADE & INDUSTRY IN INDIA—JANUARY-JUNE 1941

Administration of India 1941

Chronicle of Events—Jan.-June 1941

Notes on Indian History

&

India in Home Polity—Jan.-June 1941

1941-42 Budget Figures at a Glance

In Lakhs of Rupees

Government	Revenue	Expenditure	Surplus	Deficit
Central Government . .	1,45,04·83	1,58,89·38		13,84·55
Provinces—				
Madras . .	18,21·37	18,08·62	12·75	. .
United Provinces .	14,34·30	14,29·46	4·84	. .
Bengal . .	14,03·14	15,37·38	. .	1,34·24
Bombay . .	13,56·65	13,56·00	·65	. .
Punjab . .	13,28·67	12,56·35	72·32	. .
Bihar . .	6,11·08	5,79·82	31·26	. .
Central Provinces and Berar . .	5,10·76	5,08·78	1·98	. .
Sind . .	4,35·47	4,34·47	1·00	. .
Assam . .	3,13·01	3,24·90	. .	11·89
Orissa . .	1,92·74	1,90·59	2·15	. .
N. W. Frontier Province . .	1,91·25	1,90·93	·32	. .

Administration of India 1941

Reigning Sovereign—His Majesty George the VI

India Office

Secretary of State for India—The Right Hon. Mr. L. S. Amery. (*April 1940*)

Permanent Under-Secretary of State—Sir Find-later Stewart, G. C. B., G. C. I. E., C. S. I., L. L. D.

Parliamentary Under-Secretary of State—The Duke of Devonshire.

Advisers to the Secretary of State—Sir H. Strakosch, G. B. E. Sir A. A. L. Parsons, K. C. I. E., Sir H. Williamson, C.I.E., M.B.E., Sir J. Clay, K.C.I.E., C.S.I., O.B.E., E. Raghavendra Rao, Lt.—Col. Sir H. Suhrawardy, O.B.E., Sir J. A. Woodhead, K.C.S.I., C.I.E, Dewan Bahadur S. E. Ranganathan, Sir Courteny Latimer, K.C.I.E., C.S.I.

High Commissioner of India—Malik Sir Feroz Khan Noon, K.C.I.E.

Trade Commissioner for India—Sir David Meek, Kt., C.I.E., O.B.E.

Government of India

(*Area—1,808,679 Sq. miles with a population of 352,837,778 of people—nearly one-fifth of human race*)

Viceroy & Governor-General

His Excellency The Most Hon'ble The Marquess of Linlithgow, P.C., KT., G.M.S.I., G.M.I.E., O.B.E., D.L., T.D., (*18th April 1936*)

Commander-in-Chief in India

His Excellency General Sir Archibald Percival Wavell, G.C.B., C.M.G., M.C., British Service.

Executive Council

The Hon. Sir Hormusji P. Mody, K.B.E, (*Supply*).

The Rt. Hon. Sir Akbar Hydari, P.C. (*Information and Broadcasting*).

The Hon. Sir Sultan Ahmed (*Law*).

The Hon. Mr. E. Raghavendra Rao (*Civil Defence*).

The Hon. Mr. M. S. Aney (*Indians Overseas*).

The Hon. Mr. Nalini Ranjan Sarkar (*Education, Health and Lands*).

The Hon. Malik Sir Firoz Khan Noon, K.C.S.I., K.C.I.E. (*Labour*).

The Hon. Sir Reginald Maxwell, K.C.S.I., C.I.E., I.C.S., (*Home*).

The Hon. Sir Andrew Clow, K.C.S.I., C.I.E., I.C.S, (*Communications*)

The Hon. Sir Jeremy Raisman, K.C.S.I., C.I.E., I.C.S., (*Finance*).

The Hon. Dewan Bahadur Sir A. Ramaswami Mudaliar, (*Commerce*).

President, Legislative Assembly—The Hon. Sir Abdur Rahim, K.C.S.I.

President, Council of State—The Hon. Sir Maneckji Byramji Dadabhoy, K.C.S.I., K.C.I.E., L.L.D., Bar-at-Law.

Numerical Strength of Parties

(a) In Central Assembly

Congress Party	40
Muslim League Party	25
Non-Party	25
Independent Party	10
Congress Nationalists	11
European Group	9
Officials	20
Total	140

(b) In Council of State

Independent Progressive Party	10
Congress Party	6
Muslim League	6
Total	22

Government of Bengal

(*Area 82,955 Sq. miles ; Population 5,10,87,338*)

Governor

H E. Sir John Arthur Herbert, G. C. I. E. (Nov. 18, 1939)

Council of Ministers

Coalition ; formed June 23, 1938 ; Personnel:

(i) Abul Kasem Fazlul Huq (Muslim, Coalition), *Chief Minister* ; Portfolios: *Education and Publicity*.

(ii) Khwaja Sir Nazimuddin, K. C. I.E. (Muslim, Coalition), Portfolios: *Home, Constitution & Elections* ;

(iii) Sir Bijoy Prasad Singh Roy (Hindu, Coalition), Portfolio: *Revenue*,

(iv) Nawab Khwaja Habibullah Bahadur of Dacca (Muslim, Coalition), Portfolios: *Public Health, Medical & Local Self-Government*.

(v) Maharaja Srischandra Nandy of Cossimbazar (Hindu, Coalition), Portfolios: *Communication and Works.*

(vi) Huseyn Saheed Suhrawardy (Muslim, Coalition), Portfolios: *Finance, Commerce and Labour.*

(vii) Nawab Musharruff Hossain, Khan Bahadur, (Muslim, Coalition), Portfolios: *Judicial and Legislative.*

(viii) Prasanna Deb Raikut (Hindu, Coalition), Portfolios: *Forest and Excise.*

(ix) Mukunda Behari Mullick (Hindu, Coalition, Portfolios: *Co-operative Credit and Rural Indebtedness.*

(x) Tamizuddin Khan (Muslim, Coalition), Portfolios: *Agriculture, Industries, Veterinary & Rural Reconstruction.*

Parliamentary Secretaries

(i) Khwaja Shahabuddin, C.B.E., M.L.A. (Muslim, Coalition) ;

(ii) Mesbahuddin Ahmed, M.L.C. (Muslim, Coalition) ;

(iii) Nawabzada K. Nasrullah, M.L.A. (Muslim, Coalition) ;

(iv) Mrs. Hasina Murshed, M.B.E., M.L.A. (Muslim, Coalition)

Numerical Strength of Parties

(a) In Assembly..... (Total seats—250)

Coalition 108, Scheduled Caste Group supporting Government 11, European 25, Nationalist 11, Anglo-Indian 5, Congress 54, Proja 19, Scheduled Caste Group opposing Government 12, Unattached members 4 : Total—249. (Excluding Speaker).

(b) In Council—(Total seats 63)

Coalition 33, Congress 13, European 6, Independent 6, Progressive 4 : Total—62 (Excluding President).

Capital and its population—Calcutta ; 11,96,734.

Summer Capital and its population—Darjeeling ; 19,903.

Receipts and Expenditure on Revenue Account for the current year : Receipts—Rs. 14,03,14,000 ;

Expenditure—Rs.15,37,38,000.

Government of the Punjab

(*Area—13,6,330 Sq. miles ; Population—28,490,857*)

Governor

H. E. Sir Bertrand Glancy, K.C.S.I., K.C.I.E. (April 7, 1941).

Council of Ministers

Unionist ; formed April 1, 1937 ; Personnel :

(i) Khan Bahadur Major Sirdar Sir Sikandar Hayat Khan, K.B.E. (Muslim, Unionist), *Premier.*

(ii) Rao Bahadur Chaudhri Sir Chhotu Ram (Hindu, Unionist), *Minister of Revenue.*

(iii) Sir Manohar Lal (Hindu, National Progressive), *Finance Minister.*

(iv) Major Sahebzada Malik Khizar Hayat Khan Tiwana, O.B.E. (Muslim, Unionist), *Minister of Public Works.*

(v) Mian Abdul Haye (Muslim, Unionist), *Minister of Education.*

(vi) Sardar Dasaundha Singh (Sikh, Khalsa National) *Minister of Development.*

Parliamentary Secretaries

(i) Mir Maqbool Mahmood (Muslim, Unionist) ; (ii) Mrs. Jahan Ara Shah Nawaz, M.B.E. (Muslim Unionist) ; (iii) Raja Ghazanafar Ali Khan (Muslim, Unionist) ; (iv) Chaudhari Tikka Ram, M.B.E. (Hindu, Unionist) ; (v) Sheikh Faiz Muhammad, M.B.E. (Muslim, Unionist) ; (vi) Sayed Amjad Ali Shah, O.B.E. (Muslim, Unionist) ; (vii) Bhagat Hans Raj (Hindu, Unionist) ; (viii) Sir William Roberts, Kt., C.I.E. (Christian, Unionist) : (ix) Nawabzada Muhammad Faiyaz Ali Khan (Muslim, Unionist) ; (x) Khan Bahadur Mian Mustaq Ahmad Gurmani (Muslim, Unionist) ; (xi) S. B. Sardar Ujjal Singh (Sikh, Khalsa National) ; (xii) Sardar Jagjit Singh Man (Sikh, Khalsa National) ; (xiii) Sardar Gopal Singh (Sikh, Khalsa National) ; and (xiv) R. S. Thakur Ripudaman Singh (Sikh, National Progressive).

Numerical Strength of Parties

Total seats—175.

Government supporters : Unionist 95, Khalsa National 13, National Progressive 5, Total 133 ; Opposition : Congress 37. Ahrar 2, Independent Members 20 : Total 59 ; Vacant 2 :

Grand Total—174 (Excluding Speaker).

Capital and its population—Lahore ; 4,29,747.

Summer Capital and its population—Simla ; 18, 144.

Receipts and expenditure on Revenue Account for the current year : Receipts—Rs. 12,60,58,000 ;

Expenditure—Rs. 12,56,35,000.

Government of Assam

(*Area—67,334 sq. miles ; Population—1,02,04,773*)

Governor

H. E. Sir Robert Niel Reid. K.C.S.I., C.I.E., I.C.S. (March 4, 1937)

Council of Ministers

Coalition ; formed November 17, 1939 ; Personnel :

(i) Saiyid Sir Muhammad Saadullah, M.A., B.L., (Muslim, United Party), Portfolios : *Home.*

(ii) Rohini Kumar Chaudhuri, B.L., (Hindu, United Party), Portfolios : *Education & Prisons.*

(iii) Munawwar Ali, B.A., LL.B., (Muslim, United Party) Portfolios : *Agriculture and Veterinary.*

(iv) Hirendra Chandra Chakravarty, B.A., (Hindu, United Party), Portfolios : *Medical and Public Health*

(v) Khan Sahib Mudabbir Hussain Chaudhury, B.L., (Muslim, United Party), Portfolios : *Judicial and Local Self-Government.*

(vi) Dr. Mahendra Nath Saikia, L.M.P. (Scheduled Caste, United Party) Portfolio : *Excise.*

(vii) Abdul Matin Chaudhuri, B.L., (Muslim, United Party), Portfolios : *Public Works & Labour.*

(viii) Khan Bahadur Sayidur Rahaman M.A., B.L., (Muslim, United Party), Portfolios : *Finance, Revenue & Legislative.*

(ix) Miss Mavis Dunn, B.A., B.T., B.L., (Khasi Hills, Tribal, United Party), Portfolios : *Registration, Industries and Co-operative.*

(x) Rupnath Brahma. B.L., (Hindu, Plains Tribal, United Party), Portfolios : *Forest.*

PARLIAMENTARY SECRETARIES

(i) B. K. J. Sarwan (Indian Christian, Labour. United Party) ;

(ii) Benjamin Ch. Momin (Indian Christian, Hills Tribal, United Party) ;

(iii) Kalachand Roy (Scheduled Caste, United Party) ;

(iv) Dhirsing Deuri (Hindu, Plains Tribal, United Party).

Numerical Strength of Parties

(a) IN ASSEMBLY—Total seats—108) Congress Coalition 48, Assam United 54, Independent 5. Total—107 (Excluding Speaker).

(b) IN COUNCIL—(Total seats—22) Upper House : No Party system exists.

Capital and its population—Shillong ; 38,192.

Summer Capital and its population—(No Summer Capital).

Receipts and Expenditure on Revenue Account for the current year :

Receipts—Rs. 3,13,01,000.

Expenditure—Rs. 3,24,90,000.

Government of Sind

(*Area—46,378 sq. miles ; Population—48,41,000*).

Governor

H. E. Sir Hugh Dow, K.C.S.I., C.I.E. I.C.S. (April 1,1941.)

Council of Ministers

(i) Khan Bahadur Allah Buksh Mohammad Umar Soomro, O.B.E. (Muslim, Azad Party), *Premier ;* Portfolios : *Finance.*

(ii) Nihchaldas Chatumal Vazirani (Hindu, Independent), Portfolios : *Revenue (excluding Agriculture, Veterinary, Forests, Excise and Rural Reconstruction).*

(iii) Sir Ghulam Hussain Hidayatullah, K.C.S.I. (Muslim, Azad Party), Portfolios: *Home, Political Miscellaneous (excluding Labour), Legal and General (Excluding Medical, Public Health, Local Self-Government, Education and Industries).*

(iv) Rao Sahib Gokaldas Mewaldas (Hindu, Independent), Portfolios : *Local Self-Government, Agriculture & Veterinary.*

(v) Pir Illahi Bakhsh Nawazali (Muslim, Azad Party), Portfolios : *Education, Labour, Industries, Forests and Rural Reconstruction & Excise.*

(vi) Abdus Satar Abdul Rahman (Muslim, Azad Party), Portfolios : *Public Works, Medical and Public Health.*

PARLIAMENTARY SECRETARY

Khan Bahadur Allah Baksh Khudadad Khan Gaboe, J.P. (Muslim, Azad Party).

Numerical Strength of Parties

Total seats—60

Capital and its population—Karachi ; 3,58,500.

Receipts and expenditure on Revenue Account for the current year :

Receipts—Rs. 4,35,47,000.

Expenditure—Rs. 4,34,47,000.

Government of Bombay

Area—77,221 Sq. miles ; Population—1,79,92,053)

Governor

(H. E. Sir Lawrence Roger Lumley, G.C.I.E., T.D., (*Sept. 18,1937.*)

Advisory Council

The Congress Ministry having resigned the Governor assumed Administrative and Legislative Powers assisted by the following advisers :—

Council formed Nov. 4, 1939 ; Present Personal :

(i) Janandan Atmaram Madan, C.S.I., C.I.E., I.C.S. Portfolio : *Revenue.*

(ii) Henry Foley Knight, C.I.E., I.C.S. ; Portfolio : *Finance.*

(iii) Charles Holditch Bristow, C.I.E., I.C.S. ; Portfolio : *Home.*

Numerical Strength of Parties

(a) In Assembly—(Total seats—175)

Congress 86, Muslim League 25, Independents 13, Independent Labour 14, Progressive 12, Peasants and Peoples 7, Peasants and Workers 7, Democratic Swaraj 4, (Vacant seats 7) : Total—175.

(b) In Council—(Total seats—30)

Congress 10, Muslim League, 3, Independents 9, Progressive 1, Democratic Swaraj 3, Liberal 1, (Vacant seats 3) : Total—30.

Capital and its population—Bombay City ; 11. 61. 383.

Summer Capital and its population—Poona ; 2,56,003.

Receipts and expenditure on Revenue Account for the current year :

Receipts—Rs. 13,56,65,000 ;

Expenditure—Rs. 13,56,00,000.

Grvernment of the U. P.

(Area—1, 12,191 sq. miles ; Population—5, 51, 38, 000)

Governor

H. E. Sir Maurice Garnier Hallett, K.C.S.I., C.I.E., I.C.S. (December 6, 1939)

Advisory Council

The Congress Ministry having resigned the Governor assumed Administrative and Legislative Powers assisted by the following advisers :—

Council formed Nov. 4. 1939 ; Personnel :

(i) P. W, Marsh, B.A. (Oxon), C.S.I., C.I.E., I.C.S. Portfolios : *Revenue, Rural Develorment, Agriculture, Forests, Communications and Irrigation.*

(ii) Dr. Panna Lal, M.A., B.Sc., LL. B. (Cantab), D. Litt. (Agra), Bar-at-Law, C. I.E., I.C.S. ; Portfolios : *Education, Industries, Local Self-Government and Public Health.*

(iii) T. Sloan, M.A. (Glas.), C.S.I., C. I.E., I.C.S. ; Portfolios : *Home, Finance, Justice and Jails.*

Numerical Strength of Parties

(a) In Assembly—(Total seats—228).

Government supporters : Congress 147 ; Opposition : Muslim League 36, Independent 24, Unattached (generally vote with Opposition) 21 : Total 228.

(b) In Council—(Total seats—60)

Government supporters : Congress 14 ; Opposition : Nationalist 13. Independent 8, Unattached (including 11 who have not intimated Party affiliations) 24 : Total—59 (excluding President).

Capital and its population—Allahabad ; 2,57,575.

Summer Capital and its population—Nainital ; 21,313.

Receipts and expenditure on Revenue Account for the current year :

Receipts—Rs. 14,34 30,417.

Expenditure—Rs. 14,29,46,397.

Government of Madras

(Area—1, 24, 363 sq. miles ; Population—4, 93, 41, 000)

Governor

H. E. Sir Arthur Hope, G.C.I.E., M.C. ; (March 12, 1940)

Advisory Council

The Congress Ministry having resigned the Governor assumed Administrative and Legislative Powers assisted by the following advisers :—

Council formed Oct. 30, 1939 ; personnel :

(i) Sir George Boag, K.C.I.E., C.S.I., I.C.S.

(ii) H. M. Hood, C.S.I., C.I.E., I.C.S.

(iii) T. G. Rutherford, C.S.I., C.I.E., I.C.S

(iv) T. Austin, I.C.S.

Numerical Strength of Parties

(a) In Assembly......(Total Seats 215)

Congress 157, Justice 14, National Democrats 4, Muslim League 12, European 6, Anglo-Indian 2, Independents 9, (Vacant seats 11.) : Total—215.

(b) In Council—(Total seats—55)

Congress 25, Justice 4, National Democratic 3, Muslim League 2, Independents 8, Unattached 4 (Vacant seats 9) : Total—55.

Capital and its population—Madras City ; 7,77,300.

Summer Capital and its population—Ootacamund ; 24,616.

Receipts and Expenditure on Revenue Account for the current year :

Receipts—Rs. 18,21.37,000.

Expenditure—Rs. 18,08,62,000.

Government of C. P.

(Area—1,81,559 sq. miles ; Population—1,68,22,018)

Governor

H. E. Sir Henry Twynam, K.C.S.I., C.I.E., I.C.S. (Oct. 2, 1940)

Advisory Council

The Congress Ministry having resigned the Governor assumed Administrative and Legislative Powers assisted by the following advisers :—

Council formed Nov. 11. 1939 ;

Personnel :

(i) Sir Geoffrey Pownall Burton, K.C.I.E., I.C.S.

(ii) Henry Challen Greenfield, C.S.I. C.I.E., I.C.S.

Numerical Strength of Parties

Total seats—112

Government supporters : Congress 71; Opposition : Independent 17, United 5, Muslim League 10, Unattached 8 ; Total —111 (excluding Speaker).

Capital and its population—Nagpur ; 3,01,287.

Summer Capital and its population—Panchmarhi ; 6,693.

Receipts and Expenditure on Revenue Account for the current year :

Receipts—Rs. 5,10,76 000.

Expenditure –Rs. 5,08,78,000.

Government of Bihar

(*Area—69,348 Sq. miles ; Population—3,23,71,434*)

Governor

H. E. Sir Thomas Alexander Stewart, K.C.S.I., K.C.I.E., I.C.S., (*August 6, '39*)

Advisory Council

The Congress Ministry having resigned the Governor assumed Administrative and Legislative Powers assisted by the following advisers :—

Council formed Nov. 4, '39 ; Personnel :
1. E. R. J. R. Cousins, C.I.E., I.C.S.
2. R. E. Russell. C.S.I., C.I.E., I.C.S.

Numerical Stregth of Parties

(a) IN ASSEMBLY—(Total seats—152)

Congress 96, Bihar Nationalist Coalition 25, Muslim Independent 19, Unattached 7, (Vacant 5) : Total—152.

(b) IN COUNCIL—(Total seats—30)

Congress 10, Bihar Nationalist Coalition 12, Independent 1, Unattached 6, (Vacant 1) : Total—30.

Capital and population—Patna ; 1,73,948.

Summer Capital and its population—Ranchi ; 57,238.

Receipts and Expenditure Account for the current year :

Receipts—Rs. 6.11 08,000.

Expenditure—Rs. 5,79,82,000.

Government of Orissa

(*Area—32,000 sq. miles ; Population—87,14,000*).

Governor

H. E. Sir William Hawthorne Lewis, M.A. (Cantab.), K.C.S.I., K.C.I.E., I.C.S., J.P. (April 1, '41)

Advisory Council

The Congress Ministry having resigned the Governor assumed Administrative and Legislative Powers assisted by the following advisers :—

E. O. Ansorge, C.I.E., I.C.S., Adviser to H. E. the Governor.

Ministers

The following Ministers were appointed at the end of the year 1941 :—

1. Hon'ble Captain Maharaja Sri Sri Sri Krishna Chandra Gajapati Narayan Deo of Parlakimedi (*Prime Minister*)—*Home Affairs (excluding Publicity), Local Self-Government and Public Works.*

2. Hon'ble Pandit Godavaris Misra—*Finance, Home Affairs (Publicity), Development and Education.*

3. Hon'ble Maulavi Abdus Sobhan Khan—*Law and Commerce, Revenue and Health.*

SPEAKER, LEGISLATIVE ASSEMBLY

Hon'ble Sri Mukunda Prasad Das.

Numerical Strength of Parties

Total seats—60

Government supporters : Congress 35; Opposition : National 13, Independent 1, All Orissa United 1, Unattached 9 :
Total—59 (excluding Speaker)

Capital and its population, Cuttack, 74,200.

Receipts and Expenditure on Revenue Account for the current year : Receipts—Rs. 1.92,74,000 ; Expenditure— Rs. 1 90,59,000.

Government of N. W. F. Provinces

(*Area—36,356 sq. miles ; Population—25,28,165*)

Governor—H. E. Sir George Cunningham, K.C.S.I., K.C.I.E., C.B.E. (Mar. 2, '37)

Advisory Council

The Congress Ministry having resigned the Governor assumed Administrative and Legislative Powers assisted by the following advisers :—

Lt.-Col. Walter Fendall Campbell, C.I.E., Adviser to H. E. the Governor.

Numerical Strength of Parties

Total seats—50

Government supporters : Congress 21, non-Congress 4 ; Opposition : Muslim League 12, Hindu Sikh Nationalist 4, Central National 5, Unattached 3 : Total —49 (excluding Speaker).

Capital and its population...Peshawar ; 1,62.510.

Receipts and Expenditure on Revenue Account for the current year :

Receipts—1,91,25,000 ;

Expenditure - Rs. 1,90,93,000.

Government of Burma

Governor

H. E. The Right Hon'ble Sir Reginald Hugh Dorman-Smith., P.C., G.B.E.

Council of Ministers

The Hon'ble U Saw, *Premier* (also Minister of *Agriculture and Forests*) (on Tour)

The Hon'ble Sir Paw Tun, A.T.M., BAR-AT-LAW, *Acting Premier* (also Minister of *Lands and Revenue*)

The Hon'ble U Tharrawaddy Maung Maung, B.SC., *Health and Public Works.*

The Hon'ble Major Maung Aye, BAR-AT-LAW, *Home Affairs.*

The Hon'ble U Ba Than, Minister of *Commerce and Industry.*

The Hon'ble Saw Pe Tha, BAR-AT-LAW, Minister of *Judicial Affairs.*

The Hon'ble U Ba Yin, Minister of *Education.*

The Hon'ble U Htoon Aung Gyaw, M.A., LL.B., BAR-AT-LAW, Minister of *Finance.*

The Hon'ble U Ba On, Minister of Labour.

President of the Senate :—The Hon'ble Sir J. A. Maung Gyi, BAR-AT-LAW.

Speaker of the House of Representatives. U Chit Hlaing, BAR-AT-LAW,

Federal Court of India

CHIEF JUSTICE

Hon. Sir Maurice Linford Gwyer K.C.B., K.C.S.I.

JUDGES

Hon. Sir Shah Mahomed Sulaiman, Kt. M.A., L.L.D.

Hon. Sir Srinivasa Varadachary.

Bengal Judical Department

High Court—Calcutta

CHIEF JUSTICE

Derbyshire, The Hon. Sir Harold, Kt., K.C., M.C.

PUISNE JUDGES

Costello, The Hon. Mr. Justice Leonard Wilfred James, Kt.,M.A., LL.B Bar-at-Law.

Lort-Williams, The Hon. Mr. Justice John, Kt. K.C.

Ghose, The Hon. Mr. Justice Sarat Kumar, M.A., I.C.S.

Panckridge, The Hon. Mr. Justice Hugh Rahere, Bar-at-Law.

Ameer Ali, The Hon, Mr. Justice Torick, Bar-at-Law.

Bartley, The Hon. Mr. Justice Charles, I.C.S. Bar-at-Law.

Mc Nair, The Hon. Mr. Justice George Douglas, Bar-at-Law.

Ali, The Hon. Mr. Justice Syed Nasim,

Henderson, The Hon. Mr. Justice Allen Gerald,

Mitter, The Hon. Mr. Justice Roopendro Coomar,

Khundkar, The Hon. Mr. Justice N. A., Bar-at-Law.

Rao, The Hon. Mr. Justice Benegal Narsinga, Kt., C.I.E., I.C.S.

Edgley, The Hon. Mr. Justice Norman George Armstrong,, I.C.S., Bar-at-Law.

Mookerjee, The Hon. Mr. Justice Bijan Kumar. M.A., D.L.

Biswas, The Hon. Mr. Justice Charu Chandra, M.A., B L.

Lodge, The Hon. Mr. Justice Ronald Francis, B A., I.C S.

Sen, The Hon. Mr. Justice Amarendra Nath, Bar-at-Law.

Roxburgh, The Hon. Mr. Justice T. J. Y., C.I.E, I.C.S.

OFFICIATING JUDGE

Akram, The Hon. Mr. Justice A.S.M.

ADVOCATE-GENERAL

Sir Asok Kumar Roy, Kt. Barrister-at-Law.

Bombay Judicial Department

High Court—Bombay

CHIEF JUSTICE

Beaumont, The Hon. Sir J. W. F., K.C., M.A. (*Cantab*)

PUISNE JUDGES

Blackwell, The Hon. Mr. Justice Cecil Patrick, Kt, M.B.E., Bar-at-Law.

Broomfield, The Hon. Mr. Justice R. S., B.A., I.C.S. Barrister-at-Law.

Wadia, The Hon. Mr. Justice Bomanji Jamshedji, Barrister-at-Law.

Kania. The Hon. Mr. Justice Harilal Jekisondas, LL.B.

Wadia, The Hon. Mr. Justice Novroji Jehangir, I.C.S. Barrister-at-Law.

Divatia, The Hon. Mr. Justice Harsidhbhai Vajubhai, M.A., LL.B.,

Macklin, The Hon. Mr. Justice A. S. R., I.C.S.

Wasudey, The Hon. Mr. Justice K. B., LL.B.

Somjee, The Hon. Mr. Justice, M.A., Bar-at-Law.

Sen, The Hon. Mr. Justice K.C., I.C.S. (*Additional Judge*)

ADVOCATE-GENERAL

Setalvad, M. C., B.A., LL.B., Advocate

Madras Judical Department

High Court—Madras

CHIEF JUSTICE

Leach, The Hon'ble Sir Lionel., Kt. Bar-at-Law.

PUISNE JUDGES

Burn, The Hon. Mr. Justice S., Kt., I.C.S.

Mockett, The Hon. Mr. Justice V.
Pandurang Row, The Hon. Mr. Justice V., I.C.S.
King, The Hon. Mr. Justice A. J., I.C.S.
Wodsworth, The Hon. Mr. Justice S., I.C.S.
Venkataramana Rao Nayudu, The Hon'ble Mr. Justice P., Rao Bahadur
Lakshmana Rao, The Hon. Mr. Justice K. P., Diwan Bahadur
Gentle, The Hon. Mr. Justice F. W. Bar-at-Law.
Rahman. The Hon. Mr. Justice Dr. Abdur, Kt., Khan Bahadur
Krishnaswami Ayyangar, The Hon. Mr. Justice K. S.
Somayya, The Hon. Mr. Justice B.
Patangali Sastri, The Hon. Mr. Justice M.
Horwill, The Hon. Mr. Justice L. C., I.C.S.

Behar & Orissa Judicial Dept.

High Court—Patna

CHIEF JUSTICE

Harries, The Hon'ble Sir Arthur Trevor, Kt.

PUISNE JUDGES

Wort, The Hon. Mr. Justice Alfred William Ewart. Bar-at-Law.
Fazl-ali, The Hon. Mr. Justice Saiyid, Bar-at-Law.
Dhavle, The Hon. Mr. Justice Sankara Balaji, I.C.S.
Agarwala, The Hon. Mr. Justice Clifford Monmohan, Bar-at-Law.
Varma, The Hon. Justice Sukhdev Prashad, Bar-at-Law.
Rowland, The Hon. Mr. Justice Francis George, I.C.S.
Lall, The Hon. Mr. Justice Monohar, M.A. (Cantab.), Bar-at-Law.
Chattarji, The Hon. Mr. Justice Subodh Chandra,
Meredith, The Hon. Mr. Justice Herbert Ribton, I.C.S. (Acting Additional).

ADVOCATE-GENERAL

Mr. Baldev Sahay, M.A., LL.B.

Burma Judicial Department

High Court—Rangoon

CHIEF-JUSTICE

Roberts, The Hon'ble Sir Earnest Handforth Goodman, Barrister-at-Law.

PUISNE JUDGES

The Hon. Justice Sir Mya Bu, Bar-at-Law.
The Hon. Mr. Justice A. G. Mosely, I.C.S.
" " " " U Ba, Bar-at-Law
The Hon. Mr. Justice H. F. Dunkley, Bar-at-Law, I.C.S.
The Hon. M. Justice H. H. Mackney, I.C.S.
The Hon. Mr. Justice R. Taaffe Sharpe, Bar-at-Law.
The Hon. Mr. Justice Joseph Shaw, Bar-at-Law
The Hon. Mr. Justice J. B. Blagden, Bar-at-Law

ADVOCATE-GENERAL

Maung, U Thein, M.A., LL.B., Bar-at-Law

C. P. & Berar Judicial Dept.

High Court—Nagpur

CHIEF JUSTICE

Stone, The Hon'ble Sir Gilbert, Bar-at-Law

PUISNE JUDGES

Grille, The Hon. Mr. Justice Frederick Louis, Kt., M.A., Bar-at-Law, I.C.S.
Niyogi, The Hon. Mr. Justice M. Bhawani Shankar, M.A, LL.M., C.I.E.
Pollock, The Hon. Mr. Justice Ronald Evelyn, B.A., Bar-at-Law, I.C.S.
Gruer, The Hon. Mr. Justice Harold George, M.A., Bar-at-Law, I.C.S.
Bose, The Hon. Mr. Justice Vivian, B.A., LL. B., Bar-at-Law.
Puranik, The Hon. Mr. Justice Wasudeo Ramchandra, B.A., LL. B.

ADVOCATE-GENERAL

Dutt, Walter, Barrister-at-Law

Punjab Judicial Department

High Court—Lahore

CHIEF JUSTICE

Young. The Hon'ble Sir J. Douglas, B.A., Barrister-at-Law.

JUDGES

Tekchand, The Hon. Mr. Justice Bakshi. M.A., LL. B.
Dalip Singh, The Hon. Mr. Justice Kunwar, B.A., Bar-at-Law
Monroe, The Hon. Mr. Justice J. H., B.A., LL. B., K.C. Bar-at-Law.
Skemp, The Hon. Mr. Justice F. W., M.A., I.C.S.
Bhide, The Hon. Mr. Justice M. V., B.A., I.C.S.
The Hon. Mr. Justice Abdul Rashid, M.A., Bar-at-Law
Din Muhammad, The Hon. Mr. Justice Khan Bahadur, M.A., LL B.
Blacker, The Hon. Mr. Justice H. A. C., B.A., I.C.S.

Ram Lal, The Hon. Mr. Justice Diwan, B.A, Bar-at-Law.
Sale, The Hon. Mr. Justic S. L., B.A., I.C.S.

United Provinces Judicial Dept.

High Court—Allahabad

CHIEF JUSTICE

Thom, the Hon'ble Sir John Gibb, Kt., M.A., LL.B, D.S.O., M.C.

PUISNE JUDGES

Bennet, The Hon. Mr. Justice Sir Edward, Kt., B A., LL.D., Bar-at-Law, J.P., I.C.S.
Iqbal Ahmad, The Hon. Mr. Justice, B.A., LL B.
Harries, The Hon. Mr. Justice Arthur Trevor, Bar-at-Law.
Singh, The Hon. Mr. Justice Rachhpal, Rai Bahadur, Bar at-Law.
Collister, The Hon. Mr. Justice Harold James, J.P., I.C S.
Allsop, The Hon. Mr Justice James Joseph Whittlesea, J.P, I.C S.
Bajpai, The Hon. Mr. Justice Uma Shankar, M.A. LL.B.
Rai Bahadur, The Hon. Mr. Justice Ganga Nath B.A., LL B.
Khan Bahadur, The Hon. Mr. Justice Muhammad Ismail, Bar-at-Law.
Verma, The Hon. Mr. Justice Kamala Kantha, B.A., LL.B.
Braund, The Hon. Mr. Justice Henry Benedict Linthwaite, Bar-at-Law.

Chief Court of Oudh—Lucknow

CHIEF-JUSTICE

Thomas, The Hon'ble Mr. Jusice George Hector, Bar-at-Law.

JUDGES

Khan Bahadur, The Hon. Mr. Justice Zia-ul-Hasan, B.A.
Hamilton, The Hon. Mr. Justice Archibald de Burgh, B.A., J.P., I.C.S.
Yorke, The Hon. Mr. Justice Robert Langdon, B.A., J.P., I.C.S.
Srivastava, The Hon. Mr. Justice Radha Krishna, B SC., L.L.B. (*Addl. Judge*)

Chief Court of Sind

CHIEF JUSTICE

The Hon'ble Mr. Godrey Devis, I.C.S.

JUDGES

The Hon'ble Mr. Charles M. Lobo, B.A., LL B.
The Hon'ble Mr. Erec Weston, B.A., I.C.S.
The Hon'ble Mr. Hatim B. Tyabj, Bar-at-Law.

Indian States, (with Salutes)

(Area—712,508 Sq. Miles ; population—81,310,845)

Assam State

Manipur—H. H. Maharaja Sir Chura Chand Singh, K.C.S I., C.B.E. Maharaja of—
Date of Birth :—15th April, 1885
Date of succession :- 18th September 1891
Area of State in Sq. miles :—8638 (Approximately)
Population of State :—4,45,606
Revenue :—Nearly Rs. 9,59 620
Salute in guns :—11

Baluchistan State

Kalat—His Highness Beglar Begi Mir Sir Mahmud Khan, G.C.I.E., Wali of—
Date of Birth :—1864
Date of succession :—1893
Area of State in Square miles :—73,278
Population of State :—328,281
Revenue :—Rs. 17,78.000 nearly.
Salute in Guns :—19

Baroda State

Baroda—H. H. Farzand-i-Khas i-Daulat-i-Inglishia Maharaja Sir Pratapsingh Gaekwar G.C.I.E., Sena Khas Khel, Shamsher Bahadur, Maharaja of—
Date of Birth :—29th June 1908
Date of Succession —7th Febauary 1939
Area of State in Sq. miles :—8,164
Population of State :—28,550,10
Revenue :—Rs. 245·23 lacs.
Salute in guns :—21

Bengal States

Cooch Behar—H. H. Maharaja Jagaddipendra Narayan Bhup Bahadur, Maharaja of—
Date of Birth—15th December 1915
Date of Succession—20th December 1922
Area of State in Sq. miles—1318,35
Population of State—6,39,898
Revenue :—About Rs. 38½ lakhs
Salute in guns—13

Tripura—His Highness Maharaja Manikya Bir Bikram Kishore Deb Barman Bahadur, K.C S.I., Maharaja of—
Date of Birth :—19th August 1908
Date of succession :—13 August 1923
Area of State in square miles :—4,116
Population of State :—382,450
Revenue :—Rs. 33,42,104 (including the revenue of the Zamindaries in British India)
Indian State Forces :—Tripura Infantry
Salute in guns :—13

Bihar & Orissa States

Kalahandi—H. H. Maharaja Pratapkeshori Deo, Maharaja of—
Date of birth :—5th October '19
Date of succession :—19th September '39
Area of State in Sq. miles :—3,745
Population of State :—5,99,751
Revenue :—Rs. 6,43,000
Salute in guns :—9

Mayurbhanj—Maharaja Sir Pratap Chandra Bhanj Deo, K.C.I.E, Maharaja of—
Date of birth—18th February, '01
Date of Succession :—23rd April, '28
Area of State in Sq. miles :—4,243
Population of State :—9,89,887
Revenue :—Rs. 34 lacs
Salute in guns :—9

Patna—H. H. Maharaja Rajendra Narayan Singh Deo, Maharaja of—
Date of birth :—31st March '12
Date of succession :—16th January '24
Area of State in square miles :—2,511
Population of State :—16,32,220
Revenue :—Rs. 11,02,251
Salute in guns :—9

Sonpur—H. H. Maharaja Singh Deo, K.C.I.E. Maharaja of—
Date of birth :—28th June 1874
Date of succession :—8th August '02
Area of State in square miles :—906
Population of State :—226,751
Revenue—Rs. 3,74,000 nearly
Salute in guns :—9

Bombay Presy. States

Balasinor—H. H. Babi Shri Jamiat Khanji Munavvar Khanji Nawab Saheb Bahadur, Nawab of—
Date of birth :—10th November 1894
Date of succession :—31st December '15
Area of State in square miles :—189
Population of State :—52,525
Revenue : Rs. 3,50,000 nearly
Indian State Forces :—Cavalry—60, Infantry—177, Guns—10
Salute in guns :—9

Bansda—H. H. Maharawal Shri Indrasinhji Pratapsinhji, Raja of—
Date of birth :—16th February 1888
Date of succession :—21st Sept. '11
Area of State in square miles :—215
Population of State :—40,125
Revenue :—Rs. 7,98,000 nearly
Salute in guns :—9

Baria—Lt. Col. His Highness Maharaol Shree Sir Ranjitsinhji, K.C.S.I., Ruler of—
Date of birth :—10th July 1886
Date of succession :—20th Feb. '08
Area of State :—813 sq. miles
Population :—1,89,206
Indian State Forces :—1 Cavalry (Irregular) Strength 17, 1 Company Ranjit Infantry Strength 153. 1 Platoon Militia. Strength 50
Salute in guns :—9

Bhor—H. H. Meherban Shrimant Raghunathrao Shankarrao, Pant Sachiv of—
Date of birth :—20th September 1878
Date of succession :—17th July '22
Area of State in square miles :—925
Population of State :—130,420
Revenue :—Rs. 6,00,000 nearly
Salute in guns :—9

Cambay—H. H. Nawab Mirza Hussain Yawar Khan Saheb Bdr. Nawab of—
Date of birth :—16th May '11
Date of succession :—21st January 1915
Area of State in Sq. miles :—392
Population of State :—87 761
Revenue :—Nearly Rs. 10 00,000
Indian State Forces :—119 Infantry; 166 Police Forces ; 15 Body guards
Salute in guns :—11

Chhota Udepur (Mohan)—H. H. Maharawal Shri Natwarsinhji Fatehsinhji Raja of—
Date of birth :—16th November 1906
Date of succession :—29th Aug. 1923
Area of State in Sq. miles :—890,34
Population of State :—1,62,145
Revenue :—Rs 13,08,248
Salute in guns :—9

Danta—H. H. Maharana Shri Bhavanisinhji Hamirsinhji, Maharana of—
Date of birth :—12th September 1899
Date of succession :—20th November 1925
Area of State in square miles :—347
Population of State :—19,541
Revenue :—Rs. 1,75,000 nearly
Salute in guns :—9

Dharampur—H H. Maharana Shri Vijayadevji Mohandevji, Raja of—
Date of birth :—3rd December 1884
Date of succession :—26th March '21
Area of State in Sq. miles :—704
Population of State : 1,12,031
Revenue nearly Rs. 8,50,000
Salute in guns :—9

Idar—H. H. Maharaja Dhiraja Shri Himmat Singhji Sahib Bahadur, Maharaja of
Date of birth :—2nd September 1899
Date of Succession :—14th April '31
Area of State in Sq. miles :—1,669
Population of State :—30,77,98
Revenue :—Rs. 24,66,000 nearly
Salute in guns :—15

Janjira—H. H. Nawab Sidi Muhammad Khan Sidi Ahmad Khan, Nawab of—
Date of birth :—7th March '14
Date of succession :—2nd May '22
Area of State in square miles :—379

Population of State :—1,10,388
Revenue :—Rs. 11,00,000
Salute in guns :—11

Jawhar—Shrimant Yeshwantrao Maharaj, Raja of—
Date of birth :—11th December '17
Date of Succession :—11th Dec. '27
Area of State in Sq. miles :—308
Population of State :—65,291
Revenue :—Rs. 5,20,000
Salute in guns :—9

Khairpur—H. H. Mir Faiz Mahomed Khan Talpur, Mir of—
Date of birth :—4th January '13
Date of succession :—December '35
Area of State in Square miles :—6,050
Population of State :—227,168
Revenue :—Rs. 25 84 (lacs)
Indian State Forces :—Khairpur "Faiz" Light Infantry, 215 ; Khairpur Camel Transport Corps, 72
Salute in guns :—15

Kohapur—Col. H. H. Shri Sir Rajaram Chhatrapati Maharaj, G.C.S.I., G.C.I.E., Maharaja of—
Date of birth :—30th July 1897
Date of succession —6th May 1922
Area of State in square miles :—3,217·1
Population of State :—9,57,137
Revenue :—Rs. 126,86,527
Salute in guns :—19

Lunawada—Lieut. H. H. Maharana Shri Virbhadrasinhji, Rajaji Saheb of—
Date of birth :—8th June, '10
Date of succession :—2nd October, '30
Area of State in Sq. miles :—388
Population of State :95.162
Revenue :—About Rs. 5,50,000
Dynastic Salute :—9 guns

Mudhol—H. H. Srimant Raja Bhairavsinh (minor), Raja of—
Date of birth :—15 Oct. '29
Date of succession :—9th Nov. '37
Area of State in square miles :—369
Population of State :—62,832
Revenue :—Rs. 4 85 000 nearly
Indian State Force :—Mudhol Sajjan Sinh Infantry—115
Salute in guns :—9

Rajpipla—Captain H. H. Maharana Shri Sir Vijaya Sinhji Chhatrasinhji, K.C.S.I., Maharaja of—
Date of birth :—30th January 1890
Date of Succession :—26th Sept. '15
Area of State in Sq. miles :—1,517·50
Population of State :—2,48,068
Revenue :—Rs. 24,32,000 nearly
Indian State Forces :—Rajpipla Infantry 152 ; Rajpipla Bodyguard 25
Salute in guns :—13

Sachin :—His Highness Nawab Sidi Muhammad Haider Muhammad Yakut Khan, Mubarizud Daula, Nusrat Jung Bahadur, Nawab of—
Date of birth :—11th September '09
Date of Succession :—19th November 1930
Area in Sq. miles :—57·80
Revenue :—Rs. 4,00,000/-
Indian State Forces :—Sachin Infantry 80
Salute in guns :—9

Sangli—Captain H. H. Raja Shrimant Sir Chintamanrao Dhundirao alias Appasaheb Patwardhan, K.C.I.E., Raja of—
Date of birth :—14th Feb. 1890
Date of Succession :—15th June 1903
Area of State in Sq. miles :—1,136
Population of State :—2,93,498
Revenue :—Rs. 16,80,244
Salute in guns :—9

Sant—Maharana Shri Jorawarsinhji Partapsinhji, Raja of—
Date of birth :—24th March 1881
Date of succession :—31st August 1896
Area in sq. miles :—394
Population :—83,531
Revenue :—4 85,826
Salute in guns :—9

Savantvadi—(Minor) H. H. Raja Bahadur Shrimant Shivram Savant Bhonsle,
Date of birth :—13th August '27
Date of succession :—5th July '37
Area of State in Sq. miles :—930
Population of State :—2,52,170
Revenue—Rs. 6,13,478
Salute in guns :—9

Central Indian States

Ajaigarh—H. H Maharaja Sawai Bhupal Singh Bahadur, Maharaja of—
Date of birth :—13th November 1866
Date of succession :—7th June '19
Area of State in Sq. miles :—802
Population of State :—84,790
Revenue :—Rs. 5,00,000 nearly
Salute in guns :—11

Alirajpur—H. H. Maharaja Pratap Singh, K.C.I.E., Maharaja of—
Date of birth :—12th Sept. 1881
Date of succession :—14th February 1891
Area in Sq. miles :—836
Population—112,754
Revenue of the State :—Rs.5,35,000
State Forces :—Alirajpur Cavalry—23 Alirajpur Pratap Infantry—80
Salute in guns :—11

Baoni—H. H Azam-ul-Umara Iftikhar-ud-Daulah Imad-ul-Mulk Sahib i-Jah Mihin Sardar Nawab Mohammad Mushtaq-ul-Hasan Khan Safdar Jung, Nawab of—
Date of birth :—7th February 1896
Date of succession :—28th October '11
Area of State in Sq. miles :—121
Population of State :—25,256

Revenue :—Rs. 2,25,000
Salute in guns :—11

Baraundha (Pathar Kachar)—Raja Gaya Parshad Singh, Raja of—
Date of birth :—1865
Date of Succession :—9th July '09
Area of State in Sq. miles :—218
Population of State :—15,912
Revenue :—Rs. 45,000 nearly
Salute in guns :—9

Barwani—His Highness Devisinghji Rana of—
Date of birth :—19th July '22
Date of Succession :—21st April '30
Area of State in Sq. miles :—1,178
Population of State :—1,76,632
Revenue :—Rs. 11,04,510
Salute in guns :—11

Bhopal—Lt.-Col. H. H. Iftikhar-ul-Mulk Sikandar Saulat Nawab Haji Muhammad Hamidulla Khan Bahadur, G.C.I.E., G.C.S.I., C.V.O., Nawab of—
Date of birth :—9th September 1894
Date of succession :—17th May '26
Area of State in Sq. miles :—7,000
Population of State :—700,000
Revenue :—Rs. 62,10,000 nearly
Indian State Forces :—Bhopal (Victoria) Lancers—141 ; Bhopal Sultania Infantry—772 ; Bhopal Gohar-i-Taj Own Company—164
Salute in guns :—19

Bijawar—H. H. Maharaja Govind Singh Minor. Maharaja of—
Date of birth :—17th June '34
Date of succession :—11th Nov. '41
Area of State in Sq. miles :—973
Population of State :—1,20,928
Revenue :—Rs. 3,55,278
Salute in guns :—11

Charkhari—H. H. Maharajadhiraja Sipahdar-ul-Mulk Armardan Singh Ju Deo Bahadur, Maharaja of—
Date of birth :—29th December '03
Date of succession :—6th October '20
Area of State in Sq. miles :—880
Population of State :—123,405
Revenue :—Rs. 8,26,000 nearly
Salute in guns :—11

Chhatarpur—H. H. Maharaja Bhawani Singh Bahadur, Maharaja of—
Date of birth :—16th August, '04
Date of succession :—5th April, '32
Area of State in Sq. miles—1,130
Population of State—1,61,267
Gross Revenue Nearly—Rs. 12,00,000
Indian States Forces—412
Salute in guns—11

Datia—Major H. H. Maharaja Lokendra Sir Govind Singh Bahadur, K.C.S.I., Maharaja of—
Date of birth :—21st June 1886
Date of succession :—5th August '07
Area of State in Sq. miles :—911
Population of State :—148,659
Revenue :—Rs. 19,00,000 nearly
Indian State Forces :—Datia 1st Govind Infantry—200
Datia Govind Infantry (B Company)—117
Salute in guns :—15

Dewas (Senior)—His Highness Maharaja Sir Vikramsinha Rao Puar, K.C.S.I., B.A., Maharaja of—
Date of birth :—4th April 1910
Date of succession :—21st December 1937
Area of State in sq. miles :—449·50
Population of State :—89479
Revenue :—Rs, 7,00,000
Salute in guns :—15

Dewas (Junior Branch)—H. H. Maharaja Sadashivrao Khase Saheb Pawar, Maharaja of—
Date of birth :—13th August 1887
Date of succession :—4th February 1934
Area of State in sq. miles :—419
Population of State :—70,513
Revenue :—Rs. 6,83,000
Salute in guns :—15

Dhar—Lieut H. H. Maharaja Anand Rao Puar Saheb Bahadur, Maharaja of—
Date of birth—24th November, '20
Date of succession—1st August, '26
Date of Investiture—16th March, '40
Area of State in sq. Miles—1,799·34
Population of State—2,53,210
Revenue including Feudatories and Jagirs Rs. 30,00,000
Indian State Forces—Dhar Light Horse 66 ; Dhar Infantry (Laxmi Guard) 263
Salute in guns 15

Indore—H. H. Maharajadhiraja Raj Rajeshwar Sawai Shri Yeshwant Rao Holkar Bahadur, G.C.I.E., Maharaja of,
Date of birth :—6th September '08
Date of succession :—26th February '26
Area of State in sq. miles :—9,902
Population of State :—over 15,00,000
Revenue :—Rs. 1,21.81,100
Indian State Forces :—Indore Holker Escort—141
Indore 1st Battalion, Maharaja Holkar's Infantry Companies "A" & "B"—380
Indore Holkar Transport Corps—266
Salute in guns :—19

Jaora—Lt. Col. H. H. Fakhrud-Daulah Nawab Sir Mohammad Iftikhar Ali Khan Bahadur, Saulat-i-Jang, G.B.E., K.C.I.E., Nawab of—
Date of birth :—17th January 1883
Date of succession :—6th March 1895
Area of State in sq. miles :—601
Population of State :—1,16,738
Revenue :—Rs. 16,00,000
Salute in guns :—13

Jhabua—H. H. Raja Udai Sing, Raja of—
Date of birth :—6th May 1875
Date of succession :—26th April 1895
Area of State in sqr. miles :—1,336
Population of State :—123 932
Revenue :—Rs. 3,50 000 nearly
Salute in guns :—11

Khilchipur :—Raja Rao Bahadur Sir Durjansalsingh K.C.I.E.. Raja of—
Date of birth :—26th August 1897
Date of succession :- 19th Januray '08
Area of State in Sq. miles :—273
Population of State :—45,625
Revenue :—Rs. 2.42,000
Salute in guns :—9

Maihar—H. H. Raja Sir Brijnath Singhji Deo Bahadur, K.C.I.E. Raja of—
Date of birth :—22nd February 1896
Date of succession :—16th Dec. '11
Area of State in square miles :—407
Population of State :—68 991
Revenue : Rs. 5,00,000 (nearly)
Salute in guns :—9

Nagod (Unchehra)—H. H. Raja Mahendra Singhjee Deo Bahadur, Raja of—
Date of birth :—5th February '16
Date of succession :—26th Feb. '26
Area of State in Sq. miles :—501·4
Population of State :—87,911
Revenue :—Rs. 3,00,000 (nearly)
Salute in guns :—9

Narsinghgarh—H. H. Raja Sir Vikram Singhji Sahib Bdr. K.C.I.E. Raja of—
Date of birth :—21 Sept. '09
Date of succession :—23rd April '24
Area of State in Sq. miles : -734.
Population of State :—1,24 281
Revenue :—Rs. 7,09,291 (nearly).
Salute in guns :—11.

Orchha—H. H. Saramad-i-Rajaha-Bundelkhand Shri Sawai Sir Vir Singh Dev Bahadur, K.C.S.I. Maharaja of—
Date of birth :—14th April 1899
Date of succession :—4th March '30
Area of State in Sq. miles :—2,080
Population of State :—314,661
Revenue :—Rs. 13,00,000 (nearly)
Salute in guns :—15

Panna—H. H. Maharaja Mahendra Sir Yadvendra Singh Bahadur, K.C.S.I., K.C.I.E., Maharaja of—
Date of birth :—31st January 1894
Date of succession :—20th June '02
Area of State in Sq. miles :—2,596
Population of State :- 2,12,130
Revenue :- Rs. 9,50,000 nearly
Salute in guns :—11

Rajgarh—H. H. Raja Rawat Bikramaditya Singh Bahadur (minor), Raja of—
Date of birth :- 18th December '36
Date of Succession :— Do Do
Area of State in Sq. miles :—962
Population of State :—1.48,609
Revenue :—Rs. 8,63,200
Salute in guns :—11

Ratlam—Major-General H. H. Maharaja Sir Sajjan Singh, G.C.I.E., K.C.S.I., K.C.V.O.,
Date of birth :—13th January 1880
Date of succession :—29th Jan. 1893
Area of State in Sq. miles :—693
Population of State :—1,26,117
Revenue :—Rs. 10 lacs
Indian State Forces :—Shree Lokendra Rifles—Authorised Strength—161
Salute in guns —13 permanent, local 15

Rewa—H. H. Maharaja Dhiraj Sir Gulab Singh Bahadur, G.C.I.E., K.C.S.I., Maharaja of :—
Date of birth :—12th March. '03
Date of succession :—31st October, '18
Area of State in sq. miles :—13,000
Population of State :—18,20,306
Salute in guns :—17
Revenue :- Rs. 60,00,000

Sailana—H. H. Raja Sahib Sir Dileep Singhji Bahadur, K.C.I.E. Raja of—
Date of birth :—18th March 1891
Date of succession :—14th July '19
Area of State in sq. miles :—297
Population of State :—40228
Revenue :—Rs. 3,00,000
Indian State Forces :—1. Cavalry 30; 2. Infantry 44; 3. Police 130.
Salute in guns :—11

Samthar—H. H. Maharaja Sir Bir Singh Deo Bahadur, K.C.I.E., Raja of—
Date of birth :—26th August 1864
Date of succession :—17th June 1896
Area of State in square miles :—180
Population of State :—33,216
Revenue :—Rs. 3,50,000 nearly
Salute in guns :—11

Sitamau—H. H. Raja Sir Ram Singh, K.C.I.E., Raja of—
Date of Birth—2nd January 1880
Area of State in sq. miles—201
Population of State :—26,549
Revenue :—Rs. 2,55,076
Salute in guns—11

Gwalior State

Gwalior—H. H. Maharaja Mukhtar-ul-Mulk, Azim-ul-Iqtidar, Rafi-ush-Shan, Wala Shikoh, Motasham-i-Dauran, Umdat-ul-Umra, Maharajadhiraja Alijah, Hisamus-Salta-nat George Jayaji Rao Scindia, Bahadur, Srinath, Mansur-i-Zaman, Fidwi-i-Hazrat-i-Malik-Muazzam-i-Rafi-ud-Darjat-i-Inglistan, Maharaja of—
Date of birth :—26th June '16
Date of succession :- 5th June '25
Area of State in square miles :—26,367

Population of State :—3,523,070
Revenue :—Rs 241·81 lacs nearly
Indian State Forces :—
Gwalior 1st Yayaji Lancers—526
„ 2nd Alijah „ —526
„ 3rd Maharaja Madho Rao Scindia's Own Lancers—526
„ 1st Maharani Sakhya Raya's Own Battalion—763
2nd Maharaja Jayaji Rao's Own Battalion—765
3rd Maharaja Scindia's Own Battalion—772
„ 4th Maharaja Bahadur Battalion —772
„ 7th Scindia's Battalion (Training)—488
„ Mountain Battery—260
Scindia's Horse Artillery—138
„ Sappers Artillery—178
„ Pony Transport Corps—479
Salute in Guns :—21

Hyderabad State

Hyderabad—Lt.-General H. E. H. Asaf Jah Muzaffar-ul-Mulk wal Mamalik, Nizam-ul-Mulk Nizam-ud-Daula, Nawab Sir Mir Usman Ali Khan Bahadur, Fateh Jang, Faithful Ally of the British Government, G.C.S.I., G.B.E., Nizam of—
Date of birth :—6th April 1886
Date of succession :—29th August '11
Area of State in sq. miles:—100,465
Population of State :- 17,877,986
Revenue :—Rs. 894.98 lacs
Indian State Forces :—Hyderabad 1st Imperial Service Lancers. 544
Hyderabad 2nd Imperial Service Lancers, 544
Salute in guns : 21

Jammu & Kashmir State

Jammu & Kashmir :—Lieut. General H.H. Raj Rajeshwar Maharajadhiraj Maharaja Shri Harisinghji Bahadur, Indar Mahindar, Spar-i-Saltanat-i-Englishia, G.C.S.I., G.C.I.E., K.C.V.O., LL.D., Maharaja of—
Date of birth :—September 1895.
Date of succession :—September 25
Area of State in square miles :—84,471
Population of State :—40,21,616
Revenue :—Rs. 257.92 lacs
Indian States Forces :—
1. Ist Line Troops (Fighting Service) Jammu and Kashmir Body Guard Cavalry—653
2. Ist Jammu & Kashmir Mountain Battery 314
3. 2nd Jammu & Kashmir Mountain Battery 262
4. 1st „ „ „ Infantry 679
5. 2nd „ „ „ Rifles 690
6. 3rd „ „ „ „ 679
7. 4th „ „ „ Infantry 690
8 5th „ „ „ Light „ 679
9. 6th „ „ „ „ „ 772
10. 7th „ „ „ „ „ 690
11. 8th „ „ „ „ 679
12. 9th „ „ „ „ 679
Ist Line (Troops Administrative Service)
13. J&L A. T. O. 365
14. Jammu & Kashmir Infantry Training Battalion 1969
15. Jammu & Kashmir Army Training School 26
16. Auxiliary Service
17. Jammu & Kashmir Military Transport 299
18. Jammu & Kashmir State Band 68
19. „ „ Fort Dept. 117
20 Military Veterinary Crops 21
21. Military Medical Corps 40
Salute in guns :—21

Banganapalle—H. H. Nawab Saiyid Fazle Ali Khan Bahadur, Nawab of—
Date of birth :—9th Nov. '01
Date of succession :—22nd Jan. '22
Area of State in Sq. miles :—275
Population of State :—44,631
Revenue :—3,53,758
Salute in guns :—9

Cochin—H. H. Sir Kerala Varma, Maharaja of—
Date of birth :—29th Vrischigon 1039 M.E.
Date of succession :—13th April '41
Area of State in sq. miles :—1480
Population of State :—1,422,875
Revenue :—Rs. 1,21,46,238
Indian State Forces :—34 officers and 370 men.
Saulte in guns :—17.

Pudukkottai—His Highness Sri Brihadamba Das Raja Rajagopala Tondaiman Bahadur, Rajah of—
Date of birth :—23rd June, 1922.
Date of accession :—24th October, 1928.
Area in sq. miles. :—1,179.
Population :—4,38,348.
Revenue :—Rs. 20,74,000 nearly.
Salute in guns. 11.

Travancore—H. H. Sri Padmanabha Dasa Vanchi Pala Rama Varma Kulasekhara Kiritapati Manney Sultan Maharaja Raja Ramaraja Bahadur Shamsher Jang, G.C.I.E.. Maharaja of—
Date of birth :—7th November 1912
Date of succession—1st September 1924
Area of State in square miles—7,625
Population of State—5,095,973
Revenue :—Rs. 264 lacs
Salute in guns :—19

Mysore—H. H. Maharaja Sri Chamaraja Wadiar Bahadur, Maharaja of—

Date of birth :—18th July '19.
Date of Succession :—8th Sept. 1940.
Area of State in Sq. miles :—29,493.
Population of State :—73.29 lakhs including Civil & Military Station, Bangalore.
Revenue :—Rs. :—4,65,66,000 nearly.
Indian State Forces :—Mysore Lancers 495 ; Horse 136 ; Body Guard 125 ; 1st Infantry 772 ; 2nd Infantry 1130 ; Palace Guard 500.
Salute in guns :—21.

Punjab States

Bahawalpur—Major H. H. Rukn-ud-Daula, Nusrat-i-Jang, Saif-ud-Daula, Hafiz-ul-Mulk, Mukhlis-ud-Daula, wa-Muinud-Daula Nawab Al-Haj Sir Sadiq Muhammad Khan V Abbasi, Bahadur, G.C.I.E., K.C.S.I., K.C.V.O., Nawab Ruler of—
Date of birth :—30th September '04
Date of succession :—4th March '07
Area of State in sq. miles :—22,000
Population of State :—Over one million
Revenue—nearly Rs. 1,40,00,000
Indian State Forces :—Bahawalpur 1st Sadiq Infantry ; Bahawalpur 2nd Haroon Infantry ; H. H. the Nawab's Own Body Guard Lancers.
Salute in guns :—17

Bilaspur (Kahlur)—H. H. Raja Anand Chand, Raja of—
Date of birth:—26th January '13.
Date of Succession :—18th Nov. '27.
Area of State in Sq. miles :—448.
Population of State :—1,10,000
Revenue :—Rs. 3,00,000 nearly.
Salute in guns :—11.

Chamba—H. H. Raja Lakshman Singh, the Ruler of Chamba State (minor).
Date of birth :—8th December 1924.
Date of Succession :—7th Dec. '35.
Area of State in Sq. miles :—3,127.
Population of State :—168938
Revenue :—Rs. 9,00,000 nearly.
Salute in guns :—11.
Council of Administration appointed by the Government to carry on Minority Administration. President :—Lt.—Col. H. S. Strong, C.I.E. Vice-President & Chief Secretary :—Dewan Bahadur Lala Madho Ram. Member :—Rai Bahadur Lala Ghanshyam Dass.

Faridkot—Lt. H. H. Farzand-i-Saadat Nishan-i-Hazrat-i-Kaisar-i-Hind Barar Bans Raja Har Indar Singh Bahadur, Raja of—
Date of birth :—29th January '15
Date of succession :—23rd December '18
Area of State in Sq. miles :—643
Population of State :—164,346
Revenue :—Rs. 17,00,000 nearly
Indian State Forces :—Faridkot Sappers-Headquarters 8. (Field Company) Sappers & Miners 129. Bodyguard Lancers 27. Infantry 112. Band 35.
Salute in guns :—11

Jind—Colonel H. H. Farzand-i-Dilband Rasikh-ul-Itikad Daulat-i-Inglishia Raja-Rajgan Maharaja Sir Ranbir Singh, Rajendra Bahadur, G.C.I.E., G.C.S.I., Maharaja of—
Date of birth :—11th October 1879
Date of succession :—7th March 1887
Area of State in square miles :—1,259
Population of State :—308,183
Revenue :—Rs. 28,00,000 nearly
Indian State Forces :—Jind bodyguard Cavalry 112 ; Jind Infantry 411 ; Jind Training Company 289 ; Jind 2nd Line Infantry 150.
Salute in guns :—13

Kapurthala—Colonel His Highness Farzand-i-Dilband Rasikh-ul-Itkad Daulat-i-Inglishia Raja-i-Rajgan, Maharaja Sir Jagatjit Singh Bahadur, G.C.S.I., G.C.I.E., G.B.E., Maharaja of—
Date of birth :—24th November 1872
Date of succession :—5th September 1877
Area in sq. miles :—652
Population :—3,78,380
Revenue :—Rs. 34,00,000 roughly
Salute in guns :—13

Loharu—Capt. H. H. Nawab Mirza Amin-ud-Din Ahmed, Fakhar-ud-Daula Khan Bahadur, Nawab of—
Date of birth :—23rd March '11
Date of succession :—30th Oct. '26
Area of State in sq. miles :—222
Population of State :—27892
Revenue :—Rs. 1,33,000 nearly
Salute in guns :—9

Malerkotla—Lt.-Colonel H. H. Nawab Sir Ahmad Ali Khan, Bahadur, K.C.S.I., K.C.I.E., Nawab of—
Date of birth :—10th September 1881
Date of succession :—23rd August '08
Area of State in sq. miles :—168
Population of State :—80,322
Revenue :—Rs. 15,61,000 nearly
Indian State Forces :—Sappers—Headquarters 16 ; Lancers (Bodyguard) 40 ; Infantry 226 ; Field Company Sappers & Miners 295.
Salute in guns :—11

Mandi—Major H. H. Raja Sir Joginder Sen Bahadur, K.C.S.I., Raja of—
Date of birth :—20th August '04
Date of succession :—28th April '13
Area in sq. miles :—1,200
Population :—2,07,465
Revenue :—Rs. 12,50,000 nearly
Salute in guns :—11

Nabha—H. H. Farzand-i-Arjmand, Aquidat-Paiwand-i-Daulat-i-Inglishia, Barar Bans, Sarmur Raja-i-Rajagan Maharaja Pratap Singha Malvendra Bahadur, Maharaja of—
Date of birth :—21st September '19
Date of succession :—February '28
Area in sq. miles :—928
Population :—263,334
Revenue :—Rs. 24.05,000 nearly
Salute in guns :—13

Patiala—Dr. H. H. Farzand-i-Khas Daulat-i-Englishia Mansur-ul-Zaman, Amir-ul-Umra Maharajadhiraj Raj Rajeshwar Shri Maharaja-i-Rajgan Shri Yadavindra Singhji, LL.D., Mahendra Bahadur, Maharaja of—
Date of birth :—7th January '13
Date of succession :—23rd March '38
Area in sq. miles :—5,932
Population :—1,625,520
Revenue :—Rs. 1,57,00,000
Indian State Forces :—

	Combatants :	Non-Combatants
1. 1st Rajindar Lancers	475	178
2. 2nd Patiala Lancers	212	85
3. War Strength 2nd P. Lrs.	60	0
4. P. H. A.	90	28
5. 1st R. S. Infantry	732	66
6. 2nd Yadavendra "	665	61
7. 3rd P. S. "	662	51
8. 4th Patiala "	662	51
9. Training Battalion	635	45
10. Patiala Transport Corps	99	33
11. S. M. Vety. Hospital	5	9
12. Army Trg. School	39	10
13. Patiala Wireless Section	46	6
14. Duty Company	227	10
	4,609	633

Salute in guns :—17

Sirmur (Nahan)—H. H. Lt. Maharaja Rajendra Prakash Bdr. Maharaja of—
Date of birth :—10th January '13
Date of succession :—Nov. '33
Area in sq. miles :—1,141
Population :—1,48,568
Revenue :—Rs. 10.00,000 nearly
Indian State Forces—Sappers—Headquarters 5 ; Band 23 ; No. 1 Company 142 ; No. 2 Company 155 ; State Bodyguard Lancers 31.
Salute in guns :—11

Suket—H. H. Raja Lakshman Sen, Raja of
Date of birth :—1894
Date of succession :—13th Oct. '19
Area in sq. miles :—420
Population :—54.328
Revenue Rs 2,67,000 nearly
Salute in guns :—11

Bashahr—H. H. Raja Padam Singh, Raja of—
Date of birth :—1873
Date of succession :—5th Aug. '14
Area in sq. miles :—3,820
Population :—86.077
Revenue :—Rs. 3,34,000 nearly
Salute in guns :—9

Rajputana States

Alwar—H. H. Shri Sewai Maharaj Tej Singhji Bahadur, Maharaja of—
Date of birth :—19th March, '11
Date of succession :—22nd July, 37
Area in sq. miles :—3217
Population :—7,49,751
Revenue :—About Rs. 40,00,000
Indian State Forces :—
1. Jey Paltan Infantry—865
2. Pratap Paltan Infantry—331
3. Alwar Mangal Lancers—158
4. Garrison Force—28
Salute in guns :—15

Banswara—H. H. Rai-i Rayan Maharawal Sahib Shri Sir Pirthi Singhji Bahadur, K.C.I.E., Maharawal of—
Date of birth :—15th July 1888
Date of succession :—8th Jan. '14
Area of State in sq. miles :—1,946
Population of State :—2,99,913
Revenue :—Rs. 8.17,726
Salute in guns :—15

Bharatpur—Lt.-Col. H. H. Maharaja Sri Brajindra Sawai Sir Krishna Singh Bahadur, Bahadur Jang, K.C.S.I., Maharaja of—
Date of birth :—4th October 1899
Date of succession :—27th August 1900
Area in sq. miles :—1,982
Population :—4,96,437
Revenue :—Rs. 34,25,000 nearly
Indian State Forces :—Jaswant Household Infantry—772 ; 2nd Ram Singh's Own Infantry—353 ; 3rd Baretha Infantry—353.
Salute in guns :—17

Bikaner—General H. H. Maharajadhiraj Rajeshwar Narendra Shiromani Maharajah Sri Ganga Singhji Bahadur, G.C.S.I., G.C.I.E., G.C.V.O., G.B.E., K.C.B., A.-D.-C., LL.D, Maharajah of—
Date of birth :—13th Oct. 1880
Date of succession :—31st Aug. 1887
Area of State in sq. miles :—23,317.
Population of State :—12,93,000
Revenue :—Rs. 1,58,11,000
Indian States Forces :—

Ganga Risala (Camel Corps)	532
Sadul Light Infantry	773
Dungar Lancers (including H. H. 's Body Guard	342
Bijey Battery	245
Camel Battery	20
Artillery Training Centre	158
2nd Battalion, Bikaner State Infantry	697

3rd Battalion, Bikaner State Infantry 362
Training Battalion 413
Motor Machine Gun Sections 100
Salute in gun—Personal 19, Permanent 17
Local 19

Bunde—His Highness Hadendra Siromani Deo Sar Buland Raj Maharajadhiraj Maharao Raja Sir Ishwari Singhji Saheb Bahadur, G.C.I.E.
Date of Birth :—8th March, 1893
Date of succession :—8th August, 1927
Area in sq. miles 2 220
Population :—2,49,374
Revenue :—Rs. 15,50,000
Salute :—17 Guns

Dholpur—Lt.-Col. H. H. Rais-ud-Daula Sipahdar-ul-Mulk Maharajadhiraja Sri Sawai Maharaj-Rana Sir Udaibhan Singh Lokindar Bahadur Diler Jang Jai Deo, K.C.S.I., K.C.V.O. Maharaj-Raja of—
Date of birth—25th Feb. 1893
Date of succession—29th March '11
Area in sq. miles—1 200
Population—2,30,188
Revenue—Rs. 17,50,000 nearly
Indian State Forces—
Dholpur Narisingh Infantry—164
" Sappers and Miners—75
Salute in guns—15

Dungarpur—H. H. Rai-i-Rayan Mahimahendra Maharajadhiraj Maharawal Sri Lakshman Singhji Bahadur, K.C.S.I., Maharawal of—
Date of birth :—7th Mar. '08
Date of succession :—15th Nov. '18
Area of State in sq. miles :—1,460
Population of State :—2,74, 282
Revenue :—Rs. 8,00,000
Salute in guns :—15

Jaipur—H. H. Saramad-i-Rajaha-i Hindustan Raj Rajindra Sri Maharajadhiraja Sir Sawai Man Singh Bahadur, G C.I.E., Maharaja of—
Date of birth—21st August '11
Date of succession—7th September '22
Area in sq. miles—16 682
Population—26,31.775
Revenue—Rs 1,35,00.'C0 nearly
Indian State Forces—Jaipur Infantry—772 ; Jaipur Lancers—526 ; Trpt. Corps—570
Salute in guns—17

Jaisalmer—H. H. Maharajadhiraj Raj Rajeshwar Param Bhattarak Sri Maharawalji Sir Jawahir Singhji Deb Bahadur Yadukul Chandrabhal Rukan-ud-Daula, Muzzaffar Jang, Bijaimand K.C.S.I., Ruler of—
Date of birth—18th Nov. 1882
Date of succession—26th June, '14
Area of State in sq. miles—16,062
Population of State—93,246
Salute in guns—15

Jhalawar—H. H. Dharmadivakar Prajavatsal Patit-pawn Maharaj Rana Shri Sir Rajendra Singh Ji Dev Bahadur, K.C.S.I., Maharaj Rana of—
Date of birth—15th July 1900
Date of succession—13th April '29
Area of State in sq. miles—813
Population of State—1,22,375
Salute in guns—13

Jodhpur—Air Commodore His Highness Raj Rajeshwar Saramad-i-Rajai-Hind Maharajadhiraj Shri Sir Umaid Singhji Sahib Badadur, G C.S.I., G.C.I.E., K.C.V.O., A.D.C., LL.D., Maharaja of—
Date of birth—8th July, '03
Ascended the throne—3rd October, '18
Area—36.071 sq. miles
Population—21,34,848
Revenue—Rs. 157.71,521
Indian State Forces—
Jodhpur Sardar Rissala—508
Jodhpur Training Squardron—147
Jodhpur Sardar Infantry, Including Training Coy. (163) and State Military Band (39) :—864
2nd Jodhpur Infantry—669
Jodhpur Mule Troops—80
Fort Guard—94
Salute in guns—17

Karauli—H. H. Maharaja Sir Bhompal Deo Bahadur Yadukul Chandra Bhal, K.C.S.I., Maharaja of—
Date of birth—18th June 1866
Date of succession—21st August '27
Area of State in sq. miles—1,242
Population of State—1,52,418
Estimated Gross Revenue—6,28,000
Salute in guns—17

Kishengarh—H. H. Umdae Rajahae Baland Makan Maharajadhiraja Maharaja Sumair Singhji Sahib Bahadur, (Minor) Maharaja of—
Date of birth—27th January 1929
Date of succession—24th April '39
Area in sq.miles—858
Population—1,04,155
Revenue—Rs. 7.5(),000
Salute in guns—15

Kotah—Colonel H. H. Maharao Sir Umed Singh Bahadur, G.C.S.I., G.C.I.E., G.B.E., Maharao of—
Date of birth—15th September 1872
Date of succession—11th June 1889
Area in sq. miles—5,684
Population—6,85,804
Revenue—Rs. Rs. 53.68 lacs
Salute in guns—19

Pratabgarh—H. H. Maharawat Sir Ramsinghji Bahadur, K.C.I.E., Maharawat of
Date of birth—1908

Date of succession :—'29
Area of State in Sq. miles :—889
Population of State : 91,967
Revenue Rs. 5,82,000 nearly
Salute in guns :—15

Shahpura—H. H. Rajadhiraj Umaid Singhji, Raja of
Date of birth :—7th March 1876
Date of succession :—24th June '32
Area of State in Sq. miles : - 405
Population of State :—61,173
Revenue :—Rs. 3,36.762 nearly
Salute in guns :—9

Sirohi—H. H. Maharajadhiraj Maharao Sir Sarup Ram Singh Bahadur, G.C.I.E., K.C.S.I. Maharao of—
Date of birth :—27th Sept. 1888
Date of succession :—29th April '20
Area of State in square miles :—1,994
Population of State :—2,33,870
Revenue :—Rs. 11,48,771
Salute in guns : - 15

Tonk—H. H. Said-ud-Daula Wazir-ul-Mulk Nawab Hafiz Sir Mohammmad Sadat Ali Khan Bahadur Sowlat-i-Jung, G.C.I.E, Nawab of—
Date of birth :—13th February, 1879
Date of succession :—23rd June '30
Area of State in Sq. miles :—2,553
Population of State :—3,53,687
Revenue :—Rs. 19,30,000 B. C. nearly
Salute in guns :—17

Udaipur (Mewar)—Lt.-Col. H. H. Maharajadhiraja Maharana Shri Sir Bhopal Singhji Bahadur, G.C.S.I., Maharana of—
Date of birth :—22nd February 1884
Date of succession :—24th May '30
Area of State in square miles :—12,753
Population of State :—1,925,000
Revenue :—Rs. 80,00,000 nearly
Salute in guns :—19

Sikkim State

Sikkim—H. H. Maharaja Sir Tashi Namgyal, K.C.I.E., Maharaja of—
Date of birth—1893
Date of Succession :—5th Dec. '14
Area of State in Sq. miles :—2,818
Population of State :—81,721
Revenue :—Rs. 4,33,000 nearly
Salute in guns :—15

United Provinces States

Benares—H. H. Maharaja Vibhuti Narayan Singh Bahadur (minor), Maharaja of—
Date of birth :—5th November '27
Date of succession :—5th April, '39
Area of State in square miles :—875
Population of State :—451,327
Revenue :—Rs. 30.42,921 nearly
Salute in guns :—13 (Local 15)

Rampur—Captain H. H. Alijah Farzand-i-Dilpazir-i-Daulat-i-Inglishia Mukhlis-ud-Daula Nasir-ul-Mulk, Amir-ul-Umara, Nawab Sir Saiyid Muhammad Raza Ali Khan Bahadur Mustaid Jung, K.C.S.I., Nawab of—
Date of birth :—17th Nov. '06
Date of succession :—20th June '30
Area in Sq. miles :—892·54
Population :—4 64,919
Revenue :—Rs. 51,00,000 nearly
Salute in guns :—15

Tehri (**Garhwal**)—Lt. Colonel H. H. Maharaja Narendra Shah, K.C.S.I., of—
Date of birth :—3rd Aug. 1898
Date of succession :—25th April '13
Area in Sq. miles :—4,502
Population :—3,18,482
Revenue :—Rs. 18,30,000 nearly
Indian State Forces : Tehri H. Q. Infantry and Band—100
Tehri Pioneers Narendra—101
" Sappers and Miners—129
Salute in guns :—11

Western India States

Bhavnagar—Lt. H. H. Sir Krishnakumersinhji Bhavsinghji, K.C.S.I., Maharaja of—
Date of birth :—19th May '12
Date of succession :—18 July '19
Area in Square miles :—2,961
Population :—5,00,274
Revenue :—Rs. 1,09,68 620
Indian State Forces—Bhavnagar Lancers —270 ; Bhavnagar Infantry—219
Salute in guns :—13

Cutch—H. H. Maharajadhiraj Mirza Maharao Shri Sir Khengarji, Sawai Bahadur, G.C.S.I., G.C.I.E., Maharao of—
Date of birth :—23rd Aug. 1866
Date of succession —1st Jan. 1876
Area of State in square miles :—8,249.5
Population of State :—5,00,800
Revenue :—Rs. 31,00,000 nearly
Salute in guns :—17 Perm. 19 Local

Dhrangadhra—Major H. H. Maharaja Shri Ghanshyamsinhji Ajitsinhji, G.C.I.E., K.C.S.I., Maharaja of—
Date of birth :—31st May 1889
Date of succession :—February '11
Area of State in Sq. miles :—1,167
Population of State :—95,946
Revenue :—Rs. 25,00,000 nearly
Salute in guns :—13

Dhrol—H. H. Thakor Shaheb Shri Chandrasinhji Saheb, Thakor Saheb of—
Date of birth :—28th Aug. '12
Date of succession :—20th Oct. '39
Area in square miles :—282·7
Population :—27,639
Revenue :—Rs. 2 89,281
Salute in guns :—9

Gondal— H. H. Maharaja Shri Bhaga-

vatsinhji Sagramji G.C.S.I., G.C.I.E., Maharaja of—
Date of birth :—24th Oct. 1865
Date of succession :—14th Dec. 1869
Area in Sq. miles :—1,024
Population :—2,05,846
Revenue :—Rs. 50,00,000 nearly
Salute in guns :—11

Junagadh—Captain H. H. Nawab Sir Mahabatkhanji Rasulkhanji, K.C.S.I., G.C.I.E., Nawab of—
Date of birth :—2nd Aug. 1900
Date of succession :—22nd Jan. '11
Area in Sq. miles :—3,336·9
Population :—545,152
Revenue :—Rs. 1,00 00,000
Indian State Forces :—Junagadh Lancers —173 ; Junagadh Mahabatkhanji Infantry 201
Salute in guns :—15

Limbdi—Thakor Saheb Shri L. Chhatrasalji Digvijaysinhji, Thakore Saheb of—
Date of birth :—19th Feb. '40
Date of succession :—6th Jan. '41
Area of State in Sq. miles :—343.96 (exclusive of about 207 sq. miles in the Collectorate of the Ahmedabad).
Population of State :—44,000
Revenue :—Rs. 7,00,000 nearly
Salute in guns :—9

Morvi—H. H. Maharaja Shri Lakhdhirji Waghji, G.B.E., K.C.S.I., Maharaja of—
Date of birth :—26th Dec. 1876
Date of succession :—11th June '22
Area in sq. miles :- 822
Population :—1 13,023
Revenue :—Rs. 50 lacs nearly
Salute in guns :—11

Nawanagar—Lt. Col. H. H. Maharaja Jam Shri Sir Digvijaysinhji Ranjitsinhji Jadeja, G.C.I.E., K.C.S.I., A.D.C., Maharaja Jam Sahib of—
Date of birth :—1st Sept. 1895
Date of succession :—2nd April '33
Area in Sq. miles :—3,791
Population :—5,04 006
Revenue—Rs. 94,00,000 nearly
Salute in guns :—15

Palanpur—Lt.-Colonel H. H. Nawab Shri Taley Muhammad Khan Bahadur, G.C.I.E., K.C.V.O., Nawab Sahib of—
Date of birth :—7th July 1883
Date of succession :—28th Sept. '18
Area in Sq. miles :—1,774·64
Population :—3,15,855
Revenue :—Rs. 11,64,987
Salute in guns :—13

Palitana—H. H. Thakor Saheb Shri Bahadursinhji Mansinhji, K.C.I.E., K.C.S.I., Thakor Saheb of—
Date of birth :—3rd April 1900
Date of succession :—29th Aug. '05
Area in Sq. miles :—288
Population—62,150
Revenue :—Rs. 9,00,000 nearly
Salute in guns :—9

Porbandar—Captain H. H. Maharaja Shri Sir Natwarsinhji Bhavsinhji, K.C.S.I., Maharaja Rana Saheb of—
Date of birth—30 June '01
Date of succession :—10th Dec. '08
Area of State in Sq. miles :—642.25
Population of State :—1,46.648
Revenue :—Rs. 26,00,000 nearly
Salute in guns :—13

Radhanpur—H. H. Nawab Saheb Murtazakhan Jorawarkhan Babi Bahadur Nawab of—
Date of birth—10th Oct. 1899
Date of succession :—7th April '37
Area of State in sq. miles :—1,150
Population of State :—70,530
Revenue :—Rs, 8,00,000 to 10,00,000
Salute in guns :—11

Rajkot—H. H. Thakor Saheb Shri Pradumnasinhji, Thakor Saheb of—
Date of birth :—24th Feb. '13
Date of succession :—17th August, '40
Area in sq. miles—2824
Population :—1,03,033
Revenue :—Rs. 13,40,872 nearly
Salute in guns :—9

Wadhwan :—H. H. Thakore Saheb Shri Surendrasinhji, Thakore Saheb of—
Date of birth—4th January, '22
Date of succession—27th July '34
Area. 242.6 Sq. miles excluding the area in the British Indian District of Ahmedabad.
Population :—50,934
Revenue :—Rs. 6 Lacs.
Salute—Permanent 9 guns

Wankaner :—Captain H. H. Maharana Shri Sir Amarsinhji, K.C.S.I., K.C.I.E., Maharana Rajsaheb of—
Date of birth :—4th January 1879
Date of succession :—12th June 1881
Area in sq. miles :—417
Population :—55,024
Revenue :—Rs. 7,67,000
Salute in guns :—11

Indian States (without Salutes)

Baluchistan State

Las Bela :—Mir Ghulam Muhammed Khan, Jam of—
Date of birth—December 1895
Date of succession—March '21
Area in sq. miles—7,132
Population—50,696
Revenue—Rs. 3,78,000 nearly

Bihar & Orissa States

Athgarh :—Raja Sreekoran Radhanath

Bebarta Patnaik, Raja of—
Date of birth :—28th Nov. '09
Date of succession :—22nd June '18
Area in Sq. miles :—168
Population :—55,508
Revenue :—Rs. nearly 1,76,000

Athmalik :—Raja Kishor Chandra Deo
Date of birth :—10th November '04
Date of succession :—3rd November '18
Area in sq. miles :—730
Population :—59 749
Revenue :—Rs. 1,81,000 nearly

Bamra :—Raja Bhanuganga Tribhuban Deb, Raja of—
Date of birth—25th Feb. '14
Date of succession—1st January '20
Area in sq. miles—1 988
Population—1,34,721
Revenue :—Rs 5,81,000 nearly

Baramba :—Raja Sree Narayan Chandra Birbar Mangraj Mahapatra, Raja of—
Date of birth :—10th Jan. '14
Date of succession :—20th Aug. '22
Area in sq. miles :—142
Population :—52 924
Revenue :—Rs. 1,03,000 nearly

Baud :—Raja Narayan Prasad Deo of—
Date of birth :—14 March '04
Date of succession :—10th March '13
Area of State in square miles :—1,264
Population :—124,411
Revenue :—Rs. 2,72,000 nearly

Bonai :—Raja Indra Deo, Raja of—
Date of birth :—6th January 1884
Date of succession :—19th February '02
Area in sq. miles:—1,296
Population :—68,178
Revenue :—Rs. 2,36,000 nearly

Daspalla—Raja Kishore Chandra Deo
Date of birth :—16th April '08
Date of succession :—11th December '13
Area in sq. miles :—568
Population :—53,833
Revenue :—Rs. 1,41,993

Dhenkanal :—Raja Sankara Pratap Mahendra Bahadur, Raja of—
Date of birth :—5th Nov. '04
Date of succession :—16th Oct. '18
Area in sq. miles :—1,463
Population of State :—2 33,691
Revenue :—Rs. 5,13,000 nearly

Gangpur :—Raja Bhawani Shankar Sekhar
Date of birth :—14th May 1898
Date of succession :—10th June '17
Area in sq. miles :—2,492
Population :—3,09,271
Revenue :—Rs. 6,76,000 nearly.

Hindol :—Raja Bahadur Naba Kishor Chandra Singh Mardraj Jagadeb, M.R.A.S., F.R.S.A., Raja of—
Date of birth :—14th June 1891
Date of succession :—10th Feb. '06
Area in Sq. miles :—312
Population :—48,896
Revenue :— 1,45,000

Keonjhar—Raja Shri Balabhadra Narayan Bhanj Deo, Ruler of—
Date of birth :—26th December '05
Date of succession :—12th Aug. '26
Area in sq. miles :—3,217
Population :—529,786
Revenue :—Rs. 15·05 lakhs nearly

Khandpara—Raja Harihar Singh, Mardraj Bhramarbar Ray, Raja of—
Date of birth—26th August '14
Date of succession—26th December '22
Area in sq. miles—244
Population 64,289
Revenue :—Rs. 1,22,000

Kharsawan—Raja Sriram Chandra Singh
Date of birth :—4th July 1892
Date of succession :—6th February '02
Area in sq. miles :—157
Population :—44,805
Revenue :—Rs. 1,18,000 nearly

Narsinghpur :—Raja Ananta Narayan Mansingh Harichandan Mahapatra
Date of birth :—9th September '08
Date of succession :—5th July '21
Area in Sq. miles :—207
Population:—48,448
Revenue :—Rs. 1,29,000

Nayagarh :—Raja Krishna Chandra Singh Mandhata, Raja of—
Date of birth :—15th August, '11
Date of succession :—7th Dec. '18
Area in sq. miles :—552
Population :—1,61,409
Revenue :—Rs. 3,92,210/-

Nilgiri :—Raja Kishore Chandra Mardraj Harichandan, Raja of—
Date of birth :—2nd February '04
Date of succession :—6th July '13
Area in Sq. miles :—284
Population :—73,109
Revenue :—Rs. 2,14,589

Pal Lahara—Raja Muni Pal, Raja of—
Date of birth :—26th November '03
Date of succession :—18th April '13
Area of State in Sq. miles :—452
Population :—23,789
Revenue :—Nearly Rs. 75,000

Rairakhol—Raja Bir Chandra Jadumani
Date of birth :—1894
Date of succession :—3rd July '06
Area in square miles :—833
Population :—31,225
Revenue :—Rs. 75,000 nearly

Ranpur—Raja Birbar Krishna Chandra Mahapatra, Raja of—
Date of birth :—About 1887
Date of succession :—12th July 1899

Area in sq. miles :—203
Population :—41,282
Revenue :—Rs.65,000

Seraikella—Raja Aditya Pratap Singh Deo, Ruler of—
Date of birth :—30th July 1887
Date of succession :—9th Dec. '31
Area :—449 square miles
Population of State :—156,374
Revenue—Rs. 418,000 nearly

Talcher—Raja Kishore Chandra Birbar Harichandan, Raja of—
Date of birth :—9th June 1880
Date of succession :—18th December 1891
Area in square miles :—399
Population :—86,432
Revenue :- Rs. 8,97,668 gross

Maratha States—(Bombay Presy)

Akalkot—Meharban Shrimant Vijayasingh Fatehsingh, Raja Bhonsle, Raja of—
Date of birth :—13th Dec. '15
Date of succession :—4th April '23
Area in Sq. miles :—498
Population :—92,605
Revenue :—Rs. 7,58,000 nearly

Aundh—Meharban Bhavanrao alias Bala Sahib, Pant Pratinidhi of—
Date of birth :—24th Oct. 1868
Date of succession :—4th November '09
Area in square miles :—501
Population :—88,762
Revenue—Rs. 3,38.278-12-1

Phaltan—Major Raja Shrimant Malojirao Mudhojirao alias Nana Saheb Naik Nimbalkar, Raja of—
Date of birth :—11th September 1896
Date of succession :—17th October '16
Area in Sq. miles :—397
Population :—58,761
Revenue :—Rs. 8,56,000

Jath—Lt. Raja Shrimant Vijayasinghrao Ramrao Dafle, Raja of—
Date of birth :—21st July '09
Date of succession :—14th August '28
Area of State in Sq. miles :—981
Population :—91,099
Revenue :—Rs. 4,24,000

Jamkhandi—Meherban Shankarrao Parashramrao alias Appasaheb Patwardhan, Raja Saheb of—
Date of birth :—5th Nov. '06
Date of succession :—25th Feb. '24
Area in Sq. miles—524
Population—1,14,282
Revenue :—Rs. 10,06,715

Kurundwad (Senior)—Meherban Chintamanrao Bhalchandrarao alias Balasaheb Patwardhan, Chief—
Date of birth :—13th Feb. '21
Date of succession—10th September '27
Area in sq. miles—182·5
Population :—88,760
Revenue :—Rs. 3,76,000 nearly

Kurundwad (Jr)—Meherban Madhavrao Ganpatro alias Bhausaheb Patwardhan, Chief of—
Date of birth :—6th. December 1875
Date of succession :—29th July 1899
Area in Sq. miles :—114
Population :—34,288
Revenue :—Rs. 2,88,000 nearly

Miraj (Sr)—Narayanrao Gangadharrao alias Tatyasaheb Patwardhan, Chief of—
Date of birth :—6th Sept. 1898
Date of succession :—11th Dec. '39
Area in sq. miles :—342
Population :—93,938
Revenue :—Rs. 4,41,000 nearly

Miraj (Jr)—Meherban Sir Madhavrao Harihar alias Baba Saheb Patwardhan, K.C.I.E., Raja of—
Date of birth :—4th March 1889
Date of succession :—16th Dec. 1899
Area in sq. miles :—196½
Population :—40,686
Revenue :—Rs. 3,68,515 nearly

Ramdurg—Meherban Ramrao Venkatrao alias Rao Saheb Bhave, Chief of—
Date of birth :—16th Sept. 1896
Date of succession :—30th April '07
Area in square miles :—169
Population :—33,997
Revenue :—Rs 2,69,000 nearly

Savanur—Captain Meherban Abdul Majid Khan, Diler Jang Bahadur, Nawab of—
Date of Birth—7th October, 1890
Date of succession—30th January 1893
Area in sq. miles—70
Population :—16,830
Revenue :—Rs. 1,69,000 nearly

Mahi-Kantha States

Ghodasar—Thakor Shri Fatehsinhji Ratansinji Dabhi Thakor Saheb of—
Date of birth :—7th August '09
Date of succession : 31st May '30
Area in square miles :—16
Population—6,708
Revenue—Rs. 51,000

Ilol Thakor Shivsinhji, Thakor of—
Date of birth :—31st Dec. '10
Date of succession :—18th Oct. '27
Area in sqr. miles :—19
Population :—3 349
Revenue :—Rs. 41,000 nearly

Katosan—Thakor Takhatsinhji Karansinhji, Thakor of—
Date of birth :—9th Dec. 1870
Date of succession :—Januray 1901
Area in Sq. miles :—10
Population of State :—4,818

Revenue :—Rs. 51,000 nearly

Khadal—Sardar Shri Fatehsinhji Raisinhji, Thakor Shri of—
Date of birth :—1899
Date of succession :—7th February '12
Area in square miles :—8
Population of State :—2,825
Revenue : Rs. 35,000 nearly

Malpur—Raolji Shri Gambhirsinhji Himatsinhji,
Date of birth :—27th Oct. '14
Date of succession :—23rd June '23
Area in Sq. miles :—97
Population :—16,582
Revenue :—Rs. 1,10,000 approx.

Pethapur—Thakor Fatehsinhji Gambhirsinhji, Thakor of—
Date of birth :—3rd Oct. 1895
Date of succession :— 1896
Area in Sq. miles :—11
Population :—3,938
Revenue :—Rs. 34,000 (nearly)

Varsoda—Thakor Joravarsinhji of—
Date of birth :—17th April '14
Date of succession :—18th July '19
Area in Sq. miles :—11
Population :—3,424
Revenue :—Rs. 33,000 nearly

Vijayanagar—Rao Shri Hamir-sinhiji,
Date of birth :—3rd January '04
Date of succession :—27th June '16
Area in Sq. miles :—135
Population—12,000 (approx)
Revenue—Rs. 1,00,000 nearly

Rewa Kantha States

Bhadarwa—Shrimant Thakur Saheb Shree Natvarsinghji Ranjitsinhji, Thakor of—
Date of birth :—19th November 1903
Date of succession :—26th April 1935
Area in sq. miles. :—27 (excluding several Wanta villages under Baroda State)
Population :—13,520.
Revenue :—Rs. 1,14,000 nearly

Jambugodha—Meherban Rana Shri Ranjitsinhji Gambhirsinhji, Thakore Saheb of—Parmar Rajput. He enjoys full Civil and Criminal powers
Date of birth :—4th January 1892
Date of succession :—27th September 1917
Area :—143 square miles
Population :—11,385
Revenue :—Rs. 142,000/-

Kadana—Rana Shri Chhatrasalji, Thakor of,
Date of birth :—28th January 1879
Date of succession :—12th April 1889
Area in sq. miles :—130
Population :—15,370
Revenue :—Rs, 1,32,000 nearly

Nasvadi—Thakor Ranjitsinhji, Thakor of—
Date of birth :—24th March '05
Date of succession :—13th Sept. '27
Area in sq. miles :—1950
Population :—4,197
Revenue :—Rs, 33,000 nearly

Palasni—Thakor Indarsinhji, Thakor of—
Date of birth :—16th Aug. 1885
Date of succession :—30th May '07
Area in sq. miles :—12
Population :—1,766
Revenue :—Rs. 22,000 nearly

Sihora—Thakor Mansinhjee Karansinhjee,
Date of birth :—4th November '07
Date of succession :—13th June '28
Area in sq. miles :—19 (approx.)
Population :—5300
Revenue :—Rs. 36,000 nearly

Uchad—Thakor Mohomadmia Jitabawa,
Date of birth :—15th October 1895
Date of succession :—24th June '15
Area of State in sq. miles :—8 50
Population of State :—2 330
Reven e :—Rs. 41,000 nearly

Umetha—Thakor Ramsinhji Raisinhji,
Date of birth :—19th August 1894
Date of succession :—1st July '22
Area in sq. miles :—24
Population :—5,355
Revenue :—Rs. 73,000 nearly

Central India States

Alipura—Rao Harpal Singh, Rao of—
Date of birth :—12th Aug. 1882
Date of succession :—26th March '22
Area in sq. miles :—73
Population :—14,580
Revenue :—Rs. 70,000 nearly

Bakhtgarh—Thakur Rai Singh, Thakur of
Date of birth :—3rd October 1889
Date of succession :—30th May '12
Area in sq. miles :—66
Population :—10,414
Revenue :—Rs. 74,000 nearly

Garauli—Diwan Bahadur Chandrabhan Singh, chief of—
Date of birth :—2nd April 1883
Date of succession :—20th Dec. 1883
Area in sq. miles :—31
Population :—4,965
Revenue :—Rs. 36,000 nearly

Jobat—Rana Bhimsing, Rana of—
Date of birth :—10th November '15
Date of succession :—20th May '17
Date of getting Ruling Powers :—14th March '36
Area in sq. miles :—131.20
Population :—20,945
Revenue :—Rs. 81,550/-

Kachhi-Baroda—Maharaj Benimadho Singh
Date of birth :—4th October '04
Date of succession :—13th June '06
Area in sq. miles :—34.53

Population :—5000
Revenue :—Rs. 71000/-

Kathiwara—Rana Thakur Sahib Onkarsinhji, Rana of—
Date of birth—5th December 1891
Date of succession—8th June, '03
Area in sq. miles—70
Population :—6096
Revenue :—Rs. 44,880

Kothi—Raja Bahadur Sitaraman Pratap Bahadur Singh, Raja of—
Date of birth—26th July 1892
Date of succession—8th August '14
Area—169 sq. miles
Population—20,037
Revenue—Rs. 70,000 nearly

Kurwai—Nawab Sarwar Ali Khan of—
Date of birth—1st December '01
Date of succession—2nd October '06
Area in sq. miles—142
Population—19,851
Revenue—Rs. 2,64,000 nearly

Mota Barkhera—Bhumia Nain Singh of—
Date of birth—7th November '07
Date of succession—4th June '12
Area in sq. miles—39
Population—4,782
Revenue—Rs. 53,000 nearly

Multhan—Dharmalankar, Dharm-bhushan, Dharm-Divaker, Shreeman Maharaj Bharat Sinhji Sahib, Chief of—
Date of birth—1893
Date of succession—26th August '01
Area in sq. miles—100
Population—11,804
Revenue—Over Rs. 1,00,000

Nimkhera—Bhumia Ganga Singh, Bhumia
Date of birth—'11
Date of succession—27th March '22
Area in sq. miles—90
Population—5,358
Revenue—Rs. 62,000 nearly

Paldeo—Chaubey Shiva Prasad, Jagirdar of
Date of birth—1st March '08
Date of succession—3rd Oct. '23
Area in sq. miles—53.14
Population—9,038
Revenue—Rs, 50,000 nearly

Piploda—Rawat Mangal Singh, Rawat of
Date of birth—7th September 1893
Date of succession—5th Nov. '19
Area in sq.miles—35
Population—9,766
Revenue—Rs. 1.14,000 nearly

Sarila—Raja Mahipal Singh, Raja of—
Date of succession—11th Sep. 1898
Area in sq, miles—35,28
Population :—6,081
Revenue—Rs. 1,00,000 nearly

Sarwan—Thakur Mahendra Singh
Date of birth—6th November '09
Date of succession—23rd April '21
Area in sq. miles—71
Population—7,199
Revenue—Rs. 60,000 nearly

Sohawal—Raja Bhagwat Raj Bahadur Singh, C.I.E., Raja of—
Date of birth—7th August 1878
Date of succession—23rd Nov. 1899
Area in sq. miles—213
Population—38,078
Revenue—Rs. 1,04,000 nearly

Tori Fatehpur—Dewan Raghuraj Singh, Jagirdar of—
Date of birth—28.1.1895
Date of succession—7.4.'41
Area in sq. miles—36
Population—6,269
Revenue—Rs. 31,000 nearly

Central Provinces States

Bastar—Maharaja Pravir Chandra Deo
Date of birth :—25th June 1929
Date of succession :—28th Feb. '36
Area of State in Sq. miles :—13,725
Population :—6 34,915
Revenue :—Rs. 13,20,699

Chhuikhadan—Mahant Bhudhar Kishore Das of—
Date of birth :—April 1891
Date of succession :—30th Sept. '03
Area of State in Sq. miles :—154
Population of State :—26,141
Revenue—Rs. 1,22,000

Jashpur—Raja Bijay Bhushan Singh Deo
Date of birth :—11th Jan. '26
Date of succession :—8th Feb. '26
Area of State in Sq. miles :—1,923
Population of State :—2,23,632
Revenue :—Rs. :—3,62.342

Kanker—Maharajadhiraj Bhanupratap Deo, Chief of—
Date of birth :—17th September '22
Date of succession :—8th Jan. '25
Area of State in sq. miles :—1,429
Population :—1,22,928
Revenue—3,88,000

Kawardha—Thakur Dharmraj Singh Chief of—
Date of birth: :—18th August '10
Date of succession :—4th Feb. '20
Area in sq. miles :—805
Population :—72820
Revenue :—Rs. 2,93,175 nearly

Khairagarh—Raja Birendra Bahadur Singh, Raja of—
Date of birth :—9th November '14
Date of succession :—22nd October '18
Area in sq. miles :—931
Population :—157,400
Revenue :—Rs. 5,80,000 nearly

Korea—Raja Ramanuj Pratap Singh Deo, Raja of—

Date of birth :—8th December '31
Date of succession —November '09
Area in sq. miles—1,647
Population—90,500
Revenue—Rs. 7,00,199

Makrai—Raja Drigpal Shah Hathiya Rai of
Date of birth—24th September '04
Date of succession—30th October '18
Area in sq. miles—155
Population—12,803
Revenue—Rs. 2,01,000 nearly

Nandgaon—Mahant Sarveshwar Das, of—
Date of birth—30th March '06
Date of succession—24th June '13
Area in sq. miles—871
Population—1,47,919
Revenue—Rs. 7,91,000

Raigarh—Raja Chakradhar Singh, Raja of
Date of birth:—19th August '05
Date of succession :—23rd August '24
Area in Sq miles :—1486
Population—2,41,634
Revenue—Rs. 6,46,000 nearly

Sakti—Raja Liladhar Singh, Raja of—
Date of birth—3rd Feb. 1892
Date of succession—4th July '14
Area in sq miles—138
Population—41,595
Revenue—Rs. 1,20,000 nearly

Sarangarh—Raja Bahadur Jawahir Singh,
Date of birth—3rd Dec. 1888
Date of succession—5th Aug. 1890
Area in sq. miles—540
Population—1,17,781
Revenue—Rs. 3.14 000 nearly

Surguja—Maharaja Ramanuj Saran Singh Deo C.B.E., Maharaja of—
Date of birth—4th Nov. 1895
Date of succession—31st Dec. '17
Area in sq. miles—6,055
Population—5,51,307
Revenue—Rs. 7,58,500 nearly

Udaipur—Raja Chandra Chur Prasad Singh Deo, Raja of—
Date of birth—5th June '23
Date of succession—8th Dec. '27
Area in sq. miles—1,052
Population—71,124
Revenue—Rs. 3,12,000

Madras State

Sandur—Raja Srimant Yeshwantha Rao Anna Saheb, Rao Sahib, Hindu Rao Ghorapade, Mamlukatmadar Senapati, Raja of—
Date of birth—15th November '08
Date of succession—5th May '28
Area in sq. miles—167
Population—11,684
Revenue—Rs. 2,03,000 nearly

Punjab States

Dujana—Jalal-ud-Daula Nawab Mohammad Iqtidar Ali Khan, Bahadur, Mustaqil-i-Jan, Nawab of—
Date of birth—20th Nov. '12
Date of succession—21st July '25
Area in sq. miles—100
Population—25,833
Revenue—Rs. 1,65,000 nearly

Kalsia—Raja Ravi Sher Singh Sahib Bahadur, Raja Sahib, of—
Date of birth—30th October '02
Date of succession—25th July '08
Date of investiture with full ruling powers : } 6th April '22
Area in sq. miles—192
Population -59848
Revenue—Nearly Rs. 3,50,000

Pataudi—Nawab Muhammad Iftikar Ali Khan, Bahadur, Nawab of—
Date of birth—17th March '10
Date of succession—30th Nov. '17
Area in sq. miles—53
Population—18,097
Revenue—Rs, 1,40,000 nearly

Simla Hill States

Baghal—Raja Surendra Singh, Raja of—
Date of birth—14th March '09
Date of succession—13th Oct. '22
Area in sq. miles—124
Population—25,099
Revenue—Rs. 1,00,000 nearly

Baghat—Raja Durga Singh, Raja of—
Date of birth—15th Sept. '01
Date of succession—30th Dec. 1911
Area in sq. miles—36
Population—9,595
Revenue—Rs. 1,10,000 nearly

Bhajji—Rana Birpal, Rana of—
Date of birth—19th April '06
Date of succession—9th May '13
Area in sq. miles—96
Population—14,263
Revenue—Rs. 99,000 nearly

Jubbal—Rana Sir Bhagat Chandra Bahadur, K.C.S.I., Ruler of—
Date of birth—12th Oct. 1888
Date of succession—29th April '10
Area in sq. miles—288
Population—28,500
Revenue—Rs. 3,50,000 nearly

Keonthal—Raja Hemendar Sen, Raja of—
Date of birth—21st January '05
Date of succession—2nd Feb. '16
Area in sq. miles—116
Population—25,599
Revenue—Rs. 1,30,000 nearly

Kumharsain—Rana Vidyadhar Singh,
Date of birth—1895
Date of succession—24th August '14
Area in sq. miles 97
Population—12 227
Revenue—Rs. 75,000 nearly

Nalagarh—Raja Jogindra Singh, Raja of—
Date of birth—1870
Date of succession—18th Sept, '11
Area in sq. miles—256
Population—52 737
Revenue—Rs. 2,71,000 nearly

Tiroch—Thakur Surat Singh, of—
Date of birth—4th July 1887
Date of succession—14th July '02
Area in sq. miles—75
Population—4,219
Revenue—Rs, 1,30,000 nearly

Western India States

Bajana—Malek Shri Kamalkhan Jivankhan, Chief of—
Date of birth :—6th December '07
Date of succession—2nd Feb. '20
Area in sq. miles—'83,12
Population—14017
Revenue—Rs. 1,82,424 average

Bantwa-Manavadar—Babi Ghulam Moyuddinkhanji Fatehdinkhanji, Chief of—
Date of birth—22nd December '11
Date of succession—October '18
Area in sq. miles—221'8
Population—14,984
Revenue—Rs. 5,43,000 nearly

Chuda—Thakor Shri Bahadursinhji Joravarsinhji, Thakur of—
Date of birth—23rd April '09
Date of succession—20th January '21
Area in sq. miles—78'2
Population—11,833
Revenue—Rs. 2,11 000 nearly

Jasdan—Darbar Shree Ala Khachar, Chief of—
Date of birth—4th November '05
Date of succession—11th June '19
Area in sq. miles—296
Population—36632
Revenue—Rs. 6,00,000 nearly

Kotda-Sangani—Thakore Shri Pradyumnasinhji
Date of birth—5th December '20
Date of succession—23-2-30
Date of Installation—10-12-40
Area in sq. miles—90
Population—12165
Revenue—Rs. 1,50,000 nearly

Lakhtar—Thakore Saheb Shri Balavirsinhji, Karansinhji, Thakor Saheb of—
Date of birth—11th January 1881
Date of succession—8th August '24
Area in sq. miles—247,438
Population—21,·23
Revenue—Rs. 4,49,000

Lathi—Thakore Saheb Shri Pralhadsinhji, Thakor of—
Date of birth—31st March '12
Date of succession—14th October '18
Area in sq. miles—41'8
Population—8, 35
Revenue—Rs. 1,83,000

Malia—Thakor Shri Raisinhji Modji, of—
Date of birth—14th February 1808
Date of succession—20th Oct. '07
Area in sq. miles—103
Population—12,660
Revenue—Rs, 3,02,000

Muli—Thakor Shri Harichandrasinhji, of—
Date of birth—10th July 1899
Date of succession—3rd December '05
Area in sq miles—133.2
Population—16,390
Revenue—Rs. 1,57,000 nearly

Patdi—Desai Shri Raghuvirsinhji, of
Date of birth—8th Jan. '26
Date of succession—25th Oct. '28
Area in sq. miles—39.4
Population—2,508
Revenue- Rs. 1,14,000

Sayla—Thakore Saheb Shri Madarsinhji, Vakhatsinhji, Takore Saheb of—
Date of birth—28th May 1868
Date of succession—25th Jan. '24
Area in sq. miles—222.1
Population—13,351
Revenue—Rs. 2,54,000

Thana Devli—Darbar Shri Vala Amra Laxman, Chief of—
Date of birth—28th Nov. 1895
Date of succession—12th Oct. '22
Area in sq. miles—94'21
Population—11,348
Revenue—Rs. 3,00,000 nearly

Tharad—Waghela Bhumsinhji Dolatsinhji Thakore of—
Date of birth—28th Jan. 1900
Date of succession—19th Feb. '21
Area in sq. miles—1,263½
Population—52,839
Revenue—Rs. 99.000 nearly

Vadia—Darbar Shree Suragwala Saheb Chief of—
Date of birth—15th March '05
Date of succession—7th Sept. '30
Area in sq. miles—90
Population—137·9
Revenue—Rs. about 2 lacs

Zainabad—Malek Shri Aziz Mahomed Khanji Zainkhanji. Talukdar of—
Date of birth—21st June 1917
Date of succession—26th January 1923
Area in sq. miles—30
Population—3,456
Revenue—Rs. 1,200,000 nearly

Chronicle of Events

January 1941

The arrest of Maulana Abul Kalam Azad, the Congress President, under the Defence of India Rules created a good deal of sensation all throughout the country. He was sentenced to 18 months' simple imprisonment.

The National Institute of Sciences of India held its annual conference at Benares. Many distinguished scientists presided over the various sections and delivered illuminating addresses.

Mr. V. D. Savarkar, President of the Hindu Mahasabha gave his impressions and interpretation of the resolutions of the Madura session of Hindu Sabha.

Mr. M. N. Roy took a leading part in the furtherance of an Anti-Fascist organization whose chief aim was the defeat of Nazism and the rapid development of India's resources.

Trawlers of the Bassett class were being built in India for allocation by the Viceroy from his War Purposes Fund.

Congress M.L.A.'s in Bengal who repudiated Mr. Sarat Chandra Bose's leadership formed a separate group inside the Legislature and elected Mr. Kiran Sankar Roy to lead them in the Assembly and Mr. Kamini Kumar Dutt to lead them in the Council.

The Bengal Government stated in reference to a common rumour and accusation that it had no intention of reducing the number of secondary schools.

The Satyagraha campaign continued in full swing.

Sir Sikandar Hyat Khan, the Punjab Premier returned from Egypt and gave his impressions of conditions in the British and Indian units in North Africa.

The Standing Committee of the Chamber of Princes met officials of the Political Department of the Government of India.

Sir Tej Bahadur Sapru in the 'Twentieth Century' renewed his appeal for a settlement between political parties in India and with the British Government. Sir Sikander Hyat Khan also made an appeal to Congress for a six months' political holiday.

At a meeting of Sikh leaders at Lahore, it was decided to form a Khalsa League for the defence of India. One of its objects was to maintain the Sikh proportion in India's armed strength.

The Delhi Radio station introduced into its programme a daily talk to Indian soldiers serving in the Middle East.

The new Commander-in-Chief, General Sir Claude Auchinleck, arrived in India.

Congress Socialist leaders disapproved of the Satyagraha campaign.

Measures of labour reform were suggested at a conference of representatives from British India, the States and the Government of India.

Sj. Subhas Chandra Bose disappeared from his house in Calcutta.

1st. His Excellency the Marquess of Linlithgow sent a message of greetings and good wishes for 1941 to boyscouts of India.

Mr. V. D. Savarkar, President of the Hindu Mahasabha, in an interview in Madras, regarding his impressions of the Mahasabha session at Madura, said: "Not only in the Punjab, Maharastra or Bihar but in the province of Madras also, the Hindus have awakened to the consciousness of their own power and the necessity of guarding their own interests. The Congress is now bound to be, day by day, more and more afraid of sacrificing Hindu interests".

2nd. Mr. G. S. Bajpai, Education Member, Government of India, in his Presidential address at the Indian Statistical Conference held at Benares observed: "The collection of statistics would be attended with far greater usefulness if its purpose was proclaimed and its process made intelligible to the ordinary citizen."

Sir Ardeshir Dalal, presiding at the Indian Science Congress at Benares, observed: "It is not man power that counts in the highly mechanized warfare of the present day, but planes, tanks, guns, ships and the factories, plants and workshops behind them. The lesson for India is plain and she can only neglect it at her peril. It is no longer the question of a balanced economy or of mere material progress. It is necessary for India's very existence that she should be highly industrialized.

Mr. M. N. Roy, leader of the Radical Democratic Party, made an appeal in Calcutta to all progressive forces to rally round the banner of the Radical Democratic Party, whose "entire energy, for the moment, will be applied to the task of mobilizing the Indian masses in the struggle against the Fascist menace."

Sir R. N. Chopra, Director, School of Tropical Medicine, at the annual meeting of the National Institute of Sciences of India, held at Benares, made the suggestion that a Federal Ministry of Public Health should be established in India. He also made an appeal for more funds and patronage for scientific and industrial research.

Maulana Abul Kalam Azad, the Congress President, observed at New Delhi: "The Congress will always welcome Mr. Subhas Chandra Bose to come into the Congress fold provided he regrets his past activities."

3rd. Maulana Abul Kalam Azad, the Congress President, was arrested at the Allahabad railway station, while he was on his way from Delhi to Calcutta.

Presidential addresses of several sections of the Indian Science Congress which opened at Benares were delivered.—Sir Maurice Hallett, Governor of U. P. opened the session.

In the Geology section, Dr. M. R. Sahani referring to the constant changes on the earth wrought by geological forces, pointed out that in the warring world of today, continents which aggressors sought to possess are "in the infinitude of time, like the patterns of a cloud—an illusion and a chimera."

According to a message received from Sir Sikandar Hayat Khan, (Visiting the Indian units in the Sudan) the health, discipline and spirits of the Indian troops in Egypt were admirable.

Sir Sarvapalli Radha Krishnan, inaugurating the first All-India Pharmaceutical Conference at the Benares Hindu University, referred to the phase of industrial renaissance through which they were passing and pleaded that attempts should be made to convert their raw materials into manufactured drugs in their own country.

4th. His Highness the Maharaja of Kapurthala broadcast a message to his co-religionists on the occasion of the birthday anniversary of Guru Govind Singh in Calcutta.

In New Delhi, an order under section 144 Cr. P. C. was promulgated by the District Magistrate, prohibiting for two months the carrying of lathis and other weapons in public places as a precautionary measure in connexion with the Id and Muhurrum festivals.

Mr. M. N. Roy envisaged the formation of an Indo-British Anti-Fascist Labour front, in a statement he issued from Calcutta on the organization of the National Democratic Union and preparations for an All-India Convention.

The Government of Orissa decided to form a small Advisory Committee to advise the Director of Public Instruction on all matters connected with the education of Mohamedans.

5th. Mr. V. D. Savarkar, President of the Hindu Mahasabha issued a statement from Bombay, containing the correct interpretation of the two main resolutions passed by the Hindu Mahasabha at Madura on the subjects of "war situation" and the "immediate programme" of the Mahasabha.

At a meeting of teachers and guardians held in Calcutta, resolutions urging the withdrawal of the Secondary Education Bill and pledging support to the "Bengal Education Council" were passed.

Mr. M. N. Roy, addressing an Anti-Fascist Labour rally in Calcutta, declared : "The object of the campaign opened by this rally is to make the Indian workers conscious of their grave responsibility, so that they may discharge the role creditably, and having done that win for themselves as well as for India as a whole "place of honour as a free and powerful nation".

Mr. Walchand Hirachand, issued a statement from Calcutta in connection with the communique of the Government of India dealing with the schemes for the manufacture of aircraft and automobiles as well as for ship building. Mr. Walchand who was connected with all the three projects, observed that he wished the Government took as much pains to assist and encourage schemes for establishing vital industries in India as they were taking in other directions.

6th. The Constitution of the Bombay Provincial Congress Committee was suspended and a state of emergency was declared at a meeting of the provincial committee held in Bombay.—The Committee also authorized Dr. D. T. Anklesaria, its President, to nominate his successor before offering Satyagraha.

Several Satyagrahis were arrested in various provinces.

Dr. Radha Kumud Mookherji, addressing a public meeting convened by the various Hindu, Moslem, Parsi and other student bodies in Bombay, made an appeal to "build up India in the light of realities and existing problems and not mere slogans, catchwords and fancies."

Khwaja Sir Nazimuddin, Home Minister of Bengal, in an address at a meeting at Dacca, declared : "I should like Mr. Gandhi once again to consider the proposal of Mr. Jinnah and the Viceroy. That appears to me to be the only possible solution of the present impasse . ...Let us postpone our demands about the future Constitution of India till the termination of the war. Let the Congress and the Moslem League agree to join the Viceroy's expanded Executive Council ; let there be a Coalition Government in every province"

The Calcutta Radical Democratic Party decided to hold a Provincial Conference on January 18 and 19.

Mr. Edward Thompson wrote a letter to the "*Times*" stating, "I believe that Congress leaders could be persuaded to return to office even now and waive their election right and accept Moslem Leaguers into their Cabinets which of course should be greatly enlarged. That is, India would have National Government for the war period."

7th. In a Bengal Press Note, the allegation that the Government of Bengal plan to reduce the number of high schools in the Province was denied.—The Government proposed under the Secondary Education Bill to set up a board representative of varied educational interests and experience and to entrust to this board the responsibility of devising plans for future development.

Four sections of the Indian Science Congress, mamely the Psychology and Educational Science, Engineering, Geography and Geology, and Chemistry met at Benares.

His Holiness Sirdar Syedna Tahar Saifudin Saheb Bahadur, High Pontiff of the Dawoodi Bohra community, addressing the students of the Anjuman Industrial school in Madras, observed: "The advancement of Islam depends on the strict observance of its fundamentals and therefore every young Muslim should adhere to them and do everything to put them into practice."

A Press Note was issued from New Delhi stating: "Trawlers of the Bassett class costing about Rs. 7 lakhs each and fitted for mine-sweeping and anti-submarine work, of which the first three will be named "Travancore", "Baroda" and "Hyderabad" and armoured "Carriers" which are now being built in India at a cost of about Rs. 10,000 each are the objects chosen by H. E. the Viceroy for the allocation of contributions which have been made to his War Purpose Fund for the Defence of India."

8th. Maulana Abul Kalam Azad, the Congress President, was sentenced by the

City Magistrate, Allahabad, to 18 months' simple imprisonment under rule 38 (5) of the Defence of India Act.—Maulana Azad was charged with having delivered a prejudicial speech at Allahabad on Dec. 13.

Mr. P. B. Gole, a former Minister of the Central Provinces and President, Akola Town Congress Committee, was arrested and sentenced to one year's simple imprisonment under the Defence of India Rules.

Lala Shamlal, M.L.A. (Central) was arrested while addressing a meeting at Hissar.

At a meeting of the Export Advisory Council in Calcutta, a proposal to send trade delegations to various countries with which it was possible to enter into trade negotiation or to expand existing trade, was one of the subjects considered. Sir A. Ramaswamy Mudaliar, Commerce Member, Government of India, presided.

The Hon. Sir A. P. Patro, in a statement from Madras, said: "The primary duty of all sections of people in India is to help the war effort and win the present war before constitutional problems relating to India are pressed forward. To crush the enemy at the door would prepare the way for freedom".

In the Assam Legislative Council, the President, Rai Bahadur Heramba Prasad Barua modified his ruling regarding Tenancy Bills and allowed the Government to proceed with the Gaalpara and Sylhet Tenancy (Amendment) Bills 1939. Sir Muhammad Saadulla, the Premier had made representations regarding the delay which had taken place.

The seven day session of the Indian Science Congress came to a close at Benares with the conclusion of the sectional meetings.

9th. The Working Committee of the Bengal Provincial Hindu Mahasabha met in Calcutta under the presidentship of Sir Manmathanath Mukherji and considered among others the resolutions passed by the All-India Hindu Mahasabha at Madura and census operations in the province.

The Southern India Chamber of Commerce sent a communication to the Government of India urging them to take early steps to apply in all provinces the maximum limit of Rs. 50/- prescribed in respect of taxes on professions, trades and callings, by an amendment of the Government of India Act.

Mr. Sri Prakasa, M.L.A. (Central) President of the U. P. Congress Committee, was arrested under the Defence of India Rules at Benares.

Mahatma Gandhi, in the course of a letter to a prominent member of the Working Committee of the All-India Forward Bloc, said that individual civil disobedience movement had undoubtedly been on the issue of freedom of speech, but at the end of every issue there was the issue of independence of India.

10th. Mr. M. A. Jinnah, President of the All-India Moslem League, speaking at the annual meeting of the Moslem Educational Service League in Bombay, expressed the view that India would be able to lay down a "Monroe doctrine" for the country once the Hindus and Moslems made up their differences and were settled in their respective homelands.

The decision of the Government of India to constitute an Industrial Research Utilization Committee, was made known at the meeting of the Board of Scientific and Industrial Research held in Calcutta. Sir A. Ramaswamy Mudaliar, Commerce Member, Government of India, presiding.

Sir Tej Bahadur Sapru, in an article in the "Twentieth Century" under the caption "The need of the Hour", observed: "If India is to be a full-fledged Dominion after the war, why hesitate to say so, and why not do something now as an earnest of the things to come—even though it may not be perfect in every respect ?"

11th. The monthly statement of the Central Government's receipts and disbursements published in a revised form, disclosed a decline in revenues of nearly Rs. 5 crores till the end of November, 1940 over previous year's figures.

It was stated in New Delhi that portions of a Defence Department scheme, approved by the Chatfield Committee, for the expansion and modernization of the ordnance factories at a cost of some Rs. 4 crores were about to come into production.

The Government of India Labour Department's scheme for the training of technical personnel to man the expanding war industries met with satisfactory response in New Delhi.

General Molesworth in a broadcast message from New Delhi stressed the supreme importance of modern equipment and training as against more numbers.

Mr. Sri Prakasa, M.L.A. (Central) acting President of the U. P. Congress Committee was sentenced to one year's simple imprisonment.

Mahatma Gandhi sent a message on "Independence Day" from Wardhaganj, stating, "There is to be no Civil Disobedience that day. For we must not invite disturbance of our meetings, processions & Prabhat Pheris on that day (January 26)."

12th. Dr. Shyama Prasad Mukherjee, Working President of the All-India Hindu Mahasabha, presiding at a meeting in Calcutta, made an appeal for unity and solidarity among Hindus in order to defend their rights and interests.

Mr. M. N. Roy, addressing an anti-Fascist labour rally at Jamshedpur, said: "We shall be false to the internationalist ideals of the labour movement, if we fail to extend our helping hand to our British comrades in this moment of great trial."

Acharya Kripalani, General Secretary of the Indian National Congress, issued a circular to all provincial Congress Committees in the course of which he said that the celebration of "Independence Day" on January 26 had a "special significance."

Over 1,000 copies of geography books of the Allahabad district containing a map of Allahabad district (Urdu and Hindi editions) and over 800 wall maps of the United Provinces, were removed from a local press in pursuance, it was believed, of a general order issued some time ago under the Defence of India Rules banning the sale of maps of a certain size.

Mr. J. B. Kripalani, analysing the working of the Defence of India Rules in the various provinces, wrote among other things, "The Government of India and the Provincial Governments in their handling of the present satyagraha movement seem to have lost hold on reason and reality. There is some kind of imperial logic behind the rejection of Congress demand for a clarification of war aims and the refusal of a national Government. Such things have been done in the past by short-sighted imperialism, averse to parting with power. But what passes all comprehension is the way of dealing with the present movement."

13th. Sir P. C. Roy presiding over the Rural Welfare session of the Social Service Conference in Calcutta, emphasized the part that enlightened and well-to-do city-dwellers could play in the work of rural reconstruction.

Dr. Shyama Prasad Mukherjee was elected President of the All-India Hindu Youth Sabha for the year 1941.

Sir Roger Lumley, Governor of Bombay, made a survey of the voluntary war effort of the Bombay Presidency, addressing the Annual Dinner of the Rotary Club of Bombay.

The hearing of the case against Sj. Subhas Chandra Bose (in Calcutta) under the Defence of India Rules was further postponed by the Additional Chief Magistrate, Calcutta, till January 27 in view of Sj. Bose's inability to attend the Court owing to illness.

Sir Sikander Hyat Khan, Premier of the Punjab, giving impressions of his visit to the Middle East War front at a gathering at Lahore, said that the Indian troops there had done remarkably well.

14th. The Government of India's main conclusion on the railway accident at Bihta on July 17, 1937, was embodied in a letter, released for publication, to the General Manager of the East Indian Railway. It was to the effect: "The evidence now available still leaves some points obscure, but it points strongly to the conclusion that the accident resulted from a combination of three factors...engine, track and speed."

A resolution urging the Government of Bengal to withdraw the Finance (Sales Tax) Bill, pending before the Legislature, was adopted at a conference of dealers, indigenous manufacturers and consumers in Calcutta. Mr. Nalini Ranjan Sarkar presiding.

Sir Sikander Hyat Khan, the Punjab Premier, in an interview at Lahore, expressed the opinion that the responsibility for the deadlock in the country was that of the Congress, and said that he would not hesitate to make an appeal to the British Government to make a move for ending the deadlock, if there was a favourable response to his appeal to the Congress.

15th. The annual report on the working of the Co-operative Societies in Bengal for the year ended June, 30, 1939, stated that the Government of Bengal's decision fully to support the co-operative movement in the province and not to allow it to fall into any serious danger gave a real impetus to the movement. The Department carried out the policy enunciated by the Government as far as possible.

The Government of Bengal appointed a committee to examine the problems regarding the training of nurses, with Dr. B. C. Roy as the president.

The Mysore Legislative Council which met at Bangalore, considered the Mysore Elementary Education Bill.

Mr. Pattom Thanu Pillai, President of the Travancore State Congress, was released from detention. He said: "I expect hard work in many directions more than excitement at public meetings."

16th. A special bench of the Bombay High Court refused permission to the Government of Bombay to appeal to the Federal Court on the question of the validity or otherwise of the law of prohibition in Bombay, as promulgated by the Governor's Act in 1940.

Acharya Narendra Deo, the acting President of the U. P. Provincial Congress Committee, was arrested under section 129 (2) of the Defence of India Rules.

Pending Mahatma Gandhi's approval of the suggestion for wholesale withdrawal of Congressmen from local bodies, Dr. Rajendra Prasad advised Congressmen in local bodies to withhold from either resigning their seats or taking part in the Satyagraha.

17th. The view that the British Government had so far failed to unify British and Indian interests and to inspire zeal for the British cause among the people of India, and the opinion that the situation in the country, though serious, could be improved beyond recognition if the British acted with vision and courage, were expressed by prominent Indian Liberals in the course of a signed statement in reply to the message to the people of India from nine members of the British Parliament. The signatories among others, were Mr. V. N. Chandavarkar, Sir P. S. Sivaswamy Aiyar, Mr. V. S. Srinivasa Sastri.

The Government of India decided to set up a central training institute for A. R. P. particularly for the benefit of industrial areas.

18th. Mr. A. K. Fazlul Huq, Premier of Bengal, made a call to the people of Bengal interested in industrial enterprise to make the best possible contribution to the resuscitation of the dead and moribund industries of the province, when he addressed a conference of businessmen and industrialists in Calcutta. Mr, Abdur Rahaman Siddiqui, the Mayor of Calcutta, presided.

The Working Committee of the Hindu Mahasabha held its first day's sitting in the Hindu Mahasabha Bhawan in New Delhi, with Dr. Shyama Prasad Mookerjee, Working President of the Hindu Mahasabha in the chair. It was resolved that leading members of the Working Committee should undertake an extensive tour throughout India.

Mr. M. N. Roy, addressing the Bengal Provincial Conference of the Radical Democratic Party in Calcutta, observed: "Fascism being the embodiment of all the forces of reaction in the world, whoever is fighting against it, is an objectively progressive, indeed, an objectively revolutionary, force. Therefore, Mr. Churchill, who guides today the front rank fighters against the bulwalk of world reaction, whatever else he may have in his mind, is a more revolutionary force than all the Congress leaders, Right or Left, put together, who are only obstructing that fight."

A preliminary conference of Indian Christians in the city, convened under the joint auspices of the Indian Christian Association, Madras, and the Indian Christian Federation of South India, was held at Purasawalkam, with Mr. A. N. Sudarisanam, Editor of the *Guardian*, presiding.

19th. In order to prepare the Sikhs for the defence of India by all possible means such as maintaining and strengthening their special position in the armed forces—and to work for the early Indianization of all the defence forces, a Khalsa Defence of India League was formed at a meeting of Sikh leaders from all over the Punjab at Lahore.

The Working Committee of the Hindu Mahasabha resumed its sitting in New Delhi under the presidentship of Dr. Shyama Prasad Mukherjee, and considered what action should be taken in case no satisfactory reply was received from the Government to the demands contained in the resolution passed by the Hindu Mahasabha at its Madura session.

The Committee appointed by the Syndicate of the Calcutta University, re : Secondary Education Bill, expressed the opinion that the Board proposed to be set up under the provisions of the Bengal Secondary Education Bill would neither be representative in character nor be independent of Government control and would, as such, fail to command the confidence of a large section of the people.—Sir Azizul Haque, the Vice-Chancellor, Mr. Justice C. C. Biswas, Dr. B. C. Roy, Dr. Shyama Prasad Mukherjee, were among the members of the Committee.

20th. His Excellency the Governor of Bengal, addressing a gathering at Dacca, observed : "You must not imagine that defensive preparations are the business of a few. officials or experts in Delhi or Calcutta. They are a vital matter in which everyone must take a hand."

Sir K. Nazimuddin, Home Minister, Bengal, opening the Mymensingh District Muslim League Conference at Bhairab, observed : "If inspite of the serious handicaps of comparative poverty and lack of education, Muslims have been able to run a Government on such truly national lines, it can be easily imagined what greater contribution they can make to the common good of their motherland when they have achieved further economic and national progress."

Dr. Choitram P. Gidwani, President of the Sind Provincial Congress Committee, in an interview at Karachi, said ; "Mahatma Gandhi is quite happy about the way in which the Satyagraha movement is going on in this country. He is satisfied with the results."

21st. Mr. Amery, Secretary of State for India, replying to a question re : the Viceroy and the Indian Political Leaders in the House of Commons, said : "There have been no further discussions, and no substantial change in the political situation since my last statement on November 20."

Mr. H. S. Suhrawardy, Finance Minister, Bengal, presiding over the annual session of the Mymensingh District Moslem Conference at Bhairab, said : "If we are to work for the country, for the society and for the poor, we must organize the Moslems under the banner of the Moslem League." Mr. Suhrawardy expressed the hope that the people returning from the conference would form branches of the League throughout the district in order to infuse strength into the organization.

Mr. M. N. Roy, addressing the inaugural conference of the Bengal Democratic Union in Calcutta, declared : "All wishful thinking about a reconciliation between Congress and the Government should be deprecated and more realistic public men should come forward to assume the leadership of the country in these critical days."

The Punjab Assembly passed three official Bills, namely, the Punjab Fisheries (Amendment) Bill, the Punjab Courts Amendment Bill, and the Sikh Gurdwaras Amendment Bill.

22nd. Mr. Tamijuddin Khan, Minister for Agriculture and Industries, Bengal, addressing the second day's session of the Mymensingh District Moslem League Conference, referred to the scheme of jute restriction and said that the policy which the Government was pursuing was in the best interest of the cultivators as well as of the people in general.

Dr. G. S. Arundale, President of the Theosophical Society, discussing political problems of the day with representatives of certain Calcutta newspapers, advocated the establishment of an Indo-British union on the lines of the union suggested by Mr. Churchill between France and England before the collapse of the former country.

23rd. Mr. L. S. Amery, Secretary of State for India, in an interview with Sir Alfred Watson, Editor of *Great Britain and the East*, made the following observations :—The real problem today is one that only Indians can solve for themselves, said Mr. Amery, when asked if the possibility of a quick solution of the Indian problem rested with India.

Mr. Amery suggested that it was worthwhile clearly to understand how far the Government of India's policy had really gone. "As regards the future", he said, "it has met the widely expressed Indian demand for a constitution framed in accordance with Indian ideas and not dictated by the British Parliament in accordance with British views or British interests."

Sir Andrew Clow, Communications Member, Government of India in opening the Indian Road Congress in New Delhi, suggested that officials, businessmen, doctors, journalists and schoolmasters should each do a few days' voluntary labour to build and maintain roads.

It was announced from New Delhi that six members of the Council of the All-India Moslem League, three from Bengal and three from the Punjab were expelled from the League in accordance with the decision of the sub-Committee of the League set up in Bombay.

In the Punjab Assembly, Sardar Ujjal Singh informed the house that the Khaksar movement in the Punjab cost the public exchequer a sum of Rs. 1,94,730 up to November 1940.

The Hon. Sir G. S. Bajpai, Member for Education, Health and Lands, Government of India met the Council of the Imperial Indian Citizenship Association in Bombay and discussed with them the various questions arising from the position of Indians abroad.

His Excellency the Governor of Orissa addressing a public meeling at Balasore, under the auspices of the Balasore District War Committee, said : "Although very much has been done in the way of war effort, very much still remains to be done."

24th. India's new Commander-in-Chief, General Sir Claude Auchinleck reached New Delhi to take over Command from General Sir Robert Cassels on January 26th.

Mr. K. C. Mahomed Ismail, Vice-President, Madura District Congress Committee, who offered Satyagraha on January 20th was sentenced under Defence of India Rules to six months' R. I. and to pay a fine of Rs. 200/-.

25th. Mr. S. K. Basu, presiding at the annual generel meeting of the Bengal Millowners' Association in Calcutta, struck a note of optimism with regard to the cotton mill industry in Bengal.

The Bengal Provincial Board for Anglo-Indian and European Education, at a meeting in Calcutta approved the proposals made by the Inter-Provincial Board for the setting of question papers in modern Indian languages for the Cambridge Local Examinations by examiners in India and for marking the scripts likewise for an increase in the number of vocational subjects in the Junior School Certificate Examination.

The Senate of the Calcutta University, by 36 votes to 21, six members remaining neutral, adopted the report of the Committee appointed by the syndicate to consider the provisions of the Bengal Secondary Education Bill, urging the immediate withdrawal of the measure and creation of "a favourable atmosphere for a calm and dispassionate consideration of the problems of educational advancement of the province." The Vice-Chancellor, Sir Azizul Haque presided.

In Madras, an appeal to the public to carry out the constructive programme of the Congress and to bring about unity among all classes was made by speakers, at a public meeting under the joint auspices of the local Congress Sabha and the Madras District Congress Committee. Mr. T. P. M. Pillai presided.

Mr. G. L. Mehta, when he addressed the Dufferin old Cadets' Association in Calcutta, stressed the need for an adequate and efficient national merchant marine as an integral part of India's national economy as well as for commercial purposes.

A communique from New Delhi, stated : "In pursuance of an undertaking given in the Legislative Assembly in the debates on No. 22, 1940 in connexion with Mr. Akhil Chandra Datta's Bill to amend the Hindu Women's Rights to Property Act to appoint a committee to examine the Hindu Women's Rights to Property Act, 1937 with particular reference to the following non-official Bills : The Hindu Women's Rights to Property (Amendment) Bill promoted by Mr. Akhil Chandra Datta ; the Hindu Women's Rights to Property (Amendment) Bill promoted by Mr. A. N. Chattopadhya and others ; the Hindu Women's Rights to Property (Amendment) Bill promoted by Dr. G. V. Deshmukh and Mr. Kailash Bihari Lal.

26th. Congressmen in Calcutta celebrated the "Independence Day" in the manner prescribed by Mahatma Gandhi. In the morning a number of them assembled at the office of the Bengal Provincial Congress Committee. Congress flags were also hoisted on the offices of different student and labour organizations, and several private buildings in the city.—Similar celebrations were held in other parts of India.

At a meeting organized by the Radical Democratic Pary in Bombay to celebrate "Independence Day", speakers dwelt on the international situation and explained how Indian independence was closely connected with the future of the war.

His Excellency Sir Arthur Hope presided over the christening of the first trainer aircraft purchased out of the contributions made from the Governor's War Fund (Madras).

Mahatma Gandhi in a letter to Mr. M. L. Shah, General Secretary of the All-India Students' Federation, observed : "Students cannot afford to have party politics. They may hear all parties as they read all sorts of books, but their business is to assimilate the truth of all and reject the balance. That is the only worthy attitude that they can take. Power politics should be unknown to the student world. Immediately they dabble in that class of work they cease to be students and will therefore fail to serve the country in its crisis."

Dr. N. B. Khare, addressing a public meeting at Nagpur on "Independence Day", observed : "There may be many ways of gaining independence but Mr. Gandhi's constructive programme is not one of them".

27th. Sj. Subhas Chandra Bose was missing from his house in Elgin Road, Calcutta. It was also not known when exactly Sj. Bose left his house. A warrant of arrest was issued by the Additional Chief Presidency Magistrate, Calcutta.

His Excellency Sir John Herbert, Governor of Bengal, replying to the addresses presented to him dwelt on the problem of jute crop.

With the object of developing a technique for ascertaining the rate of yield of jute, the Indian Central Jute Committee at its meeting in Calcutta approved of a scheme of crop cutting experiments spread over a period of three years at a cost of Rs. 48,000 half of which would be contributed by the Bengal Government. Mr. P. M. Kharegat, President of the Committee and vice-chairman of the Imperial Council of Agricultural Research presided.

Mr. M. A. Jinnah, in reply to inquiries made by the students of the Lucknow University said : "I hope that the Muslim students will not participate in any strikes, protest meetings or any other activities directly or indirectly to support the Congress, as the latter's objective is to force the British Government to surrender to their demands which are highly detrimental to the vital interests of the Muslims in the country."

In the Punjab Assembly, a statement on A. R. P. in the Punjab was given by Mr. Maqbool Mahmud, Parliamentary Secretary to the Premier.

"There is absolutely no news here about Mr. Subhas Chandra Bose", stated a telegram received by Mr. Sarat Chandra Bose from an inmate of the Sri Arobindo Ashram at Pondichery.

28th. Her Excellency the Marchioness of Linlithgow, opening the annual conference of the Trained Nurses Association of India in New Delhi, urged better conditions of work and living for nurses and commended the proposal to establish a post-graduate college where nurses would get special courses of training.

Sir Shaafat Ahmad Khan, in a statement to the Press from Allahabad, referring to the interview given by Mr. Amery on the Indian question, said that it has removed many misunderstandings and elucidated some of the points upon which clarification was sought in the previous year by political organizations.

Mr. A. K. Fazlul Huq, Bengal Premier. in a letter he had addressed to Mr. Jinnah, President of the All-India Moslem League, requesting him to convene a meeting of the working committee or of the Council of the League to consider the communal problem, said : "Some day or other these communal differences will be made up, but I do not see any reason why the Moslem League should not take the wind out of the sails of other organizations and secure to itself the credit of having done the greatest possible service to India and her people."

Mr. S. Srinivasa Iyengar, presiding over the inaugural meeting of the Madras Provincial Gold and Silver Workers' Association, stressed the importance of trade unions being kept free from communalism.

Congress Socialists in the United Provinces, made it clear that they did not approve of Mahatma Gandhi's Satyagraha campaign.

29th. Labour reforms of a far reaching character were recommended by the conference of Provincial and States representatives and officials of the Central Government which was sitting in New Delhi under the chairmanship of Sir Ramaswami Mudaliar.

A reference to the disappearance of Sj. Subhas Chandra Bose, from his house, was made in the Calcutta Corporation.

Six official Bills dealing with labour problems were to be drafted for introduction in the autumn session of the Central Assembly embodying the results of the discussion at the second Labour Conference of Provincial Governments and States representatives.

The Government of India decided to acquire by purchase in different Provinces private load-carrying vehicles to meet the shortage of such vehicles for training purposes.

30th. The Central Jute Committee at its meeting in Calcutta, under the chairmanship of Mr. P. M. Kharegat, appointed a sub-committee of experts to recommend among other things the kind of machinery that would be required to carry on research regarding new uses for jute.

A meeting of the Munitions Productions Advisory Committee to the Government of India was held in Calcutta, in the office of the Director General of Munitions Production.

Mr. L. S. Amery, Secretary of State for India, replying to a question by Mr. R. A. Cary, in the House of Commons, declared: "The British Government have clearly set out their policy for constitutional advance in India and that policy still holds the field."

Mr. A. K. Fazlul Huq, Premier of Bengal, addressing a gathering of Muslims at Habigunj (Sylhet), made an appeal to the Muslims "to join the League and work for it heart and soul."

31st. Mr M. N. Roy, in the course of an open letter to Mahatma Gandhi, made an appeal to the Mahatma to persuade his followers "to behave less violently and more truthfully."

Mr. V. R. Kalappa, President of the All-India Trade Union Congress and Secretary of the Congress Parliamentary Party in the C. P. Assembly was sentenced at Nagpur, to nine months' rigorous imprisonment and a fine of Rs. 50 under the Defence of India Rules.

Mr. H. G. Wells, referring to India in an interview to the "United Press of India" declared: "What I want to see is India taking her place in a world Federation which we have got to work for from now on. It is a world, not a national settlement all mankind needs."

February 1941

Indo Burma Trade Negotiations began in New Delhi.

Empire Countries' purchases of Indian exports increased substantially in the first nine months of the financial year 1940-41. Exports to the U. S. A. also increased but those to Japan declined. India imported more Empire and U. S. goods.

The personnel and functions of the Industrial Research Utilization Committee were announced.

Fifty Indian technicians left for Britain to be trained under the Bevin Scheme.

Sir Sikandar Hyat Khan made a moving appeal for communal unity when addressing a *Basant* gathering.

The Bengal Legislative Assembly discussed the Sales Tax Bill.

Trade representatives of India and Burma met in New elhi. The leaders of both the countries spoke of the historic interest of the occasion.

Empire Countries took Rs. 14 crores more of Indian goods

during the first nine months of the year, and helped to swell India's trade balance to Rs. 28 crores.

In the House of Commons, Mr. Amery, the Secretary of State for India, recalled two recommendations of the Eastern Group Conference at Delhi, the first, the establishment in India of a Central Provision office to co-ordinate military requirements and secondly, the appointment of an Eastern Group Council to coordinate production and supply.

General Sir Claude Auchinleck, Commander-in-Chief to His Majesty's Forces in India, in a broadcast speech predicted the defeat of the Germans and exhorted the Indians to do their utmost in bringing about a victorious issue.

Mr. V. N. Chandavarkar, President, National Liberal Federation of India, expressed the view in Madras that solution of the Indo-British problem should be a condition precedent to the solution of the Hindu-Moslem problem.

At the 'India Day' function at the officers' Sunday Club in London, Mr. Amery, Secretary of State for India, referred to the remarkable steadiness of Indian troops in the Middle East under modern artillery and air bombardments.

In the Central Assembly, the Defence problems and the general programme of Army expansion were discussed.

The Working Committee of the All India Moslem League met in New Delhi and considered the political situation in the country: strong disapproval of Mr. Amery's pronouncement was expressed by a resolution.

The Council of the All-India Moslem League commenced its session in New Delhi. The Council approved the three resolutions passed by the Working Committee relating to Mr. Amery's "India First" slogan, observance on March 23, as a "Pakistan resolution Day" and celebrations of Moslem League week, once every three months. The Council also unanimously elected Mr. Jinnah, president.

Mr. L S. Amery, in a broad-cast speech from London, dwelt on India's place and part in the great struggle in which the Empire was engaged.

In the Central Assembly, Sir Jeremy Raisman pointed out in his Budget speech that India's defence budget for 1941-42 was Rs. 84 crores against Rs. 72 crores in 1940-41. The total strength of India's armed forces was well over 500,000 men.

1st. In the Central Legislative Assembly, the opening day of the Budget session promised to provide a short sitting, the main item being the consideration and passing of the Insurance Act Amendment Bill, which sought to provide for the reduction temporarily of the amounts payable as instalments of the sum to be deposited by an insurer under Sec. 7 of the Insurance Act.

Sir Sikander Hyat Khan, Premier of the Punjab, addressing a students' gathering in connexion with the celebration of the *Basant* festival at Lahore, made an appeal to his countrymen, particularly the younger generation, to rise above communalism and work for unity.

The first batch of Indian technicians selected to proceed to England, for training under the Bevin Scheme, arrived in Bombay, en route to Britain.

The Standing Committee of the All-India Newspaper Editors' Conference met in New Delhi in the premises of the *Hindusthan Times*. Mr. K. Srinivasan, Editor of the *Hindu*, presiding. The committee passed a number of resolutions.

Mr. I. Chengalroyan and Mr. Eranki Narayanmurti offered Satyagraha in

Madras. Both of them were charged under the Defence of India Rules. They were convicted and sentenced to undergo rigorous imprisonment for three months each.

The All-India Students' Convention, which met at Benares, passed a resolution condemning the repressive policy adopted by the Government and educational authorities against the students' movement and calling upon students to make full contribution in co-operation with other progressive organizations for the achievement of complete independence of India.

2nd. Mrs. Sarojini Naidu, addressing a luncheon meeting of the Progressive Group in Bombay, declared: "All talk of majority and minority rights becomes nonsense if we cease to approach life's problems in terms of a particular community." Mrs. Naidu said that the Congress stood for equity and justice between all communities and individuals. Its leaders and its followers might fail but the ideal of the Congress would remain the same.

The United Provinces Excise Amendment Act, which related to the policy of prohibition was promulgated for general information at Lucknow.

Sir Maurice Gwyer, Chief Justice of India and Vice-Chancellor, Delhi University, speaking at the prize distribution of Union Academy in New Delhi, referred in detail to the reorganization of University education in Delhi and the part that secondary schools should play in future.

3rd. The Standing Committee of the Newspaper Editors' Conference in New Delhi adopted a resolution assuring Mahatma Gandhi that reappearance of the *Harijan* would be welcomed.

The Additional Chief Presidency Magistrate, Calcutta, reissued the warrant against Sj. Subhas Chandra Bose and ordered the issue of a proclamation for his arrest and for attachment of his property.

In the Bengal Legislative Assembly, the Supplementary Estimates for 1940-41, was presented at the opening day's Budget session. The total covered by the estimates was Rs. 1,67,19,000.

Mr. Justice Lort Williams, in his presidential address at the Royal Asiatic Society of Bengal in Calcutta, put forward a plea that the Society should resist the tendency towards over-specialization and provide a common cultural platform upon which specialist and non-specialist could co-operate.

The first batch of 50 Indian technicians who were to be trained in England under the Bevin Scheme were entertained at a tea-party by the Government of India, in Bombay.

Charges under Sec. 38 of the Defence of India Rules, were framed by the District Magistrate, Lahore, against Dr. Choitram Gidwani, President of the Sind Provincial Congress Committee, in connexion with a speech delivered by him at Lahore on January 13.

The U. P. Women Students' Conference was held at Benares under the presidentship of Miss Kanchanlata, a Professor in the Indraprastha Girls' College, Delhi.

H. E. Sir Arthur Hope, Governor of Madras, addressing a public meeting at Mangalore, observed: "It was a folly on the part of the Congress leaders to say that although they would wish Nazism and Fascism defeated, they would not do one single thing to help to achieve it. On the contrary, they did everything to embarrass the war effort. It was neither logical nor sensible."

4th. Mr. S. A. Hydari, Secretary to the Labour Department, Government of India, wishing Godspeed (in Bombay) to the first batch of 50 Indian technicians proceeding to England to be trained under the Bevin Scheme, referred to the quick and adequate response the scheme had met with and said that the undertaking was in essence yet another instance of that comradeship which animated all units of the commonwealth in the face of a common danger.

The Additional District Magistrate of Alipore issued a non-bailable warrant for the arrest of Sj. Subhas Chandra Bose.

In the Bengal Legislative Assembly, the Motor Spirit Sales Taxation Bill, sponsored by Mr. H. S. Suhrawardy, Finance Minister, had an easy passage.

His Excellency the Governor of Sind, prorogued the Sind Assembly which adjourned sine die on December 11.

Dr. Choitram Gidwani, President of the Sind Provincial Congress Committee, was sentenced to 18 months' rigorous imprisonment and a fine of Rs. 500 by the District Magistrate, Lahore, under Rule 38 of the Defence of India Rules for a speech delivered by him at Lahore on January 13.

5th. Trade representatives of India and Burma met in New Delhi. Both Sir Ramaswami Mudaliar, Leader of the Government of India delegation and the Hon. U. Saw, Premier of Burma, who led the visiting delegation, spoke of the historic interest of the occasion.

Mahatma Gandhi, in the course of a reply to Mr. E. A. Mack, District Judge, Nellore, re: Red Cross organization, observed: "I would not regard it as a breach of discipline for a Congressman to subscribe to the Red Cross or take the necessary training. But it would be a different thing if a Congressman yielded to outside pressure and in order to avoid the displeasure of an authority and to gain a selfish end, subscribed to it."

In the Bengal Legislative Assembly, the Finance (Sales Tax) Bill, which was tabled for discussion, appeared to have given rise to a sharp difference of opinion among members of the Coalition (Ministerialist) Party. Several of them, in the course of a signed statement, presented to the leader of the party, expressed their disapproval of the measure on the ground that it did not mention the purpose for which the proposed tax would be utilized and that the Bill, if passed would operate harshly on the poor.

The Government of Madras superseded the Cuddalore Municipal Council for two years and appointed the commissioner as the Special officer to exercise the powers, discharge the duties and perform the functions of the Council and its chairman, in addition to his own duties.

Mr. J. V. Joshi, Director of Commercial Intelligence and Statistics met the President and members of the Southern India Chamber of Commerce, in Madras, for a discussion.

Empire Countries took Rs. 14 crores more of Indian goods during the first nine months of the year, and helped to swell India's favourable trade balance to Rs. 28 crores.

H. E. the Governor-General, withholding his assent to the Madras Estates Land (Orissa Amendment) Bill, in the course of a communication to the Governor of Orissa, said that it was apparent from the proceedings of the Orissa Assembly in respect of the Bill that, though complicated agrarian questions were involved, there had been no general investigation of them prior to the promotion of the Bill in the legislature. Neither had there been any preliminary negotiations conducted by the provincial Government with representatives of the two interests involved, that is to say, the landholders and the tenants.

6th. In the House of Commons, prompt progress in implementing the finding of the Eastern Group Conference at Delhi was recorded.

The Secretary for India, Mr. Amery recalled two recommendations of the conference: first, the establishment in India of a Central Provision Office to co-ordinate military requirements and secondly, the appointment of an Eastern Group Supply Council to co-ordinate production and supply.

The Governments concerned had accepted those proposals and Britain had appointed Sir Archibald Carter, formerly of the Board of Admiralty, to be their representative on the Council and Major-General W. C. Holden as Officer-in Charge of the Central Provision Office.

In the Bengal Legislative Assembly, after a debate lasting three hours, the House agreed to the proposal of the Finance Minister, Mr. H. S. Suhrawardy to take into consideration the Finance (Sales Tax) Bill 1941, as modified by the Select Committee and rejected by 90 to 54 votes, a Congress proposal that the Bill be recommitted to the Select Committee.

H. E. Sir Arthur Hope, Governor of Madras, addressing a public meeting at Calicut, made an appeal by saying, "I beg the Congress Party even now to reconsider its decision, and render all help to save this country."

7th. Ex-servicemen were coming back from their villages in ever increasing numbers to help in the expansion of India's army to half a million men.

Mr. M. A. Jinnah, President, All-India Moslem League, issued a statement from Poona, with regard to Sind affairs. He observed: "The Hindu and the Congress Press is misrepresenting the situation in Sind day in and day out. The Congress party and the Hindu Independent Party concluded an agreement with a few individual members of the Assembly who belong to the Moslem League on the basis of the so-called 21 points along with the understanding that they will maintain the Mir Ministry for the remaining period of the Assembly."

Mr. N. C. Chatterjee, presiding at the Barisal District Hindu Conference, at Barisal, said: "The Pakistan Scheme is essentially anti-Hindu, anti-Indian, anti-national. It is meant to disrupt and disintegrate the essential unity and integrity of India. It will for ever render impossible the building up of a homogeneous national life in India."

Referring to the Mahasabha's attitude towards the War, Mr. Chatterjee said: "We are not non-violent non-cooperators. Our policy is that of Tilak and Savarkar—diplomatic responsive co-operation. We realized that the whole world was organized on the basis of disciplined violence. Therefore, in order to make India's freedom a reality we must have a national army and a properly equipped defence force able to keep India inviolate."

Mr. Chatterjee characterized the activities of some of the Ministries functioning in India, as communal, and referring to the Ministry in Bengal, "the deliberate policy of attempting to weaken and suppress one community, which is being pursued in the province, is probably without any parallel in the present day civilized world. It is becoming a class war with a vengeance." He mentioned in this connexion the Secondary Education Bill and the Calcutta Municipal (Amendment) Bill.

8th. At the first meeting held in Calcutta of the Provincial Advisory Board of Forest utilization, constituted by the Government of Bengal, the necessity for immediate collection of statistics regarding the availability and cost of extraction of timber useful for making bobbins and shuttles was stressed.

The installation of about 3000 tubewells at a cost of Rs 21,00,000 at different places in Calcutta, (as a precaution in event of air raids) was decided upon at a conference between the Government of Bengal and representatives of the Calcutta Corporation.

In a special interview at Cocanada, Mr. M. N. Roy said: Evidently the war cannot come to an end in Europe. Germany cannot advance further towards the West. The invasion of England cannot be successful."

Rao Sahib N. Natesa Aiyar, presiding over the All-India Varnashrama Swarajya Sangha Conference held in Calcutta, questioned the credentials of the Hindu Mahasabha to speak for the Hindus and claimed that the all-India V. Sangha was the only representative body capable of speaking for the Hindus.

9th. General Sir Claude Auchinleck, in his first broadcast as Commander-in-Chief to India and to Indian troops abroad, declared: "That Germany's armed forces will be defeated I have no doubt, but the task is likely to be long and strenuous and to succeed in it we shall need everyman and all the material we can get."

Mr. M. A. Jinnah was unanimously nominated for the presidentship of the Madras session of the All-India Moslem League, at a meeting of the Working Committee of the Bengal Provincial Moslem League, in Calcutta.

Mr. V. N. Chandavarkar, President, National Liberal Federation of India, addressing a public meeting in Madras, expressed the view that the solution of the Indo-British problem should be a condition precedent to the solution of the Hindu-Moslem problem. Mr. Srinivasa Sastri presided.

Mr. L. S. Amery, Secretary of State for India, referred to the remarkable steadiness of Indian troops in the Middle East under modern artillery and air bombardments, at the "India Day" function at the Officer's Sunday Club in London.

Khan Abdul Ghaffar Khan, on return from tour of the southern districts, said that the aim of the civil resisters in the Frontier Province was to utilize the liberty of speech afforded to them by the Government and carry the Congress message to every hearth and home in the Province.

Mrs. Asaf Ali inaugurated in New Delhi, the Delhi Women's Political Conference. She promised "every possible assistance" to the constructive programme of the Congress.

The Government of Orissa published an Act, issued by the Governor of Orissa, making certain amendments to the Orissa Hindu Religious Endowments Act, which was passed during the time of the Congress Ministry. The amending Act did not in any way affect the general policy regarding control over religious endowments.

Acharya Kripalani addressed a meeting of students in Madras. He appealed to the students to carry out the constructive programme, instead of passing resolutions as to what should or should not be done by the leaders.

10th. In Calcutta, about 60 persons, including a police sergeant, a tramway inspector and five constables, were injured through the action of riotous mobs.

The trouble originated in connexion with the Mohurrum incident of the 8th. when tramway wires had to be cut for the passage of tazia processions.

The Travancore Government issued a communique warning State Congressmen. It stated inter alia : "The Government are not prepared to let liberty of speech degenerate into license and desire publicly to warn those concerned that they cannot but take prompt action to avoid a repetition of such tactics and such procedure."

Mr. N. A. Bechar (M.L.A.) in a communication to the Press commenting on Mr. Jinnah's statement on the Sind Ministerial position, made an appeal to Mr. Jinnab, President of the All-India Muslim League, to trust his men "on the spot" and not to disturb the Azad arrangement.

11th. In the Bengal Legislative Council, the agenda included consideration of the Official Trustees Bill (Bengal Amendment) Bill, as passed by the Lower House, and the report of the Committee on Public Accounts on the Appropriation Accounts and Finance Accounts of the Government of Bengal for 1938-39 and the Audit Reports 1939.

The Council passed the Official Trustees Bill without any discussion.

In the Bengal Legislative Assembly, the consideration of the Finance (Sales) Tax Bill, clause by clause, was taken up.

The Budget session of the Central Assembly opened.

12th. In the Central Assembly, Sir Reginald Maxwell, Home Member, speaking on an unofficial resolution asking for the appointment of a committee to examine the living conditions of detenues under the Defence of India Act, made a statement that acknowledged communists and active supporters of the communist programme of violent mass revolution represented the majority of security prisoners held in detention camps. He also said that the men formed the Central directorate of the communist organization in India and their detention was necessary to cripple the communist machinery.

In the Bengal Legislative Council, Mr. A. K. Fazlul Huq, the Premier, made a statement regarding the disturbances which took place in Calcutta on the 10th. of February. The Premier denied the allegation that arrests were made indiscriminately or that womenfolk were insulted and huts broken into.

In the Bengal Legislative Assembly, Mr. H. S. Suhrawardy, Finance Minister, presented the supplementary budget estimates for 1940-41. The estimates relating to police and jails were subjected to considerable criticism by several members of the Opposition. In the end the estimates were passed without any modification. The total covered by the estimates was Rs. 1,67,19,000 out of which 1,39,000 was charged and the balance was voted.

Sir A. Ramaswami Mudaliar, Commerce Member, at the first meeting of the Industrial Research Utilization Committee in New Delhi, dewelt on the many problems connected with the utilization of the results obtained by the Board of scientific and Industrial Research.

Dr. Shyamaprasad Mukherjee made a statement at Chittagong that if the demands of the Hindu Mahasabha were not fulfilled by March 31, direct action would be launched, with a definite programme.

Mr. L. S. Amery, Secretary of State for India, speaking at a luncheon meeting in London, said : "Preservation of the wonderful fabric which the full co-operation of our predecessors have built up and the further developement of the path of political and social progress."

13th. In the Central Assembly, the Defence problems and the general programme of Army expansion were discussed.

The employment of Moslems at Army Head Quarters, the pay of European British subjects and Indian British subjects holding commissioned rank, Indianization, the recognition of martial and non-martial classes, the progress of mechanization and the defence of India against attack by air, sea or land were among the subjects raised.

In the Bengal Legislative Assembly, a proposal by the European party to lower the "taxable quantum" provided in the Finance (Sales) Tax Bill, met with strong opposition. The Bill provided that the "taxable quantum" should be Rs. 50,000 for certain classes of dealers.

14th. The Central Assembly passed without division Sir Raza Ali's amendment supporting the Government of India's attitude in the Ceylon negotiations and appreciating the Ceylon Governor's message to the State Council.

In the Bengal Legislative Assembly, the question of the construction of a trunk road in Pabna was discussed at length. Another subject considered by the House related to the treatment of political prisoners.

The Government of India's scheme to make things easier for small insurance companies during the war period was accepted with approval in the Central Assembly.

In the Bengal Legislative Council, non-official resolutions were taken up. Of the 11 resolutions on the agenda. three were disposed of, one was withdrawn, one carried and one was lost.

The statement of monthly accounts of the Central Government published by the Finance Department gave information about revenue and expenditure up to the end of December 1940. There was a decrease of Rs. 3 crores in receipts.

Sir Manohar Lal, Finance Minister, Punjab, replying to a toast at a dinner at Lahore, observed : "Sir Sikander Hyat Khan is capable of producing men of great military strength, but men alone will not do. What is wanted is armour not less than men ; men in factories are as important as men in the fighting lines."

15th. Mahatma Gandhi made a declaration in Bombay that he did not wish well to India at the expense of Britain, in the same way as he did not wish well to Britain at the expense of Germany. He reiterared his faith in non-violence and reaffirmed its efficacy in meeting even Hitler's violence, if properly applied.

In the Bengal Legislative Assembly, Mr. H. S. Suhrawardy, Finance Minister, presenting the Provincial Budget for 1941-42, said that the estimates showed that there would be a deficit. He said : "The year starts with an opening balance of 1 crore 92 lakhs, which is the anticipated closing balance for the current year. Revenue receipts are placed at 14 crores 3 lakhs or 21 lakhs better than the Revised." Our proposals for expenditure on revenue account amount to 15 crores 37 lakhs, which is 52 lakhs more than the anticipated expenditure in the current year."

In the Bengal Legislative Council, the Government's policy in regard to jute was explained by the Finance Minister (Mr. Suhrawardy) when he presented the Budget.

At the annual Shahi Jirga durbar held at Sibi, Sir Aubrey Metcalfe, Agent to the Governor-General, Baluchistan, in his speech referred to the situation in Europe and warned against easy optimism founded on the successes in Africa or elsewhere.

Jathedar Udham Singh Nagoke, presiding over the second All-India Akali Political Conference at Lahore, under the auspices of the Shiromoni Akali Dal, observed : "Non-violence and violence are both useful in their own spheres ; in fact both of them form part of my religion."

Dr. P. V. Naidu, General Secretary of All-India Hindu Mahasabha, suggested from Madras that the Viceroy should invite a conference of the Premiers of the Provinces and the Congress ex-Premiers, along with a certain number of leaders, nominated by the Hindu Mahasabha, the Muslim League, Sikhs, Christians and the Depressed classes in order to find a way out of the political deadlock.

Mr. Thakkar Baba, Secretary All-India Harijan Sevak Sangha, addressing a public meeting at Mysore, observed : "Removal of untouchability and of restrictions, to which Harijans are subject, cannot be effctively done, merely by a State or a State legislation. Unless the efforts of the State are supplemented by its people in the same direction, much benefit cannot result from them."

16th. The Working Committee of the All-India Hindu League concluded its two-day meeting in New Delhi. A resolution was passed urging that the Government should take the initiative by inviting leading men, "who are willing to co-operate with them in their war effort to assume the responsibility for the administration of the Central Government." Mr. M. S. Aney presided.

17th. In the Central Assembly, India's export trade and the loss of European markets as a result of war was the subject of a number of questions. Grievances regarding the Census formed the subject of two adjournment motions. One was ruled out by the chair and the other fell through for want of support.

His Excellency the Governor of Bengal, addressing a gathering at an A. R. P. demonstration at Howrah, made an appeal to the people "to be prepared now while peaceful conditions still last."

In the Punjab Assembly, Sir Shahabuddin, read to the House, applications for leave from five Congress members of the Assembly.

Sir Chhotu Ram, Minister for Development, presented the report of the Select Committee on the Punjab Urban Rent Restrictions Bill.

Mr. Mohamed Suleman Cassim Mitha, member of the Bombay Legislative Assembly, disagreeing with the policy of the Muslim League, resigned his seat in the Legislature. He also resigned from the Muslim League Bombay Legislative Assembly Party.

Mr. R. K. Sidhwa, Leader of the Congress Assembly Party (Sind) observed : "Things have considerably improved and the relations between the two major communities have begun to be cordial. All the same, Hindus feel somewhat nervous because of the danger they apprehend from the surrounding Muslim villages."

Notices issued by the Additional Chief Presidency Magistrate of Calcutta, were served on a number of banks in the city directing them to stop operation of any account standing in the name of Sj. Subhas Chandra Bose.

13th. The Central Legislative Assembly discussed the Ticketless Travellers Bill as reported by the Select Committee. The President, Sir Abdur Rahim, disallowed an adjournment motion of Mr. Govind Deshmukh for the removal of a rifle range near the Peshawar Cantonment.

Mr. M. A. Jinnah, President, All-India Moslem League, issued a statement to the Press from New Delhi. He stated *inter alia* : "My attention has been drawn to a report under the heading 'Revised Pakistan Scheme Committee's Recommendations' published in a newspaper to-day. This is entirely incorrect. After the Lahore resolution, now popularly known as the Pakistan resolution, was passed last March, the Working Committee of the All-India Moslem League appointed a sub-Committee to invite any proposal on the basis of the fundamental principles embodied in the Lahore resolution."

The Foreign Committee of the All-India Muslim League published details of the Pakistan Scheme which would be discussed at the meeting of the Working Committee. Three zones were contemplated—North-West, North-East, and Hyderabad with certain additions, Sind, Baluchistan, the Frontier Province, and the Punjab, with Delhi would constitute a sovereign State.

A surplus of Rs. 14.46 lakhs was revealed in the Budget estimates of the Bombay Port Trust for the next financial year.

Another order for the issue of a proclamation for the arrest of Sj. Subhas Chandra Bose, was passed by Mr. S. G. Creek, Additional Magistrate at Alipore, when the case against Sj. Bose under the Defence of India Rules came up for hearing before him.

19th. In the Legislative Assembly, the Railway Budget presented by Sir Andrew Clow, the Railway Member, forecast for 1940-41 a surplus of Rs. 14.59 crores against a surplus of 8.29 crores originally estimated, and for 1941-42, a surplus of 11.38 crores.

After the presentation of the Railway Budget, the Assembly resumed discussion of the Ticketless Travellers Bill.

Mr. M. A. Jinnah, President, All-India Moslem League, issued a statement from New Delhi on the political pact in Sind.

In the Council of State, the Budget session opened.

A Press Communique from New Delhi stated : "His Majesty's Government in the United Kingdom have informed the Government of India that in view of heavy demands on the steel industry in the United Kingdom exports of finished steel product from the United Kingdom will in future only be permitted if they are proved to be essential to the war effort and cannot be obtained from any other source."

The death occurred of Sir John Gibb Thom, Chief Justice of the Allahabad High Court.

Mr. M. A. Jinnah, President of the All-India Muslim League, issued a statement from New Delhi : "Khan Bahadur Khuhro was good enough to come all the way from Karachi to see me and he has placed the whole matter fully before me and in consultation with Sir Abdulla Haroon, President of the Provincial Muslim League, Sind, I have come to the conclusion that the so-called Pact or Agreement is a pure myth."

20th. The Central Assembly discussed non-official resolutions. Sir Ziauddin Ahmed moved a resolution recommending the appointment of officers of a judicial mind to hear appeals of railway employees and to scrutinize the rule relating to those appeals.

Sir Md. Zafrulla Khan, replying to Sir Ziauddin, in the Central Assembly, said that the total expenditure on the Eastern Group Conference was approximately Rs. 2,15,000. This sum, he added, in answer to another question, was debitable to the Central Revenues.

A Press Note issued by the Director of Public Information, Bengal, said: "The Government desire to announce once more that regulation of the jute crop is the fundamental basis of their declared policy in relation to jute. Government will leave nothing undone to ensure effective restriction of the 1941 crop in accordance with the statutory notification that they have already issued. They will spare no effort and no expenditure for this purpose."

It was learned from New Delhi that the non-official advisers to the Government of India and the representatives of the Government of Madras, Bengal and Bombay, after fully considering the fresh proposals of the Burma Government in connexion with the Indo-Burma trade negotiations, submitted their report to the Government of India. The report was believed to have been unanimous.

Mr. M. N. Roy, at a public meeting in Madras, expressed the firm belief that India by being a willing participant in the war and winning freedom for the world from the menace of Fascism, would arrest its own freedom. Mr. E. V. Ramaswami Naicker, Leader of the Justice Party, presided.

21st. His Excellency Sir Claude Auchinleck, Commander-in-Chief, replying to an address presented to him by members of the Khalsa Defence of India League said that methods for improving the machinery for securing officers for the Army, were under his consideration.

Mr. W. A. M. Walker in his presidential address at the annual general meeting of the Indian Jute Mills Association, in Calcutta, discussed various problems relating to the Jute industry. He said: "Despite adverse trade conditions, the industry is in a sound position and I trust that the future will see even closer cooperation among ourselves."

22nd. In the Central Assembly, members of the Moslem League Party withdrew as soon as the House took up general discussion of the Railway Budget. Mr. Ghulam Bhik Nairang, Deputy Leader of the Party, made a statement before they withdrew, declaring that they were doing so in order to mark their protest against the policy followed by the Government in regard to Moslem grievances.

The Working Committee of the All-India Moslem League met in New Delhi, at the residence of Nawabzada Liaquat Ali Khan, Mr. M. A. Jinnah presiding. The main item which was considered was the political situation. The committee held a prolonged meeting and passed 5 resolutions. Strong disapproval of the latest pronouncement of Mr. Amery was expressed by a resolution.

Khan Abdul Ghaffar Khan sent a telegram to Mahatma Gandhi from Peshawar, expressing his desire to meet the Mahatma at Delhi and to discuss matters pertaining to the Satyagraha movement, with special reference to the Frontier Province.

Mr. Amery's statement in the House of Commons in reply to Sir Alfred Knox, was considered by prominent Hindu leaders of the U. P. (at Lucknow) at the residence of Sir Jwala Prasad Srivastava, President of the United Provinces Hindu Mahasabha.

23rd. The Council of the All-India Moslem League began its session in New Delhi, Mr. M. A. Jinnah presiding.—On the motion of Sir Abdulla Haroon, the council approved the three resolutions passed by the Working Committee relating to Mr. Amery's "India First" slogan, observance of March 23 as "Pakistan resolution day" and celebrations of Moslem League 'Week' once every three months. The Council also unanimously elected Mr. Jinnah president.—The main discussion centred round the non-official resolution relating to the Congress campaign of Satyagraha.

The Working Committee of the All-India States' Moslem League met in New Delhi, under the presidentship of Nawab Bahadur Yar Jung Bahadur, and passed 10 resolutions. One of the resolutions urged upon the Government of India "to take suitable steps for the augmented recruitment of the States' Moslems in the Land, and Naval Forces, and suggested that the facilities and amenities of life should be elaborately provided to the families of soldiers on active service abroad.

Another resolution stated, "Having very carefully studied the present political situation in the country and the recent views of the members of the British Parliament, the Secretary of State for India and the Viceroy and British Statesmen amplifying and clarifying the assurances contained in the declaration of His Majesty's Government of August last as well as the response and reaction by the various political parties and the public leaders in India, the Working Committee of the All-India States' Moslem League welcomes the possibilities and prospects of bringing about a constitutional settlement which is acceptable and suitable to the genius of the powerful and principal elements in the country, and urges that the present political deadlock in the country should be immediately ended."

24th. Mr. L. S. Amery, Secretary of State for India, in a broadcast talk from London, dwelt on India's place and part in the great struggle in which the Empire was engaged.

After referring to the strategic position of India on the map of the world, and to her vast resources in man power and raw materials Mr. Amery said, inter alia : "Indian reinforcements were hurried to the Middle East and Singapore. Indian troops played their part in General Wavell's initial success at Sidi Barrani and in the fighting in Eritrea and Abyssinia. They have given evidence of the fighting quality of the Indian soldier under conditions of modern warfare......

"The Ruling Princes of India have their own martial traditions and their long record of loyalty to the Crown. In the last war they placed their forces unreservedly at the disposal of the King-Emperor both in India and overseas."

"The Indian Air Force is being expanded as rapidly as it is possible to provide the machines. That is the only limit on expansion, for India is enthusiastically air minded and young men of the right quality are ready to come forward in far larger number than at present can be trained."

Mahatma Gandhi, replying to several Satyagrahis from Calcutta who sought his advice regarding their march to Delhi, said : "It would not be wrong if non-arrested Satyagrahis tour the whole district for a month or two and then proceed to Delhi. Some may tour in the district and some may go to Delhi."

25th. In the Central Assembly, a Bill was introduced by Mr. O. K. Carol, Secretary, External Affairs Department, seeking to constitute the Assam Rifles as a central responsibility.

On the motion of the Commerce Member, Sir Ramaswami Mudaliar, compensation for war injuries and damages sustained by masters and seamen employed on small vessels plying in Indian coastal waters and rivers was agreed to in principle.

The Council of State held a general debate on the Railway Budget. Before the beginning of the Budget debate, members of the Moslem League party staged a walk out, after their leader, the Hon. Mr. Hossain Imam, had made a statement.—In his statement Mr. Imam said that his party's grievances were that since the fixation of a communal ratio for direct recruitment to the superior posts, Moslems had not received even three-fourths of that quota, that large numbers of posts were filled by promotion on communal grounds to keep out the Moslems, that they did not want a 25 per cent share in promotion, but they asked for 25 percent of the total recruitment, and they wanted direct recruitment in the intermediate grades, like the lower gazetted staff.

The Bengal Legislative Assembly proceeded with the general discussion of the Budget estimates as presented by the Finance Minister, Mr. H. S. Suhrawardy.

In the Central Assembly, Mr. M. S. Aney asked whether the British Consul-General at Saigon had been instructed to take all necessary steps to protect Indian property in Indo-China in view of the unsettled conditions prevailing there. Mr. O. K. Carol, Secretary, External Affairs Department, replied : "It is the duty of His Majesty's Consuls in all foreign countries to take all proper steps to protect the interests of British subjects residing in those countries."

Sir Henry Gidney, addressing the Anglo-Indian R. A. M. C. Contingent at Lucknow, declared : "India must in the future, if she has to take a right place among the Dominions as a partner in the British Commonwealth of Nations, have a standing army of at least five hundred thousand, if not a million."

Dr. P. V. Naidu, Secretary of the All-India Hindu Mahasabha in the course of a statement from Madras, said: "As General Secretary of the All-India Hindu Mahasabha, I consider it my duty to warn patriotic Hindus against joining Mr. M. N. Roy's National Democratic Party. If any member of the Hindu Mahasabha has joined this group already, I request him to resign the membership forthwith."

26th. In the Sind Assembly, Khan Bahadur Alla Baksh, Finance Minister, envisaged a surplus of Rs. 1,00,000 in the Budget estimates for 1941-42. The anticipated revenue receipts being Rs. 4,35,47,000 and expenditure charged to revenue Rs. 4,34,47,000.

In the Bengal Legislative Council and in the Assembly discussion on the Budget continued.

The Central Assembly resumed discussion of the Railway Budget. All the cut motions moved during the day's debate were rejected. Members of the Moslem League Party did not attend.

In the Central Assembly, Sir Fredrick James raised the question of the ban on the emigration of unskilled labour to Ceylon.

Mr. V. D. Savarkar, President of the Hindu Mahasabha, in a special interview in Bombay said: "It is my honest belief that the non-violence preached during the last 20 years is responsible for the deterioration of the Hindu cause. It has emboldened the Muslim League to demand Pakistan."

27th. All the railway demands for grants were passed by the Central Assembly.

The President of the All-India Newspaper Editors' Conference received a letter from Sir Richard Tottenham, Additional Secretary, Government of India, in reply to the resolutions passed by the Standing Committee of the Conference held in February in Delhi, in which it was declared: "The Government of India recognizes the duty of newspapers to give legitimate publicity to news in which their readers are interested, and so long as newspapers will refrain in accordance with their declared intention of doing nothing to impede the war effort, from publishing news or views which will incite persons to take part in the anti-war movement and which are, therefore, "prejudicial reports" within the meaning of the law, Government see no difficulty in maintaining the Delhi Agreement and the good relations between the Government and the Press which is its purpose to preserve."

In the Council of State, a resolution was moved by Mr. P. N. Sapru to the effect: "This Council recommends to the Governor-General-in-Council to advise the Secretary of State for India to suspend British recruitment to the Indian Civil Service during the period of the war." On the assurance of the Home Secretary that he would communicate the members' views to the Secretary of State, the motion was withdrawn.

In the Punjab Assembly, Sir Manoharlal, Finance Minister in introducing the Budget estimates for 1941-42, observed: "With our position on the map of India being what it is, the question of ensuring internal security had to be firmly faced."

28th. In the Central Assembly, Sir Jeremy Raisman pointed out in his Budget speech that India's defence budget for 1941-42 was Rs. 81 crores against Rs. 72 crores in 1940-41. Charges borne by His Majesty's Government for supplies and services rendered by India were expected to exceed double of India's war expenditure for 1941-42. The total strength of India's armed forces was well over 500,000 men of all arms. Further expansion was proceeding.

Mr. J. H. S. Richardson, in his presidential address at the annual general meeting of the Bengal Chamber of Commerce, in Calcutta, remarked: What the future holds for us no man can tell. But come what may, we will meet it honestly and courageously; and in standing shoulder to shoulder, in times of adversity as in days of peace, we shall contribute in no small measure to the future of this country and to the security of the British Commonwealth of Nations."

In the Bengal Legislative Assembly, the report of the Select Committee on the Calcutta Municipal (Amendment) Bill, 1941, was presented by Nawab Habibulla Bahadur of Dacca, Minister for Local Self-Government.

In the Central Assembly, the Communications Member, Sir Andrew Clow, in a written reply stated that the number of monthly paid artists, including musicians employed at the Delhi, Lahore, Lucknow and Bombay broadcasting stations was 115 in January 1941,—of these 35 were Hindus and 77 Moslems.

Mr. A. K. Fazlul Huq, Bengal Premier, presiding over the conference of the Bengal Provincial Unemployed Federation, in Calcutta, expressed the view that a permanent solution of the unemployment problem in Bengal lay in the industrialization of the province.

Mahatma Gandhi performed the opening ceremony of the Kamala Nehru Memorial Hospital at Allahabad.

March 1941

The Chief incident of the month was the Non-Party Leaders' Conference in Bombay.

Dr. Shyama Prasad Mukherjee, Working President, All-India Hindu Mahasabha, presiding over the Punjab, Sind and the North Western Frontier Province Hindu Conference at Lahore said that so long as 28 crores of Hindus remained alive, Pakistan scheme would not operate in any part of Hindusthan.

Mr. M. A. Jinnah, addressing the special Pakistan session of the Punjab Moslem Students' Federation at Lahore, asserted that the Pakistan scheme was the only solution for India's most complex problem, for which there was no parallel in the world.

In the Central Assembly, the Congress Nationalist Party and the Moslem League Party opposed the provision in the Bill relating to the 'Ticketless Travellers', seeking to give power to the railway staff to eject a passenger found travelling in a class higher than that for which he held a ticket.

Sir Claude Auchinleck, Commander-in-Chief, moved a resolution in the Council recommending to the Governor-General in Council that the Army authorities should review sources of man power throughout the country and should exclude no class or area from consideration for recruitment.

The Central Assembly rejected the Moslem League Party's cut motion for reforms in Beluchistan.

Sir Tej Bahadur Sapru, addressing the annual Convocation of the Calcutta University, laid stress on the synthesis of different cultures and entertained the hope that the Universities might be of great help where politicians failed.

The Anti-communal Conference at Lahore, presided over by Khan Abdul Gaffar Khan, passed a resolution condemning the Pakistan scheme as "highly unpatriotic, anti-national and against the best interests of the country."

Sir Claude Auchinleck, Commander-in-Chief, paid a glowing tribute in the Council of State to the deeds of bravery of the Indian soldiers fighting against the Italians in Africa.

The Conference of Non-Party leaders for the purpose of finding a solution to the political deadlock in the country began in Bombay. Sir Tej Bahadur Sapru, the President, made an earnest appeal to the Government of India to get together the leaders of the Congress and the Moslem League, in an effort to resolve the deadlock.

The Fact Finding Committee appointed by the Government of India circulated a set of 19 questions re: spinning and handloom industry in the country.

The Central Assembly by 46 votes to 28, passed the motion to take the Finance Bill into cosideration and afterwards passed the Bill by 40 votes to 19.

The Eastern Group Supply Council, explained the general organization and functions of the Council, to the representatives of the Press.

In accordance with the wish of His Majesty the King Emperor, India observed the National Day of Prayer.

'Pakistan Day' was observed at a number of places in India, under instructions from Mr. M. A. Jinnah, President of the Moslem League.

The Central Assembly by 48 votes to 17, rejected Mr. H. M. Abdulla's resolution urging recognition of Communal Unions of Government employees.

In the Central Assembly, Mr. Govind Deshmukh moved a resolution expressing concern at the low price of Indian cotton and in the course of a debate initiated by Mr. A. N. Chattopadhya, for a supplementary grant in respect of "Commercial intelligence and Statistics",—the Meek-Gregory Mission to America was strongly criticized.

1st. Sir Henry Craik, Governor of the Punjab, when he addressed the Passing-out Parade of the third group of pupil-officers to complete their course at the Indian Air Force initial training school at Lahore, said : "You go out from here to a much more arduous and severe course of service and training."

Mr. Amritlal Ojah, President of the Federation of Indian Chamber of Commerce, criticizing the taxation proposals of the Finance Member, Sir Henry Raisman, observed in a statement : "I quite agree that the Government's need for funds is very great, but that does not necessarily mean that these have to be raised only by means of taxation, particularly direct taxation.

Dr. Shyama Prasad Mukherjee, Working President, All-India Hindu-Mahasabha, presiding over the Punjab, Sind and the North-West Frontier Province Hindu Conference at Lahore, said : "Mr. Jinnah's Pakistan scheme will remain embodied in pamphlets and reports and so long as 28 crores of Hindus remain alive, it will not operate in any part of Hindusthan."

Referring to the political situation the speaker observed that a policy of wholesale non-cooperation had landed them in disaster and said that political power was of vital importance to the people.

Sir Sikander Hyat Khan, Premier of the Punjab, addressing the annual general meeting of the Northern India Chamber of Commerce, at Lahore, declared : "Every Indian, whatever his political views, whether a Congressman or a Unionist feels that in this war India will have to make a supreme effort to crush Nazism and Fascism.

Sir Gurunath Bewoor, Chairman, Board of Directors of the Government Telephone Board Ltd. made a formal offer to purchase at a cost of Rs. 475 lakhs, the Bengal, Bombay and Madras Telephone Companies.

2nd. The All-India Manufacturers' Conference passed a resolution in Bombay urging the Government of India to provide adequate facilities for the financing of small and medium scale industries in the country.

Mr. M. A. Jinnah, addressing the special Pakistan session of the Punjab Moslem Students' Federation at Lahore, made an assertion that the Pakistan scheme was the best and the only solution for India's most complex problem, for which there was no parallel in the world.

Mr. M. A. Jinnah said that it would be in the interest of the three vital elements in India, namely, the British Government, the Princes and the Hindus, to accept this solution. Referring to the attitude of the Moslem League towards the war, Mr. Jinnah said that the League realized that whatever their complaints and grievances against the British Government it was in their interest not to place any difficulties in the way of the war efforts which were made to strengthen the defence of India. Likewise they did not wish to embarrass the British Government and were willing even to support and wholeheartedly co-operate with them provided it was agreed that the League representatives had real authority in the Centre and the Provinces.

The Moslem League's Pakistan scheme was condemned by the Punjab, Sind and the Frontier Provinces Hindu Conference which concluded its two-day session at Lahore.

Through one of the resolutions which was moved by Rai Bahadur Mehrchand Khana (Frontier) the Conference felt that the Pakistan scheme was fraught with great danger to the peace and tranquillity of the country and held that the scheme constituted a great blow to the political and national integrity of India. The conference called upon every Hindu to resist it to save India from the proposed vivisection.

3rd. In the Central Assembly, Mr. O. K. Caroe, persuaded the House to agree to remove the constitutional and administrative barriers which placed the Assam Rifles under control of the Provincial Government.

The Central Assembly disposed of three official Bills. It agreed to two amendments made by the Council of State in the bill to amend the law relating to fraudulent marks on merchandise, and passed Mr. O. K. Caroe's Bill for the regulation of and maintenance of discipline in the Assam Rifles.

In the Punjab Assembly, Sir Sikander Hyat Khan, the Premier, replying to a debate on a cut motion, expressed the view that the Conferences held at Lahore during the week-end had added to the "poison and bitterness" which he had wanted to avoid.

In the Assam Legislative Assembly, a deficit of Rs. 11,89,000 in the revenue account was revealed in the Budget estimates of the Government of Assam for the year 1941-42.

In the Bengal Legislative Assembly, the Finance Minister, Mr. H. S. Suhrawardy, in winding up the debate, referred to the jute policy of the Government. He claimed that the Government policy had benefited the agriculturists and added that those who were against the policy were "enemies of the people and the agriculturists". The remark of the Minister was followed by a walk-out by members of the Congress Party, under the leadership of Sj. Sarat Chandra Bose and the Krishak Praja Party, led by Mr. Shamsuddin Ahmed.

Mr. S. Srinivasa Iyengar, presiding over the ninth anniversary of the Madras University Students' Union, in Madras, exhorted the members to develop a true feeling of patriotism and to work hard for the elimination of communalism. He also urged that an industrial bias should be given to education.

4th. In the Central Assembly, there was a general discussion on the Budget.

In the Central Assembly, Mr. G. V. Deshmukh asked Government to supply a statement showing the allowance and accommodation received by Italian prisoners of war in India and Indian prisonors of war taken in the Sudan and France. Mr. C. M. G. Ogilvie, Defence Secretary, said: "The treatment of both Italian and Indian prisoners of war is governed by the international convention relating to the treatment of prisoners of war signed in Geneva in 1929, which has been ratified by India, Germany and Italy."

The Punjab Government prepared a scheme for the promotion of communal harmony in the province.—The scheme envisaged the collection of authentic historical incidents indicating tolerance and respect for the susceptibilities of the followers of other religions on the part of Hindu, Moslem and Sikh rulers, both past and present; organization of lecturers by eminent leaders on communal harmony and encouragement of papers and magazines of good standing which studiously refrained from indulging in communal politics and consistently advocated communal harmony.

In the Bengal Legislative Assembly, when consideration of the Sales Tax Bill was resumed, considerable opposition was offered to clause 5 of the Bill which dealt with the rate of tax. In the Bill this was put down at one quarter of an anna in the rupee on a dealer's taxable turnover.

In the Bengal Legislative Council, the Congress Party withdrew from the House, following a statement by Mr. Kamini Kumar Dutta, Leader of the Party, with the remarks: "Whenever the present Government brings forward measures to trample the fundamental interests of the province, those of us who will remain outside the prison, will come here to record our opposition."

The Punjab Assembly passed the City of Lahore Corporation Bill by 40 to 15 votes.

In the Sind Assembly, Khan Bahadur Allah Buksh, Finance Minister, replying to the general debate on the Budget, observed: "Sind has stood the test of making the Barrage Debt remunerative and the Government of India should in honour adjust the Barrage Debt if they find that the estimates do not come up to expectations."

5th. In the Central Assembly, when the debate on the Ticketless Travellers Bill was resumed, the Congress Nationalist Party and Moslem League Party concentrated their attack on the provision in the Bill seeking to give power to the railway staff to reject a passenger found travelling in a class higher than that for which he held a ticket.

In the Bengal Legislative Assembly, considerable progress was made with the Sales Tax Bill when as many as 15 clauses, relating to assessment of tax, power of the Commissioner of Commercial taxes, offences and penalties under the measure and various other matters were passed.

The Council of State held a general discussion on the Budget.—Mr. Shantidas Askuran, said that the Commander-in-Chief should appoint a special committee of the Central Legislature to scrutinize all defence expenditure. He also urged that the Army Indianization Committee should resume its work. Thirdly, he wanted the creation of a War Advisory Council representing both British India and the Indian States.

6th. Sir Claude Auchinleck, Commander-in-Chief, moved a resolution in the Council of State, as a substitute for the one proposed by Pandit Kunzru regarding recruitment to the Army: "This Council, while recognizing that to begin with, the Army could be most speedily expanded only on the existing basis of recruitment, recommends to the Governor-General in Council that the Army authorities should now review sources of manpower throughout the country and should exclude no class or area from consideration for recruitment in the formation of new units."—the resolution was passed unanimously.

In the Central Assembly, Sir M. Zafrulla Khan, in reply to a debate initiated by Sir Zia-ud-din Ahmed on a cut motion, explained the Working of the Supply Department and the relations between the Eastern Group Supply Council and the Provision Offices.

In the Sind Assembly, three Sind Ministers—Khan Bahadur Allah Buksh (Finance), Mr. Nichaldas Vazirani (Revenue) and Rai Sahib Gokuldas (Local Self-Government) announced their resignation from the Cabinet.

The Bengal Legislative Assembly passed the third reading of the Sales Tax Bill, by 71 votes to 33.

His Excellency Sir Henry Craik, Governor of the Punjab, presiding at the annual prize distribution at the Khalsa College, Amritsar, advised the Sikhs to join the army in large numbers.

7th. In the Central Assembly, the European Group decided to subordinate sectional interests to the pressing necessity for debating issues connected with war finance and war propaganda.

The Assembly rejected by 40 votes to 18 the Moslem League party's cut motion demanding reforms for Baluchistan.

The Marwari Association, Calcutta, discussed the various proposals for safeguarding the handloom industry in India and measures for reconciling the claims of the handloom and mill industries were discussed in a communication to the Secretary of the Fact Finding Committee (Handloom and Mills), Government of India.

The Bengal Legislative Assembly rejected a resolution moved on behalf of the Opposition that all political prisoners should be placed in Division 1.

It was officially announced that Khan Bahadur Allah Baksh was sworn in as Premier at Karachi Government House, and was asked to form a new Cabinet in Sind.

Sir Tej Bahadur Sapru, who was invited to Calcutta, to deliver the Convocation Address of the Calcutta University at a tea party given in his honour by the Indian Association, observed among other things: "The time has come when each one of us should ask 'what is going to happen to this country' and 'not what is going to happen to me, to this community or that community'. I want you to approach the question from that point of view."

8th. In the Central Assembly, the grant of allowances to compensate Government servants on low rates of pay in the event of a substantial rise in the cost of living, a proposal to appoint Indian Trade Commissioners in Canada and South America, and the installation of two telephone circuits were among the demands discussed by the Standing Finance Committee. Sir Jeremy Raisman, Finance Member, presided.

Sir Tej Bahadur Sapru, addressing the annual Convocation of the Calcutta University, emphasized the part that Indian Universities could play in bringing about a synthesis of different cultures and evolving "that common culture which should be the highest aim of Indian nationalism to achieve."—"Is it altogether a vain hope", he asked, "that our Universities may come to our rescue when our politicians have failed us and that out of the chaos of ideas and aspirations it may be given to the Universities to evolve a cosmos of clear thinking and generous feeling ?"

It was officially announced that Khan Bahadur Alla Baksh, the Sind Premier, presented to His Excellency the Governor, his colleagues in the new Cabinet. Sir Ghulam Hussain Hidayatullah, Pir Elahi Bux, Mr. Nichaldas Vizirani and Rao Saheb Gokuldas, the New Ministers of the Sind Cabinet, were sworn in.

Sir Abdul Halim Ghuznavi, M.L.A., Vice-President, Civil Recruitment Committee, Calcutta, presiding over a meeting in New Delhi, said : "Bengal contributed over 7000 recruits as no more was wanted in 1916-18. This time she is eager to contribute many times the 7000 if Government will only have them. I appeal to my Bengali brethren in the province of Delhi to do their part and I am sure they will do so in an organized way."

9th. The Anti-communal Conference which began at Lahore, passed a resolution condemning the Pakistan scheme, which in its view was "highly unpatriotic, anti-national, and against the best interests of the country."—The view that there never could be real Hindu-Moslem unity unless they tried to understand each other's religion and culture was expressed by Khan Abdul Gaffar Khan, presiding at the Conference.

His Excellency the Governor of Madras, addressing a public meeting at Chetinad, said, "we do not know whether the war will end in a week, or a month or ten years, but there is only one possible ending to this war and that is complete victory for Great Britain."

Resolutions condemning the anti-war activities of the Congress, characterizing the Congress leadership as reactionary and holding the party directly responsible for the political deadlock in the country were passed at the first provincial conference of the U. P. Radical Democratic People's Party held at Cawnpore under the presidency of Mr. Sirajuddin Piracha.

Sir Manmatha Nath Mukherjee, President, Bengal Sanskrit Association, at the annual convocation of the Association, held in Calcutta, said: "The Bengal Sanskrit Association has been bearing the burden of developing and encouraging the spread of Sanskrit education not only in Bengal but also in other parts of the country as well."

The Working Committee of the All-India Hindu Mahasabha was in session in Bombay, when apart from administrative matters relating to the organization, there was a general discussion on the political situation.

10th. In the Central Assembly, Sardar Sant Singh pleaded on behalf of the Congress Nationalist Party for the appointment of a Defence Advisory Committee.

In the Council of State, in a written reply to a question by Raja Yuvaraj Dutta Singh in regard to the prominent part played by Indian troops in Africa, His Excellency the Commander-in-Chief, Sir Claude Auchinleck, stated: "I welcome the opportunity afforded me by the honourable member to pay a personal tribute on the floor of this House to the magnificent part troops from India have played in destroying the threat of Italian aggression in and from North Africa."

In the Bengal Legislative Assembly, a discussion on the demand for Budget grants for General Administration began with a number of cut motions moved by the opposition parties with a view to criticize the actions and policies of the Government.

His Excellency the Governor of Bengal presided at an informal conference in Calcutta. of representatives of the parties in the Legislature. A general discussion took place with particular reference to the deterioration in communal relations.

In the Assam Assembly, non-official business was taken up. Mr. Badruddin

Ahmed's Shop Assistants' Relief Bill, Mr, Amzad Ali's Goalpara Tenancy Amendment Bill, and Mr. Abdul Aziz's Sylhet Non-Agricultural Tenancy Bill, were introduced and circulated for eliciting opinion.

In the Council of State, a resolution asking Government to withdraw their orders (1) "restricting the number of candidates appearing for the I. C. S. Examination in India and (2) fixing the provincial quote" was moved by Mr. V. V. Kalikkar.

11th. The Central Assembly began the general debate on the Finance Bill. Sir Yamin Khan, opening the debate, considered that there was no proper control over expenditure and that the country's trade was in general contracting and wealth decreasing.

The Council of State adopted four official Bills which had been passed by the Legislative Assembly. Three of the Bills, namely, the Bill amending the Petroleum Act, the Bill extending certain Acts to Berar, and the Bill providing for the regulation and the maintenance of discipline in the Assam Rifles, were passed without any opposition. Several provisions for checking ticketless Travelling, were criticized by non-official speakers during the consideration stage.

The three-day session of the Working Committee of the All-India Hindu Mahasabha concluded in Bombay with the following statement: "The Working Committee of the All-India Hindu Mahasabha went through all the correspondence which passed between the Hindu Mahasabha and the Viceroy and discussed at length the present political situation in India. It was decided to say the last word in connexion with the negotiation after March 31, in accordance with the resolution passed at Madura."

In the Bengal Legislative Assembly, the discussion on the demands for grants for General Administration was concluded. All the cut motions were lost and the entire demand for Rs. 1,27,00,000 was carried.

12th. Five thousand villagers of Ballia District (U. P.) gave three Indian soldiers who took part in the capture of Tobruk an enthusiastic welcome at a reception in the collectorate compound and heard an account of their experience. Mr. J. Nigam. I. C. S., the District Collector, congratulated them on the glory and honour they had brought to the district.

On the petition of the police for an order of attachment on the property of Sj. Subhas Chandra Bose, against whom a proclamation had already been issued, the additional Chief Presidency Magistrate, Calcutta, passed orders attaching the immovable properties of Sj. Subhas Chandra Bose as detailed in the petition.

Surpluses of Rs. 9 lakhs in 1940-41 and of Rs. 5 lakhs in 1941-42 were estimated in the financial statement of the U. P. Government.

In the Bengal Legislative Council, the Finance (Sales Tax) Bill was taken up for consideration.

The death occurred of Sir Shah Muhammad Sulaiman, Judge of the Federal Court of India.

His Excellency the Governor of Bengal opened the Coronation Bridge over the Teesta, at Sevoke.

In the Bengal Legislative Assembly, the Government's determination to enforce their jute regulation policy was stressed by Mr. Tamizuddin Khan, Minister for the Department of Agriculture when the demand for a grant for the Department of Agriculture came up for consideration. The Minister said that unless next year's crop was regulated according to the Government's scheme, the situation would be unmanageable.

Mr. M. A. Jinnah, at a meeting held at Aligarh under the auspices of the University Union, declared: "Pakistan has been there for centuries. It is there to-day, and it will remain till the end of the world."

13th. The Conference of non-party leaders for the purpose of finding a solution to the political deadlock in the country began in Bombay. Sir Tej Bahadur presided over the meeting. Nearly 40 leaders from various parts of the country attended in the camera sitting of the Conference which adjourned after adopting the draft resolutions.

Dr. P. V. Naidu, General Secretary of All-India Hindu Mahasabha, who returned to Madras after attending the meeting of the Working Committee of the Mahasabha in Bombay, expressed the hope that if Lord Linlithgow and Mahatma Gandhi made one more effort towards settling the deadlock in India, they would succeed in doing so and thus would lay themselves under a deep debt of gratitude of the future generations of Indians.

14th. H. E. the Viceroy received a gracious message to India from His Imperial Majesty the King-Emperor.

In the Central Assembly, a Bill further to amend the Excess Profits Tax was introduced by Sir Jeremy Raisman, the Finance Member, mainly to provide for the consequences of a change in the period of charge and the rate of the Excess Profits Tax.

The Fact Finding Committee (Handloom and Mills) appointed by the Government of India, circulated a set of 19 questions regarding the condition of the spinning, weaving and handloom industry in the country.

The Bengal Legislative Assembly voted the demand made by Tamizuddin Khan, Minister for Agriculture, for a grant of Rs. 43,85,000 for expenditure under the head, "Agriculture."

Sir Tej Bahadur Sapru, opening the conference of non-party leaders in Bombay, made an earnest appeal to the Government of India to take the initiative in getting together leaders of the Congress and the Moslem League in an effort to resolve the political deadlock and if that attempt failed, to mobilize the large mass of unattached opinion in the country.

The Government of Assam issued a Press note, saying, "In view of its geographical position, having one of the few accessible land frontiers of India, the Province of Assam has special interests and responsiblities in regard to the possibility of air raids, from which few countries, whether non-belligerent or neutral, are wholly immune."

The All-Travancore State Congress Workers' Conference held at Trivandrum, decided that immediate work before the State Congress should be the enlistment of as large a number of primary members as possible and the formation of primary committees throughout the State.

Mr. Srinivasa Sastri commenting in Madras, on the resolution passed at the non-party leaders' conference in Bombay, said: "To listen while there is time to the clear call sounded in Bombay is the wisest course for Great Britain at the moment."

Sir P. S. Sivasami Iyer, in an interview in Madras, said: "The resolutions passed at the non-party leaders' conference should be accepted by the British Government and carried out without delay. The refusal of the British Government to carry out the policy urged by the non-party leaders is bound to estrange even the moderate sections of Indian people and weaken India's efforts in aid of the war."

Sir Mohammed Usman, a former acting Governor of Madras, in an interview said: "The deadlock cannot be solved till the Congress and the Moslem League unite. There is no use in blaming the British Government."

15th. The Central Assembly continued the general debate on the Finance Bill. Maulana Zafar Ali said that if the Congress were in the House, Hindus and Moslems would have joined hands and made an effective demonstration against the Bill.

In the Bengal Legislative Assembly, various Government schemes for the development of industries in the province were out-lined by Mr. Tamizuddin Khan, Minister for Agriculture and Industries, when he asked for a grant of Rs. 19,19,000 for expenditure on 'Industries'.—During the discussion on the subject, Mr. J. R. Walker, made a strong plea for the fishery industry which, he maintained, offered the best prospect for increasing the wealth of the province.

16th. The Moslem League Party in the Central Assembly, at a meeting in New Delhi, decided to make an effort to throw out the Finance Bill at the consideration stage.

It was announced from Nagpur that the Working Committee of the All-India Hindu Mahasabha would meet on April 5 and 6 in Calcutta "to take final decision on the resolution regarding direct action" which was adopted by the Madura session of the Mahasabha. A meeting of the Central Council of Action as also the Conference of the Provincial Councils of Action would be held in Calcutta at the same time.

Sir Tej Bahadur Sapru, in his concluding address at the Non-Party Leaders' Conference in Bombay, declared that the right thing for India to demand was perfect equality not merely in status but in power with other Dominions of the British Common-wealth.

17th. His Excellency the Viceroy addressed the Chamber of Princes in New Delhi, urging "some pooling of cherished sovereignty" and describing the need for such sacrifices as "a stark reality".

The Council of State rejected a resolution by the Hon. Mr. Hossain Imam recommending the formation of a committee of members of the Indian Legislature to scrutinize and suggest the apportionment of defence expenses between the Government of India and His Majesty's Government and to submit a report on the transactions since the war began.

His Excellency Sir John Herbert, Governor of Bengal, presided over the annual meeting of the Bengal Tuberculosis Association in Calcutta, and announced that the Government of Bengal proposed to establish a permanent tuberculosis sanatorium at Peshok, in the Darjeeling District.

In the Bengal Legislative Assembly, when the Premier, Mr. A. K. Fazlul Huq moved that Rs. 1,68,74,000 be granted for expenditure under the Head "Education", Rai H. N. Chowdhury raised, by means of a cut motion, a discussion on Government's policy in regard to primary education.

18th. In the Central Assembly, the general debate on the Finance Bill was continued.

In the Bengal Legislative Assembly, two Budget grants for education and jails and convict settlements were discussed. The entire demands, under both heads, were voted.

Three persons were killed and many injured as a result of communal clashes and stray assaults at Dacca.

The A. I. C. C. office (Nagpur) published an article entitled "The Parting of the Ways" (between Britain and India) by Pandit Jawharlal Nehru, which, it was stated, was written on the 10th. August 1940.

The Sind Assembly passed into law the Debt Conciliation Bill.

19th. The Working Committee of the Bengal Provincial Hindu Sabha at a meeting in Calcutta, under the presidentship of Dr. Syama Prasad Mookherjee expressed its deep sympathy with the sufferers and members of the families of persons who had lost their lives and property in the riots at Dacca and Khulna.

14 people were killed and 91 injured as a result of communal rioting in Dacca.

The Government of India in a Gazette Extraordinary, published a resolution announcing "Dearness" allowances, ranging from Rs. 2 to Rs. 3 for employees of State-owned railways getting Rs. 60 and below per month.

His Excellency the Governor of Assam, addressing an open air gathering at Shillong, observed : "The obvious points of attack in this province are the oil fields of Digboi, the oil installations of Tinsukia together with the surrounding neighbourhood, and thirdly the capital of the province."

In the Bengal Legislative Assembly, Mr. A. K. Fazlul Huq, the Premier, observed during the consideration of the Police Budget, "One of the fundamental requisites of our advance depends on the maintenance of law and order and the existence of peace and tranquillity in the country."

A Press Note stated that the Conference of Leaders of various parties continued its session at Government House, Calcutta. Among the subjects discussed were the communal riots at Khulna and Dacca.

20th. The Central Assembly by 46 votes to 28 passed the motion to take the Finance Bill into consideration. The Moslem League and the Congress Nationalists voted against the motion.

Sir Jeremy Raisman, Finance Member, replying to the criticism of the Budget on the ground that there was no attempt at retrenchment coupled with economy, emphasized that there was an important distinction between the two ideas of economy and retrenchment.

Maulana Zafar Ali attempted to secure admission for an adjournment motion in the Central Assembly, to discuss "the unwarranted interference" of the local police with the lawful activities of the Khaksars near the Jumma Musjid (Delhi).

21st. In the Central Assembly, increased space for each pilgrim on any ship engaged in carrying Haj pilgrims was to be provided and marked off under the provisions of Shaikh Tazlihaq Piracha's Bill which was passed.

Mr. J. B. Ross, Chairman of the Indian Mining Association in his presidential address at the annual general meeting of the Association in Calcutta, dealt with some of the more difficult problems with which the coal trade was faced.

In the Bengal Legislative Assembly, an account of the activities of the Co-operative Department was given by Mr. M. B. Mullick, Minister in Charge, when he placed the budget of the Department before the House. The Minister also asked for a grant of Rs. 20,23,000 for expenditure under the head debt conciliation. This gave rise to a debate regarding the working the Agricultural Debtors Act.

In the Assam Assembly, a point of order raised by Mr. Kamini Sen, questioning the legality of the supplementary demand of Rs. 1 lakh which the Ministry contributed to the British war Fund was disallowed by the Speaker.

The Eastern Group Supply Council met representatives of the Press and explained the general organisation and functions of the Council. It was explained that the Council had been formed to facilitate the practical carrying out of the policy formulated by the Eastern Group Supply Conference so that the task of supplying troops in the Eastern Group Area (whether in the field or in their own countries under training or for local defence) might proceed as smoothly and with as small a drain upon shipping as possible.

22nd. The Central Assembly passed the Finance Bill by 40 votes to 19. The increased duty on matches was the first of the new taxation proposals on which an attack was launched when the House took up discussion of the various clauses of the Finance Bill.

Mr. Amritlal Ojha, President of the Federation of Indian Chamber of Commerce and Industries, in his presidential address, at the 14th annual meeting of the Federation, in New Delhi, advocated the appointment of an Indian Industrial Reconstruction Council to turn to the fullest advantage the experience gained by war conditions.

The Bengal Legislative Assembly voted Budget demands for Rs. 71,12,000 and Rs. 22,29,000 for expenditure under the heads "Administration of Justice" and "Provincial Excise" respectively.

23rd. In accordance with the wish of His Majesty the King Emperor, India, in common with the rest of the British Empire, observed the National Day of Prayer. Thanksgiving and Intercession Services were held in churches of various denominations and special prayers were offered in many temples and other places of worship.

"Pakistan Day" was observed at a number of places of India, in accordance with the wishes of Mr. M. A. Jinnah, President of the Moslem League.

Mr. A. K. Fazlul Huq (Premier of Bengal), Mr. H. S. Suhrawardy (Finance Minister), president and secretary, respectively of the provincial Moslem League, in a joint statement, explained the reasons for postponing the celebration of "Pakistan Day" in Bengal.

The Federation of the Indian Chamber of Commerce and Industry passed resolutions concerning the Eastern Group Council, taxation of incomes by Provincial Governments, exports and imports quotas and surcharge of railway freights on food grains and fodder, and concluded its session in New Delhi.

Mr. M. A. Jinnah, in explaining the Pakistan Scheme in New Delhi, said that Muslims and Hindus could not rule jointly, as there was a great difference in their modes of living, dress and language.

Mr. A. L. Ojha, in his presidential address to the Indian National Committee of the International Chamber of Commerce, (in New Delhi) urged that the opportunity created by the war should be utilized to effect permanent changes, which were long overdue in the basic economic structure of the country.

24th. The Central Assembly passed without a division, Sir Ramaswami Mudaliar's Bill to continue for another year the existing protective duties on iron and steel manufactures, sugar, and silver thread and wire.

The House also passed the Bill to extend the import duties on wheat and flour for another year.

The Budget of the Government of the Central Provinces and Berar for 1941-42, as authorized by His Excellency the Governor, was published in a Gazette Extraordinary.

In the Bengal Legislative Assembly, problems connected with the land revenue system of Bengal were discussed, when Sir B. P. Singh Roy, Minister-in-Charge of Revenue asked for a grant of Rs. 31,58,000 for the administration of the Department. Opposition members criticised the Government for failing to give relief to the tenantry by education of rents.

In the Council of State, a resolution recommending the appointment of a committee of officials and non-officials to examine the question of the strength of and posts reserved for the I. C. S., by Mr. Hossain Imam, was withdrawn after the Government's point of view was explained by Mr. Conran Smith, Home Secretary.

25th. The Central Assembly by 48 votes to 17 rejected Mr. H. N. Abdullah's resolution urging recognition of communal unions of Government employees. The resolution which was moved by Mr. Abdullah on behalf of the Moslem League Party, recommended "that the present discriminatory policy of Government as regards recognition of so-called common unions of Government employees should be abandoned forthwith and unions of employees belonging to any one particular section or community should be officially recognized.

In the Central Assembly, Mr. Govind Deshmukh moved his resolution expressing concern at the low prices of Indian cotton, especially short staple, and their result on the general economic condition on the cotton growers in India and urging that the recommendation made by the Indian Central Cotton Committee in January in Bombay should be given effect to help the cotton-growers in their present condition.

Sir Ramaswami Mudaliar, Commerce Member, pointed out that price control was instituted at the request of the Provincial Governments and did not apply to commodities like cotton, but only to foodstuffs.

26th. Mr. A. T. Luker, Chairman of the Madras Trades Association, addressing the annual meeting of the Association in Madras, stressed the need to start thinking out post war problems from now on in order to draw and form some workable plan.

Mr. C. P. Bramble, President of the Bombay Chamber of Commerce, at the annual general meeting of the Chamber, in Bombay, examined the situation in India, both political and commercial.

H. E. Sir Roger Lumley, Governor of Bombay, addressing the Bombay Chamber of Commerce, declared: "We meet this year, with a full knowledge of what we are up against and with the expectation that the sternest tests lie ahead of us."

27th. The Central Assembly agreed to circulation of the Bill to limit to a maximum of Rs. 50 per annum, the amount payable in respect of any person by way of tax on profession, trades, callings and employment.

The Council of State considered the Finance Bill.

Mr. C. E. Jones, Finance Secretary moved that the Finance Bill be taken into consideration. He said that by their Bill it was intended to give legislative sanction to all the Budget proposals, except the one imposing a 10 p.c. duty on pneumatic tyres and tubes, which being a new duty and in absence of a general excise duty required separate enactment.

The Assam Legislative Assembly by 37 votes to 8, passed the Assam Bill (1941).

A small surplus of Rs. 32,000 was anticipated in the Budget Estimates of the North-West Frontier Province for 1941-42. The total revenue for the year 1941-42 was expected to yield Rs. 1,91,25,000 against which the Expenditure was estimated to amount to Rs. 1,90,93,000.

Orissa's Budget Estimates for 1941-42 showed a surplus of Rs. 2.15,000. The total revenue was estimated at Rs. 1,92,74,000 and expenditure charged to revenue at Rs. 1,90,59,000.

In the Bengal Legislative Council, the President (Hon. Mr. S. C. Mitra) admitted an adjournment motion relating to the ban on publication by newspapers of any matter regarding any communal disturbance in the province.

28th. The Central Assembly discussed supplementary grants.

The Council of State passed the final reading of the Finance Bill without division.

In the Bengal Legislative Assembly, dissatisfaction with the working of the Medical and Public Health Departments were expressed by several opposition members, when Mr. Tamijuddin Khan, Minister of Agriculture and Industries asked for grants of Rs. 51,13,000 and Rs. 50,52,000 respectively, for expenditure for the departments.

Sir S. Radha Krishnan, George V Professor of Mental and Moral Science, Calcutta University, resigned in order to take up the newly created Sir Sayaji Rao Professorship of Indian Culture and Civilization at the Benares Hindu University.

The Assam Assembly passed the Assam Forest Amendment Bill (1940) which repealed Sec. 63 of the Assam Forest Regulation of 1891.

The Assam Revenue Tribunal Bill (1941) was referred to a Select Committee.

The Rt. Hon. V. S. Srinivasa Sastri presiding over a meeting of the Lakshipuram Young Men's Association in Madras, observed : "I am by no means certain that, just because we take a hand in this war, we shall be considered fit to take a share in the fruits of the war."

29th. In the Central Assembly, in the course of a debate on a cut motion moved by Mr. A. N. Chattopadhya under a demand for a supplementary grant in respect of "Commercial intelligence and Statistics," the Meek-Gregory Mission to America was strongly criticized.

The Council of State met to dispose of four official Bills passed by the Central Legislative Assembly.

In the Bengal Legislative Assembly, the labour policy of the Government of Bengal was explained by Mr. H. S. Suhrawardy, Finance and Labour Minister, when asked for a grant of Rs. 4,92,000 to defray the cost among other things, of Labour Department.—The House voted the grant as well as the budget demands in respect of Anglo-Indian and European education, Forests. and certain other departments. The Budget Estimates, as presented by the Finance Minister, were passed without any modification.

The Working Committee of the All-India Hindu League, met in New Delhi, with Mr. Aney in the chair and discussed the political situation in the light of latest developments in and outside the country.

Mr. S. Srinivasa Iyengar, speaking on "war and Diplomacy" in Madras, said : "Our diplomacy towards the British people is by no means perfect, and that is the reason for its failure. While we may be frank and truthful with them, we should keep our counsel and reserve an element of surprise in our tactics."

30th. The draft memorandum which was to be forwarded to His Excellency the Viceroy in explanation of the Bombay Conference resolution was considered at a meeting of the Standing Committee of the Conference in New Delhi presided over by Sir Tej Bahadur Sapru.

The Working Committee of the All-India Hindu League concluded its two-day session in New Delhi, and with the object of creating a common political platform for all political parties on matters of common concern, passed a resolution appointing a committee of nine members, with Mr. M. S. Aney as its chairman, to examine the questions from all points of view and changes that might be required to be made in the name, creed and constitution of the organization.

Sir Henry Gidney, in the course of his presidential address at the annual general meeting of the Punjab Branch of the Anglo-Indian and Domiciled European Association, at Lahore, appealed to the Anglo-Indians to join the Army in large numbers and contribute their utmost in furtherance of the war effort.

Mr. M. A. Jinnah, addressing a public meeting at Cawnpore, declared that the position of the Muslims with regard to the Pakistan scheme had been made crystal clear.

Sir Sikander Hyat Khan, the Punjab Premier, presiding over a meeting at Lahore, made a call to the youth to come forward and work for Hindu-Muslim Unity without which they could never achieve freedom.

31st. In the Central Assembly, an adjournment motion tabled by Mr. M. A. Kazimi concerning the use by provincial Governments of the Defence of India Rules was disallowed by Sir A. Rahim (President).

The Bengal Legislative Assembly by 43 votes to 37, passed a token demand made by the Premier (Mr. A. K. Fazlul Huq) in connexion with a proposal to contribute Rs. 1,00,000 to the Mayor of Calcutta's fund for the relief of London air raid victims.

Mr. S. C. Ghosh in his presidential address at the annual general meeting of the Indian Mining Federation in Calcutta, discussed various matters relating to the coal mining industry.

Sir Lancelot Graham, retiring Governor of Sind, in the course of an interview to a Karachi daily, characterized as "incorrect" the impression in Indian political circles, that the Pakistan scheme was favoured by the British Government.

The Maharajadhiraj of Burdwan, in his presidential address at the Annual Meeting of the British Indian Association, in Calcutta, observed : "We trust that the Government will for a while stop at extirpating the landlords' legitimate rights in the land and concentrate on devising some effective methods for the realisation of arrears of rent to the lasting benefit and abiding interest of all the parties in the business of agriculture."

April 1941

Mr. L. S. Amery's speech in the House of Commons regarding the political situation in India, and the session of the Moslem League in Madras were the striking features of the month.

The Bengal Legislative Assembly and the Council rejoice at the success of the Indian troops in capturing Keren and Harar. The Bhopal Legislative Council also paid glowing tributes to the "magnificent" work of the British and Indian troops in the capture of the above places.

Mr. Amery, the Secretary of State for India, in answer to a question in the House of Commons re: Co-operation in a National Government", said, "His Majesty's Government are keeping open the far reaching and constructive proposals", "and they and the Viceroy will continue to examine sympathetically any suggestion which may help to surmount the difficulties."

Mr. T. Chapman Mortimer, at a meeting of the Western Bengal branch of the European Association, dwelt with the political situation in India and criticized the Congress attitude towards the British Government.

Mr. H. Siddaiya, President, Mysore State Congress, advised his hearers to refrain from thinking of office acceptance so long as there was no sign of the change of heart on the part of the Government.

Mr. A. K. Fazlul Huq, in a statement on the floor of the Bengal Legislative Assembly assured the House that all possible steps had been taken at Dacca to bring the riot situation under control.

Mr. Mohiuddin, presiding over the second Bihar Momin Conference at Bettiah, complained that the Muslim League was an organization of upper class Muslims who had thriven at the cost of the Momins.

The session of the All-India Moslem League began in Madras. Mr. Jinnah, the President, in his address surveyed the activities of the League and expressed his determination to support the establishment of "Independent" States in certain areas in India.

Dr. Rajendra Prasad, in a Press statement from Patna on Mr. Jinnah's speech in Madras, asked "in what respect will Pakistan differ from existing independent Moslem States" and "how it will be able to give protection to the Moslem minorities."

Mahatma Gandhi refused to withdraw the Civil Disobedience movement and declared that his "unquenchable faith in the power of non-violence" was unshaken.

Mr. Rajendra Prasad expressed that no Congressman should seek re-election to a local body, even in his individual capacity, once the Congress as a Party had withdrawn from it.

Mr. L. S. Amery, Secretary of State for India, moved a resolution in the House of Commons, to extend for another year the proclamations under which the Governors of the Indian Provinces would assume the powers of Provincial Legislatures.—Referring to Mr. Amery's speech, Mahatma Gandhi remarked: "The callousness makes me more than ever confirmed in my opinion that the Congress must abide by its policy of non-violence inspite of the heavy odds facing it."

The Standing Committee of the Bombay Non Party Leaders' Conference in a statement on Mr. Amery's speech, regretted that it "displayed such an unsympathetic and unbending attitude towards the aspirations of India."

The Conference of Party leaders in the Bengal Legislature, "urged upon all communities the desirability of putting aside all communal or sectarian prejudices which might be the cause of discord."

1st. The Central Legislative Assembly adjourned *sine die* after passing the Delhi Restriction of uses of Land Bill.

The Bengal Legislative Assembly had a brief session ; the discussion on the Land Revenue (Floud) Commission Report, which had been fixed for the evening, having been postposed as all the materials connected with the subject had not been received by members.

The Bengal Legislative Council adopted a special motion rejoicing at the capture of Keren and Harar and congratulating the Indian troops on the gallant part played by them in bringing about those successes.

In the Bhopal Legislative Council, glowing tributes to the "magnificent" work of the British and Indian troops in the capture of Keren were paid by all sections, when the House unanimously passed a resolution congratulating His Highness the Nawab of Bhopal on his return after his successful tour of the Middle East.

Sir William Hawthorne Lewis was sworn in as Governor of Orissa in the Ravenshaw College Hall, in the presence of the leading noble men, officials and and non-officials of the province. The oaths were administered by Sir Arthur Harries, Chief Justice, Patna High Court.

Mr. M. A. Jinnah, President of the All-India Muslim League, before leaving for Delhi, forwarded to His Excellency the Viceroy a copy of the resolutions passed by the Council and the Working Committee of the League.

Sir Hugh Dow was sworn in as Governor of Sind. Sir Godfrey Davis, the Chief Judge of the Chief Court, administered the oath of allegiance.

The Bengal Shops and Establishments Act came into force in Calcutta and Howrah.

2nd. The death occurred of Sir Sunder Singh Majithia, Revenue Minister, Punjab, at the age of 69. He was leader of the Khalsa National Party in the Punjab Assembly.

The Council of State, without a division, adopted an official amendment to the Hon. Hridaynath Kunzru's resolution regarding industrialization of the country.

Mr. C. A. Carmichael, the Chairman, speaking at the annual meeting of the Indian Paper Makers' Association in Calcutta, referred to the effect of the war on India's paper industry.

In the House of Commons, Mr. Graham White asked Mr. Amery what steps were being taken by the Government of India to encourage and turn to the practical advantage of Britain and India the growing feeling and increasingly influential movement in favour of co-operation in a National Government.

Mr. Amery, in a written reply, said, "I have already made it clear that His Majesty's Government are keeping open the far reaching and constructive proposals which they themselves put forward last August and they and the Viceroy will continue to examine sympathetically any suggestion, within the scope of these proposals, which may help to surmount the difficulties that have stood in the way of political advance in India.

3rd. The formal ceremony of the signing of the new Indo-Burma trade agreement took place in the room of the leader of the Indian delegation, Sir Ramaswami Mudaliar, Commerce Member. Only the heads of the agreement were signed as the agreement in its final form was not ready.

The Bengal Legislative Council agreed to take into consideration the Agricultural Debtor (Second Amendment) Bill, as passed by the Legislative Assembly.

In the Bengal Legislative Assembly, the agenda consisted of 5 Government Bills but almost the entire time of the House was taken up with the discussion of the Markets Regulation Bill introduced by Mr. Tamizuddin Khan, Minister for Agriculture and Industries.

A number of schemes of road development to be financed from allocations made to the provinces from the Central Road Fund were approved by the Standing Committee for Roads at its meetings held in New Delhi.

4th. The Government of Madras issued a Press communique on the condition of the rice market. The Government warned speculators against any attempt to corner stocks with the idea of profiteering.

A communique stated: The Governor-General in consultation with the Secretary of State, appointed Mr. H. B. Hodson to be Reforms Commissioner in succession to Sir Hawthorn Lewis.

The Council of State adjourned *sine die* after passing the Delhi Ribbon Development Bill and the Insurance Act Amendment Bill as passed by the Assembly.

In the Bengal Legislative Council, non-official resolutions comprised the agenda. There was debate over a resolution by Khan Bahadur Ataur Rahaman that Government contracts should be given to Bengal Moslems on their population basis in various districts.

Sir Sikander Hyat Khan, Premier, proposing his toast at a farewell dinner at Lahore, given by the Premier and Ministers of the Punjab Government, paid a tribute to Sir Henry Craik as an ideal constitutional head of the province whose mature wisdom and sympathetic advice had been a source of inspiration to the Ministry.

Mr. T. Chapman Mortimer, speaking at Asansol at a meeting of the Western Bengal branch of the European Association, dwelt on the political situation in India and criticized the attitude adopted by the Congress towards the British Government's offer to reopen the constitutional problem after the war.

Mr. V. D. Savarkar, President of the Hindu Mahasabha, observed in Bombay, "The Working Committee of the All-India Hindu Mahasabha is the real authority to say the last word on this question. In the meanwhile, if any views are expressed for or against the preparations for direct action, they must be treated as personal or unauthorised ones."

The All-India Conference of Sanatanists under the auspices of the Bharat Dharma Mahamandal concluded its three day session at Benares. The Conference was presided over by the Maharaja of Darbhanga, the Maharaja of Dewas and Seth Ram Krishna Dalmia on April, 1, 2 and 3, respectively.

5th. His Excellency the Governor of Madras, announcing that the Madras War Fund, in the short space of nine months, reached the total of a crore of Rupees, said: "We are celebrating to-day an achievement of which our presidency may be truly proud."

His Excellency Sir Maurice Hallett, the Governor of U. P., replying to an address of welcome at Bulandshahr said: "The future constitution of India is a matter of future discussion; rather though it may be discussed now, it cannot be settled until the present threat to freedom is removed, until we are free from the threat of Nazi domination."

6th. An official communique re: the riot situation in Dacca villages stated, "The situation in Narsindi, Raipura, and Sibpur thanas of the Dacca district is causing considerable anxiety. Detailed information is still lacking, as the local officers were busily engaged in the affected area. The Inspector General of Police observed that two large villages have been burnt out as well as several smaller localities."

Nawabzada Liaquat Ali Khan, Secretary of the All-India Moslem League, in his presidential speech at the Bombay Provincial League Conference declared that it would be unfair to brush aside the Pakistan scheme on the ground that it was a communal demand.

Mr. Mahadev Desai, addressing open the Khadi Village Industries and Swadeshi Exhibition organised by the State Congress at Vinobanagar, observed: "What is urgently required throughout India at present is a network of industries to provide employment for villagers. Your State can help you considerably in this respect. But you need not depend too much on such a help and so feel depressed when such help is denied by the State. I am sure that the millions that are supporting you have greater power than the State."

7th. Sir Tej Bahadur Sapru met His Excellency the Viceroy in New Delhi.

Mr. H. Siddaiya, President, addressing the Fourth Session of the Mysore Congress, observed: "So long as the reforms continue to be what they are, so long as the attitude of the Government remains one of hostility and opposition to the Congress and so long as there is no desire or earnestness on the part of the Government to understand and befriend us, the question of office acceptance by the Congress is of no moment and need not be considered at all."

In the Bengal Legislative Assembly, the Premier, Mr A. K. Fazlul Huq, made a statement on the riot situation in the Dacca district.—The Premier assured the House that all possible steps had been taken to cope with the situation, which he said, was under control.

Mr. Fazlul Huq, Bengal Premier, in a statement on the situation created by communal riots in Dacca and several other places appealed to Hindus and Moslems to co-operate among themselves and with the Government in restoring harmony.

Mr. Mahadev Desai, addressing a ladies' meeting at Ahmedabad, declared: "Mahatma Gandhi wants women to take up the difficult work of moving stony heart." He exhorted the women of Gujrat to take to spinning and other activities which Mahatma Gandhi had advised.

The Bombay Provincial Moslem League adopted a resolution, supporting the "Pakistan" resolution adopted at Lahore and expressed the opinion that Pakistan was the only natural, peaceful and permanent solution of the constitutional problem of India." Nawabzada Liaquat Ali Khan presided.

U. Ba Than, Commerce Minister, Burma in a statement to the House of Representatives on the Indo-Burma Trade Agreement, observed: "The arrangements are likely to secure for Burmese goods in India more or less their present position. while we hope that the low tariff that will be imposed upon Indian goods in Burma is low enough to maintain the present predominant position which Indian goods hold in the Burma market. Finally, the new arrangements will enable Burma to have the much needed revenue of over a crore from the customs duty."

8th. Sir Tej Bahadur Sapru called a meeting of the Standing Committee of the Bombay Conference at Allahabad on April 20 to inform his colleagues of what transpired between the Viceroy and him.

In the Bengal Legislative Council, a Congress motion for adjournment to criticize the Government in connexion with the communal disturbance in the Dacca district was talked out.

The Government of India decided to make a grant of Rs. 24,000 to Visva-Bharati in 1941-42 in recognition of the contribution it was making to Indian culture. The Bengal Government released the grant of a similar sum to the institution.

Mr. L. S. Amery, Secretary of State for India in a speech in London, said: Indian troops were side by side with British and Australian in delivering at Sidi Barrani "the first of General Wavell's hammer blows which smashed like an eggshell all Graziani's elaborate preparations for the invasion of Egypt."

9th. The Bengal Legislative Assembly by 107 votes to 67 rejected the adjournment motion moved by Rai H. N. Chowdhury in connexion with the riot situation in the Dacca district.

The report of the Select Committee on the Secondary Education Bill was presented to the Bengal Legislative Assembly.

Mr. L. S. Amery, Secretary of State for India tabled resolutions in the Commons to extend the validity of the Proclamations under Sec. 93 of the Government of India Act for another year in the seven former Congress Provinces.

Sir Maurice Hallett, Governor of the U. P. speaking at a meeting of the Meerut War Committee at Lucknow, criticized the Congress failure to recognize the realities of the war situation.

The U. P. Government decided to ban both Shia and Sunni processions on Bara-Wafat day which they had intended to allow earlier and proclaimed curfew for April 10, between the hours of 7 A.M. and 7 P.M.

10th. At the third All-India Obstetric and Gynecological Congress which commenced in Calcutta, under the presidency of Dr. N. N. Purandare of Bombay, various problems relating to maternity and child welfare were discussed. Sir P. C. Roy in his inaugural address regretted that in India provisions for maternity services were inadequate.

11th. The Executive Council of the U. P. Hindu League at Lucknow, passed a resolution urging upon all persons and bodies to observe the "Anti-Pakistan Day" on April 17, 1941, by holding public meetings and other suitable methods in their respective district headquarters.

By other resolution the Committee expressed full agreement with the spirit underlying the demand of the Non-Party Leaders' Conference and welcomed the discussions held between H. E. the Viceroy and Sir Tej Bahadur Sapru on the subject.

Mr. Mohiuddin, presiding over the 2nd. Bihar Momin Conference at Bettiah, observed that the Muslim League was an organization of upper class Muslims who had thriven at the cost of the Momin Community. He also contested the claim of the Muslim League as the sole representative of the Muslim Community in India.

12th. The twenty-eighth session of the All-India Muslim League Conference opened in Madras. Mr. M. A. Jinnah, the President, could not deliver his address owing to indisposition. Mr. Hamid Khan, referring to the Moslem League's demands, said : "The demand for Pakistan which implies the establishment of independent and separate Moslem States on the basis of a confederation does not run counter to the idea of India's political unity, nor does it mean the vivisection of India, since the basis of Pakistan has existed at all time in this country."

The Civil disobedience started by Sunnis against the decision of the authorities at Lucknow, banning their procession on Bara-Wafat day was suspended pending the result of negotiations with the Government.

Rai Bahadur Lala Ram Saran Das, leader of the Progressive Party in the Council of State, presiding over the 22nd. session of the All-India Khatriya Conference in Calcutta, expressed the opinion that India's best interests lay in the victory of Britain in the War.

At the Bengal Provincial Medical Conference at Dum Dum, a plea for a uniform standard of medical education was put forward.

Dr. D. R. Bhandarkar, presiding over the fifth session of the All-India Cultural Conference at Bolangir, expressed the view that Indian culture was a synthesis of practically all the cultures that had come to the country in the wake of foreign invasions.

His Highness Sir Sri Rama Varma, Maharaja of Cochin, died at Chowera.

Giani Tirath Singh, chairman of the Reception Committee, addressing the Sind Akali Conference at Karachi, said : "Nationalism is the political cult of modern India, and while this cult is in the course of development, we find a separatist trend being introduced by Mr. Jinnah in his Pakistan scheme."

13th. The main points of the Trade Agreements signed by the Governments of India and Burma were published in New Delhi.

The subjects committee of the All-India Moslem League discussed amendments to the League's constitution in Madras. In the absence of Mr. Jinnah, the Raja Saheb of Mahmudabad presided.

The question of launching "direct action" as contemplated in the Madura resolution of the All-India Hindu Mahasabha was to be decided by the All-India Committee of the Mahasabha. The decision was taken by the Working Committee of the Mahasabha which met at Nagpur under the presidentship of Mr. V. D. Savarkar.

Mr. M. Yunus, ex-Premier of Bihar, presiding over the second annual session of the Bihar Mel-Milap (Bihar Provincial Unity Conference) at Hazaribagh, observed : "The perpetual source of discord and disunity will remain so long as the so-called male nations of the world do not abandon the insensate game of maintaining harems of weaker nations. To appeal to those who have lust of domination is to appeal to Philip drunk. The real question is how to make Philip sober."

Mahant Digvijayanath of the Gorakh Temple, Gorakhpur, presiding over the Hindu Conference at Allahabad, urged that the Hindus should join the Army and Police forces and prepare for the defence of the country.

14th. The second sitting of the open session of the All-India Moslem League began in Madras, when Mr. M. A. Jinnah delivered his presidential address.—Mr. Jinnah in his address, surveyed the activities of the Moslem League and referred to the determination of the organization to establish Independent States in certain areas in India. The Moslem League, he said, would not under any circumstances agree to any constitution of an All-India character with one Government at the centre.

The Subjects Committee of the All-India Moslem League adopted a number of resolutions in Madras relating to Mahatma Gandhi's civil disobedience movement and the change of the creed of the League.

Ten thousand spectators, mostly Moslems, watched the Sunnis offer civil disobedience on the grounds adjoining the Idgah.

Dr. Rabindranath Tagore received numerous congratulatory messages on the occasion of his 80th birthday which was celebrated by the Visva-Bharati at Santinikentan.

15th. At the open session of the Moslem League in Madras, an amendment to the All-India Moslem League's constitution making Pakistan its goal, was unanimously passed.

A Government communique on the riot situation in the Dacca district, issued in Calcutta, said: "The Hon. the Chief Minister and the Hon. the Revenue Minister have returned from Dacca, where they discussed the situation with local officials and with prominent members of both communities. The Hon. Nawab Khawaja Habibulla Bahadur is still in the city."

The communal situation in Sind was considered at an emergency meeting of the Working Committee of the Hindu Mahasabha at Karachi, which expressed the opinion that things had not improved at Sukkur and that there was still some sense of insecurity, particularly in villages.

16th. Dr. Rajendra Prasad when shown the suggestion made by Mr. Jinnah in his Madras speech that the Congress should examine the Pakistan scheme, said at Patna: It is no use asking the Working Committee of the Congress to consider a scheme which has not been worked out and the details of which are not known to the public."

Mr. W. A. M. Walker, chairman of the Indian Jute Mills Association, in a broadcast speech from Calcutta described the part that the Indian Jute mill industry was playing in the war effort.

17th. The United Provinces Government refused permission for a deputation of the Sind Congress to interview Maulana Abul Kalam Azad in the Naini prison. The U. P. Government replied to Mr. P. Tahilramani, Secretary of the Sind Provincial Congress Committee, regretting its inability to grant an interview for the purpose desired.

Mr. M. A. Jinnah, in a statement from Madras, in reply to the one made by Babu Rajendra Prasad, asserted that the principle of partitioning India should be accepted first and then only would come the question of details.

The progress of Satyagraha in the province (Bihar) was reviewed by the Working Committee of the Bihar Provincial Congress Committee which met at Patna under the presidentship of Dr. Rajendra Prasad. The meeting was attended by representatives of the different District Congress Committees also.

18th. At Ahmedabad, five persons lost their lives and about 70 were injured as the result of communal disturbances in the city. Several shops were reported to have been burnt.

Prominent members of the Justice Party (Madras) met Mr. M. A. Jinnah and discussed with him the general political situation and how best the Moslem League and the Justice Party could work together for the attainment of their objective.

Dr. P. V. Naidu, delivering the presidential address to the Tanjore District Hindu Mahasabha Conference held at Kumbakonam, explained the implications of the Pakistan scheme of the Muslim League and appealed to the Hindus to rally behind the Hindu Mahasabha in its fight for freedom and safeguarding the position of the Hindus.

19th. Dr. Rajendra Prasad, in a Press statement from Patna, said: "I have seen Mr. Jinnah's statement issued from Madras on April 17, in which he has sought to make two points, and charged me with turning and twisting things. The first point is that the Congress need not wait for the details of the scheme of Pakistan, but should accept the principle forthwith and then the details may be worked out. The second is that the Congress is responsible for the failure of negotiations to arrive at a settlement and that the Congress position has been most arrogant and dictatorial.........One would like to know from Mr. Jinnah how and in what respects will Pakistan differ from these existing independent Moslem States and if it will not differ, how it will be able to give protection to the Moslem minorities in the rest of India any more than these existing independent Moslem States have been able to give."

The Raja of Mahmudabad, presiding at the Malabar District Moslem League Conference at Palghat, said that if Mahatma Gandhi came to terms with the

Moslems and accepted the Pakistan scheme, the communal problem would be solved and Moslems would fight shoulder to shoulder with the Hindus for India's freedom.

His Exalted Highness the Nizam of Hyderabad issued a firman, in which he stated *inter alia*: "It can never be expedient during war time for thoughtless people to publish mischievous articles in local newspapers or for irresponsible organizations to hold meetings for making speeches and passing resolutions, nor is it proper for one community to make unnecessary remarks against another or throw ridicule over it."

Sardar Santokh Singh, leader of the Opposition in the Punjab Assembly, welcoming the delegates to the Punjab Traders Conference at Amritsar, made a detailed criticism of the legislation affecting trade and industry particularly the general Sales Tax Act, enacted by the Punjab Government.

Sardar Amar Singh, President of the All-India Sikh League, at a function arranged in his honour at Karachi, declared: We will rather be annihilated than submit to a communal raj and we would never leave our motherland, religion and community and will not permit the establishment of a communal raj."

20th. There was a further deterioration in the riot situation at Ahmedabad when trouble spread to the outlying areas of the city. The total number of casualties were over 55 killed and about 390 injured. The Governor, Sir Roger Lumley toured the riot affected areas, then proceeded to the Civil Hospital, and saw the people injured in the riots.

Sir Maurice Gwyer, Vice-Chancellor of Delhi University, addressing the annual meeting of the University Court, declared: Though the present war, in which civilization itself it at stake, demands all our energies and all the money which we can afford, yet there is one service which it would be falsest of false economy to cut down, even at a time like the present......I mean the service of education."

Mr P. V. Naidu, General Secretary, All-India Hindu Mahasabha, presiding at the Tanjore District Hindu Sabha Conference at Kumbakonam, declared that if the British Empire collapsed it would be most disastrous to Hindus.

21st. Mahatma Gandhi refused to withdrew the civil disobedience movement. In an interview in Bombay, he said: "I adhere to all that I said at the initiation of the struggle. I had no foolish illusion about a sudden miracle happening. It was conceived to be, and it remains, a silent declaration of unquenchable faith in the power of non-violence even in the midst of circumstances so terrible and so baffling as face the world today.—"I believe more in the efficacy of the incalculable force of an inscrutable Divinity than in the efficacy of the calculated and calculable forces that the combined powers of destruction can bring into play on this little planet. That incalculable force has somehow or other to act through human agency."

Mr. A. K. Fazlul Huq, the Bengal Premier, in a statement to the press, made an appeal to his countrymen not to give way to panic, but to do their utmost to prevent any breach of the peace.

In connexion with Congress Satyagraha in the Punjab, Mr. Prakash Chand of Gojra was sentenced to nine months and to a fine of Rs. 25.

The Tanjore District Hindu Mahasabha Conference. under the Presidentship of Dr. P. V. Naidu adopted a resolution, among others, recommending to the All-India Committee of the Hindu Mahasabha that the Madura resolution on direct action should be reconsidered purely from the point of view of serving and advancing the Hindu cause.

22nd. The riot situation at Ahmedabad, according to official reports, definitely improved, and apart from the mill area, the city returned to normal conditions.

The total number of arrests in the city of Dacca in connexion with the arrests was 1,046, whiie that in Narainganj Subdivision was about 875.

The "Hindu" commenting on Mahatma Gandhi's statement on civil disobedience, said: "Mr. Gandhi's reply to the suggestion that the present individual civil disobedience movement should be called off, is not surprising from one whose primary preoccupation is with those moral issues which are at the root of all conflict, and which merely find in the present war an extended and terrible illustration."

In the Bengal Legislative Assembly, when the Bengal Local Self-Government (Amendment) Bill, 1941, as passed by the Legislative Council came up for consideration, the measure met with strong opposition from the Bose Group and the Krishak Proja Party.

The Government of Bengal decided not to accept the suggestion of the Government of India to undertake prosecution themselves on behalf of Government servants when they were defamed.

Dr. Rajendra Prasad, in reply to the representation made by the Manbhum District Congress Committee, expressed the opinion that no Congressman should seek re-election to a local body even in his individual capacity once the Congress as a Party had with-drawn from it.

Mr. L. S. Amery, Secretary of State for India, moved a resolution in the House of Commons, to extend for another year the proclamation under which the Governors of the Indian Provinces would assume the powers of Provincial Legislatures.

Nawab Bahadur Yar Jung of Hyderabad, President, All-India States Muslim League, addressing a big gathering of Muslims at Bangalore, stated that Hindusthan never had been, and never could be, one political unit and there could never be one nation in India. He claimed that Pakistan was the only solution for developing the interest and culture of Muslims. The meeting was organized by the Mysore State Muslim League.

His Excellency the Governor of Bengal presided at a meeting of the Conference of Political Leaders.

23rd. The Budget session of the Bengal Legislative Assembly which began on February 3, concluded when the House was prorogued. The only item on the agenda was the consideration of the Local Self-Government (Amendment) Bill as passed by the Legislative Council. The measure was passed without any modification. Before the House was prorogued, the Speaker, Sir Mohamed Azizul Haque, read a message received from His Excellency Sir Archibald Wavell, Commander-in-Chief of His Majesty's Imperial Forces in the Middle East, in reply to the message sent by the Assembly through His Excellency the Governor of Bengal and the Commander-in-Chief in India, expressing its rejoicings at the capture of Keren and Harar, and congratulating the Indian troops and other units of the Imperial forces on the gallant part played by them in bringing about those successes.

24th. The heads of agreement arrived at by the delegates of the Governments of India and Burma concerned with the Indo-Burma trade negotiations were published. They gave details under two parts, one relating to tariff treatment of Burma goods on import into India and the other relating to tariff treatment of Indian goods on import into Burma.

Mr. Nalini Ranjan Sarkar, presiding over the All-Bengal Economic Conference in Calcutta, stressed that the problem that confronted India was essentially one of production and not distribution.

Sir Jagadish Prasad characterized the statement of Mr. Amery as "most disappointing and unhelpful."

Mr. V. N. Chandavarkar, President, National Liberal Federation of India remarked that Mr. Amery's statement "does not lead us anywhere."

Sir Chimanlal Setalvad said: "The demands put forward by the Bombay Conference have been rejected by Mr. Amery: no other result was possible.

Sir S. Radhakrishnan declared: "The way in which the proposals of the Bombay Conference have been treated by the Secretary indicates that, even in this crisis, Britain is not willing to part with power in India."

Sir P. S. Sivaswami Aiyar declared in an interview: "The latest speech of Mr. Amery in the House of Commons will not bring about any solution of the constitutional deadlock or any of the easing of the political and communal tension in this country."

A Bill to amend the Punjab Agricultural Produce Markets Act was published in a Gazette Extraordinary at Lahore.

25th. Communal riots again broke out in Bombay city and the police had to open fire at three different places along Mohamedali Road to deal with mob violence.

Mahatma Gandhi made a statement from Wardha, on Mr. Amery's speech in the House of Commons: "I have read painfully the long report of the debate in the House of Commons on India. Distress has been known to have softened people's hearts and made them mindful of facts. But Britain's distress has evidently left Mr. Amery absolutely cold and untouched. The callousness makes me more than ever confirmed in my opinion that the Congress must abide by its policy of non-violence inspite of the heavy odds facing it."

26th. His Excellency the Governor of Bombay, accompanied by the Commissioner of Police, toured the riot affected areas in the city and made enquiries at various points about the steps taken for the strict enforcement of the curfew and for the prevention of breaches of the peace.

The Audit Report, 1941, on the Administration of Finances in Orissa disclosed that the budget estimates for the year 1939-40 included a provision of Rs. 172.82 lakhs in the voted section, and the expenditure actually incurred amounted to Rs. 161.57 lakhs, showing a saving of Rs. 11.25 lakhs.

27th. Mr. S. Srinivasa Sastri, presiding over a public meeting at Mylapore (Madras) declared : "We ask the Congress people to come back, lead us and protect us in this time of great trouble. Their place today as people who hold our confidence and suffrage, is beside us, and not in prison cells."

A communique was issued regarding the deliberations at the conference of party leaders in the Bengal Legislature held in Calcutta under the presidentship of His Excellency the Governor of Bengal. It stated *inter alia* :

"The Conference desires to emphasize strongly the paramount need for maintaining unity between all classes and communities, particularly in view of the latest developments in the Near East. It urges upon all communities the desirability of putting aside all communal or sectarian prejudices which might be the cause of discord."

The members of the Standing Committee of the Bombay Leaders' Conference who were present at Allahabad, namely, Kunwar Sir Jagadish Prasad. Mr. M. S. Aney Sardar Sant Singh and Mr. B. Shiva Rao, opened informal discussions with Sir Tej Bahadur Sapru, as President, at his residence.

28th. The Standing Committee of the Bombay Conference after its deliberations at Allahabad, issued a statement observing : "The Standing Committee of the Bombay Conference have read Mr. Amery's speech in the House of Commons with the care which they deserve. The Committee very much regret that the speeches should have betrayed such an amazing misunderstanding of the real political situation in India and displayed such an unsympathetic and unbending attitude towards the aspirations of India.

"The Committee feel that Mr. Amery has missed the opportunity of winning public confidence which was offered to the British Government with the best intentions by those who have a vivid appreciation of the dangers of the international situation."

Mr. P. N. Brahma was unanimously elected as the Mayor of Calcutta for 1941-42.

29th. Sir Tej Bahadur Sapru in a statement on Mr. Amery's speech in the House of Commons, observed : "Bluntly put, Mr. Amery is mortgaging our future to certain intractable leaders. Expediencies of the hour are not always consistent with lasting policies seeking to achieve permanent good of a vast country like India. Has Mr. Amery such a permanent policy ?"

Sir Sultan Ahmed, presiding at the Bihar Provincial War Committee meeting at Muzaffarpur observed : Knowing as I do the pulse of my countrymen, I can honestly and conscientiously assert that 99 per cent of the population are not only against Fascism and Nazism but they feel that Hitler's and Mussolini's success would be the end of all India's political ambitions."

The Government of Bengal decided to appoint a committee to inquire into the disturbances in Dacca.

30th. The Dacca Chamber of Commerce at a meeting adopted a resolution requesting His Excellency the Governor to assume his special responsibilities under the Government of India Act and restore peace and order in the town with a view to the resumption of normal business conditions.

Srimati Vidyabathi Seth and Srimati Bhagwanti were convicted by the additional District Magistrate of Amritsar under the Defence of India Rules and sentenced to 9 months' simple imprisonment each.

A district "Mel-Milap" Unity Association was formed Muzaffarpore with Mr. Safi Daudi, EX-M.L.A. (Central) as its President.

His Excellency the Governor of Bengal, accompanied by the Commissioner and other local officials visited several areas in the Dacca district.

May 1941

Mr. M. A. Jinnah, President of the All-India Moslem League, in releasing the correspondence between him and Sir Tej Bahadur Sapru, remarked that he was always willing to meet Mahatma Gandhi or any other Hindu leader to have a heart to heart conversation on the political deadlock in India.

Sir Tej Bahadur Sapru, in releasing the correspondence which passed between him and Mahatma Gandhi, observed that Mr. Jinnah wanted to see "Mahatma Gandhi or any other Hindu leader on behalf of the Hindu Community". But Mahatma Gandhi was not willing to agree to the condition imposed by Mr. Jinnah.

Mr. Jinnah, in a statement observed that the Non-party leaders' Conference in Bombay was engineered by the agents of the Congress and the Hindu Mahasabha. The statement occasioned vehement protests from the Congress and the Hindu Mahasabha and Sir Tej Bahadur Sapru also emphatically contradicted the suggestion made by Mr. Jinnah.

Mr. S. C. Mookerjee, President, Indian Christian Association, Bengal, at a general meeting of the Association in Calcutta, exhorted his audience to help Britain in her hour of trial as the destiny of India and England was indissolubly bound up.

Mahatma Gandhi, in the course of a statement on the communal riots in Bombay and Bengal, regretted that the influence of the Congress was "practically unfelt during the dark days" and remarked that Congress influence was to be measured not by the number of members only but by its leavening quality.

Dr. Rabindranath Tagore's 80th. birthday was celebrated in Calcutta and in other parts of India. Felicitations were conveyed to the poet.

H. E. H. the Nizam's Government repudiated the theory propounded by a Muslim organization, that the Sovereignty of the State belonged to the Muslims only.

The Hon'ble Nawab Bahadur of Murshidabad, President of the Hindu Muslim Unity Association, in a statement issued from Calcutta strongly criticized the Pakistan Scheme as advocated by Mr. Jinnah and remarked that the scheme could never be wholeheartedly accepted by the Indians.

His Excellency the Governor-General gave his assent to the Act for the further amendment of the Madras Local Boards Act, 1920, which provided that the Provincial Government might, by notification, supersede for a specified period not exceeding three years, a district board which was dissolved and was awaiting reconstitution.

There was a representative gathering of Hindus and Moslems at Patna for discovering ways and means of bringing about a peaceful settlement of the problems of the two communities. Dr. Rajendra Prasad, Khan Bahadur S. M. Ismail and M. Yunus addressed the gathering.

Sir Henry Gidney in a message to the Jubbulpore branch of the Anglo-Indian Association, strongly advised the members of his Community to render every possible help to the King and Country.

The death occurred of Mr. S. Srinivasa Iyengar, ex-President of the Indian National Congress.

Mahatma Gandhi, in a letter to the Secretary, Gujrat Provincial Congress Committee, stated, "That people should flee for their lives for fear of the goonda should be intolerable", and advised every one to resist the evil-doers either non-violently or violently as the situation demanded.

The Duke of Devonshire, Parliamentary Under-Secretary of State for India, declared: "It is intended that the Government of India should be carried on by India, for India, in India and not from Whitehall."

Sir Mirza Ismail, Dewan of Mysore, observed at Bangalore that the bonds which united the Hindus and the Muslims were far stronger than all the differences which were stressed by interested parties.

1st. At a May Day labour rally in Calcutta, Mr. Safiatulla Khan made a call to the working classes of India to unite in order to fight the menace of Nazism and Fascism,

The Holkar Government appointed a committee to go into some of the grievances of labourers including the question of an additional allowance necessitated by the rise in the cost of living.

Mr. M. A. Jinnah, President of the All-India Muslim League released the correspondence between him and Sir Tej Bahadur Sapru and issued a statement to the Press, stating inter alia: "He (Sir Tej Bahadur) characterises me as an 'intractable leader', when by my letter dated February 10, 1941, I at once showed my willingness, as suggested by him, to meet Mr. Gandhi or any other Hindu leader to have a heart to heart conversation."

2nd. The report on the administration of Mysore for the year 1939-40 revealed the great strides made in the development of industries and commerce and the all round progress witnessed in all spheres of Governmental activity.

3rd. Dr. N. N. Law presiding over the first annual general meeting of the Bengal Banks Association held in Calcutta, referred to the difficulties which most Bengali Banks were experiencing on account of the coming into force of the Bengal Moneylenders' Act with effect from September 1, 1940.

Mr. S. C. Mukherjee, President, Indian Christian Association, Bengal, at a general meeting of the Association in Calcutta, observed: "It is our bounden duty to help Britain in every possible way in the life and death struggle with Germany. Our destiny is indissolubly bound up with that of England. If England goes under, the consequences will be disastrous to India, nay to the whole world."

The number of dead in the communal rioting in Bihar-Shareef and neighbouring villages was reported to be 21, according to official information received at Ranchi.

4th. Sir Tej Bahadur Sapru, in releasing the correspondence which passed between him and Mahatma Gandhi in his efforts to bring Mr. Jinnah and the Mahatma together with a view to solving the political dead-lock, issued a statement: "In his statement Mr. Jinnah says that he showed his willingness to meet Mr. Gandhi, or any other Hindu leader to have a heart to heart conversation. He would have been more accurate if he had drawn attention to the following sentence, in his own letter to me, 'I have always been ready and willing to see Mr. Gandhi or any other Hindu leader, on behalf of the Hindu community and do all I can to help the solution of the Hindu-Moslem problem,—"The words 'on behalf of the Hindu Community' which he has omitted in his statement, but which are found in his letter, would go to show that he wanted Mr. Gandhi to see him in that professed capacity. Mr. Gandhi as will appear from his letter, was not in a position to agree to this condition. There the matter ended, and it was no use carrying the matter further with Mr. Jinnah."

Mr. M. A. Jinnah, in a statement from Nandi Hill, observed that there was ample evidence before him to show that the Bombay Conference was engineered by agents of the Congress and the Hindu Mahasabha leaders and that also well-known and prominent Congress leaders remained in the background and that Sir Tej Bahadur Sapru consciously or unconsciously let his name be associated with the move.

At the annual meeting of the Council of the U. P. Provincial Moslem League held at Lucknow, under the presidentship of Nawab Sir Mohamed Ismail Khan, a resolution expressing disapproval of Mr. Amery's utterances on the Moslem League's demand for Pakistan and Mahatma Gandhi's statement thereon, was passed.

5th. Dr. P. V, Naidu, General Secretary of the Hindu Mahasabha, in the course of a statement from Madras made an emphatic denial that the Hindu Mahasabha had any hand in the Bombay Conference.

Mahatma Gandhi published a note in the May issue of the Sarwodaya : "The movement for the conduct of which I am responsible, may prove a vain effort. If I represent no one but myself and if I remain true to my faith, I may be satisfied, but so far world peace is concerned the effort will prove inadequate in terms of the present".—"For producing the desired result during the lifetime of the present generation it will be necessary to give an unmistakable demonstration that a substantial part of the nation is behind the effort. Much more has to happen before such a demonstration becomes possible. The present movement is a humble attempt in that direction. Man can only make an honest attempt."

Mr. K. Srinivasan issued a statement from Madras with reference to Mr. Jinnah's statement on the Bombay Conference observing inter alia : "This is the first time I have come across such a report. The allegations made therein are absolutely false and baseless."

Mr. M. S. Aney, M.L.A. (Central) at the annual meeting of the District Association, Yeotmal observed : "All political and prudential considerations combine in emphasising the importance of the youth of the country flocking to the military profession, whose gates are now flung wide open to all and sundry."

6th. Sir Tej Bahadur Sapru issued a statement in reply to the one made by Mr. Jinnah in which the latter made certain observations regarding the conference of non-party leaders in Bombay. He observed inter alia : "Mr. Jinnah finds himself at bay and that must account for the intemperate and at places vitriolic language which he has used in denouncing the Bombay Conference.—"Mr. Jinnah says that the resolution is a 'worthless document intended purely for purposes of propaganda to mislead the ignorant and credulous people of India'. I know and I regret that in this country 'ignorant and credulous people' have been very much exploited by certain parties, but if the resolution was so worthless, why is Mr. Jinnah wasting so much of his time and mine over it ?"

Mahatma Gandhi directed that Sind should be considered outside the Satyagraha Zone and Congressmen of the province should continue their normal activities.

Mahatma Gandhi, in the course of a statement on the communal riots, said : "Hindu-Moslem riots that have broken out in many important places in the country must have saddened all sane people. My grief, however, is special. Congress influence seems to have been practically unfelt during the dark days. We have proved ourselves barbarians and cowards in these places..........Congress influence is not to be measured by the number of members on the Congress register but by its leavening quality."

Sir C. P. Ramaswami Aiyar, Dewan of Travancore addressing a public meeting in Madras, said : "The end of this war will leave this world in a dreadful state of disorganisation and ruin. The world would have to be rebuilt, society renovated, philosophies reassimilated, and ways of life reshaped."

After five days' suspension of business as a protest against the Punjab Agricultural Produce Markets Act, Shops were opened throughout the province.

7th. Dr. Rabindranath Tagore's 80th birthday was celebrated in Calcutta and in various other places. Felicitations were conveyed to the poet.

Sir Henry Gidney, M.L.A. (Central) in a statement from New Delhi on the Indian political situation, pointing what should be done pending communal settlement, said : "I consider Mr. Amery's demand for a Hindu-Moslem settlement before there can be any change in the present constitution a wise decison, especially at the present time when the peace of everv country in the world is threatened from outside."

Mahatma Gandhi issued a statement to the Press, re: Bihar riots, and observed: "The account of the riot makes painful reading. I have studied the various statements regarding them also. Rajendra Babu has gone to Bihar to put the whole of his weight in favour of sanity and peace.........Peace will somehow be restored, if it has not been already, by the police and the military. But this can only be a Superimposed peace. Rajendra Babu's, as every Congressman's and, for that matter, every sane citizen's business is to find out the cause of the riots. Unless this is done, there is no likelihood of permanent peace."

H. E. H. the Nizam's Government, through a Gazette Extraordinary, repudiated the theory propounded by the 'Majlis I Hidadul Muslimeen' (a Muslim organization) that the sovereignty of the State vested in the Muslims of the State and that His Exalted Highness merely embodied "the Muslim Sovereignty" and disclaimed the charge of the Majlis that the Government's attitude was responsible for the theory,

8th. Sir Tej Bahadur Sapru issued a statement from Allahabad, with regard to the canard regarding the convening of the Bombay conference and the authorship of the resolution of the conference, and said that Mr. K. Srinivasan, Managing Editor of the *Hindu* never prevailed on him to convene the Conference and the resolution was not drafted by Mr. C. Rajagopalachari. The only person who asked him to preside over the Bombay Conference was Sir Jagadish Prasad. Later on Sir N. N. Sircar expressed his satisfaction that he had agreed to preside.

The Standing Committee of the Bombay Conference in a statement in reply to the one issued by Mr. Jinnah, said inter alia: "At the Moslem League meeting in Madras, Mr. Jinnah adopted the orthodox Delhi view towards the Bombay Conference. He had even the audacity to say that the Hindu Mahasabha had repudiated it although he must have known that Dr. Shyama Prosad Mukherji, President of the Mahasabha was a member of the Standing Committee. His attitude came very handy to Mr. Amery whe said that he was not sure who the actual supporters of the Bombay resolution were.—"Mr. Jinnah has now come out in his true colours. No scheme of Government will satisfy him even for the period of war unless it is in furtherance of the disruption of India. And yet Mr. Amery asks the President of the Conference, Sir Tej Bahadur Sapru, to address his proposals not to the British Parliament but to Mr. Jinnah."

The Committee of the Indian Chamber of Commerce, Calcutta, submitted a memorandum to the Government of India embodying their views on some aspects of the problem of post-war economic reconstruction in reference to certain observations made by the Commerce Member of the Government of India during the general discussion of the Finance Bill in the Central Assembly.

Congressmen, members of the Moslem League, the Hindu Mahasabha and others attended a meeting at Gaya to condemn communal riots. Khawaja Sir Muhammad Noor, former Judge, Patna High Court presided.

9th. It was announced that the Government of India decided to extend by another year the experimental period for the special press concessional rate for press messages sent over the trunk telephone between midnight and 6 A. M.

Millowners from different parts of India met in conference representatives of the Department of Supply to discuss matters relating to military requirements of cotton textile goods.

10th. Sir Tej Bahadur Sapru, in the course of an article in the *Twentieth Century*, under the caption, "Mr. Amery and the Bombay Conference", observed: "For the British generally to agree to the demand for the dissection of India will be, I maintain, an act of black treachery to India."

His Excellency the Governor of Bengal, by an order issued under the Defence of India Rules, rescinded from May 7 the Bengal Government order dated November 26, 1940, passed on all printers, publishers and editors of newspapers in Bengal, requiring them to submit all matters relating to military subject within the province and Assam military district, before being published in any newspaper, journal or periodical, for scrutiny to the headquarters of the province and Assam District, Fort William, Calcutta.

The Bengal Local Self-Government Amendment Act received the assent of his Excellency the Governor of Bengal.

Sir Ghulam Hussain Hidayatullah, Minister for Law and order, addressing the Unity Conference convened at Sukkur, declared: "Either the badmash elements who foment riots should be wiped out or I am fully prepared even to lay down my life for making Sind safe for peaceful citizens and am determined to maintain peace at any cost."

To discuss the situation created by the Government proposal to restrict imports of newsprint, a deputation of the Indian and Eastern Newspaper Society waited on Sir Ramaswami Mudaliar, Commerce Member, Government of India.

11th. Maulvi Yusuf Ali convened a meeting at Faridpur, with a view to devising ways and means for maintaining communal harmony. Khan Bahadur Rahamat Jan Chowdhury presided.

The Committee of the U. P. Liberal Association passed a resolution at Allahabad, urging His Majesty's Government to make a "clear unequivocal declaration that they will not entertain any proposal to destroy the teritorial integrity and unity of India". Pandit Hridayanath Kunzru was in the chair.

His Excellency Sir Hawthorne Lewis, Governor of Orissa, visited Chowdwar, the site selected in 1934 by the Orissa Assembly for the capital of the province.

12th. Sir K. V. Reddi Naidu presiding over the Meelad celebrations of the Government Muslim Servants' Association in Madras, said that there was no Hindu-Muslim problem in the Province. For years they had been living as brothers and he hoped that the relationship would continue for generations to come.

Mr. V. D. Savarkar, criticising a statement issued by Dr. Rajendra Prasad on the communal riots in Bihar, said that Dr. Rajendra Prased, just as he had admonished the Hindus in Bihar should also have given a word of advice to the Muslims in Bengal. Why had not Dr. Rajendra Prasad condemned the riots in Dacca ? "Every well-wisher of the country", added Mr. Savarkar, "should realise that the sooner peace and good-will are restored and the Hindus and Muslims come to live as good neighbours, the better for us all. But if the Muslims continue to take the aggressive, it may be that the Hindus suffer in the beginning but the Muslims shall also have to pay the bill".

13th. A press communique stated : "The Italian mountain stronghold of Amba Alagi, already in grave danger from the north by the steady advance of Indian troops, is now seriously menaced by the approach from the south of Abyssinian patriots and South African forces."

At a meeting of the Executive Committee of the Indian Association, Calcutta, strong disapproval of the manner in which the disturbances in the Dacca distrct were dealt with by the Government of Bengal, was expressed in a resolution.

The special committee appointed by the Mysore Government on March 6, 1940, (re : Prison Reforms), with Dewan Bahadur K. S. Chandrasekhara Aiyar as chairman, submitted their report to Government on April 3, 1941. The abolition of whipping and solitary confinement as forms of judicial punishment were unanimously recommended by the Committee.

The Hon. Nawab Bahadur of Murshidabad, President of the Hindu-Muslim Unity Association issued a statement from Calcutta, in which he observed inter alia : "Mr. Jinnah, whatever his ideology may be, is to be congratulated on his far-fetched proposition of building up a Pakistan edifice in India resting on a flimsy foundation which concensus of opinion will do all in its power to prevent being established. If Mr. Jinnah could have, by any contrivance, got himself promoted from the grade of a political leader to that of a despotic ruler, he might have thrust his Pakistan scheme nolens volens on the heads of the helpless people of India, who even then could not have wholeheartedly supported it."

A representative gathering of Hindu and Muslim citizens of Patna, heard Dr. Rajendra Prasad, Khan Bahadur S. M. Ismail, President of the Bihar Muslim League and Mr. Mohamed Yunus, ex-Premier of Bihar, speak on the necessity of living in harmony and peace, at a meeting held under the auspices of the Patna Peace Committee.

14th. His Excellency the Governor-General gave his assent on the 9th May 1941 to the Act further to amend the Madras Local Boards Act, 1920, which provided that the Provincial Government might, by notification, supersede for a specified period not exceeding three years, a district board which had been dissolved and was awaiting reconstitution.

The Government of Bombay sanctioned a scheme for the grant of subsidies and loans to artisans for the purchase of appliances and tools and to provide them with working capital.

15th. The Government of Madras issued a communique explaining the circumstances which led to their action in declaring the Karshaka Sanghams of South Kanara and Malabar districts to be unlawful associations within the meaning of the Criminal Law Amendment Act.

Mr. A. Rama Aiyar, presiding over the Madras Provincial Educational Conference at Rishi Valley, Madanapalle, made a comprehensive analysis of the problems facing educationists in the province. Surveying the general and all-round failure of the prevailing system, he pleaded for a vigorous and radical policy of reform. He also emphasised the imperative necessity of adopting the mother tongue as the medium of instruction.

Lord Hailey, in the course of a discussion at the East India Association, (London) declared : "If India is not providing as much war equipment as she might, it is because of Britain's own lack of preparedness and not the fault of the Indian Government.

16th. Sir Mirza Ismail, Dewan of Mysore, tendered his resignation of the dewanship of the State following an interview with His Highness the Maharaja.

The question of maintaining the supply of electricity in Calcutta and the surrounding industrial areas of the 24 Pergs, Howrah and Hooghly and the towns of Asansol, Chittagong and Dacca during a period of emergency, was under the active consideration of the Government of Bengal.

17th. An official notification was issued from Bangalore: "His Highness the Maharaja has been pleased to grant Sir Mirza Ismail a years's leave preparatory to retirement, to take effect from June 1, 1941, from which date Rajmantra-pravina N. Madhava Rao will officiate as the Dewan of Mysore."

The conference convened by the Mayor, Mr. M. H. Gazdar, to consider the question of maintaining internal security at Karachi, was attended by prominent citizens representing various organizations including the Congress, the League and the Hindu Sabha. It appointed a committee, with the Mayor as chairman, to keep vigilance and interview the Ministers for the purpose of taking adequate action in emergency.

Mr. M. A. Jinnah, in an interview with the President of the Mysore State Muslim League, at Bangalore, declared that the Pakistan Scheme of the All-India Muslim League had nothing to do with the States.

Mr. F. R. Pilot, who arrived in India, to represent New Zealand on the Eastern Group Supply Council, in the course of a statement to the Press at Simla, said that the Dominion was eager to play its part in the economic and millitary organization of the Eastern Group and of the British Empire as a whole.

Sir Henry Gidney, in a message to the annual general meeting of the Jubbulpore branch of the Anglo-Indian Association, said: "Service to the King and Country, in times of crisis like this, is an instructive attribute of the Anglo-Indian, and I have no doubt that it will continue to be so for ever."

18th. The Government's scheme for training aircraft mechanics to provide personnel for the Air forces was explained by Mr. P. H. Davy, Chief Inspector of Aircraft, in a broadcast talk from Delhi.

19th. The death occurred of Mr. S. Srinivasa Iyengar, ex-President of the Indian National Congress at "Amjad Bagh," his residence in Mylapore (Madras).

Mr. Tushar Kanti Ghosh, presiding at the fourth annual general meeting of the Bengal Film Journalists' Association in Calcutta, suggested formation of an All-India Film Journalists' Association on the lines of the All-India Newspaper Editors' Conference.

Government control of newsprint prices and issue of licenses and quotas to newspapers were urged by a deputation on behalf of the Indian Languages Newspaper Owners' Association of the Bombay Presidency, which waited on Sir Ramaswami Mudaliar, Commerce Member.

Mr. L. S. Amery, accompanied by Mrs. Amery, visited 50 Indian technicians at work in a Government training centre in London. Mr. Amery said: "The result of your training will, I hope, be an advantage to each one of you, enabling you to earn better money when you get back to India and to make a successful career in your native home. But the object of your coming here is something more than that. It is that you should serve your country, India."

20th. Mr. Mohamed Yunus, former Premier of Bihar in a Press interview at Patna, welcomed the proposal of Mr. A. K. Fazlul Huq, Bengal Premier, to convene a conference of Provincial Ministers and former Ministers with a view to solving the impasse and giving wholehearted support to war efforts.

21st. In connexion with the preparation of new electoral rolls for the Central Legislative Assembly, steps were taken by European Association, Calcutta Branch, to ensure that the name of every European who was a qualified elector was placed on the roll.

A scheme for the reorganization of the Bengal Textile Institute at Serampore was formulated by the Bengal Mill-owners Association at the instance of the Government of Bengal.

The President, Andhra Provincial Congress Committee, issued a statement regarding the progress of Satyagraha for the period of six months ending with the 5th May, 1941 from November 26, 1940. During the period, Satyagraha was carried on with great vigour and enthusiasm in the fourteen districts of Andhra, of the 2,161 approved Satyagrahis who offered civil disobedience, 1,115 were arrested, prosecuted and convicted, 1,046 were either not arrested at all or were let off some time after arrest.

22nd. In Bombay, within a fortnight of the withdrawal of all restrictive orders in connexion with communal tension in the city, Hindu-Moslem riots broke out again and within half an hour a number of cases of stabbing and stray assaults occurred.

Sir B. Rama Rau, formerly Agent-General for India in South Africa, in an interview in Bombay, said : "The present Government in South Africa is sympathetic towards the Indian problem and the presence of Mr. Hofmeyer in the Cabinet is a guarantee in itself that the Indian question will be dealt with not only sympathetically but also liberally."

23rd. The Empire Day message was sent by the chairman of the Royal Empire Society, London, to all fellows of the society in India through its Secretary, Mr. R. B. Lagden.

Sir Badridas Goenka, President of the Indian Chamber of Commerce, presiding at the quarterly general meeting of that body in Calcutta, advocated an active policy of industrialization of India.

Fourteen Satyagrahis who shouted anti-war slogans in Madras were convicted by the officiating Chief Presidency Magistrate, under the Defence of India Act and sentenced to varying terms of imprisonment. Mrs. Krishna Bai Nimbkar (wife of Capt. V. D. Nimbakar), a medical practitioner, was among the Satyagrahis who were sentenced.

Mahatma Gandhi, in the course of a letter to Mr. Bhogilal Lala, Secretary, Gujerat Provincial Congress Committee, said : "That people should flee for their lives for fear of the goonda should be intolerable. They ought to possess the capacity of resisting goondashahi (reign of the goonda) violently or non-violently. If my interpretation of the Congress creed is correct, the Congress and Congressmen may offer non-violent resistance only and they are sure to succeed. But we should tell the people, in the clearest possible terms, that running away in fear is cowardice. It is their duty to offer resistance, even violent, if they are incapable of non-violent resistance which is a worthy way."

The Punjab Agricultural Produce Markets (Amendment) Act which was passed by the Punjab Assembly, received the assent of His Excellency the Governor. His Excellency also accorded his assent to Punjab Urban Rent Restriction Act.

24th. The Government of Bengal appointed the Hon'ble Mr. Justice McNair (President) and Mr. W. M. C. Sharpe, I.C.S., District and Sessions Judge (Member) to constitute the committee of inquiry into the disturbances in Dacca city and district.

Communal tension continued in Bombay. Eight persons were stabbed.

25th. At Lahore, in response to an invitation by Mian Iftikaruddin, President of the Punjab Provincial Congress Committee, over one hundred representatives of various communities met at his residence, to explore ways and means of fostering communal harmony in the province. Sir Abdul Quadir presided over the meeting, which passed a resolution appealing to every section of the people of the Punjab to work for fostering peace and goodwill in the province. The meeting formed a committee of eleven members to give practical shape to the programme of the meeting.

The formation of a "Muslim Defence Council," consisting of "Muslim leaders and statesmen such as Sir Sikander Hyat Khan, Mr. A. K. Fazlul Huq, Sir M. Saadulla, the Nawab of Chhatari, etc. under the presidentship of H. E. the Viceroy or a Muslim ruler as suggested in a resolution at Bhopal, should be moved at the special session of the All-India States' Muslim League at Ajmere.

26th. British troops were called out in Bombay to help the police in quelling communal rioting in the city.

A further extension of the Bengal Government's youth welfare scheme was under active consideration of the authorities.

Sir R. K. Shanmukham Chetti, Dewan of Cochin, requested His Highness the Maharaja to permit him to retire from office as Dewan on June 30.

In a message to the members of the Mysore University Union, Mr. M. A. Jinnah advised them, "not to be led away by the slogans and high sounding words of leaders but to hear them and to maintain your own independent judgment on every question."

27th. A meeting of the Working Committee of the Bengal Provincial Moslem League was held in the office of the Moslem League. Mr. A. K. Fazlul Huq, President of the Provincial League was in the chair. The Committee discussed the appeal preferred by certain Moslem League members of the Calcutta Corporation against the decisions of the Calcutta District Moslem League concerning the Moslem League Municipal Association and the formation of a coalition party in the Corporation.

28th. Two persons were killed and 15 injured in the communal disturbances in Bombay City. There was no organized rioting, disturbances being mainly in the nature of stabbing or assault.

Mr. P. K. Rao, former Secretary, Servants of India Society said at Poona, "The scheme of Pakistan is a first attack on the central Government itself which at any rate, will have control over all in the geographical limits of India, whether Muslims or Hindus."

29th. Mr. V. D. Savarkar, President of the All-India Hindu Mahasabha, in a message on the occasion of his 59th birthday, observed : "Hindus should test all national and international politics and policies through the Hindu point of view alone."

The Duke of Devonshire, Parliamentary Under-Secretary of State for India, speaking with the "full authority of the Government" as Chancellor of the Leeds University, declared : "It is intended that the Government of India should be carried on by India, for India, in India, and not from Whitehall."

The potentialities of the Eastern Group Supply Council as an efficient organization for pooling the resources of the Empire Countries for the successful prosecution of the war and also for the solution of many postwar economic problems, were stressed by Sir Bestram Stevens, Australian representative on the Council, when he was entertained at a party given in his honour by Mr. G. L. Mehta, Vice-President, Indian Chamber of Commerce, in Calcutta.

Communal tension instead of abating in Bombay, spread to the north of the city, where three stabbing cases occurred.

Miss Eleanor Rathbone, M.P., in an open letter addressed to some Indian friends, said that she saw a risk that the attitude of most of her British friends who were concentrating on the question of how far the British Government might be blamed for the Indian deadlock and what they could possibly do to end it might mislead non-co-operating Indians into thinking that all progressive minded British people were with them in throwing the whole blame on the British authorities. Hence, she said, she was moved to take the opposite course by trying to set down the opposite side as she saw it—the case against non-co-operators.

A public meeting was held in Bombay, under the presidency of the Mayor, to welcome the members of the standing committee of the All-India Women's Conference.

Babu Rajendra Prasad in a letter to Dr. Syed Abdul Latiff of Hyderabad, wrote : "The Congress never refused to discuss any scheme and any proposal for bringing about a settlement of the communal problem. Our trouble has been that we have never been allowed to get to the stage where concrete suggestions could be put forward or considered."

30th. The Standing Committee of the Newspapers Editors' Conference met at Simla, with Mr. K. Srinivasan, president, in the chair, and devoted the whole sitting to a discussion of complaints of non-observance of the agreement arrived at in Delhi with regard to the Press advising on Mahatma Gandhi's statements to the Press.

Sir Mirza Ismail, Dewan of Mysore, observed at Bangalore : "I am convinced that the differences between the Muslim population in India and the much older and larger Hindu population that are stressed today, for making drastic changes, are negligible beside the bonds that unite them as children of one Universal Creator and as citizens, by ancestry, of a common country."

Khan Bahadur M. Musa Sait, President of the Muslim Chamber of Commerce, Madras, said "unless India was given full control over Finance, Defence and Foreign Affairs, a solution of the political deadlock would not be possible."

The Sikh Political Conference at Lahore adopted a resolution urging the complete Indianisation of the Viceroy's Council, and the inclusion of a Sikh among the members.

31st. The Standing Committee of the Newspaper Editors' Conference continued discussions on questions relating to the Press advising on Mahatma Gandhi's statements and agreed to address a letter to the Government setting forth its views on those questions and particularly clarifying its Delhi resolution on the subject.

A Mysore Government Gazette Extraordinary said : "Amin-ul-Mulk Sir Mirza Ismail, Dewan of Mysore, having requested His Highness the Maharaja to permit him to lay down his office, His Highness has been graciously pleased to allow him to retire from public service with effect from June 1."

The Standing Committee of the All-India Women's Conference in Bombay, in the course of a statement on the Hindu Law Committee's questionaire, stressed the need for a radical change and a complete overhaul of Hindu Law and a demand for the enactment of a Universal equitable law to replace the different personal laws.

June 1941

The chief incident of the month was the sitting of the All-India Committee of the Hindu Mahasabha, in Calcutta, which discountenanced the Madura resolution on 'direct action'.

The Riots Enquiry Committee appointed by the Government of Bengal commenced its sitting at Dacca, under the presidency of Mr. Justice McNair of the Calcutta High Court.

Dr. Rabindra Nath Tagore, in a spirited reply to the open letter addressed to Indians by Miss Rathbone, M. P., pointed out the indiscretion and impertinence of the lady in throwing out a challenge to the Indian conscience on the score of ingratitude.

The Government of India declared the Khaksar organization to be an unlawful association. The Provincial Governments were also instructed to take necessary steps to suppress the said organization.

The Government of India announced the decision of establishing a Departmental Committee to advise on Defence matters.

The Government of India decided to appoint a Reconstruction Committee, under the Chairmanship of Sir Ramaswami Mudaliar, Commerce Member.

Sardar Dasaundah Singh, Minister of Development, Punjab Government, exhorted the Sikhs to join the Hindus, Moslems and others in helping the successful operation of the War.

At a meeting, under the presidency of Dr. Rajendra Prasad, at Patna, it was decided to establish Peace Committees in the Districts of Bihar with the help and co-operation of the people of all shades of opinion.

Mr. Mahomed Yusuf Shareef, ex-Minister of the Central Provinces, presiding over the South Indian Anti-Separation Conference at Kumbakonam, strongly opposed the 'Pakistan Scheme' with all its implications.

10

Mahatma Gandhi in a statement from Wardhaganj denounced the outrages perpetrated by the rioters in Bihar and particularly the murder of a Muslim family. He advised the evil-doers to surrender themselves to the authorities for suffering any punishment which might be inflicted on them.

Second Lieut. Premindra Singh Bhagat of the Corps of Indian Engineers was awarded the Victoria Cross with the approval of His Majesty the King.

A group of Oxford youngmen, comprising Hindus, Muslims and Europeans issued a programme designed to solve the Indian constitutional deadlock.

Mr. V. D. Savarkar in an interview at Wardha, advised his countrymen to miss no opportunity of joining the Army, Navy and Air Force, especially in view of the war situation.

The Working Committee of the All-India Hindu Mahasabha recommended to the All-India Committee of the said Sabha not to give effect to the Madura resolution on "direct action".

The All-India Committee of the Hindu Mahasabha, at its session in Calcutta, passed a resolution, postponing the question of launching a campaign of "direct action" on an All-India issue as suggested by the Madura resolution.

The Government of India decided to establish an Advisory Panel of Accountants. Its function would extend over general Accountancy questions relating to the terms of contracts for war supplies.

Dr. Rajendra Prasad laid the foundation of the first ship building yard at Vizagapatam.

Mr. K. M. Munshi addressed a letter to Mahatma Gandhi discussing "organized violent resistance."

The Council of the National Liberal Federation of India met at Poona. The Council while recommending whole-hearted co-operation in the war effort at the same time urged His Majesty's Government to declare that they proposed to make India a free and equal partner in the British Commonwealth of Nations.

1st. The Standing Committee of the All-India Newspaper Editors' Conference met at Simla and ended after passing several resolutions.

An elaborate memorandum setting forth the Hindu point of view and seeking facilities for Hindus to entrol themselves in the army and navy from Mr. V. D. Savarkar on behalf of the All-India Hindu Mahasabha Militarization Board was submitted to His Excellency the Commander-in-Chief by Sir J. P. Srivastava when he interviwed His Excellency at Simla.

A deputation of a large number of newspapermen led by Mr. Devadas Gandhi, acting President, Indian and Eastern Newspapers' Society waited on Sir Ramaswami Mudaliar, Commerce Member, Government of India, at Simla, to discuss questions arising out of Government control of newsprint and the serious dearth of shipping space.

2nd. The Committee appointed by the Government of Bengal to inquire into the riots in the Dacca City and district commenced its sitting in the office of the Divisional Commissioner. The Committee consisted of Mr. Justice McNair, president, and Mr. W. Mc Sharpe.

A Press Note issued from Simla stated that discussions between representatives of the Government of Bengal and the Government of India concerning A. R. P. matters, which commenced on May 29, concluded on June 2.

The Bihar Government proposed to levy a punitive tax on the inhabitants of Bihar Sharif for the maintenance of a strong police force in that subdivision.

His Excellency the Governor of the Punjab passed an order directing that within the limits of the Punjab, no person forming part of a procession should carry any arm.

3rd. The riot situation in Bombay showed a definite improvement.

The need for organizing Moslems of Calcutta, was emphasized by Maulana Nazir Ahmad Chowdhury presiding over the conference of the General Council of the Calcutta District Moslem League.

It was learnt from Simla that one hundred instructors were being imported from Great Britain for training of technicians in India. One hundred and fifty centres were already at work and their capacity was being increased to train ten thousand candidates. The number of candidates under training was believed to be five thousand.

The Dacca Riots Enquiry Committee, accompanied by the District Magistrate Mr. J. George, and a party of representatives of the various communities and organisations and their counsel inspected the damaged places in the city.

Six fighter squadrons of the R. A. F. were named by the Air Ministry after various parts of India following the dispatch of gifts of money to the Ministry of Aircraft Production for purchase of aircraft.

4th. A fresh communal incident was reported from the Bihar subdivision which was the scene of rioting towards the end of April.

The ex-Kaiser died at Doorn.

Dr. Rabindra Nath Tagore in a statement on the open letter addressed to Indians by Miss Rathbone, M. P., said, inter alia: "The lady has ill-served the cause of her people by addressing so indiscreet, indeed impertinent, a challenge to our conscience. She is scandalized at our ingratitude—that having drunk deeply at the wells of English thought we should still have some thought left for our poor country's interests. English thought, so far as it is representative of the best traditions of Western enlightenment, has indeed taught us much, but, let me add, that those of our countrymen who have profited by it have done so despite the official British attempts to ill-educate us. We might have achieved introduction to Western learning through any other European Language."

Reuter's Diplomatic Correspondent learnt that the Duke of Devonshire's speech at Leeds, was in no sense a formal declaration of policy, and did not in any way modify the declaration already made by H. E. the Viceroy in the name of His Majesty's Government.

Dr. Syed Abdul Latif of Hyderabad (Deccan) in the course of a circular he addressed to certain political leaders in the country, said that a solution of the communal problem was possible if at least the substance of the Muslim League demand was conceded.

5th. A Government of India communique issued in Simla stated that steps were taken to declare the Khaksar organisation an unlawful association wherever necessary.—Provincial Governments were instructed to take all steps they considered necessary "to dispel the menance which the action of these misguided persons has brought into existence.

In the Assam Assembly, Khan Bahadur Sayidur Rahaman, Revenue and Finance Minister, made a statement on the floods in Sylhet district.

6th. The decision to establish a Departmental Committee to advise on Defence matters, was announced from Simla.

The Committee would consist of ten non-official members of whom six would belong to the Central Legislative Assembly and four to the Council of State. The Commander-in-Chief would be the President of the Committee.

The Khaksar organization having been declared an unlawful association by the Central Government, Khaksars were rounded up in the various parts of India.—Following the action taken by the Government of India, more provincial Governments, namely, the Punjab, Sind, Bihar, Orissa, the North-West Frontier Province and Delhi implemented the instructions from Simla and declared Khaksars an illegal organization.—A Gazette of India Extraordinary issued in Simla, announced that the Government prohibited the carrying of belchas in public places by members of the association, commonly known as the "Anjuman-i-Khaksaran."

The Government of India decided to appoint a Reconstruction Committee under the chairmanship of Sir Ramaswamy Mudaliar, the Commerce Member.

The Dacca Riots Inquiry Committee gave directions about the large number of documents called for by the Hindu Mahasabha.

Sardar Dasaundah Singh, Minister of Development, Punjab Government, in an appeal to the Sikhs to join hands with Hindus, Muslims and others, to keep the enemy away from India's boundaries, said: "The present is just the time when we (Sikhs) should make a huge effort to beat even our own every brilliant martial record of the past. Our history is full of marvellous achievements on the battlefield."

7th. Following the ban on the Khaksar organization, the rounding up of the members of the organization continued in the various parts of India.

A message from Simla stated that the strength of the Khaksar organization was believed to total something over 30,000,—of this number about 14,000 were in the United Provinces, 5,000 in the Punjab and the remainder distributed in smaller numbers in other parts of the country.

Sir Bijoy Prasad Singh Roy, Revenue Minister, Government of Bengal, addressing a public meeting at Barisal, made a statement on the basis of action which the Government proposed to take regarding relief measures in the cyclone affected areas.

The Assam Assembly concluded consideration of amendments to the Assam Motor Vehicles Rules, 1940. Before the House was prorogued, a motion moved by the Premier, Sir Mohammed Saadulla, to the effect that the Government should take steps to incorporate the amendments passed in the House in the body of rules in the light of discussions in the House, was carried.

Mr. Ram Kumar Jhunjhunwalla, President of the Marwari Association, at the annual general meeting of the Association in Calcutta, criticized Government's policy with regard to the industrialization of the country vis-a-vis the war.

In view of the communal tension prevailing in the country, it was decided to establish Peace committees in the Districts of Bihar with the help and co-operation of the people of all shades of opinion. It was also decided to organize a Shanti Dal consisting of men and women pledged to non-violence, under the patronage of Dr. Rajendra Prasad for the purpose of promoting communal harmony.—The above decisions were arrived at a meeting at Patna, Dr. Rajendra Prasad presiding.

8th. Mr. Mahomed Yusuf Shareef, ex-Mininter of the Central Provinces, presiding over the South Indian Anti-Separation Conference at Kumbakonam, entered a strong caveat that the partition scheme was wrought with grave risks and danger to the future happiness and prosperity of India.

Mr. M. A. Jinnah, at a reception held at Bangalore, advised his co-religionists to choose the leader of their community very carefully to avoid any disappointment.

The University Committee appointed by the Congress Ministry with Pandit Nilkanta Das, M. L. A. (Central) as chairman, submitted its report to the Government of Orissa recommending the establishment of a separate university for the Province.

The C. P. Government directed the district authorities not to arrest any person for merely giving intimation of his intention to offer Satyagraha. The decision of the Government was the result of a ruling by the Lahore High Court that merely giving intimation to offer Satyagraha did not constitute any offence under the Defence of India Rules.

9th. His Highness the Maharaja of Mysore, in inaugurating the joint session of the two Houses of Legislature under the reformed constitution of 1940, observed: "We will do well to remember that, in a State like ours the interests of the people and those of the Government are fundamentally identical and that the differences in ideology as between different sections are for the most part superficial and transient."

A communique from Hyderabad (Deccan) said that the Nizam's Government invested a sum of Rs. 50 lakhs in the Government of India 3 percent 1941-42 Defence Bonds.

Mahatma Gandhi issued a statement from Wardhaganj: "I have read and re-read with shame and sorrow an official account of the cool calculated and unprovoked murder of a Muslim family, including an infant girl three years old. Though Rajendra Babu is doing glorious work on behalf of communal peace in Bihar, it is impossible for me to suppress my own opinion on this cruel crime. The perpetrators, whoever they may be, have done no good either to themselves or to their religion, if they have any, or to this country. This I say apart from my views on "Ahimsa". I suggest that on no ground, even of violence, can such murders be defended......"I therefore, advise the perpetrators, with all the force my words may possess, to deliver themselves up unconditionally to the authorities for such punishment as the latter may think fit to award."

A number of resolutions were passed by the Anti-Separation Conference at Kumbakonam. Mr. M. Y. Shareef presided.—The main resolution which was unanimously carried, stated: "It is the considered view of Musalmans from all parts of South India assembled at the conference that the two-nation scheme of Pakistan, envisaged in the resolution of the Muslim League, would not only not serve the interests of the Muslim Community in India for which purpose it is avowedly declared, but would also be definitely detrimental to its growth, expansion and solidarity and would further result in the disintegration of the whole country which has all along been treated as such, and that it would eventually lead to internal strife, thereby exposing the country to foreign exploitation."

10th. A Press Communique from Simla stated, "His Majesty the King Emperor approved the award of the Victoria Cross to Second Lieutenant Premindra Singh Bhagat of the Crops of Indian Engineers."

The possibilities of fabrics produced from indigenous silk on handlooms in Bengal being used for the manufacture of parachutes were being investigated by the Government of India.

The Bengal Government decided that during the period of an emergency, the Bengal Legislative Assembly would sit from 9 A.M. to 12 noon and the Council from 2-15 P.M. to 4-15 P.M.

Mr. Gopinath Singh, General Secretary of the U. P. Congress Socialist Party was arrested at Lucknow under Sec. 129 of the Defence of India Rules.

Khan Abdul Ghaffar Khan opened another Red Shirts Camp near the Shah Alam Bridge in Peshawar district.

Dr. P. V. Naidu, General Secretary of the All-India Hindu Mahasabha, in an interview in Madras, declared: "It will be a tragedy if the Hindu Mahasabha is committed to any form of 'direct action' under the present circumstances."

Dr. Moonje observed at Nagpur: "It will be suicidal to the Hindus to embark on any programme of 'direct action, at the present moment."

The Budget session of the Mysore Representative Assembly met under the new reformed constitution.

A Press communique from Simla stated that the Government of India and the Government of Burma were anxious, if possible, to reach an agreed solution of the various problems relating to Indian immigration into Burma. As a result of preliminary discussions both Governments were of opinion that a stage had been reached where personal negotiations offered a reasonable prospect of success.

11th. Acting for the "Argonaunts"—a non-party youth movement of the Democracies—a group of Oxford Youngmen comprising Hindus, Muslims and Europeans, issued a programme designed to solve the Indian constitutional deadlock. The signatories constituted themselves into an initiative group to be known as the Indian Collaboration Committee. Their plan, *inter alia,* declared that Indian Home Rule should be vested in the Viceroy and the Viceroy should create a National War Cabinet composed of prominent Indians.

Dr. B. S. Moonje in a circular which he issued to all the members of the All-India Committee of the Hindu Mahasabha (from Calcutta) expressed the view: "That this is not the time for going to jail by launching direct action."

12th. Mr. V. D. Savarkar, President of the All-India Hindu Mahasabha interviewed at Wardha regarding the Madura resolution of the Mahasabha on 'direct action', said: "I cannot say whether it will be modified, revised or dropped in Calcutta. As a war is on and as the international situation is worsening it is essential that we should be knocking at Government's door for admission to the Army, Navy and Air Force. India, particularly Hindus, should avail of the opportunities afforded by the war and be ready for defending the country."

Responsible section of tribes in North Waziristan took a reasonable view of events in Iraq and expressed relief at the restoration of constitutional Government in that country.

His Excellency the Viceroy received a number of messages from General de Gaulle and the heads of various Allied Governments, acknowledging the contribution of Rs. 2,00,000 made from the Viceroy's War Purposes Fund and expressing keen appreciation of India's generosity.

13th. Members of the All-India Committee of the Hindu Mahasabha met in Calcutta and had an informal discussion about the questions to be considered at the meeting of the Committee.

Captain Nimbakar, General Secretary, Hindu Sabha, in a telegram to Mr. V. D. Savarkar, said: "All Madras members of the All-India Committee with the exception of one, are opposed to direct action."

Mr. B. C. Chatterjee addressed an appeal to Mr. A. K. Fazlul Huq, the Bengal Premier, stating *inter alia*: "We are at the cross-roads of history. India has to come to a decision whether her Hindu and Moslem sons shall plunge her into primeval darkness under cover of which they are to thrust the dagger into each others' hearts or they are to carry on the civilizing and nationalizing mission founded by her sons of the last generation."

His Highness the Maharaja of Patiala, presiding at a meeting of the Khalsa Defence of India League, held at Oakover, Simla, observed: "We are one, we should be one, and we must remain one."

Dr. Khan Saheb, ex-Premier of the Frontier Province replying to an address presented to him at a public meeting at Srinagar, held under the auspices of the Jammu and Kashmir National Conference, said that India could not make any progress unless communalism vanished and the people were united.

14th. The Working Committee of the All-India Hindu Mahasabha, at its meeting in Calcutta, under the presidentship of Mr. V. D. Savarkar, decided to recommend to the All-India Committee not to give effect to the Madura resolution on "direct action" for the time being in view of the deterioration in the communal situation.—The other resolutions discussed by the Working Committee related to census, communal riots in different provinces, constructive programme, organization of volunteers, military training and the havoc created by the cyclonic storm in Barisal and Noakhali.

Sir J. P. Srivastava sent a telegram to Mr. V. D. Savarkar: "United Provinces solidly against direct action in any form in existing international and internal situation; Hindus stand to lose greatly by any such precipitate move. We must concentrate all our energies on militarization and industrialization."

Acharya Kripalani in the course of an article on "Communal Riots and Satyagraha" asked: "Can an effective non-violent way to tackle the communal problem be devised when peaceful negotiations fail?" Answering the question himself, Acharya Kripalani said: "If we rule out violence and if we are not to rely exclusively upon martyrdom, we have, in my opinion, to devise some scheme of non-co-operation."

When the All-India Committee of the Hindu Mahasabha met in Calcutta, a resolution drafted by the Working Committee suggesting that the Madura resolution on 'direct action' should not be implemented, was placed before the meeting. The resolution was proposed and seconded by Dr. B. S. Moonje and Mr. N. C. Chatterjee, respectively, but its consideration was postponed.

15th. The All-India Committee of the Hindu Mahasabha, at its session in Calcutta, (as recommended by the Working Committee) passed by an overwhelming majority a resolution that the question of launching a campaign of direct action on all-India issue and scale, as suggested by the Madura resolution be postponed. —The Committee arrived at the decision taking into consideration the developments since December 1940, both national and international and particularly in view of the "widespread and organized aggression on Hindus," which, it was stated, was their paramount duty to resist and crush, and also in view of the fact that the war was rapidly aproaching India on both frontiers.

Great concern was expressed at the communal riots in Dacca, Ahmedabad, Bombay, Cawnpore, Bihar Shareef, Bhiwani (Punjab) and other parts of the country by the Working Committee of the All-India Hindu Mahasabha in a resolution adopted at its meeting in Calcutta. Dr. Shyama Prosad Mukherjee presided.

16th. The inquiry into the origin and circumstances of the Dacca riots was resumed at Dacca before Mr. Justice Mc Nair (President) and Mr. W. Mc Sharpe who constituted the Inquiry Committee.

Mr. K. M. Munshi, Home Minister in Bombay's former Congress Government, issued a statement from Bombay, drawing attention to the urgent need of restoring communal harmony in the country.

Tributes to the memory of Mr. C. R. Das were paid at a largely attended meeting in Calcutta under the auspices of the Bengal Provincial Congress Committee, on the occasion of the 16th anniversary of his death.

Mr. Mahadev Desai, addressing the students of the Gujarat Vidya Mandir at Ahmedabad, made an appeal to face any communal disturbances that might occur again with God on their lips.

17th. Sir Bertram Stevens, Leader, Australian Section, Eastern Group Supply Council, in an address on "Problems of Today and Tomorrow," in Calcutta, declared: "India can fight a total war as much as any other country. This is a war of production, and India's potential output is immense. This is a crisis of production on the Allied side and Britain's need of the production of India and the Dominions is intense. At all costs this output must be expanded, even if economic life is transformed."

Acharya Kripalani, General Secretary of the A. I. C. C. issued instructions for the guidance of Satyagrahis and Congress Committees after consultation with Mahatma Gandhi.

A Press Note from Simla stated : "The Government of India have decided to establish an Advisory Panel of Accountants, consisting of not more than ten leading members of the Accountancy profession in this country. Its function will extend over general Accountancy questions relating to the terms of contracts for war supplies such as those bearing on the system of payments, profit percentages, the scope and extent of the check to be applied on the accounts of contractors, etc. "Its functions will be purely advisory in character, but in view of its composition, the opinion expressed by it will naturally carry great weight both with the Government and Industry.

A statement on the nature and extent of Government assistance to weavers in the Mysore State was made in the Representative Assembly, in reply to a question. The Dewan-President presided.

A Press Note from Nagpur re : prohibition in the C. P. contained the observation : "There is little doubt that a considerable part of the money formerly spent on drink is now being utilized by the ex-addicts to provide better food and clothing for their families. There is also the general opinion that the prohibition of country liquor has helped many persons to reduce, or clear their debts."

18th. The anniversary of the declaration of General de Gaulle, that Free France, under his leadership, would continue the struggle side by side with her Ally, Great Britain until final victory was attained, was celebrated in all cities and towns of the Free French Empire.

At Chandernagore a meeting was held under the presidency of Lieut. J. M. Massontier, at which all the French officials and principal citizens were present.

The Government of Bengal formulated a comprehensive scheme for the control of leprosy in Bengal.

Mr. Rajendra Prasad, referring to the communal situation in the country, in the course of an interview at Wardhaganj, observed : "The best and the only effective check is mutual trust and goodwill, but the foundations of these are being sapped day by day by communal propaganda."

His Excellency the Governor of the Punjab, prorogued the Punjab Legislative Assembly.

19th. The Rao Committee on Hindu Women's rights to property signed its report at Simla.

Besides recommending an enlargement of its terms of reference the committee recommended that where provincial legislation was immediately necessary to give Hindu widows the right of succession to agricultural property, such legislation should be undertaken without delay.

A communique from Simla stated that the Government of India decided to establish an Indian purchasing mission in America.

20th. Dr. N. N. Law, presiding at the quarterly general meeting of the Bengal National Chamber of Commerce in Calcutta, outlined his ideas as to the manner in which the post-war economic reconstruction in India should be carried out.

Sir Jogindra Singh, ex-Minister, Punjab Government, in the course of a talk on "solidarity in this critical hour" declared : "Leaderless, India is dispersing its gathered harvest of a country. They who ought to mourn, rejoice at the tragedy; they who claimed to be custodians of India's united resolve to lead her from poverty to power are dumb. They are unable to utter the word which would serve India to take her full share in saving the spirit of man and his heritage, the much coveted but ever illusory freedom."

21st. The laying of the foundation of the first India-owned ship-building yard was performed by Dr. Rajendra Prasad, a former President of the Congress at Vizagapatam.

A statement issued over the signatures of Mrs. Sarojini Naidu, Mrs. Rameswami Nehru, Mrs. Vijoylaxmi Pandit, Raj Kumari Amrit Kuar and others of the All-India Women's Conference in reply to the British Women's message to India's Women, observed *inter alia* : "Let us point out the anomaly of British women asking India, though a slave nation, to help a slave owner in distress instead of asking the slave owner to undo the wrong and cure himself of the initial sin and thus ensure the moral justness of his position."

Dr. Rajendra Prasad, replying to an address at Vizagapatam, observed : "Attempts are being made by the enemies of Indian nationalism to divide our country into various sections on the ground of the existence of different races, religions and culture, but whole country had believed the theory of different races and cultures. India had not only a great part, but was destined to have a great future. We are one and shall continue to be one."

The Governor of U. P. sanctioned the payment of compensation to cane-growers in the Barabanki, Hardoi, Sitapur, and Kheri districts at the rate of Rs. 15 per acre for surplus cane.

Dr. C. R. Reddi, Vice-Chancellor of the Andhra University, in an interview in Bombay, observed: "I believe the installation of a National Government composed of representatives of the war-minded parties and organizations who are prepared to postpone consideration of the bigger issues till after the war is necessary if the country is to be roused to a proper pitch of enthusiasm and give fuller and more cordial support to Great Britain.

22nd. Mr. Jamnadas Metha, M. L. A. (Bombay) speaking at a public meeting in Calcutta, expressed the view that the Indian National Congress had practically liquidated the political work for which it had stood for nearly 50 years. The meeting was organized under the auspices of the Radical Democratic Party and the National Democratic Union.

Five persons were injured in a clash in Bombay that occurred between two crowds belonging to different communities, when the police made a lathi charge and opened fire to disperse the mob.

In a telegram to the Governor of the United Provinces, Pandit Madan Mohan Malaviya requested the Government to inquire into the Agra Jail incident and suggested that His Excellency's Government should make it clear that, until detenus were tried and convicted they should not be treated as criminals and should enjoy the privileges that detenus enjoyed before the new rules came into force.

23rd. The communal situation in the different parts of the country was discussed at a conference of Bengal Congress workers with Dr. Rajendra Prasad, a member of the Congress Working Committee and Acharya J. B. Kripalani, General Secretary, All-India Congress Committee, in the B. P. C. C. office, Calcutta.

The Chief Mining Engineer, Railway Board, handed over to the Viceroy's War Purposes Fund a sum of Rs. 79, 999 as a contribution from the officers staff and employees of the State Railway's Coal Department.

24th. The Government of Bengal sanctioned grants of Rs. 3,00,000 as agricultural loans, and Rs. 60,000 for gratuitous relief for the cyclone affected areas in the Bakarganj district. Total grants made for the district amounted to Rs. 13,00,000 and Rs 1,00,000, respectively.

Sir Ziauddin Ahmed, Vice-Chancellor of the Aligarh University and Dr. R. C. Majumdar, Vice-Chancellor of the Dacca University informed Mr. Rohini Kumar Chowdhury, the Education Minister of Assam of their decision to accept the invitation to attend the meeting of the Select Committee of the Assam Univertity Bill in the first week of July.

Dr. Shyama Prasad Mukherjee and Sir Azizul Huq, Vice-Chancellor of the Calcutta Universsty already signified their willingness to attend the meeting of of the Select Committee.

25th. The death occurred in Calcutta, of Mr. G. S. Dutt, I. C. S. (retd.) the Founder of the Bratachari movement in Bengal. He was 59 years old.

Mahatma Gandhi permitted Mr. K. M. Munshi, former Home Minister, Bombay Government, to resign from the Congress.

Mr. Walchand Hirachand, Chairman of the Scindia Company observed in Bombay, "No facilities, either for the steel required for the hulls of ships nor for ships have been secured for the proposed ship-building yard by the Government of India from the United Kingdom.

Mr. K. M. Munshi, in a letter to Mahatma Gandhi, referred to two points raised by Mahatma Gandhi, namely that those Congressmen who favour violent resistance must get out of the Congress and shape their conduct just as they thought fit and that a Congressman might not directly or indirectly associate himself with a gymnasium where training in violent resistance was given.

26th. His Excellency the Governor of Bengal, while addressing a meeting of the Darjeeling War Committee, observed : "Let the slogan be 'lend to defend."

Subscriptions to the Second Defence Loan for the week ending June 21, 1941, amounted to Rs. 50, 20, 000. The grand total of subscriptions to all Indian Defence Loans up to June 21, 1941 was Rs. 60,26,63,000.

In the House of Commons, Mr. Sorensen suggested reconsideration of the policy regarding shipping and ship-building yards with a view to considerable expansion.

Mr. Amery pointed out that enquiries were progressing as regards the earliest date when productions of ships in India would be possible. Certain provisional steps had been taken with his and the Government of India's support.

27th. There was a renewed outbreak of Hindu-Moslem rioting at Dacca. The police fired a round in order to scare away a riotous mob on Nawabpur Road. In view of the recrudescence of the communal disturbances, the Riots Inquiry Committee did not sit.

Dr. Rajendra Prasad, addressing a meeting of lawyers at Dacca, urged them to form a peace committee with men of different communities. He said that they should agree at least to maintain peace, and use no violence.

Dr. Prasad, accompanied by Acharya J. B. Kripalani, later left for Calcutta.

In the Mysore Legislative Council, Congress members, walked out as a protest against the disallowance by the Dewan of an adjournment motion which had been held to be in order by the President of the Council and for which the leave of the House was given.

28th. Disturbances continued at Dacca. The police opened fire on an unruly mob at Luxmi Bazar.

A Press Note from Simla announced that a school for the training of A. R. P. personnel on the lines of A. R. P. staff school in England would be opened in Calcutta.

Dr. Rajendra Prasad and Acharya J. B. Kripalani on their return to Calcutta from Dacca, met the local Congress and Mahasabha leaders as also leaders of the Moslem Community, to discuss with them the communal situation in the province and to devise means for restoration of communal amity.

The determination of the Indian Christian Community to do its utmost in taking its share in all measures in connexion with the successful prosecution of the war, was reiterated at the Punjab Indian Christian Conference at Lahore. Diwan Bahadur S. P. Singha presided.

The question of the privileges of the Mysore Legislative Council and its members in relation to articles in the Press was discussed in the Mysore Legislative Council. The subject arose from an editorial in a local Kannada daily imputing certain motives to the Congress Party in the House in asking supplementary questions on a question. There was a full discussion and the President promised to consider the matter and give his ruling.

The Poona Journalists' Association passed a resolution protesting against the order issued by the Government of Bombay under the Press Emergency Powers Act demanding security of Rs. 1000 each from the Yeshvant Press, where the daily Kal, Poona, was printed and from the publisher and printer of the paper respectively because of an alleged objectionable article publised in the issue of May 25, 1941.

29th. The Council of the National Liberal Federation of India which met at Poona passed a resolution affirming that India's political progress was only possible if the Democracies won the war.

The Council, while of opinion that India should co-operate whole-heartedly in the war-effort maintained that the Government had failed to create the psychological atmosphere necessary for mobilizing to the fullest extent the resources of the country in men and material. It reiterated the Federation's demand for a National Government.

The meeting further urged His Majesty's Government to declare that they proposed to make India a free and equal partner in the British Commonwealth of Nations.

30th. Mr. M. N. Roy in an appeal from Dehra Dun inquired of the rank and file of Congressmen, if it were not more honourable to be in company of Churchill than to follow the pseudo-anti-imperialists who would continue the policy of extending moral support to Fascism.

His Excellency Sir Robert Reid, Governor of Assam, in connexion with the ceremony to mark the raising of the Assam Regiment, gave a message from Shillong.

"For the first time in history a regiment of Indian Army has been raised in Assam and has been given the name "Assam Regiment." We wish the nucleus of the regiment good luck, in the name of the province of Assam."

An A. R. P. Staff School, under the auspices of the Government of India and on the lines of the A. R. P. Staff School in England, was opened by Lt. Col. E. K. Yiend, Director-in-Charge, in Calcutta.

Notes on Indian History

and

India in Home Polity

JANUARY—JUNE 1941

Notes on Indian History

It has truly been said that a history of India that reveals the whole panorama of the vast millenia of her distinctive life and civilisation in its actual shape and colour and due proportion and perspective, still remains to be written. The materials for drawing such a vast outline and making such a comprehensive and connected sketch are not yet in hand. A fairly definite outline and connected sketch which gives the promise of being some day developed into what is called "scientific history" has, however, been steadily emerging out of the mist that veils the immensity of India's past—a mist which (thanks to the labours of the investigators) has perceptibly thinned without being as yet actually lifted as far as one can now make one's incursion into the age that saw the birth of Budhism and Jainism in India in the sixth Century B. C. Beyond that there is still only "cosmic nebulae" relieved here and there by a few stray constellations of lucidly distinct historical facts. These "nebulæ" have probably, a depth and density to be measured only in terms of millenia. But from the position where we can now make our historical prospecting, these vast remote dark spaces of Indian history recede and shrink and fold up and, at last, look like a far-away blank, black spherule beyond the galaxy of human remembrance.

Ancient Indian history is, apparently, "full" of such gaps and blanks. Beyond the time when Alexander the Great invaded the Punjab (326 B. C.), the galactical system of detailed and authentic Indian history does not far extend. There are too many unexplored blank spaces and unformed, chaotic nebulæ beyond that time still. Beginning approximately with that period, we are furnished, sometimes in abundance, with fairly trustworthy material in the shape of contemporary Greek testimony bearing on Indian history, and also, as time rolls on, with inscriptional and other kinds of decipherable and dependable domestic evidence. Of course, an immense mass of "documentary" evidence and evidence in the more or less fluid, volatile state of tradition, heressay and folk-lore (written or unwritten) have always lain by the side of the historian hitherto busy with his inscriptions, plates, coins, artefacts and any corroborative evidence that may be forthcoming from outside. And that mass of ancient Indian documentary evidence and tradition has, generally, lain neglected by his side. It has been, generally, of little help to him in reconstructing, "on scientific lines," the missing skeleton of ancient Indian History. It has been, however, of great use to the comparative mythologist, philologist and anthropologist.

But even the historian who seeks to reconstruct on scientific line the missing skeleton of ancient history, whether of India or of any other country, should do well to remember that the dry bones of the skeleton he may have been able to put together will not be true, living history unless they can be made instinct with the touch of life which literature, art, tradition, 'myths', folk-lore, religious and social institutions in their earlier and later forms alone can give. From coins, tables etc., we can built a possible or even probable frame-work of chronology into which we can put our little bits of tested facts according to one possible plan or other. Such a mosaic of dates and facts (mainly relating to dynastic succession, war and conquest) is of course important as necessary ground-plan of history. But it is not the completed structure of history. It is not history as an organic process of evolution. So we have to distinguish between structural or morphological history and organic "physiological" history.

Now India has been so far poor in comparison with some other ancient countries like Egypt, Babylonia and China in her "materials" for writing the first kind of history, and the available materials, as we saw, do not carry us much beyond the time of Budha and Mahavira in the sixth century B. C. Recently, however, a very old and, apparently, a high order of civilisation has been unearthed in the Indus Valley in the Punjab and in Sind, which according to current official beliefs, is of the Sumerian pattern. The buried cities now discovered bring to light not only very interesting features of a civilisation thriving in the western part of India in so remote a past (when the Indo-Aryans had not, according to the common view, yet migrated into India), but they even put into our hands interesting clues that may eventually help us to unravel many of the riddles of our Vedic and post-Vedic history. The Tantrik cult, for instance, may have older and deeper roots in the soil of India than have so far been granted or suspected. Nothing contemporaneous with or earlier than the Indus Valley civilisation has yet been unearthed in other parts of the sub-continent. So the present trend of speculation is to regard the Indus Valley civilisation as a sort of wedge driven into Western India—the whole of which was still at the low level of aboriginal darkness (with the possible exception of some parts that might have risen to the Dravidian 'light' level)—probably by the races and civilisation of Summer.

We are still in the duskland of probabilities or even less than probabilities as to the dates, origins, early habitats and earlier forms not only of the Indus Valley but also of the Dravidians and Indo-Aryan people. We do not know for certainty when and from where the Indo-Aryans came into India. The fact of Aryan immigration into India itself, though generally accepted, is still disputed. And if immigration be admitted, we have, probably, to admit not one but several successive streams of immigration. Such theory, apparently called for to account for some of the critical turnings and "sudden mutations" in our ancient historical evolution, will lead to many unexplored avenues of enquiry as to ages and dates, origins and characteristics.

The Rigveda

The Rigveda—the earliest and the most informing and instructive "documentary" evidence that we possess—appears to set the stage amidst scenes which show the Aboriginal, Dravidian and Indo-Aryan factors fighting for supremacy first in the land of "Five Rivers" and in the Ganges Valley, and then gradually, beyond the Vindhya Range which with its impenetrable forest mantle, stood as a barrier between Northern India (Aryyavatta) and Deccan. Gradually we find the aborigines cornered and driven to the hills and forest where their descendants, more or less Aryanised, still continue to live. In considerable parts they were also absorbed into the fold of Aryan society and culture. And in being absorbed they did not fail to impart some little part of their own character of the Aryan complex. There was not so much of racial or even linguistic fusion as of cultural assimilation, The process of Aryanisation in language, culture etc. has been a process admitting, naturally, of different shades and degrees, leaving at the one end aboriginal races that have almost kept aloof from Aryan influence and having at the other others that have become part and parcel of the Aryan system. The Aryanisation of the Dravidian peoples, especially in religion, culture and civilisation, has been a much more perfected process. But on the other hand, the Dravidian impress on the Aryan system is also in many places, deep and unmistakable. The Dravidian is co-ordinated or even subordinated to the Aryan but not lost in the latter. This power of assimilation of alien races and cultures without losing the individuality of its own essential Type or Pattern and without at the same time making the diverse elements assimilated lose whatever is essential in them—has been a special characteristic of the Indo-Aryan race and culture-complex. This has meant organic unity or unity in diversity of a more fundamental and abiding nature than can, perhaps, be claimed for the political or national unity with which histories are commonly familiar. Historians, accordingly, commonly miss the unity which lies deep and sees only the diversity which lies on the surface. India to them is thus a veritable chaos of jarring elements of races, languages, religions, castes, sects and culture which have never known unity before the days of the unitary political rule of the British. Of course, the introduction, in later times, of the Semitic religions—Muhammedanism and Christianity—disturbed to some extent the ages-long unity and balance of the Aryo-Dravidian culture and social system in India. But even these elements were in the process of being slowly drawn inth the sphere of influence of what we may call the genius of India, In other words, a slow but sure process of cultural assimilation even of this "militant" factors was going apace. Buddhism, which had risen as a "revolt" against orthodox Hinduism—but yet as a revolt from within—and which dominated the situation in India for several centuries, ended in the land of its birth by being eventually absorbed and assimilated into the parent religion. Jainism and many other old or later "revolts" have thus "squared their accounts" with the same parent religion, and have been for many centuries living peaceably side by side with one another and with the latter.

This power of assimilation and co-ordination in which all the components make their own contributions and are permitted to live side by side as members of a commonwealth of cultures, has been the secret of the wonderful resisting and staying power of the Indian culture-complex against such disintegrating forces as have smashed up many an old and glorious civilisation of the world. And it can be easily shown from facts that this staying power has been in evidence not only in the realm of cultural contacts and impacts but also in that of social and political ones. There have been many raids into India and invasions before and after Christ, but it is a travesty of facts to imagine that Indian resistance has always been weak and short-lived and that such invasions are typically like the raids of Mahmud of Gazni which ever swept away Indian armies and kingdoms like cobweb or a house of cards. Before her final subjugation by the Mahammadan Power—and the final subjugation of the whole of India was anything like an accomplished fact only for a time during the reign of the great Mogul Emperors—India had been, it should be borne in mind, a mighty Power and a Model of civilisation and culture for at least three thousand years. And it should be remembered further that when the British in India turned from trade to conquest (always with native help and alliance) they had to settle their accounts not only with Haider Ali and Tipu Sultan in the South but mainly the Maharatta and Sikh Powers which had risen on the ruins of the Mahammedan Power in India,

Unitary Indian Empire

But there were and still have been other factors which, to some extent, operated against India developing a compact and coherent political and military organisation, except occasionally like, for instance, the Great Roman Empire of old or the British Empire in modern times. We possess, apparently, no connected retrospect of the remote past of which the Vedas, Epics and Purnas speak. But as far as appearances go, an unitary centralised, Indian Empire was the exception and not the rule. In later times also, an Empire like that of Asoka was not a common achievement. As we said, India has possessed deep-laid cultural and institutional unity beneath all her diversities. India has fought, and fought bravely, for the integrity of her sacred Land, her sacred religion and tradition, and for their sacred visible Symbols and Embodiment. But she has rarely fought for the "State" as such or an Empire as such. The spirit of her culture did not favour the formation and consideration of Nationalism in the sense it is commonly understood, and her basic institutions would hardly consist with many forms of centralised State control. The all-controlling and co-ordinating Principle was Dharma (the Principle of human Values and Conduct) rather than any State agency. Each village, for example, was a self-contained commune and autonomous unit owing permanent allegiance to the reign of Dharma and only temporary allegiance to any kingship that might function for the time being. So the village communes continued to live though kingdoms after kingdoms rose and fell. They were but little affected by the accidents and exigencies of politics.

Again, the sprit of Dharma (which should not be translated as religion) has definitely and systematically favoured all human or even all-living values and tendencies and a cosmopolitan outlook, and has opposed militant aggressive, "predatory", nationalism. The old Upanishads are clear and courageous in their conception of those higher values ; and the Dharmashastras (or Codes laying down social and individual conduct) were bold and consistent in their execution of those ideas. Later, Budhism and Jainism and other "reforming" movements have tended only to stress such values as non-violence and fellowship with all men and all living being. These forces operating through the ages tended to produce in the Indian classes and masses a common disposition not quite favourable to the formation and consideration of an unitary military state for purposes of offence and defence.

Of the immense back-ground of Indian History which is represented by the Vedas (Samhitas, Brahmins, Aranyakas and Upanishdas), the various Sutras (or Digests) Philosophies, Epics (the Ramayana and Mahavarata), Puranas and Tantras (our statement here is not anything like full), we possess (unless one is prepared to grant the claim of the Puranas recently put forth in their behalf that they do contain materials for reconstructing a fairly connected chronological history beginning with the very earliest times) very little precise and connected information for the purpose of writing a political history both copious and correct as to facts and their chronological order. But of the ideals and ideas, practices and institutions of the times we do possess a very full, informing and instructive presentation. And after all, what is real history but this ? Scholars have been busy with their sketches and drawings of the ancient orders and specimens of ideas, beliefs, and practices that existed in India. But oftener than not their reviews and retrospects have been made from modern standpoins, with modern notions, criteria and standards of testing facts and appraising values. This has not enabled us in any just measure, to understand much less appreciate a civilisation (not confined to India but, possibly, reaching some of its greatest heights in this country) which was essentially of a different kind, and cannot therefore, be represented as only the first uncertain and timid steps taken on the road which has, through a long, long march, at last brought us to our present advanced stage. The ideology, plan and methods of that ancient civilisation we have yet not seriously studied and rightly understood. Much of that civilisation we still regard, without understanding, as consisting of "savage" magic, meaningless ritualism, "theological twaddle" and crude superstition. Side by side with all this we find, however, the highest philosophy, deepest mysticism and pure ethics. There is also much that is of original and genuine value from the point of view of human material and mundane progress. This seems to us a curious medley of what is nearly the highest and what is about the lowest. But let us pass on.

Coming to "historical" times we find that the invasion by Alexander the Great of India proves in the result to be little more than a brilliant raid. His victorious armies could only cut off a small slice of North-Western India, and this little slice the Macedonian would ingest, but could not digest. His steam-roller of conquest speedily developed "war-weariness" on the plains of the Punjab, and he had to go back only adding a bit of India to his vast Empire. He had won some of his battles in India, but it had not been an "easy walk-over" with him.

After his death shortly afterwards, the vast Macedonian Empire practically went to pieces. Chandragupta, who became the king of Magadha, proved himself too powerful for the Greak invaders who had violated the sanctity and integrity of the sacred Land of the Five Rivers. As the result of the formidable opposition by the armies of Chandragupta, a treaty was concluded between him and the Greek which made him the supreme, undisputed lord and sovereign of the Indian Empire. Megasthenes, who was sent by Seleucus as an ambassador to the court of Chandragupta, left a very valuable record of the times, of the customs and morals of the people, and of the administration, which, though unfortunately fragmentary, bears an eloquent and admiring testimony to the high order of material and moral civilization attained by the Hindus centuries before the Christian era. And this high civilisation was evolved in India not in isolation but in commerce with other civilisations that flourished in ancient times such as the Babylonian, Greek, Persian and Chinese. Chandragupta's son was Bindusara who was succeeded by Asoka (269-231 B. C), who was undoubtedly, one of the greatest rulers of men holding their sway for the material and spiritual good of mankind. Numerous edicts and inscriptions record the noble and glorious achievements of his reign which, in its later stage, left the bloody path of war and conquest and devoted itself to the much more noble and fruitful task of the moral and spiritual conquest and redemption of ourselves and our fellow-being. With commendable catholicity and tolerance, not seeking to impose it upon others by his great imperial authority and power, he exercised that authority and power for the purpose of transforming Budhism, which had been more or less a local sect in the Ganges Valley, into one of the greatest and most potent living world religions. Asoka's reign is therefore rightly held to be an epoch in the history of the world. His edicts also show the man, his ideals and his methods. But all this had not allowed or favoured the cement of the great Maurya Empire setting into the requisite hardness. Independent kingdoms like Bacteria and Parthia took their rise in the border land, and the Greeks renewed their incursions. New races (the Yuen-chi) came in a surge of migration which swept all before them, and in the first century A. D. a considerable portion of North-west India came under their influence.

Gupta Dynasty

Kaniska, who made Peshawar his capital, proved great as a ruler and as a patron and missionary of the Budhistic religion. Under him the Kushan branch of the Yuen-chi reached the zenith of his power. But this power fell as another power in middle India rose—the Andhra dynasty. A peak like Amaravati or Ujjain would, some time, rise and shine in the midst of the moving vastness of Indian waters. In the beginning of the fourth century the centre of political influence in India was again shifted to Pataliputra in Magadha as the Gupta dynasty emerged into power. Samudragupta, who ruled for fifty years, and his son Chandragupta, greatly distinguished themselves not only in war but in the sphere of peaceful and fruitful administration, promoting general prosperity and giving liberal encouragement to art and literature, a glorious tribute to which was paid by the Chinese pilgrim Fa-hien. According to his testimony, their Empires were vast and their administration just, enlightened. Towards the end of the fifth Century—when the White Huns from Central Asia began to pour themselves into India—the sun of the Gupta dynasty set (during whose regime, it should be noted, there had been a revival and reconstruction of ancient Brahmanism and Brahmanical culture as evidenced especially by the literature of the Purans ; but this reviving process was, very largely, a process of quiet adaptation and peaceful assimilation). More than a century had elapsed after the fall of the Gupta dynasty before there rose another great and enlightened monarch who could emulate with no mean success the greatest of the Indian rulers in historical times—Asoka. Emperor Harsha, who consolidated his authority practically over the whole of Northern India in the beginning of the seventh century, was famous equally for his geeat prowess, his high intellectual attainments and for the broad catholicity of his religious outlook. An account of his times has been left by a Chinese, Huen Tsiang by name. In that, India is still painted in generally bright and even glowing colours.

Mediaeval India

After the death of Harsha, and gradually with the emergence of India into what may be called the mediæval period, the conditions which had made the political unification of India sometimes possible in the past, nearly disappeared, and India was thrown into a state of political confusion and chaos in which petty kingdoms rose like mushrooms and constant internecine strife prevailed. Some outstanding figures like Vikramaditya would occasionally appear on the stage ; but such events were few and far between. In the South of India was being enacted a very interesting but involved drama in which the Andhras, Ballavas, Chalukyas and Cholas were the principal actors. Kashmere in the North, Kanauj in the Doab and Bengal in the east were also alive with many vivid and vital scenes and events of political, cultural and social interests. But we shall not try to make a review of them here. One outstanding event in the confusion and complexity of the general Indian situation which deserves notice even passing was the rise of the Rajput power upon which the mantle of the old caste Kshatrias (the warrior and ruling caste) fell, and which was the chief opposition that the waves of Mohamedan invasion coming one after another ever since the second quarter of the 7th century had to encounter and ultimately bear down. Guzrat, Malwa, Ajmer, Kanauj and Delhi were the principal scenes of the new drama of Rajput ascendancy—a drama so full of episodes of superhuman bravery, noble heroism and sacrifice for the sacred cause of religion and liberty that they have ever since lived in human memory as models which future generations of patriots in any country might well try to emulate. Though Rajput opposition was borne down in Northern India by the end of the twelfth entury, Rajput bravery and the spirit that animated it survived the crash of the Hindu Empire of Delhi and Ajmere over which Prithvi Raj, the hero, the last of the Hindu emperors, though not the last of the Hindu rulers, had held sway. Rajput bravery and Rajput love of independence were still factors to reckon with in the days of the great Moghuls—Akbar, Jahangir, Shahjahan and Aurangzeb. Col. Todd and some others have narrated the story, and it consitutes one of his proudest annals in the vast archives of the Hindu glory in India. As to the conquest of Northern India by the Mohamedans, it should be noted, the great prize was not very easily or quickly won : that the first Mahammedan impact was in the seventh century shortly after the passing away of the Prophet, and a Mohammedan kingdom in Northern India came into being towards the end of the 12th. century. Even this did not mean either a complete or final subjugation of India. and there is another thing to be noted. Hindu power fell not because its resistance was weak and its bravery and heroism in the field was not backed by adequate tact, strategy and discipline in diplomacy, planning and preparation.

The centuries of the mediaeval age in India were marked by a conspicuous lack of political unity and solidarity. But they were by no means unimportant and barren. It was not a 'dark" Age. In the Gupta period and in the centuries before and after, a marvellous process of social, cultural and religious reconstruction was going apace. The old Vedic scheme of social economy (involving as it did the four Varnas or "caste" and the four Ashrams or "stage" of life) was being transformed through a process of adaptation, assimilation and multiplication which made society more comprehensive and at the same time more complex. The influence of Budhism, Hellenism and that of Mongoloid races also led to adaptations and assimilations, in many important directions in the older order of Indian customs and institutions. The gradual assimilation of Budhism itself was a phenomenon of the greatest importance. The Vedic religion survived but it was transformed. The Puranas and Tantras renewed and gave a new expression to the Sanatana Dharma. In the domain of literature, art (both useful and fine), science and mathematics, philosophy and metaphysics, these centuries were also productive of fruits that were and still are of the greatest interest and value. Great poets like Kalidas and Bhavabhuti, and great

Philosophers like Shankaracharya and Ramanuja and also other pioneers and masters in other fields formed a galaxy of men of genius and talents which showed that an age of political dis-equilibrium and confusion in India was yet not necessarily an age of cultural depression and darkness and social disruption. The soul of India could, apparently, function to its best advantage inspite of her troubled politics.

But whilst this was true for some time it could not be true for all time. Her politics at last began to tell on her constitution. We do not, however, propose to continue the story through the Mohammedan and British periods. The history of these periods is more settled and definite in features, and these are, generally, well-known. One special feature, which is not always clearly recognised and to which we should like to draw attention is this. From the twelfth century right up to the eighteenth, or even for some time later, the Hindu power of revival and regeneration, of initiation and execution, was never like dead or even dying. Independent and often powerful kingdoms like Vijayanagar in the South, those of Pratap, Shivaji and the Peshwas in the west (we do not mention some others e. g, those in Bengal) would, now and then, proudly lift their heads and challenge the authority of the great Moslem emperors. Under that authority, too, there flourished many great Hindu administrators, Ministers, governors, generals and financiers. In short, during the Mohammedan era, the Hindu genius was not at its best but it was not quite decadent.

The Mahammedan rule

The Mohammedan conquerors, again, from Mahomed Ghori who wrested the sceptre of the kingdom of Delhi from Prithviraj after a first unsuccessful attempt, came to India as foreigners but they did not remain here as foreigners. India was the land of their adoption. Raids like those by Chengis Khan or Nadir Shah were rare and they did not represent the normal course of events. India suffered, and sometimes badly, no doubt, from the effects of the conquering ardour and proselytising zeal of some of the Mohammedan rulers. But the great Moghuls were as much "children of the soil" as the humblest of the Hindu "heathen". And this sharing together by the Hindus and Mussalmans of a common "hearth and home" naturally tended to breed a consciousness of community of interests in both as India's offspring. There was steady assimilation of the semitic and Indo-Aryan cultures also and even a growing understanding and appreciation of one religion by the other. The religions touched and even blended with each other at their highest points—e. g. in Sufism and Vedantic mysticism. They also met and evolved a broad common "shrine" to which folk beliefs, practices and institutions would bring their united homage. Even a common dialect (Urdu or Hindusthani) was evolved between the two in Northern India which gradually blossomed into a fine literature. The patronage extended by the Mohammedan emperors to Music, Architecture etc. was also fruitful of very fine result. India's wealth attracted the trade and commerce of the whole civilised world. In fact, America or the West Indies was discovered in an attempt to discover an western route to the Indian market. British, French, Dutch and Portuguese traders all came and scrambled for market, and eventually, for political power in India. It is also worthy of note that even under the sway of such masterful monarchs as Sher Shah, Akbar or Aurangzeb, the government of the country was in the main, decentralised, allowing provincial and local autonomy —down to the autonomy of the village units—to adequately function. Even petty local chiefs—like the feudal lords of the mediaeval West—never unlearnt the art of fighting and governing. So it was always possible for a man of ambition and ability, like Shivaji for example, to evolve sanctions whereby he could implement his high political aspirations. It was the very large measure of local autonomy and local initiative that existed that rendered possible the rise of the Marhatta and Sikh Powers and also of the kingdoms of Hyder Ali and the Nizam in the south. And British Power in India in its rise to paramountcy found its most formidable rivals or powerful allies in them.

In 1599, during the reign of Queen Elizabeth, some merchants of London formed an association for the purpose of trade with India, and this association was granted a royal charter of incorporation. At first this Company was purely a trading concern establishing factories in the east and west coasts of India and in Bengal and administering its affairs in the three "presidencies" which were at first independent of one another but subordinate to the Board of Directors at home. In course of time however, chiefly with a view to preserving and consolidating its growing and extensive trade in India, in the face of the French rivalry and intrigue and the prevailing political anarchy and unrest in the land, it established military garrison of defence which soon became involved in hostilities that saddled it with territorial responsibilities. It fought some decisive battles in Madras and in Bengal, which raised a trading company to the status of a political Power in India. French intrigue failed and French rivalry practically died down in India. One of the most decisive battles fought was the battle of Plassey in 1757. The battle was won with the aid of faithful native battalions, and with the active or passive support of the generals and noblemen of the unfortunate young Nawab of Bengal. It is worthy of note that the path of British supremacy in India, and often, its influence and prestige abroad has been paved, amongst other things, with the consent, alliance and willing co-operation of the Natives of India. It was so even during the critical period of the Sepoy Mutiny, one hundred years after the battle of Plassey. It was again so during the "ordeal" of the last great War. The machinery of administration by the East India Company was from time to time modified by Acts of Parliament (1773, 1784 ; and the Charter Acts of 1793 and 1833). By these a Governor-General-in council was made the supreme administrative authority in India subject to a Board of Control at home. By the last Act, the Company ceased to be a commercial concern and became a political and administrative body only. After the Sepoy Mutiny another Act was passed by which the Government of India was transferred from the Company to the Crown, and thenceforth the Governor-General was also the Viceroy of India. The functions of the Government of India are wide and its responsibilities heavy. But its responsibilities are to the Crown and the Parliament. It has not rested on an elective popular basis. There have been legislative bodies, but its motions, resolutions and votes have not, except as regards certain matters of secondary importance under the Act of 1919, a binding effect on the Government.

India's contributions and sacrifices in the Great War were great, but "reward" that come in the shape of the Parliamentary Declaration promising her a "progressive realisation of responsible government", the stages and times of which were to be determined by the Parliament alone was not comforting to her nationalist aspirations. And the Government of India Act of 1919, which is still in actual function though it has been, apparently, broadened and amplified in some directions by a recent Parliamentary Statute, did not meet the wishes or expectations of India. By that Act dyarchy or a kind of dual responsibility was established in the provinces, where the "nation-building" subjects were "transferred" to Ministers (not responsible however to the legislature), whilst the more important subjects were "reserved". In practice the transference of certain subjects to Ministers (who were appointed by, held office under the pleasure of, and were responsible to, the Governor) meant little more than a complication of the administrative machinery which became, in consequence, more cumbrous and expansive. The Central Government continued to remain unitary under the scheme. The legislative bodies both provincial and central, were expanded with non-official majorities, but this placed little power, for construction or even for obstruction, in the hands of the popular parties. Whilst the liberals proceeded to work the scheme, the main body of nationalist forces, as represented by the Indian National Congress, would not first even look at it. But some time later, under the guidance of Mr. C. R. Das and Pandit Motilal Nehru, a Swaraj Party, analogous to the present Congress Parliamentary Party,, was formed which entered the legislatures, both provincial and central, in telling numbers and by its obstructionist tactics caused not a little embarrassment to those entrusted with the work of day to day administration. In some provinces it was even able to "wreck" dyarchy for a time. Generally, however, the system has worked, though not satisfactorily even according to official appreciation, We need not in particular refer to the unwelcome labours of the All-White Statutory Simon Commission, to which even the habitually co-operating Liberals refused to lend their co-operation. Meanwhile the Congress ideology was becoming bolder day by day, and the Lahore session adopted a resolution setting as the goal of India complete Independence or Purna Swaraj. A campaign of civil disobedience followed to create "sanctions under the leadership of Mahatma Gandhi who has been really at the helm of Congress affairs since the early twenties. The Round Table idea was broached rather too late; but Mahatma Gandhi after concluding, what is known as the Gandhi-Irwin Pact, joined the Conference subsequently. The result of the deliberations of that body fell short of the Congress demand. And the Congress again withdrew its offer of co-operation.

India in Home Polity

Introduction

The fall of France in June, 1940, startled the world into revising its ideas on men and things, on the re-distribution of the forces and resources of the world. Men and women came to realise that the philosophy of life and conduct which the National Socialism of Germany represented has got a revolutionary quality which by its strength had acquired a status that could not be ignored any longer. Another revolutionary force in the modern world was represented by Soviet Russia. When in the fourth week of August, 1939, these two forces came to some sort of an arrangement for joint action, for co-operation in the swift movement of power-politics, the world became prepared for the World War II of the 20th century. It had not long to wait. By September, 1939, German dive-bombers flew over Poland showering death and destruction, German *Panzer* Divisions rolled over the plains of Poland crushing all opposition. All the Allied Powers, Britain and France, who had guaranteed Poland's integrity and unity, who had promised her help, looked helplessly on without being able to do their little best for her. And in course of eighteen days Poland, as she had emerged out of the first World War, vanished from the map of the world.

Co-operation between Russia & Germany

The months flew by and the western States of continental Europe, the area bordered by the Artic Circle in the north to the Gulf of Biscay in the south, lay under the heels of Germany's conquering hordes. Another twelve months rolled by keeping pace with Germany's march towards the Aegean Sea and the Eastern Mediterranean. By the end of this period happened one of those events that leave their mark in history. This was the German attack on Russia in the morning of June 22, 1941. When the Russo-German Neutrality Pact was signed the Soviet Premier and Foreign Minister, Viacheslav Molotov, had recommended it to the world's acceptance as a "turning point in the history of Europe, and not only of Europe". The German Press had hailed it as "an important, active contribution to the future new order in Europe". To the world dominated by Britain and the United States this lining up of the two dictatorships, of the two revolutionary forces represented by Nazi Germany and Bolshevist Russia, was not welcome. In an article in a U. S. A. Quarterly, *Foreign Affairs,* written by a Harvard professor, the mind of this world stood revealed. The Pact had sat upon the western world as a "nightmare". But there was hardly any relief felt at the break-up of this Pact, as it started another nightmare—the prospect, "the possibility that Germany will control the resources and the labour power in the vast territory stretching from Bohemia to the Himalayas and the Persian Gulf......" Whether or not this possibility has any chance of fulfilment is still on the knees of the

Germany and Russia part company

gods. All that one can say, as we write, is that the German time-table of a 8-weeks campaign has been upset, that Russia has almost lost the use of the Black Sea, and that the centres of Soviet industrial and military productive activities in Russia proper have been rendered more than 50 per cent useless. Speculations with regard to the outcome of this fight between these two mastodans among nations have become so prolific that there is a danger of our losing our sense of perspective, and giving reins to wishful thinking. For, there is no manner of doubt that the German attack on Russia has created "mental and emotional confusion" amongst vast sections of the population in every country. The majority feeling seems to be that Soviet Russia being the "weaker of the two well-hated dictatorships," prudence should dictate friendliness to her so that the two forces of "world revolution" might get exhausted by mutual blood-letting.

British promise of help to Russia

This feeling accounts for the alacrity with which the British Prime Minister has promised all help to Soviet Russia in the fight into which she has been dragged by the audacity of German leadership. This promise was conveyed in a broadcast speech made in the evening of June 22, the day on which German forces had moved against Soviet Russia.

"Any man or State who fights against Nazism will have our aid...We have offered to the Government of Soviet Russia any technical or economic assistance which is in our power and which is likely to be of service to them...It is not for me to speak of the action of the United States, but this I will say : If Hitler imagines that his attack on Soviet Russia will cause the slightest division of aims or slackening of effort in the great democracies who are resolved upon his doom, he is awfully mistaken...The Russian danger is our danger and the danger of the United States..."

U. S. A. underlines Mr. Churchill's promises

Mr. Churchill's "swift pledge of London-Washington aid to Moscow was a shrewd play for his team" said a U. S. A. weekly, *Time*, as it robbed "the week-ending appeasers at home and isolationists in the U. S. A." of opportunity to fish in troubled waters. Colonel Charles Lindenbergh, one of the leaders of the latter, could only say that the new turn in the war was "a very, very unusual development" ; his further comment that he was "not at all surprised" at it was an assumption of wisdom that few can accept without a grain of salt. Mr. Churchill's shrewdness was underlined by the U. S. A. Under-Secretary of State for Foreign Affairs, Mr. Sumner Wells, who under the direction of President Roosevelt read a declaration to a Press Conference on June 23, which was nothing more than a paraphrase of what the British Premier had said :

"...Any defense against Hitlerism, any rallying of the forces opposing Hitlerism from whatever sources these forces may spring, will hasten the eventual downfall of the present German leaders, and will, therefore, redound to the benefit of our own defense and security."

Danger of Communist revival

But not all in the United States subscribed to this view of Russia's transformation into a friend and ally of democracy. Mr Herbert Hoover, President Roosevelt's predecessor at the White House, struck a note of dissent. To them Communism was as much an anathema as Nazism.

"Now we find ourselves promising aid to Stalin and his militant Communist conspiracy against the whole democratic ideals of the world...if we go further and join the war and we win, then we have won for Stalin the grip of Communism on Russia and more opportunity for it to extend in the world..."

Hope of the weakening of Soviet practice

But the U. S. Administration appeared to have the backing of the majority of the people in thinking that Bolshevism in conflict with Nazism deserved help as it would be giving hostages for good behaviour if it desired help from the democracies. The feeling was widely expressed that Soviet Russia must withdraw or slacken certain of the controls that it had established over individual freedom. Mr. Sumner Wells drew pointed attention to one of these deprivations—that of the "freedom to worship God as their consciences dictate." This was "the great and fundamental right of all people" which has been "denied to their peoples by both the Nazi and Soviet Governments." The hint of criticism and accusation implicit in Mr. Wells' words was taken note of by the Soviet Government, and assurance was conveyed to the world that this "right" had not been withdrawn, and that the control, if there be any in practice, would be loosened. This responsiveness of the Soviet to world opinion has been strengthening the hope that the other rigidities of Soviet philosophy and practice would be moderated so that the Soviet regime might fit into the scheme of "economic democracy" as it is practised by Britain and the United States, and that she will be brought back into "the community of Christian nations". We do not know if these hopes will be fulfilled or not. Under the stress of war, and the quickening of idealism caused by war, the world has had many such hopes, and has grieved over their vanishing.

Italian debacle in E. & N. Africa

The outbreak of the Nazi-Bolshevik war was the most significant development during the six months of 1941, the events and trends of which form the subject of study of this volume of the *Indian Annual Register*, though it burst out at the fag end of the period. We have not seen any interpretation of this event that has been able to get hold of all the facts which helped to precipitate it. We have to anticipate many of the happenings that have prepared Nazi leadership to launch on the attack on Russia with the outcome of which is bound up their hopes and dreams of world domination or fears of irrevocable ruin. We have to make an attempt to understand these if we desire to face the future with knowledge and understanding. The world has been kept enthralled during the opening months of 1941 with the epic fight of Greece against Italy, and the see-saw of Anglo-Italian alarums and excursions over east and north Africa. Antecedent to that, during the last six months of 1940, Britain had stood alone in the world facing the greatest crisis in the life of her island history of a thousand years. Alone she had fought back the German attempt at invasion of her shores ; alone she had beat back the swarms of German bombers and fighters that from a distance of twenty-two miles only flew day and night over Britain to crush the only obstacle to German hegemony over Europe, to break the imperialism that had for about two centuries skimmed the cream off the world's goods. During these months the Italian empire in north and east Africa had all but crashed under the blows of Britain's Imperial Army helped by South African, Australian, New Zealand and Indian divisions. When during the last quarter of 1940, desert warfare became possible, Italy took the offensive from Lybia and rushed to Sidi Barrani within the borders of Egypt. It almost appeared that Italy would be repeating the exploits of the German hordes in the low countries—Holland and Belgium—and in France. But they were as quickly rolled back to Benghazi by the combined attack of ground troops and naval guns. For, the Italians had adopted the thoughtless tactics of following the costal route which is badly exposed to naval bombardment and concentrated air attack, and badly confined by its escarpment parallel to the shore. They lost mobility owing to this natural restriction, and lost all the territory up to Benghazi by February 6, 1941. Further south, Italian Somaliland and Abyssinia did not show a better record. By the capture of the former the British could sweep the Red Sea free of Axis raiders, surface or underwater; and the Emperor Haile Seliasse could return to his empire. The freeing of the Red Sea enabled U. S. ships to pour into contiguous territories all the materials of war, the President having declared that the territories flanking the Red Sea to the Suez were "not a combat zone."

German mechanized forces retrieve the position

This victory sent up British prestige. But it was a short-lived triumph. German *Panzer* Divisions and *luftwaffe* squadrons regained in course of about ten days what the British had won in as many weeks. Benghazi was evacuated on April 4, and the Allied troops fell back inside Egypt. A powerful contingent of them has been holding Tobruk. And, for reasons unexplained, this Axis thrust into the heart of Egypt stands halted. In this victory General Hommel used the technique which had brought them succcess in France. A wide-fronted advance by widely-dispersed mechanized units scattered over the desert expanse west of Egypt, the use of more powerful battle tanks frustrated General Archibald Wavell's operations and snatched victory from what the Italians had made into a debacle. Vichy sources speculated that the Germans had their eyes on the oases in the regions further south—Siwa and Jarabub, Kufra and Owerat. The last two are 500 miles far in the south, near the margins of Sudan and French Equatorial Africa. Things appear to be quiet now, but at the end of the year (1941) the desert may hum, and the Allied forces required to face an Axis attack towards the Suez, towards the oil lines and wells of Iraq and Iran. In the Balkan campaign the German victory was complete not only in over-running Greece and Jugoslovia but in strategic values. The loss of Crete has caused the loss of "the only good advance operating base in the eastern Mediterranean"; the island of Cyprus which has been under British possession for more than 60 years has been placed in peril. As a military sea-way the Mediterranean has been choked by the 90 miles bottle-neck of the Straits between Sicily and Tunisia. The Lybian scene of operations would be about 250 miles distant from Crete; Alexandria—"the final big Fleet base" in the eastern Mediterranean—would be about 340 miles off, and the Suez Canal about 550 miles. The experiences at Crete have proved that any Sea Power which does not enjoy air superiority within the area chosen for its activity is liable to most dangerous risk. The destruction of the German battleship—*Bismarck*—supports the same contention.

And, by the occupation of the six Greek islands—Semothrace, Lemnos, Mytilene, Thasos, Skyros, and Melos—Germany has captured a whip-hand over Turkey. The first two can be used to choke the Dardanelles; the third and the Dodecanese islands lie very close to Turkey's western coast. German bombers have come nearer Syria and Palestine. The realisation of the threat to her own peace must have moved Turkey to sign the Treaty of Friendship with Germany on June 18, only four days before Germany opened her campaign against Russia. As the Russo-German Pact of August, 1939, had started the present war, so it may appear that the Turco-German treaty hastened the outbreak of the Russo-German war. The two signatories to this treaty "bind themselves mutually to respect the integrity and inviolability of their national territory" and not to resort to "any measures, direct or indirect", against their treaty partner. We have been told that this treaty does not in any way go against the one that subsists between Britain and Turkey, signed in October, 1939. The position of Turkey is not easy. To her south and south east Britain stands entrenched; to her west and north-west stands Germany flushed with victory over Britain's proteges and allies. It is also a historical fact to which the Turkish Foreign Minister, M. Sarajoglu, referred that Turkey and Germany had "never been in opposition in the course of the vicissitudes of world events for centuries." More than any remembrance of past friendship, the immediate needs of the Turkish State left no choice to President Ineonu and his advisers but to yield to the courting of Hitler's Germany. We should also take into account the economic reasons which must have influenced the negotiations, Only 25 per cent of the import trade and 17 per cent of her export trade were with the British Empire and the United States, while Germany and her German-dominated neighbours provided 62 per cent of her total imports and took 60 per cent of her exports.

Increasing pressure on Turkey

We have also to recognise that in signing this treaty Turkey was fully aware that her neutrality will be enabling the German High Command, if it so willed, to move from the Mediterranean area to an attack directed at the heart of Soviet Russia. In affairs of State friendships are based on considerations other than those dictated by the heart. It is true that it was Soviet Russia's support that enabled Mustapha Kemal Ata Turk to build up a national State freed from the will-o-the-wisp of Pan-Islamism or Pan-Turanianism. That help has evidently failed to give assurance to Turkey in a Nazi-dominated Europe. It might also be a consideration that weighed with Turkey that in the name of security Soviet Russia has not been above undertaking aggression against weaker States. The Finnish war, the absorption of Latvia, Estonia, Lithuania of Bessarabia and Bukovina are instances of this spirit. It might also be that German diplomats were able to convince the Turkish politicians that the Soviet Prime Minister and Foreign Minister, Viacheslav Molotov, had demanded of Germany that she should help the Soviet in gaining control over the Sea of Marmora and the Straits of Dardanelles.

Turkey has failed Russia

This was said to have been done in course of his visit to Berlin on November 12, 1940. This demand revived an old ambition of Tsarist Russia that Istanbul (Constantinopole) should be restored to Christian possession, and that Russia which contained the majority of the Christians belonging to the Greek Church should be the State which should possess this city on the Golden Horn. We know that the Soviet authorities have denied this charge.

Russia's anxiety to placate Germany

The narration has brought us to the period when the world was confronted with the great surprise by the attack of Germany on Soviet Russia. It does not, however, explain the genesis of the rupture of the Pact between the two countries that twenty-two months back had been hailed as a corner-stone of the "New Order" in continental Europe. Even as late as June 13, the *Tass*, the Soviet News Agency, was authorized to state that Germany had not presented "any demands" to the Soviet Government; that German troop movements in Germany's eastern frontiers were due to reasons that had nothing to do with the Soviet Republic; that the recent mobilization of Soviet reserves and their manœuvres had for their object the training of the reserve contingents and the checking up of the Soviet railway system. The news of the presence of 12,000 German troops in Finland within 50 miles of the Russian base at Hango bore no sinister purpose; any unfriendly interpretation put on it was the work of "war-mongers" in the capitalist democracies. There is proof that as late as June 3 (1941) the Soviet Government was anxious to conciliate and placate Germany and the other members of the Axis; on that date it withdrew recognition from Greece due to her "loss of sovereignty". Earlier, on May 12, it had recognised the pro-Nazi El-Gilaini administration of Iraq. On April 13, the Russo-Jap Neutrality Pact was signed at Moscow. M. Stalin came to the station to see off Mr. Matsuoka, the Jap Foreign Minister—an unprecedented honour. One of the visible effects of this Pact was that 26 out of the 37 Soviet military advisers stationed at the Chinese capital (Chungking) were withdrawn. On June 11, Sir Stafford Cripps, British ambassador to Moscow, returned to London, and an elaborate announcement was broadcast that "his efforts to get any understanding with the Union of Soviet Socialist Republics had been fruitless." These and other matters lent colour to the speculation that the German Government did not directly present any demand to the Soviet Government that could be interpreted as any weakening of their friendly relations. Reports coming from the Turkish capital which proved to be remarkably correct said that Germany was trying to get "control" over certain Soviet railways and industries. This concession was regarded as the only way of obtaining increased supplies from Russia. A London *Daily Telegraph* correspondent wired in the third week of March from "somewhere" in the Balkans that the Soviet had stopped from the 1st of March all export of oil. This news might refer to the announcement published in the U. S. Press that since March 18 the shipment of war materials across the U. S. S. R. had been forbidden; a later amendment to the news said that no ban was placed on the shipment of supplies directly from Russia.

These news and speculations showed Soviet Russia in a conciliatory mood. Whether or not she was unsuspecting is more than one can say from the facts available at present. We cannot say that M. Josef Stalin had received no warning of the danger that was approaching his country. In the middle of April, Mr. Winston Churchill uttered in the House of Commons words that were intended to be a warning or ought to have been accepted as such.

Churchill's warning to Russia

"There are many signs that point to an attempt to secure the granary of the Ukraine and the oil fields of the Caucasus as a German means of gaining the resources wherewith to wear down the English-speaking world."

Coming from the quarter that it did, this speculation or warning might not have carried weight. But it is no longer a secret that since the middle of April (1941) the Soviet Government had begun to evacuate modern industrial machinery and skilled workers from the Baltic States. In hundreds of cart-loads they were removed to the Russian interior. In course of his New Year's Day Message M. Josef Stalin had declared that the "U. S. S. R. was totally mobilized". On May 6, he had hoisted himself into the Premiership of the Soviet. This step was interpreted at the time as necessary for the strengthening of Soviet industrial and military organisations. The warning issued by the Soviet Government on March 3 to Bulgaria that by allowing entry of German troops into her territories she was leading not to the consolidation of peace in the Balkans but "the extension of the sphere of war" into that area was a pointer to Russian anxiety; at the same time the Soviet ambassador at Berlin pointed out in an official *demarche* that his Government regarded Bulgaria and the two Straits as "security zones for the U. S. S. R.", and that it could not remain a passive spectator of events happening in territories that affected her security. On April 5 Russia concluded a friendly agreement with the Simovitch Government of Jugoslavia that had refused to implement the treaty made with the Axis by its predecessor in office. Why the Soviet Government did not feel or express the same anxiety with regard to Rumania, and did not throw in her weight for the protection of Yugoslavia and Bulgaria where she could have had direct touch with Britain, is one of those mysteries that must await clearing till, after the end of the present war, we have the official histories and non-official memoirs of the various Governments and their leaders.

Genesis of Russo-German rupture

We are almost tempted to think that Russia had sufficient warning. We have quoted Mr. Churchill's words; Rudolf Hess, Deputy Fuehrer of the Nazi Party, landed in Scotland on May 10. These were or ought to have been sufficient indication that changes were happening in the political atmosphere. And Sir Strafford Cripp's sudden departure from Moscow and arrival at London on June 11, and the uncalled for announcement that Anglo-Russian relations were as bad as ever, would not bear the innocent construction that has been put upon his movements. As against this interpretation we have seen an American correspondent at Moscow write that the Nazi-Bolshevik

Cripp's success in his long vigil at Moscow

differences worsened into war "without even the knowledge, let alone the activity of Cripps." Yet we believe that he departed for London to report success of his 24 months' vigil at Moscow, success which Nazi audacity had placed within his hands. And to-day we have a Pact signed on July 13, 1941, between Britain and Soviet Russia. The title of the Pact indicated its limited purpose; it is entitled—"Agreement for Joint Action by the Union of Soviet Socialist Republics and His Majesty's Government in the United Kingdom in the War against Germany." A conference has been held at Moscow where British experts headed by Lord Beaverbrook and U. S. experts headed by Mr. Harriman have met Soviet Ministers to evolve a plan of common work, to draw up a detailed scheme for supplying the various needs of the Soviet Republic in the materials of war and in the instruments for the production of these materials on Soviet soil. We have been hearing enthusiastic reports of the flood of help arriving from Britain and the United States. To arrange for the arrival of these across seas and oceans is no easy task; and the little that has arrived has not enabled the Soviet soldiers to halt the Nazi tank divisions and to disable Nazi bombers. Soviet soldiers, unaided, have succeeded in delaying the Nazi advance. The world has been witness to a war between Titans.

Exchange of goods between Russia & Germany

The world does not know why Herr Hitler switched off his victorious hosts from their advance towards Egypt, the Suez Canal, Palestine and Syria; why he did not support the Vichy administration in Syria from the naval and air bases stationed in the Italian Dodecannes Islands; why he should have taken up another enemy leaving Britain undefeated in her island home and in the approaches to the oil wealth of Iraq and Iran—the oil on which tanks and bombers move to attack and victory. We have tried to trace Soviet Russia's policy confronted by a triumphant Germany—one of anxious friendliness. Up to the time of writing we have not come upon a single fact that could satisfactorily explain Germany's attack on Russia. It might be that the export of Soviet raw materials and oil to Germany was not satisfactory; it might also be that export of industrial equipment which Germany promised to Russia in exchange was as unsatisfactory. The diplomatic correspondent of the *Daily Chronicle* (London) told us sometime in May (1941) that to straighten these out Herr Hitler was anxious to meet M. Stalin who had by that time become Chairman of the Council of People's Commissars—the equivalent to Premiership. The speculation on this news was that Herr Hitler would press at this interview for large-scale access to Ukranian wheat and Caucasus oil. In exchange he would give or was prepared to give a free hand to Russia in the whole of Asia including India and Japan together with an outlet to the Persian Gulf through Iran; M. Stalin was to guarantee in return the existing (in May) frontiers in eastern and south-eastern Europe. It was given out in the same dispatch that Germany was not very pleased with the Russo-Japanese Pact, as it had relieved Russia's anxiety with regard to her far-off eastern frontiers. Herr Hitler and M. Stalin did not, however, meet. Instead came the German invasion.

Why? We have seen it stated that the German General Staff

gave it as its opinion that it did not dare seek "a radical conclusion of the war in the west", while Russia was standing intact and organized with all the wealth of experience gained at the expense of Germany and Britain in this war of machines. A correspondent of the U. S. A. weekly, *Time*, wiring from Tokyo, after the outbreak of this campaign, said :

"I was informed in early May......that the negotiations (over economic demands) were insignificant.. ...I believe that the negotiations never broke down ; the Germans simply attacked when preparations were completed, as the main strategic aim was the destruction of the Red Army which is a potential menace to Germany in the future."

Will country & town in Soviet fight well ?

This correspondent had been in Soviet Russia off and on since 1932. He was not very hopeful that the Soviet Army would be able to put up as grim a fight as it has done during these three months ; that the Soviet people would agree for long to suffer the inevitable deprivations of war. He went so far as to say that "the (Soviet) country-side was essentially unreliable", that "the city population will fight well". He elaborated this thesis by referring to his own experience of dis-illusionment with the practices of the Soviet rulers. When he first went to Russia there were many people who "believed profoundly and fanatically in the idea of Socialism" ; these people have fallen under the axes of the various purges. The general people in the country-side would not give any particular trouble to the German invaders ; most of the peasants "will be satisfied to live" under German rule, if they were supplied with certain consumer goods—"shirts, flashlights, bicycles, shoes, radios, etc..." The Soviet people have belied the pessimistic prophecies of this correspondent. For, without the support of the general population the Soviet Army could not have so superbly up-set the German time-table of a quick and easy conquest, as it has been the case for twenty-two months since the German Army and Air Force finished Poland within 18 days. Without their support and co-operation the "scorched earth policy"—the policy that dictated that every thing that could be of use to the enemy should be carried away or broken or burnt—could not have been made the success that it has been—a policy that was successful when Napoleon Bonaparte invaded Russia one hundred and thirty years back.

Centuries-old conflict between Slav & Teuton

We have seen that there has been no particular grievance of so injurious or offensive a character that could justify Germany's attack on Soviet Russia. Interpreters of inter-national affairs have been driven by the failure of their search for a reasonable cause of this war to hark back to the distant past, the far distant past, for it. One of them has said that the key to the understanding of the present titantic struggle may be sought for in the centuries-old conflict between the Slav and the Teuton, just as to the west of Germany the cause has been found in the as old contention between the Celt and the Teuton. Prof. Happer of the Harvard University who is one of the interpreters referred to above has only varied the words in diagnosing the same seat of disease—

"......When Germany and Russia do not adjoin each other they are likely to be friendly to each other and remain at peace ; and......when they are contiguous they gravitate into war".

This diagnosis suggests that there should be strong buffer States between Germany and Russia. But this arrangement does not eliminate all the causes of the conflict—one of which remains and can be expressed as follows : who will dominate these buffer States, exploit the economic wealth that lies under their ground and the labour power that brings this wealth out of the bowels of mother earth ? This analysis brings us to the heart of the problem—who—Germany or Russia—shall guide, control and regulate the life of the area from the Baltic Sea to the Black Sea which has been demarcated into the following Nation States—Finland, Estonia, Lithuania, Latvia, East Prussia, Poland, Ukraine, Rumania, Bulgaria. Germany sought a solution of the problem by the Brest-Litovosk Treaty (March 3, 1918) which forced Russia to recognise the independence of the Ukraine, to renounce sovereignty west of a line drawn from the Gulf of Riga to the proposed Ukrainian frontier ; by a subsequent treaty (August 27, 1918) Russia had to renounce sovereignty over Estonia and Latvia and recognise the independence of Georgia, M. Stalin's native province. The German negotiators of these two treaties were fully aware of the political and economic need of having small, economically weak and unorganized States between their State and Russia. In the conditions of those days (1918) it was an efficient Germany, with surplus man-power and abounding industrial capacity, that could hope to organize these weak States. Russia, broken down by the first World War and reeling under a revolution, was in no position to claim a share in this great work. Since then under Bolshevik control Russia has gained industrial experience and strength, has been organized into a modern State, militarily and industrially equipped to meet the challenges of the modern times. There has thus developed a keen competition between Germany and Russia which has been moving towards an outburst of bloody enmity by the urge of a biological force almost.

Intensified by modern developments

The Russo-German Pact of August 23, 1939, was an attempt to intercept half-way this almost inevitable conflict. For twenty-two months there was friendliness and peace between the two countries —at least this was what the world saw and the world was told. But influences must have been working which blew up the bridge of reconciliation between them on June 22, 1941. And the world has been turning for light to the pages of German history—the history of the mystical aspirations, of the political and economic ambitions, of a *Herren-volk*—a master race—out on its God-given mission of rescuing the world from the thraldom to false gods. In Herr Hitler's auto-biography of ideas—*Mein Kampf*—"My Struggle"—are to be found many an inspired talk on such material subjects as the incalculable wealth and stores of raw materials of the Ural mountains, as the unending fertile plains of the Ukraine that have been awaiting development since their creation. And this development can reach its height at the hands of the Nordic race only—the core and centre of which is represented by the Germans. This Bible of Nazism was incubated in the prison cell of Munich. Twelve years later when

Mysticism of Teutonic aspirations

Herr Hitler became Chancellor of the Third Reich he indicated to a follower of his, Herr Hermann Rauschning who later became the President of the Danzig Diet, the line of this approach to Russia. He confessed that, perhaps he could not "avoid an alliance" with that country. But when he had realised his "aims in the west," nothing would "stop" him from attacking Russia. Because

"We must win the victory of the German race-consciousness over the masses eternally fated to serve and obey. We alone can conquer the great continental spaces ; .... We shall take this struggle upon us. It will open to us the door to permanent mastery of the world."

Herr Hermann Rauschning resigned, and escaped from the Nazi Party to America. He has recorded his talks with "the master" in two books—one of which—*The Voice of Destruction*—published in 1939—quote the words uttered in 1934. We do not come across the expression of this racial mysticism in the writings of Bolshevist thinkers and leaders though there is enough of Messianic urge in them towards world revolution and the dictatorship of the proleteriat which will rebuild the world on a juster and broader economic foundation. After the experiences of the last twenty-five years, after the betrayal of the peace that was to have made the world safe for democracy, the men and women of the year 1941 are not likely to be enthused over or misled by the various slogans that have been hurtling through the ether since Democracy, Nazism and Bolshevism threw themselves into a giant embrace of mutual destructiveness.

India's Western Frontier countries

We in India whom British State policy has placed in the galleries to witness the moves and counter-moves of the combatant hosts of Teutons and Slavs—we have been warned that our fate and fortunes are bound up and interlinked with events that have been happening in the heart of European Russia. With every step nearer the Black and the Caspian Seas made by the German mechanized Army, the crescendo of warning rises higher, and we are told that we should understand the drift of affairs not only in the Russian battle-fields but in the deserts of Egypt, round about Egypt, in Syria and Iraq. Anglo-Indian strategists have made enormous efforts to teach us that the western frontiers of India were not limited by the Hindukush, by Afghanistan and the Arabian Sea, but extended beyond Egypt and Palestine ; and her eastern defence arrangements have to be organized in the China Seas. The evolution of this western frontier of India started about sixty-five years back when Benjamin Disraeli purchased on behalf of the British Government shares in the Suez Canal Company—about 176,000 shares held by Ismail Pasha, the then Khedive of Egypt, worth above Rs 30 crores. This financial deal made the Mediterranean Sea "the life-line" of the Empire to its eastern and far Eastern units forming something like a semi-circle or arch covering the Indian and Pacific Oceans. To the need for protecting this "life-line" have on many occasions been sacrificed the interests of the countries about the eastern Mediterranean and the Red Sea, and their independence as States in the modern world has been modified into protection by Britain. Egypt has been made into one such "protectorate" ; the Turkish Empire has been disrupted ; the Arab principalities have not enjoyed the freedom that was promised them when they revolted against their Khalifa; Palestine has become a battle-ground between Jews and Arabs under a "mandate" held by Britain—all these developments have taken place because it happened that the Mediterranean and the Red Seas were joined by the Suez Canal, and shares in the Company managing the Canal were held by the British Government. It is true that not all the schemes of British Imperialists have borne fruit; England's ambitious scheme for a chain of British-controlled Arab States which would link India with Egypt has refused to work according to plan; the scaffolding of this "Middle Eastern Empire" of Mr. Winston Churchill's dreams has remained hanging in the air. But the feelings of the countries concerned are not amiable towards the British Empire though hundreds of millions of the hard-earned money of British tax-payers have been sucked into by the deserts of this part of the world.

The New Egypt since 1882

The attempt of Rashid Ali El-Gilaini to get control of the State in Iraq which was baffled by forceful methods adopted by Britain with the help of troops from India was a straw which directed attention to the way of the wind. The joint attempt of British and Russian army corps in ousting Reza Shah Pelhavi from the throne of Persia has been a success. But the very attempt—the necessity for such an attempt—points to a moral. Since the days of Arabi Pasha (1882) the El-Azhar University of Cairo has through imbibing the teachings of Jemaluddin Afghani been a centre of anti-imperialist sentiment and activity. Sheik Abdoo who became later the Rector of the University was one of the earliest of Jemaluddin's disciples. At that time the Palace of the rulers did not look kindly on the halls and cells of the University which were resounding with cries of reform in religious and political life. Since then with the quickening of national feeling a reconciliation between the two appears to have been arrived at; the present Rector of the University, Sheik Muhammad Mustafa El-Maraghi, is one of the protagonists of the idea that the Egyptian King should be made the Khalifa of Islam. This is said to have cemented a new union between the Palace and the University not quite friendly to Britain. American papers have begun to write of the "Palace-Azhar clique" directed against the occupying authorities.

Saudi Arabia's ambitions

In Arabia itself the mystery man who is at present the King of the Hedjaz within which lie Medina and Mecca, Abdul Aziz Ibn Saud, is watchful, and quietly and patiently biding his time. His adviser, St. John Philby, was in the Indian Civil Service when the first world war broke out. He was sent on deputation to the Persian Gulf potentates and has chosen to remain in Arabia, a convert to Islam, a guide and friend and philosopher to the dreamer of dreams who lives in the heart of Arabia at Riyadah but whose Kingdom extends from the Red Sea to the Persian Gulf. The news that St. John Philby has been released from restraint and detention in Britain directs attention to the fact that the object of his deputation on behalf of Sultan Ibn Saud to the British Imperial Government is not looked upon with much favour by the authorities concerned. We do not know the details of his offence. His new master's ambitions might be responsible for St. John Philby's sufferings. Owing to the shroud of silence, "the deadly silence", that generally covers the desert, we may not know the nature of these ambitions. But from hints and suggestions in the Press, specially of the United States, we may make a good guess about them. Saudi Arabia and Iraq have both been trying to conquer the Emirate of Kuweit on the Persian Gulf. The former wants to absorb the various islands in the Persian Gulf, particularly the Bahrein Islands whose rich oil deposits are being exploited by American capital under the protection of Britain; it also claims Aqaba at the northern tip of the Red Rea. King Ibn Saud with all his old-worldliness is fully or has grown fully conscious of the fact that modern life moves on oil, whether for purposes of peace or for war. His anxiety, therefore, for the oil of Bahrein is a testimony to his modernism. Herein he follows the late Shah of Persia, Reza Shah Pelhavi, who is reported to have forced in August, 1940, the Anglo-Iranian Oil Company to pay about five crores of rupees annually as royalty, thus virtually absorbing all the Company's profits for 1939, leaving nothing to the share-holders. The King of Saudi Arabia has not as yet resorted to tactics like these.

United Arabia yet a scheme

The economic and political conflicts hinted at above is a reflection of the various ambitions that have been keeping the rulers and chiefs of Arabia Proper divided. Since the end of the last world war we have been hearing a lot about a United Arabia or an Arab Federation. It is a curious fact that among the men who pioneered this movement there are many who are Christians who from Indian precedent should have feared the Muslim majority in the Arabian Federation. But these dreamers of dreams and seers of visions were built in the mould of the builders of New India who had risen above creed and colour. In Arab countries the scheme of Federation has been halted by the particularistic ambitions of the many ruling families. Scions of the family of the late Sherif Hossein of Mecca are rulers in Trans-Jordania and Iraq through the grace of Britain; the Wahhabi King of Saudi Arabia is ruler partly through his own strength but mainly through the diplomatic support of British Imperialism. The Hossein family and the Ibn Saud family have been maintaining a hereditary enmity. Emir Yehia of Yemen was a friend of Italian imperialists before the present war; what he is now is difficult to understand. In Palestine the driving force of all opposition was the Grand Mufti El-Husseini who has been moving about the countries of the Middle East organising resistance to Britain. He fled from Jerusalem to Iraq; was concerned with El-Gilaini's *coup de'tat*; from Baghdad he fled to Teheran, and when Reza Shah Pelhavi bowed before combined Anglo-Russian pressure, he is reported to have left Iran for Albania. These dominating figures in Arabia have not been able to combine for the defence of their common interests, for the advancement of the political status of Arabia in the comity of modern nations. There was a "Treaty of Arab Brotherhood & Alliance" signed at Baghdad in April, 1936, providing for a "limited unity" between Iraq and Saudi Arabia to which Yemen adhered in 1937; there was the Saadabad Pact signed in 1937 whereby Turkey, Iraq, Iran and Afghanistan bound each other for concerted action. But these plans have not brought any concrete good. These failures of Arab statesmanship, these separatist influences, may have been of advantage to British Imperialism in times of peace, but in times like the present they are sources of great weakness and anxiety. It is to anxieties like these caused by the conflicting ambitions of Arab leaders that one can trace the following confession :

> "Twenty years of close contact with the Arabs have produced a reaction against the romantic notions which remained as a legacy of Lawrence and his braves."

India loses by joining wars in her neighbourhood

Into the picture of turmoil in India's western frontiers we have not brought the movements of Indian troops and the story of India's help in the organisation of these particular invasions. From what we have heard from friends who had been to Mesopotamia during the first World War, we know that the help rendered by Indian troops to the freeing of the Arab peoples from Turkish rule earned our countrymen the hatred of the freed peoples. They helped to organise the civil administration in Iraq, to organize the railway system of the country; and their reward was enmity and a quick return to India. The British authorities felt themselves helpless in protecting Indian interests and defending or asserting the self-respect of our country. Interpellations in the Delhi Assembly drew replies from official members which disclosed that injustice to Indians could not expect to be remedied by the British High Commissioners. During the present war Indian troops have marched into Iraq, into Iran, to protect particular British interests, economic and political. And we have no reasons to hope that their experience of these two countries will be pleasanter than that of their predecessors. By association with Britain's imperialist adventures in the countries east and west of India's frontiers our countrymen have not been winning the confidence and friendship of their immediate neighbours. Our rulers have no time to think of this aspect of the matter. But we have to become aware that the ill-will of our neighbours has an evil influence on our "home polity." If this awareness grows into conviction, the Government cannot ignore it altogether.

Japan moves southward

We have made an attempt to understand and explain the many developments that have been making history in India's western frontier. In her eastern frontiers Japan's "China Incident" has yielded very little profit to the schemers of "a new order in Far Eastern Asia"—of the "Greater East Asia co-prosperity sphere," to use a new and extended version of their hopes and ambitions. During the last months of 1940, Japan acted as honest broker between Thailand (Siam) and Indo-China, a French possession which has become a pawn in the market-place of Far Eastern affairs. Japan does not propose to lose the opportunity of having a bite off this pawn. In the last volume of the *Annual Register* we drew attention to what she had extorted as brokerage at the expense of Indo-China for the trouble taken to negotiate between the two countries. On April 13 (1941) Mr. Matsuoka, Japanese Foreign Minister, on his way home from Berlin stopped at Moscow and signed the Soviet-Japan Neutrality Pact. It was of mutual advantage to both the Powers. The public men and publicists of the signatory countries hailed it as a great contribution to world peace. Without sharing in any exaggerated hope we can see that one cause of conflict in the Far East was sought to be removed by this Pact. It has held good for more than six months, even when Japan's Axis partners have been doing their best to crush Soviet Russia out of existence. It was feared at that time that China would be deprived of the solid help that Soviet Russia has been rendering her these more than four years since July, 1937 when Japan started the "China Incident." This fear gained strength when it was seen that Japan had been able to move her army corps from Manchukuo, that in July she moved her navy, army and air force into Indo-China, into her harbours, barracks and air bases. This movement of weapons of offence nearer British, American and Dutch-controlled territories seemed to indicate that the hour of destiny was striking for eastern Asia. With the islands of Hainan and the Spratley group under her command, with the Indo-Chinese naval and air bases in her effective possession, Japan was well poised for a swoop either on Burma or the Phillipines. But something appeared to be holding her back.

Geography favours Japan

To understand the reason for Japan's patient diplomacy one must study the geography of this area; compare her military and financial resources pitted against those of Britain and the United States. Geography has made the Japanese pessimists with regard to their national position as a pigmy by the side of China. It has made them "a sombre and disciplined unit" imparting an element of hyper-concentration and hyper-industriousness to their make-up. Geography in its material side also is in favour of Japan. Though the distance of Nagasaki to Cam-ranh Bay is about 2,000 miles, Japan by possession of Saigon, Cam-ranh Bay and of other bases in Indo-China has come nearer to Manila and Singapore and from these advance bases can attack both as these lie at a distance of between seven to eight hundred miles only. If war should break out in this region both the combatants will have to risk attack from their flanks. Between Saigon to Batavia in Dutch East Indies—the centre of the oil wealth of this area which Japan should covet—lie 1,200 miles of water over which she will have to stretch her supply lines; on two sides of this line lie Singapore and Manila. The Allied Navy moving towards any nerve-centre of Japan's offensive and defensive arrangements will in its northern voyage have to meet almost the same danger from the Spratley Islands on one side, and Saigon and Cam-ranh bases on the other. Further east if Japan proposes to intercept the battle formations of the American Navy she has the Marshall and Mariana islands as jumping-off grounds. But it is certain that the United States has already moved her naval and air forces, kept reserved for Pacific strategy, to Manila, to Cavite, to Singapore and Surabaya—the latter too placed at her disposal by Britain and the Dutch East Indies.

These strategic dispositions are not difficult to understand. It is more difficult to get or give any idea of the air and naval forces of Japan ranged against the strength of Britain, the United States and the Dutch East Indies. We have seen an estimate which puts Japan's naval strength at 10 battleships with 3 to 4 new ones in the Navy Yards; the U. S. A. has 12 capital ships in the Pacific to which are being added two new ones, —*Washington and North Carolina.* The threat of Axis preponderance has been quickening the building of America's Two-Ocean Navy, a 70 per cent enlargement of the present battle tonnage of the U. S. A. The main battleship power in the Pacific of the great republic is concentrated at Pearl Harbour about 3,400 miles distant from Manila. Where the United States will have to fight an offensive war in the mid-Pacific lies in Japanese waters—four to five thousands of perilous miles beyond Pearl Harbour. The practical "battle radius" of a modern fleet is 2,500 to 2,700 miles. It must have been this arithmetic of distance that led one American writer to say that in effective naval strength Japan was more than a match for the combined Anglo-American-Dutch Navy. It has been estimated that the total war-plane strength of Japan was about 8,000 of all types—not a very impressive figure when one compared it to the numbers commanded by Germany or Britain. The mettle of Japanese air forces has yet to be tested; China having practically no air force has been no effective rival. Thus armed *Dai Nippon* —Great Japan—has been preparing for her southward drive. The question that is being discussed in the world's Press is whether Japan will move over the waters or strike over-land against Burma.

Strength of Japanese war force

We have a certain impression that Japan is hesitant in launching an attack against British and Dutch territories not owing to any feeling of inferiority in military strength but owing to her economic and financial weakness. It is one thing to have to fight even in a prolonged war with China which is economically unorganized; it is another to have to stand up against Britain, the United States supporting her. For four years Japan has been busy with her "China Incident" costing at least 1,200 hundred crores of rupees. This might appear to be cheap according to the standard of war expenditure followed in European countries. But we cannot forget that Asia, including Japan, can manage things cheaper than Europe and America. And even the economically conducted war must have strained the economic resources of Japan. But this element of weakness would not have mattered much if the economic and financial arrangements of Japanese life had not been bound up with those of the "democracies", specially with the United States. Appreciation of mutual interest has built up this connection. Japan is the best United States customer in the East taking 20 per cent of the latter's cotton, buying raw materials and goods worth 80 to 90 crores of rupees every year. The United States takes or took Japanese silk worth Rs. 35 to 40 crores every year. An estimate has it that during the three years 1937, '38, '39, the U. S. sold to Japan goods worth about 300 hundred crores of rupees; of this vast amount more than half was for war materials—oil, scrap iron and other metals. She bought from Japan during the same period goods worth about 150 crores of rupees. And when we remember that oil is the motive power of the

Her economic & financial weakness

arts of peace and war in the modern world, that oil products provide motive power for 50 per cent of the world's shipping, 100 per cent of the world's aircraft, and for 5,00,00,000 of the world's land vehicles, we have to realise that the U. S. holds pre-eminent position with her control of 70 per cent of the world's existing petroleum supply. In the worsening of relations that has started between Japan and the United States, Japan has got to recognise the danger of her position in the event of a major war, a war with a great power like the British Empire. She cannot get oil from the U. S. A., from the Dutch East Indies, from British-controlled areas—all joined in an "unofficial union", directed against Japanese ambitions and pretensions in the middle West Pacific area. The Russo-Japanese Neutrality Pact which "disturbed the plans of London and Washington politicians", which was intended as a "bewildering blow" at Anglo-American interests, to use the words of the *Pravda*, the official organ of the Russian Communist party, would have relieved Japan of her dependence on Anglo-American-Dutch sources. Russia was capable of meeting this Japanese demand, a part of this demand, from her Asiatic sources, as her official statistics put 33 per cent of her coal, power and iron, and 80 per cent of her copper production east of the Urals. This hope has been dashed to the ground by Japan's Axis partner Germany attacking Soviet Russia. She must have stocked many of the essential necessities of war. One estimate we have seen says that she has a 2-year pile of oil stocked. This she has been able to do by the connivance of the U. S. Government. President Roosevelt has said that his Government connived at this trade, otherwise Japan in sheer desperation would have gone for the Dutch East Indies before America and Britain had been able to organise a proper defence. But the freezing orders passed by the United States, by the Dutch East Indies, and by the countries of the British Empire, have stopped all ways of replacing these. How great is the need for this replacement is proved when we read that Japan produces only 10 per cent of her peace-time requirement of oil from within her own territories; that her coal production is barely enough for her peace-time needs; that her Steel Industry is dependent for 80 per cent of iron, pig iron and scrap on imports from other countries.

Bad example set by other Powers

We have discussed the nature of the material difficulties that confront the Powers which in the Pacific Ocean have been girding up their loins for a fight. Japanese publicists and politicians appear to be fully aware of the risk that their country will have to face if they disturb the balance of political and economic relations that has been established since the first Opium War, a century back, when British pricked the bubble of Chinese power. We will try to summarise this century-old process of exploitation in the words that we used in Volume I., 1938, of the *Annual Register*.

"The process begun in 1840 when Britain extracted Hong-Kong as 'reparation' for China's impudence in opposing the British right of introducing opium into Chinese territories; in 1860 Tsarist Russia signed a Convention with China by which she gained 3,60,000 miles of Chinese territory, including 600 miles of coast-line on the Pacific on which stands the Vladivostock of to-day; in 1862 Britain annexed Lower Burma (a tributary of China); by the Chefoo Convention of 1876 'the virtual control of the Yangtze Valley fell into her hands' ; in 1884-85 Annam became a French 'protectorate' ; in 1886 Britain annexed Upper Burma ; Portugal seized Macao in 1887 ; British overlordship over Sikkim was recognized by China in 1890 ; Great Britain and France declared Siam 'independent' in 1893-94 ; .....in 1894-95 broke out the first Sino-Japanese War out of which Japan got Formosa, and Korea was declared 'independent' ; in 1898-99 Russia, Great Britain and France reaped a bumper harvest of Chinese territories through leases terminable at the end of 25 or 99 years. Thus, to quote a Chinese writer (the present head of the Japanese-protected Nanking Administration), "by 1899 in all China's 3,000 miles of coast-line there was not a harbour she could mobilize her ships in without the consent of the......foreigner." In 1900 Russia occupied Manchuria ; in 1904 Britain invaded Tibet, a Chinese dependency ; in 1911 Japan annexed Korea.

Japan's needs frankly stated

This lifting of Chinese territories on one excuse or other by the Western Powers has been a bad example to Japan, a great temptation to her, a great threat to the integrity of her life, to her political and economic interests. Apart from the bad example set by Western Powers, there is precedent in the Japanese contention that for her economic safety she required markets linked to her Yen ; that such economic safety could not be secured in the modern world without a "sphere of influence" dominated by her. This sphere of influence lies in the mainland of Asia, in territories contiguous to Japan, in China which has proved herself incapable of protecting and defending her independence in economic and political affairs. This has been the main argument in Japan's dialectic of aggression. On January 26 (1941) Mr. Matsuoka, the Japanese Foreign Minister, was quite frank in the statement of Japan's bid for leadership in Greater East Asia.

"Time and again, Japan has stated that her avowed aims are to create a peaceful and prosperous Greater East Asia ; but suppose Japan does have the dark design implied in Mr. Hull's statement, is it really an extraordinary design ? As America exercises a dominating influence over the Western Hemisphere, it would be the more logical if she refrained from concerning herself overmuch in other regions such as East Asia where Japan enjoys the position of exercising a stabilizing influence for peace and order.

Interest of U. S. in peace in the For East

The same complaint has been made by the publicists and public men of Germany and Italy against U. S. A.'s concern for and interference with developments in Europe and Africa. But exchange of logical arguments has very little influence in guiding the policy of States and Empires. We have seen in the last two volumes of the *Annual Register* how and why the United States should have constituted herself into a defender of the British Empire which stretches over all the continents. We have seen the influence of the many factors, idealistic and materialistic, that have helped to appreciate in the eyes of the U. S. A. the value of Britain and all that she stands for. In books and pamphlets this new-born enthusiasm has found expression—even in poems. An American woman, Alice Dewer Miller, has been much quoted by many a pro-British newspaper :-

"I am an American-bred,
I have seen much to hate here and much to forgive
But in a world where England is finished and dead,
I do not wish to live."

It is sentiments like these that have been pushing the great republic to throw her whole weight on the side of Britain. In an indirect manner she has been helping the other countries that have been trying to defend their own frontiers against aggression. The least idealistic interpretation of the crusading spirit of America may be found in any newspaper that may reach one from New York. When the fall of France stirred the widespread fear of Germany's over-powering might in arms, American papers were profuse in their expression of gratitude to the British Navy. "For the greater part of its history the United States has lived under the umbrella of protection provided by the British Fleet"; the two Fleets—British and United States—have never been "rivals but complements to each other". This mood did not, however, last long. It soon came to be asserted that the U. S. A. has paid something in return.

British & U. S. Fleets not rivals

"At the back-door of Asia the U. S. Fleet has long stood guard, setting up outposts in the Phillipines and Hawaii to prevent seizure of the Orient by pushing, expansion-set Japan."

Here we are told one of the reasons why the United States has got entangled in the Pacific, why she is regarded with such great apprehension by Japan. But there are other factors that have had their influence. The great republic on the other side of the Pacific has been cultivating a great friendship for China; her citizens have poured into China more money for constructive work in the fields of education than in any other non-European country. Forty years back the then President of the United States, Theodore Roosevelt, was credited with suggesting to Baron Kaneka, the Japanese ambassador, that Japan should declare a "Monroe Doctrine" for East Asia so that the aggressive European Powers might be restrained in China just as they have been kept off the two Americas by the declaration of President Monroe made in December, 1823. Japan could not follow that advice. Even her victory over Russia did not enable her to make such a declaration. Perhaps she dared not challenge Britain, France and Germany who were entrenched in China and from which they could be dislodged only by a major war. Instead, she has been trying to go round about towards the same purpose. She grabbed Manchuria in 1932. The European Powers tolerated this; Sir John Simon, the British Foreign Minister, speaking on behalf of Japan at the League of Nations Council which condemned the aggressor. Since then she has been nibbling at China, taking advantage of the rivalry among Chinese groups, of the differences and dissensions among European Powers, of the isolationist spirit of the U. S. A. But the "China Incident" has thrown a flash light on her policy. First we heard of her ambition to establish a "New Order in East Asia". With the weakening of European Powers, with the lessening of fear of opposition from them, Japan's appetite appears to be expanding; her statesmen have begun to talk of the foundation of a "Greater East Asia co-prosperity sphere", to quote the words of Mr. Masatsume Ogura, Finance Minister in the last Prince Konoye Ministry.

Japan failed to follow U. S. advice

But the realisation of this ambition cannot be had by peaceful means. Her war in China, and its methods, have repelled decent men and women in every part of the world. And the United States has been loudest in condemnation of these, and most generous in extending help to China. In setting up China's Currency Stabilization Fund she "pledged" about 16 to 17 crores of rupees, Britain 7 to 8 crores and China herself the same amount. American papers speak of 214 U. S. cities making collections for the United China Relief Fund of about 2 crores of rupees for the relief of China's 5 crores of war refugees—men, women and children—to provide them with food and clothing, with medical supplies, to help the orphanages, to help schools that train Chinese leaders, to help the Industrial Co-operatives that had been started with a capital of about 18 lakhs of rupees. These Co-operatives now finance about 3,000 small, mobile workshops back of the war-lines, support some 5 lakhs of refugees, supply consumer goods—shoes, nails, bandages, cigarettes, books, cloth, etc.—worth more than 2 crores a year.

U. S. A. help to China

This story is an index of the mind of the United States, of her generous mood. Side by side there is the recognition that China by her gallant fight has been helping to intercept and weaken the power of Japan, one of the disturbers of the international order that has grown under Anglo-Saxon hegemony. William Bullit was U. S. ambassador in Paris when France fell; he was young when after the last world war he was sent to Russia by President Wilson as his special "reporter" of the developments in Soviet Russia. Since his return from Paris (July, 1940) he has often acted as the maker of "trial baloon speeches" on behalf of his President. In course of a speech made on behalf of the United China Relief Fund he analysed for us the self-regarding basis of the friendship of his country for China.

The element of selfishness in U.S. help to China

"We have not yet been attacked by Germany, Italy and Japan for one reason and only reason only—they have not been able to get at us. ...The Chinese have kept the Japanese so fully occupied that they have hesitated to add a sea war against Britain or ourselves to their land war with China......To help China is to help ourselves. They are fighting......on what is literally—in a strategic sense—our Western front......In self-defence, for our preservation, whatever the consequences, we must back the Chinese."

President Roosevelt has declared that his country will continue to render assistance to Britain and "to all, who with Britain, are resisting Hitlerism or its equivalent with arms." Thus we find China receiving help under the provisions of the Lease & Lend Act, just as Britain and Russia are, as well as India. The value of "the defence articles" to be disposed to various countries under the authority of Sec. 3(a) of this Act "shall not exceed" rupees four to five hundred crores; Sec. 3(b) declares that "the benefit to the U. S. A." may be payment or repayment "in kind or property or any other direct or indirect benefit which the President deems satisfactory." In order that we can have a proper appreciation of the value of the help sent from the United States—from the "arsenal of democracy"—

Nature of U. S. "aid" to the democracies

in order to understand how in practice the Act is being worked, we cannot do better than summarize what has appeared in the January 10 (1941) issue of the *Current History* of New York. The very phrase "aid to Britain" conveyed an inaccurate impression. In every-day life "aid" by one man to another usually means an actual gift or loan of money, materials or efforts. In the case of Britain, U. S. "aid" meant nothing more than permission granted to Britain "to finance expansion of private manufacturing plants in the United States in exchange for a share of the war materials produced in those plants." This was done for "cash", at prices which in all cases were "ample to cover costs and profits, including premiums for extra shifts, over-time and early delivery." Taking note of all these factors, the U. S. Magazine has been constrained to say that "the only aid that the U. S. was actually giving to Britain was its refusal to sell a similar share of products to Germany." But then, Germany was not in a position to send her ships to the U. S. A.

World leadership U. S. should not avoid

This story reveals the less idealistic side of human nature. But life being a mix-up of the good and the less good, the path of wisdom lies in accepting such a compromise It is in this spirit that American "aid" to the Allied Powers should be given its place in the scheme of the modern world. In the last volume of the *Annual Register* we tried to show how destiny had been rousing the people of the United States to the duty they owed to the world as its richest country, and as the most organized in the ways of modern industrialism. The realization of this destiny is being popularized in books and magazine articles. In one of the former—*The American Century*—occurs the pith of the argument of the book; it is rather a pamphlet.

"In the field of national policy, the fundamental trouble with America has been, and is, that whereas their nation became in the twentieth century the most powerful and the most vital nation in the world, nevertheless, Americans have been unable to accommodate themselves spiritually and politically to that fact. Hence they have failed to play their part as a world power—a failure which has had disastrous consequences for themselves and for all mankind."

Conflict between two ideologies in the U. S. A.

The writer of this pamphlet of about 80 pages, Mr. Henry Luce, is editor of the News-magazine, *Time*, and conductor of two other weeklies—*Life and Fortune*. Between them these three papers have a reading public of about two crores—the subscribers' list of each exceeding 20 lakhs. The call to world leadership, the call for acting as the saviour of the modern world—these sentiments cannot help stirring deep eddies in the mental and moral life of the people of the United States. Developments in Europe since September, 1939, specially since June, 1940, have made it clear that Germany under Herr Hitler is out to change the present order of things, and the United States has been feeling uneasy. Mr. Henry Luce represents majority feeling in this respect when he calls upon his people to "be as big as the opportunity" presented by the 20th century to them. But there is a vocal school of thought in the country which preaches the virtue and wisdom of making terms with the Totalitarianisms, with the "Forces of the Future" which Nazism, Fascism,

Communism represent. Mrs. Anne Lindbergh—wife of Colonel Charles Lindbergh, one of the isolationist leaders in the U. S. A.—in her book—*The Wave of the Future*—says that Britain, France and the United States represented the "Forces of the Past"; that "somehow the leaders of Germany, Italy and Russia have discovered how to use new social and economic forces." She thinks that her country should not resist this change, the wave of the future as that would be "a sin against life itself."

Occupation of Greenland & Iceland ends "isolationism"

This book put against Mr. Luce's makes for us a picture of the American mind as it is developing under the threat of Totalitarian over-lordship in the world. But majority feeling, that of assuming responsibility for world events outside the two Americas, seems to be gaining strength and influencing the policies and practices of the American Administration. The material interests of the country, the requirements of the defense of its frontiers, stretched all over the new world, appear to be forcing the people to recognise that "threats of aggression can best be met at a distance from our shores rather than on the sea coast", to quote the words with which President Roosevelt stressed the lesson taught by the American naval strategist, Vice-Admiral Mahan. The recognition of this threat explains the reason or reasons why the U. S. extended "protection" to Greenland, a Danish territory, in the second week of April, 1941, and to another, Iceland, during the first week of July. Reyikjavik, the capital of this island, was occupied by American marines in agreement with the island administration. In giving information of the assumption of this responsibility to the Congress, President Roosevelt spoke of insuring "the safety of communications between Iceland and the United States, as well as the seas between the U. S. and other strategic out-posts." A discussion was raised about the validity of this step. "Hemispheric defence", it was contended, may require that Greenland should be or could be included in the American plan of defense; it appeared to be conceded that Greenland fell inside the western hemisphere. But Iceland was another proposition. No geography has put Iceland inside the new hemisphere. The plea of "protection of a little country" was dismissed with a note of admiration! And with this step was decided the problem, was settled the controversy that had divided the country.

Controversy over "two kinds of maritime solidarity"

Prof. Eugene Staley in an article in the April (1941) number of the U. S. Quarterly, *Foreign Affairs*, put in a nut-shell the practical issue involved in this controversy, that between "two kinds of maritime solidarity". Some would build the defence arrangements of the U. S. A. on a continental basis—that is "confined to North and South America and their immediate vicinities", while others would "team up with Britain in a world-girdling maritime defence group." Stated in these terms the occupation of Iceland by American marines indicated that the United States Government had accepted the latter plan. And in this it was responding to the pressure of sentiment and of national needs almost without difference of opinion. Mr. Wendell Willkie, rival to Mr. Franklin Roosevelt in the Presidential election of 1940, by his declaration that he favoured "bases in North Ireland and Scotland" underlined this unanimity in America. Even Colonel Charles Lindbergh in giving evidence before the House of Representative Foreign Affairs Committee recommended the establishment of bases in Canada, in parts of South and Central America, in the Galapagos Islands, while secondary bases might be established in Greenland. And the future trend was made explicit by President Roosevelt himself in the following words:

> "You and I think of Hawaii as an outpost of defence in the Pacific...And yet the Azores are closer to our shores on the Atlantic than Hawaii is on the other side."

Axis attempt to break up Anglo-Saxon mastery of the seas

It thus came to be increasingly accepted as the best policy that the U. S. A. should regard the "Western Hemisphere defense lines as distinctly secondary, to be prepared for emergency use if the first line of defense breaks." Their first line of defense was constituted by Britain herself and the strong points possessed by her in all the seas—in the North Sea blocking passage from Europe to the north Atlantic, at Gibralter, at the Suez Canal, at Singapore. These were supplemented by the Panama Canal and the Pearl Harbour (Hawaii) under the control of the United States. This arrangement secured mastery of the seas and oceans to the Anglo-Saxon Powers. The break-up of this historic arrangement was one of the purposes of the Axis Powers. On the success or failure of this purpose depends victory or defeat in this war. The meaning of this threat has been soaking into the consciousness of American citizens. And the ways of keeping this threat at a distance have revived the cry of the "freedom of the seas." They give meaning to the words used by Admiral Stack of the U. S. A. Navy that their patrols were operating 1,000 miles out at sea, and to those used by President Roosevelt that the U. S. will patrol the North Atlantic and South Atlantic, add more ships and planes to the patrol, and warn ships of the presence of raiders on the sea, under the sea and above the sea. These words were uttered during the peak of the "Battle of the Atlantic" when German raiders were sinking every month 4,00,000 tons of shipping bringing food to Britain from Australia and South America and North America, conveying the masses of weapons, munitions and instruments of war forged in U. S mills and factories. The possession of the Atlantic ports of France—Le Havre, Laurient, Brest—by Germany, and the use of these by her 10,000 miles range *Kurier* and *Zerostorer* planes, facilitated the sinking of British ships which followed the sea-lane west of the Azores in mid-eastern Atlantic. Owing to Eire remaining neutral Britain was deprived of the use of its south and west coast ports—Cobh (Queenstown) Berehaven and Lough Swilly—to refuel her flottilas and air craft, and from them to go out for the protection of the convoys that were bringing the food stuffs and "death-stuffs" from the east and the west. This handicap was deplored by Mr. Winston Churchill as a "most heavy and grievous burden" imposed on the resources of Britain.

And as the policy adopted by the United States has linked her defence arrangements, naval defence arrangements, with those of Britain, the present war has become what a U. S. weekly—*Time*—has characterized as the "undeclared war between the time-table of Franklin Roosevelt and Adolf Hitler".

"Undeclared war" between Roosevelt & Hitler

This characterization has become more apposite since Germany, bogged in her "little war" in the heart of Russia, has had to neglect her attacks on Britain or to limit these to the Atlantic Ocean only. This phase of the war has thrown added responsibility on the United States Government for the safe arrival of her Lease and Lend goods to Britain, China and Russia. For, no self-respecting Government could allow goods made at its own expense to be damaged or sunk under the sea without making an attempt to deliver them at their destination. The logic of this policy required that the cargoes from America should be protected with "less talk and more action", as Mr. Wendell Willkie impatiently expressed his feelings; "I care not whether you call it safe delivery, convoying, patrolling, airplane accompaniment or what not", he added. Perfect immunity could not be expected in modern naval raiding. But there is reason to believe that the U. S. has shaken herself for action on the seas. Thus has started a "shooting war" between Germany and the U S. A. which the Press cannot give any information about. This development was inevitable. Grand Admiral Erich Reader, head of the German Navy, warned the world of it when he declared in June (1941): "No body can expect a German warship to look on while an American warship communicates the position of German man-of-war to the British Admiralty. Such procedure must be regarded as an act of war......" Thus have circumstances beyond its control compelled the Government of the U. S. A. to go beyond its "limited liability" warfare with the Axis Powers.

American trade not possible in Axis-dominated Europe

The world has not had to search for long to get at the reason or reasons that have induced the United States to step on the inclined plane that leads to a full-blooded war. In the two volumes of the *Annual Register* of the year 1940 we have tried to indicate certain of the material and spiritual forces that have helped to create a kinship between the United States and the British Dominions including Britain herself. The bond of a common language breeding a common culture may explain one of the strands of this kinship. Material interests also appear to be playing the same part. The fear is strong that in a world dominated over by Totalitarian economic theory and practice, the "free economy" of capitalist competition that guides British and United States life could not expect to live and flourish. The question is being featured thus—can we expect to do business with Hitlerite Germany if and when she emerges victorious out of the present war? Books are being written on the subject; pages of magazines are occupied by articles full of relevant facts justifying the fear. One, written by Douglas Miller, Commercial Attache to the U. S. A. Berlin Embassy, bears the significant title—*You can't do Business with Hitler*. Extracts from it has appeared in the *Readers' Digest*, the New York magazine. And the question was answered, and the problem was solved for the average American citizen by what the U. S. A.

Department of Commerce made public in the second week of May, 1941. It was a summary of "a technical analysis of Germany's programme of post-war economy." The post-war life was indicated in words that could not but shock American leaders of industry and trade, American bankers who dominate world trade to-day. The words gave them timely notice that the days of their leadership were numbered if Germany could come out of the war victorious. The system of barter and bi-lateral trade agreement that Dr. Saccht has developed will break the back-bone of world-capitalism whose centre has shifted since the first World War from London to New York. The words of the report that made clear this position were the following :

"Confronted by a political combination on the continent of Europe under the domination of Germany, the individual American *entrepreneur* would hardly be strong enough to find a market for his products or services except on terms laid down by the National Socialist State."

Economic life of the Americas not self-sufficient

Leaders of business—of trade, commerce and banking—are not generally moved by sentimental and ideological appeals. The Americans are no exception to this rule. The threat implicit in the above quotation must explain, explain partly at least, why they have allowed their Administration to take them step by step towards the present war, to enlist the resources of their country for the defence of the vast assets represented and controlled by Britain. Study of their trade relations, of the movement of the products of their mills and factories, have convinced them that even the fullest exploitation of the raw materials and human power of their hemisphere, of the two Americas, cannot maintain the standard of living they have been able to build up for their own people and which they hope to spread over for their fellow-Americans. In a thesis on *A Trade Policy for National Defence*—the joint work of Percy Bidwell, Director of Studies, Council of Foreign Relations, and of Arthur Upgren, Associate Professor of Economics at the School of Business Administration in the University of Minnesota—the economic basis of Western hemisphere life was studied and discussed. It was found that of the total imports in 1937 into this huge area—valued at about Rs. 1,700 crores (taking a dollar at the rate of Rs. 3 each)—only about Rs. 700 crores or 43 per cent represented the internal trade between the 22 countries of the hemisphere. On the side of export trade the value of all the shipments across the national borders was Rs. 2,000 crores ; of this about Rs. 700 crores or only 39 per cent represented the internal trade of these countries. The problem represented by these figures boils down to this—that of finding sources of supply for about Rs. 900 crores worth of imports and markets for Rs. 1,200 crores worth of exports. During recent years continental Europe took about 37 per cent of all the exports from the Central American States and about 55 per cent of those of the South American States.

British Empire can keep the Americas "a going concern"

In 1937 the 40 crores of the people of continental Europe bought Western hemisphere products of the value of about Rs. 500 crores while the 4 crores 50 lakhs population of the British Isles took the products of the two Americas of the value of about Rs. 420 crores. In other words, for American products Rs. 93 were spent per head by the people of the British Isles, while only Rs. 15 per head were spent by the people of continental Europe. These figures prove the value of the British Isles and of the British Empire to the people of the Americas, North and South. The appreciation of this value was responsible for the use of the following words in the study made by the two U. S. economists.

"The British Empire area furnishes the markets and supplies the materials which can keep the Western Hemisphere a going concern. We are interested, therefore, in preserving the British empire as a political entity so that its markets may remain open to our exporters, and so that its raw materials may remain accessible to our importers."

The economic strength and weakness of the rival powers

The United States is not a free-trade area. Its agricultural products compete with those of many South American States. The Act and Convention of Havana adopted by the 21 American republics on July 29, 1940, set up a loose sort of an arrangement for common action in defence of common interests. It is, however, a fact that the majority of the American States did not feel at ease with their giant neighbour to the north, and their attitude towards "dollar imperialism" has for decades been standing in the way of New Hemisphere unity of feeling and action. The fall of France which was a demonstration of the might of Germany must have quickened the arrival of the decision at the Havana Conference. It is now up to the United States to assure the South American States of their political integrity and economic security. Their contention appears to be that if they lose the European markets for the offence of joining the hemispheric plan of the United States, as there is every possibility of their doing so if Nazi Germany controlled European life, alternative markets will have to be found for them. In this dilemma, created by Totalitarian methods of trade, the United States can only point out to the large area of comparatively freer trade that lies within the British Empire, specially as she herself finds difficulty in pulling down her own rather high tariff walls. It is this free trade area that can become the market of the New Hemisphere as well as the supplier and source of the essential raw materials in which it is deficient. For instance, jute and manganese from India, rubber and tin from the Malaya States, chrome and tungsten from South Africa. Closer relation with this area will consolidate the economic strength of the New Hemisphere as against the rival in the economic and political world that is being organized under Axis leadership. The Axis area in Europe is self-sufficient in many things—in coal and in iron ; is equal in capacity for steel production to that of the U. S. A, and in ship-building exceeding that of the U. S. in the ratio of 4 to 1. But it is dependent for many others, essential for modern needs. In 1938, the percentage of European consumption of these things, supplied by imports, stood as follows : copper ore 81 p. c. ; manganese ore 84 p. c. ; zinc 59 p. c. ; tungsten 76. p. c. ; crude petroleum 55 p. c. ; cotton 65 p. c. ; wool 69 p. c. and crude rubber 100 p. c. This deficiency of the Nazi-dominated world underlines the strength of the economic basis of the proposed Anglo-American "co-prosperity area" covering all the continents.

This story lays bare all the selfish and materialistic influences that have been working for the further expansion of the "Anglo-Saxony" of which we wrote in the last two volumes of the *Annual Register*. Therein we confined our attention mainly to the unselfish and idealistic impulses that are common to the English-speaking world. The story presented in the present volume gives a complete picture of idealism being reinforced by materialism to make it possible for the United States to assume the leadership of one *Mandal* or sphere of influence, economic and political, among the many *Mandals* that will be dividing the world in the near future. We have seen how the safety of the United States required that the two Americas should be organized on a common platform; we have seen how the two Americas have been found to be lacking in markets for their manufactures and in raw materials for their industries within their own territorial limits. We have seen how the addition of British Empire territories has been felt to be necessary for the smooth working of the scheme of American hemispheric life. We have now to recognize that this plan, built up with such elaboration, has a reference to our own country as it happens to be included within the British Empire. This is how dreams and realities, stirred into activity in the new world, on the other side of Pacific Ocean, at a distance of about 10 thousand miles from the eastern shores of our country, threaten to affect our "home polity" even as a small island in the north-east corner of the Atlantic Ocean at almost the same distance from our shores has been guiding and moulding our "home polity" for about the last two centuries.

"Anglo-Saxony" and India's "home polity"

When the world is in a flux, when the certainties of many centuries are being made uncertain by the upsurge of revolutionary forces, when, to quote H. G. Wells, the present disorder of things appears to be "almost the end of the human story and the world will never again emerge into freedom and unity", when Herr Hitler's "New Order", the "Imperial way" of giving shape to Japan's "Greater Asia co-prosperity sphere", when the two chiefs of the Anglo-Saxon world—President Franklin Roosevelt of the United States and Prime Minister Winston Churchill of Great Britain—have promised the world an "Atlanic Charter"—when we have these three different futures waiting for us in the immediate future, we have to take note of the process of their evolution into something more substantial than paper boats on the stream of time It is a common-place in political discussion today to say that we live in revolutionary times. To understand the various factors that go to the making of this revolution in human affairs which many of us welcome and as many fear is an attempt that the student of modern human life cannot avoid. It may be a far cry from the Americas to India just as in the middle of the 18th century Britain was a long way off from us. Today at least distance is no hindrance to inter-continental relationship, just as in the days of the sailing ships it did not stand in the way of Britain founding an empire on which the sun never set. The publicist and public man of India today have, therefore, to keep a watchful mind studying the many economic and political factors that will have an influence on

India must be aware, and be wary, of this development

the fate and fortunes of his country. The days when our ancestors could dream of avoiding the *Kalapani*—the dark waters of the sea—and of founding their social polity on such avoidance—those days are gone with the arrival of the steamship and the airship. The failure of that attempt in our country is proof that the adoption of a hermit policy was unwise. Today, even with all our weaknesses and disunities we have got to face the greater world that has been knocking at our doors. Our refusal to admit it into the court-yard of our life has failed of its purpose. In our economic arrangements we have adopted a policy of give and take with the world. In other spheres of life we will be wisely guided to do so. We must not only be aware of this development, but be wary of it.

Rabindra Nath Tagore voiced India's "moral revolt"

The realization of this necessity has made India's foreign relations world-embracing, though a record of these may not find a place in the archives of the League of Nations. India has to settle her accounts with British Imperialism which under the pressure of war will have to shed many of its crudities and abnormalities. The "moral revolt" of India expressed through the *Satyagraha* Movement may not appear to deflect the purpose of British policy. It may not affect the success of British administrators utilizing the man-power of India and exploiting the natural wealth of India to fight their battles in Europe, in Africa, in Western Asia, and in countries on the Pacific; it may not stop the mills and factories of India feeding the battle-lines with modern implements of war. But with all this going unembarrassingly forward there is hardly any doubt that the nearer approach of the war cloud either from the west or from the east towards our country does not find the mind of the people strung to that tense feeling that has enabled the British people to stand up against the showers of bombs from the skies amidst the destruction of the monuments of their historic life. There is a sense of frustration, and of irritation at the absence of conditions which would call forth the heroic in the men and women of India to fight against adversity. This frustration found expression in language of noble pathos in the message entitled—*Crisis in Civilization*—which Rabindra Nath Tagore sent out to the world on the occasion of his 81st birth-day celebration held on April 14 (1941) at Santi-Niketan, the seat and centre of *Viswa-Bharati*, the world university established by the poet-philosopher of India. It has happened that this was to be his last message to the world which he left amidst the "crumbling ruins of civilization strewn like a vast dung-heap of futility." In this message he traced the vast change that he has witnessed in his own mind and in the psychology of his people during the eighty years passed on earth. He traced for us how in the opening years of his life the generation in the bosom of which he grew up had welcomed the light that had come from the west; how the Englisman who was the messenger of this light became a "source of perpetual admiration" to his people. Then came "disillusion", a sense of national grief with which his own person was identified in a real and personal sense. Because, Rabindra Nath Tagore with his sensitive faith in the dignity of man found it difficult to reconcile the highest conception of humanity, represented to him and his generation by the Englishman, with what he discovered in the character and history of the administration that was established in this country. And he left this with a tragic disappointment in his heart.

"It is no longer possible for me to retain any respect for that mockery of civilization which believes in ruling by force and has no faith in freedom at all. By their miserly denial of all that is best in their civilization, by with-holding true human relationship from the Indians, the English have effectively closed for us all paths to progress."

"Moral standing" of Britain discredited

This last judgment passed on British rule by an admirer of the English race and of their culture points to the seat of evil that has stalked by the side of Indo-British relationship through all its history. This has even at this crisis in their life stood in the way of Indian self-respect making its definite contribution to the common defense of their common interests. The present generation of Indians may fail to understand and appreciate the innocence of belief in the "large-hearted Liberalism of 19th century English politics." But Rabindra Nath Tagore by making this confession of faith has revealed a process in the evolution that has led to the progressive estrangement between the two peoples, as awakening national self-respect in India has met at every stage hindrances to the evolution of a Nation State in the country. Till to-day, when Britain is fighting for her very existence, she finds an India unreconciled and lukewarm in face of possibilities threatening their common life, built by the history of the last two hundred years. Confronted by such irreconciliation Britain appears to have persuaded herself that even without the heartfelt co-operation of the Indian people, her officials can utilize the man-power and natural resources of the country and win their war with Germany. This may be a natural human feeling, a natural human failing as well. By yielding to these they may win the war. But there is no doubt that they will lose the peace. The Government of Lord Linlithgow has not satisfied any party or school of politics in this country. Demonstration of this fact is writ large in recent Indian history, in the Press, in the proceedings of the Central Legislature. The failure of his Government to have the supplementary Budget, containing certain war taxes, passed, has received wide comment both inside and outside the country. The Congress members had stayed away from the Assembly as a mark of protest against the policy of making India a belligerent without consultation with her or without her consent. They were present on the occasion to vote down this budget. They succeeded in their attempt. But what added to the significance of this event was that the Muslim members, the majority of them members of the Muslim League, helped by their abstention "to deal this blow" to what the *New Statesman & Nation*, weekly of London called the "moral standing" of the British position in India. The paper frankly confessed that

"Bitterly as they differ, the Congress and the Muslim League agree in exposing any pretension on our part that we rule India and combat this war with her consent."

The paper discussed how by following the policy that it has been doing the Churchill Government has been losing the peace that was to end this war. Axis propaganda has seen to it that into the minds of European peoples should sink the lesson of Britain's "Indian record", and that they should have a yard-stick by which to measure British declarations about democracy and the freedom of nations. The report that "the peninsula is morally in revolt" and that the answer of the Government has been "repression" cannot enthuse the Frenchmen, the Dutch, the Poles, the Czechs, and the Austrians who have been writhing under German heels when the gospel of liberation came to them from Britain. And the humiliation of the situation was brought home to the writer of the article by an able Austrian refugee in Britain when he said: "Nothing will so certainly win Europe as the news that India was free." India is the test and remains the test of Britain's sincerity in fighting this war against Germany's threat to the freedom of nations. Britain cannot avoid this test. But the difficulty put in the way of passing this test was Britain's own creation. By every declaration made by Secretaries of State or the Governor-General of India since the representatives of the Indian National Congress put to them the question of India's place in the present war, they have placed in the hands of each of the minority "elements" in India a right of veto over the emergence of any satisfactory and self-respecting solution of the Indian problem. Every statement of theirs has encouraged the minorities to put up their claims till today nothing appears to remain of India as a political unit but a hotch-potch of disintegrated conceits. Thus has the impasse been created because "too scrupulous to coerce a minority," Britain has been "coercing a majority without a sign of hesitation." So far as one can say and see there appears to be no way out of the difficulty for Britain but to pursue her policy in silence, and for India to watch in silence the fight for "New Orders" that will be emerging out of the fire and smoke of the present war just as during the last World War, twenty-five years back, the world had been led to believe that the end of all wars was in sight and the rule of the "self-determination of nations" will prevail over the world. This hope may uphold the belligerent peoples during the excitement of the times. Perhaps, it is best so. For such a hope can never be fulfilled as long as bloodshed is accepted as the test of truth and justice in international differences.

Britain's "Indian record" will lose the peace

The agrument between Indian Nationalism and British Imperialism is part of a world-wide phenomenon. The hopes that move other peoples, the disappointments that await them after the hectic days of the war, India shares and cannot escape. The British authorities have been trying to support these hopes by saying that the future is for the people of India to decide; that British policy would not be putting any difficulties in the way of the realization of these hopes. Let the many elements of India's myriad-pointed life agree amongst themselves, and the British Government would be prepared to accept the agreement. This has been the tradition of British policy in relation to the different countries of the Empire that are to-day Dominions of the "British Commonwealth of Nations." These assurances do not,

Non-official British community is the stumbling block

however, appear to have had any effect on the clarification of the Indo-British issue, on the solution of the impasse in India. Rather, to quote the words of Dr. Foss Westcott, the head of the official Church in India: "We appear to be reaching a stage when the long connection between Britain and India is in danger of being dissolved in a flood of mutual recrimination and misunderstanding." It is not concern for the profit-and-loss account of the British household but the highest regard for the moral and spiritual issues involved in this controversy that must have moved this man of God to specially appeal to his fellow-countrymen, living in India, to apply themselves to bridge the gulf that has been yawning between the two peoples. The promotion of good will and mutual understanding between every class of the country was the surest way to re-establish Indo-British relations on a firmer basis. This appeal did not, however, have the desired effect. The leaders of the non-official British community in Bengal organized in and represented by the Bengal Chamber of Commerce made a declaration that showed that they were behind the *non possumus* attitude of the British Government refusing to go beyond the August 8 (1940) statement of policy made by Lord Linlithgow. The immediate cause of this outburst of theirs was the suggestions made by Mr. Arthur Moore of the Calcutta *Statesman* through the Press in Britain that the control of the British Parliament over India should cease and that the Crown's authority be vested in the Viceroy who would thus be thrown on his own resources in finding advisers from amongst Indians; he had also exposed the futility of the contention that at that particular time the British Parliament could not think of imposing its own solution while during all these two centuries it had overridden every Indian argument for the evolution of self-government in the country. The Clive Street leaders of the British community came out with an uncalled-for statement that in making the suggestions Mr. Arthur Moore was not giving utterance to the authentic voice of their community. Mr. Moore's reply was that he did not claim to speak as such.

Mr. Amery's "amazingly misleading" speech

This controversy reached a new tension during the days following Mr. Amery's speech made in the House of Commons on April 22 (1941) on the occasion of moving a resolution extending for another twelve months the proclamations issued under the provisions of Sec. 93 of the Government of India Act (1935). Under the terms of that Section the Governors of seven provinces in India—Bombay, Madras, Orissa, Central Provinces & Berar, Bihar, the United Provinces and the North-West Frontier Province—had assumed the powers of the Provincial Legislatures on the Congress Ministries resigning as protest against the policy of the British Government that had pushed India into the present war without giving any body in the country an opportunity to consider the issues or declare its will. The Secretary of State in giving a history of this constitutional break-down made comments that misrepresented the whole position, that were "amazingly misleading", to quote the words used in the statement made by the Standing Committee of the Sapru Conference. As it has been the habit of the British bureaucracy, Mr. Amery, without being brought up within it, put the blame on Indian differences and on the weaknesses of her social polity for the growing intensity of internal competition and conflict. He exceeded all bounds of credence when he asked his fellow-members, the majority of them ignorant of India, to believe that the "change to direct personal rule by governors and permanent officials met with general acquiescence, and indeed good will." He gave no satisfactory explanation why no action had been taken on the proposals made in Lord Linlithgow's statement of August 8, 1940. He was less than frank when he said that the Congress attitude of "All or Nothing" was responsible for this failure of the good intentions of the British Government. The months that have passed since then, and the recent announcement made on the enlargement of Lord Linlithgow's Executive Council, have exposed how unreliable were the reasons given by Mr. Amery to explain in April the difficulties in the way of accepting the proposals that had been made in the "Leaders' Conference" held at Bombay in the second week of March. More than any positive statement that he might have made which irritated, there must have been something in the spirit informing his utterances on the occasion, that led to an out-burst of public feeling in India. Mahatma Gandhi's statement that appeared in the Press on April 27, 1941 is symbolic of this wide indignation. "Every line and every word of it breathes indignation—indignation of a type somewhat unusual with the Mahatma," said the Rt. Hon'ble Srinivasa Sastri.

"Talking Points" on India—a sample of British propaganda

The Congress had recalled its Ministries from seven provinces; its leaders were within jail gates; Mahatma Gandhi had stopped his weeklies as protest against Government interference with the freedom of the Press. Congress members had withdrawn from the Central and the Provincial Legislatures were not being called. British propagandists headed by Mr. Amery, Secretary of State for India, were holding forth on the sins of India with the help of "Talking Points" supplied to speakers by the British Ministry of Information. The truth of India's climate being more unhealthy than that of the temperate zone; "the complete difference between the Hindu and the Muslim system"; the "difficulty of getting Indian officers" for the Indianization of the Indian Army; "religious prejudices" that make the opening of one school in a village for the children of all classes "impossible"; the enormous growth of the population in India which in 80 years has grown from 250 million to 350 million being a dangerous symptom; to save herself from this disease India must either slow down the growth of population or increase its food supply ("big-scale irrigation has almost reached its limits", be it remembered) or import food-stuffs and presumably pay for them by industrialization—these samples of "talking points" were being distributed free to recommend the methods of British administration of India, to justify its ways to the world, to explain the reasons why Britain found difficulty in shedding the burden that in a fit of absent-mindedness she had put on her shoulders in 1757. The campaign based on these "talking points" was clever, no doubt. It was malicious in intent. It has, perhaps, succeeded in its evil purpose. But at what cost? We are told that modern wars require the services and sacrifices of all the men women and children of a country. An India divided against itself, as it is represented to be, could not be expected to put forth such a "total" effort either for herself and for her rulers. It must be and ever remain a burden. This may be the psychology of British distrust of men and things Indian. They have been trying to broadcast this distrust all over the world, specially over America. And distrust begets distrust. The distrust of 40 crores of people weigh late or soon in the scheme of things, in the conduct of any system of government.

Leaders of "unattached opinion" in India meet

This discrediting of India which is one of the instruments for perpetuating imperialism in this country in the hands of die-hard imperialists has been increasing the sense of frustration in the country, and making the people indifferent to what happened. This was a development that could not be helpful to war effort, even though princes might send money, poverty produced soldiers and the wealth of Britain produced the goods in India, and there were foreign newspapermen to publicize these exploits. But the sharp and angry reaction to Mr. Amery's speech of April 22 revealed a state of things that neutralized all the propaganda of the "Talking Points". Even the most moderate of Indian politicians and publicists who had been denouncing the Congress for withdrawing Ministries from seven provinces could hardly control themselves. Sir Chimanlal Setalvad said that "no political party is convinced because of past experience of the British Government's sincerity as regards parting with power". The Standing Committee of the "Leaders' Conference" pointedly asked the Secretary of State what had happened to his assertion that if the Congress and the Muslim League failed to take part in the expanded Executive Council "Lord Linlithgow will of course go ahead, prepared to work with those who will work with him and with each other." They repudiated the insinuation which Mr. Amery had borrowed from Mr. Jinnah that their Conference had been held in consultation with or at the instigation of certain Congress leaders. This Conference was held at Bombay in the second week of March (1941) by leaders of "the vast mass of unattached opinion in the country." The Rt. Hon'ble Sir Tej Bahadur Sapru was president of the Conference; Sir Jagadish Prasad who had sometime back retired from the position of the member of the Governor-General's Executive Council was the moving spirit of the new movement. The proceedings of the Conference demanded that the Government should prove its *bonafides* in the matter of transference of power to Indian hands, and recommended therefor that in the proposed enlargement of the Governor-General's Council the members should be wholly Indian, that the key positions—Defence and Finance—should be held by Indians. This would be "National Government" not in the legal and constitutional sense but in the spirit of what the vast majority of the people desired. Sir Nripendra Nath Sircar in proposing the main resolution was cruelly frank in exposing the pose of anxiety for agreement among the various elements of India's population recently cultivated by the ruling classes of Britain. "Is there any provision in the Government of India Act (1935) which is the result of agreement ?", he asked. He instanced the joint and separate electorate issue to drive home his point—the issue which is hated by the vast majority of the people and from which has followed all the abomination of dissensions in India's life that are the excuse of British imperialists today for holding on to irresponsible power. The framer of "Diarchy", Mr. Lionel Curtis, had warned his people of the evil—

"India will never attain unity and nationhood so long as communal electorates remain. The longer they remain the more difficult will it be to uproot them, till in the end they will be only eradicated at the cost of a civil war. To enable India to attain nationhood is the trust laid on us and in agreeing to the establishment of communal representation, we have been false to that trust."

Question of British *bonafides*

And the Conference was sure that if the British Government could do the courageous thing, "the large, unorganized but still powerful moderate opinion which......has been at the back of India's considerable war effort" would be able to exert such pressure on the parties which were now in opposition that the face of Indian politics would undergo a healthy change. How wide-spread was the feeling of wounded national self-respect was made vivid in the speech of the late Maharaja of Burdwan, Sir Bijoy Chand Mahatab: "We are not going there (post-war conference) as Sir Tej Bahadur Sapru went or as I went in 1926 to the Imperial Conference", declared he.

Prof. Berriedale Keith's opinion

Words like these ought to have served notice that Britain will have to revise her policy. But these fell on ears that heard not or hearing understood not the significance of the words. Five weeks later Mr. Amery in the House of Commons dismissed the Sapru Conference resolutions with personal compliments to the organisers of the Conference mixed with insinuations with regard to its unrepresentative character. The demand for the complete "Indianization" of the Executive Council was dismissed with the remark that it would not be a "modification" of the existing form of government but its "suppression" by an entirely different type. The best reply to this contention came from Prof. Berriedale Keith who in a letter to the *Scotsman* said that the Federal and Provincial Governments must work on "the basis of ministerial responsibility to the Legislature", that "Ministers must be appointed for Defence and External Relations". This is what Sir Tej Bahadur has been pressing for more than a year that the portfolios of Defence and Finance must be held by Indians as a symbol of India's status as a Dominion. The acknowledgment of responsibility to the Crown ought to satisfy the most sensitive of constitutional purists. Another suggestion of Prof. Keith's went to the root of the evil. He asserted that the British Government must "abandon efforts" to use the States as a minority interest along with the Muslims. The "utmost safeguard for all minority interests must be provided." But "the unity of India must be asserted" against all challenge. He did not accept the standpoint of the Congress that India should be independent, because he thought that in the modern world there would hardly be a place for a "neutral India to play the role of Belgium in the east." The defect of this argument is that Prof. Keith could not imagine a time, far or near, when India would be fully organized for purposes of peace and war as one of the great nations of the world, with one-fifth of the human race to work for her good and for the good of humanity.

Inspiration of the *Satyagraha* Movement

The British Government has failed to conciliate India because it has lost the capacity to understand and appreciate that 40 crores of men and women unreconciled to its ways would be a handicap in the present crisis in the life of Britain, that a country of 40 crores of people has a distinct part to play in the evolution of a better world where respect for human dignity, individual or national, would be its cornerstone. Mahatma Gandhi who has by the *Satyagraha* movement been leading the "grand protest against the conduct of the war" in the name of India has always said that even in such an activity India should be inspired by a moral purpose and that the means to attain it should be "free from any injury to man's dignity." When he started the present movement he made the clean declaration that it was not "intended" to create "an appreciable impression upon the war effort." The extraordinary precautions that he has imposed on the conduct of the movement, the rigorous selection that he has made of the participants in the movement, indicate unmistakably that he did not desire to embarrass the Government and its use of the man-power and natural resources of India. He has admitted that he was prepared to accept even the verdict that his movement has been "ineffective" in so far as concrete results were concerned, that it has failed to bend the British Government to accept the demands of the Indian National Congress. He was prepared to confess that he did not expect any such "miracle." He would be content if the movement demonstrated before all the world, to the conscience of all thinking men and women of "India's dissociation from the war effort to which it was never invited to be a party." This put the matter in the lowest possible term and in the baldest political language. Gandhiji's personal standpoint was different from that of the Congress. Faith in non-violence, trust in "the efficacy of the incalculable force of an inscrutable Divinity", has sustained him through the last half-a-century of individual and national storm and stress. He believed that this Divinity must work its will through a human agency, that wars and bloodshed and the hatred and ambitions in which these germinate cannot serve the purpose of creation. He was, however, prepared, to use the Indian National Congress, "however imperfect and however wanting in faith as an organization" it may be as the thin reed to send the call out to the men and women of the world to rethink their present philosophy of conduct and to retreat from the "calculable and calculated ways of destruction." It may appear to be an act of faith and not of of reason to thus think of halting the activities of millions and of their rulers—activities that are touched by a certain magnificence of sacrifice, by a super-human endurance, and are illumined by streaks of moral exaltation and forgetfulness of self. The nature of modern wars, the character of "total wars", invite whole peoples into these streams which cleanse and purify human nature. Herein lies the dangerous fascination of wars.

Gandhiji has tried since he came into the leadership of our political life to offer a moral equivalent of wars and bloodshed, to sublimate the feelings and sentiments that supply the motive-power to the forces of destruction. All the movements that he has been associated with and has led have to be tested on this touch-stone. But apart from his personal beliefs and sentiments there are standards of judgment which require to be applied to them as political movements that have certain material purposes to reach. The present *Satyagraha* movement has not created the wide-spread fervour that takes and uplifts people out of their accustomed grooves. This fervour has been purposely controlled and limited. It is too early to speak of the effect that the present movement will have on the intellectual perceptions of the people of this country who are directly or indirectly being affected by it; it is too early to speak of the awakening of the moral sense of the world that will compel a re-examination and re-interpretation of the principles that unconsciously to the majority of us guide our actions. We have been taught all these centuries that wars and conquests have a certain moral sanction and sublimity. Gandhiji's challenge to this teaching should help us to judge these matters from new angles. The masses in every country who supply the cannon-fodder in wars have been the greatest losers. The ferment of combativeness may excite them to a disregard of the loss that falls mostly to their lot. And when the excitement ceases, and a grateful country forgets the heroes and cannot provide the homes that were promised to them, then come disappointment that can be very bitter in expression. The first World War of the 20th century was followed by this bitterness, and the second through which we have been passing cannot promise better results. Hatred which is officially encouraged, hymns of hate that receive official sanction, leave a legacy that keeps inflamed the enmity between peoples. Anger, even righteous anger, that seeks satisfaction in the blood of enemies does not lead to peace among men. The twenty years' interval between the two wars of our experience has discredited the tale of resurrection of the human spirit after it has been cleansed by blood-bath in a war or wars fought for justice and freedom. Gandhiji's challenge may not work any miracle of conversion. But it has stirred questions in every heart that looks into the horror of the times. These cannot remain unanswered. Modern civilization, threatened by a spell of universal chaos, cannot carry on with bombers and tanks as the deciding factors in the establishment of rational human relations.

Violence from which the masses suffer the most

Gandhiji's technique has woven the problem of *Swaraj* in India into the texture of a universal human need. By securing political freedom through non-violence in a country where live one-fifth of the human race he wants to demonstrate that war between nations are not worth while. And in the peculiar conditions of our country where many races and cultures have met and where their autonomies have been given a distinct place in the life of the whole—toleration of differences and diversities, and refusal to impose on one the peculiarities of the other, can only ensure peaceful social life. These differences and diversities impose on us the need for non-violence, the duty to practise it in every walk of life. For twenty years and more Gandhiji has

A propaganda that poisons relations between neighbours

been trying to implant into our minds that the material interests of the vast majority of the peoples in every country are linked with peace which can only be built on the firm foundation of toleration, of respect for the sanctity of the human personality. This work appears to have had no influence on the conduct of the men and women who claim to lead community-life in this country. The growing estrangement of feelings between peoples who are of one blood, and speak the same language, but differ in religious beliefs and practices, testifies to the failure of this call for a more rational philosophy. Fear of our neighbours, ambition to have a bigger share in the authority of the National State that is rising over the horizon of India—these two feelings and sentiments are being enthusiastically cultivated amongst us. A civil war mentality appears to have got hold of the people Ahmedabad, Bombay, Bihar-Sharif and Dacca have been scenes of a malignity of mutual destructiveness that are becoming common in India's life. In the city of Dacca, the second city in Bengal, for about six months the assassin's knife and the coward's torch have levied their victims in life and property in proportion to the percentage of the Hindu and Muslim populations. A Hindu killed has been followed by a Muslim killed, and *vice versa*. Soon the evil spirit spread over the country-side; 10 to 15 thousand men, women and children belonging to the Hindu community fled to the neighbouring State of Tripura where the Maharaja gave them shelter, fed them and clothed them. And the Government of Bengal stood discredited before the bar of history. The men and women living now know not what has happened. Through the gagged silence the full story has not been able to reach the Indian public; the public of the world has been kept ignorant of it. So, history must judge.

A hymn of hatred & fanaticism

The outburst of this fanaticism has long been anticipated since certain members of the Bengal Ministry began inflaming communal passions by appeals to mean cupidity and inflated ambitions. Encouraged by their example lesser men stepped beyond all decencies of civilized life, and spread a propaganda of hatred that could have no other result than what has happened in Dacca. It is not possible to have record of every word said and everything done to make the relations between Hindus and Muslims bitter, to make it difficult for them to live as neighbours which they have been doing for the last one thousand years. A sample of this propaganda has been rescued for our mutual shame in the translation of a Bengalee poem that was read by the chairman of the Reception Committee at the Kalihati and Ghatail Muslim League Conference in the district of Mymensingh, held in March, 1941. Two Muslim ministers of Bengal were present at this conference. The poem was published in the Bengalee daily—*Azad*—on March 10, 1941. To let the world know the nature of the poison that is being spread over Bengal, we publish a portion of this poem.

"The oppressed remain silent by seeing the hypocrisy
Of the idolatrous Hindus—oh death-like eddy!
O victorious soldiers; march forward on our
Religious pilgrimage to the Kaaba under the banner
of the League.
We shall spill as much blood as required.

* * * *

We want Pakisthan, a proper division.
If it cannot be achieved by words, Muslims
Are not afraid to use swords and spears.

* * * *

Where are the Muslim youths! We shall attain
The desire of their hearts by tying down the wild tiger.

* * * *

Come quickly—break down Somanath.
If you want freedom, Burn! Burn! Burn! the
Jatu-griha (houses made of lac), and let all trouble end."

The burning of Hindu houses, thousands of them, has carried out the behests of this exhortation. And the break-down of neighbourly relations is symptomatic of the condition of things that the Hindu and Muslim majorities in the different provinces will be creating in the country, if propaganda like the above be allowed to continue, and what is of more importance, if society encouraged it as the outlet of its deepest yearnings and highest sentiments. For, it would be short-sighted to regard such propaganda as the growth out of an individual mind, diseased by a sense of frustration. The separatist feeling amongst Indian Muslims which has expressed itself in poems like this has a history of its own. In Vol. I 1939 of the *Annual Register* we made an attempt to trace the evolution of this feeling and idea that have captured the mind of a powerful section of the Muslim community of India and which are being sought to be given concrete shape in what has been called *Pakistans*—lands of the pure. The Muslim League has made itself responsible for pushing to the region of danger such a development. Being a minority in India, the Muslim League, so far as it represents the ideas of a section of the Indian Muslims, express distrust of the majority community, the Hindus. In any scheme of representative and responsible government for the whole of India the influence of the Hindu majority cannot but be reflected in the legislative institutions and in the governments that are recruited from these. To avoid the danger of this contamination with a majority, the theory has been invented that the Indian Muslims are not a minority community but a nation which must have new centres of government. The President of the Muslim League, Mr. Mahommed Ali Jinnah, declared, therefore, that his organisation could not tolerate "a constitution of an all-India character with one government at the Centre." Hitherto the "aims and objects" of the All-India Muslim League had been "the establishment of full independence in the form of a Federation of free democratic States in which the rights and interests of the Mussalmans and other minorities are adequately safeguarded in the constitution." During its annual session held at Madras in the second week of April, 1941, the League repudiated the Federation idea, and so changed its "aims and objects". Henceforth these are to be

The Muslim League creed & practice

(a)......The establishment of completely independent States formed by demarcating geographically contiguous units into regions which shall be so constituted with such territorial readjustments as may be necessary, that the areas in which the

Mussalmans are numerically in a majority, as in the North-West and North-East Zones of India, shall be grouped together to constitute independent States which shall be free National Homelands in which the constituent units are autonomous and sovereign."

Any interpretation of ours of this scheme is difficult in the absence of the detailed scheme of territorial adjustments, in the absence of the Muslim League map of the India that is proposed to be drawn up and that will be different from what the world has known for centuries. It is useless, perhaps. Because the logicians of the Muslim League who have developed a new impatience with the Hindu majority in Hindustan cannot long remain or appear to remain blind to the illogicality of the claim for Muslim majorities in certain areas of the country. One can understand the reason or reasons for the condemnation of the principle of majority rule in States; one may join in a campaign against the thinking that counting of heads and wisdom in rulers go well together. But to declaim that a Hindu majority is a nuisance, if not an evil thing, and that a Muslim majority is the very ark of generosity or wisdom, would be going against the verdict of history and putting a strain on the intelligence of the modern man and woman. The leaders of the League would be serving themselves better and serve the world better if they could evolve out of their Islamic experiences the plan of a constitution for India that would promise better results than representative and responsible government that the modern world has learnt to value.

Separatism may be made a process in growth

In successive volumes of the *Annual Register* since 1936 we have been tracing the growth of separatist conceits and ambitions in many of the communities and provinces of India. This sense of separatism appears to be the first essay of every renaissance movement, of every freedom movement. Indian philosophy has taught us that the realization of the separateness of the Self from the Not-Self is the first step of the pilgrim soul in the enrichment of the life spiritual, in the liberation of the human spirit from the trammels of the senses. In the quickening of political life the realization of the separateness of the ruled from the rulers is the first step towards the emergence of a democratic State. When the people of India awakened to the insult and shame of their political subjection, their leaders had to strengthen that awakening by drawing attention to the conflict of interests that was implicit in the unnatural relation between India and Britain. This conflict of interests created the separateness between the rulers and the ruled in India, and had supplied the driving power to national awakening in India. The pioneers of the political movement amongst us built up the whole of their programme of work on this separateness as between the rulers and the ruled, and on the oneness of the interests of all the people of India. No communal or provincial feeling diverted their energies. The majority of them were Hindus, but in their life and conduct there was hardly any trace of narrowness.

Hindu reaction to the separatist plea

In the case of the Muslims of India also when the awakening knocked at their doors and roused them to their frustrated life they had to pass through the process indicated above. They had to separate themselves in thought from their neighbours to realize their own strength and assert their position in the composite life of India. A Muslim educationist, Principal of a Government Mahommedan College, indicated this stage of development in his community when he said that "...... a Muslim was creating an impression intellectually that he was living more as a citizen of Arabia or Persia than as a citizen of India." This type of mind was the seed-plot of Pan-Islamism which helped the Indian Muslim to regain his self-respect by the thought of past glory, and of the comparative freedom of his co-religionists outside India. He has, however, got stuck in the conceit of separatism, and has not been able to throw it off as unnecessary now. In discussing the reaction of the Hindus of India to this mentality of their Muslim neighbours we wrote in 1938 :

"As strongly do Indian Muslims assert their separateness, and kinship with the peoples of countries outside the boundaries of India, so loudly do the leaders of the Hindu Mahasabha assert that the 'bed-rock' of Indian life is the Hindu community."

"Mandatory safeguards" for minorities

In the same volume we traced the evolution of the Hindu Mahasabha Movement and of the leadership that has organized its wide ramifications of today. The feelings and sentiments that had enabled the earlier generations of public men and publicists to build up the Indian National Congress as the organ voice of the composite national life of India, as the forum for the discussion of all matters pertaining to India, as the instrument of a quickened public opinion asserting its rights to mould public policy—these feelings and sentiments are being converted into the dynamo of a consciously assertive school of thought that claimed its right to guide and control the evolution of the country as representative of the majority community in India. Confronted by a threat to the unity and integrity of the country from the people who, the majority of them, are by blood Indians, the Hindu Mahashabha Movement appears to be drawing to itself the allegiance of an increasing number of Hindus the vast majority of whom had hitherto been content to entrust their interests to the keeping of the Indian National Congress. This unfortunate development has become almost inevitable as the rising temper of Muslim separatism has been claiming "homelands" for the culture of their particularistic sentiments, conceits and ambitions. Both the Muslim League and the Hindu Mahasabha have been embodying in their constitutions "mandatory safeguards" for the protection of the religion, culture and language of every community of India. These declarations do not, however, appear to have had any reassuring effect on the minds of the people concerned. It has not also been explained by the protagonists of *Pakistans* in India why the promise of such "mandatory safeguards" for minorities made in the constitution of a Federal India should not remove the suspicions and fears of every community in the country. The President of the Hindu Mahasabha, Sri Vinayak Damodar Savarkar, has in successive speeches sought to relieve all minorities in the country of any fear or suspicion that all their legitimate rights of "liberty of speech, liberty of conscience, of worship, of association etc" will be "expressly guaranteed". The London *New Statesmen & Nation* has handsomely recognized that no one has questioned the claim of the minorities to equal rights—civil, political and cultural ; that "for these the Hindus offer every imaginable guarantee." The Indian National Congress by the "Fundamental Rights" resolution passed at the Karachi Congress, and the leaders of the Congress in every statement made have been no less emphatic in assuring minorities of every conceivable guarantee of their rights and privileges. But the Muslim League has spurned at these assurances, and the leaders of the British community in India, both official and non-official, have helped to stabilize this attitude by open encouragement.

This argument between India and Britain has had consequences in other fields of Indian life. About Rs. 80 crores worth of British orders may have been moving the machines in certain industries in India; about 10 lakhs of soldiers recruited in India may be getting trained in the modern technique of war; Britain's wealth, accumulated through the last two centuries since "the first impetus (to industrial revolution in Britain) was given by the plunder of Bengal", to quote the words of Dean Inge, might finance these war activities; the poverty of India might help to recruit cannon-fodder from India. In direct and indirect ways Rs. 84 crores might be taxed from the people to spend as India's special war budget. But British money and Indian money are not going to establish such industries that will have any other purpose than the prosecution of war. Whenever the question has been raised that the opportunity offered by the war should be utilized in India by Indians to start industries that have a permanent value to the country, the spokesmen of the bureaucracy has been quick with the reply that all such schemes should be tested on the one touch-stone—whether or not they are of immediate use in the prosecution of war. This narrow standard has halted many a scheme of industrial expansion in the country. It is a curious mentality that talks loudly of "total war" in which every human being and every material can serve the purposes of war, while refusing the best use of these in India. Indian industrialists have been coming forward to start a motor industry, an aeroplane industry to be rewarded with official discouragement. And the Government which has failed in the political field to enlist the self-respect of India on the side of Britain has been found to be as lacking in insight and foresight in organizing the forces and resources of the country for the prosecution of the war. At a time when the "Battle of the Atlantic" has been costing the British mercantile marine every week about 4 lakhs tons of ships sunk by Nazi attacks, the Government in India has declared its decision with regard to ship-building in India—they are "not to encourage actively the merchant ship-building industry in India as a part of their effort". At a time when the U. S. Government has directed its Maritime Commission to release 20 lakhs of tons for carrying to Britain the food-stuff and the "death stuff" on which she depends for her very survival. At a time when President Roosevelt described the dangerous condition of things in the following words:

Indian industries & British policy

> "The present rate of Nazi sinkings of merchant ships is more than three times as high as the capacity of British ship-yards to replace them. It is more than twice the combined British and American output of merchant ships to-day."

The Government in India, a subordinate branch of the British Government, makes itself responsible for this discouragement to Indian initiative and Indian enterprise. In Vol. II of 1937 of the *Annual Register* we made an attempt to trace the fight of national interests against the indifferentism and discouragement of the Government, and how the foundation

Scindia Steam Navigation Co.'s Ship-Yard

of Britain's proud boast of being the "mistress of the seas" was laid under the patronage of State in the days of Queen Elizabeth and her successors in the rulership of the England. This patronage has been denied to Indian leaders in trade and industry, and non-Indian interests have been allowed to strangle one after another during the last 40 years the more than 20 shipping companies that tried to carve out a share in the costal trade of their own country. But the strength of Indian sentiment in this matter, the determination of Indian interests not to be discouraged by the unhelpfulness of the Government that calls itself Indian, have triumphed over all adverse conditions. The symbol of this triumph was the foundation of the Ship-building Yard of the Scindia Steam Navigation Company at the Port of Vizagapatam in the Andhra Desha on the 21st of June, 1941. Babu Rajendra Prasad presided over this ceremony. In his speech on the occasion he dwelt on the history of Indian shipping which had sailed the seven seas in times beyond record and memory; he traced the history of the fall of this industry during British regime. Seth Walchand Hirachand, Chairman of the Board of Directors of the Company, related the story of the difficulties that had to be overcome before they could give concrete shape to their dreams and aspirations at Vizag. This story reflects no credit on the Delhi-Simla Government. The literature on the subject of Indian Shipping, both past and present, from which Babu Rajendra Prasad and Seth Walchand Hirachand enriched their speeches, is part of the wider history of Indo-British disharmony.

British Shipping losing to the Japanese

It is a story that has, however, its comic side. For, the British interests in India's sea-going trade have not been able to enjoy all the fruits of their narrow and selfish policy; they have had to agree to lose the majority of these to the Japanese shipping interests carrying on business in the eastern seas. An account we have seen give us the story of this transaction where we watch British interests progressively losing to their Japanese rivals. In 1888 the P. & O. had 66 per cent of the carrying trade of this area, the Austrian Lloyd and the Navigation Generale having 17 per cent each. The Japanese were nowhere. In about 1896 the late Jamshedji Tata, the founder of the "House of the Tatas", who had been suffering at the hands of this European monopoly in his attempt to build up a China trade, invited the Japanese shipping interests to come in and compete. There was a freight war, and the leader of the European interests, the P. & O., had to compromise by yielding 18 per cent of the carrying trade. By 1918 the Japanese managed to squeeze out another 22 per cent. And from then on it has been a triumph for them. For, in 1921 we find them occupying the position that the P. & O. did in 1888, that is, carrying 66 per cent of the trade, while the P. & O. had to content itself with 34 per cent. And in 1929 the former had secured 80 per cent, and the latter fell back on a mere 20 per cent. One could have enjoyed this reversal of the role played by the two parties which have not allowed Indian interests to take a share in this vast trade—the overseas export and import trade of India—the annual value of which is about 400 crores of rupees. But watching as one does the worsening of relations between Britain and Japan, one cannot extract the whole enjoyment out of this business.

Committees of reconstruction in India

Both the governments and the peoples of the world have been talking of "planning" the future. This "planning" cannot but affect the life of men and women who have their own plans to regulate their own life. The Government in India have set up four committees to deal with different aspects of post-war reconstruction in this country. The first committee will deal with Labour and Demobilization. The needs of war have drawn lakhs of men into war industries and into the army in India. At the end of the war when the services of most of them will not be required they will form a "problem"—the difficulty of absorbing them into "civil life". The second committee on Disposals and Contracts will deal with the problem that will be created by the rather sudden stoppage of war industries and war contracts ; many things, important and unimportant, will be accumulated that will have to be disposed of carefully and not thrown in a huge heap on the market, allowing time for war industries to be transformed into peace industries. The third Committee will deal with Public Works and Government Purchases—the problem that will be created by the two previous problems as also by the necessity to take up what is technically known as "Public Works"—the building of Government buildings, of bridges etc.—neglected or held up owing to war ; with this problem will be linked that of Government purchases that had called into being many industries and that will cease with the return of peace. The fourth committee will deal with trade, international trade policy, with agricultural developments. With the war's end will begin a scramble in the import and export markets. With shipping returning to the ways of peace the hungry markets of India will invite the many consumer goods that foreign countries will be able to throw here, and the products of Indian agriculture which had European and non-Indian markets will try to roll out to these in floods. But during these war years men and women must have learnt to do without things, to produce substitute goods ; they must have learnt the wisdom of relying on their country's soil for the satisfaction of their needs. These new conditions and the improvement in industrial machinery in the warring countries may render many of India's contrivances and much of her skill obsolete ; it may happen that many an industry in India sheltered behind tariff walls and the absence of competition due to the war will find themselves confronted by world competition where the manipulation of tariffs will render their work uneconomic, and their struggle against this competition well-nigh impossible. These after-war problems will require special treatment which it will be the business of these four committees to render. The committee of the economic experts of India is another organization specially created. Their activities will require co-ordination ; this will be the duty of a "Steering" Committee, renamed the Reconstruction Committee. The problems that these committees will have to tackle are not peculiarly Indian ; every country in every continent will have to face and solve them. The solution of these problems will require central direction and guidance ; it may require the continuation of the many "controls' or restrictions on individual or group freedoms. The continuation of these "controls' even during the period of peace, of reconstruction, may have the effect of building up habits of command, of dictation in officials, that is the bureaucracy, and those of submissiveness and obedience in the people. This development may explain the pessimism of H. G. Wells when he uttered the words that "the world will never again emerge into freedom," at least in the near future. In the background of world catastrophe our little quarrels and doubts and fears may appear insignificant. But these are the warp and woof of life. And life goes on. And the student of life has to take note of every one of its many strands. It is under the compulsion of such a duty that we have tried to trace the sources of many dissatisfactions and discontents that stir in our midst. We have discussed the various phases of the argument between Indian Nationalism and British Imperialism. We have tried to understand and explain the far-off events that are approaching the shores of our country, and the ways they may affect our life.

Lesser incomes—more expenses

We have discussed the many schemes that the Government in India has been preparing for the purpose of building the future economic life of the people. The present, however, is not an easy time; and men and women who do not understand what the *Sarkar Bahadur* is doing find themselves with lesser incomes and higher expenses. We are told that the war is responsible for these higher expenses. We find that the policy of the railways in increasing fares and rates has co-operated in bringing about this state of things. Those amongst us who have some glimmering sight of the ways of modern business have been asking questions of the industrialists of India. Why has there been an increase in the prices of the goods that are consumed by the masses of the people? Certain of the industries that supply these goods have for years—some for more than twenty-five years, some for less—been receiving protection in various shapes from the Government and from the people. The raw materials of these industries are found abundantly in India. From the people has come the protection in the shape of preferring goods made in India to goods made outside "even at a sacrifice". The first organized expression of such a protective feeling came from Bengal nearly thirty-seven years back when the Bengalees resolved to boycott British textiles as a protest against the ill-conceived attempt of the partition of their province made by Lord Curzon. Since then the feeling has deepened and widened till to-day it inspires the life and conduct of the vast majority of our people. This protection given to the textile industry of India by the people of India has helped to reduce the value of Manchester goods imported into India from Rs. 60 crores to about Rs. 14 or 15 crores. The policy of the Government in India in support of certain Indian industries has lagged far behind popular support; it has come much later. Two other big industries—iron-steel and sugar—have received protection from the State. All this protection has placed on the consumers burdens in the shape of higher costs of the goods used by them. A former Finance Member of the Governor-General's Council, Sir James Grigg, in many speeches in the Central Legislature used to make a parade of the extra burden that the masses of India bore for giving protection to Indian industries; he estimated it to exceed Rs. 25 crores a year. During a discussion on the Protective Duties Continuation Bill in the 1941 winter session of the Assembly speeches brought out that during the last 17 or 18 years the steel industry of India has received protection whose money value was about Rs. 50 crores; the sugar industry has during less than half that time received protection the money value of which has not been less than Rs. 50 crores. The question now being asked of Indian industrialists—what have the people who have been helping to nurse your industries gained by their sacrifices of these years? They have been helping you so that in times of difficulty like the present one you should be able to make repayment of that help by keeping the costs of your goods low. Have you—makers of textiles, of iron-steel, of sugar—fulfilled your part of the bargain? The spokesmen of these industries have not been able to make replies that can be called satisfactory to the masses Many economic theories may explain the causes that have disappointed the hopes of Indian consumers; it may even be that things would not have been better if the raw materials of industry that lie scattered in India had lain idle; it may be true that consumers must sacrifice and continue to sacrifice so that industries may live and thrive; that this one-sided arrangement is an irremovable and irreplacable part of the present order of things. But these arguments in support of sacrifices on behalf of the modern organization of industries appear to have lost their appeal to the reason and to the conscience of the modern man and woman. They appear to be nearing the end of their patience, to be preparing themselves to take up the entire scheme and break it into bits in a spasm of disappointment and despair. Even India with her centuries-old philosophy of earthly despair and other-worldly hopes may be nearer such a development than we can rationally explain. Even sober members of Legislative Assemblies are found to be unable to control their impatience with things as they are, their disgust of these developments.

Indo-Ceylonese controversy

There are other troubles that have been testing the temper of our people. In our immediate neighbourhood things are being done and words are being spoken in Ceylon and Burma that create bitterness in the present and plant time-bombs of trouble for the future. In the Central Assembly during the last winter session the question of Ceylon's treatment of Indians resident in the island was discussed bringing out to the light of day the many ways in which Ceylon's Council of Ministers propose to squeeze out the few lakhs of Indians that have laboured for more than half a century to transform the life of this island. The occasion for the discussion was the presentation of the report of the Exploratory Conference held at Delhi on the 4th of November, 1940, between Ceylon ministers and representatives of the Government of India. The conference held five sittings. At an early stage of the discussion one of the Ceylon ministers laid bare the purpose of the whole range of discriminating legislation that is being adopted against Indians. There are about 9 lakhs of men and women of Indian descent in the island; of these the vast majority, about 75 per cent, belong to the "estate population", that is, labourers in the tea, coffee and rubber estates—2,11,000 men, 2,04,000 women and 2,65,000 children. The Ceylon minister said that the full number of Indians, one sixth of the population of the island, could not be absorbed into their island economy. The choice lay between sending them out of "extermination" of the Ceylonese, between drastically limiting the number of Indians or "submergence which is going a so fast." This frank statement of the case, of the "question of survival" of a people has to be sympathetically studied and understood. But it is complicated by the question that when Ceylonese publicists and public men speak of "our own people" they seem to forget history, to forget that the majority of their people are descendants of Indians who had crossed over to Ceylon and peopled the island with the fruits of their loins. If the island could absorb them and was not worse for this process of mixture, why should not the 9 lakhs of Indians who have made Ceylon their home for all practical purposes, who have by the sweat of their brow built up the modern economic life of Ceylon, why should they be rejected and thrown out as aliens? The proportion of men, women and children in the "estate population" shows that these people have decided to live and work and die in Ceylon—a good enough test of Ceylon citizenship. This aspect of the question of Indians making a better place of Ceylon by their life and work has been ignored by our Ceylonese neighbours. The same failure marks the activities of our Burman neighbours that they are not prepared to give people who have helped to enrich their country time to develop into full-blown Burmans. The refusal to co-operate with Time in making the future of their nations have been accumulating for all of us—for our two neighbours and for ourselves—troubles and trials which may be the crucible of a better life. Let us end with this note of hope.

Agony of the world & ourselves

For, hope appears to be departing from the affairs of this world. As we go to the press Japan has started her undeclared war on the United States and Britain and the Dutch East Indies. This step has been wanting for about twenty-seven months to transform the war started in the plains of Poland into the Second World War of the 20th century. Why destiny prolongs this agony of humanity and does not take the sorry scheme of things into its hands and at one blow shatter it into bits is more than we can say. We are witnesses to a dissolution of one pattern of civilization. The grandeur of the theme imparts to us a dignity equal to those who watched the death and destruction enacted in the field of *Kurukshetra*, to those who watched the sunset over Athens and Rome, to those who passed through the years when on the throne of Delhi sat puppet kings, and Sunni and Shia, Marhatta and Sikh, Afghan and Rohilla, wrestled with one another for the guardianship of the descendants of Baber and Akbar and Aurangzeb. This new dignity will, perhaps, help many of us to pass through the terror of the times with serene minds, to suffer and sacrifice with equanimity, with untroubled consciousness.—(*Specially contributed by Sri Suresh Chandra Deb.*)

Proceedings of

The Council of State

The Indian Legislative Assembly

AND

Provincial Assemblies

AND

Councils

January—June 1941

The Council of State

LIST OF MEMBERS

President—THE HON. DR. SIR MANECKJI BYRAMJI DADABHOY

Nominated (Incl. the President)—26

(*a*) **Officials—11**

H. E. THE COMMANDER-IN-CHIEF SIR CLAUDE AUCHINLECK
THE HON. SIR GIRIJA SANKAR BAJPAI
" MR. L. WILSON
" " M. S. A. HYDARI
" SIR ALAN LLOYD
" MR. E. CONRAN-SMITH
" " S. N. ROY
" " A. DEC. WILLIAMS
" " C. E. JONES
" " SHAVAX A. LAL
" " H. DOW

(*b*) **Non-officials—15**

" SIR DAVID DEVADOSS
" DIWAN BAHADUR SIR K. RAMUNNI MENON
" SIR A. P. PATRO
" " RAHIMTOOLA CHINOY
" " JOSNA GHOSAL
" RAI BAHADUR SATYENDRA KUMAR DAS
" RAI BAHADUR SIR SATYA CHARAN MUKHERJEE
" SIR MOHAMMAD YAKUB
" SIRDAR NIHAL SINGH
" RAJA CHARANJIT SINGH
" NAWABZADA KHURSHID ALI KHAN
" KHAN BAHADUR SHAMS UD-DIN HAIDAR
" DR. SIR M. B. DADABHOY
" LIEUT.-COLONEL SIR S. HISSAM-UD-DIN BAHADUR
" SARDAR BAHADUR SOBHA SINGH

Elected—**Non-officials—32**

" RAO BAHADUR K. GOVINDA-CHARI
" MR. M. CT. M. CHIDAMBARAM CHETTIYAR
" MR. NARAYANDAS GIRDHARDAS
" MR. V. RAMDAS PANTULU
" SAIYAD MOHAMED PADSHAH
" MR. GOVINDLAL SHIVAL MOTILAL
" MR. SANTIDAS ASKURAN
" MR. MANOCKJI NADIRSHAW DALAL
" SIRDAR SAHEB SIR SULEMAN CASSUM HAJI MITHA
" KHAN BAHADUR A. B. MAHOMED HOSSAIN
" MR. R. H. PARKER
" " KUMARSANKAR RAY CHAUDHURY
" KUMAR NRIPENDRA NARAYAN SINHA
" MR. SUSIL KUMAR ROY CHOWDHURY
" KHAN BAHADUR SYED IHTISHAM HYDER CHAUDHURY
" MR. ABDOOL RAZAK HAJEE ABDOOL SUTTAR
" MR. J. H. S. RICHARDSON
" RAJA YUVERAJ DUTTA SINGH
" PANDIT HIRDAY NATH KUNZRU
" PANDIT PRAKASH NARAIN SAPRU
" HAJI SYED MOHAMED HUSAIN
" CHAUDHRI NIAMATULLAH
" RAI BAHADUR LALA RAMSARAN DAS
" SARDAR BUTA SINGH
" CHOUDHRI ATAULLAH KHAN TARAR
" MAHARAJADHIRAJA SIR KAMESHWAR SINGH
" R. B. SRI NARAYAN MAHTA
" MR. NIKUNJA KISHORE DAS
" " HOSSAIN IMAM
" " V. V. KALIKAR
" " BRIJLAL NANDLAL BIYANI
" MAULAVI ALI ASGAR KHAN

The Indian Legislative Assembly

LIST OF MEMBERS

President—The Hon. Sir Abdur Rahim

Elected—**Non-officials—102**

(1) Madras—16

S. Satyamurti
K. S. Gupta
Mr. Thirumala Rao
Prof. N. G. Ranga
M. Ananthasayanam Ayyangar
T. S. Avinashilingam Chettiar
K. Sitarama Reddiar
K. Santhanam
Shrimati K. Radha Bai Subbarayan
Sri K. B. Jinaraja Hegde
Umar Aly Shah
Mualavi Syed Murtuza Sahib Bahadur
H. A. Sathar H. Essak Sait
F. E. James
Raja T. Manavedan
M. R. Ry. Sami Vencatachelam Chetty Garu

(2) Bombay—16

Dr. G. V. Deshmukh
Sir Cowasjee Jehangir, Bart
Diwan Lalchand Navalrai
Bhulabhai Jivanji Desai
Hoosenibhoy A. Lalljee
S. K. Hosmani
Keshavrao M. Jedhe
N. V. Gadgil
Mahomed Ali Jinnah
Nabi Baksh Illahi Baksh Bhutto
Seth Haji Sir Abdoola Haroon
I. D. Boyle
E. L. C. Gwilt
Manu Subedar
Khan Bahadur Mian Ghulam Kadir Md. Shahban
Sir H. P. Mody
N. C. Chunder

(3) Bengal—17

Dr. P. N. Banerjee
Babu Amarendra Nath Chattopadhyaya
Pandit Lakshmi Kanta Maitra
Subhas Chandra Bose
Akhil Chandra Datta—*Deputy President*
Sir Abdur Rahim
Hajee Chowdhury Mohammud Ismail Khan
Sir Abdul Halim Ghuznavi
Chowdhury Sikander Ali
Shaikh Rafiuddin Ahmad Siddiquee
Dr. Habibar Rahman
C. C. Miller
C. P. Lawson
T. Chapman Mortimer
Srijut Dhirendra Kanta Lahiri Chaudhury
Babu Baijnath Bajoria

(4) United Prov.—16

Chandra Bhal Johri
Chodhri Raghubir Narain Singh
Pandit Sri Krishna Dutta Paliwal
Badri Datt Pande
Sri Prakasa
Shri Mohan Lal Saksena
Sirdar Jogendra Singh
Sir Syed Raza Ali
Qazi Mohammad Ahmad Kazmi
Sir Muhammad Yamin Khan
Maulvi Abdul Wajid
Dr. Sir Zia Uddin Ahmad
Mohamed Azhar Ali
J Ramsay Scott
Raja Bahadur Kushal Pal Singh

(5) Punjab—12

Lala Sham Lal
Raizada Hans Raj
Bhai Parma Nand
Syed Ghulam Bhik Nairang
Maulana Zafar Ali Khan
H. M. Abdullah
Nawab Sahibzada Sayad Sir Mohammad Mehr Shah
Khan Bahadur Shaikh Fazl-i-Haq Piracha
Khan Bahadur Nawab Makhdum Murid Hossain Qureshi
Sardar Mangal Singh
Sardar Sant Singh
M. Ghiasuddin

(6) Behar & Orissa—12

Satya Narayan Sinha
Babu Hari Sharan Prasad Srivastva
B. Das
Pandit Nilakantha Das
Ramayan Prasad
Gauri Shankar Singh
Kailash Bihari Lall
Babu Ram Narayan Singh
Muhammad Nauman
Muhammad Ahsan
Maulvi Mohammad Abdul Ghan
Maharaja Bahadur Ram Ran Vijai Prasad Singh

(7) C. P. & Berar—6

GOVIND VINAYEKRAO DESHMUKH
SETH GOVIND DAS
PANDIT SHAMBHUDAYAL MISRA
NAWAB SIDDIQUE ALI KHAN
SETH SHEODASS DAGA
M. S. ANEY

(8) Assam—4

KULADHAR CHALIHA
BROJENDRA NARAYAN CHOUDHURY
ABDUR RASHEED CHOUDHURY
P. J. GRIFFITHS

(9) Delhi—1

M. ASAF ALI

(10) Ajmer-Marwar—1

RAI BAHADUR SETH BHAGCHAND SONI

(11) N. W. F. P.—1

ABDUL QAIYUM

Nominated 39—officials—20

THE HON. SIR MUHAMMAD ZAFRULLAH KHAN
" SIR REGINALD MAXWELL
" SIR ANDREW CLOW
" SIR JEREMY RAISMAN
" DEWAN BAHADUR SIR ARCOT RAMASWAMI MUDALIAR

B. M STAIG
SIR GEORGE SPENCE
C. M. G. OGILVIE
O. K. CAROE
J. D. TYSON
SIR GURUNATH BEWOOR
SIR RAGHAVENDRA RAU
T. S. PILLAY
H. J. FRAMPTON
V. T. DEHEJIA
MOHAMMAD IKRAMULLAH
S. H. ZAHEER
B. K. MUKHERJI
MAULVI MAZHARUL ISLAM
SAHIB SHAIKH ABDUL HAMID

Non-officials—19

SARDAR BAHADUR SARDAR SIR JAWAHAR SINGH
N. M. JOSHI
DR. R. D. DALAL
DR. FRANCIL XAVIER DESOUZA
MAJOR NAWAB SIR AHMAD NAWAZ KHAN
KHAN BAHADUR SIR ABDUL HAMID
LIEUT.-COLONEL M. A. RAHAMAN
RAO SAHIB N. SIVA RAJ
"SHAMS-UL-ULAMA" KAMALUDDIN AHMAD
L. C. BUSS
LIEUT.-COLONEL SIR HENRY GIDNEY
DR. RAJAH SIR ANNAMALAI CHETTIER
MUHAMMAD MUAZZAM SAHIB BAHADUR
NAOROJI M. DUMASIA
SETH SUNDER LALL DAGA
KUNWER HAJEE ISMAIEL ALIKHAN
HONY. CAPAIN SARDAR BAHADUR DALPAT SINGH
SAIYID HAIDAR IMAM
CAPTAIN THAKUR SINGH

Secretary—MIAN MUHAMMAD RAFI
Deputy Secretary—M. N. KAUL
Assistant Secretary—KHAN BAHADUR S. G. HASNAIN
Marshal—CAPTAIN HAJI SARDAR NUR AHMAD KHAN

The Council of State

Budget Session—New Delhi—19th. February to 4th. April 1941

GENERAL DISCUSSION OF BUDGET

The Budget Session of the Council of State opened at New Delhi on the 19th. February 1941, Sir *Maneckji Dadabhoy* presiding. After the Chief Commissioner for Railways had presented the Railway Budget, the Council adjourned till the 25th. February when a general discussion of the Budget was held. Before the commencement of the debate, members of the Muslim League Party staged a walk-out, after their leader, Mr. *Hossain Imam*, had made a statement. The other members who withdrew were Messrs. *Padshah* and *Mahommed Hossain*.

Rai Bahadur *Lala Ramsarandas*, Leader of the Opposition, congratulated the Railway Member on showing a heavy surplus. He was, however, disappointed that no relief had been given to the tax-payer, and more amenities had not been afforded to the travelling public. He declared that the Government had not made up its mind to start the manufacture of broad gauge locomotives in India. The *President*, intervening, pointed out that it was difficult to procure machinery from concerned for the present with the conditions existing before the war. At present, in the United Kingdom, Officers were obtained from Officers Cadet Training Units. The same conditions prevailed in this country, where Officers were trained at Mhow, Dehra Dun and other places. Proceeding, the Commander-in-Chief said that the times were urgent and their main and only task to-day was to win the war. "If we can combine our ideas to this end, I can assure you that we will be very happy." The Commander-in-Chief said that he wanted to get the right kind of candidates with requisite qualifications for the Officer class. He would be very glad if he could obtain such candidates from the U. T. C. Even before the war, the fact that a candidate had undergone training at a U. T. C. was given due weight by the Selection Committee. He realised that members of the U. T. C. were keen to learn and serve and he had issued necessary instructions to review and revise the U. T. C. syllabus with a view to making it more attractive and suited to modern conditions. General Auchinleck said that he would not give a similar undertaking to provide equipment for the U. T. C. As was very well known, the Empire as a whole was making every effort to make up for a shortage of equipment and the first call on this equipment must lie with those who were being trained for service at the Front. This was unavoidable but necessary. Any modernisation of the system of training at the U. T. C. at the present moment would mean their providing additional instructors and equipment, both of which were required for more urgent work elsewhere. The Commander-in-Chief further said that he would not make any radical change in the system of recruitment or training of Officers during the war. The system they had to-day was the best one. He would do his best to make the syllabus for the U. T. C, training as comprehensive and attractive as was possible. He would also give his best consideration to the question of introducing the system of certificates for efficiency, which might shorten the period of training for obtaining a Commission for the members of the U. T. C. Lastly, he would also examine the possibility of a separate Interwiew Board for the U. T. C. as far as recruitment of the Officers' rank in the Army was concerned. With these assurances he hoped that the resolution would be withdrawn. The resolution accordingly was withdrawn and the Council adjourned.

Official Bills

11th. MARCH. :—The Council of State to-day passed four official Bills, which had been passed by the Legislative Assembly. Three of these Bills, namely, the Bill amending the Petroleum Act, the Bill extending certain Acts to Berar, and the Bill providing for the regulation of and the maintenance of discipline in the Assam Rifles were passed without any opposition.

Ticketless Travelling Bill

Several provisions of the fourth Bill, which made provision for the checking of ticketless travelling, were criticised by non-official speakers during the consideration stage. Moving that the Bill be taken into consideration, Mr. *L. Wilson*, Chief Commissioner for Railways, said that the number of people travelling without ticket had gradually risen. In 1939-40 ticketless traveller numbered nearly 3,085,000. The figures emphasised the magnitude of the problem which the Railways were facing. The Bill sought to achieve the same objects which the 1936-37 Bill attempted to achieve, but by provisions of more appropriate penalties. The Bill also sought to place remaining in a carriage without a ticekt on the same footing as entry into a carriage without a ticket and it reproduced a provision, containd in the previous Bill, for the ejectment of ticketless travellers.

Rai Bahadur Sri Narain Mahtha, opposing the motion, said that he was not supporting ticketless travelling. He merely opposed the methods by which Government proposed to deal with this problem. The provisions of the Bill were far more drastic than the exigencies of the present situation demanded. Far more necessary than punishment of the ticketless traveller was his detection. *Rai Bahadur Lala Ramsarandas* revealed that since the introduction of the scheme of travelling ticket collectors on certain Railways the number of people travelling without ticket had decreased. Therefore, he suggested that more travelling ticket collectors should be engaged and corridor trains built, in order to enable checking of ticket while the trains were in motion. Mr. *P. N. Sapru* did not oppose the object of the Bill, namely the stopping of persons from travelling without ticket. But, he said, before assuming more powers, the Railways must convince the House that the existing machinery for checking the evil had been perfected. They must uproot corruption in their own staff. Why should the Railways be given more powers to stop ticketless travelling than were enjoyed by owners of other forms of public transport? he asked. He, therefore, opposed the imprisonment clause. He did not mind a heavy fine being imposed. *Sir Mohd. Yakub* agreed that the existing law was insufficient to deal with the menace of ticketless travelling. He ridiculed the suggestion that a deterrent punishment would not help the checking of crime. If that were true, he argued, then it followed that the whole of the Indian Penal Code should be abolished and there ought to be no penal law. He did not think that any civilised society would approve of such a suggestion. Mr. *V. V. Kalikar* wanted that there should be some difference in the punishments for a person who merely entered a compartment without ticket and another who tried to travel on a used ticket. The latter was clearly a case of cheating, and did not deserve to receive the same punishment as the former. Mr. *Wilson*, Chief Commissioner of Railways, deprecated the destructive criticism offered by some members. He said that the Bill did not give powers to the Railways or the Railway servants to impose imprisonment instead of fine. The power still remained, as it always had been, with the Magistrates. If a Magistrate was satisfied that the crime did not deserve imprisonment he was sure that he would not impose imprisonment. Mr. Wilson agreed that the problem could not be solved by legislation alone. He was aware that it was the duty of the Railways to prevent ticketless travelling without resorting to law, but the House knew of the difficulties involved. Nevertheless, improvement in the existing machinery was necessary. The motion for consideration was passed. The remaining stage of the Bill evoked no discussion and the House passed the Bill in the form it had emerged from the Assembly and adjourned till the 17th. March.

Defence Expenses Apportionment

17th. MARCH :—The Council of State rejected to-day a resolution by the Hon. Mr. *Hossain Imam* recommending the formation of a committee of members of the Indian Legislature to scrutinize and suggest the apportionment of defence expenses between the Government of India and His Majesty's Government and to submit a report on the transactions since the war began. Mr. *Hossain Imam* quoted figures from the Finance Member's budget speech to show that in the war expenditure vast amounts were involved. There was, he said, an insistent demand among the people of India for greater association of Indians with the war effort. They did not object to the expenditure but before agreeing to it they wanted to be satisfied and it was being incurred in the interests of India. The appointment of a committee would dispel many misgivings.

The Hon. Mr. *P. N. Sapru* moved the next resolution recommending the Governor-General in Council to take such steps as might be necessary to enlarge the Appellate Jurisdiction or the Federal Court to the extent permitted by Section 206 of the Government of India Act. 1935. Mr. *Sapru* said that the principle of establishing a Supreme Court of Civil Appeals had been accepted in the Government of India Act. The Privy Council had done most useful work. It was a great tribute to its judges that without having visited India they were able in 99 cases out of 100 to arrive at satisfactory decisions. But Indians experienced hardships particularly in war-time in going to the Privy Council whose machine in many cases was found to be expensive. The Indian Judicial system had improved very considerably. India had sufficient talent for a Supreme Court of Appeal. Mr. *E. Conran Smith*, Home Secretary, explained that the matter had been engaging the attention of the Government of India and a reference had been made to the Secretary of State for India. The consultations were still in a preliminary stage and therefore it was not possible for him to divulge their nature. He assured the House that when concrete proposals emerged from the present preliminary consultations, the Government would consult public opinion including that of commercial interests. He pointed out that it was not possible for him to accept the resolution in its present form, and Government at this stage would not like to tie themselves down to any particular principle. Mr. *Sapru*, replying to the debate, maintained that the resolution had behind it the unanimous support of Indian commercial opinion. He disputed Sir *A. P. Patro's* view that the Federal Court had very little work to do and pointed out that the Court had pronounced some important decisions in favour of the provinces. He expressed his readiness to withdraw the resolution provided the Government agreed to forward the debate to the Secretary of State. On Mr. *Conran-Smith* accepting the suggestion, Mr. *Sapru* withdrew the resolution. The Council then adjourned till March 24.

POSTS RESERVED FOR I. C. S.

24th. MARCH :—A resolution recommending the appointment of a committee of officials and non-officials to examine the question of the strength of and the posts reserved for the I. C. S. moved to-day by Mr. *Hossain Imam* was withdrawn after the Government's point of view was explained by Mr. *Conran-Smith*, Home Secretary. Mr. *Hossain Imam*, moving the resolution, said that the leave reserve of the Indian Civil Service were out of all proportion to actual requirements. Too large a number of the superior posts in the Central and Provincial Governments were being given to the I. C. S. and therefore other services such as Posts and Telegraphs, Customs, Accounts and Audit Services did not get their legitimate share of these posts. The strength of the I. C. S. too was far beyond requirements. Mr. *Conran-Smith*, opposing the resolution, revealed that the strength of the service was fixed after taking fully into consideration the acturial calculations. It was as near as possible the approximation of the Government's requirements. The leave and the training reserves were necessary for maintaining the full service. He advised the mover to withdraw the resolution as it was not proper to suggest reduction in the I. C. S. at a time like this when the strain on the service was admittedly very high. Mr. *Conran-Smith* promised to consider the question of making available to the members the acturial calculations on which the strength of the service was based. The resolution was withdrawn.

INDUSTRIAL DEVELOPMENT

Pandit *H. N. Kunzru's* resolution recommending the planning of a comprehensive and co-ordinated industrial development of the country, was postponed to a later date on the suggestion of Sir *G. S. Bajpai* who said that the Commerce Member would not be able to take part in its discussion to-day, being busy somewhere else.

MASJIDS ADMINISTRATION BILL

The House referred to a joint committee of twelve members of the Council and Assembly Mr. *Hossain Imam's* Bill to make better provision for the administration of masjids and the endowment of the Jamma Masjid, Fatehpuri Masjid and Kalan Masjid of Delhi.

LIMITATION ACT AMEND. BILL

Mr. *Chidambaram Chettiyar's* Bill to amend the Indian Limitation Act IX of 1908 was referred to a select committee of the Council. The House then adjourned till March 27.

DEBATE ON THE FINANCE BILL

27th. MARCH :—The Council of State considered the Finance Bill to-day. Mr. *C. E. Jones*, Finance Secretary, moved that the Finance Bill be taken into consideration. He said that by this Bill it was intended to give legislative sanction to all the Budget proposals, except the one imposing a 10 per cent duty on pneumatic tyres and tubes, which being a new duty and in absence of a general excise duty required separate enactment. "As has been explained in the objects and reasons and the various clauses of the Bill," said Mr. *Jones*, "this Bill provides for continuance unchanged during the coming year of existing rates in respect of the salt duty, inland postage, income-tax and super-tax, but provides for the increase of existing rates of duties on matches, mechanical lighters, artificial silk yarn and thread, increases in the Central surcharges on income-tax, super-tax and rate of excess profits tax." These proposals, he said, had been explained in the Budget speech and at this stage required no elaboration.

Sir *David Devadoss* said that India must win the war otherwise her fate would be worse than that of Poland, Norway, Belgium or the Netherlands. No sacrifice was too great for achieving that end and, therefore, he heartily supported the proposals for additional taxation.

Mr. *M. N. Dalal* was of the opinion that the proposals for new taxation were not badly framed and that the burden was fairly disturbed. He trusted, however, that the surcharge on income-tax and the increase in the excess profits tax were no more than war measures. He wished that artificial silk yarn was not proposed to be taxed quite so highly without a corresponding import duty on artificial piecegoods. Doubling the excise duty on matches appeared to him to be rather harsh because that was likely to fall in a relatively greater measure on the poorer classes.

Pandit *H. N. Kunzru* explained at considerable length the Bombay resolution of the Non-Party Conference. He said that the Bombay resolution demanded complete Indianization of the Governor-General's Executive Council plus a declaration by his Majesty's Government that India would be accorded political equality with the United Kingdom and the other self-governing Dominions within the shortest period after the war. The resolution also demanded transfer of the Defence and Finance portfolios to Indians. He assured the House that the Bombay resolution could not be regarded as making excessive demands on the Government. It demanded a declaration about the future constitutional goal of India and demanded the complete Indianization of the Executive Council as an earnest of that declaration. The Bombay resolution, he said, had not been adversely commented on either by any responsible leader or by the Press. Government, however, had not given any indication of their reaction to the Bombay resolution. Their attitude had been that they had often described the non-party politicians as most representative of the Indian masses when the Government desired support for their war effort. But these very people were characterized as 'nobodies' when they demanded political and constitutional liberty for their fellow countrymen. Analysing the likely reactions to the adoption by Government of the Bombay resolutions, Pandit Kunzru said he did not believe that any major political party in the country would be so unwise as to forget its duty to the country by making the proposed constitutional changes unworkable or that it would go to the electorates with an uncompromising opposition to the Indianized Executive Council. On the other hand, he firmly believed that even the major political parties were waiting to see whether Government would make any gesture and give sincere proof of a genuine desire to secure the whole-hearted co-operation of the Indian people. He reminded the Council that, but for the war, the Indian Federation might have been working at present and it would have been Indians who would have been in charge of Defence and Finance. There would have been a completely Indianized Executive Council responsible to the Indian Legislature. The Bombay resolution had asked for much less. It had asked for an Indianized executive not responsible to the Legislature.

Mr. *W. N. P. Jenkin*, on behalf of the Government, replied to Pandit Kunzru's charge that the Government had not acted on the recommendations contained in the resolution accepted by the Government in November last regarding the Supply Department. He said that the Government were recruiting Indians at present for the posts that were being created from time to time. Recently, some eleven appointments were created and eight or nine of them were filled by Indians. *Pandit Kunzru* had criticized mainly the working of the Directorate stationed in Calcutta. Mr. Jenkin explained that the work done in that directorate, was a very difficult one and it was therefore necessary to employ officers who had practical workshop experience. He gave an assurance to the House that efforts had been made to train the Indian personnel.

28th. MARCH :—Resuming the debate in the Finance Bill to-day, Mr. *V. V. Kalikar* thanked the Government for not having imposed more taxation. His complaint was that Indians had not been associated with the spending of the money for war purposes. He said that it was not the Congress or the Moslem League alone but the British Government that was responsible for the political deadlock. If it were really the desire of the Government to end the deadlock then it should have come forward with an offer to those who were willing to co-operate.

Rai Bahadur *Lala Ramsarandas* began by expressing pride and satisfaction at the successes of the Indian troops at Keren and Harar. He suggested that the incomes derived from compulsory war insurance should be utilised for the benefit of industries and something should be done to find employment for the educated unemployed.

Sir S. Hissamuddin said that the defence measures mentioned by the Finance Member called for their wholehearted support. He expressed satisfaction that His Majesty's Government had recently agreed to a standing arrangement under which India would receive a substantial fixed proportion of the output of equipment available from the United States.

His Excellency *Sir Claude Auchinleck*, the Commander-in-Chief, intervening in the debate, replied to various criticisms levelled against the Defence Department. Before doing so, however, he expressed his appreciation of the congratulations of the House to him and said that he had received a cable from General Wavell this morning extolling the bravery of Indian troops in the capture of Keren. He had every desire to keep in touch with public opinion and he stood by every word of what he had said in regard to associating the Legislature with the Defence Department. He assured that he and the Defence Secretary were working towards one and the same end ; and means of implementing his undertaking were being worked out at present. He expected to make an announcement shortly on that subject. He categorically denied the allegation of differentiation between Britons and Indians, particularly in the matter of recruitment, and said that no differentiation existed as he remained the Commander-in-Chief in India. Efficiency and suitability were the only two criteria for recruitment to the army. As for post-war reconstruction of the Indian Army, he asserted that neither he nor any one else could foresee what the Indian Army would be after the war. Personally speaking, he thought it unlikely that Indian commissioned officers would only be trusted with the platoon commander's job, thought there was nothing derogatory in being a platoon commander. It was just the same system in the British Army. In India the difference arose, because the Viceroy's commissioned officers used to hold the post of platoon commander. He next dealt with the question of supply of officers for the Indian Army and said that means were being worked out not only for obtaining the eight type officers but also of giving them proper training. He, expected to make an announcement on this subject in the near future. He however, reiterated that there were no two sets of efficiency, one for British and the other for Indian officers. Similarly the system of recruitment was identical for the British and the Indian.

The Commander-in-Chief admitted that there were few Indians in the ordnance factories and Indian Army Corps, but ordnance factories were prepared to recruit 100 per cent Indians, provided Indians of the right qualifications were available. His regret was that Indians of proper qualifications were not forthcoming, and during the War they were not prepared to expose themselves to risks by taking in persons without proper qualifications. He assured that there was no bar against Indians provided they had the necessary qualifications. As for the U. T. C. the matter was receiving his most earnest attention and ways and means to make the U. T. C. more useful for providing officers for the army were being worked. Here too he expected to make an announcement in the near future. Speaking on broadening the bases of recruitment to the army, he assured that the question was under close examination. Here the House should not expect spectacular results at once. He assured that any subject pertaining to the Department, if raised in the House, was bound to receive his attention.

Both Sir *Mohammed Yakub* and Mr. *Mohammed Hussain* expressed themselves against the removal of the "martial" and "non-martial" distinction from the army. Sir *Mohammed Yakub* also asserted that there was no political deadlock in the country. After the resignation of the Congress Ministries the administration in the Congress Provinces had gained in efficiency. Mr. *Mohammed Hussain* warned the Communications Member that unless the grievances of the Moslems were satisfactorily settled they would have to take effective steps to secure their demands. He also warned the British Government against their policy of appeasement of the Congress.

Mr. *P. N. Sapru* denounced Hitlerism and Fascism and emphasized India's determination to help Britain in the creation of a new world order, in which all countries, big or small, could live a free and peaceful life. Therefore, he did not wonder at the heavy expenditure on defence. But the people who were being asked to make a heavy sacrifice, and to identify themselves wholeheartedly with the cause for which Britain was fighting had the right to expect that they should have a controlling voice in the war policy.

Mr. *Hossain Imam* complained that a part of the excess profits tax was allowed to the provinces. It was a war tax and should be utilized solely for war purposes by the Centre. He also urged equalization of the burden of defence beween British India and Indian States.

Sir Girija Shankar Bajpai in a brief speech replied to some of the criticisms made. The leader of the opposition, he said, had complained that an agent for India had not been appointed in the West Indies. As explained that before, the Government were in favour of appointment of such agents and agent in the West Indies and it was suggested by the Royal Commission which sat in connexion with the future Government of the West Indies. The war intervened and the Government felt that no action would be taken on the report during the war. Recently, however, His Majesty's Government had been evolving certain decisions with regard to the future of the West Indies. In the circumstances the Government of India could legitimately ask His Majesty's Government to take up again the question of the appointment of an agent there.

The House divided on the motion for consideration, which was adopted by 27 votes to 11. The Bill was passed without division and the House adjourned,

Protection to Iron Bill

29th. MARCH :—The Council of State met this morning to dispose of four official Bills recently passed by the Central Legislative Assembly. These were:

(a) The Bill to extend protective duties by another year to iron and steel manufactures, silver thread and wire, and sugar ;

(b) The Bill continuing the protective duties on wheat and wheat flour.

(c) The Bill providing for imposition and collection of an excise duty on tyres ,

(d) And the Bill to further amend the Excess Profits Tax Act.

When *Sir Alan Lloyd* moved that the Bill to extend protective duties by another year to iron and steel manufactures, silver thread and wire, and sugar be taken into consideration, Mr. *Hossain Imam* protested that the duty on sugar was too high and therefore, was against the interests of the cultivator. *Sir Alan* gave the assurance that Government proposed during this financial year to proceed with their inquiries into the possibility of coming to some definite conclusions as to what was in the present conditions the proper rate of import duty. The motion for consideration was adopted and the Bill, as passed by the Assembly, was passed.

Protection to Wheat Bill

The second Bill, namely, the one continuing the protective duties on wheat and wheat flour, was passed without any opposition.

Tyres and Tubes Duty Bill

The motive for consideration of the third Bill, which imposed excise duty on tyres and tubes was opposed by Mr. *Hossain Imam* and Mr. *P. N. Sapru* on the ground that it was a finance measure and, therefore, did not deserve other treatment from their parties than that accorded to the Finance Bill. The Finance Secretary maintained that the duty imposed on tyres and tubes was a revenue duty and no question of protection arose, it was being imposed in the interests of public revenue. The motion for consideration was put to the vote and carried by 24 votes to eight. The third reading was passed without a division.

Excess Profits Tax Act

The Bill further to amend the Excess Profits Tax Act was also passed, Mr. *Kunzru* opposing it at the consideration stage on the ground that the Government had not accorded recognition to the constitutional rights of Indians. The House then adjourned to April 2.

India's Industrial Expansion

2nd. APRIL :—The Council of State to-day, without a division, adopted an official amendment to the Hon. Pandit *Hridaynath Kunzru's* resolution regarding industrialization of the country. The amendment which was moved by the Commerce Secretary, *Sir Alan Lloyd* read: "The Council recommends to the Governor-General-in-Council that he should review the industrial development of the country, and taking into account the post-war conditions as far as possible bear in mind the desirability of filling up the lacunae in the existing industrial system and of bringing about the co-ordinated industrial progress of the country".

Pandit *Hridaynath Kunzru's* resolution recommended a review of the industrial development of the country and the formulation of a plan, taking into account post-war conditions as far as practicable to fill up the lacunæ in the existing industrial system and to bring abont a comprehensive and co-ordinated industrial development of the country. The Pandit stated that the industrial development of India had so far been lopsided and the country still depended upon outside assistance for many of its essential needs. The last Great War and the present one had amply demonstrated that the industrialization of India was not only necessary for its self-sufficiency and higher standard of living, but also for its national security. Pandit *Kunzru* made particular reference to shipbuilding and automobile industries in this country, and said that shipbuilding had been undertaken on behalf of His Majesty's Government both in Australia and Canada. In India, on the other hand, the Government declined to recognize shipbuilding as a war industry and had, on that account, declined to give any assistance to it. Meanwhile, ships on the Indian Register had been requisitoned, resulting in shortage of tonnage for coastal trade.

The Hon. Sir *Ramaswami Mudaliar*, Commerce Member, replying, reiterated his statement in the Assembly that the Government were seriously considering the question of post-war adjustment and that an inter-departmental committee might shortly be constituted which would from now on consider what plans could be evolved for re-adjustment of industries which expanded owing to war requirements and for the re-employment of technical labour now employed in these expanded and expanding industries. Referring to the Supply Council, the Commerce Member said there was no justification for the apprehensions that the Council would not allow the start of industries in this country but that it would allow other countries to steal a march over us. It was true, however, that if we were not in a position to supply a particular article we would not wait till that supply is found in this country but would get it from where it was available. In this connexion he explained a statement made by the Commerce Secretary in the Council in answer to a question. The Commerce Secretary had stated that Government had no intention of encouraging ship-building industry as a part of the war effort. The emphasis, said the Commerce Member, was on the words "as a part of the war effort," for ships built in India would not be ready for three or four years and war needs obviously could not wait for anything like that length of time. But the Government of India had done everything possible to encourage ship-building programme not merely by leasing sites but by using their good offices with His Majesty's Government for the supply of materials. He hoped that when the proposed inquiry into gaps in the industries in India was complete, it would be possible to give to industrialists an idea of what new ventures to start. He asked the mover to withdraw the resolution.

The Hon. Mr. *P. N. Sapru* urged that there should be a member of the Executive Council in charge of post-war problems, to be known as the Minister of Reconstruction, and that an Economic Advisory Council should be set up to advise him. Emphasising the need for planning ahead, he said that by planning he meant planning for an India which would have a balanced economy, and which would be able to utilize her raw materials and resources to better economic advantage.

The Hon. Rai Bahadur *Lala Ramsarandas* gave concrete instances in which he said Government have failed to give encouragement to the growth and development of Indian industries.

Pandit Kunzru said that the speech of the Commerce Member had shown that the Government and the non-officials held identical views on the resolution and yet he was surprised to see the opposition of the Government to the resolution. Pandit Kunzru dealt at length with the speech of Mr. Richardson and said they had never asked for economic isolation of India, All they had asked was for a balanced economy.

Replying Sir *Alan Lloyd* said that the wording of the resolution went much further than the Government of India could commit itself. He reminded the House that industries was a provincial subject but the wording of the resolution would have the effect of the Government of India usurping the functions and powers of the Provincial Governments. Sir Alan suggested an amendment to the resolution.

The amendment was ascepted by Pandit *Kunzru* and as stated above was adopted by the House which at this stage adjourned till the 4th.

DELHI RIBBON DEVELOPMENT BILL

4th. APRIL :—The Council passed to-day the Delhi Ribbon Development Bill and the Insurance Act Amendment Bill as passed by the Assembly. During discussion on the Bill, Sir *Girija Sankar Bajpai* referred to an amendment, tabled by Rai Bahabur *Sri Narain Mahtha* designed to restrict the definition of "interested persons" in connexion with certain Land, and said that the provision as it stood had been objected to in the Assembly as being so wide as to permit a Moslem from Bockhara or Samarkand to interfere with the exercise of control under the Bill. Actually, however he doubted if the so called "wide definition" was likely to cause any practical difficulties in the administration of the Bill. It was Government's intention to watch the working of the Act in this as in other respects and should the Act disclose any inconvenience of the kind apprehended, then undoubtedly the Government would consider the matter. The Bill was passed.

INSURANCE ACT AMEND. BILL

During the discussion of the Insurance Act Amendment Bill, moved by Sir *Alan Lloyd*, Commerce Secretary, Pandit *H. N. Kunzru* raised a number of points regarding the interpretation of the provision that 55 per cent of policy liabilities of an insurance company should under Section 27 be invested in Government and other approved securities. The question in which the insurance companies and the general public were interested, he said, was whether the deposits to be made by every insurance company and the amount granted as loans to insured persons on the security of life policies were to be excluded from the 55 per cent referred to above. The Commerce Member in the Assembly had referred to differences in interpreting the section and had offered to meet the expenses of a test case in a court of law on the matter.

He was not concerned with the mere interpretation of the Act. It was a question of policy, and that could only be decided by the Government and not by a court of law. He also drew attention to the illogical effect produced by the explanation to Section 27 as a result of which while a company incorporated or domiciled in an Indian State would be exempted from any of the provisons of the Act, a company one-third of the members of whose governing body were, or one third of whose share capital was held by people living in an Indian State, would be subject to the disability that it had to invest all its assets in Government and other approved securities. Referring to the amendment made in the Assembly to Section 45, *Pandit Kunzru* said it conferred a power on insurance companies which might easily be abused. Dealing with the new Section 3 A, which increased the charges for renewal of registration, he declared that if it was intended that the increase in expenditure involved in the administration of the Act should be met by a call for further contributions from insurance companies. It was seriously objectionable.

Mr. *Hossain Imam* criticized the appointment of a non-Indian as the Superintendent of Insurance. Referring to the provision for increase of charges for the renewal of registration, he said that it was a form of taxation. It was the primary duty of the government, he said, to safeguard the interests of policy-holders. Mr. *Imam* strongly supported the plea made by Pandit *Kunzru* in regard to insurance companies in Indian States.

Sir *Ramaswami Mudaliar*, Commerce Member, replying first to the point raised by Pandit *Kunzru* about Section 27 explained the circumstances in which it was incorporated in the Bill "more or less as an agreed provision," after a thorough discussion both in the Legislature and outside in 1933. The policy embodied in that section dealt with the interests of insurance companies and those of policy-holders alike and he personally felt somewhat timorous of touching a section which if not sacrosanct, had received the blessings of both the Houses only two years ago. If they were certain that Government's interpretation of the Section was wrong and if they went to a court of law and had their own interpretation vindicated, he gave the assurance that Government would not have that section amended so as to restore the original interpretation. Explaining why he gave that assurance the Commerce Member said one reason why parties were unwilling to go to a court of law was that the moment they took all the trouble of having their interpretation vindicated, Government came along the next day with an amending Bill to restore the original interpretation. thereby nullifying even the decision of the Privy Council. Having this in mind, he gave the assurance referred to above.

As regards the point about the disadvantageous position of companies incorporated in British India with one-third of the shareholders in an Indian State, the Commerce Member confessed that it had not been brought to his notice by any company or insurance interest. That was an anomaly which had not been provided for but when the next amending Bill was before the House—he hoped it would not be in his time—he was certain this question would be given consideration. As regards Section 48, it was brought to his notice that in some policies it was provided that the assured must prove his age and if so there was no reason why the section should prevent such proof of age being given. It was not fair to other policy-holders who gave their age correctly that a fellow policy-holder should get the benefit of a policy although he did not give the correct age.

Referring to Mr. Imam's suggestion that the Superintendent of Insurance should be an Indian actuary, the Commerce Member said there was no want of Indian actuaries; but it might not have been possible for Government to get one on the terms and conditions on which they were prepared to get him, and when the criticism of the House was about bloated salaries that sort of difficulty would always continue to exist. Members would have to revise their ideas, he said, particularly now that this country was becoming more and more industrialized and the best brains were being diverted to industry; in any case they could not subscribe

England. *Lala Ramsarandas* pointed out that that could be imported from America. "Where there is a will there is a way," he added. Proceeding, the speaker said that the Government should have set up workshops for manufacturing other railway materials and spare parts. His information was that even rails were not being made in India, and Government was hoping to order them from England at the end of the war. Lala Ramsarandas criticised the policy of recruitment to the services. He deplored the acceptance by the Government of a policy of recruitment on communal basis. He said that the railways being commercial concerns, Government should have relied solely on merit. He objected to the grant of more representation to Anglo-Indians in the services at the expense of Hindus. Concluding, the speaker advocated an increase in the emoluments of the low-paid staff and the grant of special facilities to pilgrims going to Kumbha Melas and reiterated his demand for giving more amenities to passengers.

Mr. *Shantidas Askurn* said that the large surplus was independent of railway efficiency. He hoped that despite the surplus the need for constant watch to ensure right economy in all Railway Departments would be borne in mind by those at the top of the administration, more than ever at the present juncture. "We have been told of the possibility", said he, "of bringing suburban season ticket fares up to the level of the enhanced passenger fares of last year. I should leave this traffic untouched ; in fact, I am in favour of further concessions being made". Sir *M. Yakub* said that no Indian would object to any measure which helped the prosecution of the war. They were even prepared to suffer personal inconvenience and discomforts. But in the matter of dismantling certain lines which were likely to result in grave wrong being done to the affected people, they must take objection. It was particularly so in the case of Chandpur-Bajnaur line. By removing that line, Government had done a great disservice to the sugar industry. He hoped that the Railway Department would take greater care in future in dismantling such lines.

Kumar N. N. Sinha said that he would have been pleased if an attempt had been made in the budget to decrease even to a limited extent, the rates of fares and freights, especially the fares of third class passengers. The grievances of the third class passengers were many and longstanding. Government were eager to pass the Ticketless Travellers Bill, but were not solicitous for granting additional facilities which would enable third class passengers to purchase their tickets in time. Mr. *Kalikar* congratulated the Railway Member, Sir *Andrew Clow,* on his stand against the demand of the Muslim League for promotions on communal basis. Criticising the attitude of the Muslim League Party, Mr. Kalikar said that Mr. Hossain Imam sought to mislead the House in the morning by alleging that their fight was against preferential treatment to Europeans and Anglo-Indians. If that were so, the best thing the Muslim League would have done was to join hands with them. The speaker, however, blamed the Government for its policy of recruitment on communal basis, and urged that they should reverse that policy forthwith. Sir *David Devadoss* advised the Government to spend the railway surpluses carefully. He protested against the preferential treatment given to Anglo-Indians in the matter of recruitment. "If a Ramaswami becomes Ramson and Subramanyan becomes Sanderson, he has an easy walk over the qualified members of other communities". Sir David particularly protested against the preferential treatment accorded to the Goanese, who were foreigners and yet were recruited in preference to Indians on the M. S. M. Railway. *Pandit Hriday Nath Kunzru* congratulated the Railway Member and the Chief Commissioner for Railways on acquiring two of the company lines, and suggested that they should also give notice during the current year to the Bengal and North-Western Railway for the termination of their contract. The B. N. W. Railway Company should also be made to hand over to the Government the management of Tirhut and Kumayun Railways. The contracts for these latter lines, he thought, would come to an end in 1942. There was no reason why the Government of India should hand over these lines again to the company. Mr. *P. N. Sapru* said that the construction of the lines which had been dismantled was sanctioned by the Central Legislature. Therefore, it was the duty of the Government to have taken the approval of both Houses before dismantling the lines. By the removal of these lines, the Government had caused great inconvenience and loss to the poor agriculturist and thereby committed an act of vandalism. Mr. Sapru was glad that the Railway Authority had not yet come into existence. If it had been in existence there would have been no public criticism of railway administration and therefore no Indianisation and improvement of travelling conditions. Since railways played a great part in the national economy, it was essential that they should be State-managed.

Sir *Andrew Clow* replying to the debate assured the House that the Government were not contemplating any increase in the rates of food grains at present. He said that he merely repeated this year a warning which he had given last year. If prices did go up, which meant that the agriculturist was getting higher prices for his produce, it was not unreasonable if railways asked him to pay a higher freight. With regard to the dismantling of railways he said that the first reason for dismantling was that Government wanted the railways. That being so, Government naturally looked to those lines which were not remunerative or could be spared. Sir Andrew then dealt with the question of construction of locomotives in India. He did not agree that the scheme had been practically abandoned. The postponement was mainly due to difficulties of getting technical staff, material and workshops. Referring to the question of promotion of Muslims in railway services, he said that he had worked in a large number of offices and he and those officers who had worked with him were, he knew, most solicitous about carrying out the policy laid down by the Government. They were fully aware that small minorities of men working largely under officers of other castes and creeds might at times feel difficulties and might at times be subjected to handicaps and Government were always ready to make allowances for that. He was not prepared to say that there were no officers in subordinate grades who never yielded to communal bias. No one, he said, was perfect. But so far as he had looked into personal cases, he could testify to the fairness of mind which all officers brought to the rather invidious task of selecting candidates for promotion. Mr. De Souza had recommended certain measures which, in his view, would make the working of the promotions more satisfactory. The Railway Board and he (the speaker) were ready to consider any system which would afford those in service a greater measure of justice and also convince the men concerned that they were getting justice. So far from having any bias against the Muslim community, he declared, he had taken great care to see that the officers of that community got full justice. He was anxious to see that promotions were not based on communal considerations. He was equally anxious to see that no man of any community was biassed or prejudiced. because he happened to belong to that community. The House at this stage adjourned.

Reduction of Insurance Payment Bill

26th. FEBRUARY :—The Council of State held a brief sitting of 40 minutes to-day and passed two Bills, recently passed by the Legislative Assembly. The first was a Bill to provide for a temporary reduction in amounts payable as instalments of the sum to be deposited by an insurer under section seven of the Insurance Act, 1938.

Fraudulent Mark on Merchandize Bill

The second Bill further amended the law relating to fraudulent marks on merchandize. Two amendments of a formal nature were moved by Mr. *S. Lal* on behalf of the Government to which the House agreed. The second amendment substituted sub-section 12 of clause seven. The Council then adjourned.

Segregation of Lepers

27th. FEBRUARY :—A resolution was moved in the Council of State to-day by *Moulvi Ali Asgar Khan* recommending to the Government to take adequate steps forthwith to prevent lepers and persons suffering from dangerous diseases, such as tuberculosis, from travelling in railways, steamers and also haunting public places like hotels and resturants, so that the progress of these diseases might be checked. *Sir Girija Sankar Bajpai* said that the resolution had the sympathy of everyone in the House, but the question was how to make that sympathy effective. The mere existence of rules and regulations could not achieve the object. What was necessary was to find how there should be co-operation between the various parties. He suggested that the subject-matter of the resolution be placed before the Central Advisory Board of Public Health on which the Public Health authorities as well as the Railways were represented. There, the question of making the existing rules and regulations more effective could be considered. The mover thereupon withdrew the resolution.

Suspension of Br. Recruitment to I. C. S.

"This Council recommends to the Governor-General-in-Council to advise the Secretary of State for India to suspend British recruitment to the Indian

Civil Service during the period of the war. This resolution was next moved by Mr. *P. N. Sapru*, who said that he was not moving the resolution in a spirit of hostility to the British members of the I. C. S., whose ability, integrity, character and devotion to duty nobody could challenge. Proceeding, he said, that if Mr. *Amery* was to be believed about the grant of Dominion Status to India at the end of the war, it was necessary that the position should now be reviewed in the light of that goal. If the Government continued to recruit non-Indians into the Service it would be mortgaging the future of India. The recruiting and controlling authority hereafter must be the Government of India. Mr. *Hossain Imam* moved an amendment deleting the word "British" from the resolution. He complained that no cogent reasons had been given by the speaker for changing the present system, nor had he heard anything as to what protection was to be given to minority interests under the resolution. He did not know what would happen to the Moslem community if the administration was entrusted to Indians. Mr. Imam could not accept Indianization of the Service without a definite guarantee for the security of the minorities. To-day everything was being done under the direction of the "saint of Sabarmati" and that was why Moslems were wanting to have *pakistan*. He did not deny that Indians including Moslems were very able officers but there was a big question of policy involved which could not be settled in a haphazard manner. Mr. *E. Conran-Smith*, Home Secretary, said that he did not wish to comment on the communal aspect of the question. Therefore he had just one remark to make regarding Mr. Hossain Imam's amendment. Mr. Hossain Imam wanted to make the position with which the future authorities in this country after the war would be confronted as difficult as possible by giving them a thoroughly depleted Indian Civil Service. The mover of the resolution wanted that the recruitment of Europeans should be stopped during the war. From the point of view of practical administration, he said, the war should not provide any argument for tinkering with the Service. There was imperative need for keeping the Services, specially security services, intact. If the vacancies that would have been given to Europeans were filled by Indians then the effect would be that they could not maintain the existing proportion. The authorities who would be considering the future Constitution of India would naturally reach a decision whether Europeans in the Services were required. The mover asked the Government to impose a decision on those authorities, and prejudge the issues which they had to consider. As regards recruitment to the Service of those who were now holding Emergency Commissions, the speaker said that the Government were fully conscious of the problem and were in communication with the Secretary of State on this subject. An acceptable solution would be to leave a percentage of vacancies occurring during the war for candidates with war service to be filled after the war. Mr. *Conran-Smith* said that he was prepared to communicate the texts of the motions and the substance of the debate to the Secretary of State. Mr. *Sapru*, after replying to the debate, said that he was fully satisfied with the assurance given by the Home Secretary that he would forward the substance of the debate to the Secretary of State and asked leave of the House to withdraw the resolution. The leave was granted. The House then adjourned till the next day, the 28th. **February** when the Budget statement was made by *C. E. Jones*, the Finance Secretary.

General Discussion of the Budget

5th. MARCH :—The Council of State held a general discussion on the Budget to-day. Mr. *Shantidas Askuran* who was the first speaker demanded that the Commander-in-Chief should appoint a special committee of the Central Legislature to scrutinize all defence expenditure; that the Army Indianization Committee should resume its work and that a War Advisory Council representing both British India and the Indian States should be created. Sir. *A. P. Patro* expressed satisfaction that the gap between revenues from taxation and the uncovered deficit was being covered by means of loans. That meant, he said, that the future also would share in the burdens of the present. This was really a welcome feature of the Budget. "I am glad also to say, that the increased rate of Excess Profits Tax and supertax and other indirect taxes are such that they do not affect the masses and the lower middle class", he added. Mr. *J. H. S. Richardson* (European Group) expressed his general approval with the Budget subject to the remark that since the same sources of revenue were being further taxed it was obvious that the time was approaching when serious consideration would have to be given to raising further sums, which would undoubtedly be necessary by other means, and especially by broadening the basis. He said that he had nothing to say against the increase in the Excess

Profits Tax since he had accepted the main principles of the Bill when it was passed. The *Maharaja of Darbhanga* complained that the Government had failed to produce a war atmosphere in this country. He continued :—"It is true that taxation is mounting up and donations to War Funds are coming in : but there is a lack of that feeling of making the cause one's own which is so very essential for the success of a struggle such as this. The non-officials who finance the war do not count at all. They have no position or status. As a result of this attitude people in general do not realize that it is their own battle that they are fighting. There is a feeling of distrust, and I am afraid, it is growing. *Rai Bahadur Lala Ramsarandas* asked the Finance Member not to impose further taxation as India was a poor country. High taxation, he said, would prove detrimental to the growth of industry, because after the war industry would not be left with any reserve to stand on its own legs. Mr. *Hossain Imam* welcomed the repatriation of sterling debt to India and the Government's decision to purchase Calcutta, Bombay and Madras telephone systems, and said that the Government had reduced its sterling liability and also the silver contents in the rupee. It was time for them to transfer the Silver Redemption Fund from London to India and maintain it in rupee securities. Similarly he wanted the Government to amend the Reserve Bank of India Act in order to statutorily raise the rates of rupee securities from 25 per cent to 33 per cent. *Pandit H. N. Kunzru* also welcomed the repatriation of the sterling debt to India and said that the additional deficits and additional taxation were the results of a policy in the framing of which Indians had no voice. He inquired about the arrangements made in regard to the defence expenditure between India and the United Kingdom and said, "We want to know, and we are entitled to know, how much money His Majesty's Government were paying to India towards the cost of defence expenditure". *Sir C. Auchinleck*, Commander-in-Chief, said that there were one or two things about which misapprehension existed in the minds of members. The first was in regard to the Viceroy's Commissioned Officers. Their interests, His Excellency said, were close to his heart and he would always watch them. It would be his duty to see that they did not suffer in any way. It was not true that they were not being used in units officered by Indians. The second was the question of utilizing the University Training Crops in regard to recruitment to the army. This was also receiving his careful consideration. There was one main point about which there was universal and insistent demand and that was the demand for closer co-operation between the Legislature and the Defence Department, specially in respect of giving advice to the Defence Department and receiving information from them. Sir Claude said that this had his full sympathy, but added that it was not an easy matter to arrange. He hoped that before long it might be possible to arrive at a suitable compromise which would be useful both to the House and to the Government. In conclusion His Excellency said that he proposed to give this matter his immediate and personal consideration. (Loud Cheers). Sir *Jeremy Raisman*, Finance Member, replying said that Mr. *Hossain Imam* had objected to the expenditure of Rs. 60 lakhs for building a new mint in Calcutta. He said that the position was that the Government was almost in a desperate situation. They were working night and day on new plants. It was vital that they should take steps now to change over from the existing Calcutta mint to another. They could not stop minting suddenly and must lay down plans so that they could pass over from one place of production to another. It was bound to be a very difficult transaction to carry out. Their object was to meet all demands in time. He mentioned other factors and concluded by saying that the Government had no option but to embark on the project. The Finance Member said that having been the recipient in this House and in another place of many complimentary remarks he was in a mood to hand some to others. He complimented Pandit Kunzru "on the interesting way in which he dealt with the main essential points which emerged from the Budget, points which appear to me to be most suitable for a general debate of this kind." Pandit Kunzru had wanted precise information regarding the debiting of His Majesty's Government's expenditure in this country. The Finance Member explained the whole progress of debiting the expenditure and said that the expenditure was not exhibited in sufficient detail in England and it would, therefore, be unfair if the details were made public here. Pandit Kunzru had raised the question of charging commission on purchases made in India by the Supplies Department for His Majesty's Government. His Majesty's Government was purchasing for the Indian Government considerable quantities of material which it would not be possible to obtain from the open market, particularly at a time when industries that produced those articles were under the control of the Ministry of Supply. The Government of India were getting those supplies at exactly the same price which His Majesty's Government paid for them, although in many cases the organizations which made these purchases were much more elaborate and expensive than the one which purchased material for His Majesty's Government in India. His Majesty's Government did not recover from the Indian Government the cost of their organization. Mr. *P. N. Sapru* appreciated the attitude of the Commander-in-Chief. He hoped that a Defence Council of the Legislature would soon materialize which would result in greater co-operation in the future. The House then adjourned.

Recruitment to the Army

6th. MARCH :—The *Commander-in-Chief's* amendment to *Pandit Kunzru's* resolution, regarding recruitment to the Army was passed unanimously by the Council of State to-day. Pandit Kunzru's resolution recommended that "the additional forces required to expand the Army which have hitherto been recruited from a few classes and areas only, be in future raised from all classes and provinces in adequate numbers." Opening the debate on his resolution, Pandit Kunzru traced the history of the Indian Army to the time when the Committee known as the Simla Organization Committee recommended that the mixed system should be given up in the Bengal Army and that recruitment should be made on the basis of class system. This recommendation was not fully carried out for some time : but it was developed and vigorously advocated by Lord Roberts. Subsequently, it continued to be the policy of the Government, and was completed during the time of Lord Kitchener. The result of resorting to the class system of recruitment was that recruitment was confined more and more to certain areas. Thus fewer and fewer people of this country got the opportunity of serving their country in a military capacity. Pandit Kunzru continued that in reply to a question in the Council in November last he was told that out of 94,000 persons recruited nearly 60 per cent were from the Punjab and only a little over 12 or 13 per cent from the United Provinces. That showed that the recruitment being at present carried on in connexion with expansion of the forces was on the same basis on which the main army was recruited. "If India is to be a Dominion", he added, "the British Government should evolve such policy as would enable all the provinces to take part in the defence of India. We are becoming responsible for maintaining the integrity of our country. Is it not necessary that the area of recruitment should be widened and an increasing number of men should become acquainted with the idea of rendering service to the country, and that our potential enemies should know that if they follow a policy of aggression, India will be able to put forward sufficient men to enable them to realize that aggression should not take place."

Sir *C. Auchinleck*, Commander-in-Chief, moved the following amendment :—This Council, while recognizing that, to begin with, the Army could be most speedily expanded only on the existing basis of recruitment, recommends to the Governor-General-in-Council that the Army authorities should now review sources of man-power throughout the country and should exclude no class or area, from consideration for recruitment in the formation of new units." After reviewing briefly the existing situation, Sir Claude said : "As you know for the last 30 years or so there have been no wars worth the name, civil or otherwise, within the frontiers of India proper. Before this time there were three distinct armies of Madras, Bombay and Bengal. The cessation of armed strife in the country itself and the removal of war and the threat of war to the north-western approaches of India resulted to some extent in the rusting, as it might be called, of the two southern armies and particularly perhaps of the Madras Army." Proceeding, His Excellency said that the large-scale conversion of Madrassi into Punjabi regiment was carried out by Lord Kitchener, and he had considerable justification for his action. The soldiers of northern India made the fullest use of the opportunities thus offered to them. Their record of gallantry and devotion to duty is second to none. India owes a great debt to them. In spite, however, of the greater opportunities for service and training afforded to the men of the north, the war of 1914-18 showed very clearly that many of the older, but by that time less well known, classes had by no means lost their spirit. In the war of 1914-18 expansion, generally speaking, followed the line of the existing class composition of the Army. After the war the Army was drastically reduced, becoming much smaller than it had been in 1941, or inded for a very long time. In these circumstances one can hardly blame them for clinging to those races and classes which had proved themselves as soldiers for a long period of years, instead of launching out into experiments with less well-tried material.

"Speaking generally, the class composition of the Indian Army at the beginning of this war did not differ very much from what it was in 1941. It soon became obvious that in India, as in other parts of the Commonwealth a speedy and vast expansion of the armed forces would be necessary. Here I would like the House to consider for a moment how technical and complicated is the process of expanding or raising an army. To form new units one must have a leaven of trained Officers and Non-Commissioned Officers. One cannot just collect a thousand men and say let there be a battation. The idea that all that is required in the forming of new units is to collect the requisite number of men, clothe them, arm them and train them to stand in line, or march is quite erroneous. A modern unit, say a battalion of infantry, is a complicated and intricate fighting machine which takes months to put together in running order. Generally speaking the Indian Army is organized on a class basis : that is to say we have units, which may be battalions, companies, squadrons or platoons, each composed of one class. This system is of long standing and owes its existence to the difficulties which are involved in the administration of a unit comprising men of all classes and creeds and of widely different habits. I do not say for one moment that this system is immutable. It has been and is being modified in certain directions already. The Indian Military Academy at Dehra Dun is an outstanding example, and I believe that considerable progress in the abolition of class exclusiveness among the rank and file has been made in the Royal Indian Navy and the Indian Air Force. "These services, however important as they are, are relatively small forces compared with the Indian Army, which, more-over, has its own very strong and ancient traditions. To attempt to change these traditions and to introduce radical alterations in the system of army organization in the middle of a war, would, I think, be a most hazardous experiment. In theory a common system of enlistment irrespective of caste and creed has undoubtedly much to recommend. For the moment, however, we must build on what we know to be a firm foundation. "It is for these reasons that the first expansion of the Army followed traditional lines and consisted largely, but by no means altogether, in the duplication of existing units of the regular army, and the enlisting of many additional men from the classes already enlisted in the army. But progress has been made in the enlistment of other classes. Last week, during a tour of Bihar and Bengal, I was privileged to see at work the first regular Bengal unit—a battery of heavy artillery charged with the task of defending a most important post of our coast line. I also saw a territorial force battalion of Hyderabad Regiment, which is enlisted solely from the province of Bihar. I also saw a Madras Territorial Battalion which, though it has been in existence for barely six months, showed every sign of becoming a most useful acquisition to the army. I may perhaps mention that since the war began the strength of the Madrasis in the Army has risen from something like 4,000 to well over 10,000 and is being still further increased at a rapid rate. The same process is proceeding in respect of other classes, but it is a slow process, because there are no established units from which the nucleus of Viceroy's Commissioned Officers and Non-Commissioned Officers can be drawn. These must, therefore, be drawn from other classes and retained with the newly-raised units until these can find their own junior leaders. With our present system of class composition I think it is essential that men of each class should have its own leaders with whose speech and temperament they are familiar, rather than that they should have over them men, who though Indian, may perhaps be alien to them in speech, creed and habits." The Commander-in-Chief announced that he had already issued instructions that the old Madras Regiment, which finally disappeared in 1926, is to be revived and restored to its rightful place in the Army List. The first battalion of this regiment, which will be a regular battalion, is to be raised forthwith and will carry on its Colours the battle honours of the old Madras Army some of which go back to nearly 200 years. I hope before long to be able to ensure the permanent representation of other provinces hitherto not mentioned in the Army List in the same way.

Pandit Hriday Nath Kunzru, replying to the debate, said that the very fact that the Commander-in-Chief had tabled the amendment made it clear that he meant to do something.

Winding up the debate, the *Commander-in-Chief* said that there was a certain amount of misapprehension in the minds of some of the members that by recruiting men from all the provinces there would be an even distribution of the military expenditure among them. He explained that a very small part of the military expenditure went to men in the form of salaries. Most of the money was spent on equipment, ammunition and clothing. This money was being spent in factories situated all over the country. The Commander-in-Chief also emphasized that his primary task was to get on with the war, and that before he did anything which altered the existing organization or arrangement, he must think about it very carefully. He assured the House, however, that he would give full consideration to the suggestions made by the members. Pandit *Kunzru* then withdrew his resolution and the Commander-in-Chief's was passed. The House then adjourned till **March 10.**

Indian Troops in Africa

10th MARCH :—In the Council of State this morning, in a written reply to a question by Raja *Yuverai Dutta Singh* in regard to the prominent part played by Indian troops in Africa, His Excellency the *Commander-in-Chief* stated :—

"I welcome the opportunity afforded me by the honourable member to pay a personal tribute on the floor of this House to the magnificent part the troops from India have played in destroying the threat of Italian aggression in and from North Africa. Both British and Indian troops, sent from this country, some of them as far back as the Summer of 1939, have shown and continue to show a quality of training and fighting spirit, second to none.

"For many months, these troops had to fill a role involving waiting on the defensive in anything but comfortable conditions on the hot desert plains of Western Egypt and the Sudan. They faced an enemy, immensely superior in numbers and possessed at that time of overwhelming superiority in the air. In conditions far from inspiring, our troops never flagged in their zeal and, as more and more equipment of the most modern type was supplied to them, they trained. day after day, with a remarkable will and cheerfulness. The result is already history. When the time came, General Sir *Archibald Wavell* was able, despite the numerical superiority of the enemy, to take the initiative with confidence and to turn defence into attack,

"The North African campaign will go down to history as one of the greatest achievements of the armies of the Commonwealth. British and Indian troops had the honour of dealing the initial blow which shattered the Italian threat to Egypt. When these troops, under the command of Lieutenant-General Wilson, made that swift sweep forward from Mersa Matruh in the early days of December, the Italian morale in North Africa was unshaken. The forward troops of Marshal Graziani's army were encamped in force in and around Sidi Barrani, waiting for the moment to launch an attack. Suddenly in one of the most carefully planned battles of all time, they found themselves overwhelmed in less than 48 hours. It must, I think, be recognised that, against a stouter enemy, the almost miraculous perfection of what is now known as "the Battle of Sidi Barrani" might have been less overwhelming. Nevertheless, it was the surprise achieved which was the main factor in that victory, and that surprise could only be gained and exploited by troops who knew their business down to the last man.

"After a short and well-earned rest, many of the units from India who had played so decisive a part at Sidi Barrani were rapidly transferred to the south, where their experience on the North-West Frontier of this country would be of special value. This experience was peculiar to them. Their appearance in the Sudan was the signal for a general onslaught on Italian East Africa.

"When I broadcast shortly after my arrival in India a few weeks ago, I quoted a warm message of congratulation from General Wavell on the wonderful performance of Indian troops in what he described as 'the most brilliant pursuit of the Italians from Kasaola to Keren.' I have lately received from him the following confirmation of that message—'As detailed information of fighting in Eritrea reaches me, it confirms the magnificent performance of Indian troops at Agordot, Barentu and Keren. India may well be proud of these fine troops.'

"At Karen, the Italians have concentrated the cream of their East African Army in an attempt to stave off collapse. Details of the part played by the troops from the country in the swift drive which took our forces from the vicinity of Kassala to the precipitous and strongly fortified heights around Keren have been published in a series of press notes as fast as they have become available here. The story as it unfolds fully, justifies the warm praise General Wavell has accorded our soldiers. The many acts of individual gallantry and determination by Indian troops of all classes are too numerous for me to mention here, and it would be invidious to select any particular one. Suffice it to say this. We all know in India how, in an inhospitable country with few communications, like the tribal areas of our North-West Frontier, bold tribesmen, armed only with rifles, can and do give considerable trouble to better armed troops. It does not require much imagination therefore to visualise the difficulties of overcoming an enemy fully equipped with all modern weapons of war and firmly established in mountain fastnesses with his own internal lines of communication. When added to this, we realise that here again the Italian possesses numerical superiority, the attack which has driven him back through Eritrea to the defences of Karen can be fully appreciated.

"I will not at this stage say more, but I would like to pay a tribute to the Air Forces who have been operating with our troops in this campaign. Their efforts have been so effective that, whereas only a few weeks ago, Italian aircraft continually harassed our troops on the borders of the Sudan, enemy machines now rarely appear and the perilous operations of our troops are being conducted without the additional handicap of inferiority in the air.

"The campaign in North Africa can well be described as one of the greatest co-operative enterprises of the forces of the Commonwealth. Indian and British troops cracked the morale of Marshal Graziani's forces at Sidi Barrani, British and Dominion troops have swept the Italians from Eastern Libya. That splendid corps, the Sudan Defence Force, have led the van of the British and Indian assault on Eritrea, while South African forces have swept the Italians north from Kenya and have already captured the capital of Italian Somaliland. Indian troops are also, I am proud to state, giving invaluable support to the heroic activities of the patriot forces of Abyssinia, which are now harassing the enemy in the heart of that country.

"I would like, Sir, to remind honourable members that Africa is not our only battle-front. The Royal Indian Navy have, since the outbreak of the war, and particularly since Italy entered the war, performed an arduous and dangerous task in the closest co-operation with the Royal Navy. Its ships and its sailors have been continuously employed in guarding our trade routes and convoys in all conditions of weather and climate, and the climate of the Red Sea and the Persian Gulf is not too pleasant in the height of summer. I speak from experience. We must not forget them.

"Then we have our troops in Malaya and the Far East, who, though not actually in a theatre of war, are many of them living under active service conditions, and enduring hardship and discomfort as well as separation from their relations and homes.

"Lastly, let us remember our land and air forces on our western frontier. Officially they are not at war and they get none of the privileges and concessions which quite rightly fell to the lot of their comrades the border beyond. Now as always they carry their lives in their hands and can never relax their vigilance. A soldier or an airman on the frontier needs to be an expert at his work, and should be thankful that we have such soldiers and airmen who without fuss or advertisement, guard our marches for us, day in and day out, and in all weather".

U. T. C. AS OFFICERS' CORPS

Pandit Kunzru next moved a resolution recommending that the University Training Corps in India be trained and utilised like the Officers' Training Corps at the British Universities. *Pt. Kunzru* observed that the central purpose of his resolution was to ask that the training of members of the U. T. C. should not be limited to that given to the rank and file. Advantage should be taken of their education to fit them for the performance of more responsible duties. The regulations laid down for the training of the U. T. C.'s were in theory compatible with that idea. The regulations pointed out that the purpose of the training was to fit cadets for taking initiative and for developing qualities of leadership. But in practice, the training had fallen far short of the ideal. The Shea Committee had recommended that the Indian U. T. C. must be regarded as the most important section of the Territorial Force and that it should be viewed as the foundation stone of a National Army. Far from having been dealt with as its importance required it had never received any attention. In the Allahabad University the U. T. C. had not been given even uniforms. Sir *Claude Auchinleck*, Commander-in-Chief, replying to the debate announced that he had issued instructions for reviewing and improving the syllabus of the U. T. C. and this work was now in hand. He was also considering the proposal of introducing the system of certificates for efficiency, which might shorten the period of training taken by a cadet to get his Commission. His Excellency said that he would deal with the spirit and not with the letter of the resolution. Furthermore, he did not want to give any undertaking which he might not be able to carry out. It was war time and therefore he was not

Mr. *N. M. Joshi* said it was his experience that often the sense of prestige of the officer concerned stood in the way of appellate authorities dealing with him impartially where his actions in respect of subordinates were in question. Hence the need of disinterested judicial men handling appeals. Mr. Joshi asked that the Labour Commission's recommendations in this connection should be given effect to. He also asked that in hearing appeals, a representative of the trade union should be heard. In addition to a judicial officer to be attached to general managers, Mr. Joshi advocated the appointment of such an officer attached to every Divisional Superintendent.

Sir *Yamin Khan* said what the resolution aimed at was to ensure that appeals by subordinates were heard by officers who had the time and the frame of mind necessary to go through the whole file and hear both sides before arriving at a decision. It was commonly known that officers were guided by personal likes and dislikes in judging subordinates. It was to avoid injustices arising from this that judicial officers were needed.

Mr. *M. S. Aney* disagreed with the Communications Member that judicial officers were not fitted for the work of declaring appeals from subordinates in an organisation like the railways. It was well known that judicial officers often dealt with cases involving technical matters and gave decisions. What was needed was some machinery by which orders passed by officers on their subordinates were tested to see if they were in accordance with the rules and regulations or whether they were arbitrary. The trouble seemed to him to be that the Railway Board felt that railways were a commercial undertaking and therefore the Agents should have unfettered discretion to deal with the staff. The Communications Member seemed to think it wrong that members of the railway staff should approach members of the House. The very fact that these members of the staff felt the need to approach someone outside their offices was, declared Mr. Aney, sufficient proof of dissatisfaction with the existing system of hearing appeals. If the Communications Member would consider the appointment of a committee of experienced administrators instead of judicial officers, the debate would have served its purpose, but these officers should be men who could approach a case with a judicial mind.

The Assembly rejected Sir Ziauddin's resolution by 39 votes to 22.

Communal Unions of Govt. Employees

Mr. *H. M. Abdulla* moved a resolution recommending abandonment of the Government's present policy of non-recognition of communal unions of Government employees. Mr. *Abdullah* declared that Government did in practice recognize communal unions as in the case of the Anglo-Indian and European community and in the case of the Railwaymen's Federation which he alleged was a Hindu body. Why then not recognize Moslem unions also, he asked. Sir *Henry Gidney* said the mover was incorrect in saying that there was an Anglo-Indian union, The National Union of Railwaymen in India and Burma, with which he was connected, was not a communal organization. It had numbers of Indian, Hindu and Moslem, as members. He nevertheless expressed sympathy with the mover, because Government, he said, toyed with the All-India Railwaymen's Federation, which he regarded as a more or less Hindu Union. The Government should insist on the Federation being representative of an adequate number of Moslems and other communities. If Government were prepared to do that he would advise the mover to withdraw the resolution. The debate had not concluded when the House adjourned till the 22nd.

General Discussion of Railway Budget

22nd. FEBRUARY :—Members of the Moslem League Party withdrew from the Assembly this morning as soon as the House took up the general discussion of the Railway Budget. Mr. *Ghulam Bhik Nairang*, Deputy Leader of the Party, made a statement before they withdrew, declaring that they were doing so in order to mark their protest against the policy followed by the Government in regard to Moslem grievances.

"Whether we take into consideration the position of Moslems in the Railway Board or various State-managed railways" the statement said, "we are faced with the old tale of Moslem interests being neglected and little or no effort being made to improve their position in various railway services." Mr. *Nairang* said that the party would not take part either in the general discussion or in the discussion of demands for grants under the Railway Budget.

Sardar Sant Singh opening the general debate on the Railway Budget characterized the budget as a great disappointment. It showed a large surplus yet the increase made in freights and fares had not been removed, or reduced nor had any provision been made for relief to the peasantry, who had to pay a higher freight on the movement of their produce on which their livelihood depended. He also dwelt on the grievances arising from the favouritism shown to the Anglo-Indian community and declared that if the railways were claimed to be run on commercial lines, such special treatment of any community was reprehensible.

Mr. *L. C. Buss* said that for the first time for many years the railways have been able to make their full contribution to general revenues under the terms of the convention. In addition to that, it was proposed that half the balance that would normally have gone to Railway Reserve Fund shall be diverted to central revenues. "The financial position of Government being what it is, there is no doubt in our mind as to the wisdom of this course and this brings me to the question of the moratorium under which the railways are now working. This moratorium is due to lapse on March 31. 1942, and it seems more than likely that, before that time has elapsed, this House will have to agree to yet another extension of this moratorium.

Sir Abdul Halim Ghaznavi regretted the action of the Moslem League party in walking out from the House. "They have done a distinct disservice to the Moslem community and I hope that the Moslems of India would take note of their action this morning" he added. Speaking on the budget, Sir Abdul Halim said that in spite of the phenomenal increase in the railway surplus the Government had not reduced railway rates and fares. The export trade of the country was at a standstill and yet no measures were taken to encourage inter-provincial trade. He particularly referred to the case of coal and said that the promised reduction of a per cent in surcharge of coal from April to October did not mean any concession to the trade because there was no coal traffic during that period. In regard to dismantling of uneconomical railway lines, the speaker urged that before taking action the Government should give due consideration to cases where no alternative means of mechanical transport existed.

Sir *Henry Gidney* asserted that the large increase in the surplus was not due to any increased efficiency in the Railway Administration but to the conditions created by the war and on account of increase in rates and fares. He alluded to the dismantling of railway lines and asked why such uneconomical lines were permitted to be constructed and why they were allowed to continue for such a long time. He also urged the amalgamation of East Indian and Eastern Bengal Railways and immediate steps to be taken for the manufacture of broad-gauge locomotives in this country.

Mr. *Lalchand Navalrai* blamed the Government for the Moslem League party's action this morning, for it was the Government who issued orders for recruitment on a communal basis. He however felt that the present Communications Member did not deserve the censure, which the walk-out was intended to convey. Sir *Andrew Clow* had for the first time appointed a Moslem member on the Railway Board, who was in charge of establishment, and had also set up the Desouza inquiry committee as a result of which it had been shown that Moslems received their due share in railway services. Mr. Navalrai declared that the time had now come for the withdrawal of the circular under which recruitment on a communal basis was being made. He also stressed the need for a reduction if not removal of the surcharge in freights and fares. The surcharge was, he said, unjustified so long as economy measures such as reductiou in high salaries were not attempted.

Mr. *Govind Deshmukh* referring to the dismantling of railways which had been declared to be uneconomical, said it was not much consolation to agriculturists or other users to be told in the present circumstances that they could rely on the motor bus as an alternative form of transport. He put forward a special plea on behalf of cotton growers who he said had received no form of help or subsidy from the Government so far and must now be given some assistance by way of reduction of freight.

Dr. *P. N. Banerjee* said it would be a superficial view to take to regard the phenomenal surplus with satisfaction. The surplus, he said, had been secured by means of taxation which had placed an additional burden on the masses. The most unsatisfactory feature of the budget was the decision not to give up the surcharge on the rate and fares which had yielded Rs. 6¼ crores out of the surplus.

Mr. *M. S. Aney*, dealing with the decision to dismantle certain railways, characterized it as an act of vandalism, which in his view was "a political blunder, an economic wrong and a constitutionally inappropriate method." These lines, he said, had been built after the House had given its sanction to it, and, he declared, no one, not even the Railway Board had the right to decide to pull those lines up without the sanction of the House for that purpose. As it was, the Railway Board's action amounted to an usurpation of the rights of the House. The Government also did not seem to realize what an alarming impression the act of pulling up the railway lines was creating in the minds of the public. The impression was that it was being done because nothing could be manufactured in England. Such a moral effect should be counteracted, and he deemed it his duty to bring the matter to the notice of responsible officers of the Government.

Replying to the debate, *Sir Andrew Clow* expressed regret at the attack on his policy made by the Moslem League party's spokesmen in the Assembly and at the fact that members of the party had not remained in the House to hear his reply. The attack related to the question of appointments by recruitment and appointments by promotion. In the case of the first class of appointments, Government had laid down their considered policy in a resolution designed to safeguard the interests of the minority communities. That was not his (the speaker's) policy but had been laid down before he became the communications Member, and it was a policy which it had been his constant endeavour to fulfil in the letter and in the spirit. In view, however, of allegations that it was not being carried out properly an inquiry into the matter was entrusted to an experienced and impartial officer and a Moslem officer was later attached to that officer. "I have heard nothing since, said *Sir Andrew*, "to suggest that the facts elicited by Mr. *DeSouza* are incorrect. They appear to me to vindicate the method that my predecessors and I have followed." Eleven appointments to the superior services had been mentioned in the statement made in the House on behalf of the Moslem League party, These appointments, *Sir Andrew* pointed out, were made on the recommendation of the Public Service Commission. The real issue, however, lay in the second class of appointments, namely. appointments by promotion. There was a debate last session on this issue and the divison on it showed that the House endorsed the policy of making promotions without fear and without favour (cheers). "On this point the Hon. members of the Moslem League party and I admittedly do not see eye to eye: but the policy is not my policy. It is one followed in every department and by every member of Government. So long as it is our policy to make promotions by merit, I shall regard it my duty to see that every man serving under me, whatever his class or creed, has a fair chance of advancement to posts for which he is eligible and qualified." Replying to the criticism of the decision regarding locomotive construction, he referred to the difficulties in the country regarding men and material. It was not a simple matter to train technical labour. The Commerce Member had been doing everything possible to get as many technicians as possible. We had suffered in India for years from shortage of technical labour and he hoped that the efforts now being made by the Labour Department would leave the country after the war in a far better position with regard to this most important element of industry.

It was true that the existing locomotive would be used more intensively, but it must be remembered, he suggested, that the more our locomotives become obsolete the better would be the prospect of embarking on manufacture of locomotives in India, because the successful establishment of the industry depended on a large and continuing demand. He expressed agreement with the view that the divergence between the salaries at the top and in the lower rank was great, but any attempt to even them up must be undertaken by the country as a whole. The railways' steps were guided by the rates of pay prevailing outside the railway services. Further, having seen railways in other parts of the world, Sir Andrew thought, that the remuneration given to the top men in Indian Railways compared favourably with those elsewhere. The question had been asked why if the lines were unremunerative they were not dismantled earlier. There were two answers, Sir Andrew said. "Firstly, we do not exist entirely for economy. We exist for service : we are always reluctant to dismantle a line even if it shows a small loss. There are other lines which we believe to be unremunerative but we still keep them going for this reason." The other reason was that most of these lines were comparatively recently constructed. Owing to a further change in the situation, Sir Andrew proceeded, the Board had cancelled the notice given for the removal of one line, namely the one between Fort Abbas and Kuv-el-Amara, on the North-Western Railway. The House at this stage adjourned till the 25th.

COMPENSATION FOR SEAMEN

25th. FEBRUARY :—Compensation for war injuries and damage sustained by masters and seamen employed on small vessels playing in Indian coastal waters and rivers was agreed to in principle by the Assembly to-day, on the motion of the Commerce Member, *Sir Ramaswami Mudaliar*. He explained in the course of the debate that the vessels concerned numbered some 77,000 and ranged from 300 to 200 tons. Details of the scheme for compensation, he said, would be placed before the Standing Finance Committee for its approval. Sir Ramaswami Mudaliar's resolution ran : "This Assembly recommends to the Governor-General-in-Council to take steps to establish schemes providing for the payment from Central revenues of compensation in respect of war injuries and war damage to effects sustained during the period of the present emergency by masters and seamen employed on sea-going services on ships registered in British India under the Bombay Coasting Vessels Act. 1838, or under the Indian Registration of Ships Act, 1941."

The Commerce Member explained that rates of compensation had been provided for by His Majesty's Government for seamen on British ships registered in the United Kingdom, and these rates had been extended to Indian seamen on ships on the Indian register but coming under the British Merchant Shipping Act. These ships were big ones and the scheme of compensation did not apply to smaller vessels numbering over 77,000 which plied in Indian coastal and inland waters. The possibilities of war damage to these were still remote no doubt, but if danger should come nearer, a scheme for extending compensation to seamen on these craft analogous to the one applicable to the bigger vessels, should be ready to be applied. The resolution sought the Assembly's sanction for the establishment of suitable schemes for this purpose.

Mr. *M. S. Aney* said that the beneficent nature of the scheme proposed would be readily realized but he suggested that even if the House gave general approbation to the proposal, it would be necessary for Government to approach the House or at least the Standing Finance Committee with the detailed scheme.

Sir *Mohamed Yamin Khan*, supporting the demand for an opportunity for the House to consider the detailed scheme, asked that if any ship on the Indian register was chartered by the British Government for its own purposes and if Indian seamen on it suffered damage, compensation should be paid by His Majesty's Government. Why should the Indian exchequer, he asked, bear the loss of a ship, say, in the Atlantic or Pacific Ocean ?

Mr. *N. M. Joshi* wanted the assurance that the rates of compensation paid under the proposed scheme would not be less than those paid to European sailors under the British Act and not less than the rates paid under the legislation passed in Simla in 1939. He did not care who paid the compensation, so long as compensation was paid. He was not against the British exchequer paying Indian seamen but under present conditions it would be extremely difficult to recover compensation from the British Government.

Pandit *L. K. Maitra* stated that it would be unwise to make the recommendation contained in the resolution without a clear idea of the magnitude of the financial commitment involved.

Sir *Cowasji Jehangir* suggested that figures should be given in the budget of the extent of the liabilities under the proposed scheme. So long as the House was assured that compensation now proposed would be no more and no less than that paid under the British Act, they should be satisfied.

Sir *Ramaswami Mudaliar*, replying, said, that the Government had the power to frame the scheme, allot the money to be paid under it, put the allotment in the next budget and ask for the sanction of the House. But he wanted the approval of the House for the proposal, and it was hard lines to be accused of doing something wrong when he asked for that approval. He wanted the vote of the House for another purpose also. Two kinds of compensation were proposed : one an immediate grant and the other a pension, which would be a continuing liability. He wanted to strengthen himself by a vote of the House to agree to such a recurring grant. He made it clear that he proposed, when the scheme was actually framed, to put it before the Standing Finance Committee for its approval. The Commerce Member further explained that for Indian seamen on British ships registered in the United Kingdom, His Majesty's Government paid all the compensation ; and for Indian seamen on ships on the Indian register the Government of India had to pay compensation. The proposed scheme now, however, related to small coastal vessels ranging from 300 to 200 tons. In the case of these as in that of the bigger vessels, the owners would be relieved of the responsibility of paying compensation. The House passed the resolution.

PETROLEUM ACT AMED. BILL

Earlier Sir *Ramaswami Mudaliar's* Bill to amend the Petroleum Act was passed. The Assembly then adjourned.

DEMANDS FOR RY. GRANTS

26th. FEBRUARY :—The war should not be made an excuse for the postponement of locomotive manufacture in India, urged *Sardar Sant Singh* and those who supported his "cut" motion in the Assembly. this morning, to discuss the suspension of the pledge for the manufacture of locomotives for the period of the war". Members of the Muslim League Party were absent from the House.

Sardar Sant Singh asked that the question should be looked at from the point of view of whether a railway system of the size of India's could afford to depend, in the matter of an important part of its equipment, upon foreign supplies. It should also be considered as one concerned with the establishment of a key industry which would relieve unemployment and add to the wealth and taxpaying capacity of the people. He declined to accept the *bona fides* of the plea that all the materials were not available in India. It was lack of will and not of materials, he asserted, that stood in the way.

Sir Henry Gidney, while fully sharing the view that India's present position in the matter of major industries, was the cumulative result of Government's "studied bigotry", urged that the past should be forgotten and just at the present juncture the Empire's needs must take the foremost place. Manufacture of locomotives, he declared, was nothing compared to the need to help win the war. He called upon the Railway Member to make a definite statement that he would not lose a single moment after the war in throwing open workshops for locomotive manufacture.

Pandit L. K. Maitra quoted the opinion embodied in the latest Government report on the subject, published after the outbreak of the war, that the time was most opportune now for starting locomotive manufacture and that the start could be made without a subsidy or protective tariff. It was not suggested that the manufacture of munitions should be stopped in order to undertake locomotive manufacture, proceeded Mr. *Maitra*, but it must be remembered that locomotive manufacture was in itself an important part of war supply, because, without sufficient locomotive power, the railway system would be inefficient and might break down and the result might be that the transport of war materials would stop.

Mr. *Navalrai* urged that if it was admitted that locomotives could not, for the present, be imported, then the need to build them in India must also be admitted. As it was, the supply of engines was not sufficient, and the result was already seen in the unpunctuality of passenger trains.

Sir Andrew Clow referred to the view expressed by experts, who had investigated the question, that India had in the past gained by purchasing her locomotives abroad instead of manufacturing them herself. As regards the present, he referred to the very real difficulty of securing skilled labour. The Commerce Member had difficulty even in getting sufficient men for training as technicians. The same difficulty existed with regard to materials. An order for 25 broad-gauge locomotives had actually been placed for manufacture at the existing Ajmer workshop, but the materials were not available. It was true that the report of Messrs. *Srinivasan* and *Humphries* was presented and published after the war, but the situation to-day was very different from the situation in January 1940.

As regards the future, *Sir Andrew* did not desire to speak in terms of pledges, but of predictions. Assuming that the work could not be undertaken now, there was no doubt that, whatever the position might have been when the two officers mentioned above went round the country two years ago, the demand for locomotives would be greater after the war than it was now and while he was not proposing to pledge his successor, who must be guided by conditions that would actually face him, he himself had ample confidence in the future. There would be a surplus of skilled labour. India would be more self-sufficing as regards materials and there would be a larger market for locomotives. The motion was rejected without a division and the House adjourned.

27th. FEBRUARY :—All the railway demands for grants were passed by the Assembly to-day. During the debate on the question of a dearness allowance for railway employees, on a cut motion moved by Mr. *C. C. Miller*, (European Group), Sir *Andrew Clow*, Communications Member, announced that in order to remedy the difficulties felt by the Court of Inquiry, owing to scantiness of statistical evidence, the Government contemplated setting up machinery of a more or less permanent character, which would include experts in economic and statistical investigation. It would not be fitting at this stage, he said, to give any indication of the Government's views on the conclusions reached by the Court of Inquiry. The Railway Board had been in consultation and correspondence with the All-India Railwaymen's Federation on the subject and were awaiting their views. The discussions were proceeding not exactly on the basis of the report: and it would be recognized that if a solution could be reached by the method of negotiation it would form a sounder basis than investigation on academic economic lines. He would endeavour to keep the Standing Finance Committee in touch with any important changes in the situation. In reply to Mr. *M. S. Aney*, the Communication Member said that members were entitled to draw what inference they could from the fact that a provision was made in the Railway Budget for any possible increase in wages.

Mr. *Miller* moving the cut made a detailed criticism of the Court's handling of the statistical evidence, particularly of the figures complied by the Bombay Labour Office and contended that the evidence in support of the Court's finding that an 11 per cent increase to the cost of living had occurred was flimsy. He indicated the European Group's opposition to any suggestion that allowances given should be included as an integral part of wages and he stressed the advisability of maintaining a permanent or semi-permanent panel of persons with experience of labour conditions, who could act on courts of inquiry such as the one presided over by Sir B. N. Rau. Mr. *Miller* withdrew his motion.

Sir *Henry Gidney* raised a discussion on the policy of selection for certain posts in railway administrations and the Railway Board with particular reference to medical appointments. After this cut motion was rejected by the House Sir Henry brought forward another motion to discuss the control by the Railway Board and Communications Member over company-managed railways with special reference to the south Indian Railway. The motion was rejected. Another cut motion by Mr. *N. M. Joshi* who raised a discussion on the grievances of railway workers, was also rejected. The House then adjourned.

Financial Statement for 1941-42*

28th. FEBRUARY :—The Finance Member, *Sir Jeremy Raisman* in introducing the Central Budget, India's second War Budget, in the Assembly, to-day disclosed a deficit of Rs. 8,42 lakhs for 1940-41 and a prospective deficit of Rs. 20,46 laks for 1941-42.

The strengthening of all arms of India's Defence Services which is now going forward with speed and energy is estimated to cost approximately Rs. 24 crores this year and Rs. 35 crores additional expenditure next year.

---

*Following are the main points which emerged from Sir Jeremy Raisman's Budget speech to-day :—

India's defence budget for 1941-42 is Rs. 84 crores against Rs. 72 crores in 1940-41.

India's war expenditure is Rs. 35 crores in 1941-42 against Rs. 24 crores this year.

Charges borne by His Majesty's Government for supplies and services rendered by India are expected to exceed double India's war expenditure for 1941-42.

The total strength of India's armed forces is now well over 5000,000 men of arms. Further expansion is proceeding.

Provision has been made for raising new armoured and mechanized cavalry regiments, new Indian field artillery regiments, regular infantry battalions, engineer units and more mechanical transport sections.

The year 1941 will witness the appearance of the first "made in India" aeroplanes ; a number of modern aircraft and equipment is expected from American sources.

Vehicles, machine tools and other essential war requirements are now permitted to be purchased in the United States and Canada.

Workmen employed in Ordnance and clothing factories in India have increased from 17,000 to 45,000, and those in the Government dockyards from 1,168 before the war to nearly 5,000.

The benefit to India from the recent repatriation of sterling loans, it was explained, lies in the reduction of the Government of India's external debt by about Rs. 120 crores the decrease in sterling interest charges and an immediate gain to revenue.

CHANGES IN TAXATION

Announcing a prospective deficit of Rs. 20,46 lakhs, the Finance Member proproposed to increase the rate of the Excess Profits Tax from 50 per cent to 66⅔ per cent to yield two and a half crores.

He also proposed to raise the central surcharge on income-tax and supper-tax from 25 per cent to 33⅓ per cent to yield an additional 190 lakhs.

The Finance Member proposed to double the excise duty on matches to produce 150 lakhs.

He proposed to increase the import duty now leviable on artificial silk yarn and thread. The duty stands at 25 per cent ad valorem or three annas per pound, whichever is higher and he proposed to increase the alternative specific duty to five annas per pound to yield 36 lakhs.

The Finance-Member also proposed to introduce a new ten per cent ad valorem excise duty on pneumatic tyres and tubes to yield 35 lakhs.

The total estimated yield of new taxation is 6,61 lakhs which brings the estimated revenue for 1941-42 to 113,00 lakhs and reduce the prospective deficit to 13,85 lakhs.

The uncovered revenue deficit will be met by borrowing.

The salient points in the budget statement are :—

India's defence budget for 1941-42 is Rs. 84 crores against Rs. 72 crores in 1940 41. India's war expenditure will be Rs. 35 crores in 1941-42 against Rs. 24 crores this year.

The charges borne by His Majesty's Government for supplies and services rendered by India are expected to exceed double India's war expenditure for 1941-42.

The total strength of India's armed forces is now well over half a million men of all arms : and further expansion is proceeding. Provision is made for raising new armoured and mechanised cavalry regiments ; new Indian field artillery regiments, regular infantry battalions, engineer units, more mechanical transport sections.

The year 1941 will witness the appearance of the first "Made in India" aeroplanes. A number of modern aircraft and connected equipment are expected from American sources. Vehicles, machine tools and other essential war requirements are now permitted to be purchased in the United States and Canada.

The number of workmen employed in ordnance and clothing factories has increased from 17,000 to 45,000, and those in the Government dockyard from 1,168 before the war to nearly 4,000.

The Supply Department carried out orders for his Majesty's and other Allied Governments valued at over Rs. 82 crores by the middle or January. Orders placed on behalf of overseas Governments last year included two and a quarter

---

The Supply Department had carried out orders for H. M. G. and other Allied Governments valued at more than Rs. 82 crores by the middle of January.

Orders placed on behalf of overseas Governments last year included : 2,250,000 yards of jute canvas, 3,250 000 yards of a new jute and cotton fabric ; 12,000,000 yards of khaki materials and 14,000,00 yards of canvas.

The production of army boots, harness, saddlery and leather equipment is now thirty times the pre-war average.

Medical stores imported have decreased from 77 per cent to 46 per cent.

New manufacturing plant to meet the requirements of chemicals formerly drawn from Europe are under construction.

War equipment, lubricating oil, bichromates and acetic acid, formerly imported, are now being produced in India.

Cotton canvas has been substituted for flax canvas, fish oil for codliver oil and various Indian drugs for imported ones.

Four thousand tons of timber and more than a million railway sleepers have been purchased for military requirements.

With the completion of the sterling repatriation, India's sterling obligations will have been reduced by more than Rs. 220 crores since 1935.

The provinces' share of the incometax pool is expected to reach Rs. 4,46 lakhs in 1941-42 against Rs, 3.73 lakhs this year

million yards of jute canvas, three and a quarter million yards of a new jute and cotton fabric ; twelve million yards of khaki materials and fourteen million yards of canvas.

Production of army boots, harness, saddlery and leather equipment is now thirty times the pre-war average. Web equipment, lubricating oil, bichromates and acetic acid formerly imported are now being produced in India. Cotton canvas has been substituted for flax canvas, fish oil and various Indian drugs for imported ones.

With the completion of the sterling debt repatriation, India's sterling obligation will have been reduced by over Rs. 320 crores since 1935.

The provinces' share of the incometax pool is expected to reach Rs, 4,46 lakhs in 1941-42 against Rs. 3,73 lakhs this year.

Review of Economic Situation

The Finance Member took an hour and twenty-five minutes to deliver his speech, which was frequently applauded, particularly the passages in which he referred to the tributes paid to the training of Indian soldiers and the part they played in recent victories, announced that the year 1941 would witness the appearance of the aeroplane produced in India and his confident declaration about India's financial strength.

A hum expressive of alarm went round the members when *Sir Jeremy Raisman* gave the estimated deficit for the coming year as Rs. 20,46 lakhs.

The new taxation proposals were for the most part received in undemonstrative silence, except for an occasional gasp from some parts of the House.

The following is the text of *Sir Jeremy Raisman's* speech :

The task which falls to me of placing before this House an account of the main developments since the last annual budget was discussed, has on the present occasion been somewhat lightened by the fact that I made a financial statement during the last session in November 1940, in the course of which I drew the picture of our finances as it then presented itself. As the facts then brought out will be relatively fresh in the minds of Hon'ble Members I shall to-day devote myself largely to bringing that account up to date, and in particular to a description of the progress of India's war effort in the field of the defence services and of supply. This course, in addition to meeting what I am sure is the desire of this House, will also furnish the most suitable basis for an understanding of our financial position. I shall also take this opportunity of furnishing a fuller explanation of the operation recently announced in connection with the repatriation of a large part of our sterling dept.

Improvement in Exports

2. When speaking of the Indian economic situation in my first Budget Speech, I qualified my reference to the favourable features which were then manifest by emphasising the extent to which the continuance of prosperity was dependent on our ability to export freely overseas. The events of last spring and summer deprived us of our markets on the European Continent and caused a serious deterioration in the volume and facility of the shipping services available for our use. These factors, together with a temporary decline in confidence, which reduced the willingness to hold stocks, resulted in a marked fall on prices in the summer of 1940. This recession has, however, been magnified in some quarters to undue proportions, and it is well to view the facts in proper perspective. In the first nine months of the fiscal year 1938-39, our exports to all destinations amounted to 122 crores : in the first nine months of the present fiscal year they amounted to 144 crores. Thus the development of new export markets very largely compensated for the loss of old ones. In the second place, prices as a whole are still some fifteen per cent higher than they were at the beginning of September 1939 and those of certain commodities, e. g., raw materials, are considerably higher. Thirdly such indices as are available of general economic conditions in India, such as railway traffic and postal receipts, continue to reflect an improvement over pre-war conditions.

Post-War Prospects

3. To this improvement the steadily growing war effort most powerfully contributes. Last year that effort, on the side of the production of stores and of commodities required in connection with the war had barely begun : the tide of production is now rising rapidly and may be expected to exercise a generally beneficial effect upon the volume of employment and therefore upon the size of the national income. The holding of the Eastern Group Conference in this country and the establishment, consequent upon the deliberations of that Conference, of an inter-Imperial

to the Rs. 500 limit which had been considered desirable in some quarters until recently. As regards the cost of administration of the Act, he said that the present contribution from general revenues was Rs. 1.50,900 and the present contribution by way of fees, etc., from insurance agents and companies was about Rs. 50,000. He said that under the present circumstances for the purposes of a growing deportment, they wanted more money and it was not possible to get that money from the general tax-payer. The Bill was passed and the House, as already stated, adjourned *sine die.*

The Central Legislative Assembly

Budget Session—New Delhi—11th. Feb. to 1st. April 1941

Insurance Act Amend. Bill

The Budget Session of the Central Legislative Assembly commenced at New Delhi on the **11th. February 1941** with Sir *Abdur Rahim*, President, in the chair. The proceedings would have been ended at the usual hour but for a batch of adjournment motions which were disallowed and members' disapproval of Government's method of reporting on the recent Indo-Ceylonese negotiations.

Sir A. Ramaswami Mudaliar, Commerce Member, introduced a Bill to amend the Insurance Act and a Bill to provide for the reduction temporarily of the amounts payable as instalments of the sum to be deposited by an insurer under Section 7 of the Insurance Act. At the suggestion of several members, consideration of the Bills was agreed to be taken up on the next official day. The House then adjourned.

Treatment of Detenus

12th. FEBRUARY :—Sir *Reginald Maxwell* made an outspoken declaration on detenus in replying to the debate which was concluded in the Assembly this morning on Mr. *N. M. Joshi's* resolution, moved in the November session, recommending the appointment of a Committee to examine and report on the conditions in which detenues under the Defence of India Act lived, and whether and what provision should be made for the families of these detenus. He said :—

"Where the Government have the tremendous responsibiliy of maintaining the security of the country in a time of grave emergency such as this, they cannot divest themselves of it, but must deal with the matter solely from the point of view of what is needed to win the war. Several speakers have spoken as though these prisoners were deserving of special sympathy—as though the Government had almost to apologize to them for depriving them of their liberty to carry on their plots. It is suggested that the action of the Government can only be justified if these persons are made so comfortable that they have nothing to lose from their detention. If we wished to encourage others in carrying on such plots, there could be no better way. The Government, however, have nothing to apologize for taking action which was necessary in the urgent interests of the country."

Earlier in his speech Sir Reginald gave figures of security prisoners detained under Rule 26 of the Defence of India Act and said that according to the latest available figures these numbered about 700 at the end of the last month. Of these some 102 persons were detained in connexion with the satyagraha movement. Leaving these aside, the number of prisoners with whom the resolution was concerned was about 600. A figure of this order, he said, after 18 months of war and in a population such as that of India, did not indicate an excessive readiness of the authorities to use the powers of detention. The majority came from the provinces of Madras, Bombay, Bengal, U. P. Bihar and the Punjab. Excluding certain ex-military prisoners, the number detained by orders of the Central Government was 29 and the rest were detained by orders of Provincial Governments. Of the prisoners mentioned, 155 were detained in Deoli, including 11 of the Central Government prisoners, and the rest from the United Provinces, the Punjab, Bihar and the N. W. F. P. He said he could speak with authority only of prisoners at Deoli ; but the provinces had supplied him information about specific points. Detailing the conditions under which these prisoners were detained, he said that of the two classes into which they were divided, class I corresponded as regards diet and accommodation to those of B class convicts, and class II to those of C class convicts. Seventy-seven were in class I and 89 in class II. They received no allowances, but class I prisoners might receive up to Rs. 10 a month from relatives or friends, to supplement their amenities and class II prisoners up to Rs. 5 a month. As regards family allowances the principle followed was that Provincial Governments might in exceptional cases grant allowances to dependents of security prisoners when it was necessary on the ground that the detention had deprived the family of its income and left it in such destitute circumstances as to make assistance necessary, So far as information was available allowances had been granted in about dozen cases, the amount varying from Rs. 35 to Rs. 10 a month. The number of applications received was comparatively small and all cases were carefully investigated. "The House must, however, remember," declared Sir *Reginald*, "that if a person engages in revolutionary activities, it is he who lets his family down and not the general taxpayer who is expected to pay the allowances. We sympathize with the family but the person who is responsible is the offender. In most cases the persons detained did not earn anything much by honest work of which they are now deprived. They were paid agitators. Let them go to their masters, to the persons who paid them for carrying on subversive activities." (Mr. *M. S. Aney* : Can you prove who are their masters ? *Sir Reginald* : I know some of their masters.) The Home Member, in conclusion, said that there was no useful function which a Committee of the kind suggested in the resolution could perform.

The House divided and rejected the resolution by 40 votes to 23, the Moslem League party, the Congress Nationalists and some unattached members voting for the resolution,

Port Trust Boards

Sir Abdul Halim Gaznavi moved that the Chairman of the Karachi, Bombay and Calcutta Port Haj Committees be appointed "ex-officio" members of the Port Trust Boards of Karachi, Bombay and Calcutta, respectively. He said that this was necessary in order to remove the difficulties of nearly 20,000 pilgrims who embarked and disembarked from these ports. Opposing the resolution, Sir *Andrew Clow* said that, on inquiries made in all the three port trusts, he had found that no case relating to Haj pilgrims had come up before any port trust so far and there was no case concerning pilgrims which any of the trust had refused to consider sympathetically, Moreover, the percentage of pilgrim shop to other ships handled by the trusts, was infinitesimal. In Calcutta port last year out of the 4,000 ships which has been cleared only one was of pilgrims. The proportion in other ports was similarly small. The mover was replying to the debate when the House adjourned.

Relief to Ry. Employees Taxation Bill

13th. FEBRUARY :—Non-official Bills were discussed in the Assembly to-day. Mr. *Md. Azhar Ali* moved consideration of his Bill to amend the Indian Railways Act to give relief to certain low-paid railway employees from certain district board or municipal taxes. After some discussion during which the Bill was opposed by *Sir Andrew Clow*, Communications Member and Mr. *M. S. Aney*, the Bill was withdrawn. Mr. *Azhar Ali* pointed out that in 1922 the Railway Board exempted all subordinate railway staff irrespective of pay, from payment of all taxes (except electric power lighting charges) whether the services were rendered by the railway or by a municipality. But the United Provinces Government held that the liability of railway employees to pay properly taxes levied by district boards was not affected by the exemption. District Boards had, therefore, imposed and levied these taxes. He said that if the Railway Board had the power to exempt subordinate staff in certain places, exemption should be granted to all of their subordinate staff. *Sir Andrew Clow*, opposing the Bill said that the mover was in error both as regards law and the facts. The House had no power to exempt servants of the Central Government, or anyone from provincial taxation, and the provision of the Bill would be held to be *ultra vires*. Nor was there any reason why railway servants should be placed in a privileged position in comparison with others getting the same salary. It was true that the Railway Board had granted exemption but the Board in those days were in some obscurity as regards Provincial and Central spheres of taxation. They had later discovered the error and were now paying the tax for subordinates. The Railway Board were hesitating to take away the privilege because it would be regarded as a hardship.

Criminal Procedure Code Amend. Bill

The House next agreed to the circulation of Mr. *Lalchand Navalrai's* Bill to amend the Code of Criminal Procedure so as to repeal the provision allowing private unqualified persons to appear and act as pleaders in criminal cases with the permission of the court. The provision, Mr. Navalrai said, served some purpose in the old days when qualified pleaders were not easily available, and could be engaged only at a heavy cost. At present, there was no dearth of pleaders, and the provision had, therefore, outlived its object. *Sir Reginald Maxwell*, Home Member, moving the circulation of the Bill for the purpose of eliciting public opinion by July 1, 1941, pointed out that the administration of justice was a provincial subject, and it would not be proper to proceed with this Bill without giving the provinces an opportunity to comment on it.

Mr. *Lalchand Navalrai* next moved that the Bill to amend the Land Acquisition Act be taken into consideration. He said that granting of power to the courts of first class sub-judges in the Bombay presidency and the courts of sub-judges in other presidencies would avoid the delays now taking place in the decision of cases arising out of the Land Acquisition Act. *Sir M. Zafrulla Khan* opposed the Bill on the ground that the Centre had no jurisdiction to pass such legislation. The subject, he said, fell exclusively within provincial jurisdiction according to the Government of India Act. The *President*, ruling the objection out of order, said that he was not aware of any rule, procedure or practice which required that any objection to a motion being moved must be taken at any particular stage. The House rejected Mr. Navalrai's motion.

After a number of other Bills had been introduced, the House adjourned.

Indo-Ceylon Relations

14th. FEBRUARY :—Support to the attitude of the Government of India representatives at the recent Indo-Ceylon conversations and appreciation of the Governor of Ceylon's message to the State Council were expressed in an amendment moved in the Assembly to-day by Sir *Raza Ali*, former Agent-General to the Government of India in South Africa, to a Government motion that the documents relating to the Indo-Ceylon conversations be taken into consideration.

Sir Raza Ali's amendment ran as follows : "And this Assembly regrets the failure of the Indo-Ceylon conversations as revealed in the verbatim report and supports the attitude adopted by the representatives of the Government of India, which faithfully represents the point of view of Indian public opinion ; and while recognising the desire of the Ceylon State Council to maintain its independence of action, appreciates the message sent by the Governor of Ceylon to that body with respect to the undertaking given by His Majesty's Government and by the Government of Ceylon to the Government of India and expresses the hope that it will serve to emphasise the importance, particularly under the present circumstances, of nothing being done by the Government and people of Ceylon which will endanger the good relations which should exist between the two countries, whose interests are so intimately bound together".

Mr. *J. D. Tyson*, Education Secretary, moving the motion for consideration, briefly referred to the papers laid on February 11 before the Assembly and the Ceylon Council, and said that subsequent to that the Governor of Ceylon had sent a message to the Ceylon State Council reminding that House of the existence of certain undertaking given by Ceylon to India. Mr. Tyson regretted that the Government had not yet received from Ceylon the exact text of His Excellency's message. From press message, he said, it appeared that His Excellency considered that the Government of Ceylon were bound by their undertakings and he went on to say that he held that as Governor he was required to withhold ratification or consent in respect of any measures depriving Indians of their right to which the Government of India did not agree. (Applause). Mr. Tyson trusted that the Governor's reminder would be regarded as timely and reassuring by Indians in Ceylon and elsewhere and as a sequel, better counsels would prevail. *Sir Raza Ali*, moving his amendment, regretted that there had been consistent attempts on the part of the Government of Ceylon to impose disabilities on Indian residents there. The Village Communities Ordinance and the Fisheries Ordinance were designed to achieve their political and economic strangulation. There was now a proposal to deprive Indians of the monopoly of the rice trade on the pretext of controlling food in war-time. Various other attempts were also being made, he said, and while he appreciated the attitude of the Government of India and the manner in which they had stood up for the rights of the people, he hoped they realised that they should not relax their efforts to keep careful watch over all that was happening in Ceylon. "I can say that we should not do anything really to disturb harmonious relations between any two countries of the British Commonwealth : but we must also realise that it is not only our duty to continue them : it is equally the duty of the Government of Ceylon not to do anything to disturb harmonious relations. Writings that have appeared in the Ceylon Press and the speeches made by Ministers leave no doubt that whereas there is very little anti-Indian feeling in Ceylon, interested persons want to take advantage of the present position by enacting anti-Indian legislation both in the political and economic fields. That impression is supported by a number of writings and speeches. I hope the debate in this House will serve a useful purpose. It will remind the people of Ceylon that not only the Government of India have very rightly stood up for the rights of the people of this country, but this House, which is the representative of this country, is able to give its unqualified support to the action of the Government of India. This House also reminds the Government of India not to relax its efforts and not to be a party to any concession whatsoever which is sure to be demanded by the Government of Ceylon in future to the detriment of our people." Sir Raza Ali was grateful to the Government of India for their moderate and reasonable attitude in the past which was appreciated by every Indian. The Government would have won more admiration from the people if they had associated with the negotiations one or two representives of the people of India.

Dr. P. N. Banerjee, supporting the amendment said : "We have often criticised the Government of India for their failure to do their duty by Indians in other colonies, but a better state of things seems to have commenced now and I hope that the Government of India in future will be as strong and as firm as they have been with regard to the Ceylon negotiations. We appreciate also the attitude taken up by the Ceylon Governor". (Applause). As regards the suggestion for the association of non-official Indians with negotiations of this kind, Prof. Banerji said: "The negotiations are not yet finished. I believe there will be further negotiations, because the interests of the two countries are intertwined and when these negotiations take place again, I hope Sir Girija Sankar Bajpai will think fit to have some representatives of this Assembly associated with the negotiations".

Mr. *F. E. James*, supporting the motion, said that the dominant feeling left in his mind after a perusal of the documents was one of profound regret at the whole business. The conversations were held for the purpose of exploring the ground and to try to find some common measure of agreement on which a structure of reasonable formal agreement between the two countries could be erected. It was surprising that even at this stage no common basis was found. "Yet when we read the documents, we realise that judging by the attitude of the Ceylon Ministers, there was no hope of arriving at any common agreement even in the early stages. It is most regrettable that the Ministers should have come to this country in no better frame of mind. It is clear that unless there is a radical alteration in the attitude of the Ministry in Ceylon to the question of the important Indian minority in that Island, there is no chance of any agreement being reached." (Cheers).

The Assembly passed without a division Sir Raza Ali's amendment of India's attitude in the Ceylon negotiations and appreciating the Ceylon Governor's message to the State Council.

Fraudulent Marks of Merchandise Bill

17th. FEBRUARY :—The Assembly held a brief half-day sitting this morning and passed the Bill further to amend the law relating to fraudulent marks of merchandise, as reported by the Select Committee.

Insurance Act Amend. Bill (contd.)

The House also referred to a Select Committee further to amend the Insurance Act. The Commerce Member, *Sir A. Ramaswami Mudaliar*, making the Select Committee motion on the Bill, explained that the amendment embodied in the Bill had been necessitated by the working of the Act enacted three years ago. Before the Bill was drafted, the Government held a Conference with the insurance interests and discussed various proposals, which the Government had received in recent months. The Bill, however, was not designed to be the last word on the subject and the Select Committee would consider if any important changes were necessitated in the Bill. *Dr. Banerjee* moved that the Bill be circulated for eliciting public opinion by July 31, 1941. He said that it was true that the Government had consulted insurance interests before having the Bill drafted. No final agreement had, however, been reached at the Conference. The Bill was of a technical nature and affected large sections of people. It was, therefore, necessary that ample opportunities should be given to all sections affected by the Bill to express their views. The *Commerce Member* added that the amendments embodied in the Bill were no reflection on the legal acumen and the care bestowed by the then Law Member, Sir *N. N. Sarcar* on the Insurance Act. The amendments were to remove certain defects in the Act, which could not be foreseen by the framers of the Act. Referring to the motion for circulation, the Commerce Member said that circulation procedure were not the rule but the exception in the matter of legislation. Ordinarily, Bills were referred to Select Committees and were passed by the House. He, however, assured the House that he had no intention to rush the Bill through. He intended to consult insurance interests before the Select Committee considered the Bill. He further assured the House that he would give the utmost consideration to any suggestion made by the Select Committee on the Bill. Referring to the Simla Conference, he said that there was a consensus of opinion on certain matters. On certain matters there were differences, and on such matters Government had to come to certain decisions. The House divided and the motion for circulation was lost by 43 votes to 26. The House then adjourned.

Ticketless Travellers' Bill

18th. FEBRUARY :—The Assembly to-day adopted without a division *Sir Andrew Clow's* motion for consideration of the Bill to check ticketless travel as reported upon by the Select Committee. Sir Andrew Clow, replying briefly, agreed with Pandit Maitra that legislation alone would not achieve the object in view. He had never been under any such illusion nor did he believe that the administration was not capable of improvement. Pandit Maitra had further referred to the smallness of the percentage of ticketless travellers detected. What, asked Sir Andrew, was the deduction he drew from it ? The percentage of murder was much smaller, and he had never heard any suggestion that those who were detected should be treated leniently. He had been charged with having changed a civil liability into a criminal liability. He had done nothing of the kind. It had already been done by the Act as it stood which made travelling with intent to defraud a criminal offence. He was only trying to make the punishment more deterrent. Mr. Nauman had stated that he, (the speaker) had somehow maligned or condemned this country by this Bill. Surely, suggested Sir Andrew, no country could be said to be maligned because of provisions in the Statute Book against murder or other offences. As regards the statement that punishment of this kind did not exist in any other part of the world, the Communications Member pointed out that attempts to cheat were punishable in all parts of the world. He went on to give the example of Ceylon, Federated Malay States, etc. as countries which had legislation providing more stringent punishment for ticketless travelling than was attempted in the Bill. He also explained in reply to Prof. Banerjee that the punishment prescribed in the Bill was the maximum, and any Magistrate who felt so inclined had the power to award less. As for the suggestion to instal slot machines, if Sir Abdul Halim Ghaznavi would go to the Delhi Station he would find them there but experience had been that they had to keep a man to look after these machines (laughter). More-over, they were used only for issuing tickets of small denominations. Sir Ziauddin's suggestions, proceeded Sir Andrew, were all of an administrative character and were, therefore, not strictly relevant to the Bill ; but members of the Railway Board would be delighted to discuss those suggestions with the member.

The House passed without a division the motion for consideration and took up the clauses. Dr. *P. N. Banerjee* moved an amendment for the omission of a sub-clause inserted by the Select Committee to provide that no excess fare shall be payable by a person travelling without a ticket if he has obtained from a Railway servant permission by means of a certificate to proceed without having a ticket. Dr. Banerjea said that this Sub-Clause did not improve the Bill. If the Sub-Clause were deleted, then, a Railway servant would have the power to give verbal permission for continuing the journey. When there was no time to purchase a ticket how could a passenger have time to get a certificate, he asked. If it was intended to protect an honest ticketless traveller, then either the Sub-Clause should be omitted or at least re-worded in order to lay down that a Railway servant "shall" grant to the passenger a certificate and not "may" grant as the sub-clause stated. Sir *Yamin Khan*, supporting the amendment, gave instances of delays caused in the purchase of tickets. On one occasion, he said, it took twenty-five minutes for a booking clerk to give him a return ticket. Under such conditions, he said, it would be almost impossible for a person to get a certificate when the time at his disposal was short. The House at this stage adjourned.

Railway Budget for 1941-42

19th. FEBRUARY :—Railway estimates presented by Sir *Andrew Clow* in the Assembly to day forecast for 1940-41 a surplus of 14.59 crores against a surplus of 8.29 crores originally estimated.

Revised Estimates

Revised estimate of surplus on railways for 1940-41 is more than the actual surplus of last year by about 10¼ crores. Total traffic receipts of State-owned lines are expected to reach 109½ crores, about 11½ crores more than last year and 6¼ crores more than the original estimate. Total working expenses, including 12¾ crores for depreciation, are a little below 66¾ crores, or about 1¾ crores more than last year. The surplus expected is 14.59 crores. The balance in the depreciation fund will stand at a little over 35 crores.

Budget Estimates

Budget estimate for 1941-42 assumes traffic receipts of 108½ crores, 1 crore less than in the current year. Total working expenses will amount to a little less than 68¾ crores and will be about 2 crores more than the current year. The surplus is expected to be 11.83 crores. Balance of depreciation fund at the end of the year will be about 41 crores.

Capital Position

As regards 1941-42, dwelling first on the capital position, Sir Andrew Clow referred to the provision of 2 crores for the purchase of the Assam-Bengal Railway and 2¾ crores for the purchase of the Bombay, Baroda and Central India Railway.

Works Programme

The gross total works programme is slightly over 19½ crores. Estimates for track renewals amount to 6 crores, and those for rolling stock to 4½ crores. 3½ crores are provided for bridges and other structural works, and a little over ¾ crore for increase in stores balance. Programme includes provision of 2,265 wagons, of which 1,550 are broad gauge general service wagons to be added to the general pool. After deducting, from the above figure, about 1½ crores for credits on account of released materials and an allowance (about 2½ crores), based on past experience, for unforeseen delays in the execution of works or in obtaining supplies in the conditions created by the war, the net amount of the open line works programme (including the purchase of the Bombay, Baroda and Central India and Assam-Bengal Railways) is a little over 15½ crores.

War-Effort of Railways

Referring to the war-effort of railways, he mentioned that, besides the men who had joined the fighting forces, many were employed in the production of various war requirements, for which some railway workshops had been wholly made over. He also alluded to the fact that about 305 miles of branch lines, which had been found unremunerative, would be dismantled by the end of the year for shipment overseas of materials required for construction of railways.

Freights and Fares

In stating that the figure of receipts allowed for no important changes in freights and fares, Sir Andrew Clow mentioned Government's intention to reduce the surcharge on coal by 5 per cent. for the months from April to October inclusive with a view to encouraging the placing of orders at times when the wagon position was easier. Government were examining the question whether the rebates designed to encourage export of coal and wheat were still justified and whether suburban season tickets fares, which were not altered when the passenger fares were enhanced last year, were giving fair returns at their present levels.

Manufacture of Locomotives

In referring to the question of the manufacture of broad gauge locomotives in India, which was mentioned in his speech last year, Sir Andrew Clow stated that the heavy demands for skilled labour, machine tools and materials resulting from the immense expansion in the production of munitions and other military requirements, made it out of the question to embark at this stage on a new large scale industry, and the workshop, which had been selected for the purpose, had been completely turned over to war work. Orders for 10 broad-gauge locomotives for the North-Western Railway and 15 for the Great Indian Peninsula Railway had been placed with the Bombay, Baroda and Central India Railway Company, but it had not yet been possible to secure all the necessary materials for these.

Allocation of Surplus

Sir Andrew Clow then explained how it was proposed to allocate the surplus of the current and the next financial years.

General revenues would receive in 1940-41, 9.96 crores in all, and in 1941-42, 10.13 crores including the advance payment of 1.82 crores.

Sir Andrew Clow said he realized that this result would come as a disappointment to many who were interested in railways as, though a record surplus was expected, the railway reserve gained very little. He felt confident however that, when it was realized that the needs of general revenues were war needs and that the alternative to an arrangement such as he proposed, would be an even heavier burden on the general taxpayer than he must in any case he called upon to bear, the justification for this arrangement would be recognized.

Ticketless Travellers' Bill (contd.)

After the presentation of the Railway Budget, the Assembly resumed discussion of the Ticketless Travellers' Bill. The House rejected without a division the amendment moved yesterday by Dr. Banerjea for omission of the sub-clause providing for the grant of a certificate to bonafide passengers who, for exceptional reasons, could not purchase a ticket, the certificate being to the effect that the passenger had been permitted to travel upon condition that he subsequently paid the fair payable for the distance travelled.

Sir *Andrew Clow* accepted and the House passed Pandit *L. K. Maitra's* amendment to the effect that a railway servant authorized to give permission to the passenger to travel in the circumstances referred to above "shall ordinarily" instead of "may" grant the certificate.

A full discussion followed on the provision in Clause Four laying down that any servant appointed by the railway administration in this behalf may apply to any magistrate for recovery of the sum payably by a passenger as if it were a fine, and the magistrate shall order it to be so recovered, and may order that the person liable for the payment shall in default of payment suffer imprisonment of either description for a term which may extend to one month. The clause also provided that any sum recovered shall, as it is recovered, be paid to the railway administration.

Pandit L. K. Maitra attempted by an amendment to provide that the railway servant appointed for this purpose should not be a ticket collector or a ticket inspector and should not be below the rank of a station master. He emphasized the necessity to qualify the railway servant who was to be entrusted with this task and pointed out that the ticket collector or inspector was an interested party and should not therefore be authorized to approach the magistrate.

Sir *Andrew Clow*, opposing the amendment, referred to the fact that the humblest person in the land could apply to a magistrate and said there was no reason why that right should be denied to any railway servant. The complainant should in this case be the person who was in a position to know the facts. Nor was there any danger in the existing provision, provided the decision rested with the magistrate and provided also the magistrate was satisfied on the facts that the sum was payable. He was prepared to accept a later amendment which sought to make it clear that the magistrate shall decide on the facts.

Mr. *M. Nauman*, Mr. *A. C. Dutta*, *Sir Ziauddin Ahmed*, Mr. *Azhar Ali*, Mr. *M. S. Aney*, *Maulvi Abdul Ghani* and Mr. *Lalchand Navalrai* supported the amendment. Mr. *Aney* pointed out that even among the police a responsible officer called the prosecuting sub-inspector was entrusted with the work of prosecution.

Mr. *J. H. F. Raper*, member, Railway Board, explained that the cause substantially reproduced the existing section which had been in force since 1890 authorizing any railway servant to make the complaint. In actual practice the ticket collector where he felt the necessity to take action, reported to the station master and received instructions from him. No single instance had been mentioned, he said, of abuse or difficuly under the present arrangement. The amendment was negatived.

Mr. *Essak Sait's* amendment to lay down that only magistrates of the first or second class shall be empowered to act under the clause was accepted by Sir Andrew Clow and passed.

In accordance with the earlier understanding the Communications Member accepted the same member's amendment to the effect that the magistrate shall order recovery of the sum "if satisfied that the sum is payable." The amendment was passed.

The House divided on the next amendment moved by Mr. *A. N. Chattopadhyaya* to provide that the magistrate should satisfy himself "after proper investigation." The amendment was rejected by 42 votes to 19.

Mr. *Navalrai* attempted the deletion of all the words in the clause giving power to the magistrate to order imprisonment which might extend to a month.

Sir *Ziauddin Ahmed*, *Pandit Maitra* Mr. *Nauman* and *Maulvi Abdul Ghani* supported the amendment. The amendment was rejected by 40 votes to 19.

The Congress Nationalists and Moslem League members combined once again to oppose the next clause which gave power to any railway servant with the help of any person to eject a passenger who attempted to travel in a carriage without a ticket or refused to produce his ticket for examination.

The House rejected by 38 votes to 18 Mr. *Navalrai's* amendment to provide that the railway servant could only obtain the help of a railway sub-ordinate and not of "any person." The House at this stage adjourned.

Port Trust Board (contd.)

20th. FEBRUARY :—The Assembly discussed non-official resolutions to-day and rejected by 34 votes against 16 Sir *Abdul Halim Gaznavi's* resolution recommending that that Chairmen of the Karachi, Bombay and Calcutta Port Haj Committees, be appointed ex-officio members of the Port Trust Boards of those Ports. Sir Abdul Halim, replying to the debate on the resolution on the earlier non-official day, referred to the paucity of Muslims on all Port Trusts and said that British interests had opposed discrimination at Round Table Conferences and at meetings of the Joint Select Committee and yet there was discrimination against Indians in the composition of Port Trusts in spite of the fact that three-fourths of the business was owned by Indians.

Appeals of Railway Employees

In the absence of Dr. *Habibur Rahaman*, *Sir Ziauddin* moved a resolution recommending the appointment of officers of judicial mind to listen to appeals of railway employees and to scrutinise the present rule relating to those appeals. Sir Ziauddin said that there was a great deal of dissatisfaction with the manner and method of attending to these appeals. The whole thing had been left to the discretion of one man who was often guided by the notes of his immediate subordinates. Sir Ziauddin gave details of a number of cases in which, he alleged, injustice had been done because the officers who dealt with those cases had no idea of weighing evidence and coming to conclusions supported by facts.

Sir Henry Gidney, strongly supporting the resolution, which he considered reasonable, much-needed and urgent, said the trouble was that the Communications Member was not in a position to know what was happening in the lower ranks. There was enormous discontent, he said, among these ranks, and although some improvement had occurred recently, what was needed was wholesale correction. This could not be brought about unless a fully fledged judicial committee was attached to each railway : but if that was not possible at least a Magistrate should be attached to each railway. The injustice of the present conditions must be corrected.

Sir Andrew Clow, opposing the resolution, said it was and should be the aim of every officer to have a judicial mind, using that word in the ordinary English meaning of it, namely, a mind able to form sound judgment. The Railway Board did their best to have such men. But a judicial officer in the technical sense was, in his view, really not qualified for the work which the resolution sought to give him. The objection was that the whole method of approach and the training of the judicial officer in that sense were such that he would deal with one incident in the life of the man before him, and come to a decision on evidence, whereas the officer who has to deal with subordinates every day came to form certain judgments about each which was based on experience but for which there might not be any palpable evidence. It was a very definite handicap to efficient administration that officers could not give quick promotion to efficient men because it would mean superseding others who might take their grievances to a member of the Assembly. We were in danger, declared Sir Andrew, of concentrating on individuals, who were adversely affected.

CIVIL ESTIMATES

29. Our Civil expenditure estimates show increases amounting to Rs. 2,61 lakhs in all as compared with the current year's revised estimates. There are first the additional sums on account of the full year's working of the various schemes arising out of the war which were started in the course of the current year. Thus next year the training of the Air Force Reserve is expected to cost Rs 33 lakhs and the Scheme of Technical Training to provide the needs of skilled labour of the technical branches of the Defence Services and Ordnance and Munitions factories a further Rs. 93 lakhs. Under this scheme which provides for the training of 15,000 men by the end of March 1942, nearly 2,000 men are already being trained at different training centres and their number is increasing every day. Of the total cost of Rs. 1 crore, over 85 per cent of which is for stipends to trainees and their training fees, it is now estimated that Rs. 7 lakhs will be spent in the current year and the remainder next year.

PROVISION FOR NEW ITEMS

Then there are a number of new items of essential expenditure which the Standing Finance Committee have approved for inclusion in the budget. These include the share of the subsidy to this year's Haj pilgrimage to be paid by the Government of India to meet the extra cost attributable to war conditions, the establishment of a new Broadcasting station at Karachi, and a further programme of Civil Aviation Works. Rs. 5 lakhs are to be spent in the course of next year on the new Broad-casting House to be built at Delhi. Rs. 9 lakhs are being provided for a new high power transmitter for broadcasts to countries outside India, intended for the benefit of Indian nationals abroad and to enable India to present her point of view, as well as to counteract enemy broadcasts in those countries. A third Mint is to be constructed to cope with the present large coinage demand, which has increased so enormously as the result of the war. As soon however as the situation returns to normal, it is proposed to close down the existing Calcutta Mint and to transfer all serviceable plant to the new Mint so that the present valuable but congested site can be sold to defray a large part of the cost of the scheme.

EXPANSION OF SUPPLY DEPARTMENT

A substantial share of the new expenditure included in the Budget is on account of the Department of Supply which has continued to expand throughout the year to meet the ever growing demands. The great developments in the production of war material, as well as the reorganisation of the Department carried out last December have already been described in connection with Defence. As regards the effect on industry of the orders placed on behalf of overseas Governments it may be mentioned that these have included 2¼ million yards of jute canvas, 3½ million yards of a new jute and cotton fabric, 12 million yards of khaki materials, as well as 14 million yards of canvas valued at over Rs. 1,40 lakhs. At the same time the woollen industry's whole production has been absorbed to meet war demands. The production of army boots, harness, saddlery, and leather equipment which is now 30 times the pre-war average, has resulted in large orders for the tanning industry and increased demands for hides. New manufacturing plant to meet the requirements of chemicals formerly drawn from Europe are under construction, 400,000 tons of timber and over a million railway sleepers have been purchased for military requirements while wooden articles like tent poles, camp furniture and packing cases to the value of Rs. 60 lakhs have been made by Indian workmen from timber grown in the country. The total value of all these orders placed on behalf of His Majesty's Government and other allied Governments up to the middle of January exceeded Rs. 82 crores. This gives some indication of the necessity for the expansion of the Department's purchasing organisations. The expenditure on this account has increased from the figure of Rs. 23 lakhs originally provided in the budget for the current year to Rs. 58 lakhs as now estimated for next year.

RS. 20,46 CRORES DEFICIT

30. I can now summarise the figures for 1941-42. The expenditure detailed in the civil estimates comes to Rs. 42,72 lakhs as compared with Rs. 40,11 lakhs for the current year, and with the provision for the Defence Services placed at Rs. 84,13 lakhs, our total expenditure estimates amount to Rs. 126,85 lakhs. The figures are therefore—

		(Lakhs)
Revenue	... ...	106,39
Expenditure	... ...	126,85
Prospective Deficit	... ...	20,46

Defence Loans

At this stage I propose to deal with the Ways and Means position at it has developed in the course of the last twelve months, when despite the grave repercussions of the war the credit of the country has been fully maintained at its previous high level.

31. Defence Loans.—Our loan programme for the year was merged in the Indian Defence Savings Movement which was launched early in June with the issue of Six Year Defence Bonds, Ten Year Defence Savings Certificates and Interest free Bonds. From the 1st August we made these Six Year Defence Bonds the mainstay of our loan programme and removed the previous maximum on individual holdings. These Defence Bonds met with a ready and increasingly popular reception, and when we closed them on the 25th January, subscriptions totalled nearly 45 crores, 31½ crores having been tendered in cash and the balance by conversion of the 5 per cent Loan, 1940-43. As from 1st February we issued on terms slightly more favourable to the tax-payer a second 3 per cent Defence Loan with longer currency and repayable at par. The results of these Defence Loans, the total receipts from which in a period of eight months have amounted to over Rs. 80 crores, testify to the strength of India's financial credit and are a good augury for the future. But I must take this opportunity of emphasising the desirability of an even more intensive mobilisation of the country's savings if India's war effort is to continue to be financed in the most satisfactory way. However generous the donations for war purposes may be—and no one can fail to be impressed with the response so far made—it is obvious that the total of sums received as donations can only form a very modest fraction of the amount required to finance the war effort. The fulfilment of that requirement calls for the efforts of every individual to save to the best of his capacity and to invest his savings in one or other of the different types of Defence Loan, which we have instituted to serve different needs. In addition to the Loans already described we have started a Defence Savings Provident Fund for all Government servants which makes it easy for these classes to make regular investments. Subscriptions to this are already approaching the scale of half a crore a year. We shall shortly have in operation a simple system of facilitating popular saving by means of a new scheme of Post Office Savings Bank Accounts, the amounts in which will be repayable not on demand but a year after the end of the war. This will afford further facilities to those of limited means who desire to invest their savings so as to assist the war effort. In order to encourage deposits of this kind, the rate of interest has been fixed at 1 per cent higher than the existing rate on ordinary Postal Savings Banks Accounts.

During the current year Government exercised their option of repaying the 5 per cent Loan, 1940-43 and thereby effected an appreciable saving in our interest charges. Next year we are making provision for the repayment of the 3 per cent Bonds, 1941, the outstanding balance of which, about Rs. 10½ crores, falls due for payment on the 15th September next.

Sterling Position

32. Sterling Position.—Owing to the continued improvement in the country's balance of trade, the Reserve Bank have been able to purchase large amounts of sterling which in the first ten months of the current year aggregated approximately £ 47 millions. At the same time with large payments being received in the United Kingdom on account of recoverable war expenditure and the cost of supplies made to His Majesty's Government the amount of remittance required by Government has diminished to vanishing point. For our ordinary sterling requirements, excluding the amount that will be required to finance the debt redemption operation now pending, are now expected to amount to no more than £ 1 million in the current year, while next year instead of having to remit funds to the Secretary of State we actually expect a refund of £ 26 million.

REPATRIATION OF STERLING DEBT

33. Repatriation of Sterling Debt—As I explained in my Budget Speech last year, these acquisitions of sterling continued to enable the Reserve Bank to put large amounts at our disposal for the repatriation of our sterling debt. Considerable open market purchases were made in London, particularly in the early months of the year and the total acquired in this way now stands at approximately £28½ million. As the securities market improved, however, and as the floating stock was removed, it became increasingly obvious that purchases on this scale would no longer be possible except at a cost of pushing prices up beyond a reasonable level. In these circumstances, the British Government came to our help by issuing orders under their special war powers compelling holders resident in the United Kingdom to sell their stock to them for delivery to us at the market prices prevailing at the time of the order. The Reserve Bank agreed to provide the sterling and to guarantee the immediate financing of scheme framed on these lines to cover all our terminable obligations, that is to say, all our sterling debt which has to be repaid on fixed dates, amounting to a total which at the prices of acquisition may be taken as approximately £90 million or Rs. 120 crores. The whole of this, will of course, not have to be paid in sterling because a certain amount, though how much we do not know yet, is held by persons who are not legally considered as resident within the United Kingdom, and to whom, therefore, the order does not apply. These may be residents either in India or elsewhere. As regards the latter, the Reserve Bank has made arrangements with the Bank of England that, subject to the English regulations regarding export of capital abroad they will make an offer to non-resident holders to sell their securities on the basis of the prices fixed for their compulsory acquisition. I anticipate that many of the holders will avail themselves of this offer because once the bulk of the debt has been paid off the remaining stocks will not be easily marketable in London and it would therefore be to the advantage of the holders to dispose of them and choose some other investment. We had also to decide what terms should be given to these stocks when held by residents in this country and we decided that we would pass a corresponding compulsory order of acquisition at the same price as those fixed in London. To avoid disturbing the portfolios of insurance companies and other investors, however, we decided that we would elaborate the scheme which I mentioned to you last year of creating rupee counterparts so as to give Indian holders the option of taking over such counterparts to the extent of the nominal value of their holdings worked out at the rate of 1s. 6d. to the rupee. I hope that this offer will be largely accepted as it will be both to the holders' advantage and ours : it will be to our advantage as it naturally lessens the immediate payments which we have to make and it will be to theirs, because the sterling prices of these loans were slightly lower than those of corresponding rupee securities, so that they should gain to a slight extent on the change.

RUPEE COUNTERPARTS TO BE ISSUED

34. This brings me to the machinery for financing the operation. There are clearly two stages ; first, we buy the sterling from the Reserve Bank and secondly, we have to obtain rupees to pay for that sterling. It would be obviously quite impossible to attempt to borrow this immediately from the market even apart from our Defence borrowing requirements, and it would be inconsistent with the policy which we are following with the co-operation of the Reserve Bank of maintaining money at as cheap a level as is possible without inflation so as to minimise the burden of the war. We have found it impossible, within the limited time at our disposal, and in the absence of more definite information than is available at present of the amounts held by investors in the United Kingdom, in India and elsewhere to decide on the permanent arrangements for this purpose, but for budgetary purposes and as an interim measure pending more detailed consideration, we are adopting the procedure of maintaining the *status quo,* and of issuing in lieu of these sterling loans rupee counterparts which will bear the same rate of interest and be payable on the same dates, the only difference being that, in future, they will be payable in rupees and not in sterling. Later we shall have to determine, in consultation with the Reserve Bank, a procedure which will be simple and fair both to the general tax-payer and to the Bank, which has co-operated so readily and promptly with the Government in financing this important transaction, and which will at the same time avoid any necessity for an automatic increase in our short-term debt which might entail dangerous inflationary consequences later.

RESERVE BANK'S ETERNAL ASSETS

35. The proportion in which the Reserve Bank will distribute the securities taken up by it between its Issue and Banking Departments as a longer range holding is for that Bank to determine in the light of circumstances as they develop and in co-operation with Government. It is obvious, however, that the cancellation of this large block of sterling liabilities with its reduction in our overseas obligations to the extent of well over £ 3 million a year does permanently strengthen our external position and consequently makes it reasonable for the Reserve Bank to hold a somewhat lower proportion of external assets than previously. There is of course, no necessity or intention of reducing the minimum percentage of the external assets which they must hold under the Act, that is to say, 40 per cent of their note liabilities, nor is there any necessity, as has been suggested in some quarters, to effect a statutory revision of the prices at which they hold their gold. All that was necessary was to remove the restriction on the maximum amount of Government securities which the Reserve Bank can hold in their Issue Department and that has been effected by the abolition of the proviso to Section 33 (3) of their Act. This does not in any way affect their statutory responsibilities under the Act. It merely gives them a freedom of choice which they did not have in the past, as to the proportions in which they should hold Government securities or internal trade bills. It is also unnecessary, and we do not propose, to alter the limits on the Government securities which they can hold in the Banking Department.

I am afraid that it will not be possible to give precise figures until the 10th March when the returns asked for by the Bank of England and ourselves will have been received, but we are confident that the Indian securities market is so healthy that the finance of this large operation can be effected without detriment to Indian security prices and that, on the contrary, the effect on them is more likely to be stimulating.

INDIA'S GAINS FROM REPATRIATION

36. The House will no doubt appreciate fully to what extent this single operation, which is the largest of its kind ever carried out in this country, will improve the financial position of India. When it is complete, we shall not only have reduced the Government of India's external debt by about Rs. 120 crores, by replacing the sterling liabilities cancelled with corresponding rupee liabilities, but shall also have reduced such of our interest charges as are payable in sterling by as much as 50 per cent over the last six years. Taking the whole period since 1935, and including the amounts of sterling Railway annuities and debentures discharged each year and the transfer of our liabilities in respect of sterling family pensions, we shall have reduced our sterling obligations by over Rs. 220 crores of which about Rs. 145 crores will have been repatriated since the beginning of the war.

STRAIN ON RESERVES REDUCED

37. In the past, Indian opinion has been much pre-occupied, perhaps unduly so, by the so-called "drain", that is, the sum-total of the external obligations, on capital and interest account, which had of course to be met by providing sterling in London—the counter-part of the physical exports out of the sale proceeds of which these amounts were raised. It will be obvious to the House that the conversion of external into internal debt will diminish the strain upon the ultimate cash-reserves of the country—our holdings of gold and other external assets—which tends to manifest itself when, in consequence of world events over which we have no control, the value of our overseas trade declines. There has been in certain quarters a disposition to doubt the value of these conversion operations, since they have involved a reduction for the time being, at least, in the size of the sterlings of the Reserve Bank. These holdings have risen greatly since the outbreak of the war, an increase which has given rise to much criticism. Even after the reduction involved in the present operations, our sterling reserves will still be in the neighbourhood of Rs. 80 crores, a figure almost exacly the same as the average sterling holding during the last full pre-war year. But, in fact, it is not the absolute size of the reserve which matters but the size of the reserve in relation to the magnitude of the most pressing liabilities against which it is held. Our cash reserves are held in the first instance as a protection against external liabilities, failure to meet which would instantly react upon India's finanancial credit. By these operations we reduce the size of our external obligations and therefore permanently strengthen our position. I may emphasise again that these operations do not affect the size of our

gold reserves in the least and do not involve any change either in monetary policy or in the day-to-day operations of the currency system.

What the Exchequer Gains

38. The immediate object of the transaction was the replacement of sterling by rupee obligations and the real gain to the country lies in the liquidation of external obligations which might prove an embarassment in failure. Even otherwise Government are likely to be immediate gainers though at present it is not possible to estimate with any approach to accuracy the immediate effect on our revenue position. The profit due to the difference between the rate of interest earned by the Reserve Bank on its sterling investments and the redemption yield of the securities acquired at the prices paid must ultimately accrue, practically entriely, to Government either through the increase in the profits of the Reserve Bank, to the extent to which these securities are held by it, or directly to the extent to which Government hold these in their own portfolio, or cancel them from the funds which they borrow from the market. Later as the market gradually absorbs these liabilities in whatever form they will ultimately take, whether as rupee counterparts of the sterling loans they replace, or in the form of a simpler scheme of converted loans of suitable maturity, the gain may be reduced but against such reduction will, of course, be set off the increased receipts from income-tax.

India's Credit Strengthened

39. In my judgment these operations cannot fail greatly to strengthen India's credit. There can be few countries in the world to-day fortunate enough to possess sufficient liquid resources to repatriate a large portion of their external debt, whilst leaving their Central Bank in a position of unchallengeable strength. In relation to the growing resources of India our external debt will now be of remarkably modest proportions. Should a situation ever arise in which India were required to raise capital abroad—a contingency which I for one do not foresee—the fact that our existing external liabilities are so small would obviously be of the greatest importance in determining the rate of interest which we would be required to pay.

Assistance to Britain

40. There is of course another aspect of our repatriation operations at the present time and that is the manner in which they assist His Majesty's Government to finance the prosecution of the war. It is obvious that if India repays her creditors in London, then particularly at the present time and in the present conditions of the London money market the greater part of the sums so disbursed will be re-lent to His Majesty's Government probably in the form of investment in the Defence loans and will thus become available for Britain's use in a more permanent form than when they formed part of the balances of the Reserve Bank and were invested in sterling Treasury Bills. To this extent we may well feel gratified that India in improving her own position and has also contributed to facilitating the war-time problems of Britain.

41. Treasury Bills —Apart from financing these repatriation operations we would have reduced the value of treasury bills outstanding by about eight crores in the current year, despite the large expansion in Defence expenditure and the heavy outgo from Postal Savings Banks and Cash Certificates which would ordinarily have necessitated a large increase in our floating debt. For these factors have been largely offset by the favourable response given to our Defence Loans, the capital receipt of Rs. 12 crores from the Reserve Bank on account of the Re 1 notes and silver rupees issued to them and the fact that the payment of five crores to the Reserve Bank provided for against a return of surplus rupee coin was not required. For the moment we are reckoning on a decrease in Treasury Bills of Rs. 3½ crores during the two years taken together.

42. Post Office Cash Certificates and Savings Banks.—It will be observed from the Ways and Means statement, which is printed with the Explanatory Memorandum on the Budget, that the figure for net repayments of Post Office Cash Certificates has been increased in the revised estimate for the current year from Rs. 1½ crores to Rs. 10 crores, while for Postal Savings Banks deposits we are providing for a net outgo of Rs. 19 crores against the receipt of Rs. 2 crores taken in the budget. For during the period of uncertainty following the fall of France last summer there were large withdrawals from Postal Savings Banks and heavy discharges of Cash Certificates, coupled with a tendency to hoard savings in the unproductive form of silver rupees. Since then however there has been a marked and

progressive improvement and for next year we are assuming a net deposit of Rs. 2 crores in Postal Savings Banks and a net repayment of Rs. 6 crores of Cash Certificates, the popularity of which has naturally been affected by the issue of Defence Savings Certificates, which provide a very similar and in some ways more attractive form of investment."

NEW TAXATION PROPOSALS

Announcing his Budget proposals, Sir *Jeremy Raisman* said :

"I return now to the estimated revenue position for the next financial year, which as I indicated a few minutes ago reveals a prospective deficit of Rs. 20,46 lakhs. I would at this point remind hon. members of the extent to which the Railway Contribution has come to our assistance and how greatly it has mitigated our difficulties. It remains for me to place befoie the House the proposals which I have formulated in regard to the deficit.

INCREASE IN RATE OF EXCESS PROFITS TAX

" I deal first with direct taxation, namely, the Excess Profits Tax and the Income-Tax. It is true on the whole that at the present moment the main economic advantage which is derived from India's war supply activities accrues to the industrial and commercial sections of the country, and the direct tax-payer may fairly be called on to shoulder the larger share of any further burdens which are to be imposed. I propose that the profits of a further period of one year shall now be subjected to the Excess Profits Tax, and that the rate applicable to such profits shall be 66⅔ per cent. I think it relevant to remind the House of the remarks which I made regarding the effect on the incidence of this tax, of the important modifications which were made in the clauses of the E. P. T. Bill dealing with the optional standard periods, and also the special provisions for new industries and for such matters as abnormal depreciation. I have little doubt that with these features of our system the new level of the tax will neither cause substantial hardship to existing industries nor operate to impede the growth of new ones. The change in the percentage will, however, introduce a complication where adjustments have to be made for the assessment of the previous year, and to regulate this aspect a small amending Bill will be brought forward. The yield of this enhancement of the Excess Profits Tax is estimated at two and a half crores.

SURCHARGE ON INCOME-TAX RAISED

"As regards Income-tax and Super-tax, I propose that the present Central surcharge of twenty-five per cent should for the year 1941-42 be raised to 33⅓ per cent. This is expected to yield an additional Rs. 190 lakhs.

DUTY ON MATCHES DOUBLED

"In the field of indirect taxes, my main proposal is to double the excise duty on matches. I may observe here that the present duty was fixed in relation to a certain retail price, and that changes in that price must be in terms of the lowest unit of currency in common use and are thus not susceptible of fine gradation. Over large parts of the country the retail price has already advanced to the next higher point, yielding a large uncovenanted profit to the trade. The increase in duty now proposed will appropriate for the exchequer a due share of the enhanced retail price which the consumer has to pay. A corresponding increase will automatically ensue in the duty on imported matches, and a similar increase will be made in the duty on mechanical lighters. The yield of the additional duty on matches is estimated at Rs. 150 lakhs.

HIGHER TARIFF ON ARTIFICIAL SILK

"I have two other smaller proposals. One is to increase the import duty now leviable on artificial silk yarn and thread, an item in our import trade which unlike most others, appears to offer, even in wartime conditions, the possibility of higher revenue. The duty on artificial silk yarn and thread stands at 25 per cent *ad valorem* or As. 3 per pound, whichever is higher and I propose to increase the alternative specific duty to As. 5 per pound. The yield of the increased tax on these yarns and thread is taken at Rs. 36 lakhs.

NEW EXCISE DUTY ON TYRES AND TUBES

"The second of my smaller proposals is to introduce a new excise duty of ten per cent *ad valerem* on pneumatic tyres and tubes. The manufacture of these tyres and tubes in India was set up a few years ago, and the domestic supply now fills a large proportion of the demand which formerly was met by imports on which a revenue duty of 25 per cent *ad valorem* is levied. The yield of this new duty, for the imposition of which a separate Bill will be introduced, is estimated at Rs. 33 lakhs.

"The new duties on matches and on artificial silk yarn and thread will take immediate effect, by virtue of a certificate under the Provisional Collection of Taxes Act.

Uncovered deficit To Be Met From Loans

"The total estimated yield of this new taxation is Rs. 6 61 lakhs, which brings the estimated revenue for 1941-42 to Rs. 113,00 lakhs and reduces the prospective deficit to Rs. 13,85 lakhs. This is still a formidable gap in relation to the scale of Indian finances, and I must confess that I shall be more sensitive to the criticism of that smaller and less vocal body who may feel that the contemporary contribution by taxation to the cost of the war is too little than of the doubtless large multitude who would say it is too great. It is not merely that the estimated gap is large, but the unforeseen contingencies of the year ahead are obviously far more likely to widen than to narrow it. On the other hand, it must be remembered that our expenditure estimates still contain a provision of Rs. 3 crores for the reduction and avoidance of debt. Again, there is a factor at present incalculable, which may emerge from the Indo-Burma trade negotiations now proceeding, since any modification of the existing free trade regime must result in some increase of revenue. In any case it is not the proportion of the next year's deficit to be met by taxation which is important, but the share of the whole additional cost of our war measures which is so provided. Judged by that criterion, I feel that the position is fully defensible. The uncovered revenue deficit will, of course, be met by borrowing which will be part of the larger programme the necessity of which I have explained at an earlier stage.

"Greater Sacrifices Await Us"

"I have little doubt that greater sacrifices await us but it is indisputable that the inherent soundness of India's financial position entitles her to face the future with courage and confidence. This is no time for complacency, but whatever may be in store in the weeks and months that lie ahead, there is reason for satisfaction in the way in which the financial and economic structure of India has withstood the strains and stresses of one and a half years of war, while enabling her to play a part of which she may be justly proud, in this mortal struggle for the ideals of enlightened humanity."

Finance Bill Introduced

After the presentation of the Budget, *Sir Jeremy Raisman*, introduced the Finance Bill embodying the new taxation proposals, except the one relating to rubber tyres and tubes. When he asked for leave to introduce a separate Bill to impose an excise duty on pneumatic rubber tyres and tubes, several members objected on the ground that the agenda for the day made no mention of this Bill. *Sir Jeremy Raisman* explained that if it had been included in the agenda it would have amounted to premature disclosure of a part of his new taxation proposals. The *President* referred to a precedent during the time of President Patel when a Bill was permitted to be introduced in similar circumstances. He ruled that the Finance Member was in order. *Sir Jeremy Raisman* thereupon was allowed to introduce the Bill. The House then rose till the 3rd. March.

Fraudulent Marks on Merchandise Bill

3rd. MARCH :—The Assembly, in a brief sitting to-day, disposed of three official Bills. It agreed to two amendments made by the Council of State in the Bill to amend the law relating to fraudulent marks on merchandise.

Regulation of Assam Rifles

Mr. *O. K. Caroe* next moved his Bill for the regulation of and maintenance of discipline in the Assam Rfles. He explained that the Assam Rifles was a force of which approximately three quarters was normally employed for purposes with which the provincial Government were not concerned ; and it was incongruous that such a force should continue to be governed by a provincial Act. It was, therefore, being constituted into a Central responsibility with the consent of the Assam Provincial Government. *Maulavi Abdur Rashid Chaudhury* attempted a number of amendments in the Bill designed principally to provide that men of the force should be dealt with under the penal provisions of the Bill for durkenness or similar offences in public places. Mr. *Chaudhury* alleged that riflemen had often proved themselves a source of nuisance to women vegetable and fruit sellers in bazars. Mr. *Caroe* explained that ordinary offences such as those which Mr. *Chaudhury* had in mind could be dealt with under the ordinary law. The amendment was thereupon withdrawn. Mr. *Chaudhury* also tried to restrict the meaning of "hostile tribe" to a tribe which was at war with Government. The tribes in Assam, he claimed, were docile. Mr. Caroe disputed Mr. Chaudhury's assertion and referred to a recent incident in which a certain head-hunting tribe in Assam collected 50 heads of men of another tribe. Thre had been also cases of tribesmen raiding places in the plains. It was, therefore, not desirable to circumscribe Government's powers of dealing with the tribes in the manner suggested either by Mr. *Chaudhury* or by Mr. *Aney*. He could however, say that all expeditions against tribesmen in Assam required the Government of India's sanction, so that no action was taken without the fullest consideration. The Bill was passed.

Madras Port Trust Bill

On the circulation motion on the Madras Port Trust Bill. Mr. *Esak Sait* pleaded for a seat, if necessary, by enlarging the membership, for the Moslem Chamber of Comerce of the city. *Sir Andrew Clow*, replying, said that the claim put forward by Mr. *Esak Sait* for the Muslim Chamber of Commerce was one for the select committee, which would be appointed, but he pointed out that the Skin and Hides Merchants Association to which a seat had been given was largely, though not exclusively, a Muslim body. As regards *Sir Frederick James'* point, *Sir Andrew* said that representation was not being given on a racial basis. What had to be recognized was that, unfortunately, commercial interests were not represented by one chamber but were divided into different bodies, some of which were predominantly European and tended to reflect the attitude of European commerce, while others were exclusively Indian. As he had said, an attempt was being made to give representation based on direct interest. The Royal Commission's recommendation, said *Sir Andrew Clow*, was that labour should have a voice in the trusts. If Mr. *Joshi* wanted that the nominee of labour should be selected in consultation with trade unions, that was a point for the select committee to consider. As regards Mr. *Aney's* point about the exclusion of the Piecegoods Merchants Association, his view was that these particular trades, especially retail trades, were, normally, better excluded. Leading chambers of commerce were able effectively to represent their interests. An exception had been made in the case of the Skin and Hide Merchants Association, because of exceptional circumstances. The House agreed to the circulation of the Bill and adjourned.

General Discussion of Budget

4th MARCH :—The absence of the Congress Party from the Assembly was keenly felt by more than one member to-day during the general discussion on the Budget. *Mr. Chapman-Mortimer* expressed sympathy with the tax-payer, but emphasised that this was the right time for additional taxation for the prosecution of the war. At the moment, he said, capitalists were making substantial profits. At the end of the war they might not make any profits at all, or might incur very serious losses. With regard to the suggestion that the deficit should be met by loans, Mr. Chapman-Mortimer said that that course would merely "postpone the evil days". It would help the rich now and make the mass of the poor pay the interest on the loans ultimately. "It has been suggested by Sir *Halim Gaznavi*", said Mr. Mortimer, "that the excess profits tax at the present level is a crushing tax on new industries. I am afraid, he has over-looked that special concessions have been provided for new industries in the Excess Profits Tax Act, and they are allowed a return of more than 12 per cent before their revenue is subject to excess profits tax. I, for one, should be very glad if I can get 12 per cent for every one hundred rupees." There was ample scope, in spite of the Excess Profits Tax for capitalist enterprise, he declared,

Sardar Sant Singh emphasised that if the war must be financed by the people of India, then the people of India must have a voice in the control of war expenditure. This was the grievance which was responsible for the political deadlock in India. In fact, said the speaker, with the growth of military expenditure there was growth of military rule over India. At present, it was the military rule which was crushing the political life of the country. They wanted an assurance from the Finance Member that the money raised by the Government would not be

Supply Council at Delhi, illustrate in striking manner the position of India in the present war. No one would wish to see repeated the period of hectically inflated prices which ruled towards the end of the last war, but we can rely upon steadily increasing industrial effort during the present one, with consequences which seem likely permanently to effect India's position among the industrial nations of the world. The expansion in the demand for the products of Indian industry and the organized efforts which Government are making to increase the supply of trained workers must create an enhanced productive power which will be available in the period after the war, to improve the standard of life in India and to help to lessen the dependence of its growing population upon agriculture and secondary employment.

FINANCIAL YEAR 1939-40

4. I will now recapitulate briefly the results of the financial year 1939-40. As I explained in the course of my statement last November, the surplus of that year which in our revised estimates we had taken at Rs. 91 lakhs, actually increased to Rs. 7,77 lakhs and the amount transferred to the Revenue Reserve Fund was thus augmented by as much as Rs. 6,86 lakhs. This was the result of an improvement of Rs. 6,81 lakhs in revenue and a reduction of Rs. 5 lakhs in expenditure.

On the revenue side Customs receipts, after the short drop that had occurred at the outbreak of the war, not only recovered to their previous level but during the part closing months of the last financial year, were abnormally high. This was in large measure due to the laying in of stocks, the effect of which is seen in corresponding decreases in the receipts of the following year, so that for a fair comparison the estimates and returns of both years should be considered together. In the same way the very large receipts from the abnormal Salt clearances of last winter were off-set by a corresponding reduction in receipts in the current year : the actual receipts last year exceeded our revised estimate by Rs. 1.86 lakhs while those for the current year are likely to be half a crore below the budget estimate based on the normal annual consumption.

The profits from small coin increased by a further Rs. 37 lakhs. Railway earnings also recorded a further improvement so that the surplus payable to general revenues, though still short of the full contribution, increased by Rs. 72 lakhs.

In addition there were increases of Rs. 21 lakhs under Corporation Tax and Rs. 1,07 lakhs under Income-Tax over our revised estimates, which themselves allowed for an appreciable rise over the new high level established by the actuals for the previous years. To some extent this increase may be taken to reflect the additional revenue due to the provisions of the Income-Tax Amendment Act, the yield from which was bound to be a matter of conjecture.

This increase in Income-Tax raised the divisible pool of the total taxes on income other than Corporation Tax from Rs. 13,76 lakhs to Rs. 14,66 lakhs. While we had expected that Rs. 2,38 lakhs would be payable to the Provinces from 1939-40 the amount turned out to be Rs. 2,83 lakhs. In addition to this the arrears due on account of 1938-39 were finally certified as Rs. 39 lakhs instead of Rs. 41 lakhs as provisionally reported. As the sum distributed to the Provinces in March 1940 was Rs. 2,79 lakhs, there is a balance of Rs. 43 lakhs to be paid to them along with their share for the current year.

FINANCIAL YEAR 1940-41

5. I come now to the current year 1940-41. Our revised estimates for revenue, excluding the additional Rs. 6,86 lakhs available in the Revenue Reserve Fund show a net improvement of Rs. 4,21 lakhs compared with the Budget estimates. Against this, however, our revised estimates for expenditure show a net increase of no less than Rs. 19,54 lakhs, of which Rs. 18½ crores are on account of the Defence Services and Rs. 1,04 lakhs are for expenditure borne by the Civil Estimates, mainly on account of schemes connected with the war. Thus while the budget estimates provided for a nominal surplus of Rs. 5 lakhs and last November I put the estimated deficit, before taking into account the revenue from the fresh taxation then imposed, at about Rs. 13 crores, we now estimate that the deficit on the current year will be Rs 8,42 lakhs. The improvement is due to the additional revenue that has since accrued, including the further payment of Rs. 2,81 lakhs from the Railways as a refund of arrears of contribution, which has already been explained to the House in the speech of the Railway Member.

EFFECTS OF WAR ON REVENUE

6. War time conditions are naturally reflected in our reduced receipts from Customs. Against actuals of Rs. 45,88 lakhs for 1939-40, we had estimated for 1940-41 a total of Rs. 39,16 lakhs, while we now estimate this year's receipts at only Rs. 37,75 lakhs. Our receipts under this head are of course affected not only by the cessation of trade with enemy countries but also by the interruption and deflection of shipping. In addition we have had to conserve our resources by restricting imports of many commodities in order that the foreign exchange so saved may be available for the more urgent requirements of the war. Under Excise there is a drop of Rs. 2,10 lakhs from Sugar. As the House is aware, the sugar industry in the main producing areas of the United Provinces and Bihar has during the present year been beset with difficulties. The maintenance in the previous season of artificially high prices for cane together with over-production led during the summer months to a situation in which large stocks were held up in the factories. The industry accordingly found itself in difficulties in the matter of finance and revenue was slow to come in. As a remedy for this it was urged upon us that there should be either a reduction in the duty or that collection of a portion of it should be postponed. After negotiations with two Provincial Governments a scheme was finally adopted under which the Government of India undertook to lend to the Provincial Governments funds sufficient to enable them to advance to the industry a sum equal to Re. 1 per maund on existing stocks, to be used in part payment of duty. This, combined with some lowering of prices, helped to alleviate the position, though the industry in those two provinces continues, for resons unconnected with the Central Excise, to be faced with problems of great difficulty. In consequence we do not now expect that the collections of sugar excise duty in the current year will exceed Rs. 3,15 lakhs as compared with our budget estimate of Rs. 5,25 lakhs.

IMPROVED RAILWAY EARNINGS

7. I have already mentionel that our revenue from Salt in the current year is expected to be Rs. 50 lakhs less than the budget estimate. Railway earnings have, however, come to our assistance and the sum they are now expected to pay to Central Revenues under the Railway convention is Rs. 7,15 lakhs, which with the additional refund of Rs. 2,81 lakhs is Rs. 4,65 lakhs more than was provided in the budget estimates. The sum of Rs. 7,15 lakhs is made up of the full contribution of Rs. 4,63 lakhs, which is 1 per cent of the capital at charge less the loss on strategic railways, Rs. 30 lakhs as arrears of contribution from the previous year, and a further Rs. 2,22 lakhs as one-third of the excess over the first Rs. 3 crores of the remainder which would normally be transferred to the Railway Reserve Fund. Other increases are Rs. 92 lakhs under Currency and Mint mainly from the larger circulation of small coin and Rs. 65 lakhs in the surplus of the Posts and Telegraphs Department; while Taxes on Income, including Excess Profits Tax and the Central surcharge imposed during the year show a rise of Rs. 3,30 lakhs, a part of which goes to increase the share of the Provinces from the budgetted sum of Rs. 3,00 lakhs to Rs 3,73 lakhs.

E. P. T. RECEIPTS

As regards Excess Profits Tax the extent of the preliminary work proved even greater than had been expected with the result that returns were not due from assessees before the end of November. The subsequent stages of the assessment proceedings bristle with practical difficulties owing to the complexity of the computations. And to the difficulties ordinarily associated with E. P. T. there is the added difficulty of a separate depreciation computation owing to the change over in the Incometax law to the written down value basis for depreciation. For these reasons the progress of E. P. T. assessment work has been, and is, very slow and therefore the actual receipts in the current financial year are not expected to exceed Rs. 2 crores. A substantial portion of the original estimated receipts for 1940-41 will accordingly go to swell the collections of 1941-42. This sum may be taken as of the order of Rs. 1 crore.

PROGRESS OF WAR EFFORT

8. Defence Services.—Turning to the expenditure side of the current year, I will now deal with the aspect which overshadows all others, namely, the Defence Services. In my speech introducing the Supplementary Finance Bill last November I gave the House an indication of the extent to which our budget estimate of

defence expenditure for 1940-41 was likely to be upset as a result of the momentous developments in the war situation during the early months of that year. I described in some detail the various activities in which India was engaging to meet the direct and indirect threats to her security arising out of the changed conditions. At that time it was estimated that India's share of the financial commitments involved in those activities would amount eventually to roughly Rs. 33 crores on account of initial outlay and Rs. 16 crores per annum on account of recurring charges, while the budget estimate of Rs. 53½ crores for defence expenditure during 1940-41 would be exceeded by at least Rs. 14½ crores. The three months that have passed since then have been a period of steady and rapid progress in the development of India's war effort and I propose at this stage to give the House some particulars of this progress and the achievements already secured or in prospect.

In the interests of security it is not possible for me to bring the figures in every case up to date but what I am going to say will, I hope, show clearly enough that the immensely complicated business of producing efficient modern forces is going forward with speed and energy. In some directions we are, it is true, still held back by the difficulty in obtaining materials which we cannot as yet produce in India and also by the shortage of skilled personnel of various categories. Subject however, to these limitations, the resources of India are being intensively utilised and developed.

HALF A MILLION UNDER ARMS

9. The total strength of our armed forces is now well over half a milion men of all arms and further expansion is proceeding. Provision has been made for the raising of new armoured and mechanised cavalry regiments, new Indian field artillery regiments, regular infantry battalions, engineer units, more M. T. Sections and all the highly trained and specialised ancillary troops required for modern warfare. The Fighting Vehicles School has continued to expand; a new Cadet Wing has been opened at the Artillery School and an anti-aircraft training centre has been established which is designed to train several hundred students a month. The R. I. A. S. C. Officers Technical School has been further expanded and its output is now seven times what it was at the outbreak of war, Mechanical transport training establishments have still further increased and apart from mechanised cavalry, artillery and infantry who train their own men, the output of trained drivers has grown to 40 times what it was in August 1939. Two new Signal Training Centres have been opened and the training establishments of Sapper and Miner Units have more than doubled since November last.

TRAINING OF THE ARMY

10. It is impossible to exaggerate the importance of adequate training establishments in an expansion of the scale of that which we are now carrying out. Troops may be gallant and well equipped but they are not likely to succeed in modern war unless their standard of training is very high indeed. The training of the Indian Army has, it is admitted on all sides, been shown to be excellent. This has been proved beyond question by the part which they have played in the recent great victories, where they overcame a well armed and numerically far stronger enemy at surprisingly small cost to themselves. I have dwelt at some length upon this aspect of our war efforts as it is upon this that the pace of our expansion depends. We have no intention of sacrificing efficiency for mere numbers but are determined to follow as closely as possible the high standards which have been set and which have so dramatically and decisively proved their value in the past few weeks.

11. Many of the new units we have raised are now completing their training and a number have already taken up active roles. When the expansion of the army in India began, owing to difficulties in obtaining equipment, the number of armoured units and artillery regiments included was less than we would have desired. Improvements in the supply situation, however, both in India and the United Kingdom, have now made it possible to remedy this deficiency and our plans include the transformation into armoured and light-armoured regiments of the whole of the existing cavalry and the raising of additional regiments of this kind. With regard to artillery, increasing assistance from His Majesty's Government, both in personnel and equipment, has made it possible to ensure that we do not fall short in this component.

12. With regard to equipment generally His Majesty's Government have recently agreed to a standing arrangement under which India will receive a subs-

tantial fixed proportion of the output of the United Kingdom. As a result of this arrangement, steady supplies of all kinds of equipment unobtainable in India such as guns, machine tools, optical instruments, wireless and other signalling equipment and anti-gas equipment are now forthcoming and will enable us to push forward with the modernisation of our normal defence garrison, and with the equipment of the forces now being raised on a scale adapted to the requirements of moderrn war.

GROWTH OF NAVY AND AIR FORCE

13. The growth of the Royal Indian Navy which I summarised last November, has continued unchecked ; the programme of ship-building in India has been further expanded and the recruiting and training of officers and men to man the new construction is proceeding apace. All instructional establishments have been greatly increased in capacity ; a new Signal School is being built and a start has been made with a large new Gunnery School. Other new Naval establishments are in process of development. Some idea of the increase in work being carried out in the Government Dockyard may be gathered from the figures of workmen of all classes and trades employed there. Before the war, the figure was 1,168 ; it has now risen to nearly 5,000. In addition to meeting our own requirements, a great deal of work has been carried out on behalf of His Majesty's Government in connection with the arming and protection of both British and Indian merchant shipping, and also in the provision of repair facilities to ships of the Royal Navy.

14. As regards the Air Force the difficultiesarising from deficiencies of equipment and experienced technical personnel which I mentioned on the last occasion as holding up the expansion of this Arm have recently been considerably lessened. A number of modern aircraft and connected equipment are in sight from American sources and further supplies are expected which will go a considerable way towards completing and modernising the equipment of the squadrons now in India, as well as setting free machines for the training of new squadrons. The arrangements for training personnel have also been considerably improved. Close liaison between the civil and air force training schemes has been established and a proposed amalgamation and reorganization of all available facilities will provide Air Force elementary flying training schools formed around existing flying clubs and an expanded service flying training school. All these institutions will be operating to full capacity in the near future. A start has been made with the formation of the reserve to which I alluded and the training both of officers and airmen is being pushed forward as rapidly as the capacity of the schools permit and as fast as instructional and maintenance personnel and equipment become available. The scheme for establishing aeroplane manufacture in India has reached a new stage and there is now little doubt that the year 1941 will witness the appearance of the first aeroplanes to be produced in India. This achievement, memorable in itself, should prove of great value in speeding up the expansion of India's air force—a development to which we attach supreme importance.

SUPPLIES POSITION

15. The position in regard to the vital matter of supplies has, I am glad to say, substantially improved since I last addressed the House. The Government Ordnance and Clothing factories have been working at the highest pressure for some time past and an indication of what this means can be gathered from the fact that whereas before the war the avarage number of workmen employed in those factories was under 17.000, the number has now risen to over 45,000 and the curve of production is still rising. Steps have recently been taken to supplement the output of these factories by taking over railway and private workshops and utilising their resources for the production of munitions of war. The Roger Mission which has been investigating the possibilities of expediting India's output of war supplies has now submitted its reports to His Majesty's Government who are giving them their urgent consideration. We hope that the result will be that India will before long be able substantially to increase her output of munitions.

With a view to stimulating private enterprise and co-ordinating the resources of the country to the fullest extent possible a thorough reorganisation of the Supply Department has been carried out during the last few months and this is already resulting in an increasingly close liaison and co-operation between that Department, other Departments of Government and Indian industry.

16. Mention may also be made here of another important development which is likely to lead to a great improvement in the supply field. Until recently the work of the Supply Department in so far as it related to compliance with overseas

demands was seriously hampered by the fact that the placing of orders in this country to meet such demands was dependent on the receipt of firm indents. Owing to the enormous fluctuations in the demands so placed on the Supply Department and the immediate urgency attaching to most of them it was found impossible to ensure prompt compliance or to make forward arrangements in such a manner as to prevent dislocation of the productive activities of the country and ensure that supplies were obtained at reasonable prices. These difficulties were presented to His Majesty's Government who have now agreed to a forward programme of supply covering the estimated requirements over a period of about two years ahead. The Department of Supply is thus able to enter into forward commitments within the limits of this programme and so maintain an even flow of production.

PURCHASES IN AMERICA

17. A further improvement in the supply position has been rendered possible by the receipt of authority from His Majesty's Government to purchase vehicles, machine tools and other essential war requirements in the United States and Canada, to the extent necessary to meet our needs for a considerable period ahead. The restrictions previously placed on such purchases owing to the difficulties regarding dollar exchange had been seriously hampering the process of modernising our Army in India and equipping the newly raised units. An officer has been placed on special duty in America with the object of discovering and effecting purchases of such supplies as are available to India from this source.

EASTERN GROUP SUPPLY COUNCIL

Last, but certainly not least in this tale of progress, the deliberations of the Eastern Group Conference will shortly bear fruit in the shape of the institution of an Eastern Group Supply Council to be located in India which will in due course co-ordinate the requirements of various Empire countries and forces operating east of Suez and will ensure that the resources of the participating countries are utilised to the fullest advantage for the successful prosecution of the war.

18. These tremendous developments in the supply field must necessarily give a great stimulus to Indian industries. One of the most important results has been the investigation of the possibilities of establishing new industries in India for the production of stores that have hitherto been imported. The list of stores required both in India and to meet overseas demands is constantly under review and items formerly placed in the category of imported stores are continually being transferred to the indigenous category, a result of the discovery either of methods of producing them in India or of suitable domestic substitutes. As typical examples of this I may mention web equipment, lubricating oil, bichromates, and acetic acid, which formerly imported, are now being produced in India, while the substitution of cotton canvas for flax canvas, fish oil for codliver oil and various Indian vatieties of drugs for those previously imported has enabled us to transfer their source of supply from abroad to India. This process has been particularly marked in the case of medical stores and whereas prior to September 1939, 77 per cent of the items included in the priced vocabulary of medical stores were imported, the corresponding percentage after 18 months of war is only 46.

From this brief review, it will, I think, be realised that India has in addition to providing for her own local defence been able to make a noteworthy contribution to the success of the common cause in the provision both of highly trained troops and high grade materials. That contribution is increasing rapidly in quantity and is not diminishing in quality.

COST OF NEW DEFENCE MEASURES

19. I must now revert to the purely financial aspect of this remarkable picture of India's war activities. As a result of the further measures which I have just described coupled with the general improvement in the supply position, the estimates of extra cost that were given to the House last November, are out of date. Our latest assessment of the cost of all measures to which we are now committed and which were not envisaged at the time of preparing the defence budget for 1940-41, indicates that they will ultimately involve initial outlay of approximately Rs. 52 crores and Rs. 19 crores additional recurring expenditure per annum. The initial outlay and full recurring cost will not of course all come forward in the first year but it is estimated that during 1940-41 the increase in India's defence expenditure on account of these measures will amount to roughly Rs. 17¾ crores.

REVISED DEFENCE ESTIMATE

20. I may perhaps remind the House here that the allocation of war expenditure between India and His Majesty's Government is still governed by the settlement arrived at between the two Governments which was fully explained in my budget speech of a year ago. In accordance with the principles underlying this settlement any forces now being raised that India may agree to send for service overseas cease to be an Indian liability on leaving India and the whole initial cost of raising, training, and equipping such forces as well as the subsequent recurring charges are borne by His Majesty's Government. The details of the revised estimate of defence expenditure for 1940-41 amounting to Rs. 72,02 lakhs are as follows :—

	(Rs. in lakhs)
(1) Basic normal budget	36,77
(2) Effect of rise in prices on (1)	2,53
(3) India's war measures	24,31
(4) Non-effective charges	8,41
	72,02

The increase of Rs. 53 lakhs in item (2) over the corresponding budget figure is mainly due to the increase of emoluments granted during 1940-41 to British and Indian troops as a war concession. In so far as these increases would have raised the cost of India's normal garrison the extra cost is included under this head. The increase of Rs. 17¾ crores in item (3) has already been explained. Out of the total provision of Rs. 24,34 crores for India's war measures approximately Rs. 15 crores represents the initial cost of such measures : the balance consists of recurring expenditure. The revised estimate for non-effective charges item (4)—has for the present been fixed at the normal budget level of 1939-40 but discussions are in progress with His Majesty's Government with a view to reaching a settlement that will regulate the allocation of these charges as has already been done for effective charges. The effect of the war on these charges obviously cannot be foreseen though happily there has so far been no appreciable increase owing to the absence of heavy casualties. I should here point out that the increase of Rs. 24,31 crores shown against item (3) over our normal defence expenditure by no means reflects the full magnitude of India's war effort since it excludes the cost of supplies and services rendered by India to His Majesty's Government which is substantially greater than this amount.

I should also mention here that His Majesty's Government besides paying in full for all such supplies and services are providing free of charge much of the equipment needed for the modernisation of the Army in India and for the initial equipment of units now being raised in pursuance of our expansion scheme.

INCREASE IN CIVIL EXPENDITURE

21. The principal items mainly responsible for the increase in Civil expenditure, such as the schemes for the training of the Air Force Reserve and that for war technicians, were explained in some detail in my Statement last November and I will not repeat the account which I then gave to the House. Though the additional civil expenditure then accounted for was approximately Rs. 2,30 lakhs, the actual net increase in civil expenditure works out at only Rs. 1,04 lakhs. In the first place, there is a reduction of Rs. 71 lakhs in Interest charges. This is mainly due to smaller payments on account of Post Office Cash Certificates and Savings Bank Deposits and to lower interest rates on our short-term debt, the volume of which has also been reduced in recent months by the success of the Indian Defence Loans. Again, on account of a change of accounting procedure, which also brings about a corresponding reduction on the revenue side, the amount of Rs. 67 lakhs received from Burma as her share of pensionary charges is now to be taken in reduction of expenditure instead of as a revenue receipt under Payments by Burma.

22. Thus our Revised Civil Estimates for the current year are accepted to amount to Rs. 40,11 lakhs as compared with the Budget Estimate of Rs. 39,07 lakhs. With the net Defence Expenditure placed at Rs. 72,02 lakhs our total expenditure is estimated at Rs. 112,13 lakhs as against our total revenue of Rs. 103,71 lakhs. We are therefore left with a deficit of Rs. 8,42 lakhs in the current year. As, however, the amount provided for the reduction or avoidance of debt was Rs. 3 crores, the net addition to our indebtedness is only of the order of 5½ crores.

Financial Year 1941-42

23. I now come to the financial year, 1941-42. Our total revenue estimates amount to Rs. 106,39 lakhs as compared to Rs. 103,71 lakhs in the revised estimates of this year. Though there is no further balance available in the Revenue Reserve Fund, which provided Rs. 7,77 lakhs in the current year, this is more than made up by the first full year's receipts from Excess Profits Tax and the Central Surcharge imposed last November. We have to allow for a further drop of 3 crores under Customs, but larger receipts are anticipated from Central Excise Duties and Salt. Also the contributions to be paid to General Revenues by the Posts and Telegraphs Department and Railways are estimated at Rs. 38 lakhs and Rs. 22 lakhs respectively higher than their increased contributions in the current year.

Revenue

24. Against our current year's estimate of the yield from Customs duties of Rs. 37,75 lakhs, we have taken for 1941-42 the still lower figure of Rs. 34,75 lakhs. War time factors already described in connection with the current year's receipts must be expected to continue to affect our revenue from Customs adversely, and under present conditions no one can foresee when the process will end, or the extent to which these factors may operate in the coming year. I can only say that our estimates are based on the assumption that present tendencies will continue and that there will be no violent change.

Income-Tax Receipts and the Provinces

25. Our total estimates for Central Excise Duties show an increase of Rs. 1,75 lakhs almost entirely on account of sugar. We have raised our next year's estimate of the total yield from ordinary Corporation Tax and Income-tax by approximately half a crore to Rs. 21½ crores taking account of the fact that the assessments will be based on incomes derived from a full year of war profits. At the same time the surcharge imposed for Central purposes is expected to produce Rs. 5,68 lakhs. In the light of general trading conditions during the current year the yield from Excess Profits Tax for the year 1941-42 is estimated at Rs. 7½ crores, which with the carry-over of Rs. 1 crore from the current year gives a total estimate of Rs. 8½ crores. Though Excess Profits Tax receipts are included in the total Taxes on Income, the share payable by Companies, which is roughly estimated at five-sixths, falls under Corporation Tax and thus goes in full to Central Revenue. The Excess Profits Tax on incomes other than those of Companies is expected to yield Rs, 1,42 lakhs and the divisible pool of Income-tax to increase on account of this from Rs. 16,47 lakhs to Rs. 17,93 lakhs. The share of the Provinces is thus expected to reach the figure of Rs. 4,46 lakhs as compared with Rs. 3,73 lakhs this year.

Profits from Coinage

26. There is also an increase of Rs. 60 lakhs under Salt as compared with the Revised. With the utilisation of the large stocks carried over from last year, we count on the usual demand for fresh supplies next year and in consequence take our estimate of Salt revenue at the average figure of Rs. 8,30 lakhs. We are allowing for a decrease of Rs. 1,21 lakhs in Mint receipts as compared with our revised estimates for 1940-41. We have now decided that from next year an average figure of Rs. 46 lakhs from the profits from the circulation of small coin is to be taken to Revenue and any balance over this figure credited to a Suspense Account which will be available to even out the receipts over a series of years. For in years when there is a large demand for small coin the profits are abnormally high, while in others when there is a net return from circulation there is a loss to Government. The new procedure will tend to keep the revenue receipts from this source stable from year to year and will mitigate instead of aggravating the difficulties experienced in years of depression on this account. Under Currency however there is an increase of Rs. 1,25 lakhs. We are taking the Government's share of the Reserve Bank's profits, Rs. 1,17 lakhs higher on account of the higher interest which will be earned on the rupee securities held by the Bank in place of their sterling balances, and the receipts from the Currency Note Press are expected to improve by Rs. 8 lakhs. Included under Other Sources of Revenue are Rs. 68 lakhs on account of War Risk Insurance premia, the payment of which into the Fund created for this purpose is provided under expenditure.

Revenue from Posts and Telegraphs

27. Posts and Telegraphs.—For next year the revenue of the Posts and Telegraphs Department is expected to be Rs. 13,49 lakhs and expenditure Rs. 12,09

lakhs. The larger revenue is almost wholly due to the effect of the increases in rates. The expenditure reflects the normal growth of pay and pensionary charges in an expanding service, with some additions to maintenance charges, and to the contribution to the Renewals Reserve Fund due to the rise in the prices of stores and in the value of the assets.

In my last Budget Speech I reminded Hon'ble Members that under the system of commercialisation of accounts of the Posts and Telegraphs Department the surplus of the Department forms a reserve for it on which interest has to be paid by General Revenues. I also indicated that the procedure by which the general tax-payer obtains immediate relief by incurring a future liability could not be extended indefinitely. The recent increase in rates being a measure of taxation the Posts and Telegraphs Department cannot claim the extra revenue on this account as part of its ordinary surplus. The estimated extra revenue due to this factor, namely, Rs. 33 lakhs in 1940-41 and Rs. 1,00 lakhs in 1941-42, will therefore be transferred outright to general revenues. Further the recent surpluses of the Department are due largely to war conditions, and Government traffic has contributed substantially to them. It has been decided that on the accumulated surplus beyond Rs. 1,00 lakhs the Department will not be credited with any interest. For the present this change in the former procedure is considered a sufficient adjustment to war circumstances.

PURCHASE OF TELEPHONE COMPANIES

The licences of the Bengal, Bomay and Madras Telephone Companies expire in 1943. It has been decided not to renew the licences and negotiations are in progress to acquire by purchase the shares of the companies in order that the change-over may be effected smoothly. A "Government Telephone Board" has been formed to run the business in the interim period. The new arrangement is expected to start functioning about the beginning of the next financial year. An addition of Rs. 475 lakhs to the Telephone Development Fund will be necessary to finance the "Government Telephone Board." A proposal for a supplementary grant for this purpose will be brought forward later in this session.

INCREASE IN DEFENCE ESTIMATES

28. Defence Services—The Defence Budget for 1941-42 amounts to Rs. 84,13 lakhs made up as follows:—

	Rupees in lakhs
(1) Basic normal budget	36,77
(2) Effect of rise in prices on (1)	3,55
(3) India's war measures	35,40
(4) Non-effective charges	8,41
	84,13

The increase over the revised indicated at item (2) is due to the fact that the the increases in emoluments granted as a war concession to British and Indian troops took effect from various dates in 1940-41 whereas they will be in force throughout 1941-42.

The growth of expenditure on India's war measures has already been explained at length. The effect of this growth on the defence budget for 1941-42 is shown at item (3) the increase over the revised being Rs. 11,09 lakhs. Approximately half the total amount of Rs. 35.40 lakhs provided for India's war measures represents the initial cost of these measures, the balance consisting of recurring charges. I should like here to impress upon the House the fact that in these estimates of Defence Expenditure only such specific schemes and measures as are definitely under way or in sight have been provided for. Our Defence plans have to be adapted from time to time to meet the ever changing war situation, which means that additional projects are constantly being undertaken, and it is clearly impossible to make any forecast of the cost of such unforeseeable items. The provision for non-effective charges has been retained at the normal figure for 1939-40 for the reasons already given. Here too, as I have remarked in connection with the revised estimates, the figures exclude the value of supplies and services rendered by India to H. M.'s Government. The charges borne by that Government on this account during 1941-42 are expected to be more than double the amount of India's war expenditure.

India? Otherwise why was the Defence of India Act being used against every form of activity? The Punjab Government, he said, had issued a communique under that Act banning all processions. Did that not amount to curbing all political activity in the Province? Sardar Sant Singh also commented on the speech recently made by Sir Douglas Young in Lyallpur, and proceeded to allege that Sir Douglas on December 9 issued an order that Indian Judges should no longer try cases under the Defence of India Act. Indian Judges, both Hindu and Muslim, resisted this order with all their might and after a good deal of correspondence, the matter was going upto His Majesty the King. Sardar Sant Singh said that the Leader of the House, if he liked, could go down to Lyallpur and make enquiries to satisfy himself of the truth of his statements. The speaker added that the present relations between Sir Douglas Young and Indian Judges were so bad that there was a complete boycott. He asserted that the Defence of India Act was being used to suppress legitimate religious activities also; and the Sikhs had taken the strongest possible exception to this through the Shiromani Gurdwara Committee. He demanded the appointment of a Committee to enquire into the working of the Defence of India Act. He was so sure of his ground that he was prepared to accept the verdict of a Committee, composed of a majority of officials and presided over by an official.

Dr. *R. D. Dalal* referred to the heavy expenditure on detenus and said that the expenditure could be saved by ending the political deadlock. He was suggesting methods of solving the deadlock, when the Assembly adjourned till March 14.

14th. MARCH :—In the Assembly to-day, the second day of the general discussion on the Budget, Mr. *Navalrai* said that the doubling of the duty on matches would operate harshly on the cottage industry. The Government, in fact, recognised this when in 1934 they allowed a rebate to the cottage industry on the original rate of excise duty. He suggested that as the excise duty was being doubled, the rate of rebate should also be doubled. He urged the Central Government to use their powers of supervision to see that the Provincial Governments enforced the Defence of India Rules in the proper spirit.

Mr. *Mahomed Azhar Ali* advocated the flotation of internal loans to finance war expenditure and said that India was capable of giving lavishly. At the same time he asked highly paid officials to forego a great part of their emoluments. Retrenchment and economy, he said, should be the two principal governing policies at a time like the present. He dwelt at length on the treaty relations of His Majesty's Government with Oudh and declared that the British Government had no right to throw the burden of further taxation on the people of Oudh. The Viceroy, he asserted, was incompetent to legislate for Oudh or impose taxation on that territory. "The fact," he said, "is that I represent the Province of Oudh".

Mr. *Gwilt* visualised a possible unfavourable trade balance after the present war was over and suggested one remedy, namely, a service of highly trained Trade Commissioners. India in the past, Mr. Gwilt went on, had appointed Trade Commissioners at Hamburg, Milan, New York, Alexandria, and Mombasa and was appointing them in Australia and South America. But the mere appointment of Trade Commissioners would not be sufficient. He suggested that India should set a standard of Trade Commissioners not frequently to be found, those with a thorough grounding in the interpretation of economic data and a capacity to understand businessmen, their methods and the problems which faced them. They should also be students who had adequate training in economics, a knowledge of one European language other than English, and Accountancy. He asked what machinery existed for co-ordinating the work of Trade Commissioners already in existence.

Mr. *Nauman*, raising the question of Muslim grievances in the matter of representation in the Services, strongly urged that not only should the 25 per cent reservation be maintained as regards personnel, but care should be taken to see that the percentage was maintained as regards the emoluments given to them. He complained that in the matter of promotion. Muslims had not received a fair deal and he wanted to know what was the reason for the small number of Mussalmans in the top posts. Was it that inefficient Muslims were recruited, or was it that there was some defect in the administration which stood in the way of Muslims? After asserting that the political deadlock in the country was not the responsibility of the Muslim League, Mr. Nauman went on to declare that no sacrifice had been made by the I. C. S. which was the steel frame. They should have imposed a cut on their salaries.

Maulana Zafar Ali said that the deadlock in the country was a greater calamity than the war in Europe. To a certain extent, it was correct to accuse the British Government of having created the deadlock, but the chief share of the blame attached to us. The story of our differences was a painful one, he went on. It reminded him of the story of two brothers, who had been left a magnificent mansion to divide between themselves. The elder brother, who had the characteristic idiosyncracies of Mahatma Gandhi, said to the younger, who was somewhat like Mr. Jinnah (Laughter), "From the floor to the top of the house is mine, and from the top of the house to the highest heaven is yours." (More Laughter.) The scheme of Pakistan, he proceeded, was a plain and simple one. It is the only remedy for India's troubles. When the Muslims saw what was happening in Orissa. United Provinces, Bihar and other Provinces, in which the Congress had the upper hand, they came to the conclusion that there was no hope for them so long as there was an irresponsible Centre and under that Provinces in which the interests of minorities went unprotected.

15th. MARCH :—*Maulana Zafarali*, resuming his speech to-day, gave a lengthy exposition of the ideas underlying Pakistan and said that what Muslims wanted was a region in which they could develop spiritually, mentally and morally, unhampered by laws which were fundamentally opposed to Islamic conceptions. The Sharda Act and the law of limitation were, he said, two examples of un-Islamic laws. Under the latter law, a mosque which was in a non-Muslim's possession for twelve years became the property of the non-Muslim. Shahidganj, he said, was dismantled under the protection of British bayonets, but under God's law of compensation a thousand churches, he read the other day, had been destroyed by those "scientific savages". the Nazis. The British, he hoped, would now appreciate the state of mind of the Muslims when their mosques were pulled down. Muslims, nevertheless, did not want to embarrass the British Government in their present calamity and they were, therefore, prepared to postpone the realisation of their object of Pakistan till the war was over. Referring to the Finance Bill, he said that if the Congress were in the House, Hindus and Muslims would have joined hands and made an effective demonstration against the Bill.

Sir *H. P. Mody* in a racy and vigorous speech lasting about half an hour, covered a great number of financial and political questions. He said that the Finance Member's transaction relating to the repatriation of the sterling debt deserved to be commended (cheers), but he asked for information whether this was the right time for repatriating the debt on such a heavy scale and whether the transaction could not have been done earlier with greater advantage to the country. ("Hear, hear"). Sir Homi went on to express the opinion that direct taxation could not go much further ; the country had had a great deal more of direct taxation than indirect during the last few years, and that process could not go on endlessly. He accused the Government and many in the Legislature also of lack of "clear-cut courage" to face the political issues bound up with the question of tapping those vast fields of indirect taxation at present left untapped. He commented on the "unhappy spectacle" of most of the moneys raised in the provinces and in the Centre being devoted to objects which did not promote the moral and material strength of the country. Whatever the necessity for military or civil expenditure, only an inadequate share of the revenues was being devoted to nation-building activities. While taxation increased, the moral and material position of the country did not improve *pari passu.* Referring to the duty on artificial silk yarn, he said there were thousands of power and handlooms in this country which would be affected by the increase without earning a corresponding benefit. If the duty was merely for revenue purposes, then let the Finance Member halve the increase, put one anna on yarn and an additional anna on imports of artificial silk fabrics. It would yield the same return and an industry which was widespread in the country would be protected. Sir Homi said he did not cavil at the increase in the excess profits tax, but he wanted the Finance Member to take steps to see that in no case were profits taxed which did not arise out of the war, whether directly or indirectly. He felt that in spite of many safeguards introduced in the E. P. T. Act many loops-holes had been left and he wanted instructions to be issued that in no case in which a concern's profits arose from causes unconnected with the war would an attempt be made to tax those profits simply because they happened to be in excess of those of the standard period. Sir Homi Mody said that if the Finance Member was going to lay his hands on profits not arising from the war it was an immoral taxation. He quite realised the difficulty of distinguishing the two sets of profits, but it was feasible to establish the distinction and so long as the principle was recognised that it was war profits which were to be taxed, the Central Board of Revenue had resources to find out what were war profits and what were not. As regards the yield from the tax, he had once offered to underwrite the whole of it for Rs. 3 crores ; but that was not accepted. He was now prepared to underwrite it for six crores and even nine crores (Laughter). As regards the matches duty he said that if it had been fixed at twelve annas, then boxes containing forty stick,—which comprised the bulk of those sold commonly,—could be sold at two for three quarters of anna. But if the Finance Member insisted on the duty, of full one rupee, he should arrange, in consultation with the trade, that different units might be evolved so that the consumer who bought one or two boxes at a time might not be unduly penalised.

Dr. *P. N. Banerjee* suggested that a fifty-five ratio would be the correct division between the burden on the present generation and the burden on posterity for financing war expenditure. He welcomed Government's decision with regard to repatriation of a substantial part of the country's external obligations ; but he declared that the decision was not arrived at in order to help India but was beneficial to India only incidentally.

Mr. Hoosainbhai Lalji referred to the argument that the larger the Government expenditure the greater the national income and taxable capacity of the people. He said that that might be true of other countries but not of India where a large proportion of the Government expenditure was taken out of the country by British employees of the Government and also by British and other foreign commercial interests. Mr. Hoossainbhai Lalji criticized the Government's policy relating to the export trade. He said that a Japanese got every facility to export articles from India to his country, but an Indian had to depend on British banks to finance him, on foreign ships to carry his products, and on foreign insurance companies to insure his goods. "After the last war, the British became agents of German shipping companies and of German insurance and banking firms. I want to know whether the same thing will happen after this war." He then referred to the Swedish match combine in India. He said that the moment protection was given to the match industry, the foreigner came out to India with his factories and succeeded in cutting down all Indian competition. To-day, he controlled the match industry in India and had taken steps to see that no match machinery was sold to Indians. He got all the advantage of protection, designed to promote Indian industry in the interests of India. If the Government could run the Railways, the Posts and Telegraphs Deparment and salt and opium works, why not the match industry which alone, he estimated, would bring in Rs. 3½ crores per year. In this connexion he stressed the need for controlling profiteering in matches.

Mr. *Ghulam Bhik Nairang*, speaking on the census operations, referred to the debate in the House on the cut motion on the subject and expressed surprise that the Government did not give any assurance that they would in a spirit of seriousness and responsibility, look into the complaints made in the course of the debate. Instead of any such assurance, the House was treated by the Government spokesman to a most edifying homily on the great demonstration of public spirit India had made on the occasion of the census. Mr. Nairang went on to refer to a letter received from the Premier of Bengal alleging that for months past an extensive and intensive campaign had been carried on to spread the impression that the census was for the purpose of recruiting every able-bodied male for the war. Moslems being illiterate, were reluctant in many cases to give particulars to the census enumerators. The result, he said, was that the figures of Moslems had been deflated by a million and a half while the Hindu figures had been inflated by about 200,000 in Calcutta alone. The House then adjourned till the 17th.

17th MARCH :—Sir *Cowasji Jehangir* further elaborated the arguments in favour of borrowing to meet the deficit. He gave a number of figures to prove that the amount of the deficit met from loans in England was 116 per cent of the revenue as compared to the corresponding figure in India of 7¾ per cent of the revenue. Thus, the deficit met from loans in England was fourteen times that in India. The comparative result was that while in England the Defence Budget had risen eight times more than in India, the deficit financed out of loans was fourteen times more in England than in India. India was thus paying out of loans for her war effort 44 per cent less than England. Sir Cowasji quoted further figures and pointed out that the Government's cash balance with the Reserve Bank on March 31, 1940, was Rs. 20,25 crores, which rose on February 28, 1941 to Rs. 32,5 crores.

This was a rise of Rs. 12.25 crores. Thus Rs. 8.33 crores utilised to replace Treasury Bills plus Rs. 12.25 crores, being the extra cash balance, making Rs. 20.58 crores, must have been the result of excess borrowing. There must, he said, be some explanation how the Government meant to utilise all this money outside war expenditure, when at the same time it insisted on extra taxation. He contended that extra taxation was not necessary. Government had the money to pay the whole of the deficit of Rs. 20 crores. It was rashly contended that meeting more of the deficits out of loans would only be postponing the evil day. It was admitted that some portion of the deficit must be met from loans. To that extent the postponement of the evil day was agreed to. It was only a question of the proportion between loans and taxation. He contended it was not postponing the evil day, but it was certainly spreading the burden over two or more generations instead of making the present generation bear the whole burden. In a war like this anybody who contended that the present generation should bear the whole burden must be out of his senses.

Sir *Ramswami Mudaliar*, Commerce Member, in a speech lasting over an hour and a half, made a number of announcements. Among these were a proposal to set up a central advisory committee on sugar; an inter-departmental committee to plan the readjustment of industries and industrial labour to meet conditions which must come with the restoration of peace; a small committee to survey the situation with regard to gaps in the industrial fabric and report to Government from month to month; machinery to examine during the period of protection whether the progress of protected industries was in accordance with the Tariff Board's recommendations and whether any revision of the quantum of protection, either in the upward or in the downward direction, was necessary. He also said he was prepared to examine whether it was possible to turn Indian Trade Commissioners in different parts of the world into a self contained service, so that their experience might not be frittered away. He uttered a note of warning against industries, protected or otherwise, frittering away their resources now, and asserted that all the resources which they could accumulate now would be necessary to meet post-war conditions and if it was found that industries had not dispensed their profits wisely now, no Government would be justified in giving them help, if they were in difficulties after the war. He appealed to industrial magnates to contribute liberally to the funds of the Scientific and Industrial Research Board and said he was prepared to open a fund for the purpose. Replying to critics of the Meek-Gregory Mission to the United States, the Commerce Member explained that on the information given by the Mission about America's plan to build up stock piles of mica, an agreement had been entered into between India and the United States whereby very large quantities of mica would be sent from India to America. On that one commodity, the expenses of the Mission had been met a thousand-fold, said the Commerce Member,

The Commeree Member began by uttering a note of warning against slogans, such as "Industrialise or perish," which he said embodied an extremism of thought. He commended the wisdom of those who adopted the policy of discriminating protection for key industries but, he said, protection and yet more protection was not the panacea for all the country's economic ills, nor was the slogan of economic national self-sufficiency to be blindly adopted. It must be remembered that other countries also might have the same slogan. and it was the pursuit of this ideal of self-sufficiency that had brought on the war. Further, industrial nations during the last ten years had suddenly found deficiencies in their agriculture and had started on a policy of agricultural development while agricultural countries had started on the path of industrialisation. But at the end of the war there would be other forces at work, a more chastened frame of mind would prevail and he believed that the call would come to India to make a contribution to the world effort that would be made for a greater and more scientific adjustment of the resources of the different parts of the world. For that we must prepare ourselves, he said. A balanced adjustment between agriculture and industry should be brought. He was against the extreme nationalism that insisted that everything possible should be made in India and that trade should be made in India and that trade should be crried on on a system of one-way traffic. If India's agricultural products should find a market outside India—as they must even after all the industrialisation possible—that market could not be found unless we were prepared to allow room for imported commodities. This was a point which was apt to be lost sight of and it was necessary to give a warning against the principle that we should industrialise in this country, paying little regard to the agricultural products which must find a market abroad. Proceeding to refer to the problem of export of surplus raw products, the Commerce Member said, he was happy to state that with reference to several commodities the problem of disposal was not as serious as he had once thought. Thanks to the work of the Supply and the Defence Departments, more and more raw products were being consumed in the country. He referred in this connection particularly to wheat, cotton and rice. Alluding to sugar, he said that practically all the Governments had now accepted the principle that a flat rate should be paid to cultivators during the whole season, and a bonus should be paid on the basis of profits actually derived by the industrialist from the sale of sugar. All the replies from the interests concerned had not yet been received regarding the proposal to form a Central Advisory Sugar Committee; but he hoped that such a committee would be formed. The idea was to have a body predominantly consisting of representatives of provincial and states' governments with a small representation for sugar-cane producers and the mill industry. The Commerce Department, he went on, had been seriously thinking of the problem of the essential difference between production in peace time and production in war time and of the certainty that immediately peace came, all the industries attuned to war purposes must readjust themselves, and a large number of technical men in the industries would be thrown out of employment. Plans must be made now to meet that situation. In the Commerce Department, the economic Adviser to the Government of India had been at work for some months on the possibilities of readjusting industries and industrial labour and it was the Commerce Member's hope that examination on a wider scale than at present would shortly be taken in hand by means of an inter-departmental committee. He also hoped that that committee would get the benefit of the knowledge and advice of industrial magnates in connection with the preparation of the plan for the future.

It had been suggested that the Government's expenditure on Public Works might not be undertaken now when technical labour was abundantly employed otherwise, but that such expenditure then might assist in the solution of the problem of surplus technical personnel. It might also be that private individuals could help by postponing their building schemes till after the war, so that they could benefit by the availability of trained technical men. The Commerce Member made it clear that whatever their plan now was it would require constant re-examination. There was nothing static about it. It was true that at present there were gaps in the industrial development. The instance has been mentioned of the absence of the production of eyelets and shoelaces to complete the boot-making industry. He had been thinking over the problem and had been considering whether the time had not come when a kind of survey might not be made to find out the gaps caused by the absence of small industries, as a result of which big industries got thrown out of gear. The Roger Commission had made a survey of the industrial position, and he was having the question examined whether it was necessary to have a small committee to survey the situation and report to the Government from month to month instead of having an elaborate survey.

Referring to the suggestion made for the setting up of machinery for bringing about tariff reform, which was more speedy in its work than the Tariff Board, the Commerce Member said he would examine the question later. The suggestion had also been made that while protection was granted by Government on the recommendation of a Tariff Board, there was no machinery to examine during the period of protection whether the industry concerned was carrying on according to the recommendations of the Board and whether any change in the quantum of protection was called for. He was prepared to have that question examined at the proper time. He went on to mention a number of small industries which had come into existence on account of the war, such as, drugs and chemicals—more than seventy per cent of India's requirements were being produced in the country—the manufacture of surgical instruments, boots, and shoes, and canning.

Giving a word of caution to industrialists, the Commerce Member said that while industry had found opportunities of expansion which were not there before the war, there was a responsibility resting on industry and industrialists to look to the future. If they frittered away their resources now, they would find themselves in a difficult position after the war, whatever the Government then in power.

After the war, the position would be such that the starving millions in Europe would find it necessary to get most of our new raw products and the sufferings of the agriculturist now would to some extent be then compensated ; but exactly the contrary would be the case with regard to manufactured goods. Released from the war effort, the industries would turn out cheap goods which would invade our markets. Our industrialists must therefore have something to fall bock upon at that time, and all the resources they could accumulate now would be necessary for them.

Sir *F. E. James* was glad that the Government of India were appointing overseas representatives in several countries. He hoped that the question of appointing such representatives in Ceylon, Burma and Malaya would not be overlooked. There were already India's representatives in these countries but their duties were circumscribed to dealing with questions of population. He suggested that their functions might be widened to include all matters relating to trade and commerce. Sir Frederick said that some people had thought that the speeches of the members of the European Group had not been marked by criticism of the Finance Member's proposals. Some had suggested that Mr. Chapman-Mortimer had almost acted as a Parlimentary Secretary to the Finance Member in defending his case. Sir Frederick said that there was justification for that because the Finance Member's case was a good one. But there was in the European community a note which had not been given full expression to. That was the problem of private and public expenditure. They realised that it was extremely difficult for a secular government to give a satisfactory lead in the matter of private expenditure. But their demand related not only to private expenditure but also to public expenditure—expenditure concerning not only the Central Government on matters directly connected with war, but also the expenditure of the provincial governments and of those authorities which were functioning without legislative control or scrutiny.

The speaker preferred taxation to loan for financing. "If loans reach more than a certain proportion of the revennes which are required for the prosecution of the war," he said, "then in my view, the finances of India being as they are to-day, a distinct injustice would be done to the future. That is why I should like personally to see for greater reliance on taxation for war purposes. But in order to understand the policy of the Finance Member, the House must appreciate the political background." Referring to the present political situation, Sir Frederick said : To-day the policies of the major political parties are aiming or have already aimed a vital blow at the settled policy of successive British Governments for the last twenty-five years with regard to India. What is that settled policy ? First of all, the achievement of the organic and constitutional unity of India as a whole ; secondly, the establishment in this country of representative institutions on a democratic basis." The House at this stage adjourned.

18th. MARCH :—Resuming his unfinished speech to-day *Sir Frederick James* referred to the observations made by Sir Tej Bahadur Sapru at the recent Bombay Conference and to his suggestion that for the solution of India's difficulties there should be personal contact between representatives of Britain and India, and said that such contact between representatives of Britain and India was necessary. That contact should be made not in India but in England. The Government of India should, the speaker said, send someone with undoubted authority, patriotism and integrity and with a capacity for presenting an objective view of the country and at the same time enjoying confidence of the British people. Such a person was the Leader of the House. In the meantime as long as the deadlock continued, it was the duty of all to carry on, seizing every opportunity to guide and to educate Indian public opinion. It was possible to mobilize a surprising amount of support even for the present Executive. The Commander-in-Chief by his speeches and imaginative touches within a short time had won for himself and his department a remarkable degree of support and interest.

Sir Ziauddin Ahmed added his own slogan to the many that he said had been referred to by earlier speakers, such as "why pay debts during the war ?" and "why not meet the entire deficit by a loan ?" His slogan was "we should pay what we can pay : the balance be left to future generations. He referred to the difficulty of maintaining a proper proportion between taxation and borrowing, and said that if the war expenditure continued to increase, the proportion of borrowing would also increase. But it must be remembered that as Government expenditure increased. the national income also increased and within the taxable capacity of the people. Sir Ziauddin added that an attempt should be made to determine the maximum taxable capacity of the country. He pointed out that in determining this it must be borne in mind that, in addition to all the taxes being paid, there was in India an invisible tax, that is to say the expenditure incurred by every employed man in India in supporting a number of unemployed relations. This was a form of tax unknown in European countries. He referred to an estimate which put the burden of this tax in India at between five and ten annas in the rupee. The speaker alluded to the Commerce Member's defence of the Meek-Gregory Report, and said any person of commonsense would have known that a country embarking on a programme of increased munitions production would require mica. Sir Ziauddin maintained that it was not necessary to send a mission to America to find this out.

Sir Ziauddin advocated an excise duty on textile and iron and steel industries which, he said, were at present in a prosperous state and could therefore easily bear the burden. Emphasizing the importance of fixing prices of staple commodities, the speaker suggested that wider powers in this matter should be given to local authorities and district magistrates. He also suggested that where cotton dealers made more than, say 25 per cent profit, over the prices paid by them to the cultivators, steps should be taken to see that the excess profit was utilized to stabilizing prices. The House at this stage adjourned till the 20th.

20th. MARCH :—By 46 votes to 28 the Assembly to-day passed the motion to take the Finance Bill into consideration. The Moslem League and the Congress Nationalists voted against the motion. During the debate on the motion, Sir *Henry Gidney* protested against what he alleged to be the sudden stoppage of recruitment of Anglo-Indians to the Postal Department. He said that in 1925 he led a deputation to the Secretary of State and in 1928 received the reply that the reduction of Anglo-Indian personnel from the Postal Department would be gradual. Instead of implementing that promise the Government of India had completely stopped their recruitment. Why should such a step be taken against a community that had served the department loyally, he asked. By their action he said, the Government had violated Section 242 of the Government of India Act. He said that after the war he would take the matter to the Federal Court if the Government did not take action at an early date to remove the "injustice."

Sir *Raza Ali* suggested that the Commerce Member should immediately settle down to the tackling of the problems of post-war industries. In the course of his speech the Commerce Member had used the term "key industries" but had not mentioned which industries he considered 'key industries." Sir Raza Ali said that the match industry continued to enjoy protection, but four-fifths of it was controlled by foreign capital. He also asked why a duty of 10 per cent should be imposed on tubes and tyres without imposing a countervailing duty on their imports. Giving his personal views on the present political deadlock, Sir Raza Ali made two suggestions. First, he wanted the establishment in London of a Commonwealth Advisory Committee with representatives of the Congress, the Moslem League, the Indian States and the Government of India, along with representatives of other Commonwealth countries, the Congress and Moslem League members to be nominated by their respective bodies. Secondly, he urged the setting up in India of a Defence Advisory Committee with representatives of the Assembly and nominees of Indian States with the object of assisting the Commander-in-Chief in the conduct of the war.

Syed Murtaza Sahib complained against the reduction in the expenditure on the Pilgrim Department from about Rs. 30,000 a year to about Rs. 12,000 and contrasted this with the fact that Rs. 38 lakhs was being spent on the Ecclesiastical Department, which was a non-votable subject.

Nawabzada Liaqat Ali Khan explained why the Moslem League had decided to oppose the Finance Bill. Proceeding, he said that after the largest party had retired from the House, the Government with the help of the nominated officials and non-officials and with the obliging and ready support of the European Group had carried everything they wanted to carry. The House knew that even if the Opposition had been able to throw out the Finance Bill, the Government would have drawn on their reserve powers and would have certified the measure. Under the constitution, the only method of protest they could select was the refusal of supplies before their grievances had been redressed. The speaker said that the Moslem League had not tried to embarrass the British Government nor hinder their war effort. "If we had wanted to do so, we could have demanded the immediate granting of Pakistan. Our attitude could not be called that of bargaining or of taking advantage of Britain's difficulty. What we said was that it was difficult to create the right type of atmosphere and make the people feel that it was their war, unless and until the representatives of the principal political parties had a real share in the administration of the country. This will be evident from the Bombay resolution of the League. We then said that war committees were not sufficient for associating people with the war effort and yesterday Sir Homi Mody endorsed our view".

Sir Jeremy Raisman, replying to the criticism of the Budget on the ground that there was no attempt at retrenchment coupled with economy, emphasized that there was an important distinction between the two ideas of economy and retrenchment. Retrenchment was a policy which had to be faced at a time when society could not support the full volume of the "overheads" of Government and when it was necessary for the country to make up its mind that it was going to cut down "overheads" and that with that cutting down would go a reduction in the scale of Government activity ; in other words, you cut some branches of the trees. This, he declared, was not a time of that kind. Now, when by general consent the scope of Government activities was daily widening, the whole conception of retrenchment in that sense was out of place. What, however, was intended was economy in the day-to-day administration of Government, and with that he entirely agreed. He agreed that it was the duty of the Government and it was his duty to see that the activities which Government must undertake at this time were carried out with the maximum regard for economy. He had already explained, he said, what endeavours had been made in the sphere of supply to secure the maximum economy concurrently with the execution of the duties of that Department. To prove that over a large field of contracts placed by the Supply Department or with the assistance of that Department were not such as to leave scope for excess profits. He mentioned that he had received suggestion from more than one firm completely engaged in war contracts that the excess profits tax should be placed at 100 per cent. This was an extraordinary thing and he later discovered that these firms had their full capacity booked up by Government at prices which would not leave them liable to excess profits tax (laughter) and these firms were concerned to see that their rivals who were taking their civil and non-war business and making handsome profits paid excess profits tax. As regards the question of how the Finance Department had equipped itself to bear the greater burden of controlling expenditure now, the Finance Member gave figures of the increase in the staff in the Military Finance Department, the Military Accounts Department and the Controller of Supply Accounts, the increases varying from 60 to 200 per cent. He assured the House that Government had not ignored the importance of equipping themselves to carry out the additional responsibilities thrown upon them by the greater volume of expenditure and the greater number of places in which such expenditure arose. Another aspect of economy was touched upon in the question raised as to whether those provinces which found themselves in a position to do so, should not be asked to undertake a larger share of certain war activities such as air raid precautions and civic guards. The Finance Member referred to the Niemeyer Award and the amendment of it and said it was still the position that the Central Government was a good deal worse off and faced a more difficult position than it would, of course, if war had not broken out. While he had a year ago felt it proper to undertake certain liabilities occurring in the provinces which were not, strictly within the orbit of defence but belonged rather to the sphere of passive preparations to be taken by local Governments, he now felt it would be reasonable to approach the provinces with a request that they should take a larger share of these liabilities, and he felt that the response from the provinces would not be unreasonable. Most of the provinces now found themselves comparatively well off.

Ban on Sagotra Marriage Bill

21st MARCH:—The Hindu rule of Law prohibiting marriage between two persons of the some gotra (spiritual ancestry) and between persons belonging to different sub-divisions of the same caste was sought to be removed by a Bill which Mr. *Govind Deshmukh* moved reference to Select Committee in the Assembly to-day. Mr. Deshmukh explained that the rule had become archaic and did not subserve any eugenic purpose; it did not prevail among the Sudras and was modified by custom among certain sections of Brahmins and Kshatriyas. The ban was often circumvented by getting the girl adopted by someone of a different gotra ; but there was no legal adoption of a girl under the Hindu Law. Legislation removing the ban had been passed in Baroda and Indore States. Marriages between persons belonging to different sub-divisions of the same caste, though not legally prohibited, were rare, because of the general belief that they were not lawful A solution of the two sets of difficulties, said Mr. Deshmukh, was civil marriage, but many had conscientious objection to such civil marriage. Hence the Bill. He suggested that this measure also might be included among those which had been referred to the Committee presided over by Sir *B. N. Rau.*

used for the aggrandisement of some people. The Assembly had asked for the control of this expenditure by a committee of elected members of the House at the beginning of the war, but the Government, Sardar Sant Singh continued, did not pay any heed to their request. He could not understand why the request was being ignored.

Seth Baijnath Bajoria, stressing the need for popular control over Defence Expenditure, urged the immediate establishment of a War Advisory Council. Replying to the Finance Member's claim that the country had prospered on account of war, he said that though exports had risen, they were almost entirely made up of war material to Great Britain ; the export of other merchandise would be found to have fallen. Similarly, it was unjust to compare the slump prices with the present prices and base on it the conclusion that India was having a period of prosperity. Mr. Bajoria protested against the frequent levy of additional taxation. The Finance Member's motto seemed to be "Six crores, every six months." Last year, it was matches which had attracted the attention of the Finance Member.

Mr. *Hossainbhai Lalji* said that the question of questions was how the Government were going to get money to finance the war. "The whole thing depends on the terms on which the Government gets this money." He asserted that high rates of income-tax would not leave much capital for the starting of new industries. "A day will come when the Government will not be able to get money on present terms, if they continue their present policy." Mr. Lalji advocated the financing of war borrowings, as "the war was not being fought for the present generation only, but also for posterity."

Sir Jeremy Raisman, replying to the debate, dealt first with the controversy on the question whether war expenditure should be financed by borrowing or by taxation. It was not a question, he said, on which one could hope to find agreement but there was one point to be borne in mind. In the United Kingdom, only about a third of the total war expenditure was met by taxation and the rest was met by borrowing. Supposing, he went on, that total normal expenditure in a country was of the order of one hundred crores and the country was involved in a small war costing some additional ten crores, there was no reason why the additional ten crores should not be met by taxation in the ordinary course. But, if the war budget was twice or thrice the size of the normal budget, it was impossible to meet it by taxation. In the conditions of India to-day, he went on, there were obvious factors operating to increase the income of important taxable classes ; and it would be a serious dereliction of duty to refrain from levying on those classes taxation as a current contribution to the cost of the war. It was true that no fiscal machinery could be so perfect as to ensure that only those individuals who were able to pay were called upon so to do ; but he claimed that taxation in India was, for the most part, directed to the classes who might justly be called upon to contribute. Referring to the arguments advanced by the Federation of Indian Chambers of Commerce against the increase in the Excess Profits Tax, the Finance Member commented that the case as presented by the Federation was overstated and that the effect on industry and business was not likely to be as serious or as detrimental as the Federation would have them believe. Referring to the remarks made by speakers on the effect of the doubling of the Excise duty on matches, Sir Jeremy Raisman said: "I do not want at this moment, to anticipate what I have to state when the Finance Bill is under discussion. I recognise that it is an important responsibility of the Government in relation to the tax, to ensure that the consumer is not exploited under the guise of increased taxation, and some measure of price control may be necessary." (Cheers). As regards the increase that had already occurred, he suggested it was not so much a question of exploitation by the producer as by the retail trader. Several speakers, the Finance Member proceeded, had in dealing with the duty on artificial silk asked for an assurance that the duty would be kept in force for a considerable time. In other words, they wanted him to convert this into a protective duty. He pointed out that the object of a revenue duty was to raise money, and the moment that duty was converted into a protective duty, it sounded the death-knell of the yield from it. There was no case for protection for artificial silk, yarn and thread, and in any case it had to be investigated in a proper manner and could not be disposed of in a casual way in the course of a taxation measure. In regard to the Sterling debts repatriation scheme, some speakers had expressed anxiety as to whether the operations might lead to stringency of the money market and to deflation. "Inflation and Deflation are words which are bandied about somewhat carelessly," he said, "and I must confess, I find it difficult to follow the line of argument. All that I can adduce is a simple commonsense argument. We ourselves will be large borrowers during the course of the next year or the year after that. We have obviously an important interest in keeping money cheap. It is, therefore, not likely that we would so act as to make money dear either for Industry and Commerce or for ourselves. That is only a matter of enlightened self-interest." (Hear, hear). Mr. *Chapman Mortimer* had asked for an assurance in regard to stability of prices. "I can assure him", said the Finance Member, "that that is a matter of constant concern to the Government, and it is one which my honourable colleague the Commerce Member as well as myself are not likely to overlook. At the same time, I have no doubt that members will realise that price control is not an easy matter. There is always the danger that intervention may do more harm than good unless it is very carefully thought out." The House at this stage adjourned.

TICKETLESS TRAVELLERS' BILL (CONTD.)

5th MARCH :—The debate on the Ticketless Travellers Bill was resumed in the Assembly this morning. The Congress Nationalist Party and Moslem League Party concentrated their attack on the provision in the Bill seeking to give power to the railway staff to eject a passenger found travelling in a class higher than that for which he holds a ticket. What was to happen to the passenger so ejected, was a question raised and discussed on an amendment moved by *Pandit Lakshmi Kanta Maitra* and supported by Sir *Zia-ud-din Ahmed*, Mr *Lalchand Navalrai* and *Sir Yamin Khan*. They asked that the passenger so ejected should not be prevented from continuing his journey in the class for which his ticket was good. His position, they contended, would be most difficult if the railway staff chose to put him down at any wayside station. The power of ejection was a new one being given to the railway staff and it was necessary, they declared, to circumscribe it with proper safeguards. *Sir M. Zafarulla Khan*, Leader of the House, intervening in the debate, expressed the opinion that the apprehension was unjustified, that the passenger ejected in the circumstances referred to by the speakers would be prevented by the staff from travelling in the class for which he did hold a ticket. There was nothing in the section which purported to vest railway servants with authority to deal with the passenger in that way. But in order to meet the apprehension, he proposed a proviso which read: "Provided that nothing in this section shall be deemed to preclude a person removed from a carriage of a higher class from continuing his journey in a carriage of a class for which he holds a pass or ticket." The proviso was unanimously accepted by the Opposition and passed. The House passed the following further amendment affecting the power of ejection :—"Provided that women and children, if unaccompanied by male passengers, shall not be so removed except either at the station at which they first enter the train or at a junction or terminal station or station at the headquarters of a civil district and only between the hours of 6 a. m. and 6 p. m. Mr. *Esaak Sait* moved and Dr. *P. N. Banerjee* supported the amendment. The Bill was passed and the House adjourned.

Voting on Budget Demands (contd.)

WORKING OF SUPPLY DEPT.

6th MARCH :—Voting on Budget demands for grants commenced to-day. The working of the Supply Department and the relations between the Eastern Group Supply Council and the Provision Offices were explained by *Sir M. Zafrulla Khan* to-day in reply to a debate initiated by *Sir Zia-ud-Din* Ahmed on a cut motion. Sir Zia-ud-Din made it clear that he was not against the war efforts, but he wanted that Indias' limited resources should be well-organized and well co-ordinated. He directed his criticism to cases of what he regarded as too rapid promotion from one military rank to another, and declared it was an insult that one who could not handle a rifle should become a Lieutenant-Colonel. The speaker criticized the existing system of tenders, pleaded for constant watch by the Finance Department, suggested a tribunal at the Secretariat of the Supply Department to listen to appeals and asked for rules providing that every person engaged in the Department should disclose half yearly his immoveable property, bank deposits and shares. *Sir M. Zafrulla Khan* disclaimed any attempt to pretend that there might not be or was not room for improvement in the Departments in various directions. In fact, changes were continuously effected in organizations and methods as improvements suggested themselves. He has been hoping that in the debate suggestions might come to the surface which might be worth investigating further ; and he was somewhat disappointed that the debate had not revealed any number of suggestions of that character. With reference to the complaints of too rapid promotion, he pointed out that, generally, there was some justification for such promotion because the Department had to expand rapidly ; but in fact only two cases had been brought to his notice which required consideration. He had looked into the matter and come to certain arrangements with the Master-General of Ordinance which should obviate similar cases recurring in the future. Referring to rumours that certain sections of the Department were not working entirely "above board," he said he too had heard rumours but he could not condemn anybody on the basis of rumours. If representatives of the commercial and industrial community would bring before him concrete cases he would take the most drastic steps to put them right. He would also guarantee that no such firm or individual would suffer any prejudice on account of the fact that they brought matters to his notice. *Sir Zia-ud-Din* withdrew his cut motion.

Civil Aviation

Sir Raza Ali moving a cut motion to discus the general policy of the Civil Aviation Department gave figures to prove his contention that the progress made in India was unsatisfactory compared to that registered in other countries. India, he said, only had a total of 76 aircraft up to March 31, 1939. Any one who had seen the fleets of commercial aircraft taken off from the great air ports of Munich, Hamburg and Marseilles could easily figure out for himself that from each of these stations more aircraft took off than India's total. Mr. *F. Tymms*, Director of Civil Aviation, explained that because of lack of ground organization and owing to retrenchment of funds, it was found necessary to start the operation of air services with small aircraft, without wireless and with only one crew. In 1934 Government created a fund of Rs. 19 lakhs to enable the work of improving ground organization to be put in hand. Later in 1939, partly influenced by the war, further money was provided at the rate of Rs. 25 lakhs a year for a period of seven years for the establishment of ground organization, the underlying idea being to meet the immediate needs of defence while building up assets for civil aviation. Some of that work was now in hand. Sir Raza Ali's motion was rejected.

Reforms in Baluchistan

Syed Ghulam Bhik Nairang, by a cut motion, urged the grant of provincial autonomy in Baluchistan. He said that this question had been raised on other occasions as well, and on all those occasions Government put forward excuses. But he was not daunted by the Government's attitude. There was no substance in the Government's reasoning that because Quetta stood on Kalat territory it could not be governed under a reformed system of Government.

7th. MARCH :—The Assembly rejected by 40 votes to 18 the Moslem League party's cut motion moved yesterday, demanding reforms for Baluchistan. The Congress Nationalist party voted with Government against the motion, while Mr. *Kazmi*, a member of the Congress party, voted with the League party. Sir *Abdul Halim Ghuznavi* and Maulvi *Abdur Rashid Chaudhury* abstained from voting. Before the vote was taken, Mr. *S. M. Aney* and Mr. *Azharali* spoke. Mr. *Aney* asked whether a highly developed system of responsible Government could safely be introduced in a backward area like Baluchistan. He drew attention to the fact that the total income of the province amounted to Rs. 20 lakhs against the present rate of expenditure of one crore and a quarter. Reforms of the type advocated for the province would result in a great addition to expenditure which, in turn, would mean an addition to the general taxpayers' burden by way of subvention. Mr. Aney went on to refer to the interpretation put upon the motion by earlier speakers who had suggested the amalgamation of the province with Sind or the Punjab. On the mere question of introducing reforms suited to Baluchistan, he was in agreement with the movers but if they insisted on a larger interpretation they had sought to give, then he would oppose it. Mr. *Azharali* declared that Mr. Aney had misunderstood the object of the motion, which was only to place the people of Baluchistan on a level with other people in India. The speaker asserted that what the Moslem League opposed was not true democracy that Islam stood for but the democracy which the British Government attempted to impose on India. The House divided and rejected the motion.

War Finance & War Propaganda

The Moslem League Party's motion was talked out, and the House passed on to the European Group's cut motions of which the first was moved by Mr. *Chapman*

Mortimer to discuss financial policy with special reference to war finance. Mr. Chapman Mortimer made his observations under three heads, constitutional financial and economic. It was difficult, he said, to find patience with the follies and futilities of the Congress opposition that had brought things to their present pass. Great financial magnates might continue to issue statements on the Budget and pass resolutions outside the House, but until they realized that the place to discuss India's financial policy was here in this House, until they had the courage to defy the ban on the Congress "high command" and challenge policies, in which, he said, the great majority of Hindu opinion had no faith, the outlook for responsible government was very poor indeed. Nor was the outlook likely to improve so long as the official Congress policy continued to represent the members of this House as so many marionettes dancing to a tune played outside. It was no wonder, he said, that under the present circumstances the cry of "pakistan" was raised. It was no wonder also that while on the one hand His Majesty's Government had gone steadily forward as they promised to do so, preparing the ground, in its financial aspect, for the next stage of constitutional advance, we saw on the other hand a steady backward movement in India against the whole idea of responsible government. Speaking on the financial and economic aspects, Mr. Chapman Mortimer expressed general agreement with the financial policy of Sir Jeremy Raisman and said that the Budget revealed a policy which was in India's best interests. The Finance Member referred to the suggestion that the country had fixed, limited taxable capacity and if Government expenditure was unlimited, then their loss must increase accordingly. That was not the way he looked at the question. Government's deficit arose from expenditure most of which took place in this country so that money went out of the Treasury and went into private pockets. That amount of money helped to create a much larger taxable capacity in the country. So, as Government's expenditure increased, the national income increased too. That was an important thing to be borne in mind and if it were possible to devise an ideally perfect system of taxation, we ought to be able to recover for the Treasury an ever-growing sum as Treasury expenditure increased. That was what was happening even in India where we had an imperfect tax system, where there was not merely a minimum below which incomes were not taxed but there was a whole field of taxation such as agriculture which was not subject to the central tax system. Passing on to refer to the criticism of "the past sins of the present Government," in the matter of war preparedness, *Sir Jeremy Raisman* considered that it went to the root of the moral position in this war.

The point was that Hitler and his friends had been preparing for the war for five or six years, and it was obvious that if the British Empire were even as strong as they were to-day 18 months ago, the whole complexion of the war would have been different. But unfortunately, all those in charge of policy went on hoping that the aggressor did not mean business. That was a mistake which lay on the shoulders of not one Government or two, and not one hundred or one thousand but on many millions. It was the opinion of millions of people that nothing should be done on our side to precipitate the outbreak of war : and so the enemy got a mechanical and technical advantage. Mr. *Chapman Mortmer* on this suggestion withdrew the cut motion.

A spirited plea for more energy and drive and more money for war propaganda was made by Mr. *P. J. Griffiths* in moving the next cut motion. He said the Government of India had not yet begun to treat propaganda with the seriousness which it deserved. Neither the Provincial Governments nor the Central Government had yet accepted propaganda as a vital weapon in modern warfare, second only to defence. He complained that there were still tracts in India where no propaganda was being carried on, and particularly mentioned Assam in this connexion. The amount of money that the Central Government was spending, namely, about Rs 14 lakhs, was hopelessly inadequate to achieve any results in a population of 400,000, 000 people. *Sir Reginald Maxw ll* explained that the propaganda for which the Government of India were providing finance was only the central aspect of the question. He could not say what the Provincial Governments were spending for the propaganda they were conducting. Propaganda being a provincial subject, the Government of India could only provide the provinces with material which they could use, and that the Government of India were doing. That stimulus to the provinces had gone fairly far. Before the war, very few provinces had their own publicity officers, but now all of them had one and also local publicity committees. The Home Member next explained how the propaganda machinery at the Centre had developed, culminating in the creation of the Board of Information whose aim was to control all the publicity of the Centre through all possible media—through the Press, broadcasting and films. He then explained the machinery set up after the commencement of the war for the use of the cinema in propaganda. There was considerable difficulty at first in this sphere, but he was glad to say that news-reels were now being shown in more than half the Indian cinemas. The cut motion was withdrawn and the House adjourned till the 10th.

Control over Defence

10th. MARCH :—A reference to the political deadlock was made in the Assembly to-day when the Congress Nationalist Party moved two 'cut' motions, one urging the formation of a Defence Committee and the other, recruitment to the army from all classes and provinces. Mr. *Sant Singh* put forward a forceful plea for the appointment of an Indian Defence Member and a Defence Committee purely of an advisory character, with which the Defence Department could share its difficulties and secrets. Sir *F. E. James*, in effect, opposed the motion, and argued that if what was required was more information about the activities of the Defence Department, then, the present Public Relations Officer, himself a journalist, was doing very useful work, and making available to the public detailed information about various Defence matters. Mr. *Ogilvie* said that he was sure he would be voicing the opinion of the Defence Member when he said that His Excellency would be most grateful for the words of welcome and tributes paid to him by the speakers. He said he would acquaint His Excellency with what the speakers had said and he knew that His Excellency would deeply appreciate the honour done to him. The motion was rejected without division.

Army Recruitment Policy

Mr. *Govind Deshmukh* moved the next cut motion to discuss "the recruitment to the Army, Navy and Air Forces in India." He strongly objected to the present class basis of recruitment and the distinction between martial and non-martial classes. He declared that the distinction had been made to create prejudice and it was time that propaganda was used to spread the conception that the sword was mightier than the pen instead of the reverse. He complained that C. P. and Berar had no Recruiting Centres before the war and if anyone wanted to enlist, he had to come all the way to Delhi at his own expense. Mr. Ogilvie reiterated the declaration that Government did not recognise the distinction of martial and non-martial and what distinction was at present observed was not immutable. He should be the last person to call anyone non-martial: but on the other hand everybody would admit that a large and even supply of excellent military material was not readily obtainable from all places. It was not merely a question of physique or courage but of that type of character which combined boldness with caution, swift decision and capacity to see the weak point in the enemy, which made the true soldier. People of this kind could be got from all parts of the country ; in some parts they got more of them than in others. He went on to explain that, when in peace time the needs were restricted to a comparatively small Army and when it was obviously impossible to mingle the classes, the classes from which recruits were obtained must be comparatively speaking few. As the Army expanded so those classes also expanded and as His Excellency the Defence Member said recently, a beginning had already been made to break new ground. His Excellency had also said that breaking of new ground did not mean that they threw overboard those who had served India so valiantly and successfully in the past. (Cheers.) No reply was given, and the motion was rejected without a division.

War Allowances to Govt. Pensioners

Mr. *N. M. Joshi* by a 'cut' motion raised a debate on grievances of Government employees, with particular reference to the demand for compensation on account of a rise in the cost of living. Mr. Joshi said that some sections of industrial workers had got increases but in the case of Government employees nothing had been done. It was reported that the Central Government proposed to give some grain compensation to their employees in Provinces where Provincial Government employees had been allowed such compensation. He asked the Government of India to follow one policy and stick to it. He also asked them to accept the Rau Committee's recommendations and set a good example to the provinces by applying those recommendations in the Centrally-administered areas. Government, he said, should also consider the question of those getting a little more than inferior servants but not sufficient to maintain families. He referred to those getting up to Rs. 100. *Sir Jeremy Raisman*, Finance Member said that the Government of India's proposals to apply to Central Government employees in the Provinces the dearness allowance granted by Provincial Governments to their employees had been placed before the Standing Finance Committee and in that Committee there was remarkable unanimity of opinion on those proposals. A number of Provincial Governments had already published their schemes, and they were quite well known to the Government servants affected. It was true that several of these schemes had not yet come into operation for the simple reason that they were based on a criterion that had not yet materialised, that is, the cost of living as measured by the price of staple food grains had not risen to a point at which Provincial Governments considered that any compensation whatever was called for. The Finance Member expressed strong agreement with that point of view. The cut motion was rejected without division.

Govt.'s Repressive Policy

Mr. *Kazmi*, moving a 'cut' motion, sought to discuss the "repressive policy" of the Government. He declared that Government were using immoral means to crush a moral revolt. The speaker went on to give instances in which he alleged a satyagrahi aged sixty-five years had been sentenced six times already, and Government had interfered with elections to this House by arresting Congressmen who stood as candidates, and releasing them after elections were over. He referred to cases in which satyagrahi prisoners had been put in fetters and handcuffs while being removed from one place to another, and one prisoner, Mr. Garg of Ajmer, who was in frail health, had been given flour-grinding and in doing that work fainted. He suggested to the Home Member to shout the Congress slogan, get himself arrested, and put in jail, and then he would be in a position to understand what the satyagrahis suffered in jail.

Sir Reginald Maxwell, Home Member characterising the debate as a confusing discussion, declared that he did not exactly know what case he was called upon to meet. He could disentangle three main objects underlying the motion. Firstly the mover and Mr. *Joshi* wanted that civil liberties ought to be allowed to the extent of permitting conscientious objectors to say what they liked regardless of the effect. The object of the Defence of India Act, said the Home Member, according to its preamble, was "to provide for special measures to ensure public safety and interests and the defence of British India." The Government were interpreting it in the highest interests of the country. The rules which the Government were authorised to frame under the Defence of India Act were rules for securing the defence of British India, public safety, maintenance of public order, for efficient prosecution of the war or maintaining supplies and the services of India. In other words, the Defence of India Act was not primarily a penal enactment, but it recognised the fact that, in time of war and national emergency, liberties of the ordinary citizens had to be circumscribed in certain directions. That point had in an earlier session been stressed by the Leader of the House who gave the assurance that Government should regard themselves as guardians of those rights so far as it was possible. The Home Member gave the assurance to the House that, in all matters connected with the Defence of India Act, the Government were fully conscious of their responsibilities. "I must repeat that no assurance has ever been given that the Rules would not be used against any form of activity designed to impede successful prosecution of the war," declared Sir Reginald. Sir Reginald next dealt with the treatment of satyagrahis, the second object underlying the motion. He said that the total number of persons actually undergoing imprisonment under all sections of the Defence of India Rules on February 1, 1941, was 3,094 in the whole of India. Of this number, about 2,042 were convicted in connection with the civil disobedience movement. "These are the persons who have actually invited Government to arrest them. When a person asks to be arrested, am I doing repression ? (Laughter.) If we do not arrrest a satyagrahi, then we are regarded as unsympathetic." The Home Member next gave some cases in which satyagrahis made it a grievance that they had not been arrested. A 'bidi'-maker of Bihar was now on the road to Delhi walking three and a half miles a day imploring the local police to arrest him. (Laughter) (*Sir F. E. James* "He may get here next session." (renewed laughter). Another case was that of a young girl satyagrahi in Madras who was almost illiterate. She did not know what she was doing. She gave her age to be 19. But she appeared considerably younger. In court, when she was asked to cross examine a prosecution witness, she did not understand what was cross-examination and began shouting slogans. To the Magistrate she admitted that she did not understand the slogans and told him that the present war was between Britain and Poland (laughter).

Referring to the third object of the mover, the Home Member assured the House that no distinction was being made between satyagrahis and other prisoners in the matter of classification. All were being classified according to their status and mode of life before their arrest. The Government of India had informed the Provincial Governments that satyagrahis were eligible for "A" class. A good many of them were getting "A" class, he added. The Home Member opposed the motion which was rejected.

The guillotine was applied at 5 p. m. and all the demands were voted. The House then adjourned.

Debate on the Finance Bill

11th. MARCH :—The Assembly began the general debate on the Finance Bill to-day. Sir *Abdul Halim Gaznavi*, who took part in the debate, pleaded for revision of the Port Trust Acts in the interests of Indians, while *Sardar Sant Singh*, in a vigorous speech, criticised the working of the Defence of India Act. Sir *Yamin Khan*, opening the debate, considered that there was no proper control over expenditure, and that the country's trade was in general contracting and its wealth decreasing. He objected to the increased surcharge on small incomes. Men with an income of Rs. 2,000 a year were now spending more because of the increased cost of living. The increased surcharge should, therefore, have been put on higher incomes, such as Rs. 10,000 or Rs. 15,000 and the Finance Member should have imposed the excess profits tax on incomes of Rs. 20,000, instead of Rs. 40,000 as at present. People with these incomes could afford to pay, unlike those getting Rs. 2,000 a year; and, he said, if his suggestions were accepted, the yield, in terms of revenue, would probably be the same as the Finance Member tried to get by his present proposals. Referring to the doubling of the duty on matches, Sir Yamin Khan said that the day after the Budget proposals were presented, he sent his servant to all the shops in New Delhi and was informed that the price per box had gone up to one anna. Sir Yamin Khan said that it might be possible if he purchased from the factories direct but not from retail dealers. He suggested that if the Finance Member had before announcing the new taxes taken the local authorities into his confidence, then any rise in price above what was justified by the new duties could have been prevented. He also suggested that instead of matches the Finance Member should have chosen a luxury, like cigarettes, on which to put an increased duty. He expressed the Muslim League Party's dissatisfaction with the Government's policy of trying to please a party which could not be pleased and ignoring another party which was ready and willing to cooperate. He said the Muslim League Party had decided to lodge their protest against this policy by opposing consideration of the Finance Bill. Accordingly he opposed the motion.

Mr. *J.Ramsay Scott* dealt mainly with the Road and Rail transport systems, which he called the Siamese twins, and asked the Communications Member to give an assurance that he was co-ordinating the two and that he had the power to do so. He asked for equality of treatment for the two, and said that both were equally necessary for India's development. He reminded the Finance Member that although this year he had received a wonderful return from the Railway twin, there had been a year when he had reveived nothing, while the Road twin brought in a steady revenue every year, which the speaker believed to be Rs. 12 crores from excise and customs on such articles as petrol, motor cars, tyres and tubes, paints, varnishes, etc. The member referred to the shortage of wagons and of engine power on certain railways, and said that, in spite of it, there was a desire to restrict long-distance traffic by road. This, he considered a dog in the manger policy. After calling attention to the change in transport policy in the United Kingdom since the war began, he said that he would not like to see anything done now which would circumscribe road transport facilities and long distance traffic. He emphasised the need for maintaining roads in proper repair ; otherwise, he said, new road building programmes would have to include large reconstruction schemes. He asked the Government to get reports of the position from each province, and added that the question was of the utmost and immediate importance, for we might be faced with the position that our war effort was paralysed by a breakdown or interruption of our slender Railway communications. He also dealt with the duty on artificial silk yarns, and urged a counter-balancing duty on art silk piece-goods,

Sir *Andrew Clow* explained that he had not the power to co-ordinate Road and Rail systems. Owing to the constitutional position, he said, there was no authority that had co-ordinating control over road and rail. The Motor Vehicles Bill, as introduced in the House, might have gone a considerable distance in that direction, but the House must remember that it was modified considerably in the Assembly, and the Central Government was left with very little power in that respect. He said that Railways would not follow a dog in the manger policy, and added that the advent of the war had changed circumstances, and that if the present conditions continued, we might find that both road carriers and railways had as much as they could to manage. "We have recently been making an experiment on the North-Western Railway," he said, "by co-operating with road traffic companies to provide an efficient road tratsport. That, I think, is the better line, a line which, if pursued, may enable both road and Railways to eliminate the more dangerous forms of competition, such as cutting down rates and fares to a level which for the road interests involves serious danger." "War", he went on "was bringing new problems, and it was very far from the desire of the Government of India to curtail facilities for the public either on the roads or Railways." He made it clear that the Road Fund was intended primarily for new developments and Government had tried their best to limit grants to new work, although in moments of weakness, funds had been given for repair and maintenance. The whole question, he said, was expected to be discussed by the Transport Advisory Council and before that, the Standing Committee on Roads would be consulted.

Sir *Abdul Halim Ghaznavi*, in the course of a speech lasting over an hour and a half, asked for three assurances: First, that the Government of India would only enter into such commitments as were justifiable from the point of view of Indian interests and for Indian Defence; second, that the Government would take the Indian public into confidence regarding the manner in which the total expenditure on Defence was shared between the Government of India and His Majesty's Government; and third, that the Government would satisfy Indian public opinion that the expenditure debited to India was incurred primarily to safeguard Indian interests. He wanted the Finance Member also to bear in mind that, at any rate, the non-recurring part of the Defence expenditure should, to a reasonable extent, be met by borrowing rather than by imposing further burdens on the already heavily burdened tax-payer. Sir Abdul Halim quoted from the observations made by Sir William Meyer, Finance Member, in 1915, in support of his contention that additional taxation would only be justified to meet expenditure of a permanent character. War expenditure, he said, was of a temporary and special character, and should, therefore, be met by borrowing, the burden of which would properly be spread over a number of years and would be shared by posterity who, no less than the present generation, was benefited by our Defence measures. The speaker then went on to criticise the excess profits tax, which, he said, was likely to incapacitate the industries now being built up from forming reserves out of which they could meet the slump that must come with the end of the present war. The speaker also deprecated the way in which the Calcutta Port Trust, with its preponderance of European members, had decided not to assist an Indian firm in establishing a shipbuilding yard at Calcutta, with the result that Vizagapatam was chosen by that firm. He demanded a revision of the Port Trust Act in Calcutta, where out of the 19 members, it could be said 15 members were Europeans and only four Indians elected to represent Indian industries, whereas taking the share of the trade of the different communities, he found that out of the total trade of Rs. 130 crores, 38 was controlled by Indian Chambers of Commerce and 26 by Muslim Chambers of Commérce and the balance, though nominally in the name of British firms, was almost entirely on account of Indian dealers, because the Lancashire industry, for instance, would not deal directly with Indian merchants who must, therefore, get their orders executed through British firms in Calcutta. The constitution of the Port Trust, he declared, represented an example of discrimination against which the British people in India themselves wanted safeguards in the Act. He asked that the Port Trust Acts, which were half a century old, should now be knocked on the head.

Sardar Sant Singh then went on to interpret the Home Member's speech yesterday as containing an assurance that the Defence of India Rules would only be used to deal with activities likely to impede war effort. He asked whether the stopping of the Guru Gobind Singh Day procession in Sargodha and the arrest of 31 persons in that connection were in conformity with that assurance. Had the Home Member abdicated his position as member in charge of Law and Order in

The Bengal Legislative Assembly

LIST OF MEMBERS

Speaker—Hon'ble Khan Bahadur M. Azizul Haque, C.I.E.

Deputy Speaker—Asraf Ali Khan Choudhury, Bar-at-Law

Elected Members

Jatindra Nath Basu
Santosh Kumar Basu
Iswar Das Jalan
Dr. J. M. Das Gupta
Jogesh Chandra Gupta
Sarat Chandra Bose
Barada Prasanna Pain
Tulshi Chandra Goswami
Rai Harendra Nath Chaudhury
Dr. Nalinaksha Sanyal
Surendra Mohan Maitra
Pratul Chandra Ganguli
Maharajkumar Uday Chand Mahatap
Adwaita Kumar Maji
Pramatha Nath Banerji
Banku Behari Mandal
Dr. Sarat Chandra Mukherjee
Debendra Nath Das
Ashutosa Mullick
Manindra Bhushan Sinha
Kamal Krishna Ray
Debendra Lall Khan
Krishna Prasad Mandal
Kishori Pati Roy
Harendra Nath Dolui
Dr. Gobinda Chandra Bhawmik
Iswar Chandra Mal
Nikunja Behari Maiti
Dhirendra Narayan Mukherjee
Radhanath Das
Sukumar Dutta
Manmatha Roy
Pulin Bihari Mullick
Rai Jogesh Chandra Sen Bahadur
Hem Chandra Naskar
P. Banerjee
Anukul Chandra Das
Haripada Chattopadhyay
Lakshmi Narayan Biswas
Sasanka Sekhar Sanyal
Rai Sahib Kirit Busan Das
Atul Krishna Ghose
Rasik Lal Biswas
Nagendra Nath Sen
Hon. Mr. Mukunda Behari Mullick
Patiram Ray
Satyapriya Banerjee
Atul Chandra Kumar
Tarinicharan Pramanik
Premhari Barma
Shyama Prosad Barman
Nishitha Nath Kundu
Khagendra Nath Das Gupta
Hon. Mr. Prasanna Deb Raikut
Upendra Nath Barman
Jotindra Nata Chakrabarty
Kshetra Nath Singha
Puspajit Barma
Narendra Narayan Chakrabarty
Madhuśudan Sarkar
Atul Chandra Sen
Dhananjoy Roy
Kiron Sankar Roy
Charu Chandra Roy
Amrita Lal Mandal
Birendra Kishore Rai Choudhury
Monomohan Das
Surendra Nath Biswas
Birat Chandra Mandal
Promatha Ranjan Thakur
Narendra Nath Das Gupta
Upendranath Edbar
Jogendra Nath Mandal
Dhirendra Nath Datta
Jagat Chandra Mandal
Harendra Kumar Sur
Mahim Chandra Das
Damber Singa Gurang
Hon. Khwaja Sir Nazimuddin, K.C.I.E.
M. A. H. Ispahani
K. Nooruddin
Khan Sahib Maulvi Md. Solaiman
Hon. Mr. H. S. Suhrawardy
" Nawab K. Habibullah Bahadur
Maulvi Abul Hashim
" Md. Abdus Rasheed
Khan Bahadur Dr. Syed Muhammad Siddique
" Maulvi Alfaz-ud-din Ahmed
Maulvi Abdul Quasem
Khan Sahib Maulvi S. Abdur Rauf
Jasimuddin Ahmed
Yousuf Mirza
Khan Bahadur A. F. M. Abdur Rahaman
M. Shamsuddin Ahmed
Mohammad Mohsin Ali
Maulvi Aftab Hosain Joarder
Hon. Khan Bahadur M. Azizul Huq, C.I.E.
Syed Badrudduja
Sahibzada Kawanjah Syed Kazem Ali Meerza
M. Farhad Raza Chowdhury
Syed Nausher Ali
Maulvi Waliur Rahman
Serajul Islam

Khan Bahadur Maulana Ahmed Ali Enayetpuri
Abdul Hakeem
Syed Jalaluddin Hashemy
" Mostagawasal Haque
M. Ashraf Ali
Maulvi Maniruddin Akhand
" Mohammad Amir Ali Mia
" M. Moslem Ali Molla
" Mafizuddin Choudhury
" Hafizuddin Choudhury
" Abdul Jabbar
Khan Bahadur Maulvi Mahatabuddin Ahmed
Hon. Khan Bahadur Nawab Musharraff Hossain
Khan Bahadur A. M. L. Rahaman
" Shah Abdur Rauf
Haji Safiruddin Ahmed
Kazi Emdadul Haque
Mia Abdul Hafiz
Maulvi Abu Hossain Sarkar
Ahmed Hossain
Maulvi Rajiruddin Tarafdar
" Mohammad Ishaque
" Azhar Ali
Dr. Mafizuddin Ahmed
Khan Bahadur Mohammed Ali
A. M. Abdul Hamid
Abdur Raschid Mahmood
Abdullah-Al-Mahmood
Md. Barat Ali
Maulvi Zahur Ahmed Chowdhury
" Idris Ahmed Mia
Khwaja Shahabuddin, C.B.E.
Maulana Muhammad Abdul Aziz
S. A. Salim
Maulvi Mohammad Abdul Hakim Vikrampuri
Razaur Rahman Khan
Maulvi Aulad Hossain Khan
" Abdul Latif Biswas
" Mohammad Abdus Shaheed
Syed Shah Alum
Fazlur Rahman
Mahammad Abdul Jabbar Palwan
Giasuddin Ahmed
Abdul Karim
Maulvi Abdul Majid
" Abdul Waheed
Maulana Shamsul Huda
Maulvi Abdul Hakim
Al-Hadz Maulvi Masud Ali Khan Panni
Mirza Abdul Hafiz
Syed HassanAli Chowdhury
Khan Bahadur Maulvi Kabiruddin Khan
Abdul Hossain Ahmed
Maulvi Md. Israil
" Abdul Hamid Shah
Khan Sahib Hamiduddin Ahmad
Shamsuddin Ahmed Khandarkar
Maulvi Ahmed Ali Mridha
The Hon. Mr. Tamizuddin Khan
Yusuf Ali Chowdhury
Mahammad Abul Fazl
Al-Hadj Gyasuddin Ahmed Choudhury
Hon. Mr. A. K. Fazlul Huq
Abul Kader
Khan Sahib Maulvi Hatemally Jamadar
Khan Sahib Maulvi Syed Md. Afzal
" Bahadur Maulvi Hashem Ali Khan
Sadaruddin Ahmed
Abdul Wahab Khan
Maulvi Mahammed Mozammel Huq
Haji Maulvi Tofel Ahmed Chowdhury
Maulvi Mustufa Ali Dewan
Nawabzada K. Nasarullah
Maqbul Hossain
Maulvi Mafizuddin Ahmed
Ramisuddin Ahmed
Asimuddin Ahmed
Maulvi Mahammed Hasanuzzaman
" Jonab Ali Majumdar
Khan Bahadur Maulvi Abidur Reza Chowdhury
Mr. Shahedali
Maulvi Mohammad Ibrahim
Khan Sahib Maulvi Aminullah
Shah Syed Golam Sarwar Hosaini
Syed Ahmad Khan
" Abdul Majid
Maulvi Abdur Razzak
Khan Bahadur Maulvi Jalaluddin Ahmed
" " Mohammad Anwarul Azim
Maulana Md. Maniruzzaman Islamabadi
Dr. Sanaullah
Khan Bahadur Maulvi Fazlul Qadir
Miss Mira Dutta Gupta
Mrs. Hemaprova Majumdar
" Hasina Murshed
Begum Farhat Bano Khanam
Miss P. B. Bell-Hart
J. W. Chippendale
L. T, Maguire
C. Griffiths
I. A. Clark
Sir Henry Birkmyre, Bart
R. J. Hawkins
Curtis Millar C.I.E.
A. O. Brown
G. Morgan
H. Brabant Smith
William C. Patton
J. W. R. Steven
F. J. Marindin
Dr. H. C. Mukherji
S. A. Gomes
P. F. S. Warren
Rogers Haywood
M. A. F. Hirtzel
F. H. French
R. M. Sassoon

DAVID HENDRY	HON. MAHARAJA SRISCHANDRA NANDY OF COSSIMBAZAR
W. C. WORDSWORTH	KUMAR SHIB SHEKHARESWAR RAY
K. A. HAMILTON	MAHARAJA SASHI KANTA ACHAJYA CHOUDHURY OF MUKTAGACHHA
H. R. NORTON	RAI KSHIROD CHANDRA ROY BAHADUR
W. A. M. WALKER	J. N. GUPTA
I. G. KENNEDY	AFTAB ALI
C. W. MILES	DR. SURESH CHANDRA BANERJI
G. G. MACGREGOR	NIHARENDU DUTTA MAZUMDAR
B. B. WHITEHEAD	SIBNATH BANERJEE
SIR HARI SANKAR PAL	A. M. A. ZAMAN
NALINI RANJAN SARKAR	B. MUKHERJI
DEBI PRASAD KHAITAN	BABU LITTA MUNDA SIRDAR
RAI MOONGTU LAL TAPURIA BAHADUR	DR. SYAMAPRASAD MOOKERJEE
ABDUR RAHAMAN SIDDIQI	FAZLUR RAHMAN
HON. SIR BIJOY PRASAD SINGH ROY	

Proceedings of the Legislative Assembly

Budget Session—Calcutta—3rd. February to 23rd. April 1941

MOTOR SPIRITS SALES TAXATION BILL 1941

The Budget session of the Bengal Legislative Assembly commenced on Monday the 3rd. February 1941 in the afternoon. The Hon. Mr. *H. S. Suhrawardy*, Finance Minister, circulated a statement to the House which showed that he expected a deficit of Revenue account of Rs. 1 crore and 7 lakhs for 1940-41.

On the motion of the Hon. Mr. *A. K. Fazlul Huq* the date for the submission of the report of the Select Committee on the Secondary Education Bill was extended to April 15 next. The date for the submission of the Select Committee's report on the Calcutta Municipal (Second Amendment) Bill was extended to February 28 next.

Considerable progress was made with the consideration of the Bengal Motor Spirit Sales Taxation Bill, 1941, which proposed to levy on all retail sales of motor spirit a tax at the rate of one anna and six pies per gallon. In moving that the Bill be taken into consideration, the *Finance Minister* briefly indicated the chief changes proposed by the select committee. He said that the definition of motor spirit had been amended to exclude diesel and any other heavy oils used as fuel for industrial machinery. The select committee thought that these should not be brought within the scope of a tax whose object was to provide funds to advance the construction of new roads. An amendment by Mr. *P. Banerji* (Congress party) that the Bill be recommitted to the select committee, having failed the House proceeded to consider the measure clause by clause. With reference to the clause relating to the levy of tax, Mr. *J. F. Sinclair* (European) proposed by way of amendment that "no tax shall be levied under this Act on the sale of any motor spirit for the purpose of aviation." This amendment was accepted by the Finance Minister and passed by the House. After several other amendments had been disposed of further consideration of the measure was held on the next day, the 4th. February when the *Minister* proposed certain minor changes to some of the clauses which evoked little discussion. The only important alteration effected was in respect of the preamble. Originally, the preamble only mentioned the imposition of a tax on retail sales of motor spirit in Bengal without specifying the purpose to which the money was to be appropriated. By an amendment moved by Mr. *Suhrawardy* yesterday, it was made clear that the proceeds of this tax would be utilized for the construc- of new roads in the province. The object of this fund, Mr. *Suhrawardy* explained, was not merely to supplement the Central Road Fund but also to provide for new roads for which there was considerable demand. There appeared to be little change of getting money for the purpose from the Central Road Fund in the near future. The Minister indicated that the roads proposed to be constructed would be in the nature of trunk roads, feeder roads or marketing roads which would be taken up in accordance with the advice of the Board of Communication. He made it clear that no roads outside Mr. King's report would be taken in hand. Another important amendment was incorporated by which it was provided that the proposed tax would not be levied until October 1, 1941. The third reading of the Bill was passed by the House with the modifications mentioned above.

Bengal Finance (Sales Tax) Bill 1941

6th. FEBRUARY :—An account of the financial position of the Bengal Government was given by the Finance Minister, Mr. *H. S. Suhrawardy*, while moving in the Assembly to-day that the Bengal Finance (Sales Tax) Bill, as reported by the Select Committee be taken into consideration. Emphasising the imperative necessity of the Bill, Mr Suhrawardy said that there might be some tinkering with it, some increase or decrease of the rate, some inclusion or exclusion in the schedule, but its necessity so far as the purpose of administration was concerned, could not be denied. "This year" the Finance Minister proceeded, "we had a deficit of one crore and seven lakhs. This has been met from the closing balance, but the closing balance has now gone down to such a proportion that it cannot stand the strain of any deficit budget, as the next budget is bound to be, without this taxation." Out of one crore and seven lakhs, thirty lakhs approximately represent the jute that has been purchased by Government. Therefore, there is an increased expenditure of 75 lakhs which will have to be carried on to this year. Along with the seventy-six lakhs, further expenditure has been provided for the next year's budget. I am not in a position to give details to this House before the budget is presented." The Finance Minister emphasised that the tax would not affect the poor to any appreciable extent. After nearly three hours' discussion, the Assembly, by ninety to fifty-four votes, rejected the Congress Party's (Mr. *P. Banerjee's*) amendment urging recommittal of the Bill to the Select Committee, and the House agreed to take the Bill into consideration. The Assembly at this stage adjourned till Monday the **10th. February** when it was adjourned again by the Speaker in memory of the sudden death of Mr. *Surendra Mohan Maitra*, a member of the House.

11th. FEBRUARY :—The consideration of the Finance (Sales) Tax Bill, clause by clause was taken up by the Assembly to-day. The Opposition efforts were mainly directed to postponing the operation of the measure until six months after the termination of the war or to limiting it to three years. Amendments to that effect were defeated by overwhelming majorities and the House agreed to Clause 1, defining the extent and the date of commencement of the Bill. The claused provided that the measure would come into forces "on such date as the Provincial Government may, by notification in the official Gazette, appoint". The Assembly was considering Clause 2 the definition part of the Bill when it adjourned.

Supplementary Budget Estimates

12th. FEBRUARY :—When the supplementary budget estimates for 1940-41, presented by the Finance Minister, Mr. *H. S. Suhrawardy*, at a previous meeting of the legislature, came up for consideration to-day, the various provisions, particularly those relating to police and jails, were subjected to considerable criticism by several members of the Opposition. The total covered by the estimates was Rs. 1,67,000 out of which Rs. 1.39,000 was charged and the balance was voted.

The demands related to 15 grants, two of which, namely, "interest free advances and loans" and "advances" were outside the revenue account. These two grants between them accounted for a total of Rs. 90½ lakhs.

Under the 'revenue" heads, the largest single demand was under "Agriculture" for which 55,35,000 had been provided. This included an expenditure of Rs. 29.25,000 on the purchase of jute in June and July last with the object of maintaining an economic price level for the new crop in the current year. The rest of the additional expenditure under "Agriculture" was due mainly to the registration of jute lands and the regulation and licensing of jute. In addition, there was a provision of Rs. 70,000 to secure a stock of seeds in connextion with a scheme for making available to cultivators substitute crop seeds which might be shown on areas released by the impending restriction of jute cultivation. There were moreover charges in connexion with an expert inquiry which was now in progress in regard to the jute and hessian future markets.

The next largest demand was on account of "Education—General" for which Rs. 6,83,000 had been provided to implement the scheme of development of primary education.

Under "Police" the demand was for Rs. 5,82,000 due mainly to extra staff to maintain law and order in the province. Included in the demand was a provision of Rs. 51,000 for Civic Guards who had been organised in terms of the Civic Guard Ordinance, 1940. It was pointed out in an explanatory memorandum that the duties of civic guards were mostly in the provincial field but there were some items outside this field for which the Central Government had agreed to contribute one-third of the total cost of the organization. The provision in respect of "Other Contingencies—Arms, Accoutrements and Ordnance Stores"—under this head, represented the cost of equipment and training of three additional tear smoke squards in the Bengal Police the formation of which had been undertaken after the original budget had been passed.

The grant under "Jails" came next with a demand of Rs. 2.16,000. More than half of this was for the purchase of raw materials for jail manufactures and the balance was on account of the increased dietary charges owing to a rise in number of prisoners as well as in the price of foodstaffs. The demands under the remaining heads were comparatively small

Initiating a general discussion on the budget estimates, Mr. *Syed Jalaludoin Hashemy* (Proja) said that he thought it his duty to criticize some of the budget provision although he was sure that he would not succeed in making any impression on the minds of the members of the Coalition Party or on the Finance Minister. At a previous meeting of the Assembly the Finance Minister replying to a question, had stated that the Government of Bengal had not contributed nor were they considering any proposal to contribute any sum out of provincial revenues towards the prosecution of war or the defence of India. But a little scrutiny of the provisions of the supplementary estimates would reveal that some of the items were at least indirectly connected with the defence of India. Roundly criticizing the police, Mr. Hashemy referred to the disturbances which took place in Calcutta on Monday and remarked that tear-gas bombs had been used on innocent Moslems. He suggested that in view of the use made by the Government of tear smoke squads they would not vote the demand made in this respect. Mr. *Abu Hossain Sarkar* (Praja) said that the police force had been used by the Ministry in order to "suppress public opinion" and also to "oppress the Moslem public" of the province. Alluding to the disturbances on Monday, he said that the police had been used on that occasion in a matter which could not but be regarded as objectionable. Proposing a cut motion in connexion with the demand made under the head "Jails" *Rai Harendra Nath Choudhury* (Congress) criticized the Government for the alleged inadequacy of the dietary charges. Mr. Chaudhury's cut motion as well as several others moved in connection with certain other demands were rejected by large majorities, and, as stated, the supplementary estimates were passed without any modification.

THE SALES TAX BILL (CONTD.)

13th FEBRUARY :—A proposal by the European party to lower the "taxable quantum" provided in the Finance (Sales) Tax Bill, met with strong opposition to-day. The Bill provides that the "taxable quantum" should be Rs. 50,000 for certain classes of dealers. To this, an amendment was moved by Sir *Henry Birkmyre* (European) seeking to reduce the figure to Rs. 25,000. The Rs. 50,000 limit, observed Sir Henry, made it easier for the Government to collect the tax, but the lower limit of Rs. 25,000 would equally certainly bring in more money to the treasury. The lower limit, Sir Henry asserted, would in no way affect cottage industries or the cultivators selling their own produce in *hats* and markets. It would, on the other hand, reduce the opportunities of evasion of payment of this tax. Opposing the amendment, Mr. *Sasanka Sekhar Sanyal* (Bose group) said that he failed to appreciate the anxiety of the European members to bring down the level of the taxable quantum. He expressed his apprehension that the Government would, in view of the war requirements, want more money and larger revenue and that the Government would try to get as much money as they could, presumably for nation-building departments, but really to help the war effort. Therefore, his party set their face against this proposal. Mr. *Niharendu Dutt Majumdar* (Bose group) also condemned the amendment.

Several other amendments were moved by the Opposition, most of which aimed at reducing the incidence of taxation proposed in the Bill. Mr. *H. S. Suhrawardy*, Finance Minister in charge of the Bill, opposed all the amendments, excepting the one moved by Sir Henry Birkmyre, which, he said, he would like to consider further. The amendment, Mr. Suhrawardy said, really did not matter to the Government.

The registered dealer was not a tax-payer. He regretted the manner in which the discussion had proceeded as if the small dealer had to pay the tax from his pocket and so the figure had to be reduced. They had found that there were more people in the category of Rs. 25,000 (as the taxable quantum) in the mofussil. If the Government accepted this figure of Rs. 25,000. it would mean that they would have to appoint a larger staff for inspection. This would involve considerable expenditure for collecting the tax. It was for this reason, Government should like to consider this amendment further. The amendments proposed by the Opposition were, on division, defeated by overwhelming majorities. The Assembly then adjourned.

Financial Statement for 1941-42

15th. FEBRUARY:—The hon. Mr. *H. S. Suhrawardy*, Finance Minister, presented the Budget estimates of the Bengal Government for the year 1941-42 today. On the basis of the Budget estimates for 1941-42, Bengal is faced with a deficit, on Revenue Account, of one crore and thirty-lakhs.

The Finance Minister in presenting the Budget for the year 1941-42, said that the year would start with an opening balance of one crore and ninety-two lakhs, which was the anticipated closing balance for the current year (1940-41). "Revenue receipts are placed at fourteen crores and three lakhs, or twenty-one lakhs better than the revised. Our proposals for expenditure on Revenue Account amount to fifteen crores, thirty-seven lakhs, which is fifty-two lakhs more than the anticipated e penditure in the current year. On the basis of these estimates, there will be a deficit on Revenue Account of one crore thirty-four lakhs. The working of the Capital and Debt Deposit section of the Budget is also expected to result in a deficit of twenty-five lakhs. The joint effect of these deficits is to reduce the opening balance by one crore fifty-nine lakhs, so that the estimated closing balance stands at thirty-three lakhs only".

The Finance Minister emphasised that the Budget estimates did not include any receipts from either of the new taxation measures, which still awaited the final verdict of the Legislature, nor did they include any provision for the charges of collection. The increase of twenty-one lakhs in Revenue receipts was due, among others, to an anticipated improvement of five lakhs under jute duty, and five lakhs under income-tax. The increase under jute duty was based on the assumption that shipping facilities would improve to some extent. Some growth was allowed under the income-tax on the latest advice received from the Government of India.

On the side of expenditure, the Finance Minister said that the Budget provided for expenditure on Revenue Account fifty-two lakhs in excess of the Revised Estimates for the current year. If, however, they took into account the expenditure of twenty-eight lakhs included in the Revised Estimates for the purchase of jute, for which no provision was included in the coming year's estimates, the expenditure contemplated in next year's estimates was eighty lakhs more than they were likely to spend in the current year. It was, however, emphasised that practically the whole of this increase was under the nation-building departments.

The Finance Minister placed before the House the more important items of new expenditure with a view to enabling the House to know the main directions in which Government proposed to apply the new revenues that the Government had asked the Legislature to make available.

Dealing with the increase of fourteen lakhs under Education, the Minister said that out of it, a sum of one and a half lakhs had been set apart for the advancement of education of the members of the scheduled castes. A similar amount had been provided as the initial instalment of a grant to the Dacca University towards the cost of construction of the additional Muslim hall. There was also a provision of Rs. 71,000 for opening B. A. and I. Sc., classes in the Lady Brabourne College and a capital grant of Rs. 67,000 to the recently started Fazlul Huq College at Chakhar. There was an increase of two lakhs under Police. The bulk of this was due largely to the anticipated employment of the emergency force throughout the coming year.

In connection with the Government scheme for giving financial relief to low paid Government servants, who would be affected by a substantial rise in the cost of living caused by the War, Government considered that the price level of the cheapest common rice had now been reached, which was eight seers per rupee, and the scheme had accordingly been put into operation from the beginning of the current month. The cost of the scheme in a full year was likely to be eight lakhs of rupees.

The Finance Minister observed that the closing balance of thirty-three lakhs was hopelessly inadequate as a working balance and was less even than the minimum balance that they were required to maintain with the Reserve Bank and in Treasuries. In these circumstances, he said that the only course open to him was to assume that the Legislature would pass the Sales Tax Bill (now before the Assembly) in a form that would give Bengal sufficient additional new revenue to balance its budget.

Emphasising that the new revenues were essential, the Finance Minister said that in the unlikely event of the Legislature refusing to empower Government to raise the necessary additional revenues, it would, of course, be necessary to subject the whole Budget to drastic reductions, reductions "that will not only paralyse any attempts to extend our beneficent activities, but will seriously jeopardise the continuance of a number of essential services now in operation."

The Finance Minister remarked that no responsible Government could mark time and it was inevitable that expenditure on nation-building departments would increase year by year. "I hope I shall not be misunderstood or thought to be disturbing needlessly the peace of mind of potential tax-payers if I say that we shall have to explore still further means of increasing our revenues at no distant date. I know full well that taxation in any form is most unwelcome. There is, however, no use our attempting to shut our eyes to the fact that without further taxation, we cannot hope to satisfy the requirements of a province so starved and so ill-equipped as Bengal."

The Finance Minister continued: "The year that is now drawing to a close has seen momentous happenings beyond the boundaries of India. No thinking man can be indifferent to those happenings or to the varying course of the great struggle between the Democracies and the Dictator Powers, but this morning my reference to the War must naturally deal mainly with the effect of the War upon the economy of this Province.

"I have been told that to other Provinces the War has brought comparative affluence. In Bengal, the effect has just been the opposite and the reason is not far to seek. The loss of the continental markets has been a serious blow to the jute trade and the life blood of this Province's economy is jute."

Before resuming his seat, the Finance Minister made some general statement of the Ministry's policy in relation to India's war effort. He said: "We fully recognise that until victory is finally won, it is essential to subordinate the needs of the Province to the paramount claims of the Centre's war effort, but in our opinion, though at the present time to hold in abeyance all ideas of development may be appropriate enough in the case of those Provinces that have for many years enjoyed standards of administration considerably higher than those obtaining in the nation-building department in Bengal, such a course is not possible in the case of Bengal, where the administration of the Province is only just beginning to recover from the effects of years of starvation. Nor can we agree with the view that every rupee spent in this Province over and above that necessary to maintain the administration at last year's level is a rupee diverted from India's war effort. That is a short-sighted view. This Province is playing no small part in India's war effort, and it is our view that to the extent that we can raise the standard of living and, in particular, can improve the conditions of those on the subsistence level—workers and peasants alike—we increase the efficiency of the Province and thereby, contribute materially to the Centre's war effort."

After the presentation of the Budget, the Finance Minister taking forty-five minutes to finish his speech, the Assembly adjourned for nine days in order to enable the members to be present in their constituencies during the Census operations.

General Discussion of Budget

25th. to 27th. FEBRUARY :—The House reassembled to-day when the general discussion on the Budget commenced. Proceedings were dull, manuscript eloquence being mainly the order of the day. Altogether about a dozen members took part in the discussion and they either criticized or praised the budget according to their party affiliations. One of the principal contributors to the debate was Mr. *W. A. M. Walker*, Leader of the European Party, who congratulated the Finance Minister on his "clear and comprehensive budget statement." While agreeing that the Finance Minister had established a case for the two taxation measures—the Sales Tax Bill and the Motor Spirit Sales Taxation Bill—he emphasized the need for caution as regards new commitments and avoidance of fresh taxation. "There is a limit to the capacity of the tax-payer," he said, "and I think while he must be prepared to meet the Bill which the Finance Minister has presented to us, he is entitled to expect that there will be no further calls in the near future." Criticising the budget estimates, *Rai Harendra Nath Choudhuri* said that they furnished another example of the old trick of under-estimation of receipts and undue provision of expenditure just to work out an exaggerated prospective deficit. Thus receipts had been revised to the extent of 45 lakhs and the result anticipated on revision was that the total receipts on revenue account would go down by 15 lakhs. Next day, the 26th. February, Mr. *J. C. Gupta* (Congress) said that a budget to be worth anything must be correlated to the needs of the province, but the present budget could not be described as such from any point of view. He had no doubt that the Finance Minister was fully aware that the most crying needs of the province were the provision of two square meals a day for the masses, the prevention of death from malaria and other preventible diseases, and the removal of illiteracy which prevented the growth and development of the inhabitants of this province. *Sahibzada Kazem Ali Mirza* (Coalition) congratulated the Finance Minister, Mr. H. S. Suhrawardy, on this "excellent budget" which showed the boldness of his conception and the courage of his conviction. When the war, he said, had vitally affected the economic life in Bengal, Mr. Suhrawardy had not thought it fit to apply the brakes but true to his instinct as a real nation-builder he was determined to pursue his programme, undaunted by war conditions. He had shown a deficit of Rs. 1,34,00,000 banking on the goodness of this House to pass his Sales Tax Bill in an acceptable form to balance his budget. He (the speaker) appealed to the House to help him (Mr. Suhrawardy) towards the realization of his plan. *Miss Mira Dutt Gupta* (Congress) said that a progressive Government must explore new sources of revenue but one failed to discover anything progressive in the outlook and activities of the present Government. They were continuing the old traditions of British Imperialism in all its aspects. She emphasized the need of a Central Women's Hostel in Calcutta which might accommodate the large number of women students of the city who had so far been left completely to themselves to manage as best as they could with regard to hostel accommodation. This was an urgent and immediate necessity which deserved their utmost consideration. Continuing, Miss Dutt Gupta said "From the budget proposals as laid before this House, the baselessness of the professions of the Finance Minister about nation-building is apparent to everyone in this House. I think, I shall be voicing the considered opinion of the largest section of this House, when I say that the people of this province are unwilling to submit to further burdens of taxation on promises of nation-building activities which are entirely illusory." The budget, said Mr. *Surendra Nath Biswas* (Congress) did not disclose any serious attempt on the part of the Ministry to solve the various urgent and vital problems of Bengal. Examining the budget proposals in the light of the requirements of the nation-building departments. Mr. Biswas pointed out that for primary and adult education an additional expenditure of Rs. 8,35,000 and Rs. 79,000 had been provided. This was quite insufficient considering the vastness of their needs. Next day, the 27th. February, two of the main speakers were Mr. *A. R. Siddiqui* (Coalition) and Mr. *R. M. Sassoon* (European). The former said he saw in the Budget a want of vision on the part of the Finance Minister, while the latter stressed the need for economy and avoiding fresh commitments. Mr. Siddiqi remarked that the time when big industries should be developed by recourse to borrowing but he found no proposal of that kind in the Budget. He commented on the meagreness of the grant for river training which was an urgent problem. He pointed out that the Hooghly was fast silting up and unless its sandbanks were removed, Calcutta was likely to share the fate of Pataliputra at no distant date. The difference between income and expenditure *per capita* was the measure of a people's prosperity. He had read the whole of the Finance Minister's statement and had been unable to find a single suggestion for widening the margin between the two. Mr. Siddiqi drew the Finance Minister's attention to the "injustice" that was being done to the Calcutta Corporation in the matter of their share of the Motor Vehicles Tax. They had been allotted only Rs. 4½ lakhs out of the proceeds with which they were expected to keep in trim 100 miles of metalled roads. Mr. *R. M. Sassoon* said that his party were anxious that the actual working of the Budget, when it was passed, with or without reductions, should be carefully watched. A suggestion to which his party attached importance was that in this very critical year Government should abstain from any endeavour to enlarge this Budget by seeking supplementary grants in later sessions. This should be possible if a proper degree of restraint was exercised. Another means of economy open to

Sir *Reginald Maxwell*, Home Member, moving circulation of the Bill, observed that the measure was not only possibly controversial, but would profoundly affect Hindu social life and the structure of Hindu Law. It dealt with an item on the Concurrent Legislative List, and it had been the rule when legislating in that field that public opinion should be called in before the House dealt with the Bill. He was not averse to consulting Sir B. N. Rau with regard to the question of including it among the group of measures referred to him, but in the Home Member's view this Bill did not deal with the same principle as the others did. The House agreed to the circulation of the Bill.

Comforts for Haj Pilgrims

Increased space for each pilgrim on any ship engaged in carrying Haj pilgrims is to be provided and marked off under the provisions of *Shaikh Fazlihaq Piracha's* Bill which was passed by the Assembly this morning. Syed *G. B. Nairang*, Diwan *Lalchand Navalrai*, Maulvi *Abdul Ghani* and Sir *Abdulla Haroon* supported the Bill as reported upon by the select committee and expressed the view that pilgrims would not seriously object to any slight increase in fares in return for the additional comfort which would result from greater space and separate marking of space. Diwan *Lalchand Navalrai* and Maulvi *Abdul Ghani* felt that competition between the shipping companies concerned would prevent any rise in fares. Mr. *J. D. Boyle*, European Group, said he was glad that this point of view had been recognized by the supporters of the measure, namely, that marking of space for pilgrims would limit the carrying capacity of ships and was bound to result in an increase in the fares. Mr. *J. D. Tyson*, Education Secretary, said that the Government had decided to remain neutral on the Bill. He felt that the effect of the Bill might not be beneficial to the pilgrim public. He also announced that the Bill could not be enforced during the period of the war.

Debate on the Finance Bill (contd.)

22nd. MARCH :—During the discussion of the clauses of the Finance Bill this morning, Dr. *P. N. Banerjee* sought the doubling of the amount of the rebate allowed to the cottage match industry since 1934. He said this was only reasonable in view of the decision to double the duty on matches. His suggestion would not result in any substantial loss of revenue, because the quantity of matches produced by the cottage industry was very small.

Mr. *J. D. Boyle*, opposing, quoted the Tariff Board's observation that the manufacture of matches organised as a cottage industry had hardly any future ; and that the dangerous character of the materials used in it made it unfit to be a cottage industry. He also said the industry hardly deserved to be called a cottage industry ; the wages were wretched, the conditions of work were wretched and the match produced were also wretched. These matches, he said, could safely be struck within the Assembly Chamber without danger of a breach of the rules ; for they would not light (Laughter). He had himself tried it.

Mr. *Hussainbhai Laljee*, speaking as one who had once been engaged in the industry, strongly defended the cottage industry, which (he said) served to give the poor villagers employment and saved them from starvation. The cottage industry had been there for the last ten years and could not have survived if the matches produced by it were not saleable. He knew of matches produced by the most up-to-date machinery becoming damp and failing to light.

Sir Jeremy Raisman said that the amendment would have appealed to him if he had not taken some care to enquire into the conditions in which the cottage industry operated. Any subsidy for the cottage industry, he said, must be related to the cost of producing matches and not to the duty levied. He was also convinced that any money given would not find its way to the poor workers but to a class who did not deserve it. The amendment was rejected.

Dr. *Bannerjee* and Babu *Baijnath Bajoria* tried to secure a reduction in the Income-tax and Excess Profits Tax surcharges but failed, as also Mr. *Lalchand Navalrai* in his efforts to reduce the postal charges. All the clauses were passed without an amendment.

During the third reading, Maulvi *Abdur Rashid Chaudhury*, who had complained of having been denied an opportunity to speak on the first reading, was cheered when he rose. He said that since the last Finance Bill was rejected, nothing had happened to make the House change its attitude. Neither the Viceroy nor the Secretary of State had done anything to induce the House to change its view, nor to create any war enthusiasm in the country. He complained that taxation introduced as a war measure had continued after the war. The super-tax imposed during the last war was an instance. There was the suspicion that the taxation now imposed would also continue for ever. After Mr. *Chaudhury*, one or two other members wanted to speak, but the Leader of the House reminded the members of the agreement among the parties not to make any speeches during the third reading and of the President's statement that he would see to it that that agreement was carried out. Closure was, therefore, moved and accepted and the House divided on the motion that the Bill be passed. The Bill was passed by 40 votes to 19. The Muslim League and the Congress Nationalist Parties voted against the Bill. Sir *H. P. Mody* and Sir *Cowasji Jehangir* did not vote.

Duty on Tyres & Tubes Bill

During the discussion on the Bill to levy an excise duty on tyres and tubes, the *Finance Member* announced that he contemplated that if it was possible to do so administratively, tyres for bullock carts would be exempted from the duty.

Tyres for bullock carts, Sir *Jeremy Raisman* said, represented an innovation, which must be encouraged by every means possible because of the beneficial effect on roads and on the animals. For that reason, he was prepared to make every effort to prevent any increase of the price in the case of tyres used for these carts. (Laughter.)

In reply to the argument put forward by Sir *Homi Mody* and Sir *Raza Ali* in favour of an equivalent import duty, Sir *Jeremy Raisman* pointed out that without a proper examination of the position of the industry, an equivalent import duty could not be levied, as it would have a protective effect. He declared he was satisfied that there was no necessity to increase the existing import duty in the present circumstances. Circumstances, he went on, might arise in which this industry might be able to establish a claim for protection, and in that case, the duty should be changed from a revenue to a protective duty and from that time onwards, it would be necessary to maintain a margin between the revenue duty and excise. Both the excise and the import duty on tyres and tubes at present were revenue duties, and he claimed he was entitled to fix them independently at the level most suitable for revenue purpose.

Sir *Raza Ali* strongly urged that the conditions under which Indians were employed in the tyre factories established in India should be investigated, so as to prevent any discrimination between Indian and European employees. It was scandalous, he declared, that any such discrimination should be permitted, or that there should be no law in the country to enforce equality of treatment in this matter. Sir *Jeremy Raisman* explained that he had not enquired into the detailed constitution of these companies. Matters to which Sir Raza Ali had referred must come under examination if and when protective considerations came up. In answer to Babu *Baijnath Bajoria*, the Finance Member said there were four tyre companies established in India and gave their names. The Bill was passed without an amendment.

Excess Profits Tax Amend. Bill

The House passed the Bill further to amend the Excess Profits Tax Act, mainly to provide for the consequences of a change in the period of charge and the rate of the Excess Profits Tax.

Iron & Steel Protection Bill

Sir *Ramaswami Mudaliar* moved consideration of his Bill to continue for another year the protective duties on iron and steel manufactures, silver thread and wire and sugar. The Commerce Member, referring to the iron and steel industry, observed that it was possible that this industry had, after all the years of protection it had enjoyed and after all the sacrifices made by the consumer, might find itself in a position to stand on its legs, and the long period of protection for the industry might either come to an end, or the quantum of protection, if at all, might very materially be reduced. But the present was not the time to come to any settled conclusion on this question. Hence the decision to continue the *status quo* for another year. Further discussion was continued on Monday, the **24th. March** when Sir *Ziauddin Ahmad* moved its reference to a Select Committee which was rejected. The House passed the consideration motion, as also all the clauses of the Bill without a division. The Bill was passed without a division, as also the Bill to extend the period of the import duty on wheat and wheat flour by another year.

Import Duty on Broken Pice

The Commerce Member, moving that the second Tariff Bill be taken into consideration, referred to rice and said that, owing to the bad crop of rice, the Government had decided not to extend the import duty on broken rice this year. He, however, warned the rice trade not to take advantage of rice shortage by raising prices. If they did that, they would be making the chances of a future import duty on broken rice extremely slender.

As for wheat, the Commerce Member reiterated what he had announced last year, namely, that the Government would carefully watch the prices of wheat and would not hesitate to remove or lower the quantum of import duty or take other steps to bring down the prices if they were satisfied that speculative tendencies were responsible for higher prices of wheat at any time during the year. The Bill was passed.

Income Tax Tribunal

During discussion on demands for supplementary grants, Messrs. *Bannerji*, *Maitra* and *Lalchand Navalrai* sought information relating to the composition of the Income-tax Tribunal. They enquired whether the recruitment to the Tribunal was made through the Public Service Commission, whether the persons selected were the best available in India and whether they had any experience of income-tax law. The discussion had not concluded when the Assembly adjourned.

Non-Recognition of Communal Unions

25th. MARCH :—By 48 votes to 17, the Assembly rejected to-day Mr. *H. M. Abdullah's* resolution, recommending "that the present discriminatory policy of the Government as regards recognition of so-called common unions of Government employees should be abandoned forthwith and unions of employees belonging to any one particular section or community should be officialy recognised."

Mr. *P. J. Griffiths*, vigorously opposing the resolution, declared that the extension of the principle of communalism to trade unionism was fraught with danger to organised labour in this country. Once the principle was accepted, it must spread to the general industrial sphere ; in fact, some of the speeches had made it abundantly clear that it was intended to be applied to all unions. As a member of a minority community he was bound to have sympathy with the demands of another minority community for separate representation in various spheres of life as a form of protection, but in industrial and other spheres there were two criteria for considering the question of separate representation. Firstly, was there any conflict of interests between the minority and the majority communities with regard to any particular matters under discussion, and secondly, even if there was no conflict of interests, was it in fact the case that there was serious danger of discrimination in practice being made against the minority ? Applying these two tests, he found there was no justification for the demand made in the resolution. There was, he declared, no difference between Hindus and Muslims in matters with which trade unions dealt, namely, wages, hours of work and amenities of life.

Mr. *Aney* emphasised that the fundamantal principles of all religious faiths were the same and so if a Christian or a Hindu or a Muslim lived up to the true tenets of his faith, he would be the ideal citizen. There was nothing special with regard to any particular faith ; but what had to be remembered was that service unions were also a part of the big movement in the world to consolidate the working classes ; and if anything done in India had the effect of introducing in that movement the communal or separatist spirit, it would be not only detrimental to the employees, but to the wider world movement. The resolution called upon the Government to take a reactionary step which they should not take the responsibility of accepting. He alluded to the fact that three members of the House, who had experience of running trade unions, had spoken against the resolution.

Mr. *L. K. Maitra* vehemently opposed the resolution. He said that he had never heard even a whisper of criticism against the policies of service unions even by those for whose benefit the resolution was sought to be passed. He assured Dr. Ziauddin that the service unions could not take up the question of prayers or meals, nor could these unions take up individual cases. Such cases could be ventilated in the Assembly. He challenged the statement that these unions were a close preserve of Hindus and gave instances in which Muslims were elected presidents of these unions. Mr. *Azhar Ali* and Sir *Abdul Halim Ghuznavi* were presidents of unions whose members were predominantly Hindus.

Sir *Raza Ali* explained that the main grievance of the Muslim employees of the Government was that the Home Department Resolution dated 6th July 1934 was not being given effect to in letter and spirit, in regard to appointments, promotions and dismissals. Most of the Muslim Unions had been set up to concentrate on such grievances. He was quite prepared to advice the Union, of which he was the President, to join a common union, provided an assurance was forthcoming from a responsible authority of the latter union that they would help their Muslim members to ensure that the resolution dated 6th July 1934 was properly given effect. If the common union was not prepared to help the Muslim members, then surely, there was a conflict of interests. and therefore there was discrimination against the Muslims. That being so, it was the duty of the Government to be just and act courageously by accepting the resolution under discussion.

Sir *Abdul Halim Ghuznavi* declared that he detested communal unions, but they could not shut their eyes to facts. The feeling among the Muslim employees was that by joining a common union their grievances could not be removed. That feeling was based on facts aud past experience.

Sir *Reginald Maxwell*, Home Member, said that in considering their attitude, the Government had approached the question with an open mind, had endeavoured to give due weight to the feelings of those in favour of the resolution ; and if he had to oppose it, it was only because, after a full consideration, the Government remained of the opinion they had previously held, that it was not either in the best interests of the employees themselves nor of the general public that communal unions should be given official resignation.

Explaining the circumstances under which the Government agreed in 1920 to give recognition to Associations of Government servants, the Home Member said that it was agreed that these Associations could only be for the purpose of making representations on matters of common interest to a whole class of Government employees. On other matters, Government employees were able to submit individual memorials. The principles of recognition then adopted were that an Association should consist of a distinct class of Government employees and every Government employee of the same class must be eligible for membership of the Association. These conditions had remained unchanged ever since 1920 ; in 1932, these principles were reaffirmed. These, in his view, were sufficient to protect the interests of whole classes of Government servants as such, because where major issues were at stake, even the majority community would recognise that the solidarity of the Service or the Association was essential, and the Association could not afford to neglect the interests of any section of the members without detriment to the membership strength.

Mr. *Abdul Rashid Chaudhury*, supporting the resolution, declared that the present common trade unions were concerned with every other interest except that of Muslims. The House divided on the resolution and rejected it by 48 votes to 17.

Profession Tax Bill

27th. MARCH :—The House agreed to-day to circulation of *Sir Frederick James'* Bill to limit to a maximum of Rs. 50 per annum the amount payable in respect of any person by way of tax on profession, trades, callings and employments. Sir Frederick James said that the Bill sought to remove what they in Madras felt to be an anomaly and an injustice. After referring to the circumstances leading to the passing of the India and Burma (Miscellaneous Amendments) Act by Parliament, he said the new section added by the Amending Act, while continuing the right of provinces to impose a tax on professions, trades, callings and employments, limited the incidence of that tax in respect of any one person to a maximum of Rs. 50 per annum, save in the case of those provinces in which a tax of this kind was levied at a higher rate prior to March 31, 1939. In such cases exemption was granted from the operation of the limit of Rs. 50. The result was that whereas in most provinces taxes of this nature were limited to Rs. 50 maximum, in Madras Presidency the maximum rate was an high as Rs. 1,000 per annum in the City of Madras and Rs. 550 per annum in the districts outside the City.

Sir Jeremy Raisman, moving that the Bill be circulated, said that a measure of this kind necessitated the survey of a number of existing taxes, and the taking of action to replace these taxes by alternative sources of revenue and, on that ground alone. time must be given to all the Provincial Governments and local bodies affected to consider the possible effect of the measure and state their views upon it. As regards the general object of the mover, it was no secret that the Government of India had, for many years, discouraged this type of tax. He himself had pointed out the Provincial Governments that they were erecting a superstructure of local taxation on a foundation of doubtful validily, and that it was highly objectionable that the field of income-tax should be invaded in this surreptitious way.

Sir Henry Gidney, on behalf of the newly formed Independent Party, Mr. *Aney and Syed Murtaza Saheb* supported the motion, which was passed.

Federal Courts Appeal Bill

The Assembly referred to a Select Committee *Dr. Banerjee's* Bill to simplify the procedure in appeals to the Federal Court. The mover said that the rules at present made applicable to appeals to the Federal Court were complex and dilatory and also expensive. They were suited to appeals to the Privy Council, situated 6.000 miles away, but not to appeals to the Federal Court situated in India. He stressed the desirability of giving to the Federal Court full powers to regulate its own practice and procedure under Section 214, Government of India Act, and quoted the opinions given in support of the suggestion by *Sir Maurice Gwyer* and the late *Sir Shah Sulaiman*. *Dr. Banerjee* made it clear that the Bill made no attempt to extend in any way the Federal Court's jurisdiction.

Meek-Gregory Mission

29th. MARCH :—The Meek-Gregory Mission to America was strongly criticised and as strongly defended in the course of a debate on a cut motion moved by Mr. *A. N. Chattopadhya* under a demand for a Supplementary Grant in respect of Commercial Intelligence and Statistics."

Dr. P. N. Banerjee, supporting the cut motion, made references to *Dr. Gregory*, suggesting that he was not fully acquainted with the economic needs and conditions of India but on a point of order raised by *Sir Frederick James*, the Chair ruled that it was not desirable to discuss in the House the merits of individual officers. Dr. Bannerjee declared that it was not his intention to disparage Dr. Gregory but wanted to lodge a strong protest against the non-appointment of Indians. If an Indian Delegation had been sent to America, he asserted, they would have carried out the work better ; they would have given their attention not only to the question of export from India but to imports from America and to the question of machinery for key industries which America alone could supply at present. *Dr. Banerjee* referred in support of his criticism of the Mission's work to an Editorial in the *Hindu*, Madras.

Sir A. Ramaswami Mudaliar, Commerce Member in a spirited defence of *Dr. Gregory*, declared that Dr. Bannerjee's remarks were thoroughly unjustified. Dr. Gregory was one of the few officers on whom, he, the Commerce Member, had constantly depended and whose advice had been of invaluable help to him in trade and economic matters. As regards Dr. Gregory's suitability for this mission, the Commerce Member was convinced that he could not have made a better selection. (Hear, hear). The Commerce Member said that some commercial bodies had criticised the Mission but they had done so under the impression that the Mission was sent to negotiate a trade pact ; but when it was explained to them that this was a purely fact-finding mission sent to survey the situation and to make a report to the Government of India on the situation at that time, most of the commercial bodies recognised the reasonableness of Government's action. *Dr. Banerjee* had ignored all this. The Commerce Member went on to explain that Dr. Gregory had been in the United States before associated with an important mission which the United Kingdom had sent there, and had established contact and acquaintance with officials of the United States Treasury, and these contacts were invaluable in the carrying out of his mission on behalf of India. The Report of the Mission could not be published in its entirety, because it contained confidential matters relating to America's key industries and requirements. The published Report was an expurgated edition but even so, its value could not be questioned. The Commerce Member remarked upon the incongruity of a Professor of Economics like Dr. Bannerjee taking lessons in economics from editorials in daily newspapers.

Sir Raza Ali thought it unfortunate that Dr. Banerjee should have brought in the question of the fitness and the suitability of Dr. Gregory. From what he (Sir Raza Ali) knew of Dr. Gregory's work, it had given entire satisfaction to the people with a reasonable frame of mind. As for Sir David Meek, Sir Raza Ali bore testimony to his sincere and earnest desire in dealing with industrial and economic questions to find out the course of action really beneficial to India. But, said Sir Raza Ali, on the question of appointment of Indians, he was entirely in accord with Dr. Banerjee. The Commerce Member on his question had committed himself to a policy with which non-official members of the House could never be in sympathy. He had justified Dr. Gregory's appointment on the ground that Dr. Gregory was well-known in America and had access to officials because of his previous knowledge of the country. If that logic was true, there would, considering the difficulty of Indians as a race in countries like America, be a perpetual argument against the appointment of Indians.

Sir A. Ramaswami Mudaliar, intervening, said that Sir Raza Ali was reading more into his remarks than was justified. All that he (the Commerce Member) had said was that, in the conditions of that time and for the purpose intended and in order to get a report within the time available, Dr. Gregory was the best man available. There was no policy behind it. The Commerce Member reminded the House that every Trade Commissioner appointed by the Commerce Department had been an Indian, except in the United Kingdom.

Sir Raza Ali said that if that was the Government of India's policy he did not have much to say; but he asked why it should not have been possible for the Commerce Member to send a delegation of one Englishman and one Indian? Sir A. Ramaswami Mudaliar pointed out that the Indian Trade Commissioner in New York, Mr. *H. S. Malik*, was associated with the Mission, while as regards Sir *David Meek*, he was on his way to England through America, and the Government of India took advantage of that to use his services in connection with the mission. Sir *Raza Ali* observed that, to be in the position of an Adviser was not the same thing as to be a member of the Delegation. He emphasised that unless on these delegations there was, if possible, a majority of Indians, the reports of these delegations were not going to command the country's confidence. As regards daily newspaper editorials, Sir Raza Ali said that he had been a careful reader of some of the leading articles and he must say he took off his hat to the writers. Sir Raza Ali asserted that in no case should a Delegation of this kind have less than a fifty-fifty Indian representation. The cut motion was rejected and the demand was assented to.

INSURANCE ACT AMEND. BILL

The Assembly agreed to all demands for Supplementary Grants and then took up the Insurance Act Amendment Bill.

In moving that the measure be taken into cosideration, the *Commerce Member* dealt with the main Amendments adopted by the Select Committee. He said that they had removed from the Bill the provision relating to the power of prescribing the manner of making an application for renewal of a registration and had by inserting a new sub-section laid down in the Act itself, what was to be done in making such an application. He said that the scale of charges contemplated would be such as to fix the fee at Rs. 100 where the annual premium income of the insurer in the class of business concerned was Rs. 1 lakh or less, Rs. 200 when it exceeded one but did not exceed two lakhs, Rs. 300 when it exceeded two but did not exceed four lakhs, Rs. 500 when it exceeded four but did not exceed six lakhs, Rs. 750 when it exceeded six but did not exceed ten lakhs and Rs. 1,000 when it exceeded ten lakhs. The scale would also secure that the total of the fees payable in respect of all classes of business exclusive of life insurance business did not exceed Rs. 1,500.

Mr. *Chapman-Mortimer* supported the Bill, while Messrs. *Chattopadhyaya* and *Nauman* wanted more time for the consideration of the Bill. They felt that the Bill was being rushed through in unnecessary hurry.

The motion for consideration was adopted and the House took up the clauses.

The provision increasing the registration fee for each class of business from Rs. 100 to Rs. 500 for new insurance companies was attacked by Mr. *A. C. Datta*, who moved an amendment to omit the provision and was supported by Dr. Banerjee, Mr. Aney and Dr. F. De Souza. The speakers objected to the provision which, in their view, made the Bill "a taxation measure." The Commerce Member, they suggested, had himself admitted this when he said that the contribution from the General Revenues towards the cost of administration of the Act would be limited to Rs. 1,50,000 and the balance of the cost would be met from the proceeds of the fees. The speakers expressed the fear that the increased fee would "kill" young and small insurance companies and as the department would be dependent on the contribution made by insurance companies, the bigger companies which contributed more would exert a greater influence on the department. The department would, therefore, lose its independence, and would become extravagant because the Finance Department, which only made a fixed contribution, might not exercise a rigid and strict control.

Sir *Cawasji Jehangir* gave the assurance that the Select Committee on the Bill constantly had before it the interests of the smaller companies, but he agreed that there was the danger of extravagance owing to the lack of Finance Department's Control.

Mr. *Chapman-Mortimer* said that his Group protested against the principle of making the insurers pay for the cost of administration ; and he made it clear that unless the Commerce Member gave an assurance that as the Department grew, more money would, if necessary, be forthcoming from the General Revenues. He could not support the provision.

Sir *Ramaswami Mudaliar* reminded the House that the fee of Rs. 500 was with reference to new insurance companies which might, hereafter, come into existence. On the question whether the Government had been committed to the policy of making the Department self-supporting, he made it clear that that was not the policy. It had already been emphasised that the fees were to be charged in order to increase the realisations under the Act so as to cover the present direct cost of administration. He laid stress on the words 'present' and 'direct' and said he was not committing the House to any proposition that Rs. 1,50,000 was the maximum which the general tax-payer would bear towards the cost of administering the Act. The amendment was lost.

During the discussion on Clause 4, prescribing a graduated scale of charges for renewal of registration, the Commerce Member reiterated that the Government had no intention of making any profit out of the Bill. They only wanted to raise the bare minimum necessary amount for the Department of the Superintendent of Insurance. He anticipated that the Rules which were expected to be published during the year would contain a lower scale of charges than were incorporated in the Select Committee's report, to which he had referred in his speech earlier in the day. He, however, declared that having regard to the finances of the Government, he would not be able to carry on the responsibilities of the Department unless the House agreed to the Bill and thereby enabled him to raise money. On the point raised by Mr. *Aney*, the Commerce Member stated that the Government had power to grant exemption from stamp duty on renewal fees, and they would do so if it was found that renewal of licences required additional payment on account of stamp duty. Sir Ramaswami Mudaliar accepted and the House passed an amendment adding to the Clause a proviso to the effect that an appeal shall lie to the Central Government from an order passed by the Superintendent of Insurance imposing a penalty on the insurer.

Clause 4 was allowed to stand over for further consideration of an Amendment moved by Dr. Bannerjee, and the House passed Clauses 5 to 12 and adjourned till Monday the 31st. March when the Congress Nationalist party gained a point on which they had laid great stress, namely, that the powers of the Superintendent of Insurance were too exhaustive under the Act and should, to some extent, be curtailed.

Dr. *P. N. Banerjea* supported by Mr. A. N. Chattopadhyaya and Mr. A. C. Datta had, on Saturday, moved an amendment to the effect that the renewal of registration of an Insurance Company should be automatic on the fulfilment of the requirements of the proposed new Section 3 A, and that the discretion left to the Superintendents by the following sub-clause should be removed :

"The Superintendent of Insurance, shall, on being satisfied that the insurer has fulfilled the requirements of this section, renew the registration and grant him a certificate of renewal of registration."

Sir *A. Ramaswami Mudaliar*, Commerce Member, on behalf of the Government, had accepted the idea, but not the wording of the amendment, and further consideration was left over till to-day in order to enable an agreed amendment to be drafted.

The agreed amendment was moved and passed this morning.

With the amendment the subclause reads :—

"The Superintendent of insurance, shall, on fulfilment by the insurer of the requirements of this section, renew the registration and grant him a certificate of renewal of registration."

The House passed the Bill to amend the Insurance Act.

DELHI RIBBON DEVELOPMENT BILL

1st. APRIL :—The house continued to-day the discussion on Mr. *J. D. Tyson's* Bill to control ribbon development in Delhi, described by him as the first measure of its kind in India. Sir Yamin Khan, Mr. Kazmi, Mr. Abdul Ghani, Mr. Azhar Ali and Pandit Nilakanta Das spoke generally supporting the provisions of the Bill but demanding relaxtion of some of the powers proposed to be taken under it. Messrs. *Azhar Ali* and *Kazmi* argued that the Government had ample powers already to exercise the control which they wanted to do by means of the Bill. Mr. Kazmi urged the establishment of a Planning Authority, and said that without such an Authority no restriction on development should be placed.

Mr. *Ghani* expressed grave doubts about the policy of those in power in Delhi in the matter of improving or preserving graveyards and religious buildings and complained that even permission for ordinary repairs and whitewashing of these religious buildings had been refused by the authorities. *Sir Yamin Khan* complimented the Government on deciding not to make use of their voting power to pass the Bill but to carry the House with them. He said that he originally entertained apprehension about the Bill but he was now convinced that it was a beneficial measure.

Mr. *Tyson*, replying to the suggestion that powers already existed which, without recourse to legislation, could have been utilised to give the Government the control which they wanted pointed out that apart from the fact that the more democratic course was to introduce a Bill in the House and not to adopt measures without reference to the House, this was the first measure of its kind in India and even had the Government wished, they could not have adopted from any province the privisions that were being introduced in the Bill. The consideration motion was passed.

During discussion of the clauses, Mr. *Tyson* accepted and the House passed a number of amendments moved by Mr. Kazmi, Mr. Ghani, Mr. Nairang and Mr. Aney. Among these amendments was one laying down that a person shall be deemed to be interested in land if, among other things, he is a Muslim and the land is one occupied by or for the purposes of a mosque, Imambara, Dargah, Karbala or Muslim graveyard. Another amendment accepted excluded from control under the Bill places of worship, the tomb, samadhi, cenotaph or the graveyard or the wall enclosing these, and also the construction of an unmetalled road intended to give access to land soley for agricultural purposes. A proviso was added to the effect that, in case the Chief Commissioner decided to acquire land, the claimant to it shall be entitled to be repaid by the acquiring authority the amount of expense which he might have properly incurred in connection with the preparation and submission of his claim for compensation and in default of agreement, such amount should be determined by the authority deciding the value of the land in the proceedings under the Land Acquisition Act. In the course of the discussion, Mr. Tyson made it clear that control under the Bill was not intended to apply to areas where Improvement Trust Schemes were in operation.

During the third reading, Mr. Aney expressed regret that Government should have agreed to the wide definition of an "interested person." The definition in his view was so wide that it was open to a Muslim from Bokhara to come and enter a claim. The Bill, as amended, was passed. The House was then *prorogued*.

THE FLOUD COMMISSION REPORT

1st. APRIL :—The Assembly to-day had a brief session, the discussion on the Land Revenue (Floud) Commission Report, which had been fixed for the evening, having been postponed as all the materials connected with the subject had not been received by the members. When the matter came up for consideration, Mr. *Sasanka Sekhar Sanyal*, chief whip of the Bose Party, complained that members had not been supplied with either the volumes containing the evidence collected by the Floud Commission or the report of the Special officer appointed by the Government to examine the recommendations of the Commission. Unless these materials were available to them, they were not in a position to discuss the report and give their considered views on the subject which was of such vital interest to all sections of the community.

Mr. *J. N. Basu*, leader of the Hindu Nationalist party, remarked that the Floud Commission's report related to matters of far-reaching importance and should therefore be subjected to very careful scrutiny. This could not be done unless the evidence collected by the Commission and the report of the Special Officer was available to them.

Rai D. N. Choudhury (Bose Group) remarked that if the Government were unable to make up their minds regarding the recommendations of the Floud Commission without examining Mr. Gurner's report, how then could they expect members of the House to express their considered views on the subject without studying that report? Members of his party were as anxious as the Government that a decision on the recommendations of the Floud Commission was reached as early as possible, but in order that this might be done members must have all the materials connected with the subject.

The Premier. Mr. *A. K. Fazlul Huq*, said the occasion was intended to give members an opportunity of expressing their views on the subject. There was no question of the Government being unable to make up their minds on the matter. The report of the Floud Commission was not only a matter of vital importance to various sections of the people but also touched certain constitutional questions, including the Permanent Settlement which was of great historical importance, and should, therefore, be considered from all points of view. There was no doubt that the Commission had taken great pains to collect a vast amount of useful materials affecting the land revenue system of the province. The report of Mr. Gurner was the report of an officer appointed specially to go through the Floud Commission's recommendations, summarise its conclusions and suggest means that should be adopted to implement those recommendations. The report was submitted by Mr. Gurner for the benefit of the Government. If, however, members thought that they should also have copies of Mr. Gurner's report to enable them to discuss the matter, he had nothing to say against it.

Mr. *Santosh Kumar Basu* (deputy leader of Bose Party) said that if the Government considered that Mr. Gurner's report was very helpful to them why should they deny members an opportunity of studying that report. On a previous occasion the Government promised to place at the disposal of members all materials connected with the subject. In the circumstances, he could not understand this anxiety on the part of the Government not to circulate that report.

Sir *B. P. Singh Roy* said that there was no question of not publishing the report. The position was that at the present moment the Government were considering Mr. Gurner's report, and until they had thoroughly studied the report they were not in a position to place it before the House.

The Speaker, *Sir Azizul Haque* said that he felt it desirable that members should go through the volumes containing the evidence before they were called upon to express their opinion on the recommendations of the Commission.

INDIAN SOLDIERS' VICTORY REJOICED

2nd. APRIL :—The Assembly adopted a special motion moved by the Hon. Mr. *A. K. Fazlul Huq* conveying rejoicing at the capture of Keren and Harer and congratulating the Indian soldiers through His Excellency the Governor of Bengal and His Excellency the Commander-in-Chief. Mr. *Jalaluddin Hashemy* opposed the motion on the ground that there was no occasion for rejoicings as the capture of these towns would mean only the displacement of the Italians to be substituted by the British Imperialism. He further said that there was nothing to congratulate the Indian soldiers who were nothing but merceneries and had been used on former occasions in enslaving other peoples. There would be occasion for rejoicings when their soldiers would achieve success in defending their own motherland. Mr.

Niharendu Dutta Majumdar said that if there was any nation responsible for the conquest of Abyssinia by the Italians it was the Britishers. Mr. *J. N. Basu* regretted that altogether a different issue had been raised. In fighting in Africa these Indian soldiers were really fighting for the defence of India. Mr. *W. A. Walker* said that the Imperial armies in the middle east had gone from one success to another. These victories only could have been achieved by the brilliant strategy of General Wavell and his staff. He would hardly stress the importance of these successes from the point of view of the defence of India. They particularly rejoiced at the gallant part played by the Indian soldiers. Theirs had been a new record of courage. The Hon. Mr. *A. K. Fazlul Huq* said that there was no occasion made by the Opposition on the occasion. In the first place the motion referred to the fact that it was a case of Indian achievement and therefore a matter for the pride of Indians and secondly Abyssinia was a country of vital importance to the defence of India. The motion was put to vote and carried, 175 voting for it as against 46.

Markets Regulation Bill

3rd. APRIL :—On the motion of the hon'ble Mr. *Tamijuddin Khan*, Minister for Agriculture and Industries, the Assembly to-day referred the Markets Regulation Bill to a Select Committee. An Opposition motion, urging circulation of the Bill for eliciting public opinion, was rejected without a division. The Bill seeks to define the market charges and fees which may be levied by the proprietors of markets and the rates at which they may be levied ; to maintain sets of standard weights and measures in markets ; to compel a proprietor of a market to provide adequate shelter, conservancy, water-supply, sanitation, etc. The Opposition criticism against the Bill was that it did not provide for the control of prices of commodities and that there was no definite proposals in the Bill.

The Dowry Restriction Bill

4th. APRIL :—Non-official Bills were considered in the Assembly to-day. None of the legislative effort of the non-official members, however, proceeded beyond the circulation stage. Mr. *Surendra Nath Biswas* moved for reference to Select Committee the Bengal Dowry Restriction Bill, the object of which was to put a stop to the dowry system among the Bengalee Hindus. The main provision of the Bill is that no person shall at any time offer or accept any dowry whose money value exceeds the sum of Rs. 51, which sum shall not include the value of ornaments or anything in kind given by brides' parents or guardians as a gift out of free will. The Bill was circulated for eliciting public opinion.

The Fisheries Bill

Mr. *Narendra Nath Das Gupta* and Mr. *Amrita Lal Mandal* moved for reference to Select Committees two bills for legalising the rights of fisherman. Mr. Mandal in moving his Bill—Bengal Fisheries Bill—said that the Bill had been introduced with a view to rationalise the settlement of fisheries on the basis of fair and equitable rent and stabilise the fish industry which formed a vital part in the economic structure of the province. Hon. Mr. *Tamizuddin Khan*, replying, said that there was no gainsaying the fact that rights of fishermen who had to suffer from various exactions and oppressions had to be protected by some sort of legislation. Government, he asserted, was not sitting idle in the matter. Government were anxious to bring forward a comprehensive measure to deal with the rights of the fishermen. With that end in view they had appointed a special officer on the basis of those reports. They would bring forward a Bill, which the Minister hoped would remove the outstanding grievances of fishermen. There were defects in the Bills which he opposed. The motions for the circulation of the Bills for eliciting public opinion were defeated.

Relief to Tenants' Bill

Maulvi Abdul Hakim (Coalition) introduced a Bill giving relief to non-agricultural tenants by way of giving protection from eviction and arbitrary enhancement of rent. Hon. Mr. *T. Khan*, replying on behalf of Government, said that the Chandina Committee had submitted their report and on the basis of that report Government proposed to bring forward an appropriate measure.

The Wakf Amendment Bill

Dr. *Sanaulla* (Coalition) introduced the Bengal Wakf Amendment Bill. He said that the taxation which had been introduced by the Wakf Act, was according to eminent Moslem divines illegal. Government, he pleaded, should provide for funds for the supervision and management of Wakf properties. His amending Bill was for the elimination of this taxation. Hon. Mr. M. B. Mullick said that the Government wanted some time to consider the matter and had asked the statutory Wakf Board for their opinion. The Bill was circulated for eliciting opinion.

TARAKESWAR TEMPLE BILL

Mr. *Taraknath Mukherjee* introduced the Tarakeswar Temple Bill. Mr. *Atul Chandra Kumar* opposed the Bill. He said that the provision in the Bill asking for Government interference in the management of Hindu temples was a dangerous principle. The present committee was doing work satisfactorily and the present *Mahanta* was a man of high character against whom so far nobody had any complaint to offer. The motion for circulation of the Bill was defeated and the Bill was killed. The House then adjourned.

THE DACCA RIOTS—ADJ. MOTION

9th. APRIL:—The adjournment motion tabled by *Rai Harendranath Chowdhury* (Bose Group) to discuss the Government's failure to control the extension of rioting in the Dacca District was lost to-day, 67 voting for and 107 against. The official Congress party attended the meeting and supported the motion. The Krishak Projas and Independents also supported the motion, while the European bloc supported the Government. There was a large attendance of members and the public galleries were full. Several members of the Upper House were present in the enclosures reserved for them.

Rai Harendra Nath Choudhuri (Congress), in moving the motion, referred to the statement made by the Chief Minister, Mr. A. K. Fazlul Huq, that the Government was taken unawares by what had happened in the Narayanganj Sub-Division. Mr. Rai Choudhuri pointed out that the riot had been continuing in the city of Dacca from March 17 and that ought to have constituted a sufficient warning to the Government to take precautionary measures so that the disturbance might not spread to other areas. According to the speaker, there was perfect abdication by the authorities responsible for the maintenance of law and order in that area for a certain period. He referred to the large number of people that had taken shelter from the affected area in Tripura State and remarked that this bore witness to the fact that an "unworkable and imperfect" constitution was being attempted to be worked and that, by "worthless and inefficient hands."

Participating in the debate, Mr. *Nalini Ranjan Sarker*, Ex-Finance Minister, referred to the situation created by the communal disturbances in the Narayanganj Sub-Division and remarked that in the affected area "the rule of law seemed to have given way to the rule of the outlaw." So far as the subject matter of the motion was concerned, he thought that Government had admitted that they had failed to control the situation and to ensure protection to life and property. This truth, remarked Mr. Sarker, was writ large over the many communiques the Government had issued on the riot situation. Proceeding, Mr. Sarker said that the Government were unpardonably indifferent, and that they were not taking up the matter seriously, was clear from their attitude to the forced large-scale migration. The Maharaja of Tripura had shown great generosity and sympathy in sheltering the refugees at considerable expense. Mr. Sarker said that the Government had banned the publication of news. There might be justification for some control of news at a time like this, but the censoring of news agencies and the non-publication of any authentic news by the Government themselves at the same time had been producing certain most undesirable effects. Mr. Sarker thought that the Government had failed to keep adequate touch with the actual situation in the affected areas.

Mr. *Shamsuddin Ahmed*, Leader of the Krishak Proja Party, deplored the situation that had arisen and emphasised that all the Ministers ought to have gone to Dacca to tackle the situation and that the sitting of the Assembly ought to have been suspended, so that the members of the legislature might go to the affected area to try to restore normal conditions. He maintained that rioters, whether Hindus or Muslims, should be dealt with drastically. He deplored some of the speeches made recently by Dr. S. P. Mookerjee and the hon. the Chief Minister, Mr. A. K. Fazlul Huq.

Dr. *Syama Prasad Mukerjee*, in supporting the motion, referred to the observations made by the previous speaker, and said that it was only during the last 18 months that it had been his lot to speak inside the legislature and outside it in defence of the rights and liberties of the Hindus of this province. He would like to give the assurance to the Hindus that whatever attempts might be made by interested persons to disort his speeches, in none of them he had attacked the Muslim community as such. It was no question of talking of the Muslim community as such, Dr. Mookerjee proceeded. But it was a question of exposing the policy of the present Ministry which, according to him, had been deliberately aimed during the last few years, at the curtailment of the rights and liberties of the Hindus. Dr. Mookerjee then referred to what had appeared in a Muslim daily of the City a few days ago. It was written in that paper that "the time has come to show the little rats that the lion is not dead, only sleeping. They will see to whom Bengal belongs. They shall be taught the lesson they need." Dr. Mookerjee remarked that what was happening in Dacca and Narayanganj was the lesson, which they (the Hindus) were to be taught. Proceeding, the speaker said that he was ashamed as much of the desecration of Mosques as he was ashamed of the repeated desecration of Hindu temples during the last three years. "I do not want that any religious institution should be touched by any community. I want communal concord and harmony in India. We have to live as brothers and as men who understand each other's point of view and not with one community trying to subordinate the interests of the other communities for the purpose of advancement of its own interests." He referred to the official figures of deaths in the Dacca disturbance and said that according to information received by him the official figures were not correct and the number of persons killed among the Hindu and Muslim communities was almost equalised to-day. The heart of every man went out in sympathy with a person killed, whether he was a Hindu or Muslim or Christian.

Speaking on behalf of the Government, the Chief Minister, Mr. *A. K. Fazlul Huq*, said : "When I was a boy at school, I had a classmate who was responsible for a disturbance in the classroom and as soon as he committed any offence, he used to shout the loudest in order to say that everybody but himself was in the wrong. The attitude that has been taken up by some of my friends speaking in support of this motion has reminded me of the case of that old classmate of mine. For four years, they have been singing a hymn of hate against the Ministry and the Muslim community ; they have encouraged people to come out and set at defiance the Government. I cannot help quoting a passage from a speech of Dr. Syama Prasad Mookerjee intended to make the peaceful administration of Bengal impossible. After having done that, after having prepared the ground and after having perfected their plan, things naturally began to develop themselves."

Proceeding, the Chief Minister said that it was not on March 17 that the trouble began at Dacca. The real trouble in Dacca began on the afternoon of March 14 when some Hindu boys sprinkled coloured water on some Muslim boys on the day of the Holi festival. An old man, who was passing by, protested against this. This old man was caught by the beard and his whole body was sprinkled with coloured water. Blows were given on his head and he was removed to hospital. After the incident for two days, namely, the 15th and 16th, the whole of Dacca was in tense excitement. Although stabbing was going on and Muslims were being freely stabbed, not one Hindu was stabbed in retaliation. It was on March 17 that mosques began to be desecrated. The Holy Koran was torn to pieces and leaves of the Koran were strewn on the floor. Immediately after this, continued Mr. Huq. Hindu youths dressed in 'lungies' (cloths generally worn by Muslims), with red caps on, went to various villages in the District of Dacca exciting Muslims to rise against the Hindus, saying Mosques had been desecrated and the Holy Koran had been torn to pieces and that it was time for the Muslims to rise against the Hindus. (Laughter in Congress Benches). "You may laugh, but it was part of a preconceived policy. The Hindus knew that once the Muslims were roused they would go to excesses and the Hindus knew how to retaliate afterwards," Mr. Huq remarked. In conclusion the Chief Minister assured the House that the Government had taken every possible step to meet the situation, which was now under control. He expressed the grateful thanks of the Bengal Government to His Highness the Maharaja of Tripura for the shelter that he had given to a number of people from the affected area and announced that the Government had sanctioned an expenditure of Rs. 10,000 for the relief of the victims and, if necessary, the Government would be prepared to spend more. The Assembly thereafter adjourned till April 22.

Local Self-Govt. Amend. Bill

22nd APRIL :—The Bengal Local Self-Government (Amendment) Bill. 1941, as passed by the Legislative Council, came up for consideration to day. The measure met with strong opposition from the Bose Group and the Krishak Proja Party. A suggestion that the Bill had been brought forward in the interest of certain "stalwarts" of the Coalition Party was emphatically repudiated by the Revenue Minister, Sir *B. P. Singh Roy*, member-in-charge of the Bill, who explained that its object was that the reconstitution of district boards might not be unduly delayed.

The Bill seeks to provide for a special machinery for the decision of disputes relating to elections held under the Bengal Local Self-Government Act of 1835 and at the same time oust the jurisdiction of civil courts in respect of such disputes as has been done under the other Acts relating to the administration of local self-government in the province. It is further proposed that the principles of the Bill, when enacted into law, should apply to elections which have already been held and in respect of which disputes are still pending in civil courts, so that the new boards to which elections have been made may come into existence and function without avoidable delay.

23rd. APRIL :—The Bill was strongly opposed both at the second and the third readings to-day. The Opposition, through amendments, fought stoutly for making a provision in the Bill for an appellate authority against the decision of the district or subordinate judge on the election petitions. *Sir Bijoy* opposed the amendments and the Opposition's attempts proved futile against the weight of number which the Coalition Party commanded. The Opposition also fought against the principle of giving retrospective effect to the enactment and wanted the deletion of the provision. Mr. *Sanaka Sanyal* pointed out that it was a wellknown convention that the existing laws of the land should be treated with respect. By the passing of the present bill into Act all election suits, now pending before courts, would automatically become null and void. It was now almost an admitted fact that the bill was a Dacca enactment,—the election suits regarding Dacca District Board which were now pending decisions were the main pivot of the present measure. With the passing of the bill into Act those suits would become null and void. This was against all principles of democracy and progressive Government. The election suits at Dacca were instituted under the existing law and with reference to the existing conditions. Now they wanted to arrest the powers of the courts under the existing laws by the passing of this bill. This was, Mr. Sanyal remarked, more than robbery. Sir *Bijoy*, replying to the point, merely stated that he did not want to waste the time of the House by repeating his arguments in regard to this matter. He formally opposed it. The amendment was lost.

During the third reading of the bill, *Rai Harendra Nath Chaudhury* said that he would be speaking on it in order to record his emphatic protest against the 'pernicious measure'. Sir Bijoy, he said, had taken shelter under the Bengal Municipal Act of 1922 for the principles introduced in the bill in ousting the jurisdiction of the civil courts. But he would only remind him that the measure, when first introduced, was thrown away by the then Council and was only passed when the Congress had withdrawn from the legislature. Was it not a fact, he enquired, that this piece of legislation was going to be a scandalous abouse of the legislative machinery ? It was unfortunate, Mr. Rai Choudhury remarked, that an experienced minister like Sir Bijoy Prasad Singh Roy should allow himself to be influenced by the reactionary coterie of Dacca in the matter of local self-governments. He, on behalf of the Opposition, strongly opposed the passing of the measure. In reply, Sir *Bijoy* stated that there was no justification for so much excitement. He asked the House to pass the bill. The bill as settled in the House was passed by 150 to 55 votes. The Assembly was then *prorogued.*

The Bengal Legislative Council

LIST OF MEMBERS

Presid nt :—Hon'ble Mr. Satyendra Chandra Mitra

Deputy President :—Mr. Hamidul Huq Chowdhury

Elected Members

Shrish Chandra Chakravarty
Kanai Lal Goswami
Rai Manmatha Nath Bose Bahadur
Rai Satish Chandra Mukherjee Bahadur
Ranjit Pal Chowdhury
Rai Sahib Jatindra Mohan Sen
Rai Brojendra Mohan Maitra Bahadur
Rai Keshab Chandra Banerjee Bahadur
Rai Sahib Indu Bhusan Sarker
Lalit Chandra Das
Alhadj Khan Bahadur Shaik Muhammad Jan
Khan Bahadur Naziruddin Ahmad
" " S. Fazal Ellahi
" " Ataur Rahaman
Humayun Reza Chowdhury
Khan Bahadur Mukhlesur Rahaman
" " Mohammad Asaf Khan
" " Mohammad Ibrahim
Alhadj Khan Bahadur Khwaja Mohammad Esmail
Khan Bahadur Kazi Abdur Rashid
" Sahib Abdul Hamid Chowdhury
" Bahadur M. Abdul Karim
Moazzemali Chowdhury (*alias* Lal Mia)
Khorshed Alam Chowdhury
Khan Bahadur Syed Mohammad Ghaziul Huq
Khan Bahadur Rezzaqul Haider Chowdhury
Nur Ahmed
H. C. A. Hunter
W. F. Scott-Kerr
W, B. G. Laidlaw
Dr. Radha Kumud Mukherjee
Khan Sahib Sabidali Molla
Kamini Kumar Dutt
Mohammed Hoossain
Amulayadhone Roy
Rai Radhika Bhusan Roy Bahadur
H. G. MacKay
J. B. Ross
H. P. Poddar
Bankim Chandra Dutta
Naresh Nath Mukherjee
Maulana Muhammad Akram Khan
Sachindra Narayan Sanyal
Hamidul Huq Chowdhuri
Mesbahuddin Ahmed
Kader Baksh
Saileswar Singh Roy
Narendra Narayan Roy
Hon. Mr. Satyendra Chandra Mitra
Khan Bahadur Saiyed Muazzamuddin Hosain
Narendra Chandra Dutta
Humayun Kabir
Raja Bhupendra Chandra Sinha Bahadur of Nashipur
Nawabzada Kamaruddin Haidar
E. C. Ormond
Khan Bahadur M. Shamsuzza
Rai Surendra Narayan Sinha Bahadur
Begum Hamida Momin
K. D'Rozario
Latafat Hossain
Dr. Arabinda Barua
Dr. J. Cohen

Proceedings of the Council

Budget Session—Calcutta—11th. February to 8th. April 1941

Public Accounts Committee Report

The opening meeting of the budget session of the Bengal Legislative Council on the 11th February 1941 was short, lasting a little more than an hour. After questions had been answered and some formal Government business disposed of, the House adjourned as a mark of respect to the memory of Mr. *Surendra Mohan Moitra*, a member of the Bengal Assembly.

11th. FEBRUARY :—The Council had another short sitting to-day. The agenda included consideration of the Official Trustees (Bengal Amendment) Bill, as passed by the Lower House, and the report of the Committee on Public Accounts on the Appropriation Accounts and Finance Accounts of the Government of Bengal for 1938-39 and the Audit Reports 1939.

The Council passed the Official Trustees Bill without any discussion. As regards the report of the Committee on Public Accounts, Dr. *Radhakumud Mookerjee* (Congress) objected to the consideration of the report on a point of privilege. He maintained that the Council had nothing to do with this report submitted by a committee which had no connexion with this House. He felt that a definite breach of privilege of the House had been committed in this matter and remarked that the Finance Minister was not justified in taking the time of the House by asking it to give its opinion on something which did not come within the purview of the Council. A discussion followed on the point raised by Dr. Mookerjee and eventually the House agreed to refer the matter to its Privilege Committee. The House then adjourned.

The Raza Bazar Disturbances

12th. FEBRUARY :—The President, Mr. *S. C. Mitra*, ruled out of order to-day an adjournment motion sought to be moved by Prof. *Humayun Kabir* to discuss the situation arising out ot the disturbances at Raja Bazar on Monday. The motion sought to discuss "a matter of urgent and definite public importance namely, the action of the police in making indiscriminate arrests in the early hours of Monday morning,and the ruthless lathi charges on members of the public in the forenoon and afternoon of the same day and the failure of the Government, in spite of repeated requests on the floor of the House, to supply adequate information or explanation of the incident, which arose out of the action of the police."

Narrating the circumstances leading to the disturbances, the *Chief Minister* said that in the first place the matter arose out of a case which had been already started under Section 143, I. P. C. and the arrests on Monday morning were made in pursuance of that case. He reminded the members that on the afternoon of February 8, a number of "tazias" were passing through the Circular Road with unusually long poles which were obstructed by the telegraph and tram wires and the taziawalas could not proceed further. They demanded that the wires should be cut. The police tried to argue with them and urged them to move on one side, but they would not listen to any request. The situation was then such that the police had either to use force or to adopt some other means to meet the wishes of the taziawalas. The use of force then would have meant "perhaps nothing less than slaughter". Hundreds of persons would have been injured or killed. The police, therefore, thought that the best way to deal with the situation was to cut the tram and telegraph wires and allow the "tazias" to proceed. Proceeding, the Chief Minister said that cases under Section 143, I.P.C., and also under the Police Act for obstruction were then started against persons who insisted on the wires being cut and on Monday morning these persons were arrested. There were a number of police officers when the arrests were made. The arrests were made not indiscriminately, but on the identification of police constables. The identifications were made by Muslim constables and under the supervision of Muslim superior officers. After these arrests were made, they were taken to the thana and they were subsequently released on bail. The Chief Minister added, "At about noon when we were in office we received information that people had collected at the Raza Bazar Tram Depot and were obstructing tram cars, hurling stones and indiscriminately assaulting people. The Home Minister, the Finance Minister and myself, accompanied by the Commissioner of Police and other persons, went to the Moulali where I met a crowd. They listened to me and dispersed. We then moved on to the Raza Bazar and when we came near the Calcuttta Medical School, we were met by a number of persons brandishing lathis, shouting slogans and throwing stones. They, in fact, surrounded my car. I got out of my car and wanted to speak to them, but I was received with a fusillade of stones. I came back to my car. Stones were thrown at my car and it was an accident that I did not get stones on my head. I went home. "Since I came away, I had personally no knowledge of what took place later. But I was told that in some places the crowds were unruly : when Sir Nazimuddin was speaking to them, stones were thrown on all sides." The Chief Minister declared, "I can bear testimony to the fact that during the time I was there, the mob behaved in an unruly manner and the police dealt with them there with extreme patience." Mr. *Fazlul Huq*, proceeding, observed that it was not a fact that indiscriminate arrests were made. Neither was it a fact that huts were broken into or any woman molested. He said that a case had already been started under Section 143, I. P. C., against some persons for riotous behaviour in the Raja Bazar area. The *Premier* added that the number of people injured in the disturbances were : on the police side 24, tramway employees 18 and on the mob side 9, including a Hindu.

Better Control of Trust Funds

14th. FEBRUARY :—Non-official resolutions were taken up to-day. Of the 11 resolutions on the agenda three were disposed of, one was withdrawn, one carried and one was lost. The House resumed discussion of the resolution moved by the *Raja Bahadur of Nashipur* (Progressive) on September 13 last that a representative committee, consisting of members of the Hindu community, be appointed to draft a Bill to provide for better governance, administration and supervision of Hindu public religious charitable funds to which the Hindu public customarily has to contribute and has contributed. The motion was withdrawn.

Help for Weaving Industry

Mr. *Nur Ahmed* (Coalition) moved that the Government of Bengal be requested to make early steps to encourage and help in all possible ways the handloom industry in Bengal and to make a strong representation to the Government of India to continue on a large scale their grant-in-aid to the handloom weaving industry in Bengal at least for another period of ten years. Khan Bahadur *Saiyd Muazzum-uddin Hossain* (Coalition), Mr. *Lalit Chandra Das* (Congress), Mr. *Dhirendra Lal Barua* (chosen by the Governor) and Mr. *Humayun Kabir* (Proja) supported the resolution which was carried. The Council then adjourned till the 15th. February.

Financial Statement for 1941-42

15th. FEBRUARY :—In the course of his Budget speech to-day, the *Finance Minister*, referred to the jute policy of the Government and said that the keystone of the whole policy was regulation and they would leave nothing undone to secure effective regulation of this year's crop. Nothing was more certain than that the growing of another large jute crop in 1941 would not only cause total collapse even of the present price, but would result in making jute of all kinds, of the very finest quality possible, unsaleable this year and the next. Referring to the record of jute lands prepared this year, the Finance Minister said that Government had admitted that the records were not free defects and mistakes and were not perfect. But he assured the House that Government had taken steps to see that the effect of such inaccuracies and any hardship that might arise out of them, should be reduced to a minimum. The Finance Minister added that Government had taken special steps in this connection and had appointed special staff to deal with the errors in recording. The total cost of the year and the next would amount to Rs. 2,50,000 As this decision was taken after the supplementary budget estimates for the current year were placed before the House and the preset budget estimates were in print, this item of expenditure could not be included in either of them and would have to be regularised in due course. The Finance Minister referred to the two taxation measures now awaiting the final verdict of the Legislature and remarked : "Without additional revenues for which the Legislature has been approached, it will not be possible to undertake any expansion of our constructive programme or even to balance our budget." The House at this stage adjourned till the 25th. February.

General Discussion of Budget

25th. to 27th. FEBRUARY :—Divergent opinions on the budget for 1941-42 were expressed to-day when the general discussion of the budget began. Dr. *Radha Kumud Mookerji* (Congress) congratulated the Finance Minister on the businesslike manner in which he had presented the budget but criticized its plan and the principle on which it was based. While agreeing with the Finance Minister that the fundamental weakness of Bengal's financial position was due to the deductions from its revenue made at the Centre, he asked what steps the Government had taken to have this injustice remedied. *Begum Hamida Momin* (Coalition) while she was glad that an increase of over Rs. 14,00,000 had been provided under the head "Education" regretted that no provision had been made for the Sakhwat Memorial Girls' High School which was at present in a rented, unsuitable house. She drew attention to the need of a suitable grant for Government Moslem women training schools, and said that for want of proper middle English and Middle Vernacular schools for Moslem girls it was difficult to set qualified candidates for the training classes. Rai *Monmatha Nath Bose* Bahadur (Progressive) twitted the Government with bringing about a deficit despite a windfall in the shape of revision of the Meston Award, Mr. *Birendra*

Government was to insist on surrender of funds, wherever it was found that the sum provided in the Budget was in excess of what turned out to be actually needed the measures for which provision was made ; in other words, to set its face against financing, by reappropriation, items not included in the Budget simply because there happened to be some surplus money to spare. Examining some of the detailed provisions in the Budget, Mr. Sassoon referred to the Rs. 7 lakhs allotted for commutation of pensions. He asked the Finance Minister if he considered that in the present circumstances of financial stringency that provision was justified. "Is he in fact working on a wartime plan concentrating on what is essential and urgent and cutting out what may be postponed ?" This finished the budget discussion and the House adjourned.

Calcutta Municipal Amend. Bill 1941

28th FEBRUARY :—The report of the select committee on the Calcutta Municipal (Amendment) Bill. 1941, was presented to-day by *Nawab Habibullah Bahadur of Dacca*, Minister for Local Self-Government. The committee made certain modifications, particularly in respect of the provisions in the Bill relating to the appointment of the executive and the proceedings of the Corporation and suggested the lowering of the franchise.

The Bill, it may be stated, seeks to make definite provision in the Act for the supersession of a department of the Corporation and the dissolution of the body of councillors and alderman—in case of incompetency and default in the performance of the duties imposed on them by the Act. The Bill also provides for the appointment of a Government officer as the Chief Executive Officer by the Government and the setting up of a service commission. It also provides safeguards against abuse of power and proposes the lowering of franchise in certain respects "so as to allow the poorer section of the community to vote in Corporation elections" and also "to enfranchise the occupiers of huts in a bustee."

The select committee while retaining the clause giving power to the Provincial Government to supersede a department of the Corporation, suggested the deletion of the provision vesting the Government with power to dissolve the Corporation.

In the opinion of the committee, "the existing provisions of the Act together with the reformatory and penalizing provisions introduced by the Bill, including the control of important appointments and supersession of a department under certain circumstances, are expected to provide sufficient safeguards against the charges usually made against the Corporation." They considered "it expedient to give the new condition a fair trial before thinking of a clause for dissolution of the Corporation." They had, therefore, recommended the deletion "of this prima facie drastic provision from the present Bill."

As regards the appointment of the Chief Executive Officer, they have restricted the appointment to a member of the executive branch of the Indian Civil Service having at least 15 years' service to his credit.

The committee were of opinion, "without casting any reflection on the capacities of the members of the Bengal Civil Service (Executive) that the Chief Executive Officer to be appointed by the Government must, for the first few years at any rate, be a member of the Indian Civil Service. Other sources of recruitment for the post should be considered only after the affairs of the Corporation have been brought to a smooth and satisfactory working order."

The committee have also limited the proposed power of the Executive Officer to sanction estimates up to Rs. 5,000 only instead of Rs. 10.000 as originally provided.

As regards franchise, the committee suggested the lowering of the rent-qualification of people occupying huts in bustees. The committee further proposed the addition of a new clause laying down the special procedure to be adopted in election petitions for further scrutiny and recount of votes.

The committee consisted of 13 members, seven of whom have signed the report subject to separate notes of dissent.

In a joint note of dissent, Mr. W. C. Wordsworth and Mr. C. W. Miles, while generally approving of the provisions of the Bill, pointed out "that the inclusion of provisions extending the franchise in a Bill, the primary object of which is to improve the administration of the Corporation, is inadvisable and inappropriate." In their opinion, "the extension of franchise is a separate problem."

As regards the clauses regarding building regulations, they recommended that these provisions should be omitted from this Bill and that Government should immediately take up the revision of the building rules with a view to introducing a separate amending Bill dealing solely with this question.

NON-OFFICIAL BILLS

Following the presentation of the Select committee's report on the Municipal Bill, the Asembly proceeded with the consideration of several non-official bills, covering a variety of subjects. They were, the Putni Taluks Regulation (Amendment) Bill (introduced by Khan Sahib Abdul Hamid Chowdhury) ; Land Revenue Sales (Amendment) Bill (by Syed Abdul Majid) ; Medical (Amendment) Bill (by Mr. Anukul Chandra Das) ; Tenancy (Amendment) Bill (by Mr. Khagendra Nath Das Gupta) ; the Adi Ganga Improvement Bill (by Mr. P. Banerjee) ; the Marriage Dowry Prohibition Bill (by Mr. Idris Ahmed Mea) and the Rent Reduction (Temporary Provisions) Bill (by Mr. Abdul Hakim).

The first two Bills were passed. The Medical Bill, the Marriage Dowry Provision Bill and the Rent Reduction (temporary Provisions) Bill were circulated for eliciting public opinion. As regards Mr. Khagendra Nath Das Gupta's Tenancy (Amendment) Bill, the House refused to refer it to a select committee ; while the Adi Ganga Improvement Bill was withdrawn. The Assembly then adjourned till the 3rd. March.

GENERAL DISCUSSION OF BUDGET (CONTD.)

3rd. MARCH :—The concluding portion of the *Finance Minister's* speech, in reply to the general discussion on the budget this evening led to uproarious scenes, following which the opposition withdrew from the House. Towards the end of his speech, the Finance Minister was explaining the jute policy of the Government. He claimed that the policy pursued by the Government in regard to jute had benefited the people and the Government and the Government would continue that policy. He accused the Leader of the Krishak Proja Party in opposition of being responsible for a fall in the price of jute, remarking that members of the Party had gone about in the country telling the people that the Government would give up the policy of jute restriction. The Finance Minister characterised them as the "greatest enemies" of the people in general and of the agriculturists in particular. The Finance Minister's remark evoked a storm of protest from the Krishak Proja Party and the Sarat Bose group and there were further interruptions as he proceeded with his speech. The uproar in the Opposition benches continued in the midst of which the Finance Minister remarked that crores and crores of rupees had flowed into the pockets of the agriculturists as a result of the action taken by the Government in regard to jute.

There was then some exchange of words between the Chair and several members on the Opposition benches about the former's decision in "naming" Mr. *Dutta Majumdar* following which Mr. *Sarat Chandra Bose* said that the only thing they could do by way of parliamentary protest, was to withdraw from the House. Mr. Bose and the members of his group then withdrew from the chamber and they were followed by the members of the two other Opposition parties, namely the Krishak Proja Party and the Independent Scheduled Castes Party. The Finance Minister continued his speech for another ten minutes and after he had concluded the House adjourned.

THE SALES TAX BILL (CONTD.)

4th. to 6th. MARCH :—Consideration of the Bengal Finance (Sales Tax) Bill,clause by clause, was resumed in the Assembly this evening. The Opposition made several unsuccessful attempts to reduce the rate of tax proposed in the Bill. The rate of tax as recommended by the Select Committee, was one pice in the rupee on the taxable turnover. The Opposition point of view was that in no country in the world had a sales tax started with such a high rate. They further contended that the tax would ultimately fall on the consumer and they suggested that if, after the actual working of the budget next year, they found that it was necessary to raise the rate of tax, they might do so. The Finance Minister, Mr. *H. S. Suhrawardy*, said that the Government must have money if they wished to expand its activities. There must also be a certain surplus and closing balance which was necessary for the financial stability of any government. He claimed that the tax, proposed in the Bill, would not touch the poor at all, because most of the articles, used by the poor, had been exempted from the purview of the Bill. He told the House that the tax would fall on the middle classes and the richer people. The Assembly adjourned till the next day, the 5th. March when excepting clauses 6, 23 and the schedule, all other clauses were disposed of. Clause 23 relates to the rule-making power of the Provincial Government for the administration of the taxation measure, while the schedule deals with the list of goods that are to be exempted from this tax. The clauses that were disposed of related *inter alia* to assessment of tax, keeping and production of accounts, penalty for the breach of the provisions of the measure. The clauses were passed with minor modifications. Next day, the 6th. March, by 71 votes to 33 the Assembly passed the third reading of the Bill. The House sat till 9-45 p.m. to finish the discussion. The late sitting was necessitated by the Opposition tactics who demanded no less than eight divisions involving a loss of time of about 50 minutes.

The Bill was passed practically in the form in which it emerged from the Select Committee with the exception that a few more articles were included in the list of exemptions. One of the important articles thus exempted was newspapers. The amendment in regard to which was moved by Mr. *C. W. Miles* of the European Party. Mr. *H. S. Suhrawardy*, Finance Minister, who sponsored the Bill said that he gladly accepted Mr. Miles's amendment. From the representations that he had received from newspaper-owners and others, the Government had been convinced that it would be impossible for them (newspaper-owners) to pass on the tax to others. They had already been compelled to bring down the size of their papers to an extent which admitted of no further reduction. Moreover, the amount of money that the Government would be able to collect from this source through the tax would not be more than Rs. 30,000, which they could afford to forego.

Among the articles which the Opposition pressed for exemption were biri and coarse cloth. Giving reasons why he could not include these in the exemption list Mr. Suhrawardy said that he had excluded hooka tobacco as it was a necessity for the agriculturists, but biri was not. Moreover, a labourer who was rich enough to buy a rupee's worth of biri could surely pay one pice more by way of tax.

As regards coarse cloth, he said, he was anxious to try and exempt such cloth as was usually worn by the poorer people; but there were difficulties in classifying such cloth. If they tried to make any such attempt it would lead to evasion, to detect which they would need a huge staff of inspectors and watchers.

But the Government, the Finance Minister said, proposed to compensate the poorer classes by setting apart an adequate sum of money out of the yield of the Tax for giving them relief.

After the schedule and the preamble of the Bill had been passed, Mr. Suhrawardy formally moved that the Bill, as settled in the Assembly, be passed.

Mr. *Sarat Chandra Bose*, Leader of the Opposition, said that in the light of their experience in the past and the absence of proper definition of the Government's existing schemes, it would be dangerous to put more money in the Government's hands or more power to impose further taxation. In case further taxation was to be imposed, the Government must satisfy two criteria, namely, they must put before the legislature and the people a clear-cut programme of social and economic reconstruction based on sound economic lines: and the Government must satisfy them about the merits of the proposal and the urgent necessity of the Sales Tax. The Government had up to now satisfied neither of these two criteria. The declared object of the Government, Mr. Bose continued, was to raise additional revenue to enable them to maintain the natural development of the programme of nation-building departments already in progress, and for the purpose of financing other beneficient schemes. These were

---

The following is the schedule showing the list of articles exempted from the tax:—

All cereals and pulses (including all forms of rice raw or cooked). (Except when sold in sealed containers).

Flour (including atta, suji and bran).

Bread.

Meat which has not been cured or frozen.

Fresh fish.

Vegetables, green or dried. (Except when sold in sealed containers).

Coocked foods, other than cakes, pastries and sweetmeats. (Except when sold in sealed containers).

Gur, sugar and molasses, Salt, mustard oil, milk, butter and cheese. Livestock, including poultry. Agricultural implements. Fertilizers. Yarn. Bullion and specie.

Gold ornaments manufactured from bullion or specie. (When sold by the manufacturer who charges separately for the value of the gold and the cost of manufacture).

high-sounding' words. But they had seen what the record of this Government's nation-building schemes had been in the past. What the Government really wanted from them was a blank cheque or an overdraft. He added that this measure would give no corresponding benefit to the people at large. If the Government really intended to spend on nation-building programmes, there was nothing to prevent them from declaring that clearly in the premble of the Bill.

Replying to criticism, Mr. *H. S. Suhrawardy* said that though he had tried to meet the responsible wishes of all sections of the House, there was no proof that his spirit of compromise had not been appreciated. He pointed out the tax was very low, indeed lower than anywhere else. It was only a one-point tax and not a general sales tax. He maintained that the tax would not affect poor people adversely, but would fall primarily on the middle and the richer classes. He repeated the assurance that the money received through the tax would be spent in ameliorating the conditions of the poor.

The Bill, as setled in the Assembly, was passed and the House adjourned.

Special Class for Political Prisoners

7th. MARCH :—The question of placing all the political prisoners in Bengal Jails in Division I or in a special class similar to Division I to be created for them, was raised in a non-official resolution discussed to-day. The motion, after discussion, was lost without a division.

On behalf of Mr. Pratul Chandra Ganguly, a Congress member of the Assembly now in detention under the Defence of India Rules, Mr. *Atul Chandra Sen* (Congress) moved a resolution expressing the view that all persons convicted in Bengal under the Defence of India Rules and the Indian Penal Code for offences against the State should be placed in Division I in jails. Mr. *Surendra Nath Biswas* (Congress) moved an amendment to the resolution to the effect that, "all prisoners in Bengal jails, whether detained or convicted under the Defence of India Rules or kept under trial or convicted for offences against the State under the Indian Penal Code should be placed in Division I or that a new special division similar to Division I should be created for them and new rules should be framed in respect of their ration, interviews, letter-writing, supply of books, newspapers and other reasonable amenities." Opposing both the resolution and the amendment, *Sir Bijoy Prosad Singh Roy*, Revenue Minister, who now holds the portfolio of jails in the absence of the Home Minister, informed the House that some Security prisoners' rules had been published. But as regards other classes of prisoners, draft rules had been framed and as these involved financial questions, they were being examined. He explained that Government in this country since the advent of the British had never accepted the motive of a crime as the basis for classification of prisoners. He pointed out the difficulties in accepting such a basis for

---

Coal and coke.

Country liquor (including tari and pachwai), potable foreign liquor (including medicated wines, ganja), excise opium (excluding preparations of opium), bhang and charas.

Water, but not aerated or mineral waters when sold in bottles or sealed containers.

Electrical energy.

Motor spirit, that is to say, any liquid or admixture of liquids which is ordinarily used directly or indirectly as fuel for any form of motor vehicle or stationary internal combustion engine, and which has a flashing point below 76 degrees Fahrenheit.

Rape oil and mixtures of mustard and rape oil.

Handloom woven cloth sold by a dealer who does not sell any other kind of cloth.

Kerosene oil.

Tobacco for hookah.

Matches.

Quinine and febrifuge.

Text-books approved for primary classes and such sacred books as may be prescribed.

Coal gas—when sold by a gas supply company for consumption, (a) by Government or any local authority or (b) in respect of any industrial undertaking (other than in residential or office premises) or (c) in any place declared by the Provincial Government to be exclusively used for public charity, and Newspapers.

classification of prisoners and told the House that the present Government did not propose to change the policy that had been pursued so long in this regard.

Mr. *Biswas'* amendment was rejected by 76 to 42 votes and the original resolution was negatived without a division.

VOTING ON BUDGET DEMANDS

10th. to 29th. MARCH :—Discussion on the Budget demands for grants commenced on the **10th. March** the first item to come under discussion was that on General Administration. To criticise the general policy of the Government 3 principal cut motions were moved, (1) by Mr. *Sasanka Sekhar Sanyal* (Bose group) urging the need for a comprehensive and progressive policy on the part of the Government with a view to secure peace and prosperity of the people, (2) by Mr. *Jonab Ali Majumdar* (Krishak Proja) stressing the need for freedom of holding meetings to discuss parliamentary matters and to carry on election propaganda, and (3) by Mr. *Prem Hari Barma* (Independent Schedule) pointing out the failure of the Government to strictly adhere to the service ratio in the case of the scheduled caste candidates. The first two amendments were pressed to division and were lost by 40 to 91 and 37 to 81 votes respectively. Mr. Barma whose motion was also lost did not divide the House on it. Next day, the **11th March**, the House sanctioned without any cut the Government's entire Budget demand for the grant of a sum of Rs. 1,27,00,000 for expenditure in the coming year under the head "Administration". Mr. *Nishit Nath Kundo* (Congress) moved a cut motion to raise a discussion on the "methods of realisation of war contributions from the people of the Province, particularly of the district of Dinajpur." He referred to some instances in which he alleged that war contributions were being realised by coercion. Speaking on the motion, the Chief Minister, Mr. *A. K. Fazlul Huq*, pointed out that Government looked with extreme disfavour on any attempt on the part of any officer to have recourse to any coercion in regard to raising money for war funds. Government would make an enquiry into the allegations that had been made on the floor of the House and if they found that any officer had acted in contravention of the distinct orders of the Government and of the instructions issued to them from time to time, Government would take sufficient steps to see that these things were not repeated. The cut motion was rejected without a division. Mr. *Surendra Nath Biswas* (Congress) moved another cut motion to raise a discussion on the "policy of the Administration with special reference to the application of the Defence of India Rules in the Province by the Government and the granting of allowances to the victims thereof and the classification and treatment of the political prisoners". Opposing the motion, *Sir Bijoy Prosad Singh Roy*, Revenue Minister, emphasised that the first and foremost concern of any body in India and the British Empire at the present moment was to win the war and if anybody tried to hamper the war efforts of Government or did anything which created an atmosphere inimical to such war efforts of the Government, the Government in the wider interests of the country, was bound to take action. He repudiated the charge that there had been any discrimination in the matter of application of the Defence of India Rules. The cut motion was rejected without a division. The House adjourned till the next day, the **12th March**, when the jute policy of the Government was discussed during consideration of the agricultural budget. The hon' *Mr. Tamizuddin Khan*, Minister for Agriculture and Industries, moved that a sum of Rs.43,85,000 be granted for expenditure under the head, "Agriculture" in the coming year. Mr *Abu Hossain Sarker* (Krishak Proja) moved a cut motion to criticise the jute policy of the Government. The opposition speeches stressed that mere regulation of jute cultivation would not succeed in securing an economic price of jute for the cultivators. It was also maintained that there were various inaccuracies in the record of jute lands prepared by the Government on the basis of which the jute restriction policy was going to be enforced. It was further maintained that Government had "bungled and mismanaged" the whole thing in regard to jute. Replying, the *Minister* said that the policy of the Government with regard to jute was to make every attempt huma ly possible, to give the growers the best possible prices for this commodity. The first step towards this end was the adjustment of supply to demand. Previous attempts to do this by voluntary restriction of production having proved ineffective, the Government had ultimately decided to regulate the production of jute on a compulsory basis. This had necessitated a comprehensive survey of the entire jute area of the province, and the work of issuing licences to more than fifty-five lakhs of jute growers was now proceeding apace. This was an experiment which, in its boldness, far surpassed any similar attempt made anywhere else in the world. The Government, he emphasised, were determined to carry on this policy of regulation because they were convinced that unless the next year's crop was regulated, the situation would be absolutely unmanageable. The Minister added that circumstances might arise when it might be necessary to fix the minimum price of jute and he could not say that the proposition of fixing a minimum price for jute was outside the purview of Government policy. If necessary, the Government would do so, but the Government could not do that until the obvious difficulties in the way were solved. Mr. *Sarker's* motion was rejected by the House by 65 to 30 votes. The House then adjourned till the **14th. March** when a demand for a grant of Rs. 43,85,000 for expenditure for the coming year under the head, "Agriculture" was sanctioned by 62 to 27 votes. A cut motion moved to discuss the "absence of a comprehensive policy" with regard to the vital problems of agriculture was rejected by 76 to 28 votes. Maulvi *Janab Ali Majumdar's* (Krishak Proja) cut motion to emphasise "the desirability of exempting from the operation of the jute Regulation Act those jute growers whose jute lands were below one acre in all" was rejected by 87 to 45 votes. The House then adjourned till the next day, the **15th. March**, when various Government schemes for the development of industries in this province were outlined by Mr. *Tamizuddin Khan*, Minister for Agriculture and Industries, when he asked for a grant of Rs. 19,19,000 for expenditure on "Industries." During the discussion on the subject, Mr. *J. R. Walker* made a strong plea for the development of the fishery industry which, he maintained, offered the best prospect for increasing the wealth of the province. Two cut motions were moved by Messrs. *Surendra Nath Biswas* and *Sasanka Sekhar Sanyal* of the Bose Party to criticize the industrial policy of the Government. Both motions were lost. Next day, the **17th. March**, the Education Budget of the Government of Bengal for the year 1941-42 was discussed. Rai *Harendra Nath Chaudhury* (Congress) moved a 'cut' motion to discuss the policy that was being pursued in the sphere of primary education in the province. He alleged that there had been a phenomenal rise in the past few years in the number of Maktabs at the sacrifice of general non-denominational primary schools and that Hindu boys had been compelled to read in Maktabs for want of general primary schools. The hon'ble Mr. *A. K. Fazlul Huq*, Education Minister, pointed out that there was no difference in the curriculum of studies in the Maktab and the general primary schools throughout the province at present. The only difference was that religious instruction was made compulsory in the Maktab and he added that not only Muslim students but also Hindu students received religious instruction there. He told the House that the Government had until now received no complaint whatsoever either from the guardians of the Hindu boys or from the Hindu boys themselves reading in such Maktabs. It was a happy sign of the time, he remarked, that even now in spite of the communal atmosphere prevailing in the country Hindu and Muslim boys, at least in their tender years, sat together in the same class room and received education from the same set of teachers. On the question of deprovincialisation of Government institutions, the Education Minister remarked that the analysis of the results of different examinations showed that the percentage of success in Government institutions was much higher than that in non-Government institutions. The 'cut' motion was rejected without a division. The House then adjourned till the **18th. March** when the Education (General) grant amounting to Rs. 1 68,74,000 and Jail and Convict Settlements grant amounting to Rs. 36,94,000 were passed. The non-release of the grant to the *Viswa Bharati* which was provided for in the last year's budget and absence of any provision in this year's budget was raised during the discussion on the Education grant. The European party also lent their support to the proposal for grant to the *Viswa Bharati*. The *Chief Minister* replying said that he was releasing the last years's grant immediately, but did not mention anything with regard to future grants. The House divided only once in connection with the Jail demand on the cut motion of Mr. *Charu Roy*, which was defeated by 36 to 72 votes. Next day, the **19th. March**, when the demand for Police grant was under consideration, the discussion mainly centred round the desirability of financing the Chowkidari cost from out of the provincial revenue. There was unanimity of opinion regarding giving relief to the rural population, even the Coalition party members according their support to the proposal. The Chief Minister who was temporarily in charge of the Police Department in the absence of Sir Nazimuddin said that the report of the Chowkidari Committee was still under consideration and that the Government now had accepted the policy that the entire cost of the rural police should not fall on the rural people. The entire Police grant amounting to Rs. 2,20,53,000/- was passed by the House. Next day, the **20th. March**, the Budget demands for Rs. 32,13,000 for Irrigation and Rs. 1,55,71,000 for Civil Works, placed before the House by the Hon. Maharaja *Srish Chandra Nandy* of Cossimbazar, were voted. In the course of his speech, the Maharaja stated that the Bengal Government, in co-operation with other provincial governments concerned, set up two interim committees, one for the Ganges and the other for the Brahmaputra and the Meghna rivers to frame the necessary constitution of the proposed Inter-Provincial River Commission. These interim committees had since finished their labours and submitted their reports. With regard to the Brahmaputra-Meghna River Commission, the hon. Minister said that both the Bengal and Assam Governments had accepted the recommendations of the Committee and the Bengal Government had been authorised by the Assam Government to address the India Government on the subject with a request to constitute the commission on the lines of these recommendations. It was expected that the constitution of the Brahmaputra-Meghna River Commission might be a settled fact in the course of the coming year. The progress with regard to the constitution of the proposed Ganges River Commission had not, however, been so satisfactory. Opposition members and some of the Coalition members criticised the Government for lack of any comprehensive irrigation scheme, while the European members congratulated the Minister on the achievements of the department. Next day, the **21st. March**, an account of the activities of the Co-operative Department was given by Mr. *M. B. Mullick*, Minister in charge, when he placed the budget of the Department before the House. The Minister also asked for a grant of Rs. 20.23,000 for expenditure under the head debt conciliation. This gave rise to a debate regarding the working of the Agricultural Debtors Act. The budget demands relating to both the Co-operative and Rural Indebtedness Departments were passed. Next day, the **22nd March**, the budget demands for Rs. 22,29,000 for the Excise Department, and Rs. 71,12,000 for the administration of justice were voted. The Congress Party moved a cut motion in order to emphasise the necessity of separation of the judiciary from the executive. Opposing the motion *Nawab Musharraf Hussain*, Judical Minister, said that complete separation of the judiciary from the executive was not a practical proposition. The motion was rejected without a division. Two other cut motions were moved on behalf of the Congress and the Krishak Praja Parties to emphasise the desirability of introducing complete prohibition in the province. Opposing the resolutions, the Excise Minister, Mr. *P. D. Raikut*, said that in the present circumstances complete Prohibition was not feasible on various grounds. He, however, reiterated the Government's policy of gradual enforcement of total Prohibition throughout the province. Both the cut motions were rejected by 74 votes to 31. The House then adjourned till Monday, the **24th March** when the Government were charged by the Opposition with failure to give sufficient relief to the peasantry by the reduction of the rate of rent when the Land Revenue demand for grant was under consideration. The Krishak Proja Party who fought the election under the leadership of Hon. Mr. *A. K. Fazlul Huq*, reminded the Chief Minister of his election pledge and his "failure" to implement the pledge. *Sir Bijoy Prosad Singh Roy*, Minister, Land Revenue, in reply refused the charge and said that the Government took their stand on the Bengal Tenancy Amendment Act, by which piece of legislation, he asserted, the Ministry would go down to prosperity. Next day, the **27th March**, a tribute to the good work being done by the Calcutta Society for the Prevention of Cruelty to Animals was paid by the Premier Mr. *A. K. Fazlul Huq*, when replying to a debate on the working of the Society. The debate was raised on a cut motion in respect of the Budget demand for Rs. 7,19,000 for the Veterinary Department. On the **28th March** Medical grants amounting to Rs. 51,13,000 and Public Health grants amounting to Rs. 50,52,000 were voted. The demands were moved by Hon. Mr. *Tamijuddin Khan* in the absence of Hon. Nawab Bahadur of Dacca, Minister-in-Charge of the Departments. Next day, the **29th March**, the remaining budget demands were voted. The labour policy of the Ministry was discused in connection with the Budget demand for Rs. 4,92,000 for "Miscellaneous Department." The demand which includes a provision of Rs. 54,000 for the Labour Department, was placed before the House by the hon. Mr. *H. S. Suhrawardy*, Labour Minister. Opposing the entire demand Mr. *A. M. A. Zaman* (Congress Labour) severely criticised the labour policy of the Ministry and the activities of its Labour Department. He alleged that the money meant for labour welfare work had been utilised in bringing into existence a large number of 'bogus' trade unions. Mr. *J. Kennedy* (European) supported the demand on behalf of the European Group. He emphasised that the year that had passed, since the Labour Minister last presented his demand to the House, had been singularly free from major labour troubles and, in the opinion of his Party, this was due in no small measure to the Minister's solicitude for the workers of Bengal and his determination to safeguard their rights. Replying to the debate, Mr. *H. S. Suhrawardy*, Minister for Labour, said that Mr. Zaman had cast aspersions against the constitutional trade unions that had grown up in pursuance of their policy of encouraging trade unions in this province which conducted themselves in a reasonable and constitutional manner. Replying to the criticism that they had been encouraging the formation of trade unions on communal lines, the hon. Minister said that they had done nothing of the kind. The policy of the Government was that so far as labour was concerned they considered the Hindus and Muslims as one. They deprecated the formation of trade unions on communal lines. They refused to recognise any trade union which was of an exclusive character, that is, either of Hindus or of Muslims. The demand was passed and the Assembly adjourned till Monday.

Relief of London Air-raid Victims

31st. MARCH :—Following debate lasting two hours, the Assembly this morning sanctioned by 130 votes to 47, the supplementary demand for a token grant of Re. 1 to enable the Government to pay one lakh of rupees to the Calcutta Mayor's Fund for the relief of London air-raid victims. The demand was placed before the House by the Chief Minister, Mr. *A. K. Fazlul Huq*. The money was proposed to be paid in the current year out of the saving under the head "Miscellaneous". An Opposition cut-motion moved by Mr. *Sasanka Sekhar Sanyal*, the Chief Whip of the Congress Party, to discuss the principle underlying the proposal was rejected by 121 to 41 votes. The Opposition also raised a point of order, maintaining that the contribution could not be made under Section 150 of the Government of India Act and that the money could not be "for the purposes of India or some part of India" as was laid down in the Section.

Mr. *Sarat Chandra Bose*, Leader of the Opposition, said that Section 150 of the Government of India Act laid a territorial restriction on the powers of the province in respect of imposing any burden on the revenues of the Federation of the Provinces. The question of courtesy of humanitarian sentiment did not arise. He maintained that, so far as the present demand was concerned, it was entirely out of order under Section 150.

The *Chief Minister* pointed out that legal opinion received by the Government showed that the grant could be made under the Government of India Act. He referred to the opinion which the Secretary of State for India had forwarded to the Government of India for communication to the Provincial Governments which had been obtained in consultation with the best legal opinion available in London. The opinion of the Secretary of State was that, "For the purposes of India" under Section 150 could in practice be construed as including any activities, the pursuit of which was in the country's interest. Such interests need not be in the nature of specific and measurable benefit and could include many other things of broader consideration in respect to the reputation and dignity of India in the comity of nations. The Chief Minister also referred to the opinion of the Advocate-General of Assam in this connection and remarked that the members of the Bengal Cabinet were fully satisfied that the demand could be made under the Government of India Act.

The *Speaker* (*Sir M. Azizul Huq*) pointed out that it was a well-known international custom to send relief. Supposing India was affected by a severe famine, as a matter of courtesy she would get relief from others. "Are we to be debarred from sending relief to others under similar circumstances ?" He considered that the sending of such relief would be "for the purposes of India" for the simple reason that they were merely reciprocating feeling of humanity as other countries had done. He admitted, however, that the question of interpretation of the Section was not free from difficulty. Whether the phrase "the purposes of India" meant restricted purposes of India, or the wider purposes of the country which included the existence of India as a nation in the comity of nations was a matter which was to be decided by a Court and he thought that he should not intervene by ruling out the motion. He, therefore, held that the motion was in order. Concluding, the Speaker said that the whole principle behind the Government of India Act was provincial autonomy in financial matter and if autonomy meant that we could do everything but extend international courtesy, then the Section had been rather badly drafted. "But" he added: "As I say, I do not hold that this Section is such as to preclude an item of this nature—unless a Court declares otherwise."

Shaik Faiz Muhammad
Chaudhri Faqir Chand
„ Faqir Hussain Khan
Subedar Major Raja Farman Ali Khan
2nd. Lieutenant Bhai Fatehjang Singh
Khan Sahib Raja Fateh Khan
Mian Fateh Muhammad
Malik Fateh Sher Khan
Khan Bahadur Nawab Chaudhri Fazal Ali Khan
Khan Sahib Chaudhri Fazal Din
Main Fazal Karim Bakhsh
Mr. E. Few
Raja Ghazanfar Ali Khan
Khan Bahadur M. Ghulam Mohy-ud-Din
„ „ Ghulam Qadir Khan
Chaudhri Ghulam Rasul
Khan Sahib Khawaja Ghulam Samad
Mahant Girdhari Das
Dr. Sir Gokul Chand Narang
Rai Bahadur Lala Gopal Das
American Sardar Gopal Singh
Dr. Bhargava Gopi Chand
Sardar Bahadur Gurbachan Singh
Malik Habib-Ullah Khan
Khan Haibat Khan Daha
Bhagat Hans Raj
Rai Sahib Hari Chand Rai
Munshi Hari Lal
Sardar Hari Singh
„ Harjar Singh
Lala Harnam Das
Captain Sodhi Harnam Singh
Rai Sahib Chaudhri Het Ram
Sardar Indar Singh
Mr. Jafar Ali Khan
Beddi Tikka Jagjit Singh
Sardar Jagjit Singh Man
Mrs. Jahan Ara Shah Nawaz
Chaudhuri Jalal-ud-Din Amber
Sardar Jogindar Singh Man
Chaudhri Jugal Kishore
Master Kabul Singh
Sardar Kapoor Singh
Shaikh Karamat Ali
Chaudhri Khetar Singh
Sardar Kartar Singh
Mr. Khalid Latif Gauba
The Hon. Major Nawabzada Malik Khizar Hayat Khan Tiwana
Seth Kishan Dass
Sardar Kishan Singh
Chaudhri Krishna Gopal Dutt
Sardar Lal Singh
The Hon, Mr. Manohar Lal
Mir Maqbool Mahmood
M. Mazhar Ali Azhar
Sayed Mohy-ud-Din Lal Badshah
Sayed Mubarik Ali Shah
Chaudhury Muhammad Abdul Rahim Khan
Khan Bahadur Raja Muhammad Akram Khan
Dr. Shaikh Muhammad Alam
Khan Sahib Shaikh Muhammad Amin
Chaudhri Muhammad Asaf
Sardar Muhammad Azam Khan
Nawabzada Muhammad Faiyaz Ali Khan
Chaudhri Muhammad Hassan
Khan Bahadur Sardar Muhammad Hassan Khan Gurchani
Khan Bahadur Makhdum Sayed Muhammad Hassan
Nawab Sir Malik Muhammad Hayat Khan Noon
Sardar Muhammad Hussain
Chaudhri Muhammad Hussain
Main Muhahmad Iftikhar-ud-Din
Khan Bahadur Nawab Sir Muhammad Jamal Khan Leghari
Major Sardar Muhammad Nawaz Khan
Main Muhammad Nurullah
Chaudhri Muhammad Qasim
Makhdumzada Hazi Sayed Muhammad Reza Shah Jeelani
Khan Sahib Khan Muhammad Saadat Ali Khan
Chaudhri Muhammad Sarfraz Khan
Raja Muhammad Sarfraz Khan
Khan Sahib Chaudhri Muhammad Shafi Ali Khan
Chaudhri Muhammad Sarfraz Khan
Raja Muhammad Sarfraz Khan
Khan Sahib Chaudhri Muhammad Shafi Ali Khan
Makhdumzada Haji Sayed Muhammad Wilayat Hussain Jeelani
Chaudhri Muhammad Yasin Khan
Khan Muhammad Yusuf Khan
Rai Bahadur Mukand Lal Puri
Sardar Mula Singh
Pandit Muni Lal Kalia
Khan Bahadur Main Mushtaq Ahmed Gurmani
Sardar Muzaffar Ali Khan Qizilbash
Khan Bahadur Captain Malik Muzaffar Khan
„ „ Nawab Muzaffar Khan
Chaudhri Nasir-ud-Din
Pir Nasir-ud-Din Shah
Rana Nasrullah Khan
Lieutenant Sardar Nau Nihal Singh Mann
Sayed Nawazish Ali Shah
Khan Bahadur Mian Nur Ahmad Khan
Sardar Pratab Singh
Khan Sahib Chaudhri Pir Muhammad
Rao Pohop Singh
Chaudhri Prem Singh
Mahant Prem Singh
Siddhu Sardar Pritam Singh
Srimati Raghbir Kaur
Chaudhri Ram Sarup

Chaudhry Ranpat Singh
Begum Rashida Latif Baji
Khan Bahadur Chaudhri Riasat Ali
Rai Sahib Thakur Ripudaman Singh
Sir William Roberts
Sardar Rur Singh
Shaikh Sadiq Hassan
Khan Sahib Chaudhri Sahib Dad Khan
Chaudhri Sahib Ram
Sardar Sampuran Singh
Sardar Sahib Sardar Santokh Singh
Dr. Sant Ram Seth
Dr. Satya Pal
Khan Sahib Rai Shahdat Khan
Nawab Sir Shah Nawaz Khan
Pandit Shri Ram Sharma
Khan Bahadur Major Sirdar Sir Sikandar Hyat Khan
Diwan Bahadur S. P. Singh
Lala Sita Ram
Rai Sahib Lala Sohan Lal
Sardar Sohan Singh Joshi
Seth Sudarshan
Sultan Mahmud Hotiana Mian
Chaudhri Sumer Singh
The Hon. Sardar Sir Dr. Sundar Singh Majithia, Sardar Bahadur
Chaudhri Suraj Mal
Khan Talib Husain Khan
Sardar Tara Singh
" Sardar Tej Singh
Chaudhri Tikka Ram
Sardar Bahadur Sardar Ujjal Singh
Sardar Uttam Singh, Dugal
" Wali Muhammad Sayyal Hiraj

Budget Session—Lahore—21st, January to 28th April 1941

The Sales Tax Bill

The Budget Session of the Punjab Legislative Assembly which met after the Christmas recess on the **21st. January 1941** passed three official Bills, namely, the *Punjab Fisheries (Amendment) Bill*, the *Punjab Courts Amendment Bill* and the *Sikh Gurdwaras Amendment Bill* and postponed discussion on the *Punjab Jagirs Bill*, as doubts were expressed about its legality.

Earlier, *Sir Chotturam*, Development Minister, presented the report of the Select Committee on the *Punjab General Sales Tax Bill*. The most important change made by the committee seeks to empower the Provincial Government to prescribe the points in the series of sales by successive dealers at which any goods or class or description of goods may be exempted from payment of tax. Another change recommended by the Committee reduces the penalty for an offence under the Bill from Rs. 1,000 to Rs. 500 or double the amount of the tax recoverable, whichever is greater.

Import Duty on Foreign Cotton

23rd. JANUARY :—A strong plea for the imposition of a heavy duty on the import of foreign cotton and wheat at least for three years, was made by *Sir Chhoturam*, Development Minister, speaking on a non-official resolution to day recommending to the Government to press upon the Government of India, the urgent need of imposing a heavy import duty on foreign cotton. The resolution received unanimous support from all sections of the House and was passed.

After referring to fluctuations in the prices of agricultural produce and other commodities consequent on the war, *Sir Chhoturam* complained that while the United Kingdom had purchased the entire cotton crop of Egypt, no attention had been paid to the Punjab either by the United Kingdom or the Government of India. He, therefore, urged that the Government of India should come to their aid and impose a heavy duty on the import of foreign cotton as well as wheat at least for three years. The Minister stressed that at a time, like the present, when the Punjab was liberally assisting in the prosecution of the war, it was necessary for the Government of India to satisfy the Punjab peasant. He pointed out that the Punjab was not only supplying recruits but had made liberal contributions to the War Purposes Fund and the War Loans Fund.

Labour Welfare Legislation

The House also adopted another resolution recommending to the Government to undertake legislation which will promote labour welfare without adding to the direct financial commitments of the State. *Sir Chhoturam*, while welcoming the resolution, stated that Government were contemplating to bring forward legislation on the subject shortly, if the Government of India did not introduce such legislation in the Central Legislature.

Seven non-official Bills which figured on the agenda were either rejected or not moved.

THE PUNJAB JAGIRS BILL

24th. JANUARY :—After question-hour the Speaker, *Sir Shahabuddin* gave his ruling on the Punjab Jagirs Bill to which an objection was raised by the Opposition that the Bill was repugnant to the provisions of the Government of India Act and, therefore, could not be proceeded with. The *Speaker* said that the matter had been fully examined by him and the Law Officers, and he was satisfied that the Legislature was competent to proceed with the Bill, and that a provincial legislature could legislate on the subject of alienation of revenue. The House, after a brief discussion, referred the Bill to a select committee.

THE GENERAL SALES TAX BILL

27th. to 31st. JANUARY :—The Assembly discussed this afternoon the Punjab General Sales Tax Bill clause by clause. The House carried two official amendments, moved by *Chaudhri Tikkaram*, Parliamentary Secretary, to Clause III, which relates to the rate of taxation payable by the dealers. The official amendments accepted by the House seek to levy a graded tax instead of the uniform rate as proposed in the original Clause. During the debate on Clause 3, several members including Sir William Roberts, Mr. Guest and Sir Gokal Chand Narang, ex-Minister, warned the Government that the Bill would not only retard the development of trade and industry in this province but industry would migrate to the neighbouring provinces. Sir *Gokal Chand Narang* complained that the Government was out to help a particular class at the cost of others and declared that zamindars were not paying any tax to the exchequer but were paying rent of their land. Replying to the debate, Sir *Chhotturam*, Minister for Development asserted that the sales tax dated back to ancient times and that there was nothing new in it. Referring to Sir Gokal Chand Narang's statement, Sir Chhotturam said that the land belonged to those who tilled it and the Government was not collecting rent from zamindars, but tax. He assured the House that the proceeds of this tax would be utilised in providing relief to zamindars and in expanding the beneficent departments. Next day, the **28th. January** a number of agricultural commodities including wheat, wheat flour, gram, gram flour, maize, maize flour, bajra, bajra flour, and cotton ginned and unginned, were exempted from the operation of the Bill, on an amendment to clause 5 of the Bill, moved by *Sir Sikander Hyat Khan*, the Premier. On the 31st. January, the third reading of the Bill was passed. *Sardar Santokh Singh*, Leader of the Independent Party, and others protested against the provisions of the Bill and described it as discriminatory. Sardar Santokh Singh regretted that fuel, milk and other commodities of daily use had not been exempted. *Sir Chhotu Ram*, Development Minister, explained that poor traders as well as the primary producers of agricultural produce had been exempted from the operation of the Bill. Moreover, the Bill would not affect wheat, wheat flour, and similar necessities. Regarding exports, he pointed out that Government had been empowered to remit the tax partly or wholly in case of commodities exported from the province.

PRIMARY EDUCATION BILL

The House also passed the Punjab Primary Education Bill in the form recommended by His Excellency the Governor. The amendments suggested by the Governor related to the exemption of Cantonments from the operation of the Bill. The Education Minister, *Mian Abdul Haye*, explained that the House could not legislate as regards local self-government in Cantonment areas.

Major Khizar Hayat Khan, Minister of Public Works, then introduced the restriction of Urban Rents Bill which was referred to a Select Committee, The Minister said that the Bill was designed to prevent the shifting of the incidence of urban immovable property tax to poor tenants.

PUNJAB JAGIRS BILL

14th. FEBRUARY :—The Assembly pssed this afternoon the third reading of the Punjab Jagirs Bill. Under the Bill, the Government shall have power to make in any one year new assignment of land revenue by way of jagirs not exceeding in value of Rs. 5,000. A Jagir created under this Bill may be continued after the death of the original Jagirdar but its term shall be so expressed as to provide that the amount assigned to the next holder shall not exceed half the amount assigned to his predecessor and that the Jagir shall be extinguished after the death of the second holder. During discussion, *Sir Sikandar Hyat Khan*, the Premier, pointed out that the Government had power to assign land revenue but he thought it advisable to take the House into confidence. He announced that 30,000 acres of land had been earmarked for war services and would be distributed to soldiers on their victorious return home.

City of Lahore Corporation Bill

17th. FEBRUARY :—The Assembly, this afternoon, made rapid progress with the City of Lahore Corporation Bill, disposing of over 300 clauses in four hours. Most of these clauses were a reproduction of the Punjab Municipal Act and were passed without discussion. The House deferred consideration of two clauses relating to the imposition of Property Tax by the Corporation of not less than ten per cent of the annual valuation of lands and buildings in the city including lands and buildings belonging to the Crown. Next day, the 18th. February, a motion to a new clause to the Bill, introduced by *Sheikh Faiz Mohammad*, Parliamentary Secretary, empowering the Provincial Government, until March 31, 1943, to make an order to modifying the provisions of the Act, was withdrawn after leave for its introduction had been granted by the House. Opposition members pointed out that it would amount to taking away the right of the Legislature to enact laws. *Major Khizar Hyat Khan*, Minister for Public Works, said that though the clause was not common in India Acts, a similar provision existed in the Local Self-Government Act in England. He, however, would withdraw the clause if the Opposition unanimously felt that it was undesirable. Sir *Gokul Chand Narang*, a former Minister for Local Self-Government and a leading member of the Opposition, said that the provision, if introduced, would create unnecessary alarm and the Opposition members were unanimous in requesting the Minister to withdraw it in the interest of public peace. The Minister thereupon withdrew the clause and the House adjourned for one hour to allow time for consultation between the Minister and the Opposition members on some of the contentious clauses of the Bill whose consideration had been deferred.

The Assembly discussed clause 7 of the Bill which lays down that the Corporation shall consist of sixty-eight councillors of whom not less than three-fourths shall be elected. A number of amendments suggesting increase in the number of elected councillors had been tabled, while another standing in the name of Begum *Rashida Latif Baji* sought to eliminate altogether the nominated element from the Corporation. Participating in the debate on the amendments several speakers urged increase in the number of elected councillors and protested against the retention of the system of nomination. The debate had not concluded when the House rose for the day.

Supplementary Budget

25th. FEBRUARY :—*Sir Manohar Lal*, Finance Minister, presented to-day supplementary estimates aggregating to Rs. 53,77,750. These included over Rs. 13 lakhs for the retention of the additional police, establishment of tear smoke squads and organisation of civic guards in each district of the province, etc.; Rs. 4,74,600 for a air raid precaution ; Rs, 50,000 contribution for the relief of air raid victims in the United Kingdom and Rs. 13 lakhs for transfer to the special development fund of the province.

The House adopted without much discussion the report of the Public Accounts Committee on the appropriation accounts and finance accounts for the year 1938-39 and voted the excess grants recommended by the Committee. Moving the consideration of the report the Finance Minister said that the Committee had examined the accounts of the province with utmost care and thoroughness. He was glad to announce that in spite of heavy expenditure on famine relief the general financial position of the province remained very sound.

Financial Statement for 1941-42

27th. FEBRUARY :—"With our position on the map of India, the question of ensuring internal security had to be firmly faced, and in a province which furnishes the most distinguished soldiery in the country destined to cover themselves with glory in the campaigns of the Middle East, in what may justly be called the Battle of India, the repercussion of the war on finances must necessarily be considerable." With these observations, *Sir Manohar Lal*, Finance Minister, introduced this afternoon the budget estimates for the year 1941-42 which forecast a surplus of Rs. 4 lakhs.

The revenue receipts are estimated at Rs. 1,260 lakhs, very nearly the same as the revised estimate for the current year, while the expenditure is Rs. 1,256 lakhs, Rs. 17 lakhs more than the estimate for the current year. The receipts constitute a big advance of Rs. 90 lakhs on the year 1939-40 which is mainly due to increased land revenue (Rs. 53 lakhs), share of income-tax under the Niemeyer Award (Rs. 13 lakhs) and other taxes and duties (Rs. 13 lakhs).

New expenditure includes an additional provision of Rs. 21 lakhs for beneficent departments. Two significant items under public health are the grant of Rs. 1½ lakhs towards the improvement of Simla and the provision of about Rs. 75,000 in connection with the Solar Eclipse fair at Thanesar during 1941. The allotment from the Special Development Fund will go in the main towards improving drinking water supply in 216 villages. Once again there is special provision of Rs. 10,000 for wells for the scheduled castes.

A lakh of rupees has been provided for the promotion of communal harmony in the province, a provision of nearly one lakh has been made for the next general elections and of a lakh and a half for war publicity. A sum of Rs. 14 lakhs, provided for additional police in the revised estimates for the current year, are being retained in the coming year.

After referring to the revised estimate of extraordinary receipts of Rs. 83 lakhs which were intact to improve the balance and meet capital expenditure, the Finance Minister observed that it would be difficult to discover any year in the history of Punjab finance that showed so characteristically and unmistakably the essential soundness of their finances.

Explaining the effect of famine on provincial finance, Sir Manohar Lal said that the famine in the southern districts, which appeared in 1938 and was within fair sight of coming to an end, had cost Rs. 275 lakhs in four years—stupendous figure considering the Punjab's limited finances.

The Finance Minister next referred to the strikingly liberal scale of suspensions and remissions of land revenue and water rate since 1937 when the present Government came into power and said that the aggregate for the five years was Rs. 7 crores as compared with Rs. 4,27,87,000 during the five years proceeding the inauguration of Provincial Autonomy.

Dealing with the extraordinary receipts during the coming year, the Finance Minister said that the budget estimate was Rs. 68 09 000 while the aggregate for the three years was Rs. 1,92,23,000. These extraordinary receipts had in the main gone to the building up of big capital works.

In connection with the debt position, Sir Manohar Lal pointed out that during the past four years loans amounting to Rs. 630 lakhs were raised by Government while the debt of the province increased only by Rs. 449 lakhs during the period. This gratifying situation, he added, was due to the rigour with which the sinking and deprecation fund had been duly applied to the cancellation of existing debt.

City of Lahore Corporation Bill

3rd MARCH :—The Assembly this afternoon passed the second reading of the City of Lahore Corporation Bill. A new clause added to the Bill provides that no injunction shall be granted by any civil court to interfere with the public duties of the Corporation, the Standing Committee or the Chief Executive Officer.

The House then proceeded with the third reading of the Bill. Sardar Santokh Singh Leader of the Opposition, characterised the Bill as a negation of the principles of local self-government. He said that most of the reactionary provisions of the various Corporation Acts in other provinces and of the Punjab Municipal Act had been embodied in the Bill, ignoring the recent progressive amendments in the Bombay and Karachi Acts. Most of the important features had been left to the rule-making power of the Government and even the method of election had not been decided upon. Next day, the 4th. March, the Assembly passed the third reading of the Bill by 40 votes to 15. The Bill, which contains over four hundred clauses and has been before the House for over 16 months, was described by the Minister for Public Works as the longest and bulkiest piece of legislation ever placed before the House. In the course of the debate, several members urged that the legislation should be enforced as soon as possible. *Begum Shah Nawaz* urged the enfranchisement of women. Replying to the debate, *Malik Khizar Hyat Khan*, Minister for Public Works, said that what they wanted was good Government for the city of Lahore. He assured the House that if they had any objection to the rules framed by the Government under the Act, they would have an opportunity of placing their point of view before the House.

General Discussion of Budget

6th. MARCH :—General discussion of the budget was taken up to-day. Sir *Gokulchand Narang*, a former Minister, was the first speaker. He said that so far as bold schemes or big planning for the development of the province were concerned the budget was disappointing. He severely criticised insufficient provisions for industrialisation of the province and suggested that, to advance the industrial status of the province, Government should borrow and then advance loans to reliable industrialists or they should come forward with their own schemes. Sir Gokulchand spoke for three hours and fifty minutes when he touched on almost all spheres of the provincial administration. He particularly drew attention to what he described as "the cruel and relentless crusade" undertaken by the Punjab Government against the non-agricultural classes." Sir Gokulchand pointed out that the present policy of the Government was not one of equal treatment to all communities, and urged for a revision of Government's policy. Referring to the Mandi Hydro-Electric Scheme, Sir Gokulchand suggested that at this stage without apportioning blame, efforts should be made to minimise the evils resulting from the failure of the scheme. Next day, the 7th March, the policy of the Punjab Government regarding recruitment in services was explained at great length in the course of a two-hour speech by Sir *Sikandar Hyat Khan*, Premier. After analysing the figures for various communities in different departments, Sir Sikandar Hyat Khan said that, taking into consideration all Gazetted appointments in the province the share of Muslims was 44 per cent ; Hindus 36·2 per cent and Sikhs 19·6 per cent. Hindu agriculturists were only 9 per cent and the rest went to non-agriculturist Hindus. The Premier assured the House that in future recruitment due share would be given to agriculturist Hindus. As regards cultural and semi-religious matters, Sir Sikandar Hyat said that Government would adhere to *status quo* in the absence of any agreement between the communities concerned. Referring to the criticism against the Education Bill, the Premier reaffirmed that *status quo* would be maintained regarding the medium of instruction.

Voting on Budget Demands

10th. MARCH :—No satyagrahi prisoner will, in future, be fettered by the jail authorities while on transfer from one jail to another :—This announcement was made by Sir *Manohar Lal*, Minister for Finance and Jails, in reply to a debate on a cut motion under the demand "general administration" this afternoon. He added that instructions to this effect had been issued by the Punjab Government and the necessary amendment had been carried out in the Punjab Jail Manual.

Earlier, an attempt was made by *Mian Nurullah*, a member of the Opposition, to reduce the Premier's salary by Rs. 100, when the Finance Member moved the demand for grant of Rs. 94,67,500 in respect of general administration. The object of the cut was to censure the Government for failure to effect to the recommendations of the Darling Committee regarding reduction in land revenue. The Speaker, Sir *Shahabud-din* ruled out the cut on the ground that the Premier's salary was non-votable.

Future Constitution of India

11th. MARCH :—An exposition of his scheme for a future constitution of India was given by Sir *Sikandar Hyat Khan* in the Assembly this afternoon speaking during the debate on a cut motion to criticize the Government for its alleged failure to bring about communal harmony in the province. Referring to the Lahore resolution of the Moslem League he admitted that he had drafted the original resolution, but there was a difference between his resolution and the amended resolution as adopted by the League. The latter part of his resolution relating to a centre for co-ordination of the various units had been omitted. Therefore the resolution as passed could not be called his resolution. The Premier sounded a note of warning to those who were exploiting the word "Pakistan," and said that he was prepared to listen to all advice but it was for him to accept it or not. He declared : "Let everybody have freedom but not freedom to dominate" Defining his attitude towards Pakistan Sir Sikandar said that a number of Pakistan schemes had been drafted by various persons beginning with Jamaluddin Afghani, and he wondered if the critics realized which scheme they had in mind. There were Moslems who did not believe in the scheme of Jamaluddin Afghani ; Mr. Jinnah himself did not believe in extra-territorialism. He stood by the Lahore resolution. The confusion was due to the fact that a scheme which should be considered on its merits was being exploited because of the word Pakistan. It was the greatest mistake to use that name as it was likely to make confusion worse confounded. He was not worried about the words ; it was the substance that mattered. Explaining how a new constitution should be set up, Sir Sikandar said that he believed that every unit should have complete freedom, and it was fortunate that the population of India was so divided that there were Moslem majorities in certain provinces and Hindu majorities in others. It would give the fullest opportunity to every community within its own sphere to rule as a majority with the help of the minority. Neither community should seek to thwart and dominate the other. Proceeding, Sir Sikandar Hyat Khan asked Moslems to accept the Hindu majority in seven or eight provinces and the Hindus to accept the Moslem majority in four provinces. Once they decided to look at it from the All-India point of view all difficulties and clouds would disappear and sunshine would appear. Let them have full autonomy in the units and let the units then devise a control agency to administer comment or a co-ordinating committee by whatever name they liked. They would come to the conclusion that a centre agreed upon by the units of their free will would be stronger than if two-thirds of India were fighting against it. The Premier claimed that under his scheme they would get not only independence for the provinces but it would also add solidarity and strength to India as a whole. Once they gave up the idea of dominating or interfering from the Centre the problem would be simple. Moslems must be assured that there would not be a dominating Centre. He therefore suggested that there should be an elastic centre which they could demolish. Such a Centre should have power to administer subjects like customs, defence, currency, etc. If after some years they found that it was not working satisfactorily they could then cut adrift but not without making a serious effort to work it. Sir Sikandar added that the future destiny of India lay in accepting a position of freedom within the British Commonwealth. It would be a criminal folly for India to cut adrift from the Commonwealth at a time when they stood in need of protection from external aggression which Britain alone could give them.

Voting on Budget Demands

20th. MARCH :—After two day's debate the Assembly rejected without division the 'cut' motion moved to discuss the industrial policy of the Punjab Government and voted the entire demand for the Industries Department. Several members urged the need for industrial development of the province. Mr. *P. H. Guest* (Commerce) advocated three fundamentals of sound industrial development, namely, security, confidence and technical education. These were long view requirements. he said, and would take time to mature, but were essential if industries, started by war necessities, were not to die after the artificial stimulus and protection produced by the war ceased. Mr. Guest said that the present Government had taken steps to increase the atmosphere of confidence essential for the development of industries but regretted that the recent taxation measures had caused this sense of confidence to be severely shaken. To recreate that feeling of confidence he strongly supported the suggestion for the appointment of a small committee of experts to find out the actual incidence of taxation on urban and rural classes. Replying to the debate, *Sir Chhoturam*, Development Minister, said that he had been thinking of requesting the Premier to transfer the Industries Department to Sir Manoharlal because he enjoyed in a far greater measure, confidence of the industrialist class than he did. He had no doubt that the industries could grow and make greater progress under Sir Manoharlal, who was an economic expert. Sir Chhoturam controverted the allegation that the Punjab Government had no sympathy with industrialisation or that they had no policy. Any man, who had even an iota of sense, would agree that industrialisation was a necessity and in industrialisation lay the prosperity of the zamindars and the labourers. In the year 1932, the provision for industries, he said, was Rs. 14 lakhs which, to-day, had increased to Rs. 22 lakhs. This was in spite of the difficulies which the Punjab Government had to face on account of acute famine conditions to meet which they had to spend Rs. 270 lakhs. They could not start any heavy industry because they could not get machinery on account of the war. The factories which manufactured that machinery were busy preparing war materials. The policy of the Punjab Government, he added, was clear. The House had given its verdict in a resolution which the Government was pledged to implement. As conditions permitted steps would be taken to implement that resolution.

21st MARCH :—The large number of I. M. S. officers in civil employ in the Punjab considerably exceeding the quota reserved for them by the Secretary of State, was criticised in the Assembly to-day during discussion on the Budget for the Medical Department, which amounts to Rs. 45,66,400. The Opposition was led by *Malik Barkat Ali* (Muslim League), who recalled a notification of the Government of India dated 25th March 1937, according to which it was obligatory on the Punjab Government, after the introduction of provincial autonomy, to employ seventeen I. M. S. officers, eight of whom would constitute the Army Reserve. Malik Barkat Ali pointed out that the number of I. M. S. officers serving in the Punjab in 1938 was 34, which had increased to 36 in 1939, while in 1941-42, their number would be 30. He criticised the Government for unnecessarily burdening the provincial Exchequer and maintained that Section 246 of the Government of India Act, on which the Education Minister took his stand last year, could not be applied to posts beyond the quota of 17, reserved for the I. M. S. by the Secretary of State He said that the I. M. S. was essentially a military service and these officers should go to the army making room for private medical practitioners who had distinguished themselves in the profession. Malik Barkat Ali urged a revision of the scale of pay of the provincial civil medical service to bring it on a par with the other provincial services. Several members, including Mian Abdul Aziz and Sheikh Sadiq Hassan, pleaded for encouragement of the indigenous system of medicine. *Raja Ghaznafar Ali*, Parliamentary Secretary, while agreeing that the number of I. M. S. officers should be reduced, pointed out that the Education Minister deserved credit for Indianising important posts in the Medical Department.

SUPPRESSION OF INDECENT ADVERTISING BILL

27th. MARCH :—The Assembly held a brief sitting, lasting twenty-two minutes, this afternoon, when it passed all the three readings of the Punjab Suppression of Indecent Advertisement Bill. The Bill, which was sponsored by Sir *Sikandar Hyat Khan*, sought to penalise the exhibition of indecent advertisements. Offenders under the provisions of the Bill shall be punishable with imprisonment for a term which may extend to one year or with fine which may extend to Rs. 500, or with both.

URBAN RENT RESTRICTION BILL

1st. APRIL :—The Assembly passed this afternoon the third reading of the Punjab Urban Re t Restriction Bill which seeks to restrict the increase of rents on certain premises situated within the limits of urban areas in the Punjab. The Bill will remain in force for a period of five years from the date of its enforcement in particular areas unless such period is extended by a resolution of the Punjab Assembly. The Bill provides a restriction on raising rent which was charged on January 1. 1939.

The Assembly next referred the Punjab Weights and Measures Bill to a Select Committee. On a motion of the Premier, the Assembly adjourned for Easter recess.

DEATH OF SIR SUNDAR SINGH MAJITHIA

21st APRIL :—The Assembly. which met to-day after the Easter recess, was adjourned without transacting any business as a mark of respect to the memory of the late Sir Surendra Singh Majithia, Revenue Minister. A condolence resolution moved by *Sir Sikandar Hyat Khan* was adopted all standing. The Premier paid a touching tribute to Sir Sunder Singh who, he said, had died in harness like a soldier in war. While Sir Sundar Singh was a vigilant custodian and champion of the rights and interests of the Sikh community, he was never unfair to other communities and it would be difficult to find another leader of his calibre. He was profoundly religious and lived up to the great traditions of the Sikh Gurus. The Premier expressed his profound and heartfelt sympathy to Sir Sundar Singh's son and other members of the bereaved family. Sardar Dasunda Singh, Development Minister, Sardar Santokh Singh, Leader of the Opposition, Sardar Bahadur Ujjal Singh, Leader of the Khalsa National Party, Nawab Muzaffar Khan and Sir William Roberts associated themselves with the sentiments expressed by the Premier. *Sir Shahabuddin*, Speaker, while undertaking to convey the resolution to the bereaved family remarked that it would be difficult for the Sikh community to replace Sir Sunder Singh Majithia.

ELECTRICITY POWERS BILL

24th. APRIL :—The House resumed discussion to-day on the Punjab Electricity (Emergency Powers) Bill and passed all the three readings. *Malik Khizar Hyat Khan*, Minister of Public Works, said that the Punjab Government had decided that, wherever circumstances favoured, the licensed electric supply undertakings in the province should be purchased when the next option of purchase fell due. It was, therefore, considered that the period of notice required to be served on a licensee under the Electricity Act should be curtailed from two to one year which

Kishore Roy Chowdhury (Congress) characterized the budget as disappointing. Dealing with the Government policy regarding college education in Bengal, he said that Government should consider its needs as a whole and allot its grants for the benefit of all. Hindu students, he complained, were being neglected in many areas. Referring to the jute restriction scheme, he said that while in Bengal the cultivation of jute was restricted yet in other provinces it was being grown on an increasing scale. Khan Bahadur *Saiyed Muazzamuddin Hossain* (Coalition) thought that the budget could not be described a deficit one as there was a closing balance of Rs. 32,91 lakhs. Poverty and illiteracy, he said, were the two deadliest enemies with which they had to wage war and if they were to succeed they must equip themselves properly no matter it meant fresh and heavy taxation. But in imposing taxation they should take care that the method they adopted for raising money did not defeat the very object for which the money was being raised. Next day, the **26th. February**, about half a dozen speakers participated. Mr. *J. B. Ross*, Leader of the European Party, congratulated the Finance Minister on the "clear, cleaver and comprehensive" manner in which he had presented the budget this year. He, however, maintained that while his party had every sympathy with the desire of the Government to improve the work of the nation-building department, they, nevertheless, felt that in the present abnormal times the utmost caution should be exercised in controlling expenditure in view of the recent progressive decline in certain items of revenue, such as, jute export duty, land revenue and stamp. Next day, the **27th. February**, the Finance Minister, Mr. *H. S. Suhrawardy*, replying to the debate, maintained that substantial amounts of money had been allotted to the different nation-building departments. As an instance, he pointed out that, whereas in the previous budget, hardly any money was set apart for primary education, this year the budget provided approximately forty-five lakhs of rupees for the purpose. Speaking on the grants under head, "Police", the Finance Minister said that keeping in view the area and the population of Bengal, he could say that "the cost of Police in Bengal is less than in any other province. The increase in Police is not meant for the purpose of making inroads into the liberties of the people with a political bent of mind; it is for the purpose of saving these honourable gentlemen from any difficulty that may arise in case of an invasion of this country or trouble on the countryside." The Government had to issue an Ordinance, pointed out Mr. Suhrawardy, for fixing maximum and minimum prices of jute, because if the Government had not stepped in, say towards the beginning of August, 1939, jute would have been purchased by millowners and others at no price "whatsoever". Of course, the Ordinance was issued at a time when jute had virtually passed out of the hands of the agriculturists, but the Ordinance had served to maintain the price of the old crop and to ensure a satisfactory price for the new crop.

LAND REVENUE SALES AMEND. BILL

28th. FEBRUARY :—Non-official bills were considered in the Council to-day. As many as 20 bills were circulated for eliciting public opinion, one was passed while four others were introduced. The Bengal Land Revenue Sales (Amendment) Bill, 1940, for which Mr. *Nur Ahmed* was responsible was passed. It provided some opportunities to the owners and the persons having interest in the immovable property which were sold at auction under the provisions of the Bengal Land-revenue Sales Act or the Public Demands Recovery Act of 1913. The bill provided that such owners and interested persons would be entitled to apply for the setting aside of the sale within 30 days.

MOSLEM MARRIAGE EXPENDITURE BILL

The Bengal Moslem Marriage Extravagant and Superfluous Expenditure Regulation Bill, 1940, moved by Mr. *Nur Ahmed* was circulated for public opinion on the motion of *Nawab Musharuff Hossain*. The Nawab remarked that it was a social legislation which would affect all sections of Moslems and as such he thought that public opinion should be gathered before enacting such a legislation.

LOCAL SELF-GOVT. AMEND. BILL

Mr. *Humayun Kabir's* Bengal Local Self Government (Amendment) Bill, 1937, was circulated for eliciting public opinion on the motion of Sir Bijoy Prasad Singh Roy. Mr. Kabir's bill sought to do away with the system of nomination in the local bodies, introduce adult franchise and provided that no chairman either of municipality or district board should be eligible for the membership of either house of the legislature. Mr. Kabir remarked that the bill was circulated previously for public opinion. High Government officials had expressed opinion in favour of the measure and Mr. Kabir hoped that government would accept the bill.

4th MARCH :—Mr. *Kamini Kumar Dutta*, Deputy Leader of the Congress Parliamentary Party and Leader of the Party in the Upper House, withdrew from the House with his followers to-day in accordance with the directions of the All-India Congress Parliamentary Sub-Committee. Prior to this, Mr. Dutta made a statement similar to the one made by his leader, Mr. Kiron Shankar Roy in the Assembly yesterday. Khan Bahadur *Naziruddin Ahmad* (Coalition), rising on a point of order, enquired of the hon'ble President whether it was constitutional to proceed with the business of the House without any Opposition or without a Leader of the Opposition. The *President* in giving his ruling, said that if a particular party decided to abstain from the proceedings of the House, it would be constitutionally correct to continue the Government. His Majesty's Government must be carried on, he remarked.

Motor Spirits Sales Taxation Bill

The House then on a motion moved by the Finance Minister. Mr. *H. S. Suhrawardy*, took the Bengal Motor Spirits (Sales Taxation) Bill, as passed by the Assembly, into consideration, which was passed on the next day, the 5th March.

The object of the Bill is to levy a tax of one anna and six pies per gallon on retail sales of petrol and a tax of six pies per gallon on retail sales of motor spirit other than petrol. It is the intention of Government to use the proceeds of the tax to supplement the annual receipts from the Road Fund in order that the present scale of expenditure on new construction may be maintained. The discussion centred on three amendments seeking to reduce the tax on petrol to six pies per gallon, and to exempt passenger transport vehicles from payment of the tax on motor spirit or in the alternative to pay a tax of six pies per gallon of motor spirit. These proposals were negatived. There were a large number of amendments. The majority of them which were formal and consequential and made clear certain provisions of the Bill were accepted by the Government. An equally large number were not moved while one was ruled out of order.

The Sales Tax Bill

12th. MARCH :—The Finance (Sales Tax) Bill was taken up for consideration to-day. Moving that the Bill be taken into consideration, Mr. *H. S. Suhrawardy*, Finance Minister, said that the general election was approaching and if he had brought forward such a measure of taxation now it was because of an impelling necessity. They were passing through difficult and extraordinary times. A war was on and they should like as much of their available resources as possible to be devoted towards the prosecution of the war. But while war efforts must be supported, he continued, the work of the province had also to be carried on. The revenues of the province were insufficient for maintaining the standard of administration, and providing even ordinary amenities for the poor. They were unable to make adequate provision for nation-building works. Since the Ministry took office, they had embarked on various nation-building schemes but in the absence of sufficient funds they could not make the desired progress. The ordinary resources of the province were insufficient to meet this growing task, and it was their duty to make suitable provision for it. The Government had chosen this kind of taxation because they hoped to obtain thereby a large amount of revenue. He was aware that this proposal had engendered a certain amount of agitation in the province. but he was also aware that such agitation came mainly from traders and merchants. The general consumers, in particular the vast agriculturists, had not protested against the proposal because they realized that it was to be levied in the best interest of the province—and for the benefit of the masses. From the exemptions proposed, he added, it would be seen that it would hardly touch the proper classes.

Rai Bahadur *Keshab Chandra Banerji*, moved that the Bill be circulated for eliciting public opinion. The measure, he said, was of such a far-reaching character that it should be carefully considered. He suggested that every possible retrenchment should be effected before the Government brought forward such a measure. The motion for circulation was lost.

Following this. Mr. *B. K. Roy Chowdhury* moved for reference of the Bill to "the Committee of the whole Chamber," and Rai Bahadur *Keshab Chandra Banerji* asked for reference to a select committee. The House rejected both the proposals and agreed to the consideration of the Bill. The Council then adjourned until March 19.

Supplementary Budget

19th. MARCH :—A supplementary estimate of expenditure of rupee one for the current year was presented by the Chief Minister, Mr. *A. K Fazlul Huq*, this afternoon, for the purpose of obtaining the assent of the House to the payment of Rs. 1,00,000 to the Calcutta Mayor's Fund for the relief of the London air raid victims, the balance being available from the savings made under the head "Miscellaneous."

Local Self-Govt. Amend. Bill

The House agreed on a motion moved by the hon. Revenue Minister, Sir Bijoy Prosad Singh Roy, to take into consideration the Bengal Local Self-Government (Amendment) Bill (1941), which *inter alia* "seeks to provide for a special machinery for the decision of disputes relating to elections held under the Bengal Local Self-Government Act of 1885 and at the same time oust the jurisdiction of civil courts in respect of such disputes, as has been done under the other Acts relating to the administration of local self-government in the province." The House then adjourned.

Purchase of Bengal Made Goods

21st. MARCH :—The Council considered non-official resolutions to-day. A proposal sponsored by Khan Bahadur *Saiyed Muazzamuddin Hosain* (Coalition) urged that, in order to encourage the industries of the province, the Government of Bengal should purchase, as far as possible, "all articles of furniture, stationery, uniforms and other articles required for Government offices and institutions or for Government purposes in any department from locally manufactured articles of Bengal, if available." Mr. *Tamizuddin Khan*, Minister for Agriculture and Industries, accepted the proposal and explained the Government's policy in regard to the matter. Their policy was to make purchase of stores in Bengal in such a way as to encourage the development of industries in the country to the utmost possible extent, consistent with economy and efficiency.

Encouragement of Fishery in Bengal

The *Minister* also accepted Mr. *Nur Ahmed's* resolution requesting the Government to encourage and help the fishery industry in Bengal. The Minister recognized the need for the development of the fishery industry and pointed out that a sum of Rs. 82,000 had been provided in the Budget for the establishment of a fishery department. He assured the House that when that department was established they would take into consideration the various suggestions made on the floor of the House. Both the resolutions were passed.

Dacca Riots—Official Statement

24th. MARCH :—The Premier Mr. *A. K. Fazlul Huq*, made a statement to-day regarding the Dacca riot situation in reply to a short-notice question by Mr. *Lalit Chandra Das*. The Premier said :—According to the latest report the situation has improved. There were five stabbing cases on Saturday (March 22) and two up to midday on Sunday (March 23) ; but there is a little looting and shops are opening. Vegetable sellers, for example, are again taking up their customary places. It has, however, been reported that this (Monday) morning there was a fire in the cooly lines of the Dacca Cotton Mills and some looting in Naya Sarak. Sporadic cases of stabbing continue. These must unfortunately be expected for some time yet and till they stop confidence cannot be fully restored. The following are the figures so far reported, of deaths and admissions to the Mitford Hospital with injuries :—

	Moslem	Hindu	Christian	Unidentified	Total
Deaths	21	6	—	1	28
Injured	99	55	2	1	157

The Premier added :—Every effort is being made by political leaders, officials and non-officials to restore peace between the communities. Executive action included :—The curfew order, an order under Section 144 Cr. P.C, banning the assembly of five or more persons : drafting from other district of 400 extra police, four sergeants and two officers of the Indian Police Service ; pickets at the more important street junctions and patrols through different parts of the city. The number of arrests so far made are as follows :—Moslems 77 ; Hindus 157. The Premier assured the house that all possible action was being taken to restore peace and order.

PRIMARY EDUCATION IN BENGAL

The Premier next made a statement about the action taken by the Government on the resolution regarding additional provision of one crore of rupees for the expansion and improvement of primary education in Bengal, that was passed by the House on August 30, 1940. "Government," he said, "are unable to accept the resolution in toto on the ground that there are practical difficulties in the way of accepting it as it stands. "The problem of primary education is not merely a question of provision of funds but the question of the supply of trained teachers as well. At present there are a little over 30,000 trained teachers only. The existing training schools (including 32 centres) turn out annually a little over 3,000 trained teachers and with the opening of new training centres the number can be raised at best to 6,000 or 7,000 per annum ; whereas for the successful solution of the problem of primary education in Bengal, Government require about 148,000 trained teachers. Money spent on untrained teachers will be a sheer waste. "The resolution has, however, been partially implemented by Government by agreeing to the additional provision of Rs. 35,00,000 recurring for primary education and of over Rs. 18,00,000 non-recurring for the training of teachers of primary schools"

THE SALES TAX BILL

The House then proceeded to consider the Bengal Finance (Sales Tax) Bill, as it emerged from the Legislative Assembly, and passed four clauses, two with certain slight modifications and the other two without any change. Clause 5, relating to the rate of tax, was under discussion when the House adjourned till the **27th. March**, when clauses 5 to 26 were passed. Amendments mostly of drafting character were carried to different clauses while by carrying an amendment to clause 22 it was provided that all offences punishable under this Act should be cognisable and bailable. The Schedule which deals with articles to be exempted from the tax remained to be dealt with.

NON-OFFICIAL RESOLUTIONS

28th MARCH :—The House proceeded to consider non-official resolutions, to-day the first of which was sponsored by Mr. *Nur Ahmed* (Coalition) and read : "An address be presented to His Excellency the Governor of Bengal through the Hon. the President of the Bengal Legislative Council requesting His Excellency to make a strong representation to the proper authorities to revise and reduce at an early date the scales of pay for the All India Services." The resolution was passed.

The following resolution moved by Mr. *Humayun Kabir* (Krishak-Proja) was also passed : "An address be presented to His Excellency the Governor of Bengal through the Hon. the President of the Bengal Legislative Council requesting His Excellency to move the proper authorities for definitely abandoning the proposal to abolish the Kalukhali- Bhatiapara section of the Eastern Bengal Railway."

Following this, Raja Bahadur *Bhupendra Narayan Sinha* of Nashipore, Leader of the Progressive party, and Mr. *Nur Ahmed* introduced the Bengal Hindu Religious Endowment Bill and the Bengal Suppression of Immoral Traffic (Amendment) Bill respectively. Three other non-official Bills, namely, the Court-Fees (Bengal Amendment) Bill, the Bengal Pasture Bill and the Bengal Non-Agricultural Tenacy Bill, were circulated for public opinion. The Council then adjourned.

ALLEGATIONS RE. DACCA SITUATION

31st MARCH :—Government order imposing restrictions on the publication of news, comments etc. relating to communal disturbances in the province under the Defence of India Rules was characterized as 'distinct encroachment' upon the liberty of the Press by the Opposition to-day. The situation arising out of the promulgation of the order was discussed on an adjournment motion moved by Mr. *Sachindra Narain Sanyal* when the Opposition pointed out that by keeping back information from the public Government were indirectly aggravating the situation. Sooner the order was withdrawn, the Opposition emphasised, the better. Government took strong objection to the reading out of a statement purported to have been written by Dr. *Shyamaprasad Mookerjee* regarding the communal clash at Dacca and eventually in order to stop its publication in the newspapers the press gallery and the visitors' galleries were 'cleared' by the Hon. President at the instance of Government. Sir *Bijoy Prasad Singh Roy* declared that Government thought that the publication of the statement concerned of Dr. S. P. Mookherjee would not be in the interest of the public.

The House then took up the consideration of the Bengal Finance Sales Tax Bill, 1941, and passed it with modifications and then adjourned.

ADDRESS TO GOVERNOR

1st. APRIL :—The House adopted a special resolution to-day moved by the Leader of the House, Sir *Bijoy Prasad Singh Roy* to the effect: "This Council is of opinion that an address be presented to His Excellency the Governor of Bengal through the Hon. President of the Bengal Legislative Council that a message of sincerest rejoicings may be conveyed through His Excellency the Commander in Chief to His Excellency Sir Archibald Wavell, Commander in Chief of his Majesty's Imperial Forces in the near East at the capture of Harrar and Keren and that this Council further conveys its warmest congratulation to the Indian soldiers for the conspicuous gallant part played by them in bringing about the success."

The Council next considered the Bengal Local Self-Government Amendment Bill, 1941, clause by clause and had not concluded the debate when the House rose.

AGRICULTURAL DEBTORS' AMEND. BILL

3rd. APRIL :—The Council to-day agreed to the consideration of the Agricultural Debtors (Second Amendment) Bill, 1940 as passed by the lower House. The bill seeks to provide a machinery for the restoration of such holdings which were hurriedly sold away about the time when the original bill was published in the official gazette, to as many as possible of their former possessors, subject to the payment of proper compensation to the decree holders. A subsidiary object of the bill is to place the Calcutta High Court outside the general scope of the Act and to make provisions for the procedure to be adopted as regards, and the effect of appellate and revisional applications to, and proceedings in, the High Court when such applications and proceedings relate to debts which are the subject of applications made to Boards. The Hon. Mr. *M. B. Mullick* pointed out that there was an insistent demand for a measure of this kind. A large number of holdings passed out of the hands of the agriculturists due to economic depression and Government sought to rectify the apparent injustice done to these agricultural debtors whose properties were hurriedly sold. He added that the question of jurisdiction of the High Court was still under the consideration of the Government and this provision might be taken out of the bill. Mr. *B. K. Roy Choudhury* moved an amendment for the circulation of the bill. He said that as a result of the operation of the Act not only a considerable section of the people had been defrauded of its rightful savings in the name of affording relief to another but the entire credit system in the rural areas had been completely broken down. Therefore, before they proceeded with the measure, they should carefully consider its provisions. *Raja Bahadur of Nashipur* moved that the bill be committed to a select committee. He said that the measure was of great importance to the agriculturists and this bill when passed into law would be a permanent Act and as such its various clauses should carefully be scrutinized, in the cool and dispassionate manner in the select committee. Both the amendments were lost and the House agreed to the motion of the Minister that the bill be taken into consideration.

CONTRACTS ON POPULATION BASIS

4th. APRIL :—Non-official resolutions comprised the agenda in the Council to-day. The debate arose over a resolution by Khan Bahadur *Ataur Rahman* (Coalition) that Government contracts should be given to Bengal Moslems on their population basis in various districts after properly advertising for tenders. He said that the Government had fixed the ratio of Government appointments. Some more facilities should be given to people who could undertake Government contracts. Mr. *J. B. Ross*, Leader of the European Group, said that it was not the custom of his party to take part in communal debates but a resolution of a communal character should not be ignored. The resolution was of such a one-sided character, that his party felt they would be failing in their duty if they did not express their view on it. It showed a trait of irresponsibility in the mover which he (Mr. Ross) had not noted before. The *Maharaja of Cossimbazar*, Minister for Communications and Works, said that Government had given equal facilities to every community to submit tenders. There was no denying the fact that the number of contracts given to Moslems was small. With a view to giving every community an opportunity to submit tenders, Government in their approved list of contractors wanted the communities to be on the 50-50 basis as in the case of the service ratio. As a result in the last few yea s there had been a steady increase in the number of Moslem contractors throughout Bengal. Unfortunately, the Minister continued, the majority of Moslem contractors were poorer than other contractors. To give Moslem contractors better facilities to compete with others, Government had classified contractors according to the amount of work they could take up at a time. While they had started with the lowest tender, they had been very careful to see that there was no unfair treatment and no rate cutting. Their experience so far of the present system of working had been fairly satisfactory. Government would do their best to see how far they could give effect to the spirit of the resolution but they could not deviate from the principle of the lowest rate. The resolution, as amended, was carried.

COMMUNAL PEACE

Mr. *Nur Ahmed* (Coalition) moved that the Government of Bengal be requested to prepare and put in operation a suitable scheme for the promotion of communal harmony in Bengal as early as possible. He deplored the differences that had arisen between Hindus and Moslems and appealed to members of the Council to consider the question from all points of view. It was unfortunate for Hindus and Moslems that they did not understand one another. The discussion had not finished when the Council adjourned.

DEBATE ON DACCA RIOTS

7th APRIL :—Congress members attended the Council today when two of their party moved adjournment motions in connexion with the Dacca riots. After the motions had been admitted and their discussion fixed for the next day, they left. Mr. *Kamini Kumar Dutta*, Leader of the Congress Party, moved :

"This Council do adjourn its business for the purpose of discussing a definite matter of urgent public importance, namely, the situation arising out of the burning and the looting of the houses of Hindu residents in a large number of villages exceeding 30 in number comprised in Raipura and Shibpur thana in the district of Dacca and of Hindu shops in the bazars in the same area from April 1 to 4, and of the complete failure of the police and of the authorities concerned to prevent these outrages committed in daylight and by organized mobs and to give any protection to the oppressed Hindus and the consequent evacuation of the residents from the affected area and taking refuge in an Indian State—namely the State of Tripura outside British India—and failure of the Government to take any measure of protection for Hindu residents of that area.

Mr. *Lalit Chandra Das* (Congress) moved :

"This Council do adjourn its business to discuss a definite matter of urgent public importance, namely, the failure of the Government in giving due protection to the lives and properties of non-Moslems in the villages of Raipur, Baripur, Meratoli, Serampur, Methikandi, Brahmandi, Radhaganj Bazar, Ranimaad, etc., in all about 40 villages within the subdivision of Narainganj in the district of Dacca, where as from the beginning of this month news whereof reached here yesterday, uncontrolled acts of organized loot, arson, plunder, forcible conversion to Islam, outraging the modesty of Hindu women, with cases of deaths and suicide have gone on with the result that several people of those localities have left their hearths and homes and crossed over to Tripura and many thousands of whom again left British India and sought the protection of the Maharaja of Tripura and taken refuge in Agartala."

LOCAL SELF-GOVT. AMEND. BILL

Sir B. P. Singh Roy, Revenue Minster, next moved that the Bengal Local Self-Government (Amendment) Bill, 1941, as settled in the Council, be passed.

Mr. *W. F. Scoot-Kerr* (European) supporting the motion, said that his party were in complete agreement with the principles and objects of the Bill. But they must again protest against the way in which the Bill had been settled in this House. The Bill, which originated here, was sent to a select committee the members of which failed to reach unanimity. Eventually, a series of amendments were drafted by members of the Coalition party, moved on the floor of the House and certain additions were made to the Bill. In many cases the House did not have an opportunity of considering those amendments as carefully as they should have been. The inclusion or exclusion of a small word, the displacement of a comma, might alter the whole meaning of a clause or sub-section. If the Bill was given to a expert draftsman he would have made it far simpler and half the length, without altering any of the principles at all. Khan Bahadu. *Nazimuddin Ahmed* (Coalition) supporting the motion, remarked that the Bill was an improvement on the existing state of affairs and would have to be passed. Supporting, the *Raja Bahadur of Nashipur*

(Progressive) observed that his party were in favour of the Bill. Khan Bahadur *Syed Muazzamuddin* (Coalition) in supporting the passage of the Bill, suggested certain modifications. Mr. *Nur Ahmed* (Coalition) also supported the motion. Mr *Humayun Kabir* (Krishak Proja) said that his party were in general agreement with the principles of the Bill. Mr. *Abdul Quasem* (Coalition) said that the Coalition Party had their own views and did not follow the Government blindly as was evidenced by the large number of amendments moved by them. When members of the Coalition party were not convinced that the Government were right they moved amendments. He supported the motion. Sir *B. P. Singh Roy*, in reply, assured the House that as regards legislation the Government would see that more attention was paid to drafting. The motion that the Bill as settled in Council be passed was carried. The Council then adjourned.

DEBATE ON DACCA RIOTS

8th. APRIL :—The adjournment motion on the Dacca Riots was talked out this afternoon. After a discussion for about ninety minutes, the Ministerialist Coalition moved closure which was accepted by 22 to 12 votes. Following this, the mover stood up to give his final reply and before he could finish the two-hour time limit expired and the motion was, therefore, talked out. In moving the adjournment motion, Mr. *Kamini Kumar Dutta* assured the Muslim members of the House that he had not tabled the motion in a narrow communal spirit. He thought it was his duty to appraise all the members of the House of the real situation prevailing in the villages in Dacca district and to give them a true picture of the situation so that they might be conscious of the failure of the Ministry to give protection and security to the life and property of those people over whom they practically ruled.

Mr. Dutta said that on April 1 three villages were looted and burnt and on April 2 eight villages were raided and burnt and on April 3 nineteen houses and eleven pucca buildings were burnt. These place, he said, were not jungle areas, where all sorts of crime could be committed and from which the miscreants could melt away as the Chief Minister had wanted them to believe in the Government Communique. As a matter of fact these places, said Mr. Dutta, were the most prosperous portions of Dacca district and they were within one and a half hour's journey from Dacca, and easily accessible by rail and steamer. Speaking about the refugees, who had taken shelter in the Tipperah State, Mr. Dutta said that he had been in that native State and found several thousands of Hindu refugees there. Among the refugees were men and women, children and even babies a few days old with their mothers. Among the refugees there were also graduates of the university, respectable members of society, such as members of Union Boards, District Boards and other public institutions, merchants, zamindars, big cultivators and people of all classes. A greater condemnation of the Ministry, he said, could not be imagined. From the facts gathered by him, he said, it seemed that the outrages committed in the locality were engineered by outside agency. Many houses were set fire to with combustibles which could not be obtained by ordinary villagers. That showed that the looting and arson were carried out under the direction of intelligent brains.

Mr. *Lalit Chandra Das* (Congress) in supporting the motion said that from information available, from the method of operation of the rioters it was clear that the whole thing was preconceived and organised. He suggested that if they were to bring in an atmosphere of peace and harmony, the present Ministry must be dissolved and a new Cabinet set up in its place, composed of Nationalist Hindus and Muslims.

Replying to the debate, *Sir Bijoy Prasad Singh Roy* said that the Government sincerely regretted the situation that had arisen as a result of the communal trouble and deplored the fact that the peace and tranquillity of the province, in the maintenance of which the present Ministry during the last four years took a sincere pride, had at last been disturbed. He repudiated the statement made by Mr. Kamini Kumar Datta that Moulvis and mischief-makers were going about exciting communal feelings in that particular area for some time past and that they were allowed to carry on their nefarious activities unchallenged. The Government, he said, had no information in support of this allegation. It was a fact, however, that communal feelings were running high because of the incidents that had happened at Dacca, and they suddenly burst out. Sir Bijoy said that the moment they got the information of the trouble, the machinery of the Government was set in motion and all available help was sent at once. It was indeed a fact that many people had suffered seriously and houses and properties of many were destroyed and that a large number of people had taken refuge in the Tipperah State. He informed the House that the situation had been brought under control and refugees were beginning to come back to their respective homes. The whole communal situation, the Minister continued, however unfortunate it might be, should be studied against the background of the activities of some of the communal leaders during the last few years and of the press generally. The fact that the present Ministry had been in power had given a great shock to certain section of the Hindu community, although the Ministry consisted of an equal number of Hindu and Muslim Ministers, barring the Chief Minister, to begin with. If the Opposition wanted to play the part of a constitutional Opposition it was up to them to help the Ministry to tackle the situation and not embarrass the Government. That was unpatriotic. In any independent country in a similar situation the leaders of the different groups would have put their heads together and pulled their resources and would never have tried to embarrass the Ministry or the party in power. It had been suggested, the Minister proceeded, that His Excellency the Governor of Bengal should intervene under a certain section of the Government of India Act. He would put to those who had made this suggestion, where were they when a similar situation arose in the Congress-governed provinces ? Did they at that time suggest that Governors of those provinces should assume responsibility for the administration of those provinces ? He would beg of the members of the House not to embarrass the Government in their attempt to deal with the situation. If the Opposition was prepared to advise the Government and make suggestions as to how they should deal with the situation, the Government would readily accept them. He would like to put it to the House that it was very difficult for the Government alone to deal with the situation unless the full and sincere co-operation had been forthcoming from a certain section of the community. That co-operation was unfortunately lacking. If the establishment of peace and the improvement of the communal situation was their sole object, they (the Opposition) should give up for the time being the cry of Ministry-breaking which had gone too far and too long. By that cry they had created a situation in the country, for which they themselves were largely responsible.

The Council at this stage was *prorogued.*

The Punjab Legislative Assembly

LIST OF MEMBERS

Speaker :—Hon. Chaudhury Sir Shahab-ud-Din

Deputy Speaker :—Sardar Dasaundha Singh

Elected Members

Mian Abdul Aziz
Sufi Abdul Hamid Khan
The Hon. Mian Abdul Haye
Mian Abdul Rab
Chaudhury Abdul Rahim
Chaudhury Abdul Rahim
Syed Afzaalali Hasnie
Chaudhri Ahmad Yar Khan
Khan Bahadur Mian Ahmad Yar Khan Daulatana
Sardar Ajit Singh
Pir Akbar Ali
Chaudhri Ali Akbar
Khan Bahadur Nawab Malik Allah Bakhsh Khan
Syed Amjad Ali Shah
Chaudhri Anant Ram
Captain Ashiq Hussain
Qaderi Sayed Badr-Mohi-ud-Din
Rao Bahadur Captain Rao Balbir Singh
Sardar Baldev Singh
Sardar Balwant Singh
Malik Barkat Ali
Lala Bhagat Ram Choda
Pandit Bhagat Ram Sarma
Rai Bhagwant Singh
Lala Bhim Sen Sachar
Diwan Chaman Lall
Sardar Chanan Singh
Hon. Rao Bahadur Sir Chaudhri Chhotu Ram
Lala Deshbandhu Gupta
Mr. Deb Raj Sethi
Captain Dina Nath
Lala Duni Chand
Mrs. Duni Chand
Rai Faiz Muhammad, Khan

Budget Session—Karachi—26th. February to 2nd. April 1941

FINANCIAL STATEMENT FOR 1941-42

The Budget session of the Sind Legislative Assembly commenced at Karachi on the **26th. February 1941.** A surplus of Rs. 1,00,000 is envisaged in the Budget estimates for 1941-42 presented to-day by *Khan Bahadur Alla Baksh*, Finance Minister, the anticipated revenue receipts being Rs. 4,35.47,000 and expenditure charged to revenue Rs. 4,34,47,000. The main features of revenue receipts are increased land revenue, totalling Rs. 180 lakhs and excise revenue Rs. 34 lakhs. The other items of receipts are : Subvention from the Central Government Rs. 105 lakhs and income tax contribution of Rs. 8½ lakhs. A provision has been made for capital expenditure of Rs. 35,42,000 and repayment of dept to the central Government to the extent of Rs. 40 lakhs of which Rs. 36 lakhs is to be credited towards the Lloyd Barrage debt account. New items of expenditure include expansion of education in Mullah schools, Rs. 38,100 ; and literacy campaign Rs. 25,000. A provision of Rs. 3 lakhs has been made for the expansion of the Government Press. The major irrigation work to be undertaken under capital account is the Pyari canal project, which marks the completion of a comprehensive scheme called the Karo Canal works estimated to cost Rs. 34,80,148 and Rs. 7 lakhs is allotted for it. The opening balance for the year 1941-42 is Rs. 9,97,000 exclusive of investments in Treasury Bills.

With regard to the debt position. Sind will be able to pay in the next financial year in addition to interest charges Rs. 35,97,000 towards the refunding capital. During the current year, she will be paying, besides interest charges in full, about Rs. 44 lakhs towards the capital. Since the beginning of provincial autonomy, the province has liquidated a debt of Rs. 135½ lakhs and on March 31, 1941 the debt figure will stand at Rs. 2,398 lakhs on the Lloyd Barrage account and Rs. 406 lakhs for other purposes. The revised estimates for 1940-41 show a surplus of Rs. 2,84,000, revenue receipts being Rs. 4,59,99,000 and expenditure charged to revenue Rs. 4,57,15,000. The actuals for 1939-40 showed a surplus of Rs. 23,79,000.

The Khan Bahadur dealt at great length with the debt position of the province and considered that the position would have been vastly improved if the Government of India had cancelled the debts of all Provinces and allowed them to start on clean slates as had been done in the case of certain Provinces. Not only was this not done, he added, but the financial settlement made in respect of Sind, in his opinion, was unfair to the Province. He said that instead of giving an annual subsidy and insisting on repayment of the Barrage debt with interest the Central Government could have written off the entire Barrage debt in which case the Province would have been saved high interest charges which it has to pay at present. The Finance Minister quoted the findings of various committees to support his view and drew attention to the fact that arrangements in force at present for the repayment of debt had been based on the Government of India forecast in 1936, and pointed out that experience had shown that the assumptions made in the forecast were unduly optimistic and had not been realized in actual practice. Despite the rising tide of expenditure and the necessity of providing for certain major works, he concluded; the Government had been able to include in the budget certain proposals for development and improvement of the social and economic welfare of the Province.

SPECIAL CLASS FOR POLITICALS

5th MARCH :—An interesting debate took place to-day on a resolution, moved by recommending "special class" for political prisoners in Sind. The resolution found all-round support. Members of the Congress benches urged the necessity for greater prison reforms, while Sir *Ghulam Hussain Hidayatulla* urged the enactment of special legislation for the definition of " political offences." He said that decency required special treatment for political prisoners ; they should not be lodged with ordinary criminals. The Minister for Prisons, *Sheikh Abdul Majid*, agreed with the principle of the resolution, and supported Sir Ghulam's view. Khan Bahadur *Allah Baksh*, winding up the debate, assured the House that the Government would bring in legislation for the purpose of classification of prisoners, and informed them that the Government had called for a list of prisoners convicted under the Defence of India Rules so as to classify them under "B" class. Concluding, he said that the Government would also bear in mind the question of interviews and supplying of newspapers to political prisoners.

Resignation of Ministers

6th. MARCH :—The Premier, *Mir Bundeh Ali Khan*, *Khan Bahadur Khuhro* and *Sheikh Abdul Majid*, three League Ministers, tendered their resignations to the Governor to-day. This followed the action of Mr. *Allah Baksh*, Mr. *Nichaldas Vazirani* and *Rao Bhahadur Gokuldas*, the other Ministers, in announcing their resignation and crossing the floor during the session to-day. *Mir Bundeh Ali Khan* informed the House that "as he had no majority in the legislature and as the members of the Cabinet had resigned he was submitting the resignation of the whole Cabinet." *Khan Bahadur Allah Baksh* was summoned by the Governor this evening, and he agreed to form a new Ministry.

The announcement of the decision of the Ministers, Khan Bahadur Allah Baksh, Mr. Nichaldas Vazirani and Rao Saheb Gokuldas, to resign and cross the floor to-day, took their three colleagues by surprise. The Ministerial benches were practically deserted except for the presence of half-a-dozen Muslim supporters of the League Ministers and two European members. The public, expecting a battle royal to-morrow when the no-confidence motion against the Premier was due to be discussed, was totally unprepared for the dramatic turn of events, and this was evidenced by the spare attendance in the gallery. An inkling of the coming storm was however provided by the good attendance on the Opposition beenches, 34 members being present, comprising sixteen Muslim supporters of Khan Bahadur Allah Baksh, eleven Hindus and seven Congressites. In accordance with a pre-arranged plan, the Opposition members withdrew all the one rupee cut motions. Mr. *M. H. Gazdar* (Muslims League) also withdrew his one rupee 'cut' motion under the head Land Revenue. General discussion of the entire demand did not take more than one hour.

Towards the end of the discussion, Mr. *Nichaldas Vazirani*, Minister in charge, replying said, "I am quite convinced that the whole House is fully satisfied with my policy and my department." He then suddenly announced the resignation of himself and his two other colleagues in the following words. "Now, Sir, the position is this, You know very well that the Premier made a statement here that some of his colleagues were not seeing eye to eye with him and he has been desiring my resignation. I therefore have submitted my resignation to the Governor. With your permission, I may be allowed to cross over."

Rao Saheb Gokuldas, Minister for Local Self-Government, then announced: "I also have resigned and submitted my resignation to the Governor."

Khan Bahadur Alla Baksh next addressed the House. He said that he would have liked to continue till the time of moving of the "no-confidence" motion against the Premier fixed for to-morrow, but unfortunately he had received a leaflet in which the Muslim League had tried to intimidate and threaten members not remaining in their fold, and expressed its intention of staging a demonstration at the Secretariat. "It is not possible for us." he said, "to submit to coercion. Coercion being there, we decided that there should be no further talks, and we therefore tendered our resignation." Immediately after his statement, Mr. Allah Baksh walked over to the Opposition benches.

New Ministers Sworn-in

7th. MARCH :—It was officially announced to-day that Khan Bahadur *Alla Baksh*, the Premier, presented to His Excellency the Governor his colleagues in the new cabinet ; Sir Ghulam Hussain Hidayatullah, Pir Elahi Bux, Mr. Nichaldas Vazirani and Rao Saheb Gokuldas, who were then sworn in as Ministers.

The following will be the portfolios in the new Government : Khan Bahadur Alla Baksh (Premier : Finance and Excise and P. W. D. until a sixth Minister is appointed) ; Sir Ghulam Hussain Hidayatullah (Law and Order) ; Mr. Nichaldas Vazirani (Revenue) ; Rao Saheb Gokuldas (Agriculture and Local Self-Government) ; Pir Elahi Bux (Education, Public Health, Prisons and Labour).

The Premier, *Khan Bahadur Allah Baksh*, sought the adjournment of the Assembly for the day soon after it met to-day. He announced that he undertook to form the Government when he was called upon by the Governor to do so, and that he had been sworn in. He, however, had not presented to the Governor the names of his colleagues, and therefore proposed adjournment of the House till to-morrow. Mr. *Gazdar* wanted to know the difficulties the Premier was encountering in forming a Cabinet, while Sheikh *Abdul Majid* suggested that the Premier, Khan Bahadur Allah Baksh, was "not in a position to form a Ministry to-day", as he was unable to command a majority and wanted to know whether he would be feeling confident by to-morrow to form a Cabinet. Strongly refuting the suggestion, Khan Bahadur *Allah Baksh* stated that when he agreed to form a

Ministry it was because he knew he was having a majority. There was absolutely no question of negotiations going on between parties which wished to join ; it was only a matter of selecting the personnel. The Speaker thereupon adjourned the House till to-morrow.

Ex-Premier's Statement

Detailing the events at length till the resignation, *Mir Bundeh Ali* said that he assumed office when Sind was plunged into utter confusion, lawlessness and disorder owing to serious omissions and commissions of the last Government. The formation of a new Government ushered in a new era and by his firm action, respect for law and order was restored. He, however, felt surprised that the Congress group, despite their solemn pledge, had tried to break with the Ministerial Party within two weeks. Referring in detail to the political discussions which took place during Maulana Azad's visit to Sind, Mir Bundeh Ali admitted having told Maulana Azad that, with a view to resolving the deadlock, he would probably resign withinin a couple of months' time and that the Governor had been appraised of his intention. Mir Bundeh Ali characterised as wicked the suggestion that he had joined the Muslim League to escape the implication of the secret letter as he had always looked upon himself as a Leaguer. Moreover, he added, no Muslim Leaguer would continue to work in a Cabinet the head of which was a non-Leaguer, and to avert any unpleasant developments he had joined the League. Mir Bundeh Ali said that he was fully prepared to implement the Azad Arrangement, the spirit of which was that Khan Bahadur Allah Baksh and Sir Ghulam Hussain should be brought in but his Party did not want him to resign, as by his resignation the two Muslim Leaguers would be ordered to go and sit in the Opposition. He also disclosed that he had been trying for an alternative and acceptable formula but the Party had not be n given the opportunity. He added, "If I have been guilty of not implementing the Azad Arrangement, my three colleagues have been equally guilty by refusing to tender resignation for upholding its sanctity.". Mir Bundeh Ali stated that he considered that the Pact did not disqualify him from offering himself as a candidate for the Premiership. Continuing, Mir Bundeh Ali Khan declared that the Congress Party was doing nothing but sabotaging the very mission which occupied Maulana Azad for ten days by supporting the 'no-confidence' motion and thus upsetting what he had laboriously reared up, namely, an all party government.

8th. MARCH :—An invitation to *Sheikh Abdul Majid*, the former Moslem League Minister, to join the Cabinet was extended this morning by the Premier, *Khan Bahadur Allah Baksh*, when replying on a debate on a cut motion sponsored by Dr. *Popatlal* (Congress). The invitation followed the Sheikh's offer of responsive co-operation in case the Ministry adopted his five-year plan for achieving prohibition. The Ministerial benches were well attended, the entire Hindu block of 12 members and 17 Moslem supporters of the Ministry occupying them. With the suport of the Congress party (seven) and the Europeans (three) the Ministry appeared to command a strength of about 40.

After question time the House granted the Land Revenue demand. The rest of the day was devoted to a discussion of the Excise demand. Criticism was mainly directed against the reported appropriation of the proceeds of certain taxes, specially imposed for purposes of prohibition, to general revenue and the Government's alleged failure to take adequate steps strictly to enforce prohibition measures. The cut motion was eventually withdrawn and the demand passed.

Debt Conciliation Bill

18th. MARCH :—The Assembly to-day passed into law the Debt Conciliation Bill, the second and third readings of the Bill occupying hardly two hours. The main features of the Bill are: It seeks to establish conciliation boards in districts which will bring about an amicable settlement between agricultural debtors and creditors and provides that in any scheme of debt conciliation, no creditor will be allowed a greater amount in satisfaction both of principal and interest than twice the amount of the principal originally borrowed, and if a creditor has received twice or more than twice the amount of the principal, no interest will be allowed on the unpaid principal.

Based on the Madras and Bengal legislation, the measure differs from them in minor details. The Sind Bill provides for appeals against the decisions of conciliation boards which will consist of one officer assisted by two advisers, to district courts. The board is also empowered to determine the extent of debt. The maximum rate of interest to be taken into consideration while effecting a settlement is fixed at nine per cent. The bill brings within its scope and benefit all agricultural debtors who pay up to Rs. 8,000 land revenue and whose debt does not exceed Rs. 50,000. Conciliation officers are given wide powers to determine the nature of offers of settlement and compel any settlement.

The bill received all round support and the only dissentient note sounded was by *Khan Bahadur Khuhro*, who felt that the Bill had not gone far enough. He maintained that the establishment of conciliation boards under the present Act would not avoid litigation, which it sought to eliminate in view of the provision of appeal against the decision of the boards. Mr. Khuhro also wanted the lowering of the rate of interest from nine to three per cent and its application to all agriculturists. Replying to the debate, the Revenue Minister, Mr. *Nichaldas Vazirani* admitted that the full utility of the legislation depended on the establishment of morgtage banks and protection against alienation of lands and small khatedars through legislation, both of which questions were under the active consideration of the Government.

The Sind Jagirdars Bill

19th. MARCH :—An interesting debate took place to-day over the rights of Jagirdars when it considered the Second Reading of the Bill, seeking to introduce the survey and settlement of Jagir lands in the province. The Bill, which was introduced in the last session, is based on the recommendations of a special officer appointed for investigation and examination of the relations between Jagirdars and their tenants. The Bill was circulated for public opinion, which is mainly in favour of the legislation. While the Government spokesman held that it was an inoccuous measure based on equity and justice and affecting only unscrupulous Jagirdars, who tried to deceive the Government in regard to water-rates payable to it, the Oppositionists characterised the Bill as a class legislation aiming ultimately at expropriation of Jagir rights. The Congress Benches complained of the limited scope of the Bill and wanted direct collection of rents by the Government from 'Haris' of Jagir lands. The Second Reading was postponed.

Non-official Bill

24th. MARCH :—The Assembly disposed of to-day as many as 47 private members' Bills on the agenda. Most of them lapsed due to the absence of movers, and many others were dropped. Four Bills passed the first reading, and were referred to select commitees, while a minor amending Bill to the Weights and Measures Act was passed. The most important among the measures referred to select committees was one moved by Mr. *R. K. Sidhwa* (Congress), seeking to regulate the powers and privileges of members of the Assembly. The other Bills related to prevention of gambling by seeking to prohibit the publication of astrological forecasts regarding movements of market prices, and the abolition of funeral feasts.

Ministers' Salary Bill

31st. MARCH :—An increase in the salary of Ministers from Rs. 500 to Rs. 1,500 was sought in a new Bill which was introduced to-day. The salary will be inclusive of car allowance and house-rent. The Ministers will be however entitled to prescribed travelling and daily allowances while on tour on public business. The Bill also seeks to increase the salary of the Speaker from Rs. 800 to Rs. 1,250 per month and membe s' salaries from Rs. 75 to Rs. 150 a month and their daily allowance from Rs. 2 to Rs. 5 during sessions. It will be remembered that the Ministers are at present receiving Rs. 500 a month and are given cars which are maintained by the State and a free furnished house. The attitude of the Muslim League was expressed by *Khan Bahadur Khurro* who said that the party had decided to remain neutral on the issue and pointed out that the League had not fixed the maximum salary of Ministers as the Congress had done. He added that it was a matter between the Congress and the *Allah Baksh* Ministry which came to power in complete violaton of the Azad Pact and through the machinations of the Congress and Hindu parties. Mr. *R. K. Sidhwa*, Leader of the Congress Assembly Party, strongly opposed the measure on principle and held that the Alla Baksh party had raised itself in the estimation of All-India by accepting the Congress principles and by their sacrifices and hoped it would continue to do so. He, however, declared that the Congress supported the Ministry and would continue to support it and would not fall into the trap which was laid for them by the League for the purpose of defeating the Ministry. Discussion was not concluded when the House adjourned.

The Assembly passed to-day three Bills including one regularising the notification banning the sale of charas which was held to be *ultra vires* by the Chief Court.

1st. APRIL :—The Sind Ministers' Salary Bill was passed into law this afternoon. The new salaries which have retrospective effect from the date of assumption of office on March 8 by the new Ministry, will be inclusive of the present car allowance and house rent. Opposition to the measure mainly came from Congress benches while the Muslim League remained neutral. Replying to criticisms, *Sir Ghulam Hussain Hidayatulla*, Home Minister, maintained that the Congress Ministers in Bombay were getting about Rs. 1,500 if the rent-free furnished houses and car allowances were taken into account. The Bill merely sought to consolidate the present salary of Rs. 500 with free houses and car allowances which the Ministers were now getting.

The Assembly also passed the bill seeking to raise the Speaker's salary from Rs. 800 to Rs. 1,250.

Members' Salary Bill

After the recess, it was stated that the Government did not desire to proceed to-day with the Bill relating to the increase of members' salaries from Rs. 72 to 150 per mensem. Minister *Nichal Das Vazirani* declared that there was difference of opinion among Government benches over this question and in order to bring round all members of the party to the Government view, he moved the adjournment of the House, and the House adjourned.

Sind Barrage Debt

2nd. APRIL :—The Assembly adopted a resolution to-day recommending advanced payment of thirty lakhs of rupees from the free balance towards the Barrage debt in the Government of India. Explaining the implications of the resolution about the Barrage Debt, Khan Bahadur *Allah Bakah*, the Finance Minister, said that it was purely a matter of investment, as the amount was lying idle. Maintaining that this did not mean that the Province would be able to repay the debt according to the Niemeyer Award, the Premier said that at present all the income from the Barrage-unified system after charges were deducted would be given to the Government of India towards the debt and after 1940-43, the whole revenue of the Province would become pledged for funding the Barrage debt on an equated scale with interest charges on the balance. Unaccelerated payment was allow d and the Government of India were good enough to agree to advance re-payment from the free balance amount to be replenished next year from the Barrage revenue. Adverting to the Niemeyer Award, the Premier declared that he did not think that it would be fair if the Barrage did not pay its way as expected, and the non-Barrage area be called upon to pay the debt and on that reason alone apart from others, the Award was unreasonable.

Members' Salary Bill

The Assembly earlier passed the first reading of the Members' Salary Bill as amended by the Government, retaining the present scale of Rs. 75 of the members, but increasing the allowances and railways fares for moffusil members. The Congress Party opposed the measure at every stage and demanded three divisions, the last one over the first reading, resulting in the narrow majority of one for the Government, with 23 votes against 22.

Debt Conciliation & Jagirs Bills

The session which concluded to-day was marked by the passage of two bills of far-reaching importance besides others, namely, the Debt Conciliation Bill and the Jagirdars' Bill. With regard to non-official Bills, the most important among the measures referred to a Select committee was the one moved by Mr. *R. K. Sidhwa* seeking to regulate the powers and privileges of the members of the Assembly. The House then adjourned *sine die*.

The Government of Orissa

Financial Statement for 1941-42

Orissa's Budget estimates for 1941-42 issued from Calcutta on the 27th. March 1941 show a surplus of Rs. 2,15,000. The total revenue is estimated at Rs. 1,92,74,000 and expenditure charged to revenue at Rs. 1,90,59,000.

It was estimated that 1940-41 would begin with an opening balance of Rs. 11.67 000 but actually the year opened with a balance of Rs. 15 90.000 The revised estimate of revenue for 1940-41 is Rs. 2,01,66.000 against the current estimate of Rs. 1,95,21,000—Rs. 6,45,000 more than was anticipated. An improvement of Rs. 2.20.000 is anticipated in the province's share of income-tax. Improvements of Rs. 3,05,000 are expected under. "Excise" of Rs. 33,000 under "Stamps" and of Rs. 96,000 under "Forests."

On the other side of the account the revised estimate of expenditure debitable to revenue is Rs. 1,99,52,000 against Rs. 1,99,88,000 originally estimated. The revenue for the year according to revised estimates, is expected to exceed expenditure charged to revenue by Rs. 2,14,000.

Besides the revenue account, the net transactions on account of debts deposits, remittances and similar heads are expected to result in a net disbursement of Rs. 13.79,000 with the result that 1940-41 is expected to close with a balance of Rs. 4,25,000.

The balance is less than the minimum cash balance of Rs. 9,00,000 which the province has to maintain with the Reserve Bank and in the Treasuries. The cash balance on March 31, 1941, is actually not likely to be less than the minimum of Rs. 9.00,000. however, This apparent anomaly is explained by the fact that the accounts are kept open for interprovincial book adjustments for 15 days after the close of the year and past experience shows that considerable adjustments against the accounts of a financial year were made in the first 15 days of the next financial year. The estimated closing balance of Rs. 4,25,000 provides for such adjustments.

The Government of N. W. F. Province

Financial Statement for 1941-42

A small surplus of Rs. 32,000 is anticipated in the Budget Estimates of the North-West Frontier Province for 1941-42, published from Peshawar on the 27th. March 1941. The total Revenue for the year 1941-42 is expected to yield Rs. 1,91,25,000 against which the Expenditure is estimated to amount to Rs. 1,90,93,000.

The estimates for Expenditure include Capital Expenditure totalling Rs. 3.64,000, on account of irrigation works (Rs. 44,000) and the Malakand Hydro-electric scheme (Rs. 3,20 000) which is being met from revenue. If this is excluded the total revenue surplus would amount to Rs. 3,96,000.

The major items of new expenditure occur under Land Revenue on account of the appointment of a civil estates officer and the resettlement of the Hazara district under General Administration on account of provision for the preparation of electoral rolls for elections to the provincial Legislative Assembly ; under Administration of Justice on account of the creation of a separate sessions division at Abbottabad ; and under Irrigation and Civil works, due to the usual activities of these departments.

The total provincial balance at the end of 1941-42 is estimated at Rs. 30,45,000, It is, therefore, unlikely that the province will have to borrow money for Ways and Means purposes during the course of the year.

In the Revised Estimates for the year 1939-40, prepared last year, it was anticipated that Revenue would amount to Rs. 1,84,86,000 and expenditure to Rs. 1,87.66,000 and that there would be a small deficit of Rs. 2,80,000 which would reduce the cumulative surplus of Rs. 15,30,000 brought forward from the previous year to Rs. 12,50,000 at the close of the year.

Actually, however there was a deterioration of Rs. 1,70,000 which was due to a drop of. Rs. 2,25,000 in revenue, counter-balanced by a saving of Rs. 55,000 in expenditure. The anticipated deficit on the year's transactions thus increased to Rs. 4,50,000 and the cumulative balance at the close of the year fell to Rs. 10,80,000.

The Government of Central Provinces

Financial Statement for 1941-42

The budget of the Government of the Central Provinces and Berar for 1941-42, as authorised by His Excellency the Governor was published in a Gazette extraordinary on the **24th. March 1941.** The year 1939-40 closed with a revenue surplus of Rs. 32·90 lakhs. This was the first surplus year after a series of deficit years. The first two years of provincial autonomy ended with a revenue deficit of Rs. 55·90 lakhs which was reduced to Rs. 23 lakhs at the end of 1939-40.

The revised estimate for 1940-41 shows a surplus of Rs. 21·11 lakhs as against Rs. 22 lakhs in the budget. The improvement of Rs. 20,89 lakhs is brought about by the increase in revenue of Rs. 13,79 lakhs and the decrease in expenditure of Rs. 7,10 lakhs. The largest increase in revenue is under "taxes on income" and "forest" and is directly attributable to war. The decrease in expenditure is only nominal.

A sum of Rs. 8·50 lakhs representing the excess collection of land revenue over the standard figure which was to be carried to the deposit head "Revenue Reserve Fund" is now reduced to Rs. 29,000 on account of the deterioration in the land revenue position resulting from the prolonged drought in September and October in the Chhattisagarh division. Suspensions and resuspensions of land revenue have been granted to the extent of Rs. 14 lakhs and Rs. 81 lakhs, respectively. The allotment under the Land Improvement Loans Act and the Agriculturist Loans Act have been increased to Rs. 4 87 lakhs and Rs. 12·3 lakhs respectively. The provision for famine relief has been increased from Rs. 8 800 to Rs. 1,24,000. A sum of Rs. 10,000 has been ear-marked for cutting and stacking of fodder for cattle. As a result of the prolonged drought in the Chhattisgarh division there was a great rush of cultivators to come under rice irrigation agreements, particularly in the areas served by the Kharung and Maniari Canals. The total area under agreement has risen from 3,89,000 acres to 6,50,000 acres and the irrigation revenue from Rs. 7·15 lakhs to Rs. 9·00 lakhs. Government has sanctioned a grant of Rs. 16,000 during the current year and provided for a sum of Rs. 26,000 in the ensuing year for the publication of the war bulletins "Yuddah Varta" and "Yuddah Samachar". A Provision of Rs. 25,000 has been included in the budget for 1941-42 for meeting the out-of-pocket expenses of members of the provincial and district war committees for conducting propaganda tours. The expenditure on Civic Guards including the pay of the officers on special duty is estimated at Rs. 24,000.

The budget estimate for the year 1941-42 provides for a revenue surplus of Rs. 1,08 lakhs. Revenue is estimated at Rs. 510,76 lakhs or an increase of Rs. 1 84 lakhs over the revised Estimate of 1940-41. The expenditure against revenue is estimated at Rs. 508,78 lakhs or an increase of Rs. 20,97 lakhs. The expenditure includes Rs. 14 60 lakhs to be appropriated to the head "appropriation for deduction of avoidance of debt", being the excess of land revenue collection over the standard figure of Rs. 220,41 lakhs. Total new expenditure is Rs. 15,45 lakhs of which Rs. 10,24 lakhs is only technically new and represents more or less recurring commitments, such as grant of Dufferin Fund Hospitals Rs. 68,270, the Indian Red Cross Society Rs. 32,500, the co-operative institutes Rs. 25,600, and the general purposes grant to District Councils Rs. 5,38,000. The provision for real new expenditure is Rs. 5.21 lakhs the greater portion of which has been allotted to nation-building departments like education Rs 48,708, Medical Rs. 63,643, Agriculture Rs. 33,659, and Co-operation Rs. 1,38,961. Only such proposals have been included in the budget as are revenue yielding or unavoidable or are of great importance. Special mention may be made of Rs, 50,000 for housing accommodation for forest subordinates ; Rs. 10,500 for grants to the Scout Associations in the province ; Rs. 25,000 for a grant to the proposed opthalmic hospital to be built out of the King George V Memorial Fund ; Rs. 38,887 for improvements to the Mental Hospital, Nagpur ; Rs. 12,323 for grants to the leper homes ; Rs. 10,470 for the expansion of the open pan sugar factory and the development of cane cultivation in the Bilaspur district ; Rs. 1,10 lakhs for grants to meet the deficit in the working expenses of certain central banks in accordance with the scheme of rehabilitation of the co-operative movement and Rs. 11 560 for the continuance of the scheme for the encouragement of hand-spinning and hand-weaving in the rural areas.

The budget is framed on the level of the existing taxation. It has been possible to avoid new taxation on account of the increased share of the province in income tax and larger receipts under forest. Certain taxation measures due to expire during the year will be redewed as in the current year.

The percentage of renenue contributed by Berar is 34,3 as against 35,2 in the budget for the current year. The percentage of total expenditure in Berar is expected to be 32,9 against 33 in the current year while that of new expenditure in Berar is 45.

The year 1941-42 is expected to commence with an opening balance of Rs. 1,16 lakhs including the treasury bills outstanding of Rs. 50 lakhs. The revenue section of the budget provides for a surplus of Rs. 1,98 lakhs while the net result of the capital and debt head transactions is expected to be a deficit of Rs. 19 lakhs. Thus the year is expected to close with a balance of Rs. 98·98 lakhs. If the budget anticipations are realised the revenue deficit which was Rs. 23 lakhs at the end of 1939-40 will have been reduced to Rs. 1·89 lakhs at the end of 1940-41 and completely wiped out at the end of 1941-42.

The Government of Madras

Financial Statement for 1940-41

The Budget Estimates of the Madras Government for the year 1941-42, as authorised by His Excellency the Governor, was published from Madias on the **8th. March 1941.**

The Budget shows that the year 1939-40 closed with a surplus of 28·51 lakhs; that in 1940-41, the surplus according to the revised estimates is expected to be 4·81 lakhs; and that for the year under budget a surplus of 12·75 lakhs is budgeted.

The following table gives the figures of revenue and expenditure at a glance:

In Crores of Rs.

	Accounts. 1939-40.	Revised Estimate. 1940-41.	Budget Estimate. 1941-42.
Revenue	16·66	18·04	18·21
Expenditure	16·37	18·00	18·09
Surplus	·29	·04	·12

. A notable feature of the budget is the creation of a Revenue Reserve Fund, being the surplus yield of commercial taxes, after meeting the cost of collection and loss of revenue due to Prohibition, "so that it may be available to give a future Ministry time to adjust its finances to policy." An amount of 91·14 lakhs will accrue to the Reserve at the end of 1941-42.

Another feature is the allocation of 10·65 lakhs in the current year to distribute to elementary schools the full grants earned according to the Grant-in-aid Code and 13·29 lakhs in 1941-42.

A Sum of 7·41 lakhs has been provided for the Poondi Reservoir scheme.

From the revenue of the two years 1940-41 and 1941-42, a sum of Rs. 75 lakhs has been allocated to capital expenditure, thus avoiding borrowing.

The Government of Behar

Financial Statement for 1940-41

The budget estimates of the Bihar Government for the year 1941-42, issued in a memorandum from Patna dated **20th. March 1941** anticipate a net revenue of Rs. 6,11,08,000 and expenditure of Rs. 5 79.82,000 leaving a surplus of Rs. 31.26 000.

This surplus, it is pointed out, is largely illusory as no provision has been made for the re-habilitation of the co-operative movement, and for compensation to the growers of surplus sugarcane and the grant of a cost of living allowance to low-paid employees of the government, to all of which Government are committed. The Budget also does not provided for any new measures of taxation.

The revised estimate of revenue for the year 1940-41 is Rs. 6 16,12,000 against the current estimate of Rs. 55,008 000 and expenditure of revenue Rs. 6,09,62,000 against the original estimate of Rs. 5,46,34,000.

The improvement in revenue is mainly due to an anticipated increase of Rs. 11½ lakhs in the Province's share of the income-tax revenue form the Government of India and Rs. 16 lakhs under "Industries" on account of special cess on sugarcane. Increase also occurs under 'Excise' (14 lakhs) and 'Stamps' (10½ lakhs).

period should be sufficient to enable the licensee to wind up his concern. This Bill, he added, was intended to give effect to the above decision. The Bill was referred to a Select Committee, the circulation motion having been rejected without a division.

AGRICULTURAL PRODUCE MARKET BILL

25th to 28th APRIL :—Sir Sikandar Hyat Khan, intervening in the debate on the Agricultural Produce Markets Act Amendment Bill, which was introduced to-day, uttered a warning to those who had bolstered up an unconstitutional and unwarraned agitation. He said that if the growers and consumers, who constituted 90 per cent of the population, took upon themselves to flout the law there would be bloodshed, the responsibility for which would lie on the shoulders of the agitators. *Sardar Santokh Singh* assured the Premier that those directing the agitation had issued instructions to traders not to organise any processions, raise slogans or otherwise infringe the law. If they were compelled to carry on agitation it would be carried on strictly within constitutional limits. After the consideration of all except the penal clause, had been concluded, the House adjourned till Monday, the 28th April. Surprise at the attitude of the Standing Committee of the Punjab Trader's Conference after the concession of their main demands by the Government was expressed by *Sir Sikander Hyat Khan*, when Clause three of the Bill, which debars dealers who do not take licences by September 1 from taking them for three years was taken up for discussion. The Clause also provides that the Government may, in their discretion, issue a licence to such a person and may, before using such a licence impose such penalty, not exceeding Rs. 2,000, as they may think fit. Before the Clause was taken up, the Premier renewed his offer to Sardar Santokh Singh, Leader of the Opposition, that he would not press the Clause provided an assurance was given to him that the deadlock would end. He further expressed the Government's intention not to use the provision unless they were forced to do so in an emergency. *Sardar Santokh Singh* said that he could not go beyond the decision of the Standing Committee. Opposing the Clause, *Sardar Santokh Singh* said that the Clause was ill-advised. It was a threat of coercion and traders would not take that threat lying down. They would rather ruin themselves than submit to a threat of coercion contained in the Clause.

Intervening in the debate, the *Premier* said that the attitude taken by the traders' meeting last night was a threat to the Government established by law and order. While declaring that the Government was prepared to listen to all legitimate grievances and redress them, the Premier emphasised that the Government would not be cowed down by coercion or threat. The traders had thrown a challenge to the growers, the consumers, the law of the land and to the representatives of the people in this House. If they had thrown the gauntlet in that spirit, the Government must accept the challenge. This might mean a certain amount of hardship for small growers, but the Premier assured the House that the Government would do all they could to help the growers as well as consumers. Continuing, the Premier said that those dealers who would be prepared to continue their business would be provided the fullest protection by the Government against coercion. He pointed out that if anything untoward happened, the responsibility would lie on the shoulders of the leaders of the movement. As regards the demands for traders' majority on the market committees, the Premier expressed his inability to accept it on the ground that it would undermine the principle of the Act. He, however, assured the traders that if the rules or any other provisions in the Act were found to operate harshly the Government would be prepared to amend the Rules and, if necessary, bring another fresh amending bill later on.

Later, the House accepted an amendment moved by *Mir Maqbool Mahmood*, Parliamentary Secretery to the Premier, that Clause 3 shall not come into force until notified by the Punjab Government in the Gazette.

After some discussion the Clause as amended was passed by 72 votes against 18 and the House proceeded with the third reading of the Bill. As soon as the Bill was disposed of, the House adjourned *sine die*.

The Assam Legislative Assembly

LIST OF MEMBERS

Speaker :—THE HON. BASANTA KUMAR DAS

Deputy Speaker :—MAULVI MUHAMMAD AMIR-UD-DIN

Elected Members

SJ. JOGENDRA NARAYAN MANDAL
" SANTOSH KUMAR BARUA
KUMAR AJIT NARAYAN DEV
SJ. PARAMANANDA DAS
" JOGENDRA CHANDRA NATH
" GHANASHYAM DAS
" KAMESWAR DAS
" GAURI KANTA TALUKDAR
" SINDHI NATH SARMA
" BISNURAM MEDHI
" BELI RAM DAS
HON'BLE SJ. ROHINI KUMAR CHAUDHURY
SJ. GOPI NATH BARDOLOI
" PURANDAR SARMA
" BIPIN CHANDRA MEDHI
" OMEO KUMAR DAS
" MAHADEV SARMA
" HALADHAR BHUYAN
" MAHI CHANDRA BORA
" PURNA CHANDRA SARMA
HON'BLE DR. MAHENDRA NATH SAIKIA
SJ. RAJENDRANATH BARUA
" SANKAR CHANDRA BARUA
" KRISHNA NATH SARMAH
" RAMNATH DAS
" DEBESWAR SARMA
" BHUBAN CHANDRA GOGI
" JADAV PRASAD CHALIHA
" LAKSHESVAR BOROOAH
" JOGES CHANDRA GOHAIN
" RAJANI KANTHA BAROOAH
SJ. SARVESWAR BARUA
BABU AKSHAY KUMAR DAS
" BEPIN BEHARI DAS
" KARUNA SINDHU ROY
" SHIBENDRA CHANDRA BISWAS
" NIRENDRA NATH DEB
" DAKSHINA RANJAN GUPTA CHAUDHURI
BABU LALIT MOHAN KAR
THE HON'BLE MR. BASANTA KUMAR DAS
BABU HARENDRA NARAYAN CHAUDHURY
BABU RABINDRANATH ADITYA
" BALARAM SIRCAR
" KAMINI KUMAR SEN
HON. SJ. HIRENDRA CHANDRA CHAKRAVARTY
MR. ARUN KUMAR CHANDA
BABU KALA CHAND ROY
MAULVI GHYASUDDIN AHMED
MAULANA ABDUL HAMID KHAN
MAULVI JAHANUDDIN AHMED
" MATIOR RAHAMAN MIA
" MUHAMMAD AMJAD ALI
" SYED ABDUR ROUF
HON. SIR SAIYID MUHAMMAD SAADULLA
MR. FAKHRUDDIN ALI AHMED
MAULVI SHEIKH OSMAN ALI SADAGAR
" MUHAMMAD AMIRUDDIN
" BADARUDDIN AHMED
" KERAMAT ALI, KHAN BAHADUR
HON. KHAN BAHADUR MAULAVI SAYID RAHMAN
MAULVI DEWAN MUHAMMAD AHAB CHOWDHURY VIDYABINODE
MAULVI ABDUL BARI CHAUDHURY
MAULVI DEWAN ALI RAJA
HON. KHAN SAHIB MUDABBIR HUSSAIN CHAUDHURI
MAULVI ASRAFUDDIN, MD. CHAUDHURY
MAULVI ABDUR RAHMAN
" NAZIRUDDIN AHMED
" ABDUL AZIZ
" MD. ALI HAIDAR KHAN
SHAMSUL-ULAMA MAULANA ABU NASR MD. WAHEED
MAULVI MD. ABDUS SALAM
KHAN BAHADUR DEWAN EKLIMUR ROZA CHAUDHURY
HON. MAULVI ABDUL MATIN CHAUDHURY
KHAN BAHADUR MAULVI MUFIZUR RAHMAN
MAULVI MUBARAK ALI
KHAN BAHADUR HAZI ABDUL MAZID CHAUDHURY
KHAN BAHADUR MAULVI MAHMUD ALI
MAULVI MAZARROF ALI LASKAR
" NAMWAR ALI BARBHUIYA
HON'BLE MISS MAVIS DUNN
MR. A. WHITTAKER
" COMFORT GOLDSMITH
HON. SRIJUT RUPNATH BRAHMA
SRIJUT RABI CH. KACHARI
SJ. KARKA DALAY MIRI
" DHIRSING DEURI
MR. BENJAMIN CHANDRA MOMIN
" JOHANG D. MARAK
REV. J. J. M. NICHOLS-ROY
" L. GATPHOH
SRIJUT KHORSING MAUZADAR
MR. A. H. BALL
" A. F. BENDALL
" F. W. BLENNERHASSETT
" N. DAWSON
" D. B. H. MOORE

Budget Session—Shillong—3rd. March to 29th. March 1941

Financial Statement for 1941-42

The Budget session of the Assam Legislative Assembly commenced at Shillong on the **3rd. March 1941.** A deficit of Rs. 11,89,000 in the revenue account was revealed in the budget estimates for the year 1941-42. The estimates were presented to-day by the hon. Khan Bahadur *Sayidur Rahaman*, acting Finance Minister. No fresh taxation proposals were announced.

The year 1941-42 is estimated to start with an opening balance of Rs. 51,47,000. It is pointed out, however, that this substantial balance is mainly the result of the loan of Rs. 50,00,000 floated during the current year (1940-41).

The receipts are estimated at Rs. 6,37,95,000 (revenue receipts Rs. 3,13,01,000 and capital receipts Rs. 3,24,94,000). The estimated expenditure has been taken at Rs. 6,42,45,000 (revenue expenditure Rs. 3,24,90,000 and capital expenditure Rs. 3,17,55,000) thus leaving a closing surplus balance of Rs. 46,97,000. The revenue budget shows a deficit which is estimated at Rs. 11,89,000.

The following are the figures :—Receipts : Opening Balance Rs. 51,47,000, Revenue Receipts Rs. 3,13,01,000, Capital Receipts Rs. 3,24,94,000, Total Rs. 6,89,42,000 ; Expenditure : Revenue Expenditure Rs. 3,24 90,000, Capital Expenditure Rs. 3,17,55,000. Total Rs. 6,42.45,000, Closing Balance Rs. 46,97,000.

Under the head "Police" a sum of Rs. 64,600 has been included under Section 78 (2) of the Government of India Act, 1935, for the due discharge of the special responsibilites of His Excellency the Governor. The amount has been earmarked for the "Criminal Investigation Department".

"Assam's position on the north-eastern frontier has in recent days, brought her more prominently within the sphere of a possible danger and it is satisfactory that preparations have satisfactorily advanced in the area primarily concerned." observed, the *Finance Miuister*, presenting the budget estimates in the Assembly. Referring to the war efforts of the province, the Finance Minister stated that after a lengthy correspondence on the widely expressed desire of the people of the province to take a combatant part in the defence services, an agreed solution of the problem was achieved by the end of 1940, and the Defence Department of the Central Government announced the formation of the first Battalion of the Assam Regiment. Speaking on the budget proper, which disclosed a deficit, the Finance Minister observed that he was not altogether hopeless about the financial condition of the province but it was expected that they would be able to make up the loss within the next two years. The Ministry has provided a sum of seven lakhs for expenditure for the purpose for which it was floated. Giving his reasons why the Government had strengthened the Criminal Investigation Department, the Finance Minister said that subversive elements from Bengal were found to be penetrating into Assam in order both to stir up trouble here and use Assam as a base for continuing their nefarious activities in Bengal. Assam, he added, was indeed on the point of becoming a refuge where plotters might pursue their schemes as enemy agents do in neutral countries. Many societies and political organisations had sprung up in the province whose harmless titles were merely cloaks for action against the very basis of the society. The Government would be failing in its duty towards the people of Assam if it did not make adequate provision for watching these organisations. With the advent of the war came the likelihood of elements in the ordinary population being exploited by enemy states and evidence was by no means lacking that this possibility had not been overlooked by hostile Powers. The Government of India had adequately provided for the surveillance of aliens but could not be responsible for the conduct of the people of a province. The Finance Minister announced that the Intelligence Branch of the Criminal Investigation Department, which was abolished in pursuance of the vote of the Assembly in 1937, had been revived by the Governor for the purposes of discharging special reponsibilities. The House then adjourned.

General Discussion of Budget

7th. to 8th. MARCH :—Budget discussion was continued in the Assembly to-day. Mr. *Kaminikumar Sen* characterized the budget as disappointing and lacking in sound principles of budgeting. Assam, he pointed out, had 12 deficit budgets in the last 13 years and Government was following a policy of drift with no hope for the future. The Government was only thinking of retrenchment but that would not bring much relief. He condemned the appointment of parliamentary secretaries for Assam for whom there was, he said, practically no work. Mr. *Arnold Whittaker* (Leader, European Group), congratulated the Finance Minister for the lucid manner in which he had expounded his budget. The deficit of over Rs. 11 lakhs, he said, was a large one and while recognizing the urgent needs of the welfare departments, the European Group did not share the Finance Minister's view that expenditure on these departments must continue to increase even at the cost of increasing these deficits. The gap of Rs. 12 lakhs was not a very large figure but clearly some means must be found bridging the gap in the future. Mr. *Balaram Sircar* did not approve the appointment of parliamentary secretaries. He brought to the notice of Government the deplorable condition of subsidized dispensaries for which about Rs. 200 was paid for medicines every year which was insufficient in these days of increasing prices of medicines. The subsidized doctors were also ill-paid. Mr. *Nabakumar Dutt* characterized the budget as disappointing and urged that some relief be given to small tea estates. The brightest spot in the budget was, he said, the total prohibition of opium but this to be successful must enlist public co-operation. Regarding the mass literacy campaign the high expectations raised at the beginning had died out. Villagers had stopped going to school. To make the scheme successful the speaker suggested that the services of voluntary workers should be enlisted. He concluded by requesting the Government to keep lands for future expansion without disposing all land to the landless people. Mr. *Bepin Behari Das* said that the budget did not provide adequately for schedule caste people. He did not approve of the plan for appointing parliamentary secretaries. There was no provision for water supply. The crying need of the people of the Surma Valley was the establishment of a medical school at Sylhet. Mr. Das urged that the pay of subsidized doctors be raised to at least Rs. 50 a month and the allotment for medicines should also be raised. Assam was a agricultural province but the money set apart for agriculture was, the speaker said, very poor. *Maulavi Motior Rahaman Mia* brought to the notice of the Government the deplorable condition of agriculturists caused by the low prices of jute. He requested the Government to safeguard the interests of immigrants who numbered about 1,000,000 in Assam. He pointed out that the opening of an unemployment register would not solve the unemployment problem. Next day, the 8th. March, Mr. *D. B. H. Moore* (European Group) expressed doubts on the possibility of success of the total opium prohibition scheme launched by the Government. As the largest employers of organized labour in the province, the Europeans, he said, were seriously concerned with the welfare and physical well-being of the workers many of whom were unhappily opium addicts. He said he had seen the suffering experienced by addicts in their desperate but fruitless attempts to give up the habit. Some of them were taking to ganja and bhang, resulting in a marked deterioration both morally and physically. He questioned the value of prohibition propaganda for which Rs. 90,000 was alloted in the Budget. *Maulavi Abdul Bari Chaudhury* regretted the Government's delay in starting a medical school at Sylhet. Regarding the mass literacy campaign he said he was doubtful of its success. In the Sunamganj sub-division 100 schools had been started but not even five were functioning properly. The efforts of teachers to ensure the attendance of adult pupils had failed. The correct procedure, he said, was to amend and give effect to the Assam Primary Education Act. 1926, which would have afforded compulsory primary education to children. The Government could have utilised this money for starting primary schools in every district. *Maulavi Muhammad Maqbul Hussain Chaudhury* also expressed doubts about the success of the opium prohibition and mass literacy schemes. He urged the expansion of primary schools in the province and asked that more money be given for improving communications in the backward areas. *Khan Bahadur Mahmud Ali* deprecated the spending of more money on higher education in preference to primary education. *Maulavi Abdur Rahman* referred to the deplorable condition of the co-operative movement in Assam where most central banks had already stopped paying depositors their money. The people in the village areas were not getting credit since the passing of the Money Lenders Act and the Temporary Postponement of Decrees Act and unless the Government came to their rescue by rehabilitating the co-operative movement the position of agriculturists would be hopeless. Mr. *Akshay Kumar Das* said the provision of scheduled caste community was inadequate. He doubted the success of the opium prohibition and mass literacy schemes. *Khan Bahadur Soyidur Rahman*, Finance Minister, replying to the discussion assured the members that all possible action would be taken on constructive criticisms. Referring to Government's talking of a loan of fifty lakhs of rupees for the current year, he said the Government had to repay a debt of Rs. 46,78,000 which they had inherited on the inauguration of the reforms on April 1, 1937. They inherited also a debt of Rs. 90,00,000 for officers' provident fund liabilities on April 1, 1937. He could, of course, produce a balanced budget if he cut down new schemes meant for the province's welfare. He expressed the hope that with a better realization of the Agricultural Income-tax, finances may be improved and at the end of the year there may be a surplus instead of the deficit of Rs. 12,00,000 that was anticipated. He could not without land revenue remission as agriculturists particularly in Nowgong, Kamrup and Goalpara were having a hard time owing to the reduction of the price of jute from 16 per maund to Rs. 2-8 a maund and also on account of the war there were rises in the prices of necessary foodstuffs. At present he saw no necessity for fresh taxation. If the necessity arose he might consider the desirability of introducing a Bill like the Bengal Sales Tax. Regarding the opium prohibition scheme, he would accept members' suggestions for increasing the inspecting staff to prevent smuggling for which already official and non-official vigilance parties had been formed. The Government were trying also to cope with the evil of ganja and bhang. Regarding education many had criticized his sponsoring of the University Bill as election propaganda, but he pointed out that the proposal for a university was not new and it was the legitimate desire of all people to have a university in Assam. Regarding the question of its location he suggested that the matter be placed for decision before the Senate of the proposed University or the Cabinet. Referring to the mass literacy campaign, the Minister quoted figures to prove its success. Regarding the plan for a medical school for Sylhet he said that every possible step was being taken for its establishment and he hopped that the institution might be started in 1942-43. Dealing with the position of the co-operative movement he said the Government had provided Rs. 1,00,000 for financing the provincial bank.

Assam University Bill

11th MARCH :—After discussions lasting about five hours, the Assembly adopted to-day without a division the *Education Minister's* motion for reference of the Assam University Bill to a Select Committee. In the meantime, the Bill was also circulated for eliciting opinion which will be placed before the Select Committee for its consideration. The Select Committee was directed to submit its refort by June 30.

Air Raid Precaution

15th MARCH :—The whole territory of Assam was more vulnerable to attack by virtue of its proximity to a potential war theatre than most of the provinces, said the *Premier* moving his resolution to-day urging that the Assam Government do take the necessary steps to carry out air raid precautionary measures considered necessary and expend a sum, not exceeding Rs. 5,000, in advance of the sanction of the Government of India. The degree of the danger, the Premier pointed out, was a matter of speculation. The Assam Government had for some months been planning precautionary measures for those areas which would be most inviting to the enemy air force while also giving due attention to all parts of the province not so seriously threatened. All Air Raid Precaution Officers had already been appointed and the Central Government had undertaken to meet the cost of all such measures which meet their approval. Mr. *Baidyanath Mukherjee*, supporting the resolution, complained that the amount was too inadequate. Mr. *D. B. H. Moore*, who also supported the motion, reminded the House that they in Assam might be attacked, with the development of modern aircraft, within three hours by air from Japanese bases. Mr. *Jobang Morak* wanted to know whether Assam was really in danger and expressed the opinion that the measures contemplated might frighten the civil population. Discussion was continued on the next day, the 17th. March, when the resolution was passed.

The House passed to-day demands for Rs. 22,69,100 on general administration and for Rs. 15,71,900 on land revenue.

Grant to The War Fund

17th. MARCH :—The one-lakh grant of the Assam Government to the War Fund came before the Assembly in the form of a Supplementary demand for grant. The grant is to be discussed and voted upon on March 20 next. In the explanatory note, the *Premier* explained that since the demand for grant was referred back by the Hon'ble Speaker in November last for expert legal opinion on the validity of the contribution already made, the Advocate-General of Assam has given the opinion that the grant was legally under Section 150 of the Government of India Act, 1935. The amount has already been sent to England and a sum of Rs. 299 is shown as loss by exchange due to exchange rate for the payment of this contribution of one takh of rupees.

Govt. Decision Re-Apointments

The Government of Assam have decided to reserve 20% of the appointments to be made purely on consideration of merit, said Sir *Muhammad Saadulla*, Premier, in replying to a cut motion brought forward by Mr. *Baidyanath Mukherjee* to criticise the Ministry's policy of appointment. The *Premier* explained that this policy the Ministry had to determine in spite of a fair deal of opposition and the policy which at present was confined to recruitment made directly by Government to the Provincial Service is being further examined for its extension in spheres of subordinate appointments also. The Premier instanced one specific case in which a recent appointment of an Assistant Surgeon in the Public Health Department of Government has been made solely on consideration of merit and has gone to a caste Hindu of Sylhet though, he said, they were 200 per cent over-represented in the cadre. Mr. Mukherjee withdrew his proposed cut.

The Assembly also passed the demands for grants under heads "General Administration" (Rs. 22,69,100) and "Land Revenue" (15,71,900). 19 cut motions under each head were tabled but only a few were discussed and the rest not moved. Mr. *Baidyanath Mukherjee* and *Maulvi Abdur Rahaman*, Chief Whip of the Government Party, figured prominently in moving cut motions in course of which they criticised the Government policy of appointments, the utility of the services of the Parliamentary Secretaries and the policy of the Government with regard to the Publicity Department.

Grant to The War Fund (contd.)

20th. MARCH :—The *Premier* moved a supplementary demand for Rs. 1 lakh which the Government of Assam contributed to the British Exchequer in July 1940 to help Britain in her present struggle on behalf of Democracy. Mr. *Kamini Kumar Sen*, ex-Judicial Minister in the Congress Coalition Ministry, raised a point of order questioning the legality of the grant. Mr. Sen contended that the grant was not covered under sections 150 and 81 of the Constitution Act referring to the Speaker's ruling during the November session. He said that the Government ought to have obtained an interpretation from the Federal Court on this issue. The *Premier* at this stage informed the House that the question was placed before the Governor-General, and the Government of India had since intimated the Assam Government that there was no case to resort to section 213 of the India Act and to obtain the opinion of the Federal Court. The question was very simple as India was a belligerent country. The *Advocate-General* said that now that India was declared a belligerent country any grant for the defence of India came within the purview of section 150. He said that a grant by the province for the purpose of the whole of India was legal. He added that it was for the House to decide whether the purpose was covered by section 150, and requested the Speaker to have the question decided by a vote of the House. The *Speaker* reserved his ruling till the next day, the **21st. March**, when in a lengthy statement he discussed the implications of the various points raised, and pointed out that it was now represented that the amount was required for the defence of India and that since India was at war with Germany the whole aspect of the question was changed. The defence of India, the Speaker held, was certainly a purpose within the meaning of section 150 of the India Act. The Speaker, continuing, said Mr. Kamini Sen pointed out that the old case on which the demand was brought had now been changed, and in its place moral support for the defence of India was being urged. This certainly was a question of fact and one for the House to decide. With regard to the question of "necessity" the Speaker held the same view and allowed the supplementary demand moved by the Premier to be considered by the House. When the demand was put to the vote it was passed without division amidst applause.

The Assam Rifles

22nd MARCH :—The decision of the Government of India to take over the entire liability of the Assam Rifles and the proposal of the Assam Government to replace the detachment of Assam Rifles in the Garo Hills by a smaller armed force would result in a net saving of about Rs. 60,000 to the Provincial Exchequer.

This statement was made by the Premier, Sir *Mahommad Saadullah*, in the Assembly to-day. The Premier said that under the Assam Rifles Strength Bill, now under consideration of the Central Legislature, the cost of the force would become definitely a Federal obligation towards which the Province would contribute an account of the services rendered to Assam. The Government of India, continued the Premier, had agreed to reorganise the force with fifty-four platoons, but at the same time, it would reduce the provincial share to twelve platoons provided that no detachment be posted in the Garo Hills.

The House passed to-day the grants under the heads, "Education", 'Medical' and 'Agriculture'. and on the next day, the **23rd. March**, the demands for grants under Education (Rs. 41,44,900), Medical (Rs. 11,76,300), and Agriculture (Rs. 6,47,100) were passed. The cut motions moved were either lost or withdrawn after discussions and assurance given by the Government.

THE FINANCE BILL

27th. MARCH :—The Assembly by 37 votes to 8, passed the Assam Finance Bill (1941) to-day.

The House agreed to the amendments made by the Council on the Goalpara and Sylhet Tenacy Amendment Bills (1935), and the Assam Embankment Drainage Bill (1940) and passed the Assam Temporarily Settled Districts Tenancy Amendment Bill (1940) and the Assam Maternity Benefit Bill (1940).

The Assembly also considered the report of the Privilege Committee and adopted the first part of its recommendations, but rejected the second and third parts which recommended that the arrested or convicted members of the Assembly should attend to exercise their rights and privileges.

GOALPARA TENANCY AMEND. BILL

27th. MARCH :—The Assembly to-day to the surprise of all passed the Goalpara Tenancy (Amendment) Bill 1939 as amended by the Upper House, in spite of inconsistencies in the provisions of the Bill pointed out by Mr. *Baidya Nath Mukherjee* and admitted by Khan Bahadur *Maulavi Sayidur Rahaman*, Revenue Minister in-Charge of the Bill. Mr. Mukherjee pointed out that the Hon. Revenue Minister by an amendment in the Upper House to Clause 31 of the Bill as passed by the Assembly relating to suspension of provision of enhancement of rent changed the date "2nd March 1930" to "the date on which this Act comes into force" perhaps from an impression or belief that this Clause as passed by the Assembly militates against Section 292 of the Government of India Act which says that all the laws in force in British India prior to 1st April 1937 shall continue to be in force until altered, repealed or amended by a competent legislature. Mr. Mukherjee contended that according to Section 292 all the provisions of Goalpara Tenancy Act 1929 shall continue to be in force till the date on which they are either altered or repealed or amended. As the present Tenancy Amendment Act will come into force at date subsequent to 2nd March 1939, the Provisions of the Goalpara Tenancy Act 1929 cannot be altered, amended or repealed with effect from the 2nd March 1939 by this amending Act. Mr. Mukherjee then pointed out that if the wordings of the proposed section 93A are critically examined then it will be found that in the Sub-section (1) certain provision relating to enhancement of rent have been 'suspended' and not altered, amended or released and as such Mr. Mukherjee submitted this clause does not militate against Section 292 of the Government of India Act. Mr. Mukherjee then asked the House to consider whether by making a provision for suspension of certain sections of the Act they acted against the provision of Section 292 of the Government of India Act and also whether there was any justifiable reason to rescind its own verdict. Mr. Mukherjee further explained that Clause 5 of the Bill gives retrospective effect to the abolition of occupancy, transfer fee and as such militates against the Section 292 of the Government of India Act. Mr. Mukherjee further explained that the 'division of tenancies' in accordance with section 24 of the Goalpara Tenancy Act were either meaningless or had no sense at all. This Section 24 deals with liability for arrears of rent on transfer. Concluding Mr. Mukherjee appealed to the House whether the Hon'ble Members of the Assembly with their eyes wide open will pass this Bill with such palpable incongruity and asked the Hon. Speaker as the custodian of the dignity and prestige of the House whether it would advance the dignity and prestige of the House if such a Bill with such patent imperfections is passed. But by sheer force of majority the Bill was passed, the Revenue Minister having assured that he would come forward with an amending Bill soon to remove the inconsistencies.

ASSAM FOREST AMEND. BILL

28th. MARCH :—The Assembly to-day passed the Assam Forest Amendment Bill (1940) which repeals Section 63 of the Assam Forest Regulation of 1891.

The Assam Revenue Tribunal Bill (1941) was referred to a select committee which would submit its report by June 30, 1941.

29th. MARCH :—Khan Bahadur *Maulvi Sayidur Rahaman*, Revenue Minister, presented to-day the authenticated schedule of authorized expenditure amounting to Rs. 2,53,66,300 for 1941-42, and also the authenticated schedule of authorized expenditure in relation to the supplementary demands for grants for 1940-41 amounting to Rs. 2,66,622. The House then adjourned *sine die*.

The Sind Legislative Assembly

LIST OF MEMBERS

Speaker :—THE HON'BLE SAYED MIRAN MUHAMMAD SHAH ZAINULABDIN SHAH

Deputy Speaker :—MISS JETHIBAI TULSIDAS SIPAHIMALANI

ABDUL MAJID LILARAM SHAIKH
ABDUS SATTAR ABDUL RAHMAN PIRZADA
AKHJI RATANSINGH SODHO
K. B. ALLAH BAKHSH KHUDADAD KHAN GABOL
THE HON'BLE K. B. ALLAH BAKHSH MUHAMMAD UMER
S. B. MIR ALLAHDAD KHAN IMAM BAKHSH KHAN TALPUR
K. B. HAJI AMIR ALI THARO KHAN LAHORI
ARBAB TOGACHI MIR MUHAMMAD
MIR BANDEHALI KHAN MIR HAJI MUHAMMAD HUSSAIN KHAN TALPUR
C. T. VALECHA
DIALMAL DOULATRAM
DOULATRAM MOHANDAS
GHANSHYAM JETHANAND SHIVDASANI
GHANUMAL TARACHAND
MIR GHULAM ALI KHAN BUNDEH ALI KHAN TALPUR
MIR GHULAM KHAN MIR HAJI HUSSAIN BAKHSH KHAN TALPUR
THE HON'BLE SIR GHULAM HUSSAIN HIDAYATULLAH
MAKHDUM GHULAM HYDER MAKHDUM ZAHIR-UD-DIN
PIR GHULAM HYDER SHAH SAHIBDINO SHAH
K. B. GHULAM MUHAMMAD ABDULLAH KHAN ISRAN
SAYED GHULAM MURTAZA SHAH MUHAMMAD SHAH
K. B. SAYED GHULAM NABI SHAH MOUJALI SHAH
MUKHI GOBINDRAM PRITAMDAS
THE HON'BLE R. S. GOKALDAS MEWALDAS
LALLA MENGHRAJ BAHRUMAL
DR. HEMANDAS RUPCHAND WADHWANI
DR. CHOITHRAM P. GIDWANI
R. B. HOTCHAND HIRANAND
THE HON'BLE PIR ILLAHI BAKHSH NAWAZ ALI
ISSARDAS VARANDMAL
K. B. JAFFER KHAN GUL MUHAMMAD KHAN BURDI
LOLUMAL REWACHAND MOTWANI
S. B. HAJI JAM JAN MUHAMMAD KHAN JAM MUHAMMAD SHARIF JUNEJO
MRS. JENUBAI GHULAM ALI ALLANA
K. B. SARDAR KAISER KHAN GHULAM MUHAMMAD KHAN
SAYED KHAIR SHAH IMMAM ALI SHAH
COL. H. J. MAHON
SAYED MUHAMMAD ALI SHAH ALLAHANDO SHAH
K. B. MUHAMMAD AYUB KHAN SHAH MUHAMMAD KHAN KHUHRO
MUHAMMAD HASHIM FAIZ MUHAMMAD GAZDAR
MIR MUHAMMAD KHAN NAWAB GHAIBI KHAN CHANDIO
MUHAMMAD USMAN MUHAMMAD KHAN SUMRO
MUHAMMAD YUSIF KHAM BAHADUR KHAIR MUHAMMAD
NARAINDAS ANANDAJI BECHAR
NEWANDRAM VISHINDAS
THE HON'BLE MR. NIHCHALDAS CHATUMAL VAZIRANI
SAYED NUR MUHAMMAD SHAH MURAD ALI SHAH
J. FRASER
PARTABRAI KHAISUKHDAS
DR. POPATLAL A. BHOOPATKAR
LT. COL. W. B. HOSSACK
RAIS RASUL BAKHSH KHAN SAHIB MUHAMMAD KHAN UNER
K. S. PIR RASUL BAKHSH SHAH MAHBUB SHAH
RUSTOMJI KHURSHEDJI SIDHWA
SHAMSUDDIN KHAN ABDUL KABIR KHAN AFGHAN BARAKZAI
SITALDAS PERUMAL
K. S. SOHRAB KHAN SAHIBDINO KHAN SARKI
MUHAMMAD AMIN ABDUL AZIZ KHAN KHOSO

ment of decrees civil or of any other kind in the Province of Assam.

The Assam Shop Assistants' Relief Bill, '41 :—To regulate the hours of work in shops and improve and determine the condition of employment of shop assistants.

The Goalpara Tenancy (Amendment) Bill, '41 :—To make provision for the protection of some valuable rights of the tenants of the permanently-settled estates of the Goalpara district by amending the Goalpara Tenancy Act, '29.

The Sylhet Non-Agricultural Tenancy Bill, '41 :—To provide against eviction of non-agricultural tenants of the district of Sylhet and to give them relief by reducing their excessive rents and to control enhancement of rent.

Government of Sind

The Public Inquiries Act, '40 (26-2-40) :—To provide for the constitution of Courts of enquiry for holding public enquiries into matters of public importance affecting the Province.

The Sind Consumption of Intoxicants Restriction Act, '40, (26-2-40) :—To prohibit the consumption of intoxicants.

The Sind Zamindars' Children Education Act, '40 (26-2-40) :—To provide for the compulsory education of the male children of Zamindars.

The Sind Agriculturists' Relief Act, '40, (30-3-40) :—To provide for the reduction of debts payable by an agriculturist.

The Sind Medical Practitioners Act, '40, (5-4-40) :—To enact in order to encourage the study and spread of Indian system of medicine, and to amend the law relating to medical practitioners generally.

The Bombay Municipal Boroughs (Sind Amendment) Act, '40 (X of '40). (15-4-40) :—To introduce joint electorates with reservation of seats on population basis in the Municipal Boroughs.

The Sind Agricultural Produce Markets Act, '40, (22-4-40) :—To provide for the better regulation of the purchase and sale of agricultural produce and the establishment of markets for such produce.

The Sind Holy Quran Act, '40 (26-4-40) :—To penalise the printing, publishing or sale of the Holy Quran (Arabic text) by any person other than a Muslim or otherwise than through a Muslim Agency.

The Sind Frontier Regulations (Extending) Act, '40, (18-5-40) :—To apply to the district of Sukkur with retrospective effect from September 19, 1939, the provisions of the Sind Frontier Regulations of 1872 and 1892. In force until March 15, 1941.

The Sind Shops and Establishments Act, '40, (19-12-40) :—To regulate the conditions of employment of shop assistants and commercial employees.

The Sind Opium Smoking Act, '40. (20-12-40) :—To provide for prohibition of opium-smoking except in the case of addicts who will be exempted subject to certain conditions to be prescribed by rules.

The Sind Wild Birds and Wild Animals Protection Act '40. (20-12-40) :—To provide to preserve the small game of Sind from indiscriminate shooting and netting by prescribing an additional licence for killing or capturing the birds and animals.

The Sind Cattle Diseases Act, '40. (20-12-40) :—To provide to prevent the spread of contagious diseases among the cattle in the Province of Sind.

The Bombay Land Revenue Code (Sind Amendment) Act, '41. (15-4-41) :—To provide for the surveying of jagir lands and the recovery of cost of survey from the jagirdars.

The Bombay Abkari (Sind Amedment) Act, '41. (21. 4. 41) :—To prohibit the import export, transport, manufacture, sale and possession of charas.

The Sind Debt Conciliation Act, '41. (21-5-41) To provide for the setting up of Debt Conciliation Board to relieve agriculturists from indebtedness.

Government of Bombay

Bombay Agricultural Debtors Relief Act, '39 (Bom. XXVIII of '39. 19-1-40) :—To relieve the agricultural debtors from the burden of their indebtedness. It applies to such debtors who hold and cultivate lands personally and whose annual income from sources other than agricultural and manual labour does not ordinarily exceed Rs. 300 and whose debts do not on 1st January, 1939, exceed Rs. 15,000. The indebtedness is to be relieved by the adjustment of debts by the Debt Adjustment Board, by scaling them down and by making them payable by instalments.

Bombay Tenancy Act, '39 (Bom. XXIX of '39. 27-3-40) :—To give special protection to the tenants of six years' standing on the 1st day of January '38. Under certain conditions tenants evicted after 1st day of April, '37, are deemed to be protected tenants for the purposes of the Act. It provides that all future agricultural leases shall be for not less than 10 years. The legitimate rights of the landlords have been protected, provision being made for the resumption of the land, by the landlord in certain contingencies including non-payment of reasonable rent by the tenant, need for personal cultivation, etc.

Governor's Ordinances

Bombay Fodder and Grain Control Ordinance, '39 (Ordinance No. 1 of '39), (12-8-39) :—To control the prices both of fodder and grain and to stop the removal of the existing stocks from certain areas which were then affected by famine or scarcity on account of absence of rain.

Bombay Options in Cotton Prohibition Ordinance, '39 (Ordinance No. II of '39). (22-9-39) :—To declare the teji mandi or option business void in the whole of the Province of Bombay and to take power to impose by-laws on a recognised association on the authority of Government and without preliminary publication.

Governor's Acts

Bombay Options in Cotton Prohibition Act, '39 (Bom. XXV of '39), (11-12-39) :—To put the provisions of the Bombay Options in Cotton Prohibtion Ordinance, '39 (Ordinance No. II of '39) on the Statute Book in the form of amendments to the Bombay Cotton Contracts Act, '32 as it was essential in the interests of the cotton trade that the provisions of the said Ordinance should continue.

Bombay Finance (Amendment) Act, '40 (Bom. I of '40). (19-3-40) —To provide for extension of the Bombay Finance Act, '32, for a further period of one year. The Act also carries out certain amendments in Part VI of the Bombay Finance Act, '32 to meet the objections raised in the arguments in XLII B. L. R. 10 (Sir Byramjee Jeejeebhoy VS, the Province of Bombay).

Bombay Rent Restriction (Amendment) Act, '40 (Bom. II of '40). (19-3-40) :—To extend for a futher period of twelve months the life of the Bombay Rent Restriction Act, '39, which was enacted to restrict the increase of rent of certain premises in consequence of the levy of the urban immovable property tax, since the tax was to be continued for one year more.

Bombay Motor Vehicles Tax and Bombay Local Boards (Amendment) Act, '40 (Bom. III of '40. 26-3-40) :—To bring the provisions of the Bombay Motor Vehicles Tax Act, '35 in line with the provisions of the new Motor Vehicles Act, '39, and to remedy certain defects experienced in the working of the former Act.

Bombay Village Panchayats (Amendment) Act, '40, (Bom. IV of '40), (27-3-40) :—To provide that the panchayats and benches which were in office on the date on which the Bombay Village Panchayats (Amendment) Act, '39, came into force should continue in office, notwithstanding that the term of their members may have expired, till the date they are dissolved by the Collector.

Bombay Small Holders Relief (Amendment) Act, '40 (Bom. V of '40. 27-3-40) :—To extend the operation of the Bombay Small Holders Relief Act, '38, up to 31st March, '41.

Bombay Abkari (Amendment) Act, '40 (Bom. VI of '40. 11-4-40) :—To amend the Act of 1878, with retrospective effect from the date on which the provisions so amended were enacted. It includes among the purposes of the Act of 1878, the promotion and enforcement of the policy of "prohibition"; and enables the Provincial Government to prohibit the possession of any excisable article by any individual or class or body of individuals or the public generally. (This Act was necessitated by a High Court decision to the effect that the provisions of the Abkari Act of 1878 could not be used for the purpose of enforcing "prohibition", and that the prohibition of possession of foreign liquor by any person or of possession of any liquor by all persons in any area could not be enforced under that Act).

Bombay Legislative Council (President and Dy. President) and the Bombay Legislative Assembly (Speaker and Dy. Speaker) Salaries Act, '37 and the Bombay Legislature Members' Salaries and Allowances Act, '37 (Temporary Repeal) Act, '40. (Bom. VII of '40). (25-6-40) :—To provide for the temporary repeal, with effect from the 1st July, '40, for so long as the Proclamation under Section 93 is in force, of Acts II and III of '37, which fixed the rates of salaries and allowances payable to officers and members of the Provincial Legislature.

Bombay Legislature Members (Removal of Disqualifications (Amendment) Act, '40 (Bom. X of '40. 24-9-40) :—To permit officers of the Army in India Reserve of Officers, the Auxiliary Force, India, the Indian Territorial Force or any branch of His Majesty's Naval, Military or Air Forces to become or remain members of the Bombay Legislature.

Bombay Local Authorities Census Expenses Contribution Act, 41. (Bom. III of '41. 10-3-40) :—To make provision for contribution by local authorities of a portion of the expenses to be incurred in connection with the taking of the census in British India during the year '41.

Bombay Finance (Am ndment) Act, '41 (Bom. IV of '41. 22-3-41) :—To extend the life of the Act of '32 by one more year with certain further amendments. One of them is to increase the stamp duty on gifts and settlement even with a revocation clause as if the revocation clause did not exist. The other is to reduce the rate of Urban Immovable Property tax by 1/5.

Bombay Rent. Restriction (Amendment) Act, '41 (Bom. V of '41. 19-3-41) :—To extend the life of the Act of '39 by one more year.

Bombay Agricultural Debtors Relief (Amendment) Act, '41 (Bom. VI of '41. 20-3-41) :—To provide for piecemeal application of the Act of '39 to such districts and areas as Government may select, so that the experiment of its working in those districts and areas may be watched.

Bombay Tenancy (Amendment) Act, '41 (Bom VII of '41. 20-3-41) :—To provide for piecemeal application of the Act of '39 to such districts and areas as Government may select, so that the experiment of its working in those districts and areas may be watched.

Bombay Small Holders Relief (Amendment) Act, '41 (Bom. VIII of '41. 26-3-41) :—To extend the life of the Act of '38 by one more year.

Bombay Abkari (Amendment) Act, '41 (Bom. IX of '41. 18-4-41) :—To repeal Sections 42-E and 43-A of the Act of 1878 containing provisions for prohibition of advertisement of intoxicants.

Government of Madras

The Madras Local Boards (Amendment) Act, '40 (Madras Act I of '40 30-1-40) :—To take away the power of panchayats to to determine the fees to be levied on and the conditions to be inserted in licences issued under the places of Public Resort Act, 1888.

The Madras Finance Act, '40 (Madras Act II of '40 4-3-40) :—To reduce the general sales tax payable for the year beginning on the 1st April, '40 from Rs. 5 to Rs. 4 a month in the cases of persons whose turnover does not exceed Rs. 20,000 and from onehalf of one per cent to one-quarter of one per cent of the turnover in other cases.

The Madras Commercial Corps Markets (Amendment) Act, '40 (Madras Act III of '40. 23-3-40) :—To confer on Collectors of Districts the power to grant, suspend or cancel licences under Section 4 of the principal Act and to enable the Government to appoint members in the case of market committees established for the first time.

The Madras Tobacco (Taxation of Sales and Licensing) (Amendment) Act, '40 (Madras Act IV of '40 30-3-40) :—To introduce intermediate stages in the scale of annual fees prescribed for licences to wholesale dealers, to draw a distinction between a broker and a commission agent and to remove certain other defects found to exist in the previous law.

The Prisons (Madras Amendment) Act, '40 (Madras Act V of 40 2-4-40) :—To provide a penalty for escape or attempt to escape by a prisoner from a hospital or asylum where he has been sent for treatment and to make the provisions of Chapter XLII of the Code of Criminal Procedure applicable to a bond executed by a prisoner (or his relations or friends) who is sent to a hospital or asylum for treatment.

The Madras Irrigation Cess (Amendment) Act, '40 (Madras Act VI of '40 12-4-40) :—To validate with retrospective effect the practice of levying enhanced cesses in cases where there is unauthorised irrigation of lands with Government water.

The Madras Suppression of Immoral Traffic (Amendment) Act, '40 (Madras Act VIII of '40 20-5-40) :—To enable any police officer entering a brothel to rescue a praticular minor girl in pursuance of a Magistrate's order under section 6(1) of the principal Act to rescue also other minor girls found in the brothel and to confer a similar power of rescue on a police officer entering any premises under section 14.

The Madras Payment of Salaries and Removal of Disqualifications (Temporary Repeal) Act, '40 (Madras Act X of '40 10-6-40) :—To repeal the Madras Payment of Salaries and Removal of Disqualification Act, '37 during the continuance in force of the Proclamation issued under section 93 of the Government of India Act, 35.

The Mettur Township Act, '40 (Madras Act XI of '40 25-6-40) :—To provide for the better administration and governance of the Mettur township.

The Madras Legislature (War Service Removal of Disqualifications) Act, '40 (Madras Act XII of '40 16-7-40) :—To remove the disqualification imposed on membership of the Madras Legislature in the case of persons holding any office in the Army in India Reserve of officers, the Indian Territorial Force etc.

The Madras City Municipal, District Municipalities and Local Boards (Amendment) Act, '40 (Madras Act XIII of '40 14-8-40) :—To extend up to the Ist November, '41, the term of office of the councillors and aldermen of the Corporation of Madras, of the councillors of every municipality who were to vacate their offices on the 1st November, '40 and of the members of all local boards who were to vacate their offices in '40.

The Madras District Municipalities and Local Boards (Amendment) Act, '40 (Madras Act XIV of '40 29-8-40) :—To disqualify a person from being elected or from continuing as a member of a municipal council or a Local Board if he is in arrears of any kind due by him (otherwise than in a fiduciary capacity) to the local body concerned.

The Madras Live-stock Improvement Act, '40 (Madras Act XV of '40 29-8-40) :- To provide for the improvement of live-stock in the Province of Madras.

The Andhra University (Amendment) Act, '40 (Madras Act XVII of 1940). (7-11-40) :—To empower the Syndicate of the Andhra University to delegate any of its powers to the Vice-Chancellor or to a committee from among its own members or to the Finance Committee.

The Madras Village Courts (Amend.) Act, '40 (Madras Act XVIII of 1940). (11-11-40) :—To enable village courts to take cognizance of suits for taxes and other sums due to municipal councils and other local authorities and to permit the attachment of movable property by the president or by any other member of the panchayat court to whom the president may delegate his powers in this behalf.

The Madras Rinderpest Act, '40 (Madras Act XIX of '40). (11-12-40) :—To provide for the prevention and control of rinderpest in the Province of Madras.

The Indian Medical Degrees (Madras Amendment) Act, '40 (Madras Act XX of '40). (11-1-41) :—To penalize the unauthorized use of titles etc., implying qualifications in any system of medicine.

The Madras Hackney Carriage (Amend.) Act, '41 (Madras Act I of '41). (4-1-41) To empower the Commissioner of Police to limit the number of hackney carriages (including rickshaws) which may be registered in the City of Madras under the principal Act.

The Madras State Aid to Industries (Amendment) Act, '41 (Madras Act II of '41). (15-1-41) :—To empower the Govt. to delegate to the Board of Revenue the power to grant aid to cottage industries up to a maximum of Rs. 500 in each case.

The Madras Electricity Duty (Amend.) Act, '41 (Madras Act III of '41). (8-2-41) To exempt sales of electrical energy to the central Government, the Federal Railway authority, or a railway company operating a federal railway, from the levy of tax under Section 3 of the principal Act.

The Madras City Municipal (Amend.) Act, '41 (Madras Act IV of '41). (12-2-41) To disqualify a person from being elected or from continuing as a councillor or alderman if he is in arreas of any kind due by him (otherwise than in a fiduciary capacity) to the Corporation of Madras.

The Factories (Madras Amendment) Act, '41 (Madras Act VI of '41). (7-2-41) To restrict the examination of children and adolescents on their own application or on that of their parents or guardians, to those cases where they are able to produce a certificate from the manager of a factory that they will be employed in the factory if a certificate of fitness is granted to them.

The Madras City Municipal (Second (Amendment) Act, '41 (Madras Act VII of 1941). (26-2-41) :—To provide for applications for a licence or permission or for Registration or for a renewal thereof being made in all cases within a specified period.

The Madras City Municipalities, District Municipalities and Local Boards (Amendment) Act, '41 (Madras Act VIII of '41). (27-2-41) :— To empower the Government to modify from time to time or cancel any decision given by them in regard to dispute between local authorities.

The Madras Finance Act, '41 (Madras Act IX of '41). (18-3-41) :—To reduce the general sales tax payable for the the year beginning on the 1st April, '41, from Rs. 5 to Rs. 4 a month in the cases of persons whose turnover does not exceed Rs. 20,000 and from one-half of one per cent to one-quarter or one per cent of the turnover in other cases.

The Madras Districts Municipalities (Amendment) Act, '41 (Madras Act X of

'41). (17-3-41) :—To confer on the Govt. the power to make rules rgarding the conditions on which and in which of contracts may be made by or on hehalf municipal councils.

The Madras Prohibition (Supplementary Act, '41 (Madras Act XI of '41). (16-4-41) :—To rectify a defect pointed out by the Madras High Court, namely that the provisions of the Madras Prohibition Act, 1937, so far as they related to dangerous drugs, were void by reason of the fact that the Act was not reserved for the consideration of the Governor-General or for the signification of His Majesty's pleasure under section 107 (2) of the Government of India Act. '35.

The Madras District Municipalities and Local Boards (Amendment) Act, '41 (Madras Act XII of '41 19-4-41) :—To empower the municipal council and the panchayat to farm out the collection of fees for the use of cart stands.

The Madras City Police (Amendment) Act, '41 (Madras Act XIII of '41 28-4-41):- To minimize the beggar nuisance in the City of Madras.

The Madras Local Boards (Amend.) Act, '41 (Madras Act XIV of '41 9-5-41):— To empower Government to supersede district boards for a maximum period of three years.

The Madras Pawn-brokers Bill, '40 :— To regulate and control the business of pawnbrokers in the Province of Madras.

The Madras Proprietary Estates Village-Service and Hereditary Village Offices (Amendment) Bill, '40 :—To make solvency a condition precedent to appointment to certain village offices, to provide for the suspension or removal of officers who have ceased to be solvent, to provide for second appeals to the Board of Revenue against orders removing certain village officers and to empower the Revenue officer in charge of the division to disapprove the appointments submitted to him by the proprietor on the general ground of unsuitability for office.

The Madras Registration of Births and Deaths (Amendment) Bill, '41 :—To make the registration of the name of a child in the register of births obligatory in non-municipal areas within thirteen months from the date of the birth of the child.

The Madras City Police and towns Nuisances (Amendment) Bill, '41 :—To deal with the menace of Pathan money-lenders in the City of Madras. Another object of this Bill is to prevent the annoyance caused to neighbouring residents by the indiscriminate use of loud-speakers in public places both in the City and in the mofussil.

The Madras Elementary Education (Amend.) Bill, '41 :—To free Govt. from the obligation to make the contribution in respect of taxation which may be sanctioned after the amending Act comes into force and to remove the statutory limit to the rate of tax.

The Madras Public Health (Amend.) Bill, '41 :—To remove certain difficulties which have been experienced in giving effect to the provisions of the Madras Public Health Act, '39, since it came into force in March, '39.

The United Provinces

The United Provinces Stayed Arrears of Rent (Remission) Act, '39. (30-1-40) :— To remit, with certain exceptions, arrears of rent the recovery of which had been stayed by the United Provinces Stay of Proceedings (Revenue Courts) Act, '37.

The United Provinces Tenancy (Amend-) Act, '40. (30-4-40) :—To remove or remedy accidental omissions in the original Act and to restore certain provisions which existed in the original Bill as introduced in the Assembly.

The United Provinces Encumbered Estates (Amendment) Act, '40 (18-5-40) :— To clarify how pre-slump profits and post-slump profits shall be calculated in districts which have been re-settled or in which assessment has been revised.

The United Provinces District Boards (Amendment) Act, '40. (4-6-40) :—To postpone elections.

The United Provinces Municipalities (Amendment) Act, '40. (4-6-40) :—To postpone elections.

The United Provinces Legislature (Suspension of Salaries) and Emoluments Act, '40, (13-6-40) :—To discontinue the payment of salaries to officers and members of the Legislature of the United Provinces in view of the suspension of the constitution.

Temporary Postponement of Execution of Decrees (Amendment) Act, '40, (22-6-40) :—To extehd the period of the term of the original Act of '37 pending measures for the relief of indebtedness.

The United Provinces Legislative Members Removal of Disqualification Act, '40. (26-6-40) :—To remove the disqualification which the members of the United Provinces Legislature would incur by accepting an office of profit in

His Majesty's Naval, Military or Air forces.

The United Provinces Power Alcohol Act, '40. (28-7-40) :—To control the production supply and distribution of power alcohol.

The Code of Criminal Procedure (United Provinces Amendment) Act, '40. (26-8-40) :—To restore the validity of Section 27 of the Indian Evidence Act of 1872.

The United Provinces Power Alcohol Amendment) Act, '40 (10-11-40) :—To exempt all military requirements from the operation of the original Act to enable the enforcement of the Act in any part of the province and in piecemeal when needed, and to make Provision for a contingency when there is a breakdown in the supply of the prescribed mixture of power alcohol and petrol.

The United Provinces Sugar Factories Control (Amendment) Act, '40. (29-11-40) :-To provide for (1) the control of production and sales of sugar, (2) the realization of subsidy given to the industry and to empower the provincial Government to relax the conditions of the Act in certain special circumstances.

The United Provinces Special Powers (Amendment) Act, '40. (10-12-40) :—To extend the period of the principal Act of '32.

The United Provinces Debt Redemption Act, '40. (21-12-40) :—To reduce agricultural debt (i. e., loans advanced prior to June 1, '40) with a view to putting agricultural credit on a sound basis.

The United Provinces Regulation of Agricultural Credit Act, '40. (21-12-40) :—To restrict loans that can be borrowed by an agriculturist on the security of his crops or land to an amount that he can pay without hardship.

The Khat Haripur Bias (Jaunsar Bawar Pargana) Tenants Protection Regulation, '40. (21-12-40) :—To protect tenants from arbitrary ejectments.

The United Provinces Sugar Factories Control (Amendment) Act, '41 15-1-41) To raise the penalty in respect of sugar produced or sold by a factory in contravention of the conditions of its crushing license from annas eight to three rupees per maund.

The United Provinces Entertainments and Betting Tax (Amendment) Act, '41 (15-1-41) :—To permit a simpler calculation of moneys paid out by book makers to bankers.

The United Provinces Excise (Amendment) Act, '41. 24-1-41) :—To set at rest doubts regarding the validity of prohibition notifications.

The United Provinces Shri Badrinath Temple (Amendment) Act, '41. (24-3-41) To extend time for decision of certain disputes by Shri Badrinath Temple Committee.

The United Provinces Intermediate Education (Amendment) Act, '41 (17-4 41) To withdraw from the purview of the Board the power of control over the curricula of the middle class of Anglo-Vernacular schools, to delete Section 17 of the original Act which has long spent itself and to substitute the words "Provincial Government" for the words "Minister of Education."

The United Provinces Redemption (Amendment) Act, '41. (21-4-41) :—To make provision of Sections 17 and 19 of the original Act applicable to such members of agricultural tribes in Bundelkhand as have applied under the United Provinces Encumbered Estates Act. '34.

The United Provinces Regulation of Agricultural Credit Bill, '39. :—To restrict loans that can be borrowed by an agriculturist on the security of his crops or land to an amount that he can pay without hardship.

The United Provinces District Boards (Second Amendment) Bill, '39 :—To entrust the administration of education in rural areas to the District Boards by abolishing Education Committees.

The United Provinces Motor Vehicles Taxation (Amendment) Bill, '39 :—To remove certain inconsistencies some amendments in Sections 4 and 5 of the Motor Taxation Act have been proposed.

The United Provinces Prevention of Adulteration Bill, '39 :—To arm Government with sufficient powers to control the sale of Ghee and Vegetable oils in particular, and other foodstuffs and drugs in general.

Central Provinces & Berar

The Central Provinces and Berar Vidya Mandir Act, '39 (III of '40 15-3-40) :—To provide for the establishment of Vidya Mandirs (defined as educational institutions established or deemed to be established for the spread of literacy in a village or group of villages).

The Central Provinces & Berar Motor Vehicles Taxation Act, '40 (IV of '40. 25-3-40) :—To extend the provisions of Act VII of '39 which expired on 1-4-40 and bring it into conformity with the (Central) Motor Vehicles Act, '39.

The Central Provinces and Berar Co-Orerative Societies (Amendment) Act, '40 (V of '40). (26-3-40) :—To provide, by means of compromise or arrangement, for repayment of liabilities of registered societies.

The Central Provinces & Berar Payment of Salaries (Temporary Repeal) Act, '40 (X of '40). (28-6-40) :—To provide for the temporary repeal of the Act IV of '37 which fixed the rates of salaries and allowances payable to ministers, officers and members of the Provincial Legislature.

The Central Provinces Tenancy (Amendment) Act, '39 (XI of '40) (5-7-40) :—(i) To enlarge the right of transfer enjoyed by "absolute occupancy" tenants. (ii) To enable absolute occupancy and occupancy tenants to acquire malik-makbuza rights. (iii) To repeal the provisions of the Act of '20 relating to ejectment of occupancy tenants for non-payment of arrears of rent. (iv) To enable a Revenue Officer to declare a sub-tenant to be an occupancy tenant. (v) To give a tenant certain additional rights in trees on his holding.

The Central Provinces Money-lenders (Amendment) Act, '40 (XIV of '40) (23-9-4o) :—To amend the Act of '34 by re-enacting the provisions of the amending Act XIII of '36, which expired on 30-9-40. The Act restricts the business of a money-lender to a district or districts for which he has been granted a registration certificate.

The Central Provinces and Berar Postponement of General Elections to Local Boards Act, '41 (II of '41). (21-2-41) :—To provide for the postponement of general elections to local boards till the 31st December, '41, owing to abnormal circumstances and conditions arising out of the war.

The All India Hindu Maha Sabha

Its Aims and Present Policy.*

The Origin

The first Hindu Sabha was established in the Punjab in the year 1907 with the following objects :—

(1) To Promote brotherly feelings amongst the various sections of the Hindu community (2) To help destitute and disabled Hindus (3) To act as trustees of such properties as may be entrusted to the Sabha for charitable, religious, educational and other purposes (4) To improve the moral, intellectual and material condition of Hindus (5) Generally protect, promote and represent the interests of the Hindu community (6) To help the establishment of similar Sabhas in other important towns. *Note* (1) The Sabha will not side with any particular system of religious thought and action, and will observe perfect toleration towards all the different religious views. *Note* (2) The Sabha will have no connection with any political body. As such the Sabha is not a sectarian, nor a denominational but an all-embracing movement, and while meaning no offence to any other movement whether Hindu or non-Hindu, it aims to be ardent and watchful in safeguarding the interests of the entire Hindu community in all respects.

It will be seen that the present aim and objects of the Hindu Maha Sabha have been evolved gradually from these primary objects. Several phrases in the first draft of objects are still preserved and continued in the aim and objects of the present Hindu Maha Sabha. Every primary member of the Hindu Maha Sabha has to subscribe in writing to this aim and the objects. The present form is as follows :—

(To organise and consolidate all sections of the Hindu society into one organic whole ; to protect and promote Hindu interests whenever and whereever necessary ; To remove untouchability and generally to ameliorate and improve the condition of the so-called depressed classes amongst the Hindus ; To revive and promote the glorious ideals of Hindu woman-hood ; to promote cow-protection ; To improve the physique of the Hindus and promote martial spirit amongst them by establishing military schools and organising volunteer corps ; To reclaim all those who have left the Hindu-fold ; To found orphanages and rescue homes for orphans and homeless women ; Generally to take steps for promoting religious, educational, social, economic and political interests and rights of the Hindus. To promote good feelings between the Hindus and non-Hindu communities in Hindusthan, and to act in a friendly way with them with a view to evolve a united and self-governing *Bharateeya* Nation based on equality of civic rights and duties irrespective of caste and creed.

Note :—The Mahasabha shall not side or identify or interfere with or oppose any particular sect or sects of the Hindu Community in respect of its religious practices amongst themselves in so far as they do nor infringe on the fundamental civic liberties of others.

The First Hindu Conference

The first Punjab Provincial Hindu Conference was held in 1909 at Lahore. Nearly 800 delegates from different parts of the Province attended the two days sitting, 21st and 22nd October 1909. Full report of this Conference was published in book form (200 pages) and copies are still preserved in Hindu Maha Sabha records. The late Lala Lajpat Rai who took a prominent part in the Hindu Maha Sabha movement afterwards attended the conference and made a long speech on the first resolution on "Desirability of feeling of Hindu Nationality and Hindu Unity."

In his speech late Lajpat Rai quoted a very significant passage from his article on the Indian National Congress written ten years before that (i. e. in 1899) in the "Hindustan Review" of Allahabad. The following extract from this article written 42 years ago, will explain the motives behind the genesis of the Hindu Maha Sabha :—

"The number of subjects upon which there is any likelihood of reasonable friction existing or coming into existence between members of different religious nationalities in India, ought to be reduced to minimum, if there is any room for the same, in the agenda paper of the general assembly, such subjects being reserved

---

*Specially contributed by Mr. G. V. Ketkar, Editor, *Mahratta*, Hony. Secretary, All India Hindu Mahasabha.

While the increase in expenditure of Rs. 63,28 000 over the original estimate is mainly due to the expenditure of Rs. 38½ lakhs under 'Industries' on account of subsidy to sugar factories and Rs. 13 lakhs under 'Appropriation' for reduction or avoidance of debt on account of part payment of the loan taken from the Central Government in connection with the re-habilitation of the sugar industry. Under 'Education' there is an increase of about one lakh, mainly, due to additional provision on account of grants to municipalities for free and compulsory primary education. Extra expenditure on account of jail manufacture, dietary charges and clothing and bedding of prisoners is responsible for an increase of Rs. two lakhs under 'Jails and Convict Settlements. Charges for Police have also gone up by Rs four lakhs mainly as a result of special arrangements in connection with the present situation. There is, on the other hand, a decrease of one lakh under 'Civil Works' and of four lakhs under 'General Administration' mainly due to decreased expenditure under 'Provincial Legislative Assembly' and on schemes financed from the Government of India's rural reconstruction grants.

The net result of the transaction is that the year 1940-41 will close with a total balance of Rs. 2,12,38,000 while the financial year 1941-42 envisages a surplus of Rs. 31,26,000. The memorandum explains that there are many heavy liabilities to be met out of this surplus but, all the ameliorative measures introduced by the popular Ministry like Prohibition, mass literacy, Basic education, free and compulsory primary education in municipalities at the Head quarters of Districts, grants to District Boards for rural water supply, the sugarcane development scheme, a lump sum provision for grants for improvements to sub-divisional hospitals, anti-malarial and anti-leprosy measures, etc., are being provided for in the Budget of the coming year.

The Provincial Government have arranged to take an advance from the Central Government for the re-habilitation of the sugar industry of the Province. The Government of India have sanctioned an advance equal to the amount of excise duty at one rupee per maund on sugar (other than Khandri and palmyrah sugar). The advance will be repaired on behalf of the sugar industry in suitable instalments within the next three years.

Laws passed in 1940-41

Government of Bengal

The Bengal General Clauses (Amend.) Act, '39 (Ben. Act I of '40 31-1-40) :—To amend the Bengal General Clauses Act, 1899 in order to bring it into accord with the provisions of the General Clauses Act, 1897 and to make certain other amendments in it which are necessitated by the passing of certain Government of India Act.

The Eastern Frontier Rifles (Bengal Battalion Amendment) Act, '39 (Ben. Act II of '40 6-3-40 :—To amend Sections 3 & 4 of the Eastern Frontier Rifles (Bengal Battalion) Act, '20 in order to omit references to Section 7 of the Police Act, 1861 as appointment of police officers is now made under Section 241 of the Government of India Act, '35.

The Bengal Public Demands Recovery (Amendment) Act, '39 (Ben. Act III of '40 6-3-40) : To discontinue the payment of double interest for the same period when deposit is made with the application for setting aside sale under the Act.

The Bengal Finance (Amendment) Act, '40 (Ben. Act IV of '40 6-4-40) :—To empower Government to make rules providing for exemption or remission of the tax under the Bengal Finance Act, '39 without reference to the legislature.

The Bengal Jute Regulation Act, '40 (Ben. Act V of '40 16-4-40) :—To provide for the regulation of the growing of jute, and for that purpose to provide for the preparation of a record of the lands on which jute was grown in any year.

The Bengal Workmen's Protection (Amendment) Act, '40 (Ben. Act VI of '40 19-4-40) :—To prevent effectively the besetting of places where workmen receive their wages by professional money-lenders for the purpose of recovering their dues.

The Inland Steam Vessels (Bengal

Amendment) Act, '40 (Ben. Act VII of '40) :—To empower the special courts for the investigation of casualties to inland steam or motor vessels to make orders respecting the costs of the investigation or any part thereof recoverable from the parties concerned.

The Bengal Agricultural Debtors (Amendment) Act, '40 (Ben. Act VIII of '40 25-4-41) :—To amend the Bengal Agricultural Debtors Act '35 in order to secure a more rapid disposal of cases and to empower boards to deal with cases including usufructuary mortgages.

The Bengal Non-Agricultural Tenancy (Temporary provisions) Act, '40 (Ben. Act IX of '40 23-5-40) :—To provide pending further legislation, for the temporary stay of proceedings for delivery of possession in execution of certain decrees for ejectment of certain non-Agricultural tenants.

The Bengal Moneylenders Act, 1940 (Ben. Act X of '40 13-7-40 :—To make further and better provision for the control of money-lenders and for the regulation and control of money-lending.

The Administrator Generals (Bengal Amendment) Act, '41 (Ben. Act XI of '40 24-7-40 :—To provide certain improvements to the Administrator General's Act, '13 in order to increase its utility.

The Official Trustees (Bengal Amend.) Act, '40 (Ben. Act XII of '40 24-7-40) :—To amend the Official Trustees' Act, '13 so as to permit a suitable fractional audit of the accounts of all estates to be made in place of the detailed audit required under Section 19 of the Act.

The Bengal Revenues (Charged Expenditure) Act, '40 (Ben. Act XIII of '40 5-9-40) :—To declare the contributions payable under certain enactments, and the grants to be made to certain local authorities by the Provincial Government to the expenditur charged upon the revenues of the Province.

The Bengal Jute Regulation (Amendment) Act, '40 (Ben. Act XIV of '40. 7-9-40) :—To amend certain Sections of the Bengal Jute Regulation Act, 1940 in order to make the sense clearer and also to provide for revision of the final record of lands for correcting mistakes and omissions.

The Bengal Patni Taluks Regulation (Amendment) Act, '40 (Ben. Act XV of '40 18-10-40 :—To provide for separate account in the names of shareholders of the Patni taluk in the sherista of the Zamindar and to provide further facilities to the patnidars.

The Bengal Shops and Establishments Act, '40 (Ben. Act XVI of '40 21-10-40) :—To regulate the holidays, payment of wages, hours of work and leave of persons employed in shops and establishments for public entertainment or amusement.

The Bengal Alluvion and Diluvion (Amendment) Act, '40 (Ben. Act XVII of '40 13-11-40) :—To enable the Revenue authorities to assess to revenue alluvial reformations within an estate in cases where abatement of land revenue had been allowed at the time of diluvion.

The Bengal Tenancy (Amendment) Act, '40 (Ben. Act XVIII of '40 6-1-41 :—To amend the Bengal Tenancy Act, 1885 and the Bengal Tenancy (Second Amendment) Act, 1939 for various purposes, the main object being to allow the mortgagor to be restored to possession of the property, the possession of which was delivered to the mortgagee at the time of the mortgage and also to exempt the movable and immovable property from attachment and sale except the property for which the arrear is due.

The Bengal Legislature (Removal of Disqualifications Amendment) Act, '40 (Ben. Act XIX of '40 10-1-41) :—To enable a person to render fulltime service in any of His Majesty's Naval, Military and Air Forces without incurring any disqualification for being chosen as or for being a member of either chamber of the Bengal Legislature until the termination of the present state of war.

The Bengal Local Authorities Census Expenses Contribution Act, '40 (Ben. Act XX of '40 10-1-41 :—To provide for the contribution of certain local authorities census expenses.

The Bengal Co-operative Societies Act, '40 (Ben. Act XXI of '40 18-4-41) :—To make further provision for the formation and working of the Co-operative Societies, and for the promotion of thrift, self-help and mutual aid among persons of moderate means.

The Official Trustees (Bengal Amendment) Act, '41 (Ben. Act. I of '41 10-3-41) To give the Official Trustees for Bengal Powers to examine witnesses on oath similar to the power contained in Section 30 of the Administrator General's Act '13.

The Bengal Rural Poor and Unemployed Relief (Amendment) Act, '41 (Ben. Act II of '41 6-5-41) :—To remove the verbal defects in Section 3(3) and in the second proviso to Section 8(2) of the Bengal Rural Poor and Unemployed Relief Act, '39.

The Bengal Local Self-Government

(*Amendment*) *Act*, *'41* (Ben. Act III of '41 7-5-41) :—To provide for special machinery for the decision of disputes relating to elections held under the Bengal Local Self-Government Act of 1885 and at the same time oust the jurisdiction of Civil Courts in respects of such disputes.

The Bengal Water-hyachinth (*Amend.*) *Act*, *'41* (Ben. Act IV of '41). (14-5-41) :—To amend the Bengal Water-hyachinth Act, '36 so as to enable Collectors or authorised officers to prepare sections, make estimates of the cost and carry out the work of construction and maintenance of fences and barriers, etc. and to recover the cost proportionately from the persons benefited.

The Bengal Motor Spirit Sales Taxation Act '41 (Ben. Act V of '41). (29-5-41) To further the construnction of new roads in Bengal, and therefore to provide for the levy of tax in Bengal.

The Bengal Finance (*Sales Tax*) *Act*, *'41* (Ben. Act VI of '41). (25-6-41) :—To make an addition to the revenues of Bengal, and for that purpose to impose a general tax on the sale of goods in Bengal.

The Bengal Non-Agricultural Tenancy (*Temporary Provision*) *Bill*, *'40*. (15-2-40) To provide for the temporary stay of proceedings for delivery of possession in execution of certain decrees for ejectment of certain non-Agricultural tenants.

The Bengal Revenue (*Charged Expenditure*) *Bill '40*. (6-8-40) :—To declare certain expenditure to the expenditure charged upon the revenues of the province.

The Bengal Secondary Education Bill, *'40*. (21-8-40) :—To provide for the regulation and control of Secondary education by establishing one Board with authority over Secondary Schools of all types throughout the province.

The Bengal Pure Food Bill, *'40*. (18-9-40) :—To provide for the better control of the manufacture and sale of food for human consumption.

The Bengal Local Authorities Census Expenses Contribution Bill, *'40*. (3-12-40) To provide for the contribution by certain local authorities to census expenses.

The Bengal Motor Spirit Sales Taxation Bill. *41*. (28-11-40) :—To provide for the levy of a Tax on retail sales of Motor Spirits in Bengal.

The Bengal Finance (*Sales Tax*) *Bill*, *1941*. (29-11-40) : To impose a general tax on the sale of goods in Bengal.

The Bengal Legislature (*Privileges*) *and Powers*) *Bill*, *'41*. (4-12-40) :—To define certain privileges and power of the Bengal Legislature.

The Bengal Markets Regulation Bill, *'41*. (3-4-41) :—To provide for the licensing and regulation of markets in Bengal.

Government of Behar

The Bihar Agricultural Income-tax (*Amendment*) *Act*, *'40* (29-2-40) :—To remove a defect in the original Act for administrative convenience.

The Bihar Tenancy (*Amendment*) *Act*, *'40* (3-4-40) :—To provide for the hearing of appeals by the Collector or by any other officer specially empowered in that behalf from orders passed by revenue officers under Section 112A of the Bihar Tenancy Act, 1885.

The Chota Nagpur Tenancy (*Amendment*) *Act*, *'40* (3-4-40) :—To provide for the hearing of appeals by the Deputy Commissioner or by any other officer specially empowered in that behalf from orders made by revenue officers under certain sections of the Chota Nagpur Tenancy Act, '08.

The Court of Wards (*Amendment*) *Act*, *'39* (12-5 40) :—To remove certain defects in the Court of Wards Act, 1879, which experience has brought to notice and to empower the Provincial Government to place under the management of the Court of Wards of trust property and of the estates of proprietors who have been declared to be unfit to manage their property owing to extravagance or failure to pay their debts.

The Bihar Legislature (*Officers' Salaries*) *Act*, *'37*, *and the Bihar Legislature* (*Members' Salaries and Allowances*) *Act*, *'38* (*Temporary Repeal*) *Act*, *'40* (26-6-40) :—To repeal the Bihar Legislature (Officers' Salaries) Act, '37, and the Bihar Legislature (Members' Salaries and Allowances) Act, '38. for the period during which the Proclamation under Section 93 of the Government of India Act, '35, is in force.

The B. & O. Motor Vehicles Taxation (*Amendment*) *Act*, *'40* (28-6-40) :—To make certain amendments in the B. & O. Motor Vehicles Taxation Act, '30, consequent on the enactment of the Motor Vehicles Act, '39, and the framing of the rules thereunder.

The Bihar Refund of Cess Act, *'40* (10-10-40) :—To provide for the refund in certain cases of amounts paid as local cess by holders of estates or tenures.

The Bihar Excise (*Amendment*) *Act*, *'40* (17-11-40) :—To remove the doubts regarding the validity of certain "prohibition" notifications of the Provincial Government which were declared void by a Full Bench decision of the Patna High Court, by including the promotion, enforcement and carrying into effect of the policy of prohibition among the objects of the main Act.

The Bihar Sugar Factories Control (Amendment) Act, '40 (20-11-40) :—To provide for the appointment of a Sugar Commissioner and a Sugar Commission and to empower the Provincial Government to regulate the price and marketing of sugar.

The Bihar Sugar Factories Control (Amendment) Act, '41 (15-1-41) :—To raise the amount of penalty from annas eight to three rupees per maund for all sugar sold in contravention of a direction issued by the Provincial Government under Section 11A of the Act.

The Bihar Tenancy (Amendment) Act, '41 (21-1-41) :—To include the Kharwars of the district of Shahabad among the aboriginals to whom Chapter VIIA of the Bihar Tenancy Act, 1885, applies.

The Bihar Refund of Cess (Amendment) Act, '41 (7-4-11) :—To rectify certain formal omissions in the original Act.

The Bihar Tenure holders' Relief Bill, '39. :—To give relief to certain classes of tenure-holders in Bihar.

The Chota Nagpur Tenure-holders' Relief Bill, '39 :—To give relief to certain classes of tenure-holders in Chota Nagpur.

The Bihar Hindu Religious Endowments Bill, '39 :—To ensure the proper administration of Hindu religious endowments in strict accordance with the wishes of the grantors or the customs and usages of the endowment concerned.

The Chota Nagpur Private Forests Bill '39 :—To empower the Provincial Government to take over in the public interest suitable private forests in Chota Nagpur for management as protected forests in order to preserve them from destruction.

The Bihar Prohibition Second Amendment) Bill, '39 :—To remedy certain defects in the original Act for Administrative convenience.

The Bihar Suppression of Immoral Traffic Bill, '39 :—To provide for the suppression of brothels and of immoral traffic in women and girls, so as to improve the tone of public morality in the province.

Government of Orissa

The Orissa Hindu Religious Endowments Act, '39 (Orissa Act IV of 1939). Received the Assent of the Governor-General on 31-8-39 :—To provide for the better administration and governance of certain Hindu religious endowments.

The Orissa Court Fees (Amendment) Act, '39 (Orissa Act V of '39, 16-10-39) :—To Amend the Law relating to Court Fees in its application to the Province of Orissa.

The Sambalpur Local Self-Government Act, '39 (Orissa Act VI of '39 20-10-39) :—To make better provision for the Local Self-Government and to provide for creation of representative institutions in rural areas in the district of Sambalpur.

The Orissa Prohibition Act, '39 (Orissa Act VII of '39, 20-12-39) :—To introduce and extend the prohibition of the manufacture, sale and consumption of liquors, toddy and intoxicating drugs in the province of Orissa.

The Orissa Legislative Assembly (War Service) Act, '40 (Orissa Act VII of '40. 21-7-40) :—To prevent membership of any of His Majesty's forces or the holding of an office in the Defence Department in connection with the present war being a disqualification for membership of the Orissa Legislative Assembly.

Govt. of N. W. F. Province

The N. W. F. P. Motor Vehicles Taxation (Amendment) Act, '39 (Act I of 1940. 21-9-39) :—To reduce the rates of taxation in the case of lorry drivers and increase it in the case of private cars.

The N. W. F. P. Amending Act, '40 (Governor's Act I of '40, 6-3-40 :—To rectify certain mistakes in the N. W. F. P. Midwives Act, the N. W. F. P. Artificial Ghee Colourisation Act and the N. W. F. P Courts Regulation.

The N. W F. P. (Adolescent) Prisoner's Relase on Probation Act, Governor's Act II of '40. 5 4-40) :—To authorize Provincial Government to release an Adolescent prisoner., viz a prisoner between the age of 18 and 25 years on certain conditions.

The N. W. F. P. Courts Regulation (Amendment) Act '40. (Governor's Act III of '40, 14-6-40) :—To give powers to the Judicial Commissioner to delegate duties of a Judicial, quasi-Judicial and non-Judicial nature to the Registrar and other Ministerial Officers.

The N. W. F. P. Speaker's and Dy. Speaker's Salaries (Temporary Repeal) Act, '40 (Governor's Act IV of '40, 14-6-40) :—To provide for temporary suspension of payment of salaries and other allowances to the Speaker and Dy. Speaker of the and N. W. F. P. Legislative Assembly.

The N. W. F. P. War Services (Exemption from Disqualification) Act. '40 (Governor's Act V of '40 6-7-40) :—To provide for the exemption of members of His Majesty's forces and persons holding office under the Defence Department in connection with the War from being disqualified from membership of the N. W. F. P. Legislative Assembly.

The Punjab District Board (N.W.F.P. Amendment) Act, '40 (Governor's Act VI of '40 7-8-40) :—To provide that the employment, promotion, transfer, suspension and dismissal of persons in Veterinary, Medical and Educational institutions of the District Board was made subject to the approval of such authority appointed by the Provincial Government.

The N. W. F. P. Motor Vehicles Taxation (Second Amendment) Act, '40 (Governor's Act VII of '40, 23-10 40) :—The period of grace allowed in the original Act (Act I of '37) for the payment of tax was withdrawn and licensing officer was empowered to recover the tax as arrears of Land Revenue.

The Code of Criminal Procedure (N.W.F.P. Amendment) Act, '40 (Governor's Act VIII of '40 21-11-40) :—To amend Section 162(2) of the Code of Criminal Procedure. 1898, and thus the conflicting provisions of Section 27 of the Indian Evidence Act and Section 162 of the Code of Criminal Procedure were reconciled.

The Punjab District Board (N.W.F.P. Amendment) Act, '41 (Governor's Act I of '41 31-3-41) :—New Section 70 of the Punjab District Board Act (Act XX of 1883) was substituted for old Section 70 and it was provided that arrears of rates, taxes and rents or any sum claimable by a District Board may be recovered as arrears of land revenue.

The N. W. F. P. (Upper Tanawal Excluded Area) Coinage Regulation, '41 (Regulation I of '41 7-2-41) :—The provisions of the Indian Coinage Act, '06 and notifications, orders and rules issued thereunder were applied to Upper Tanawal, an Excluded Area in the North-West Frontier Province.

The N. W. F. P. Motor Spirit and Lubricants Taxation Bill :—To levy a small extra tax on those who use motor vehicles for private use or business purposes.

The N. W. F. P. Motor Vehicles Taxation (Amendment) Bill :—To provide relief to the lorry drivers and increase the tax in cases of private cars, the keeping of which is more or less a luxury.

The N. W. F. P. Muslim Waqf (Amendment) Bill :—To remove the legal difficulty in convening a meeting of the Muslim members of the Provincial Legislative Assembly and to make the Legislative Assembly rules applicable to such a meeting.

The N. W. F. P. Primary Education (Amendment) Bill :—To empower courts to take cognizance of cases falling under Section 10 and 11 of N. W. F. P. Primary Education Act, '38, if prosecuted by persons authorised by School Attendance Committees in that behalf.

The N. W. F. P. Agricultural Debtors' Relief (Amendment) Bill :—To remove a clerical mistake whereby figure '500' instead of '250' was entered in explanation II to clause (i) of Section 2 of the original Bill.

The N. W. F. P. Entertainment Duty (Amendment) Bill :—To authorise the executive to change the rates of duty without amendment of the Act which was necessary under the original Act.

The N. W. F. P. Goondas Bill :—To deal with persons who are a danger to the province and to prevent the disturbances of public peace by reason of conflict between communities or sections.

The N W. F. P. Table Waters Bill :—To impose a tax on table waters and thereby to make up the loss occasioned by introduction of prohibition.

The N. W. F. P. Courts Regulations (Amendment) Bill :—To amend the proviso to Sec. 30 of the N. W. F. P. Courts Regulations and thereby remove the restrictions placed on hearing of appeals by Sub-judges.

The Punjab Municipal (N. W. F. P. Amendmend) Bill :—To repeal clause (b) of Section 51 of Punjab Municipal Act, '11, which has been rendered void by Section 136 of the Government of India Act, '35.

The N. W. F. P. Restricting the Sale of Holy Quran Bill :—To restrict the publishing, printing and sale of Holy Quran to the Muslims, who alone are prepared to show it the veneration that is due to it.

Government of Punjab

The Punjab State Aid to Industries (Amendment) Act. (5-2-40) :—To provide for development of cottage and village industries through State Aid and to make

Section 24(2) of the Punjab State Aid to Industries Act of 1935, applicable to coparceners in a Joint Hindu Family.

The Punjab Motor Vehicles Taxation (Amendment) Act. (21-2-40) :—To enable the continuance of the system under which the owner of a motor vehicle is required to display a coupon in token of his having paid the tax and to abolish the local "Wheel Taxes".

The Punjab Excise (Amendment) Act. (23-2-40) :—To secure the return of excise bottles.

The Punjab Legislative Assembly (War Service) Act. (11-4-40) :—To prevent membership of any of His Majesty's Forces or the holding of an office under the Defence Department in connection with the present War being a disqualification for membership of the Punjab Legislative Assembly.

The Punjab Relief of Indebtedness (Amendment) Act, (15-4-40) :—To Remove certain defects in the Punjab Relief of Indebtedness Act, '34, particularly in regard to the powers and procedure of Conciliation Boards and to strengthen the original Act in certain respects.

The Punjab Thal (Increase in Value) Act, (19-4-40) :—To enable recovery from proprietors of a fixed sum per acre of land, which will receive benefit from the Thal Irrigation Project.

The Punjab Pure Food (Amendment) Act, (19-4-40) :—To provide that substances resembling Ghee which are not derived solely from milk fats shall not be sold unless they are given a distinctive colouring.

The *Factories (Punjab Amendment) Act.* (24-4-40) :—To regulate the establishment of large industries for the promotion of key industries, and to levy fees for registration of factories.

The Punjab Alienation of Land (Amendment) Act. (24-4-40) :—To avoid confusion and to secure uniformity in the Punjab Alienation of Land Act, 1900, by substituting the words "Deputy Commissioner" for the word "Collector" in Sections 3-B and 3-C, and to make clear that Civil Courts have no jurisdiction over proceedings under Section 13-A and that every lease is terminable on payment of proportionate amount before the expiry of its term.

The Code of Criminal Procedure (Panjab Amendment) Act :—(29-4-40) :—To restore to the law the meaning which has generally been attached to Section 162 of the Code of Criminal Procedure and to enable the proving of so much of the confession of an accused as is permissible under Section 27 of the Indian Evidence Act.

The Punjab Trade Employees Act :—(30-4-40) :—To limit the hours of employment of persons employed in shops and commercial houses and to secure for them rest intervals, holidays, leave with pay and prompt payment of wages.

The Punjab Consolidation of Holdings (Amendment) Act :—(30-4-40) :—To enable a clear and concise record of rights to be prepared afresh with new serial numbers of each estate in order to facilitate the final confirmation of the scheme of consolidation of holdings.

The Punjab Criminal Law (Second Amendment) Act, (11-11-40) :—To extend the Punjab Criminal Law (Amendment) Act, '35, which expired on 30th. November, '40, for further period of five years.

The District Board of Gujrat (Tax Validating) Act, (25-11-40) :—To avoid financial embarrassment and save further litigation to the District Board, Gujrat, by validating the assessment and collection of Haisiyat Tax made by it.

The Punjab Legislative Assembly (Removal of Disqualification) Act :—(29-11-40) :—To remove the disqualification suffered in respect of being chosen as members of the Punjab Legislative Assembly,—(1) by working railway man in respect of Trade union Labour seat ; (2) by Government Treasurers.

The Punjab Municipal (Amendment) Act :—(29-11-40) :—To amend Sections 51 and 184 of the Punjab Municipal Act, 11, so as to make the fines realisable under clause (c) of Section 51 payable to the Provincial Revenues and to bring gramophones, wireless receivers, loud speakers and other electrically operated means of producing loud noises under the definition of 'instrument' as these are beginning to be a nuisance as well.

The Punjab Primary Education Act, (10-12-40) :—To Provide for the compulsory education of children at Primary Schools.

The Punjab Urban Immovable Property Tax Act :—(14-12-40) :—To levy a tax on urban buildings and lands on the basis of their annual value in order to raise additional revenue.

The Sikh Gurdwaras (Amendment) Act :—(21-1-41) :—To Substitute the words "the net expenses" for "all expenses" in subsection (1) of Section 75 of the Sikh Gurdwaras Act '25, in order to continue to credit to the Shrimoni Gurdwaras Parbandhak Committee a ⅔rd share in the income of the Commission.

The Punjab Courts (Amendment) Act, (21-1-41) :—To remove the restrictions laid down by subsection (3) of Section 41 of the Punjab Courts Act '18, in the matter of second appeals regarding the validity or existence of any custom or usage and thereby bring the Punjab Law into accord with the general Indian Law, contained in Section 100 of the Criminal Procedure Code.

The Punjab Fisheries (Amendment) Act, (1-1-41) :—To make all offences under the Punjab Fisheries Act '14, except those under Sections 4 & 5 of the Indian Fisheries Act '97, compoundable.

The Punjab General Sales Tax Act, (31-1-41) :—To enable Government to levy a tax on the sales of goods in general.

The Punjab Entertainment Duty (Amendment) Act, (11-2-41) :—To withdraw the concession of issuing duty-free complimentary tickets other than those issued to the representatives of the Press and to provide for the compounding of the offences committed under the Act.

The Panjab Jagirs Act, (14-2-41) :—To consolidate the law relating to grants and assignments of land revenue commonly termed "Jagirs" at present scattered over various enactments, regulations and executive instructions.

The Punjab Suppression of Indecent Advertisement Act. (27-3-41) :—To penalise the exhibition of advertisements relating to syphilis, gonorrhoea, nervous debility or other complaints or infirmity arising from or relating to sexual intercourse.

The Indian Registration (Punjab Amendment) Act, (31-3-41) :—To delete the words "not being houses in towns" from sub-section (1) of Section 22 of the Indian Registration Act '08, in order that in urban areas also, where a map has been prepared, the houses should be described by reference to the map and not only by reference to their numbers, if any or by reference to the street or road to which they front.

The Punjab Urban Rent Restriction Act. (1-4-41) :—To ensure that rent is not increased on account of payment of tax on buildings and lands imposed by Lahore Municipality within its limits and to be levied under the Punjab Urban Immovable Property Tax in urban areas throughout the province.

The Punjab Agricultural Produce Markets (Amendment) Act. (29-4-41) :—To fill certain lacunae in the Punjab Agricultural Produce Markets Act and to exempt future transactions from payment of fees.

The City of Lahore Corporation Act. (Passed on 4-3-41) :—To consolidate and amend the law relating to the Municipal affairs of city of Lahore.

The Punjab Weights and Measures Act. (Passed on 22-4 41) :—To secure the use of standard weights as well as standard measures and scales in the Punjab.

The Punjab Electricity (Amendment) Act. (Passed on 24-4-41) :—To curtail the period of notice required to be served on a licensee under sub-section (4) of Section 7 of the Indian Electricity Act, as explained by the Punjab Electricity Act No. VI of '39, from two years to one year.

The Punjab Electricity (Emergency Powers) Bill. (Referred to Select Committee) :—To enable the Government to assume control of a licensed Electric Supply Undertaking in cases of emergency and to provide for the continuance of public street lighting service for a period of six months at a time up to a maximum of two years.

The Punjab Cotton Ginning and Pressing Factories Bill. (Published in in the Punjab Gazette dated April 25, 1941) :—For licensing of ginning and pressing factories in the Punjab in order to stop the mal-practices of mixing, watering, adulteration with seed etc., which cause loss to cotton growers.

Government of Assam

The Assam Finance Act, '40 (I of '40). (19-4-40) :—To fix the rate at which agricultural income shall be taxed under the Assam Agricultural Income-Tax Act, '39 (IX of '39).

The Assam Local Authorities Compensatory Grants (Charged) Act, '40 (II of '40). (19-4-40) :—To make provision for compensatory grants to certain local authorities (mentioned in the Schedule to the Act) in view of the fact that certain revenues hitherto credited directly to local authorities and administered by them have become revenues of the province and liable to be included in the annual financial statement.

The Assam Ministers (Salaries and Allowances) Act, '40. (III of '40). (12-4-40) To provide newly for the salaries and allowances of the Ministers owing to the constitution of a new Council of Ministers.

The Assam Commissioners' Powers Distribution (Amendment) Act, '40 (IV of 1940). (12-4-40) :—To make slight amendment to the Assam Commissioners' Powers Distribution Act, '39 (I of '39).

The Assam Amusements and Betting Tax (Amendment) Act, '40 (V of '40). (19-4-40) :—To amend the Assam Amusements and Betting Tax Act, '39 (VI of '39).

The Assam Local Board Elections Emergency Provisions) Act, '40 (VI of '40). (28-12-40) :—To postpone the triennial elections of Local Boards to a later period than 1st April, '41, as the existing Law requires that such elections should be held before that date.

The Temporary Postponement of Execution of Decrees Act, '41 (I of '41). (30-1-41) :—To provide for temporary postponement, pending improvement of financial condition of agriculturists and certain other class of persons from granting relief from indebtedness to agriculturists and such other persons, of the execution of certain decrees passed against them.

The Civil Procedure (Assam Amendment) Act, '41 (II of 1941). (30-1-41) :—To amend Section 138 of the Civil Procedure Code, 1908, in its application to Assam with a view to permit the Judge to dictate in suitable cases and in districts where sufficient stenographers are available, the evidence instead of recording it in his own hand and to relieve him thereby of a laborious duty which detracts from his ability to give proper attention to the proceedings before him.

The Assam Motor Vehicles Taxation (Amendment) Act, '41 (III of '41). (30-1-41) :—To amend the Assam Motor Vehicles Taxation Act, 1936 (IX of '36).

The Assam Provincial Legislature (Romoval of Disqualifications) (Amendment) Act, '41 (IV of of '41) (30-1-41) :—To amend the Assam Provincial Legislature (Removal of Disqualifications Act 1938.

The Assam Deputy President's Salary (Amendment) Act, '41 (V of '41). (30-1-41) To amend the Assam Deputy President's Salary Act, '37 (VI of '37) with a view to allow the Deputy President while touring on public business, other than for the purposes of attending the sessions of the Council to travelling allowance and daily allowance on such conditions as may be determined by rules framed by the Provincial Government.

The Assam President's Salary (Amend. Act, '41 (VI of '41). (30-1-41) :—To amend the Assam Presidents' Salary Act, '37 (V of '37) in order to give power to the Provincial Government to frame rules regulating travelling allowance and daily allowance of the Hon'ble President and to place this matter on the same line as in the case of the Hon'ble Speaker.

The Assam Speaker's and Deputy Speaker's (Salaries and Allowances) Bill, '40 :—To repeal the Assam Speaker's Salary Act, '37, and the Assam Deputy Speakers' Salary Act, '37, and to provide for the Salaries and Allowances of the Speaker and Deputy Speaker of the Assam Legislative Assembly. (The Bill as passed by the Assam Legislative Assembly was returned by the Assam Legislative Council with amendments and the Assembly has disagreed with the amendments).

The Assam (Temporarily-Settled Dists.) Tenancy (Amend.) Bill, 40 :—To amend the Assam (Temporarily-Settled Districts Tenancy Act, '35, with a view to remove certain difficulties that are experienced in realising rents from tenants and in paying Government revenue by Managers of lands pertaining to temples or other religious institutions.

The Assam Maternity Benefit Bill, '40 :—To regulate the employment of women workers on a wage or salary basis in factories, plantations etc., for certain periods before and after childbirth and to provide for the grant to them of maternity benefits.

The Assam Forest (Amendment) Bill, '40 :—To amend the Assam Forest Regulation, 1891, with a view to abolish the presumption afforded by Section 63 of the Regulation that any forest produce as to which a question arises in any proceedings under the Regulation is the property of Government and to penalise vexatious and malicious prosecutions.

The Assam Finance Bill, '41 :—To fix the rates at which agricultural income shall be taxed under the Assam Agricultural Income-tax Act, '39.

Bills pending in the Assembly

The Assam University Bill, '41 :—To constitute a separate Unversity in and for the Province of Assam.

The Assam Revenue Tribunal Bill, '41 :—To provide for the constitution of a Revenue Tribunal for the Province of Assam by an Act of the Provicial Legislature.

The Assam Decree Settlement Bill, '38 :—To make provision for the Settle-

The Punjab, Sind & Frontier Hindu Conference

Presidential Address—Lahore—1st March 1941

The Punjab, Sind and North-West Frontier Hindu Conference was h ld at Lahore on the **1st March 1941.** *Dr. Shyama Prasad Mukherjee,* Working-President of the All-India Hindu Maha Sabha, presided.

Tales of 'suffering and misery' of the Hindus of Sind and the Frontier Province were narrated by speakers from these provinces at the Conference. Rai Bahadur *Mehr Chand Khanna,* Leader of the Hindu-Sikh Nationalist Party in the Frontier Assembly, said that the situation in respect of the life and property of Hindus in the Frontier Province was worse than the plight of Hindus in Sind. He visualised that the Pakistan Scheme would not materialise but 'Pathanistan' was sure to succeed in the Frontier. The speaker warned the Hindus of the rest of India that, if communal fanaticism, prevailing in the Frontier, was not checked in time, it would spread to the Punjab and other neighbouring provinces. Referring to the rise in kidnappings, murders and dacoities during the last two years, Rai Bahadur Khanna said that ninety.nine per cent of the victims were Hindus. It was wrong, he added, to presume that the economic condition of the people of the Frontier was the cause of the crimes. He appealed to the Conference to find a solution of this question.

Mr. *Bhojraj Rajwani,* General Secretary of the Sind Provincial Hindu Sabha, referred to what he described as the havoc caused by communal fanatics in Sind. He warned that if Hindus of other provinces did not come to their rescue they would not hesitate to migrate to the neighbouring provinces as suggested by Mahatma Gandhi,

Bhai Parmanand criticised the Congress Satyagraha and suggested that Congressmen instead of courting arrest would spend a few months in doing propaganda for Hindu Sanghathan.

"Mr. Jinnah's Pakistan Scheme will remain embodied only in pamphlets and reports and, so long as twentyeight crores of Hindus remain alive, it will not operate in any part of Hindusthan," declared Dr. *Shyama Prasad Mukherjee,* presiding over the Conference. Dr. Mukherjee detailed the grievances of the Hindus in the Muslim majority provinces, and deplored the apathy of the Hindus, who, he said, had refused to face the realities of the situation. The policy of the British Government to-day, he continued, was to deny the Hindus, who constituted two-thirds of India's population, their just political rights and to adopt a pro-Muslim attitude calculated to strengthen communal tension and bitterness throughout the country. The Hindus had, during the last half of a century, made every honest effort to create a common platform to achieve the political aspirations of India as a whole.

The policy of appeasement by Indian politicians, with the best of intentions had failed, Dr. Mukherjee went on, and they were confronted to-day with a gigantic Anglo-Muslim conspiracy to crush the liberties of the Hindus and to retard the political freedom of their motherland. Dr. Mukherjee felt convinced that if in the eight provinces where the Hindus were in a majority, there had been strong Hindu Maha Sabha Governments in office, not only would the rights and liberties of the Hindus in those provinces have been protected, but the cause of the provinces like Bengal, Sind and the Punjab would have been quickly and effectively served. Explaining the ideals of the All-India Hindu Maha Sabha, Dr. Mukherjee said: "Ours is not a communal organisation in the sense that we are anxious to realise the aims of our community as such by depriving other communities of their legitimate rights or by lowering the flag of India herself. All that we say is that the systematic and persistent sacrifice of the rights of the Hindu has created an intolerable situation, and we are not prepared to permit any constitutional edifice to be erected on the ashes of the Hindus.

"The Hindu Maha Sabha lays down" continued Dr. Mukerjee, "that one of its essential objects is to establish good relationship with all other communities and to work with them in harmonious co-operation for achieving the common good of India. We are fully prepared to offer equal rights of citizenship to all persons professing diverse religions but residing in India, subject to only one condition, namely, that they identify themselves without reservation with India's joys and sorrows, will claim no separate entity of their own, and will be sons and daughters of Hindustan first and anything else only next."

Dr. Mukerjee then made an appeal to the "great Sikhs of the Punjab who have shared the same vicissitudes of fortune for centuries as the Hindus, and who are labouring under similar communal and political disadvantages to-day," to join the Hindu Maha Sabha and to revitalise it, not only in the Punjab but everywhere in India so that "we may boldly undo the wrongs and uproot the deliberate acts of injustice and reinstal Reason and Freedom."

"A cry had been raised by a section of Muslims—and Dr. Mukerjee was glad to find that the Premier of the Punjab was not one of them—that the Indian problem could not be solved unless they accepted Mr. Jinnah's Pakistan scheme. He urged the Sikhs to collaborate with the Hindu Maha Sabha to frustrate "this unholy attempt for the vivisection of our Motherland."

Alluding to the political situation, Dr. Mukerjee observed that a policy of wholesale non-co-operatian had landed them in disaster, and said that political power was of vital importance for a people in bondage. He advised the audience to "fight relentlessly for more power and go on fighting till you reach the journey's end".

So long as the Communal Award remained, Dr. Mukerjee continued, and the Hindu-Muslim problem was not solved, the Congress should allow the disputes to be settled as between the Muslims on the one hand and a strong and virile Hindu organisation such as the Hindu Maha Sabha on the other. Circumstances had reached such a stage to-day that, even if any settlement was reached—and the Hindu Maha Sabha was not against a settlement consistent with the Indian National demand—it could be reached among spokesmen of the two respective parties speaking and acting as such.

Alluding to the war situation, Dr. Mukerjee said that the war was developing rapidly. The British Government's answer to India's demands had been unsatisfactory, and utterly inconsistent with its declared war aims. The Hindu Maha Sabha had advocated that the Hindus should join the army and be represented adequately and effectively in the task of India's freedom. Whatever their quarrels with British policy might be, he added, it would be nothing short of committing suicide if they allowed the Indian army to be manned by a vast majority of non-Hindus.

Concluding, Dr. Mukherjee referred to the present attitude of the Congress and said that its policy must undergo a radical change if it was to keep pace with the trend of Indian politics to-day.

The U. P. Hindu Conference

Resolutions—Allahabad—15th April 1941

Prevention of Cow-Slaughter

The session of the U. P. Hindu Conference was held in the Purushottamdas Park, Allahabad on the **15th April 1941**. Among the resolutions adopted by the conference were :

"This Hindu Conference abhors with indignation the prevalence of cow slaughter in India and requests the U. P. Government to adopt immediate measures for its prevention as it is against the religious susceptibilities of the Hindus and is detrimental to the economic progress of the country. (Put from the chair).

"This conference demands from the U. P. Government that no non-Hindu be allowed to keep any shop or stall or hawk about and preach or make any religious propaganda during the Hindu Melas in the province.

The resolution was moved by Mr. *Chandrika Prasad Singh* of Ballia and seconded by Mr. *Ram Mohan Lal Agarwala* of Moradabad.

Future Constitution and Hindu Mahasabha

"This open session of the U. P. Hindu Conference declares in clear and emphatic terms that the Hindu Mahasabha is the only representative body of the Hindus and the Indian National Congress has no right to represent the Hindus and as such any settlement or compromise arrived at between the British Government and the Congress and the Muslim League regarding the future constitution of India will not be binding upon the Hindus unless it has full and equivalent approval of the Hindu Mahasabha.

'A copy of this resolution be sent to the Secretary of State for India, the Governor-General in Council and the Governor of the United Provinces'.

Raja Maheshwar Dayal Seth of Kotra moving this resolution said that such a resolution was very necessary. The Congress which called itself a national organization representing the Indian Nation did not, as every-body knew, including the Government, represent the Muslims but it could safely claim to be the representative of the Hindus as at the last elections it had captured almost 90 per cent, of the Hindu seats. The Congress could itself not claim to be representative of the Muslims as it now dared not set up candidates for Muslim seats. That was demonstrated by the fact that at the bye-election Nawabzada Liaqat Ali Khan was allowed to be returned unopposed.

Continuing the Raja of Kotra said that whatever might have been the position at the last general elections the Hindu public had now realized that it was very unsafe for them to trust the Congress to safeguard their culture, religion and rights. He asserted that the sportive offer of Mr. Rajagopalachariar that he would treat it a national government if all Muslims were appointed at the Centre, the declaration of Mahatma Gandhi that he would treat the rule by Nizam as cent per cent. Swaraj, and the pamphlet issued by the Congress Ministry in the United Provinces, taking pride in what they did to suppress the Hindus' rights and interests in order to unduly favour the Muslims, had opened the eyes of the Hindus and the country must make it clear that no settlement arrived at by any body other than the Hindu Mahasabha would be binding on the Hindus. The speaker observed that if the Congress was really a national organization it was none of its business to negotiate the terms for Hindu-Muslim unity with Mr. Jinnah or the Muslim League. That work was of the Hindu Mahasabha. And, he added, even Mahatma Gandhi agreed with that view for he told the speaker when he saw Mahatma Gandhi, a couple of months ago, that he (Mahatma Gandhi) did not go to Mr. Jinnah to negotiate on behalf of the Hindus but he wanted to bring about an understanding between the Congress as an organization and the Muslim League as an organization. The speaker added that everybody knew that if such an understanding was arrived at it would be at the cost of the Hindus' rights and interests.

They could not forget, he said, that Mahatma Gandhi had given a blank cheque for the Muslim at the Round Table Conference and they could not also forget that the present demand for Pakistan was the direct result of laying too much emphasis on Hindu-Muslim unity, without which according to the Crngress, Swaraj was impossible. The Muslim wanted a price for giving support to the Hindus' demand for self-government and they had now gone, therefore, to the extent of demanding a division of India. The Hindu Mahasabha, Raja Maheshwar Dayal Seth remarked, could never allow such an obnoxious scheme to be brought into operation.

He also referred to the atrocities committed on the Hindus in the Gorakpur district.

The resolution was seconded by Mr. *Jainti Prasad*, an advocate of Meerut and passed.

MADRAS GOVERNMENT CONDEMNED

"This conference condemns in strong terms the action of the Madras Government prohibiting members of the Arya Samaj and Hindu Mahasabha from addressing public meetings or taking out procession during the anniversary of the Muslim League held at Madras in this month.' (Moved by *Swami Vidyanand* and seconded by Dr. *Satya Prakash.*)

GORAKHPUR INCIDENTS

On the motion of Mr. *Ram Mohan Lal Agarwala*, which was seconded by Mr. *Kamakhyadat Ram*, the conference passed a resolution with reference to Gorakhpur district incidents, condemning the 'pro-Muslim policy' of the British Government, demanding an impartial enquiry in connection with the Barhaj firing, and asking the Government to adopt a fair and impartial policy.

FUTURE CONSTITUTION

"This conference condemns the obstructive policy adopted by the Muslims to impede the atainment of independence for India, and urges upon the Government to make an immediate declaration that in the framing of the future constitution for India no Muslim demand, which in the opinion of the majority be frivolous and futile, will be given effect to.' (Moved by *Satya Charan Varma* and seconded by Mr. *Vithit Hriday.*)

DACCA SUFFERERS

"This Hindu conference fully sympathises with the sufferings of the Hindus of Dacca who have been made victims of the savage and brutal attacks of the Muslims and condemns the pro-Muslim policy of the Bengal Government which has ever since its formation been incessantly and intentionally inflaming and inciting communal feelings amongst the Muslims and demands from the Government of India the immediate suspension of the constitution in Bengal.'

Dr. *Tej Bahadur Surya* of Aligarh delivered a vigorous speech while moving the resolution and he gave a picture of the plight of Hindus in Dacca.

Mr. *Satya Charan Verma* seconded the resolution.

Another resolution was passed enjoining upon the Hindu youths to join the Hindu militia in large numbers with a view to defend and safeguard the Hindu interests and a committee was appointed to take steps in that direction.

NEED FOR UNITED FRONT

Mr. *Satya Charan Verma* moved and *Pandit Moolchand Malaviya* seconded the following resolution :—

"This Hindu conference recognizes the Hindu Mahasabha as the only representative body of the Hindus and requests the All-India Hindu League, Hindu Sangathan Committee and other bodies which have created separate platforms to abolish their separate existence and merge in the Hindu Mahasabha, in order to put an united front at this critical juncture. A committee of Mahant Digvijai Nath, Pandit Moolchand Malaviya, Mr. Sahkar Bahadur Jorari, Raja Maheshwar Dayal Seth and Mr. Kamkhyadat Ram, be formed to bring about unision amongst these bodies and to set at rest the controversies among the provincial organizations'.

SADHUS AND HINDU SANGATHAN

"This conference requestes the Sadhus, Mathdharis, Gurus and Acharyas, who are the spiritual leaders of the Hindus, to join the Hindu Sangathan movement and thereby strengthen the Hindu cause with a view to save the imminent destruction of the Hindu culture and religion'. (Moved by Pandit *Narmadeshwar Upadhyaya* and seconded by Mr. *K. C. Nigam.*)

LOHARU INCIDENT

The conference also adopted a resolution condemning the attack on the Arya Samaj procession made in the Loharu state last month.

The All India Hindu League

Opening Day—New Delhi—15th February 1941

The working committee of the All-India Hindu League began its two-day session at New Delhi on the **15th Feb. 1941** under the presidentship of Mr. *M. S. Aney*, the president of the League. After confirmation of the proceedings of the last meeting the provincial branches of Bengal, Kashmir and U. P. formed recenty were affiliated to the All-India Hindu League. It was resolved that provincial Hindu League conferences be held in every province under the auspices of the provincial Hindu Leagues at places suitable to the convener and Kunwar Guru Narain, general secretary of the League, was authorized to take steps.

The letter from the general secretary of the Hindu League, Srinagar (Kashmir), was read and it was resolved that every help be rendered to the Srinagar Hindu League as requested by the general secretary in his letter requesting the president of the All-India Hindu League for successfully counter-acting the activities of the Srinagar Christian missionaries. It was further resolved that steps be taken to invite the attention of his Highness the Maharaja of Kashmir with regard to certain grievances relating to the administration of the rules governing educational grants. The question of census operation was also discussed by the committee. Mr. Aney informed the committee in detail of the talk he and Bhai Parmanand had with the Home Member, Sir Reginald Maxwell. The session then adjourned.

2nd Day—Resolutions—New Delhi—16th February 1941

That the Government should take an initiative by inviting leading public men 'who are willing to cooperate with them in their war efforts to assume the responsibility for the administration of the cental Government'. was urged in a resolution pased by the working committee of the League which concluded its two-day meeting on the next day, the **16th February**, Mr. *M. S. Aney* presiding.

The commitee urges upon the Governmet 'to proceed forthwith with the formation of an expanded council consisting purely of non-official Indians representing important elements in the national life of the country and place at least one of them in charge of the Defence department.'

TEXT OF RESOLUTION

The following is the text of the resolution :—

The working committee of the All-India Hindu League views the recent developments in the International situation in Europe, Africa and America with great concern as in its opinion it is fraught with potentialities of great danger and full menace to the moral and material progress of humanity for a long time to come.

The defeat inflicted by the brave people of Greece on the Italian armies and the successes achieved at Siddi Barani and other places in Africa have to some extent removed the danger of imminent invasion of India by the enemy and also kindles the hope that the British nation will be able to defeat the totalitarian forces and win the war in the end. The committee expresses its admiration at the heroic manner in which the people of England have been fighting the enemies and standing the trials and hardships and sufferings which indiscriminate bombing raids inevitably cause.

The League desires to note with pride the part played by the Indian army in defeating the Italians in Libya, Abyssinia and other parts of Africa and offers its hearty congratulations on the heroism shown on the battlefields.

The League, however, feels certain that the United Kingdom notwithstanding her grim resolve to fight the war to the finish at all costs, cannot solely rely on her own resource in men, money and munitions to achieve this end, and it stands in dire need of active cooperation and assistance in every form in her gigantic efforts for the successful prosecution from friendly countries like India and America.

The League is of definite opinion that the British Government and the Government of India will be guilty of culpable negligence if they fail to do everything in their power to awaken the national spirit of the Indian people and enlist their active sympathies and secure their enthusiastic co-operation in the war efforts. India has unlimited resources in men and materials required for war purposes and they will be readily available to the British nation for the prosecution of the present war, provided the Indian people are approached in a right spirit and persuaded to share and shoulder with the people of the United Kingdom the responsibility of fighting the totalitarian forces, not merely for the establishment of democracy in Poland and other European countries, but for the establishment at the end of the war of a responsible government in India invested with the same powers and privileges as the self-governing colonies of Canada, South Africa or the Australian commonwealth enjoy.

The League is definitely of opinion that the British Government in order to prepare the country for the establishment of the Dominion Status type immediately at the end of the war, must necessarily carry out without delay the processes of the Indianisation of the central Government, industrialisation of the country and the militarisation of the population to the utmost possible limits during the period of the war itself.

The League urges upon the Government to take an initiative by inviting leading public men who are willing to cooperate with them in their war efforts to assume the responsibility for the administration of the central Government and proceed forthwith with the formation of an expanded council consisting purely of non-official Indians representing important elements in the national life of the country and place at least one of them in charge of the Defence department.

A bold and courageous step of the nature is, in the opinion of the League, also absolutely necessary to appeal to the imagination of the people and evoke in them a genuine sense of response in the form of voluntary and enthusiastic cooperation in the prosecution of the war effort.

This step will also inspire the people with the confidence that the work of industrialisation and the militarisation of the people which are the two indispensable conditions for the efficiency and adequacy of the defence of any country will be vigorously and vigilantly pursued and completed within a reasonable time.

The creation of a completely Indianized central Government during the period of the war, of the Government's resolve to maintain the political unity of India as one undivided nation and to establish the full responsible government of the Dominion type at the end of the war besides serving as a solvent of the Hindu-Muslim problem and the political deadlock, will give the impetus needed to the people to make supreme national effort for the defeat of the authoritarian powers and the success of democracy in the civilized world.

Other Resolutions Passed

The committee passed eight other resolutions, one of which opined that 'Congress Satyagrahis who court imprisonment should be classed as political prisoners and given all the amenities that are due to political prisoners and must not be grouped along with the ordinary prisoners. The resolution also deplored the repeal in the Central Provinces of the Act passed by the Congress Ministry regarding political prisoners, and called for its revival. The formation of a national army in India forms the subject of another resolution which calls upon the Government of India 'to abandon the policy of segregation of British from Indian units, the political prejudice confining army recruitment to particular classes, and the communal practice of giving preponderance to one particular community or province in the army.

Another resolution criticized the census operations with particular reference to the entry of the name of the religion of aboriginal tribes in Bihar and of the castes of Hinduism in the Punjab and Bengal. The committee maintained that 'the conduct of the enumerators is contrary to the instructions which the central census office had promised to issue and which they are given to understand have actually been issued also'.

The committee supported the candidature of Mr. Jamnadas Mehta for one of the two seats in the central Legislative Assembly recently declared vacant.

Pakistan

A resolution relating to Pakistan demanded the British Government 'to make an unequivocal declaration that they will summarily reject any scheme that aims at or is calculated to impair the solidarity, integrity and unity of the Indian nation', and declared that 'the Hindus cannot feel any genuine enthusiasm in co-operating with the Government in their war efforts so long as the Communal Award is allowed to corrode and destroy the spirit of nationalism in the country and the sword of Pakistan is hanging over their heads'.

The committee urged upon H. E. H. the Nizam the necessity of introducing the reforms in his state 'at the earliest date possible'.

Yet another resolution urged upon Hindu women to 'take real interest and play a fuller part in the Hindu national life by joining the Hindu movement in larger numbers.

Resolutions—Working Committee—New Delhi—29th & 30th March 1941

Platform for All Parties

With the object of creating a common platform for all political parties on matters of common concern, the Working Committee of the All-India Hindu League, which concluded its two-day session at New Delhi on the **30th March 1941**, passed a resolution appointing a Committee of nine members, with Mr. M. S. Aney as Chairman, to examine the question from all points of view and submit for consideration of the Working Committee of the League at its next meeting concrete proposals indicating changes that may be required to be made in its name, creed and constitution. The resolution reads:

"The Working Committee of the All-India Hindu League carefully considered the suggestion made by the President of the Hindu League that it is necessary to widen the sphere of its activities on the one hand and to avoid all possibilities of conflict with the work and programm of the Hindu Maha Sabha on the other. The Committee is of opinion that, so long as the League is confined to Hindus only, its activities are likely to run parallel to some extent to those of the Hindu Maha Sabha.

"The League has, during the brief period of its existence, done much useful work in giving the right lead to the people in regard to their duty towards the last Census operations and also to fight the demand for Pakistan made by a certain section of the Muslim population of India. It has established itself as an integral part in the future life of India. Many active and energetic workers in different parts of India have been fired with the desire to serve the country under the flag of this League. The Committee feel legitimately proud of this achievement.

"One of the objects of the League was to create a common political platform for all political parties on matters of common concern. In experience, it is found that unless some fundamental changes are made in the constitution of the League, any substantial progress in this line is difficult.

It is therefore resolved that a Committee consisting of the President, Mr. M. S. Aney, Kunwar Guru Narain, Rao Rajah Sham Bihari Misra, the hon. Lala Ram Saran Das, Mr, B. G. Khaparde, Kunwar Hirday Narain, Dr. Dulal Mitra, Mr. Ram Nath Kalia and Diwan Lalchand Navalrai be appointed to examine the question from all points of view and submit for the consideration of the working committee of the Hindu League at its next meeting concrete proposals indicating the changes that may be required to be made in its name, creed and constitution, for this purpose."

PAKISTAN : INVITATION TO SUICIDE

The resolution on the Pakistan scheme, passed by the Committee, reads :

"The Working Committee of the All-India Hindu League has before it the task to combat the persisting menace of Pakistan which aims at the partition of India, laying the axe at the very root of the one-nation idea and ideal. The unification of the Indian people has gone on for centuries, and at the time when we are about to reap the fruits of the labours of generations of selfless nation-builders who have sacrificed themselves at the altar of the Motherland, has come the cruel blow of the so-called Pakistan movement which is the direct outcome of the "Communal Award' as embodied in the Government of India Act, 1935. The League consider Pakistan as an invitation to the nation to commit suicide and the movement has got to be crushed. Politics may divide the various nationalist parties and leaders but Pakistan ought to unite nationalists of all shades of opinion whether those of Hindu, Muslim or other communties for, whatever the sins of the nationalists, extra-territorial patriotism is not one of them. We have nothing higher to look for than the re-building of India's future greatness on the greatness of her past, and with that end in view, the Working Committee of the All-India Hindu League enjoins that an Anti-Pakistan Day be celebrated all over the country on April 27 next and urges upon all the nationalist organisations of the country, of whatever caste or creed they may be, to celebrate the day as one of special significance by holding peaceful public meetings in all the cities and towns of the country and passing resolutions to record their strong protest against the so-called "Pakistan" and the "Communal Award".

SUPPORT FOR ANDHRA PROVINCE

The Committee supported the demand of the Andhra people for a separate Andhra Province to be carved out of Madras Presidency, and urged that particular attention should be paid to the demands of the Andhra people for representation of the Andhra Chamber of Commerce on the Madras Port Trust, for the teaching of Telugu in primary schools in Hyderabad State and the enlistment of Audhras in large numbers in regiments that are being raised in the Madras Presidency,

The Committee protested against the circular of the Punjab Government, declaring that "Adi Basis" shall not be tabulated as Hindus and urged the Census authorities to show the Addi Basis of the Punjab and other similar tribes as part of the Scheduled Classes. The Committee further urged the Punjab Government to take steps to remove defects in the enumeration of Hindus in the Punjab and in Lahore in particular in the last Census.

A resolution called upon the Government not to make any distinction between listed and non-listed classes for the purpose of recruitment to the defence forces, and suggested that recruitment should neither be confined to any particular class or particular province but should be extended to all classes of people in all parts of India.

It was decided to ascertain the opinion of the members of the Committee before the President fixed the venue and date of the second annual session of the Conference of the All-India Hindu League and the President was authorised to make announcement in this connection.

The Committee condemned the alleged attack on a peaceful religious procession of Arya Samajists, led by Swami Swatantranand, at Loharu by Muslims and urged the authorities to take suitable action in the matter. The Committee offered its sympathies to Swami Swatantranand and others injured at Loharu.

The All India Muslim League

Activities of the League from January to December 1941*

The first meeting of the Working Committee of the All India Muslim League in the year 1941 was held in Delhi to consider the situation created by Mr. Amery's speech with regard to the slogan "India First". The Working Committee in view of the resentment with which his speech was received in Muslim India, passed a resolution viewing with disapproval the pronouncement made by the Secretary of State for India, which gave an impression contrary to his previous pronouncements. The Working Committee pointed out that the term "Indian" covered three times a greater range of people than the term "European" did, and strongly criticised Mr. Amery for having indulged himself in such misleading slogans. The Working Committee further pointed out that the Mussalmans of India were proud of being Indians and firmly believed in 'India for Indians'; and further said that it was in that spirit that the Lahore resolution of Pakistan was adopted, for the Mussalmans of India were convinced that Pakistan was the only solution of India's constitutional problem.

In the same resolution the Working Committee, while expressing the views of the Muslim India, reaffirmed their adherence to the Lahore resolution which laid down the basic principles on which the future constitution of India was to be framed, before it could be acceptable to the Mussalmans of India—namely 'that geographically contiguous units are demarcated into regions which should be so constituted, with such territorial readjustments as may be necessary, that the areas in which the Muslims are numerically in a majority as in the North-Western and Eastern zones of India should be grouped to constitute "Independent States" in which the constituent units shall be autonomous and sovereign.

Mr. Amery disappointed the Mussalmans of India by the expression of the slogan "India First" as his previous speeches never gave an impression that he ever thought of India's constitutional position in that light. On many occasions before making this utterence, he had expressed himself that the differences existing between the Hindus and Mussalmans of India are greater than the differences existing among the European nations to-day. He said that unitary form of Government was not suited to India, and also pointed out that India being a vast subcontinent, it was capable of being divided into various parts. But sometime after, he began preaching political and economic unity of India and raised the slogan of "*India First*". This was the reason why this pronouncement of Mr. Amery had created grave apprehensions in the minds of the Mussalmans of India, and resulted in great disappointment.

It appeared that the British had begun to yield to Congress owing to Mr. Gandhi's campaign of civil disobedience which had been just started. It looked as though Mr. Amery had not realised that the only object of starting the civil disobedience was, 'to bring pressure on the British Government to resile from the position it had taken, in regard to the future constitution of India relating to the Mussalmans and other minorities, and concede to the Congress demands which are fundamentally opposed to Muslim India as they are detrimental to their vital interest.'

Mr. Gandhi's remarks in the columns of 'Harijan', had caused no less apprehension than Mr. Amery's statements, namely "so long as there is no workable arrangement with the Muslim League civil resistance must involve resistance against the League". It clearly showed that the starting of civil resistance without an arrangement with the League under the cloak of 'liberty of speech', was only a crude method of getting over previous statements and confusing the issues. This was further confirmed by what Mr. Gandhi was reported to have said to the secretary of the Hindu Mahasabha, that if the Hindu Mahasabha was inclined, it could partake in the reorganisation of the Central Government, but the question of the Congress doing so would not arise so long as the Congress demands remained unconceded.

It can be clearly seen from what has been stated above that the Congress is fighting the British Government for the acceptance of its demands, which made

*Specially contributed by the Secretary, All-India Muslim League, Delhi.

for separate treatment by the inclusive organisations of these nationalities. This will lead to a Hindu political or semi-political Congress or Conference being organised and the sooner it is done the better. As at present situated the absence of such an organisation places the Hindus at a distinct disadvantage, and takes away from them the chances of a united action or a united expression of opinion upon matters which affect the unity, prosperity and well-being and generally the interest of Hindus all over India. In order to leave no doubt as to the necessity of this step, I will be more specific. In my opinion, it should be the business of a Hindu Congress or Conference to support and take so far as possible such steps which might conduct to their unity and strength as a religious nationality, as for instance, the language question, the question of character, the advisability of having common text-books, the teaching of Sanskrit language and literature all over India, the taking of steps which might lead to the protection of Hindu orphans from the hands of proselytising agencies of other denominations, and if necessary, to record a protest against those confidential circulars of Government, which aim at the favouring of other communities to the loss of Hindus".

Lala Lajpat Rai also explained how the Hindus by themselves formed a Nation. He said :—

"It may be that the Hindus by themselves, cannot form themselves into a nation in the modern sense of the term, but that is only a play on words. Modern nations are political units. A political unit ordinarily includes all the peoples who live under one common political system and form a State. The words 'nation' and 'state' when thus considered are practically interchangeable phrases. That is the sense in which the expression in used in connection with the body called the "Indian National Congress". That is, no doubt, one use of the word and the one which is commonly adopted in modern political literature. But that is not the only sense in which it is or can be used. In fact, the German word 'Nation' did not necessarily signify a political nation or a State. In that language it connoted what is generally conveyed by the English expression "people" implying a community in possessing a certain civilisation and culture. Using it in that sense, there can be no doubt that Hindus are a "nation" in themselves, because they represent a type of civilisation all their own".

With regard to the attitude of the Hindu Maha Sabha towards other communities in India Lalaji said :—

"In the present struggle between Indian communities, I will be a Hindu first and an Indian afterwards, but outside India, or even in India against non-Indians I am and shall ever be an Indian first and a Hindu afterwards. That is, in short, my position in the matter.

"Holding that position, I bear no ill-will to my countrymen of other faiths. I wish them all joy and prosperity. In their efforts to ameliorate the condition of their own community, and to secure a position of advantage for their co-religionists I do not find fault with them. In the existing political conditions of India they are perfectly justified in looking to the interests of their own community so long as by doing that they do not injure the Hindus by an unholy alliance with non-Indians."

The movement was comprehensive from the beginning. Lalaji said :—"The Hindu movement inaugurated by the organisers of this conference does not contemplate the exclusion of any one who is prepared to sail under the Hindu flag and take the credit or discredit which attaches thereto."

All these statements can be made by any leader of the Maha Sabha in any Conference. These statements indicate the basis principles of the formation of the Maha Sabha. In December 1900 at a meeting of leading Hindus held at Allahabad it was decided that an all India Hindu Maha Sabha should be formed. The objects and rules were drafted and office-bearers were elected. The first Akhil Bharatiya Hindu Maha Sabha Conference was held in 1914 at Hardwar.

Till 1928 Pandit Madan Mohon Malaviya and Lala Lajpat Rai led the Hindu Maha Sabha Movement. The Sessions of the Hindu Maha Sabha were mostly held since 1922 along with the Congress Sessions. The Jubbulpur Session in 1928 under the presidentship of Shri. N. C. Kelkar marked the turning point. The Session voted against separation of Sind with an overwhelming majority against the advice of the revered Pandit Madan Mohan Malaviya, who urged that the Maha Sabha should not take the "odium" upon itself of making a settlement impossible by its l at denial but "to wait for the report of the sub-committee appointed by the Madras Congress."

The Maha Sabha leaders had till then participated in the 'Indian' politics carried on by the Congress. But it must be noted that even there they formed a group in favour of parliamentary and constitutional activities and against Non-co-operation policy and Gandhism in general. The first breaking away with the Congress began with the disapproval by Maha Sabha leaders and followers of the "appeasement" policy of the Congress with regard to the political constitution of the country. The difference became more prominent when the Congress adopted the attitude of Neutrality towards the Communal Award. The same difference was visible when with regard to the policy in legislatures, the Maha Sabha felt the necessity of setting up candidates on the Maha Sabha ticket as opposed to the Congress. After the actual experience of the working of the Congress ministries in several provinces and especially in U. P., the breaking away from the Congress in the Parliamentary programme became complete.

With the relinquishment of the ministries by the Congress, its adoption of anti-militarisation policy and Satyagraha for the principle of non-violence, the political divergence between the Hindu Maha Sabha and the Congress has become almost complete.

The creed of the Hindu Maha Sabha is 'Complete political Independence' for Hindustan. But since the beginning of this war the Hindu Mahasabha is demanding Dominion Status as a step towards the goal to be taken at the end of the war. Resolution No. 2 passed by the Working Committee on 19th November 1939 at Bombay runs as follows :—

"This meeting of the Working Committee of the Hindu Mahasabha refuses to look upon Dominion Status as an ultimate goal as H. E. The Viceroy has assured in the statement but instead insists upon it as an immediate step to be taken towards the final goal of absolute political independence and that a constitution based upon that status should be conceded to India at the end of the war at the latest. Even now it is not too late to mend. A definite declaration to that effect can alone evoke a responsible and willing co-operation on the part of India".

The first resolution on the war situation was passed by the Working Committee of the Hindu Mahasabha on 10th September 1939 at Bombay. It runs as follows :—

The Working Committee does not believe in the claims of any Power among the belligerent nations engaged in the present War in Europe, some of which are themselves Imperialistic in character and outlook, to the effect that it has been actuated solely by moral and altruistic consideration apart from its own National self-interest.

But in view of the declaration made by His Majesty's Government that it has entered the War with a desire to safeguard the vital principles of Right and Democracy as against the rule of Force which claim does not fit in well with Britain's Imperialistic Policy towards India—and in view of the fact that nowhere is there greater necessity for the application of these principles than in India, the Hindu Mahasabha declares as follows :—

Responsible Government at Centre

(1) As the task of defending India from any Military attack is of common concern to the British Government as well as ourselves and as we are unfortunately not in a position to-day to carry out that responsibility unaided, there is ample room for whole-hearted co-operation between India and England. In order to make such co-operation effective, the British Government should forthwith take the following steps :

(a) To introduce full responsible Government at the Centre.

(b) To redress the grievous wrongs done to the Hindus by the Communal Decision, both at the Centre and in Provinces, particularly in Bengal and the Punjab where they have been reduced to the position of fixed statutory minority, contrary to all principles of Democracy.

(c) To inspire the people of India to feel instinctively that the Indian Army will be the Army of the people of India and not of the British.

(d) To remove artificial distinction of the so-called enlisted and not-enlisted classes, that is, the martial and non-martial classes for complete Indianization of the Indian Army as early as possible."

These two resolutions have expressed the demands of the Hindu Maha Sabha to be satisfied after the war and during the war. These demands were also repeated in the main resolution of the Madura Session in December 1940 and the resolutions passed at Calcutta in June 1941 by the Working Committee of the Maha Sabha.

The Hindu Maha Sabha does not look at the war efforts from a moral basis and does not on that basis take sides in the European War. 'Truth' said Mr. Munshi recently was the first casualty in this war. Well it is the first casualty in every war and on each side. The only thing with which Indians need concern themselves is according to the Hindu Maha Sabha "the defence of India." The Maha Sabha is for militarisation and its support for war efforts is based mainly on that consideration of self-interest. The Maha Sabha does not believe that non-violence would help India either in the National or in the internatioual sphere. In December, 1940, at the Madura Session, the Maha Sabha decided to launch a campaign of direct action to enforce its political demands. But even then it was made clear that no direct action would affect the Militarisation programme. The political demands of the Hindu Maha Sabha are not yet fully satisfied. Still owing to the communal situation created by the Dacca, Ahmedabad and Bombay riots the Maha Sabha abandoned the idea of direct action on an all-India scale. This decision was taken at a special meeting of the All-India Committee of the Hindu Maha Sabha at Calcutta in June, 1941. The resolution as recommended by the Working Committee was adopted by the All-India Committee. It sets out the reasons that led the Mahasabha to take the decision. It makes clear that the demands of Hindu Maha Sabha were not fully satisfied, but the Maha Sabha thought it advisable to postpone indefinitely 'direct action' on an all-Hindusthan scale owing to the communal situation.

If *Satyagraha* of the mildest type could not be undertaken in Sind and was suspended in Bombay owing to the riots, and if that is regarded as justifiable the Hindu Maha Sabha decision would be equally so for similar reasons.

As the political demands of the Mahasabha agree generally with the demands of the "Non-party Leaders Conference" or Sapru Conference, Hindu Maha Sabha leadeas like Shri. Savarkar, Dr. B. S. Moonje and Dr. S. P. Mukherji took active part in the proceedings of the Conference both in Bombay and Poona and supported the demands of the Conference.

It was from the point of view of militarisation that the Mahasabha supported the scheme of expansion of the Viceroy's Executive Council. The resolution passed by the Working Committee in September, 1940 says :—

"In view of the opportunities that the present war offers for the general militarisation of the Hindus and for the organisation of the defence of India on up-to-date and modern lines so that India may be converted into a self-contained defence unit, the Hindu Maha Sabha is prepared to work out the scheme of the extension of the Viceroy's Executive Council and the War Advisory Council but on terms of equity and justice."

The terms were stated in the rest of the resolution. It mainly opposes the Muslim League's claim of 50 per cent. representation.

The Maha Sabha Working Committee has repeatedly urged that the British Government should unequivocally declare that the Government did not approve of any scheme of division of India into two different Nations and States. The Maha-Sabha opposition to Pakistan is more insistent and unequivocal than that of the Congress.

Owing to the experience of Congress Ministries and especially of the U. P. Ministry the idea of contesting elections and capturing all elective bodies on the Hindu Maha Sabha or Hindu Sanghatanist ticket which had been urged by the Mahasabha since 1934 is gaining ground. Mahasabha candidates are contesting Municipal and Local-Board elections in various provinces, and by-elections to Provincial and Central Legislatures.

The Hindu Party

It must be noted that the Hindu Maha Sabha leaders do not expect that there would be a Mahasabha Party in the Legislatures. They expect that there would be a united Hindu Sanghatanist Party which would include Sikhs, Sanatanists, Arya-Samajists, Hindu Nationalists etc. Shri. V. D. Savarkar has repeatedly explained this idea in the presidential addresses at the Ahmedabad, Nagpur and Calcutta Sessions of the Hindu Maha Sabha in 1937 '38 and '39. At the Ahmedabad Session in 1937 he said :—

"Let the Varnashrama Swarajya Sangha, the Hindu Maha Sabha, the Arya Samajists, the Shiromani Sikh Sabha, the political organisation of the Democratic Swarajya Party, that stand for an honourable unity and a truly national Indian State and the great Ashramas, Sanghas and Jatiya Sabhas that take their stand on Hindutva, form a United Hindu Party in the Legislatures."

At Nagpur Session in 1938 Shri Savarkar said :—

"The only way to chastise the anti-Hindu and anti-National policy of the Congress, the best and easiest remedy under the circumstances lies in the formation of a Hindu Nationalist Front. Let all our Sadhus, Sanatanists, Arya Samajists and Sanatanist organisations make it a point never to vote for a Congress candidate but for a Hindu Nationalist candidate."

At the Calcutta Session in 1939 Shri Savarkar said :—

"Above all, we shall have to form 'a Hindu Party' including Sanatanists, Arya Samajists and all such other Hindu bodies, sects and sections who have not as yet any formal connection with the Hindu Maha Sabha as an organisation but are as devoted Hindu Sanghatanists as the Hindu Sabhaites themselves."

Future Constitution

The attitude of the Hindu Maha Sabha with regard to the future constitution of India has been explained by Sri. Savarkar in his Presidential speech at the Calcutta Session of the All India Hindu Maha Sabha in December 1939. It was as follows :—

"The Hindu Sanghatanist Party aims to base the future constitution of Hindusthan on the broad principle that all citizens should have equal rights and obligations irrespective of caste, creed, race or religion—provided they all avow and owe an exclusive and devoted allegiance to the Hindusthani State. The fundamental rights of liberty of speech, liberty of conscience, of worship, of association etc. will be enjoyed by all citizens alike. Whatever restrictions will be imposed on them in the interest of the public peace and order or National emergency will not be based on any religious or racial considerations alone but on common National grounds.

"But as practical politics requires it and as the Hindu Sanghatanists want to relieve our non-Hindu countrymen of even a ghost of suspision, we are prepared to emphasise that the legitimate rights of minorities with regard to their Religion, Culture, and Language will be expressly guaranteed on one condition only that the equal rights of the majority also must not in any case be encroached upon or abrogated. Every minority may have separate schools to train up their children in their own tongue, their own religious institutions or cultural and can receive Government help also for these, but always in proportion to the taxes they pay into the common exchequer. The same principle must of course hold good in case of the majority too."

Over and above this, in case the constitution is not based on joint electorates and on the unalloyed National principle of one man one vote, but is based on the communal basis then those minorities who wish to have separate electorate or reserve seats will be allowed to have them,—but always in proportion to their population and provided that it does not deprive the majority also of an equal right in proportion to its population too."

Hindutva is not a religion

The Hindu Maha Sabha is not a religious organisation. Hindutva or Hinduness which includes Arya, Sikh, Brahmo, Buddhist and Jain is not a religion but a nationality. Hindutva does not depend on particular spiritual belief or system of philosophy. Before the advent of the Muslims and Christians all Hindu secular institutions, traditions, customs were 'Hindu' because they were Hindusthani or Indian. If a Sanatani Hindu becomes an Arya or a Bramho, the Hindus do not feel the need of reconversion. A conversion from Hinduism to the Muslim or Christian faith is not dreaded because of the change of "religious creed" involved in it but because it removes the Hindutva which is a nationality.

Hindu Nationalism is in ultimate analysis only another name for true Indian nationalism.

"In a country like India where a religious unit tends inevitably to grow into a cultural and national unit the Suddhi movement ceases to be merely a theological or dogmatic one but assumes the wider significance of a political and national movement." (Savarkar in the introduction to "History of the Hindu Maha Sabha" published by Hindu Maha Sabha Head Office, New Delhi, 1938).

In the secular and national sense of Hindutva all Christians and Mussalmans in this country should have been Hindu Christians and Hindu Mussalmans. A number of Christians have recently come forward to say that by religion they were Christians but by culture and nationality they were Hindus.

These religions came from outside India and brought with them non-Hindu (i. e. non-Indian) culture and customs. And proselytising in their case meant denationalising. 'Hindutva' is the nationality in Hindusthan and of Hindusthan. The Hindu Maha Sabha is not based on Hindu religion but on Hindu nationality and hence it is not a religious but a national organisation.

Hindu Sabha Activities

Owing to the fact that the distribution of seats in Legislatures and other elective bodies are made dependent on the comparative proportion of the populations of different communities, the correct enumeration at the census has assumed special importance. The year 1941 being a census year the Hindu Mahasabha called upon all Hindus to record themselves as Hindus. The Maha Sabha workers were asked to co-operate with the census authorities. In order to rouse all Hindus to the importance of the census the Mahasabha observed a census week. In Bengal the Provincial Hindu Mahasabha made tremendous efforts to ensure correct record of the Hindu population. The Mahasabha leaders have exposed the tendency of census authorities to separate the Hill tribes from the Hindus. In Assam this device of disintegrating the numerical strength of Hindus has been done systematically. Even non-Hindu Sabhaites like Shri A. V. Thakkar have come forward to expose this manipulation by Assam census authorities.

The Mahasabha started special relief funds for helping sufferers in Sukkur and Dacca riots. In Bombay the Hindu Mahasabha organised relief, guidance and help to Hindus at the time of the recent riot.

The Militarisation Committee or Mandals in different provinces are actively helping and encouraging young Hindus to join the various Defence Services which are thrown open owing to the exigencies of the war situation.

Resolutions—Working Committee—New Delhi—18th & 19th January 1941

The first meeting of the Working Committee of the All India Hindu Maha Sabha after the Madura Session of December 1940 was held at New Delhi at the Hindu Maha Sabha Bhavan on 18th and 19th January 1941. Dr. *Shyama Prasad Mukherjee* presided. The following resolutions of public importance were passed :—

COMMUNAL RIOT

"The Hindu Mahasabha views with alarm the tendency disclosed in the recent Communal riots in various Provinces such as Bihar, United Provinces, Bengal and others on the occasion of the Id Festival on the part of Muslims to perform Cow sacrifice in Hindu localities in order to offend and hurt their religious feelings. The Working Committee of the All-India Hindu Mahasabha hereby points out to the Government that time has come when the authorities in charge of Law and Order should suppress these provocative and mischievous activities of the Muslims with strong hand."

"That the General Secretary be authorised to issue a circular letter to all Provincial Hindu Sabhas to submit specific and definite instructions regarding the sacrifice of Cows in purely Hindu localities and detailed information regarding riots or disturbances arising out of it."

GHAZIABAD RIOT

"This meeting of the Working Committee of the All India Hindu Mahasabha strongly deprecates the attitude adopted by the Provincial Government towards the Hindus about the riot at Ghaziabad on 10th October, 1940, and particularly condemns the callous way in which the Police fired on an unarmed peaceful Hindu Dashehra Procession without any warning and further protests against the inaction of the Government in not ordering a judicial enquiry into this affair and against the subsequent unprecedented orders passed prohibiting all processions without licence and forfeiting licences for arms of respectable peace-loving Hindus.

CENSUS WEEK

"The Working Committee calls upon all Hindu Sabhas to observe the 1st Week in February, 1941, as the Census Week. The following programme is recommended for the week :—

(1) To get in touch with the leaders of All Hindu Communities including Aryas, Sikhs, Jains, Brahmans, Budhists, Depressed Classes, and Tribes and impress upon them the necessity of recording themselves as Hindus in the coming Census, mentioning if need be their particular nomenclature.

(2) To hold meetings, distribute thousands of pamphlets, instructing Hindus about their duty with regard to the Census.

(3) To see that Santals, Bhils, Gonds and other tribes who have so long been returned as animists record themselves as Hindus and for that purpose to broadcast hand-bills, posters, pamphlets in their lown language.

(4) To organise students and other youngmen in every union of every district for rendering honorary services during the Census fort-night with instructions that they should accompany official enumerators for ensuring accurate enumeration."

Resolutions—Working Committee—Dadar—9th to 11th March 1941

HINDU MILITARISATION MANDALS

The second meeting of the Working Committee was held on **9th. to 11th. March** at Dadar, Bombay. Dr. *Shyamaprasad Mookherji* presided on the first day, and *Shri Savarkar* presided on the next day. The following resolution about Hindu militarisation was passed :—

"With a view to give effect to the resolution passed at the session of the Hindu Mahasabha at Madura on "Immediate Programme", all provincial and district Hindu Sabhas are called upon to form "Hindu Sainikikaran Mandals" (Hindu Militarisation Mandals)

(a) To encourage Hindus to join the army, navy and air forces as well as the ammunition factories, the aeroplane factories, ship-building yards and such other factories, schools and institutions in connection with war craft.

(b) To hold public meetings, distribute literature and carry on propaganda in all ways and with all means to instil military-mindedness in the Hindu public in general.

(c) To collect, publish and supply information regarding the rules, regulations and facilities in connection with the recruiting of military, aerial and naval forces and to try to remove whatever difficulties are found to stand in the way of those Hindus who are ready to get themselves enlisted in these forces.

(d) To establish contact with all military and other departmental authorities to get information and to get removed any grievances of Hindu forces.

(e) To set on for a country-wide agitation to get the Arms Act so mended as to bring it on a par with what exists in England to-day.

(f) To bring all possible pressure on the Senates and other educational institutions in general and the Government in particular to make military training compulsory in high schools and colleges with a view to bring it up in near future to the standard of efficiency obtaining in the case of students in the powerful free countries in the world.

In order to co-ordinate and control and guide the activities of all these provincial and their subordinate district Hindu Militarisation Maldals an All-India Hindu Militarisation Mandal should be constituted under the aegis of the Hindu Mahasabha. (Tentatively) The Hindu Militarisation Mandal should be formed with Sjt. G. V. Ketkar as Chairman and Sir J. P. Srivastava, Mahashay Ratanchand, Raja Narayanlal Pitti, Sjt. Madusudan Majumdar, Sjt. S. N. Banerji, Dewan Bahadur Ramaswami Shastri, Sjt. Rambhau Rajwade, Dr. N. D. Savarkar, Rao Bahadur S. K. Bole, Kunwar Chandkaranji Sharda, Dr. Moonje, Sjt. Kalikar, Sjt. Anand Priyaji and Dr. Kaney as members, with powers to co-opt.

Resolutions—Working Committee—Nagpur—12th & 13th April 1941

THE DACCA RIOTS

The 3rd meeting of the Committee was held on the **12th and 13th April 1941** at Nagpur. *Shri Savarkar* presided. The following resolutions were passed. :—

"(A) In view of the serious situation in Dacca and villages round about Dacca, the wholesale looting and arson, and burning of villages by Muslim goondas encouraged by the incapacity of the Bengal Government to protect Hindu life and property and in view of the fact that thousands of Hindus in villages are rendered penniless and homeless and are seeking refuge in Tripura State, the Working Committee of the Hindu Mahasabha calls upon the Government to suspend the constitution in Bengal and place the administration directly in the hands of the Governor.

"(B) The Working Committee expresses its sense of gratitude and appreciation of the help which the Maharaja of Tripura is rendering to the unfortunate Hindu refugees from Dacca and villages near about by allowing the refugees entry and shelter in the State."

Resolutions—Working Committee—Calcutta—14th & 15th June 1941

VICEROY—SAVARKAR CORRESPONDENCE

The 4th. meeting of the Committee was held at the Ashutosh College Hall, Calcutta on the 14th and 15th June 1941. The following resolutions were passed :—

The All-India Committee of the Hindu Mahasabha has given its most careful consideration to the correspondence that has passed between its President Veer Savarkar and the Viceroy in pursuance of the Madura Resolution, and has also examined the pronouncements made from time to time by the Secretary of State for India in connection with the political situation in India.

The Committee observes the following points enumerated in the Viceroy's reply to the demands put forth by the Hindu Mahasabha, namely,

(a) "That the proclaimed and accepted goal of the British Parliament is to lead India to an actual and equal co-partnership with Great Britain and other self-governing Dominions immediately after the war and that as early as may be."

(b) "The Governors who are responsible for the protection of minorities in their provinces, were determined that there weuld be victimisation and that where any community commits acts of aggrestion against another, the full power of the Government would be used to maintain public order."

The Committee further notes that the Viceroy turned down some of the fantastic communal demands put forward by the Moslem League with regard to the extension of the Viceroy's Executive Council.

The Committee also notes that the Secretary of State for India had under the presure of public opinion, created by the Hindu Mahasabha criticised adversely the so-called Pakistan proposal and advocated the cause of the unity and integrity of India as a State and a Nation which evoked indignant protests from the advocates of Pakistan scheme and that only recently Sir Lancelot Graham, the Governor of Sind, made a public statement to the effect "that the impression in political circles that the Pakistan scheme was favoured by the British Government was incorrect."

The Committee also notes that the Government of India has taken action against the Khaksar movement which the Working Committee of the Hindu Mahasabha urged in 1940.

VICEROY'S EVASIVE REPLIES

The All-India Committee is still of opinion that the replies received from the Viceroy and the Secretary of State regarding the demands of the Hindu Mahasabha are evasive, unsatisfactory and disappointing. The latest utterances of the Secretary of State with regard to the Pakistan scheme practically indicate a reversal of the policy as embodied in his "India First" speech and in no way dispel the just apprehension of the Hindus of India about future British intention regarding such scheme. In other respects also, the Secretary of State's speech is reactionary and mischievous. While on the one hand, it is a direct encouragement to reactionary anti-national Moslems to persist in their attitude of obstruction for holding up the future political progress of India ; on the other hand, it indicates a refusal on the part of the British Government to part with political power and hand it over to the Indians. The decision of the Secretary of State in turning down even the immediate demand to Indianise the Viceroy's Executive Council on flimsy pretexts is another instance of the anxiety of the British Government to utilise the reactionary Moslem view-point against the best interests of India and also makes it demonstrably clear that even in this crisis the British Government is not willing to part with autocratic powers unless compelled to do so.

HINDUS GRIEVANCES IN MUSLIM PROVINCES

The Committee further notes that in spite of the Viceroy's declaration of the responsibility of Governors for the protection of the interests of minority communities, Hindu interests in Sind, North-Western Frontier Provinces, the Punjab and Bengal continue to be systematically assailed and in Eastern Bengal in particular the Hindu Community did not get any adequate protection during the recent anti-Hindu rising of the Moslems.

The All-India Committee having fully reviewed the present situation in India, and having taken into consideration the developments since December, 1940, both national and international and particularly in view of the wide-spread and organised aggression on the Hindus, which it is the paramount duty of the Hindus to resist and crush, and also in view of the fact that the War is rapidly approaching our motherland on both the frontiers, resolved :—

(I) that the question of launching the campaign of direct action on an All-India issue and scale be postponed for the present.

(II) That such postponement will not in any manner debar any action that may be required to be taken on important local or provincial issues affecting the civic, religious, cultural or political rights of Hindus, it being understood that such action, if proposed to be taken by any Provincial Hindu Sabha, will require the previous approval of the All-India Working Committee which will extend to any such movement, if approved, the active support and sympathy of Hindus from all parts of India.

Sanghatan On National Scale

The campaign of the Pakistan riots already set on foot by the Muslims, makes it imperative that Hindu Sanghatanists throughout India should organise themselves on a national scale, and should be prepared in every locality to defend their hearths, homes, temples, Hindu rights and above all, Hindu honour, consolidating all available forces to resist the dangers facing Hindusthan.

That in order to intensify a spirit of resistance against all oppression and aggression, a comprehensive, constructive programme be immediately taken in hand, stress being laid on the following aspects :—

(A) Creation of Hindu solidarity and consolidation of all classes of Hindus by adopting a social programme which will remove all artificial barriers, and will rouse spontaneous pan-Hindu consciousness among them.

(B) Effective organisation of Volunteer-Dals to be recurited from all classes of Hindus for defence of Hindu rights against all aggression.

(C) Vigorous campaign for enrolment of at least one crore of Hindu Sabha members to be completed before the next All-India Session.

Cyclone Havoc

The All-India Committee expresses its heartfelt sympathy for the cyclone stricken areas in different parts of Bengal, Assam, Malabar and other places, and calls sections of Hindus to render all possible help in relief operations. It also urges upon Government to take adequate steps so that no discrimination is made in conducting relief operations out of government funds particularly in areas where Hindus are in a minority.

Defence of India Rules

That the All-India Committee expresses its strong disapproval of the application of the Defence of India Rules by the Government to suppress legitimate expression of political opinion and activities, thereby strengthening the grip of bureaucratic control in India by taking advantage of the war situation and in particular against the Hindu Sanghatanists and the Hindu Sabha workers.

Bengal Census Bungle

The All-India Committee condemns the action of the Government of Bengal in interfering with the Census operations in Bengal and in particular the scurrilous campaign of villification carried on by the Chief Minister of Bengal against the Hindu community and calls upon the Government of India immediately to intervene and to prevent any manipulation of Census figures in Bengal so as to inspire confidence in the Hindus of Bengal with regard to Census operations in Bengal.

Communal Harmony

The All-India Hindu Mahasabha is of opinion that communal amity cannot be established in this country by pandering to anti-national communal demands of minorities, but by recognising equality of civic rights for all communities without distinction and by giving equal protection to the language, culture, religion of communities, adherence to the principle of "one man, one vote" and the integrity and indivisibility of Hindusthan as a Nation and as a State.

the 26th December, 1938, he referred to the ninety millions of Indian Muslims as a nation and stated that the Congress had dashed to the ground every possible hope of arriving at a settlement of the Hindu-Muslim question. He criticised the Wardha Education Scheme and the Vidya Mandir Scheme as having been propounded with a definite object of suppressing the Muslims as much as possible. He also complained of the singing of *Bande Mataram*, flying of the Tri-coloured Flag and the suppression of Urdu. There are many Congressmen who never approved of the Vidya Mandir Scheme and the singing of *Bande Mataram* songs. It should not be difficult to settle these questions to the entire satisfaction of all denominations and schools of thought, They, however, do not justify the division of India."

Examining the principle of dividing India into separate communal states, Mr. Shareef affirmed that it was obviously impossible that the entire Hindu or Muslim population of any province could be migrated from one region to another. If, however, that could be accomplished, he asked whether the North-Western and North-Eastern States and the Mid-Northern and Central and Southern Hindu States would attain economic self-sufficiency and develop enough political power to enable them to resist the pressure of external aggression. "How will they fare in this competitive world in the matter of international trade and protection of the rights of their nationals ?"

Proceeding, the President said : "If on the other hand, it is contemplated that the minorities will stay where they are, then how are the States to be constituted ?" There is no province, he said, where one Community was uniformly in the majority in the whole of its area. There were districts in the Punjab towards the North-West where Muslims dominated, others in the South-East where the Hindus and Sikhs outnumbered the Muslims. Same was the case in Bengal. The League's resolution no doubt provided for adequate effective and mandatory safeguards in the constitution for minorities for the protection of their rights and interests. But that would mark no change. The minorities problem would remain exactly as they existed to-day even after the creation of the Muslim and Hindu States as contemplated under the League Scheme.

Mr. Shareef, continuing, said : "It is said that after the creation of the Muslim independent states, sanctions would be forced and the minority in the Muslim States would receive safeguards and protection on the principle of reciprocity : that is, the Hindu minorities in the Muslim independent states would receive the same measure of protection as the Muslims would be given in the Hindu independent states. But this would inevitably lead to internecine wars and thus expose India to external invasions. The Muslims claim India as the land of their birth and they would be the last to wish the subjection of India by any foreign country—be it a Muslim country or non-Muslim."

Mr. Shareef proceeding said :—"From the national point of view every Muslim is an Indian. The common rights of all the inhabitants of the country and their responsibilities in every walk of life and in every sphere of activities are the same. The Indian Muslim, by virtue of these rights and responsibilities, is unquestionably an Indian national and in every part of the country he is entitled to equal privileges with all other Indian in every sphere of governmental, economic and other national activities. For that very reason Muslims owe equal responsibility with other Indians striving and making sacrifices to achieve the country's independence.

The past history of political developments in the country, said Mr. Shareef, established that it had been possible for interested parties to play the two major communities of India against each other. "It must be admitted that communalism is based on fear and suspicion. Those who have sought to win the leadership of their communities have played upon these two passions." The fears and suspicions, he said, were the result of estrangement which had been brought about between them in the course of the nineteenth century. "On the basis of facts relating to language, literature, science, philosophy, art, and religion, it can be stated with every justification that the Muslims and Hindus of India had evolved a common point of view, a common way of living, a common civilization, during the long century of their contact.

The President, in the course of his address, said that according to the Koran the Muslims should model their rules of life and the laws regulating their relations and contact with non-Muslim neighbours after those immutable laws. By dividing India into two, Muslim and Hindu, independent States, they would be limiting their sphere of activities. They were the inheritors of the worlds in the language of the holy Koran. How could they then be a party to the proposed division of India ? They should have to oppose all attempts, by whomsoever made, to segregate them.

We shall have to lay down our lives in resisting all such attempts. They should boldly declare that the proposed division of India was not in the interests of the Muslims of the country in general and much less in the interts of the Muslims living in the minority provinces. The Muslims had every right to demand and insist that their observance of their religious rites and prayers should be respected and not interfered with, that their culture and all that it implied should have unrestricted scope for development in their own way and that should have an effective voice and share. All these should be embodied in the fundamental rights.

Continuing, the president said, "Our immediate need is to consolidate ourselves and to close our ranks. We should aim at fusion of all the Muslim organisations in the country. As a first step we should establish an All-India Muslim Executive Board on which all the Muslim organizations in the country should be represented in proportion to their strength. This Board should have powers to control and guide the policies and working of the Muslim organisations, and to represent the Muslims and their interests in the negotiations with the organisation of the sister communities—the Congress and the Government of the country. The only means of building up a strong India is through the establishment of relations based on esteem and affection between the communities. All else is secondary. No declarations of rights, constitutions, agreements, pacts or treaties are of any value which are not based upon mutual trust and faith in the plighted words of man. The freedom of India and the security for the religions, cultural and material interests of individuals, groups and communities, he said, must rest ultimately on the convictions and ideals of the people of India and they would endure so long as Indians would collectively desire to maintain them. What was needed was a union of hearts which no external power would ever be able to dissolve. In so far as this union was brought about by political accommodations and agreements let us enter into them. For, after all, solemn undertakings and public declarations might produce desirable psychological conditions, but above everything else let us endeavour to roll away the dark clouds of distrust which hang over the horizon."

Proceeding, the President said, "In this endeavour the responsibility of the Hindu community is great. It is this community which in numbers, wealth and education holds a position preeminent among other communities. It is the privilege and duty of the strong to produce a sense of security among those who are less strong. In the middle ages power resided with the Muslim rulers and their retainers, and they took the initiative in promoting cultural fusion. To-day when the counting of hands is replacing other and cruder methods of determining policies it is the duty of the more numerous to remove the apprehensions which prey upon the minds of the less numerous. In the alternative, if we stick obstinately to what we regard as rights, but which cannot be dignified with that name till they have been recognised by others, and they will not be recognised by others unless the others are convinced that the so-called rights are based on a common conception of the welfare of all, and are grounded in righteousness, the relations of the communities will be based not on mutual recognition, but on its repudiation and its concommitance in violence. Violence will breed civil war. Such a state of affairs will not only jeopardise the future of India, but of the Hindu community itself. It is inconceivable that any one community in India could gain independence for itself and it is equally inconceivable that independence so gained could be retained for any length of time. If the Hindus and Muslims are ranged in opposite camps, they will exploit the weakness of each.

"Wisdom demads that the communities should adopt a policy which will heal the wounds within and obliterate the differences without. Considerations of principle and expediency equally require that the communities should follow the policy of harmony and reconciliation in order that the happiness and prosperity of the country may be established on sure foundations. If by sacrificing the present we gain the future, the bargain is wholly advantageous, for the present is transitory and the future extends far into infinity.

Continuing, the speaker said that it must be clearly realised that the Hindu-Muslim problem was not merely an economic or a political problem but a cultural problem. Policies had divided the two communities but the political differences are superficial. If they desired therefore, to build up a sovereign Indian state which would stand four square to the winds blowing from all quarters, they must not seek to establish it on the basis of political compromise merely. Political parts and understandings were useful and necessary, but the guarantee of their permanence was in the mutual confidence of the communities. Confidence could only be generated when there was mutual respect and genuine appreciation of the deals'. which the groups entertain and hold dear.

Mr. Shareef said, "For one hundred years and more we have been engaged in the suicidal task of building up exclusive organisations of Hindus and Muslims. We had sought to shut our hearts upon one another in the vain hope that exclusiveness will bring us strength. In our cultural movements we have endeavoured not reconciliation but revivalism. The writers of Marati, Bengali and Hindi have considered it part of their duty to eliminate from them words of Islamic origin. On the other side writers of Urdu have sought to fill it with Arabic and Persian expressions. Our historians have extolled the Hindu period or the Muslim period and have slurred over the common achievements of both. Our artists seek to draw inspiration from pre-Muslim monuments or from Persian models and our poets sing of the glories associated with the kingdoms of a remote time or with kingdoms equally remote in space. If India is to be built up on foundations which would last for a long time, then this process must be reversed. We must retrace our steps which, in fact, lead us along a path contrary to the genius of our race. If there is one characteristic of our history which distinguishes us from other peoples, it is the remarkable power of absorption and assimilation which we have displayed. But the task which has fallen upon our shoulders to-day is not merely to continue the work which Akbar had begun, but to complete it in the condition—economic, moral and intellectual—which the modern world has created.

"But the situation though full of difficulties is certainly not hopeless. Never before was India so closely united so far as physical and material aspects of life were concerned as it is to-day. We owe this to the discoveries and inventions of science. The Hindus and Muslims study the same branches of knowledge and learn the same methods of pursuing the truth. Powerful forces, the pressure of world-wide tendencies, of international affairs, of new menaces are shaking peoples' minds up. Congress admittedly is the largest and the best organised political organisation in the country. Its unique and well-established and acknowledged position demands that it should be alert and watchful of the rights and privileges of all men and women of all denominations and schools of thought and should leave no stone unturned to secure the confidence of all. Very grave charges have been levelled against some of the Congress Ministries. The C. P. Ministry is the most blessed of all and the Congress High Command should enquire into all the charges and if established, suitable action should be taken against the Ministries concerned. This would allay all the fears or else Congress would lose more ground, and the hope of an united India would for ever be wrecked."

Concluding, Mr. Shareef said that "the scheme to divide India into artificial states, Hindu and Muslim, would neither serve the community for which it has avowedly been conceived nor would it serve the country. The essential need is an united action among the political organisations and leaders at this supreme crisis in the affairs of the country. Many of us who have preceded us in this national struggle have been gathered to God, while some of us who are still in the field belong to fast vanishing generation. My last appeal is, therefore, addressed to younger men whom I see before me and who are taking interest in the country's struggle for freedom and emancipation to carry on the fight till our full independence is assured. Difficult as your task is, do not despair, for despair is the key-note of failure. The pendulum may be swinging forward and backward, but the invisible hand is perpetually marking its progress on the dial of destiny of our motherland. There is no royal road to freedom. Reverses there must be, but reverses should all the more stiffen your back and stimulate you into further action. I appeal to you, therefore, to carry on the national fight for the evolutionary progress of our mother country and for the attainment of our freedom till the goal is reached."

Resolutions—2nd Day—Kumbakonam—9th June 1941

Pakistan Scheme Condemned

A number of resolutions was passed by the Conference at the resumed sitting on the next day, the 9th. June, Mr. *M. Y. Shareef* presiding.

The main resolution, which was unanimously carried, stated : "It is the considered view of Mussalmans from all parts of South India assembled at the Conference that the two-nation scheme of Pakistan, envisaged in the resolution of the Muslim League, would not only not serve the interests of the Muslim community in India for which purpose it is avowedly declared, but would also be definitely detrimental to its growth, expansion and solidarity and would further result in disintegration of the whole country which has all along been geographically and politically an integral unit and has been treated as such, and that it would eventually lead to internal strife, thereby exposing the country to foreign exploitation."

The Conference, by a second resolution, strongly condemned all attempts, by whomsoever made, to vivisect India on any grounds such as ethical, religious etc.

The third resolution disputed the claim of the Muslim League to represent the Muslim community as a whole. It stated: "This Conference is emphatically of opinion that the claims of the All-India Muslim League to represent the entire Muslim community of India are not justified as a major section of the Muslim community has never subscribed to the policy of the All India Muslim League."

The Conference also declared by another resolution that "it is strongly opposed to all constitutional schemes for the future governance of India that are not based on the fact that India is an indivisible nation."

Moved from the chair a resolution was passed appealing to the Congress High Command to set up a court of inquiry to enquire into all charges that have been made against Congress Ministers in different provinces and if the same or any of them are found established to take suitable action against the Ministers or the Ministry found guilty in order to rehabiliate the confidence of the different communities, interests and schools of thought in the representative character of the Congress.

Another resolution moved from the chair expressed the emphatic opinion that the Vidya Mandir Scheme of primary education adopted by the Congress Ministry in the Central Provinces, having provoked a controversy, should be repealed. It also appealed to the Congress that with a view to realising inter-communal unity, it should guarantee continuance of Urdu and Hindi and other provincial languages. It further expressed the view that to settle questions of national song and national flag, the Congress High Command should invite representatives of different communities and schools of thought to evolve an agreed formula in this behalf.

The Conference urged the need for a separate organisation and resolved that "in order to restore unity amongst Muslims in the country, it is absolutely necessary that all Muslim organisations claiming to serve the interests of Mussalmans do establish an All-India Muslim Executive Board with plenary powers to control and guide the policy and working of different organisations and to negotiate with other organisations like the Congress regarding all matters concerning them." This resolution was also moved from the chair.

Moved from the chair a resolution was passed by the Conference condemning the inter-communal troubles and ruptures which have occurred in different places in the country and sympathising with the innocent sufferers and their dependents. It appealed to the Indian States to treat inter-communal questions as one of primary consideration and to take all necessary measures to restore inter-communal unity and homogeneity with their States, by meting out just and equitable treatment to all communities.

The Anti-Communal Conference

Presidential Address—Lahore—9th. March 1941

A plea that there could never be real Hindu-Muslim unity unless they tried to understand each other's religion and culture was made by *Khan Abdul Gaffar Khan*, addressing the Anti-Communal Conference held on the 9th. March 1941 in the Baradlaugh Hall, Lahore which was packed to its utmost capacity.

Khan Abdul Ghaffar Khan said that for a long time he had been hearing the slogan of "Hindu-Muslim Ki jai" but he regretted to observe that the communal differences, far from being resolved, had been accentuated. The gulf which existed in 1919, instead of being bridged, had been widened. No unity could be achieved until the thorn and obstacles in the path of unity had been removed. He regretted that Hindus and Muslims were not trying to understand each other's religion and culture. Unless they did so the problem would remain unsolved. The mere passing of lengthy resolutions and making of speeches would not lead them to their goal of communal unity.

Referring to the Red Shirt Movement, Khan Abdul Gaffar Khan pointed out that it was a social movement organised for the purpose of serving humanity irrespective of caste or creed. He traced the history of the movement and said that when the Government attempted to crush them they approached the Muslim League for assistance but the latter declined to help them. Ultimately they had to seek the aid of the Congress which had been given on the condition that the Red Shirts should join the Congress. He said that he was preparing a movement in the Frontier which would free the country from the chains of slavery.

The President attributed the raids and kidnappings in the Frontier to political reasons and recalled how Government had refused to permit him to visit the tribal territory to help in the solution of the problem. In conclusion, Khan Abdul Gaffar Khan pointed out that it was essential to extend Congress activities to the villages, for therein lay their salvation.

Diwan Chamanlal, M. L. A., Chairman of the Reception Committee, in welcoming Khan Abdul Gaffar Khan, said that the Conference had been primarily called to confirm, establish and evoke the sense of national unity among the different classes that inhabited this Province. He dwelt at great length on the communal problem, and pointed out that the formation of separate electorates had undoubtedly been a psychological as well as a political factor in creating separatist propaganda in favour of dividing the two communities. The remarkable electoral successes achieved by the Congress throughout India, he added, had thrown the communalists into a state of frenzy and despair, with the result that the battle ground had been shifted to suit the changing scene.

Referring to the Pakistan Scheme, Diwan Chamanlal described it as absurd and observed it was untrue to say that the Hindus and Muslims were separate nations. "Most of the Muslim population", he said, "is convert from Hinduism. Even the names of many of them are common. Mr. Jinnah's own community, the Khojas, are such converts and possess common names with the Hindus.

Continuing, Diwan Chamanlal said, "Are we in the Punjab to be told that we, Hindus and Muslims, differ in culture and dress and speech ? You may write down for Census and communal purposes that your language is Urdu or Hindi but each one of you speaks Punjabi—your and my mother-tongue. Our mothers and grandmothers knew no other language. They wore and continue to wear the same dress, live in similar style, eat practically the same food. Are we to be divided from one another in order to preserve the dignity, prestige and position of communal leaders ? The masses do not appreciate or understand such cries which pass over their heads. Their concern is with the economic struggle which is common to the masses of all communities. There is no communalism in starvation."

In conclusion the speaker observed, "A new world must dawn for us all out of the blood bath of human suffering—a new world of common endeavour, of brotherhood, of peace and of prosperity in which the supporters of communalism will vanish like the morning mist".

Resolutions

The Conference passed a resolution condemning the Pakisthan scheme which in its view, was "highly unpatriotic, anti-national and against the best interests of the country."

The Conference expressed the opinion that such schemes were serious obstacles in the path of freedom and called upon every true-minded Indian to spare no pains to explain the harmful effects of such schemes. The Conference condemned the activities of all the communal organisations and censured all such speeches, writings and acts which created inter-communal hatred and enmity and appealed to all rightminded citizens of India in general and of the Punjab in particular to resist with all their might all such activities which were communal, anti-national, unpatriotic and against the real interests of the country.

By another resolution the Conference expressed the opinion that, while the minorities should be assured of full protection of their religion and culture, there should be no communal representation in the legislature and the Services. There should be no reservation of seats on a communal basis nor should there be separate electorates. The Conference recorded its protest against the attitude of the Secretary of State for India in placing the communal issue in the forefront.

Finally, the Conference appreciated the patriotic acts and deeds of Pathans of the N. W. F. P. who had, by their sufferings and sacrifices, enhanced the prestige of the country.

The Non-Party Leaders' Conference

Opening Day—Bombay—14th. March 1941

PRESIDENTIAL ADDRESS

An earnest appeal to the Government of India to take the initiative in getting together leaders of the Congress and the Muslim League in an effort to resolve the present deadlock and if that attempt failed, mobilise the large mass of unattached opinion in the country, was made at Bombay on the **14th. March 1941** by the *Rt. Hon. Sir Tej Bahadur Sapru*, opening the conference of Non-Party Leaders.

Stressing the importance of the Conference at this juncture, *Sir Tej Bahadur* said that it was under a compelling sense of duty that he had agreed to attend it.

Those who were present at the Conference were entitled to have their own views in regard to the political situation. It was no use anybody challenging their capacity or their solution. It was enough for them that as men interested in the politics and future of the country and as men who had been watching the trend of events during the twelve months or more, they were making an earnest effort to bring about a solution of the present deadlock at this critical juncture.

This Conference, Sir Tej said, was a conference of men who were approaching the Indian question as it had tended to become not from the point of view of any particular party but from the point of view of the whole country. There were some at the Conference who were identified with strong party organisation; there were others who were not identified with any party organisation. But he had reasons to believe that even men who were identified with strong party organisations, realising the supreme importance of the occasion, had put in the background their party views and had brought themselves into line with the general feeling that everything should be done in the interests of the country which may tend to ease the situation (cheers).

Proceeding to examine the position in the country, Sir *Tej Bahadur* remarked that out of the eleven provinces, seven were at present being administered by Governors with the help of official advisers. He did not wish to shut his eyes to the realities of the situation. The situation in the provinces arose in November, 1939, because the Congress Ministries in seven provinces decided to tender their resignations. It was not, Sir T. B. Sapru said, his intention to attack any political party any more than to defend any political party, but he could not help feeling that it was a very shortsighted decision for the Congress to call out the Ministers. If the Ministers had been in their place to day, much of the trouble that had arisen in the provinces would not have arisen.

Similarly, *Sir Tej Bahadur* continued, the situation had been aggravated during recent months by the starting of the satyagraha movement. He did not want to hide the fact from any one that he was a confirmed unbeliever in that movement. He had not concealed it even from the great originator of the movement, Mahatma Gandhi. But whatever might be the convictions of Mahatma Gandhi on this point, he was fully prepared to grant that they were as deep as they were sincere. It was unfortunate that at a juncture like the present, the movement should have started and should have given rise to a great misapprehension as regards the Indian attitude towards the war.

Referring next to the war, Sir *Tej Bahadur* said that there was no one present there who did not realise the gravity of the international situation. They were beginning to realise that the war was coming nearer and nearer to the shores of India. He said that he had always maintained that the fruition of their aims and aspirations depended upon the success of England. Although he knew that in the bitterness of their hearts, some people compared Fascism and Nazism with British imperialism, yet upon reflection they would find that there was a world of difference between the two. But he did not want to enter into a theoretical discussion. From a practical point of view and from the point of view of the country, it was very necessary that Britain should come out successfully from this gigantic war effort (cheers).

Sir *Tej Bahadur* pointed out that the country had been helping in the war effort if they were to believe all those broadcasts and statements issued by the Government of India, and that was about all the Government of India told them.

Money was forthcoming in abundance from the different parts of the country and there had been no trouble about recruitment. Still many believed that there was a great deal more which might be done with the willing co-operation of educated Indians. It was with a view to helping in the successful prosecution of the war that they had assembled, to take stock of the situation and to make suggestions as to how that end might be achieved.

"Frankly speaking", he said, "I maintain and maintain very strongly that there has never been a Government of India more isolated from public opinion and from the main current of thought in the country than the present Government of India. The members of the Government of India should appear before the public, take the public into confidence and they must not assume that the Indian Legislatures, respectable bodies as they are, or one or two important political bodies constitute the whole of India. I should like to see members of the Government of India appearing on the public platform and telling us what they all knew."

Sir *Tej Bahadur*, proceeding, said that on August 8, the Viceroy had made an offer and that the Congress and the Muslim League had turned it down. Whether the reasons for the refusal were just or unjust, wise or unwise, was a mater of the past. What he would like to know was what had been done since. They had been told time after time that there were unfortunate differences existing between the two organised bodies, the Congress and the Muslim League. The natural inference to these two organised bodies and the quarrels existing between them was that unless those differences were composed, they need not expect any advance. That was an unfortunate position.

Appealing to the leaders of the Congress and the Muslim League to compose their differences, Sir T. B. Sapru said :—"No one will be more pleased than myself, and I can speak on behalf of every one here if these organised bodies compose their differences even at his stage. In your names and of behalf of those interested in true progress, I make an earnest appeal to leaders of these two organisations to review the situation, to see facts as they are, to indulge less in theoretical discussions and then grapple with the realities of the situation and to come to some settlement.

"I believe we have already exposed ourselves to a great deal of ridicule in this country and outside for our inability to compose our differences even at this critical juncture. It is, therefore, that I make an earnest appeal to these two bodies and their distinguished leaders, to meet, to discuss things among themselves and devise some formula for a settlement of the outstanding disputes, because it is imperative that some day or other these disputes should be settled. If it seems necessary for either of these two bodies or to both of them to requisition the services of any one of us as common friends, I am sure none of us will stint our services."

But if those bodies were not prepared to compose their differences, then the Conference should be prepared for some alternative, Sir Tej suggested. If the two bodies did not compose their differences, then surely it did not lie in the mouth of the British Government to say that because those two organisations could not compose their differences the rest of the country should be penalised and must wait until it pleased the leaders of those parties to be sensible and to be in mood to compose their differences. That to his mind was an intoterable situation. It was not enough for the British Government repeatedly to refer to the existence of unfortunate differences. It was also necessary for the Government to say that they had done their best and that they were ready to do their best to bring about a reconciliation between the two bodies. In that respect the British Government have done practically nothing. It was not enough for the Viceroy to call men to see them individually or in groups.

Text of the Resolution

Sir *N. N. Sircar* then moved the following resolution :—

"While India should not take advantage of Britain's difficulties in her heroic struggle, the Conference is equally desirous that India's domestic problems should not be pressed to her disadvantage. As a first step towards the removal of the present deadlock and until a permanent constitution is brought into force, the Conference desires to emphasize the immediate need for the reconstruction of the Governor-General's Executive Council.

"The conference considers that the present Council, which consists of three European members for the Indian Civil Service, and three Indians of whom two are non-officials and one is a member of the Indian Civil Service, in addition to His Excellency the Viceroy and His Excellency the Commander-in-Chief, is neither adequate nor sufficiently representative to organize and direct India's war efforts at this moment of grave peril. This Conference is anxious that India's defences should be put on a firm basis and that resources of this great country in men and material should be used to the fullest advantage not only for defending her own frontiers but for helping the British people to the fullest extent possible consistently with the best interests of India.

"For the reasons mentioned above, this Conference is of the opinion that the whole Executive Council should consist of non-official Indians drawn from important elements in the public life of the country. This would naturally involve the transfer of all portfolios, including the vital ones of Finance and Defence, to Indians.

"The Conference would be content during the period of the war that the reconstructed centre remains responsible to the Crown: and so far as Defence is concerned, the position of the Commander-in-Chief as the Executive head of the defence forces of the country should not be in any way prejudiced. At the same time the Conference is strongly of the view that the reconstructed Government should not merely be a collection of departmental heads, but should deal with all important matters of policy on a basis of joint and collective responsibility. In regard to all inter-imperial and international matters, the reconstructed Government should be treated on the same footing as the Dominion Governments.

"The Conference is further of the opinion that with a view to create a favourable atmosphere for the working of the reconstructed Central Government, it is necessary to remove the doubts and misgivings of the people of this country as regards the genuineness of the intentions of His Majesty's Government by making a declaration simultaneously with the reconstruction of the Government that within a specified time limit after the conclusion of the war India will enjoy the same measure of freedom as will be enjoyed by Britain and the Dominions.

"The Conference authorises its President, the Rt. Hon. Sir *Tej Bahadur Sapru*, to communicate the terms of the resolution to His Excellency the Viceroy and the Secretary of State for India and to take such other steps as may be necessary to achieve its objects."

Moving the resolution, Sir *N. N. Sircar* referred to the different criticisms that had been levelled at the Conference meeting in Bombay, some calling them pessimists. There were also among them some who were pointing out that the deadlock was not of their making and, therefore, there was no reason why they should take the trouble to try for a solution.

Sir *Nripendra Nath* said that repeated statements had been made during the war and was repeated for the last time on February 24 by Mr. Amery that some constitutional advance would be granted to India but up-to-date nothing had been done. The policy of drift had continued and the desire to do something was reiterated without doing anything whatsoever, and this had created the present deadlock between India and Great Britain.

Sir *Nripendra Nath* pointed out the great change in policy that had occurred in the attitude of His Majesty's Government to the question of Indian constitutional advance. He recalled that in the past, British Government spokesmen had declared that constitutional progress would not be held up even if no agreement could be found on the communal question and a scheme would be applied by the British Government. But now, after the war had broken out, he regretted that the British Government were now insisting on a settlement of the communal differences and the differences between the various parties before any constitutional advance was made. While he regretted and was ashamed of their inability to settle their own differences, he pleaded that this inability should not be held up as a bar to the grant of further constitutional advance.

Sir *N. N. Sircar* was sorry to note that the British people who were showing great courage, tenacity and resoursefulness on the field of the battle were afraid to evince the same courage and singlemindedness to the Indian constitutional question. He compared the present unhelpful attitude of the British Government to one who offered three million pounds to one pound of "hot ice"

Strongly refuting the condition that internal differences should be composed before any constitutional progress was made, Sir N. N. Sircar asked, "Is there any important provision in the Government of India Act, 1935, which is the result of agreement between parties ? What about the joint and separate electorate issues, and federation and so on ? In spite of vital differences, was not the Government of India Act enacted ? If His Majesty's Government had insisted on substantial agreement between the parties on the material questions involved, there would have been no Government of India Act at all."

the Council of the All-India Muslim League adopt the resolution stating that they "have no doubt as to the real motive and object of Mr. Gandhi, in launching and pursuing vigorously his movement of *satyagraha* and draw the attention of the British Government that if any concession to the Congress is made which adversely affects or militates against the Muslim demands, it will be resisted by Muslim League with all the power it can command and the Muslim League desires to place it on record that if the situation demands it would not hesitate to intervene and play such part in the struggle as may be necessary for the protection of the rights and interests of the Mussalmans of this country.

Evidently what Mr. Gandhi wanted was not the freedom of speech but the acceptance of the Congress demands. And what were all these demands ? Adult Franchise, Constituent Assembly and National Government. If all that was wanted was freedom of speech, then why were all these counter demands simultaneously made. It was nothing but blowing hot and cold in the same breath. Mr. Gandhi knew that if he had started his civil disobedience movement on any other plea except that of freedom of speech, he would have been immediately told that nothing could be done as the Hindus and Mussalmans are not united and there is no agreed demand and that Congress would have been considered to be acting very unwisely by countries like America. The demand for freedom of speech was an eyewash. The Congress started the Satyagraha movement to coerce the British to accept their demands irrespective of any agreement with Muslim India.

The Working Committee in a resolution passed on the 22nd February, 1941 fixed 23rd March of every year to be observed for explaining the principles of the Lahore resolution popularly known as the Pakistan Resolution. Another resolution for holding a Muslim League week every three months by the Provincial and District Leagues was passed for the purpose of explaining to the people throughout India the policy and programme of the All-India Muslim League and for making a drive to enrol more members of the League and to take up the following constructive programme for the uplift of the Mussalmans economically, socially and educationally.

(i) That the cottage industries should be promoted and encouraged and stores should be established at central places on co-operative basis.

(ii) That the Muslims should use Garha made by Mussalmans on all occasions of festivity and mourning, so that the due impetus may be given to the Garha manufacture.

(iii) That Night Schools should be opened in order to spread Adult Education.

(iv) That Un-Islamic ceremonies should be given up and discouraged.

(v) That no loans on interest be taken for marriage and funeral ceremonies.

(vi) That the use of Intoxicants and Gambling should be checked.

(vii) That the true spirit of brotherhood, based on the Islamic conception of equality and fraternity should be infused among those Muslims, who have adopted the Un-Islamic view of caste, based on profession, and occupation.

(viii) That Panchayats should be established, in order to settle ordinary disputes so that people may not suffer unnecessary monetary loss by going to law-courts.

(ix) That Muslims should be persuaded to take to Commerce and Industries.

(x) That full interest should be taken in all the schemes of rural uplift and progress.

In the first week of April 1941, the Bombay Provincial Muslim League held its session under the presidentship of *Nawabzada Liaquat Ali Khan*, Honorary Secretary of the All-India Muslim League. In his address which he delivered at this session, Nawabzada Liaquat Ali Khan Saheb dealt with the various aspects of the political activities of the All India Muslim League, with particular reference to the various methods adopted by the Congress and the Hindu Mahasabha and explained in detail the importance of the Lahore resolution popularly known as the Pakistan resolution. He expressed the belief that there was no other solution except that of Pakistan which alone solved the difficulties of both Hindus and Mussalmans and that was the only way by which both Hindu and Muslim nations secured for themselves an honoured place in the life of this country.

At the historic session of the All India Muslim League held at Madras in the 2nd week of April 1941, Mr. *M. A. Jinnah* set at rest all doubts that existed in the minds of the Hindus regarding the Pakistan scheme. He made it quite clear to them that the Mussalmans of India were determined to fight for Pakistan and achieve it at any cost and told his fellow countrymen that the Mussalmans shall never agree to anything less than Pakistan.

Following are the words in which Mr. Jinnah reiterated the demand for Pakistan at the Madras session. "We want to establish a completely independent State in the North-West and Eastern zones of India, with full control of finance, defence, foreign affairs, communications, customs. currency, exchange etc. We do not want under any circumstances, constitution of All-India character, with one Government at the centre." He further explained that the Mussalmans will never be a feudatory of any power or of any Government at the centre so far as their national home was concerned. "Democracy", he said, "means a majority rule but a majority rule in a single nation and in a single society is understandable. Representative Government in a single nation, harmonious and homogeneous, is understandable. Can such a system ever work or succeed when you have two different nations, and more than two nations in the sub-continent, when you have totally two different societies, Muslims and Hindus......particularly in this land of ours there is another nation, Dravidistan. Three percent of the high castes (Brahmins) by skillful manoeuvring and by skillful methods of electioneering have secured a majority rule. Is this democracy ?"

He explained that the ideology of the League is based on the fundamental principle that the Muslims of India are an independent nationality, and any attempt to get them to merge or give up their national and political identity and ideology in that of others will not only be resisted, but will be futile for any one to attempt as they were determined to establish the status of an independent nation and an independent state in the sub-continent.

Mr. Jinnah in his memorable and historic address at the Madras session made a passing reference to Babu Rajindra Prasad. What he is reported to have said, with regard to the Pakistan Scheme is all follows :— Babu Rajindra Prasad was asked a few days ago (April 10) about the Pakistan Scheme. He said the Working Committee of the Congress never discussed the scheme as that was never referred to it by Mr. Jinnah. Did they believe that the Congress Working Committee never discussed the scheme ? This ghost (Pakistan) had been haunting them since 1940.

"What standard of truth was that ? Congress leaders had discussed, issued statements and written volumes about Pakistan. Babu Rajindra Prasad had issued a pamphlet with regard to the Pakistan Scheme. He would tell Babu Rajindra Prasad, to ask his Working Committee to discuss it, if they have not already done so, apply his mind to it honestly and without prejudice. If there is any political wisdom or statesmanship still left in the Congress leadership."

As regards the Hindu Mahasabha, Mr. M. A. Jinnah made the following remarks in the course of his presidential speech at Madras, which are noteworthy :—"So far as the Hindu Mahasabha is concerned, it is an absolutely incorrigible and hopeless organisation. I will give you one specimen of its statesmanship. Mr. Savarker, president of the Hindu Mahasabha, sent a message to the Sikh Conference in Karachi urging them to take their due share in the Defence services of India, and added that when the Muslims woke up from the dreams of Pakistan they should see established Sikhistan instead in the Punjab. Mr. Savarker not only talks of Hindudom and Hindu Nation and Hindu Raj, but urges the Sikhs to establish Sikhistan. Mr. Savarker is not an ordinary man, he is the president of the Hindu Mahasabha."

Referring to the conference of Non-Party leaders in Bombay, Mr. Jinnah said that the Bombay proposals were nothing less than another name, another movement and second edition of the Poona proposal for a National Government. "If you read the memorandum, there can be no doubt left that Sir T. B. Sapru is entirely on the wrong line and I am sorry that he has been caught in the trap by the wire-pullers of other organisations behind this movement.

Mr. Jinnah said that "this vicious propaganda" which was being pursued and the way in which they were "harassed" was not confined only to the Press and the public in this country, but to his amazement and astonishment he found that "even the British Press was being misled." This was that the *Times*, London, one of the best informed papers, wrote on April 1. "It is fools' day", Mr. Jinnah commented amidst laughter and the *Times* "has been fooled." "While these proposal have," wrote the *Times* said Mr. Jinnah, "encountered much opposition in various quarters it is significant that the most general Press comment on them is that they offer a fresh opportunity for re-examining the political situation. Mr. Jinnah's recent statement in the Central Assembly that the Muslim League would co-operate in a reconstituted Executive, provided his scheme for partitioning British India is considered after the war, may make it easier for the two chief Indian parties to reach some temporary understanding." Mr. Jinnah remarked that this was a feeler regarding a change of attitude on his part and he could only say to "the doyen of the British Press" that his was "ingratitude stronger than any traitor's arms."

Returning to the point as to why they did not demand "Pakistan here and now", Mr. Jinnah said that it was due to one and only reason, namely, we did not wish to embarrass a British Government when they are engaged in this struggle of life and death and their own existence. That is why we said that so soon as the circumstances may permit or soon after the war, the whole problem of India's constitution must be examined de novo. Instead of the British Government acknowledging this as an honourable attitude on our part, worthy of their gratitude, I find that even the British Press is playing into the hands of the Congress and Hindu propaganda. I do not know who is responsible for this, whether it is Lord Linlithgow, or whether it is Mr. Amery, the Secretary of State for India, or whether it is His Majesty's Government. But let me once more emphasise from this platform that the policy of the British Government in India, of inaction, of weakness, and of vacillation, is going to prove more disastrous than it is even in Europe. Cannot these men see that events are moving so fast and that maps are being changed ? Look at what is happening in Europe. Look at what the Axis powers are doing—placating and placating, vacillation, weakness, inaction."

In this connection, Mr, Jinnah referred to the march of events in Yugoslavia and said that following the German capture of Zagreb, the Yugoslav Province of Croatia had been proclaimed an independent State', according to the German News Agency, and a Croat general had called on all officials, army officers and non-commissioned officers to take the oath of allegiance to the "New State." They should remember, Mr. Jinnah said, that in Yugoslavia, there were the Croats, the Slovenes and the Serbs. Their position was very much like ours in India, "Dravidastans and the Dravidians, Pakistan and the Muslims and Hindustan and the Hindus. Here is a mighty sub-continent, and the question really is, are you going to wait and allow somebody else to come here and do the job for you or are you going to do it yourself."

One of the most important features of the Madras session, apart from the memorable speech of Mr. Jinnah, was an amendment of the League constitution in the Article defining the creed of the League so as to embody the goal of Pakistan. It is essential to mention here this important amendment to the constitution of the League.

(i) "The establishment of completely Independent States formed by demarcating geographically contiguous units into regions which shall be so constituted, with territorial readjustments as may be necessary, that the areas in which the Mussalmans are numerically in a majority, as in the North Western zones of India, shall be grouped together to constitute Independent States as Muslim Free National Homelands in which the constituent units shall be autonomous and sovereign ;

(ii) That adequate, effective and mandatory safeguards shall be specifically provided in the constitution for minorities in the above mentioned units and regions for the protection of their religious, cultural, economic, political, administrative and other rights and interests in consultation with them ;

(iii) That in other parts of India where the Mussalmans are in a minority, adequate, effective, and mandatory safeguards shall be specifically provided in the constitution for them and other minorities for the protection of their religious, cultural, economic, political, administrative and other rights and interests in consultation with them :

Later political develoments consequent on the expansion of the Viceroy's Executive Council and the constitution of the so-called National Defence Council are too well-known to need enumeration. The All India Muslim League considered the changes as against the policy adopted by the League organisation. Mr. M. A. Jinnah in his interview with the Viceroy at Bombay, had clarified the position of the All India Muslim League vis-a-vis the Government in the matter and lodged his protest against the inclusion of Muslim League members in the Viceroy's Executive Council and the so-called National Defence Council.

The meeting of the Working Committee of the All India Muslim League was held on the 24th, 25th, and 26th of August 1941, at Bombay under the Presidentship of Mr. M. A. Jinnah to consider the cases of those who had joined these Councils without reference to the president or the Working Committee. Mr. Jinnah acquainted the Committee with his conversation he had with the Viceroy on the constitution of the National Defence Council and the expansion of the Executive Council.

Mr. Jinnah criticized the Government and the members of the Muslim League including the three premiers of Bengal, the Punjab and Assam, who had joined the National Defence Council. The Committee considered the position and passed resolutions calling upon Sir Sikander Hyat Khan, Sir Mohd. Saadulla and Mr. Fazlul Huq, premiers of the Punjab, Assam and Bengal respectively to resign from the National Defence Council. The resolution also announced that since Sir Sikander Hyat Khan and Sir Mohd. Saadulla had already expressed their willingness to resign, the question of taking any action against them did not arise.

Mr. Fazlul Huq had been given time to resign from the National Defence Council and Mr. Jinnah had been authorised by the Committee to deal with him in case he failed to resign. Along with these matters the Committee also considered the situation in Iran and passed resolutions dealing with the military occupation of certain Muslim States in the near east by Great Britain and her allies and also regarding the un-provoked aggression against Iran by Great Britain and Russia, contrary to the declarations of the British Government.

Following are the resolutions :—

Resolution No. 6.

"The Musalmans of India are greatly perturbed at, and view with alarm the military occupation of certain Muslim States in the Near East by Great Britain and her allies. The Working Committee of the All India Muslim League, therefore, urge upon the British Government and her allies to declare unequivocally that the sovereignty and independence of those Muslim States will be immediately restored as soon as circumstances permit and that the pernicious system of mandates and the creation of zones of influence for European powers over these countries will not be resorted to."

Resolution No. 7.

"The Working Committee have learnt with dismay the news of the unprovoked aggression against Iran by Great Britain and Russia, contrary to all the declarations of the British Government to respect the neutrality and sovereignty of non-combatant states to uphold which the British Government and her allies are fighting Nazism, and in violation of the fundamental principles of International Law : and warn the Government that this action of the allies will still more complicate the Near East situation and alienate the sympathies of Muslim India and create bitterness in their hearts, which will result in the withdrawal of every help by them to the allied cause."

The Committee also passed a resolution deploring the action of His Excellency the Viceroy in having gone out of his way to canvass the Muslim League members for securing their association with the scheme of expansion. In another resolution the Committee expressed their amazement and alarm at the pronouncements made by Mr. Amery which amounted to a breach of faith to Muslim India.

Resolution No. 8.

"The Working Committee of the All India Muslim League deplore that His Excellency the Viceroy should have gone out of his way to canvass the members of the Muslim League for securing their association with the scheme of expansion of the Executive Council and the constitution of the so-called National Defence Council within the terms of the offer of the 8th of August 1940, behind the back of the leader of the organisation, knowing full well the express decision of the Council of the League rejecting a scheme on similar lines by its resolution dated the 29th of September 1940, which was duly communicated to him by the President.

Further the Committee condemn the observations of Mr. Amery, the Secretary of State for India, made in the House of Commons in his speech on the 1st of August 1941, to the effect that he was glad "to think that regardless of party leaders and in defiance of party discipline, patriotic Indians have come forward to work for India's defence," thereby casting a serious reflection on the patriotism of those who have been deliberately and by various manœuvres wanted to commit a breach of party discipline.

The Working Committee are of the considered opinion that the recent decision to resuscitate and impose upon India, the scheme of expansion of the Viceroy's Executive Council and the setting up of a National Defence Council was undertaken as a concession to the demands of the Hindus in utter disregard of the wishes of the Muslims of India and the solemn promises made to them and is intended to mislead public opinion in Great Britain and abroad.

Resolution No. 9.

The Working Committee of the All India Muslim League are amazed and alarmed that Mr. Amery, the Secretary of State for India and a responsible minister of the Crown should be permitted to make pronouncements which amount to a breach of faith to Muslim India and to resile from the declared policy of the British Government. viz ; that the constitutional issue will in no way be prejudged by His Majesty's Government and that the solution of the constitutional issue will be dependent upon agreement between the principal parties, as the following extracts form his speeches and the announcement of the Viceroy dated the 8th of August 1940 clearly disclose :—

(1) VICEROY'S ANNOUNCEMENT DATED THE 8TH OF AUGUST 1940

"There are two main points which have emerged. On these two points His Majesty's Government now desire me to make their position clear.

"The first is as to the position of Minorities, in relation to any future constitutional scheme. It has already been made clear that my declaration of last October does not exclude the examination of any part, either of the Act of 1935, or of the policy and plans on which it is based.

"His Majesty's Government concern, that full weight should be given to the views of the minorities in any revision, has also been brought out. That remains the position of His Majesty's Government. It goes without saying that they could not contemplate the transfer of their present responsibilities for the peace and welfare of India to any system of Government whose authority is directly denied by large and powerful elements in India's national life.

"Nor could they be parties to the coercion of such elements into submission to such a Government.

"The second point of general interest is the machinery for building within the British Commonwealth of Nations, a new constitutional scheme, when the time comes. There has been very strong insistence that the framing of that scheme should be primarily the responsibility of Indians themselves, and should originate from Indian conceptions of the social, economic and political structure of Indian life.

"His Majesty's Government are in sympathy with that desire, and wish to see it given the fullest practical expression, subject to the due fulfilment of the obligations, which Great Britain's long connection with India has imposed upon her, and for which His Majesty's Government cannot divest themselves of the responsibility.

'Meanwhile they will welcome and promote, in any way possible, every sincere and practical step that may be taken, by representative Indians themselves, to reach a basis of friendly agreement firstly on the form which the post-war representative body should take, secondly upon the principles and outlines of the constitution itself."

(2) MR. AMERY'S STATEMENT DATED THE 14TH OF AUGUST 1940

"Agreement, consent indeed the foundation of all free Governments, of all true democracy. Decision by a majority is not so much of the essence of Democracy as a practical convenience which presupposes for its proper working an antecedent general consent to the constitution itself. It has indeed in most federal constitutions been limited in various ways in order to safeguard the separate interests of the federating elements. To describe the need for such agreement as a veto on constitutional progress is, I think, to do an injustice to the patriotism and sense of responsibility of those concerned. Agreement means not veto by any element but compromise, and willingness to compromise, in India as elsewhere, is an essential test of the sense of responsibility on which free government must be based."

MR. AMERY'S STATEMENT DATED THE 22ND OF APRIL 1941

"It was suggested that the framework of India's future constitution should be devised by Indians themselves and not by this House. That was a far-reaching and indeed revolutionary announcement, the full importance of which has not, I think, even yet been fully appreciated either in this country or in India.

"Even more important in this connection is the stipulation that the constitution itself, and also the body which is to frame it, must be the outcome of agreement between the principal elements in India's national life. That is an essential prerequisite to the success of the future constitution. For if Indians cannot agree upon the kind of constitution they are prepared to work, how are they likely to agree upon the actual working of it ?

"I have dwelt deliberately upon Indian responsibility in the matter ; for unless Indians are prepared to face that responsibility now, they will fail to face it hereafter. Any agreement imposed by us from without cannot survive the withdrawal of our power to enforce it. Only a real agreement, freely reached, can stand that test."

The Working Committee strongly condemn the adverse criticism and remarks of Mr. Amery in his recent speech in the House of Commons with regard to the Lahore resolution of the All India Muslim League, popularly known as the Pakistan resolution, without examining the scheme embodied therein and the circumstances which have driven the Moslems to demand the partition of India into zones predominantly Muslim.

The Working Committee calls upon His Majesty's Government to reassure the Muslims of India that His Majesty's Government will stand by their declarations and pledges solemnly given by the Viceroy and the Secretary of State for India on behalf of His Majesty's Government.

If this assurance, reaffirming the declaration, which has been shaken by the recent ill-advised utterances of the Secretary of State for India, practically prejudging and condemning the Muslim League scheme of partitioning India, is not forthcoming within a reasonable time, the Muslim League will be compelled to revise, of necessity, their policy and adopt such measures as they may deem necessary to resist any departure from the solemn pledges and assurances, and the responsibility for the consequences that may ensue on account of this gross breach of faith will entirely rest on the British Government.

A meeting of the Working Committee and the Council of the All India Muslim League was held again on the 26th and 27th of October 1941 in the Anglo Arabic College Hall Delhi, under the presidentship of Mr. M. A. Jinnah. Several matters were considered, important among them being :—

(1) The withdrawal from the Legislative Assembly Session of November, December 1941 by the Muslim League party in the Legislature.

(2) The allegations contained in Mr. Fazlul Huq's letter of the 8th of September 1941 addressed to the secretary, All India Muslim League.

(3) The entering of the British troops in the kingdom of Iran.

(4) The non-representative character of those who are the members of the Viceroy's Executive Council and the National Defence Council.

The Muslim League party in the Legislature lodged its protest against the present policy of the Government by withdrawal from the December Session of the Legislative Assemly. It is worthwhile quoting here the speech of Mr. Jinnah which he made in the floor of the house before withdrawing from the Assembly. (*See vol. II Assembly Section*)

On the 2nd of November 1941, Mr. Jinnah in his speech which he delivered at the Stratchey Hallat the Muslim University, Aligarh in which he delivered that the Muslim India need not look to the Atlantic Charter for a solution of their political problem and said that they have their own Charter of Pakistan where alone lay the remedy. Some portions of Mr. Jinnah's speech are quoted here :—

"If the British Government do not make it clear as to what their intentions are regarding the Muslim States and also that they have no designs on their sovereignty and independence, I feel that it would be very difficult to control Muslim India any more."

Referring to Mr. Gandhi's recent statement hinting at Civil War, Mr. Jinnah said that if it comes it would come as a result of the Congress policy of repression and domination over Muslim India. "Muslim India is demanding only one fourth of India, leaving the rest to the Hindus, while the Congress wants to have the whole of this vast sub-continent for the Hindus. If therefore India is plunged into Civil War it would only be on account of the Congress, and nobody else," declared Mr. Jinnah.

Giving a survey of the present political situation Mr. Jinnah said that India's politics could be divided into two parts—the present and the future. As for the future he said that the Viceroy on behalf of His Majesty's Government made a declaration on August 8, 1940 which was amplified by Mr. Amery on August 15, 1940 to the effect that no future constitution of India would be framed without the consent and approval of the Major elements in India and that it could only be adopted when there was an agreement between the principal parties in India. So far as the Muslim League was concerned they had declared that their demand had been met in that regard.

With regard to the present, Mr. Jinnah said that the Muslim League was willing as far back as November 1939 to help the British Government in the successful prosecution of the war. We had realised that there was a great danger to India. We considered that it was in our own interest that we should have power to defend our homes and hearths and, therefore, within the framework of the present constitution, we were ready and willing to co-operate with the British Government with authority and power both at the Centre and the provinces. The August declaration of the Viceroy recognized that principle but when that principle came to be translated into action it was completely frustrated. The terms of the offer were such that no self-respecting party could agree to it. The Muslim League, therefore, rejected the offer and the British Govt. slept over it. But in July last it was again revived, and inspite of our disapproval and rejection a reconstituted Executive Council and a newly formed so-called National Defence Council was forced upon us. It is sought to be justified on the ground that the proposal of the Muslim League embodied in the memorandum of July 1940 to the Viceroy was based on the two-nation theory. It is inconceivable where the two-nation theory comes in the reconstruction of the Executive Council within the framework of the present constitution, which, like an emergency national Cabinet, had to be reconstructed, not on the basis of counting of heads but what the heads contain."

Mr. Jinnah then pointed out as to how the British Govt. had tried to wean the members of the Muslim League over and above the League and how the league has been able to save its prestige and honour."

"The British Govt. have now learnt a lesseon." he said, "and I hope that the rest of India will also learn a lesson very soon, that it is futile to create disruption in the ranks of either the Muslim League or Muslim India." The reconstitution of the Central Government was forced upon Muslim India, declared Mr. Jinnah, in total disregard of the attitude of the Muslim League, and as a mark of protest the Muslim League Party withdrew from the Central Legislature which is a perfectly legitimate constitutional method for a party in opposition to adopt.

Referring to the independent and sovereign Muslim States, Mr. Jinnah said: "If the British Government do not make it clear as to what their intentions are regarding Muslim States and also that they have no designs on their sovereignty and independence, I feel that it would be very difficult to control Muslim India any more. Some of the Hindu leaders have been suggesting that Pakistan is more a danger to the British Government than to the Hindus and therefore, the only way to fight this danger is to disrupt the existing independent Muslim States, so that the Hindus could rule over the whole of India easily. I say to them, it is foolish."

Commenting on Mr. Munshi's speech at Lahore as reported in the press, Mr. Jinnah pointed out that Mr. Munshi was out to incite the Sikhs and the Hindus in the Punjab against Pakistan. His allegations were entirely untrue and baseless. "He seems to suggest," continued Mr. Jinnah, "that the non-Muslims in Pakistan will be treated as untouchables. Let me tell Mr. Munshi that untouchability is only known to his philosophy. The Pakistan scheme is based on what Islam has taught us. Islam stands for equality of manhood. It stands for justice and fairplay, nay generosity to non-Muslims who are like brothers to us, and would be the citizens of the state."

Referring to the Atlantic Charter Mr. Jinnah said, "Hindu leaders are complaining that India has been excluded from the Atlantic Charter. They are demanding that a new declaration should be made contrary to what Mr. Churchill has said. What is the use of this declaration or that declaration ? Declarations, most of them, mean nothing. They have no value at all. As for Muslim India, we have forged our own charter and that is Pakistan, and I want to make it clear that Muslim India will make every sacrifice to achieve that goal. Let us now create sanctions behind it. Pakistan is not a mere slogan or a counter for bargaining. It is a political reality and a practical solution for the most complex problem of India's future constitution. We are not going to budge an inch from our demand. We are determined to watch and guard our own interests and we are capable of doing it separately."

Unfurling the Muslim League Flag at the Lucknow Pakistan Conference, held on November 29, 1941, Nawab M. *Ismail Khan* said that it was at Lucknow that the Qaid-i-Azam hoisted the Muslim League flag and added, "Everybody knows what impetus the Muslim League got under this very flag in such a short time."

Nawab Ismail Khan reminded the audience that "it was at Lucknow for the first time, that a democratic constitution for the All-India Muslim League was framed. It was again at Lucknow that the National Guard Movement was organised for the first time with such energy." He hoped it would be soon a mighty movement.

Inaugurating the conference, *Nawabzada Liaqat Ali Khan*, General Secretary of the All-India Muslim League, hailed Pakistan as the Muslim Charter of independence and appealed to the Muslims to rally under the banner of the Muslim League and stand by their demand. The cry for Pakistan, he said, had reached beyond the frontier of India, indeed all corners of the world; it meant that the Muslims in India should break the bonds of slavery and emerge a free people in the new world.

The Nawabzada referred to the ridicule hurled at Pakistan by Congressmen and others and asserted that "even threats of bloodshed and mass murders would not swerve the Muslims from their path." Mr. K. K. Munshi, he stated, had abandoned his faith in non-violence which he had advocated for twenty years.

Mr. Munshi had stated that India had always been a united whole; the only time when India had a semblance of unity was under Moghul rule and British rule and both achieved it by force. Soon after the Pakistan resolution had been passed at Lahore, (the Nawabzada went on) Mr. Gandhi had stated that fifty thousand Muslims assembled at Lahore could not effectively represent the ten crores of Muslims in India. He challenged Mr. Gandhi to find out any method by which it could be proved that the majority of Muslims were not behind the League. He added that Mr. Gandhi should be prepared to join hands with the Muslims in securing their demand for Pakistan if it were found that the majority of Muslims were for it.

The cry had been raised that by dividing India her condition would be reduced to that of present day Europe, a prey to power politics. The Muslims had no other go but to have separate zones, he concluded. He would tell the Hindu leaders that if they thought they could frighten the Muslims, it was absurd ; he would urge them to think over and see for themselves how just and equitable were their demands.

The S. I. Anti-Separation Conference

Presidential Address—Kumbakonam—8th. June 1941

A strong caveat that the Partition Scheme was wrought with grave risks and danger to the future happiness and prosperity of India was entered into by Mr. *Mahomed Yusuff Shareef*, ex-Minister of the Central Provinces, presiding over the South Indian Anti-Separation Conference held at Kumbakonam on the **8th. June 1941.**

"The division of India into Muslim and Hindu States", said the President, "instead of pacifying and strengthening India, will create internal cauldron eternally on the boil, both with passionate recriminations and internecine wars and how long will the independence of such a country last ? No, in the division of India there is no salvation either for the country as a whole or for any community. The more India thinks in terms of separate communities the more will mutual suspicions be accentuated.

"The scheme does not offer any solution whatever for the Muslims living in parts other than the North-West and in North-East of the country. The Hindu-Muslim problem will continue to trouble nearly one-third of the Muslims of this country and if all that is said about the Congress or majority oppression of the Muslims is true the proposed division will all the more intensify the oppression. In other words, the remedy proposed by the two nations scheme would be worse than the disease itself."

Referring to the origin of the scheme for partition of India Mr. Shareef said, "The Muslim League conceived the idea for the first time in 1938, about a year after the working of the Provincial Autonomy in the seven Congress provinces. In his Presidential address, which Mr. Jinnah delivered at the 26th session at Patna on

Hindu elements and made stipulations as to the future which the Viceroy could not see his way to accepting. It was, of course, always open to the Viceroy to add to his Council individual Indians of high character and ability. But such a course would not have achieved the desired object, which was to associate representative Hindu and Moslem political leaders with the conduct of the war and so bring them closer together for the future. Very reluctantly, therefore, Lord Linlithgow decided in November to discontinue for the time being, his unwearied efforts, carried on ever since the war began, to bring the parties together, leaving the door open to further reconsideration by those directly concerned.

"No one can look upon the present deadlock with satisfaction. Least of all, patriotic Indians who, looking beyond the narrower aims of sectional leaders, are deeply concerned with India's progress towards equal partnership in our family of free nations, which is alike their goal as well as ours. They better than anyone else can help to find a solution. But they can do so only if they direct their efforts to the real source of the difficulty.

THE BOMBAY CONFERENCE DEMAND

"In the last few weeks, that distinguished veteran statesman, Sir *Tej Bahadur Sapru*, whose breadth of outlook and courageous initiative played no small part in the deliberations which led up to the existing Federal scheme, brought together in Bombay a number of eminent Indian public men outside the two main contending political organisations to consider the situation. In the end, a resolution was passed, but I am not quite clear as to how many of those who attended one or more meetings of this Conference actually concurred in the resolution. That resolution has since been discussed by Sir Tej with the Viceroy and submitted to his Majesty's Government and has been published. It asked for a complete reconstruction of the Executive Council, converting it into one consisting entirely of unofficial Indians, drawn from important elements of public life. This new Council would be responsible, while the war is still in progress, to the Crown and not to the Legislature, but it should in substance be treated in regard to all inter-Imperial and international matters on the same footing as a Dominion Government. The resolution also asked that this reconstruction should be accompanied by an announcement of a definite time-limit within which India is to attain the same measure of freedom as is enjoyed by the Dominions.

"I should be the last to approach in a critical or unsympathetic spirit proposals brought forward by men of such eminent public service as those who have associated themselves with this resolution, or animated by such a genuine desire both to promote India's constitutional progress and her active participation in the war effort. I will, therefore, only touch very briefly on some of the more obvious difficulties, which such a scheme, if it were carried into effect, would present in practice. The scheme proposed by the resolution would amount not to modification of the present form of Government but to its suppression by an entirely different type of Government. That is certainly something going beyond what we think practicable in the midst of the ever-increasing strain and urgency of the war situation. It would also create internal constitutional problems of no little difficulty, both in relation to the Provinces, whether those now enjoying self-government or those administered under Section 23 and to the Princes ; and in that ways, it would raise still unresolved issues of the constitutional future.

RESOLUTION DIRECTED TO WRONG ADDRESS

"That brings me to the underlying issues, but not faced, by the Bombay resolution, if I may say so without discourtesy to those who have sponsored it, the resolution seems to me to have been directed to the wrong address. I have already pointed out that the time-table of India's constitutional advance depends far more upon Indian agreement than upon ourselves. But the same applies to any far-reaching alteration of the present constitutional position. As, I think, I have already made clear, our existing proposal for the expansion of the Viceroy's Council is in suspense, not because those concerned—I am leaving the Congress on the one side for a moment—have condemned the proposal on the ground of inadequacy but mainly because of the difficulty of reconciling Moslem and Hindu claims for relative position. That difficulty is not lessened but inevitably enhanced by any suggestion of a new type of Executive with more extensive powers.

NO AGREEMENT FOR THE BOMBAY SCHEME

"It is unfortunately already evident that Sir *Tej Bahadur Sapru* and his friends have not been able to secure beforehand for their scheme any kind of agreement—if not between the Congress and the Moslem League—at any rate between the latter and other respresentatives of the Hindu majority. Mr. Jinnah, leader of the Moslem League, has since repudiated it as being on 'entirely wrong lines' and as a trap, to use his phrase, into which Sir Tej Bahadur Sapru had been led by Congress wire-pullers. On the other hand, the General Secretary of the Mahasabha Party has declared that it will not co-operate in any scheme in which the numerical majority of the Hindu element is not reflected in the composition of the Council. There is obviously no such agreement here as would afford the reconstructed Council political support, or even acquiescence, in the Legislature. On the other hand, if the reconstructed Council is to be composed not of leaders, who between them can secure some measure of political backing, but of men individually eminent but politically unsupported, then the objections which weighed against that course in the case of an expansion of the existing Council become much more formidable if it is a question of an entirely new Council with greatly enlarged powers.

"It would, I think, be very difficult to persuade Parliament to confer Dominion or quasi-Dominion powers on a body, so constituted. Nor would such a body, between their responsibility to the Crown on one side and in face of an unfriendly Legislature on the other, be likely for long to maintain its precarious position. My appeal to Sir Tej and his friends would, therefore, be not to cease from their efforts but to concentrate, first and foremost, on bringing the contending elements in India together. Whether they can best do that by the exercise of their persuasion upon the existing party leaders or by building up a strong central party of men who are prepared to put India first, their efforts may well be decisive in shaping the whole future of their country.

India's Record in the War

"Meanwhile, there are other fields besides that of politics in which India's future is being shaped. In Africa, in Malaya and now in Iraq, India is establishing her claim to consideration as a major factor in the war. Her troops, by their gallantry and technical efficiency, have made a conspicuous contribution to our victories in Libya and Eritrea. They have faced the trying ordeal of modern war and faced it largely under the leadership of Indian officers (Cheers), who have amply justified their training and the confidence placed in them. "Her young Navy has earned the highest commendation from the Admiralty—no easy critics—for its indefatigable work in the seas east of Suez. The expansion of her infant Air Force is only held back against the flood of recruits by a still inadequate total supply of machines. Her industries have already made an unprecedented contribution to her war effort."

Mr. *Wedgwood* (Independent) interpolated : Are they making aeroplanes ?

Mr. *Amery* : They are beginning.

Earl Winterton (Conservative) : Can he tell us what advance there has been since the last debate in the production of munitions and in the intake of men into the Army ?

Mr. *Amery* said : "I was only referring to the matter quite briefly as bearing on the political situation, I was not prepared to go into details. But, of course, Earl Winterton is at perfect liberty to raise these matters in so far as I am in a position to answer. He will appreciate, however, that on many of them it is difficult to give detailed answers but I shall be happy to do so, so far as I am able. I was about to say—and perhaps this is a large part of answer I can give—that thanks to the stimulating energies of Sir Alexander Roger's technical mission, which was sent out by the Ministry of Supply, and to the policy of mutual cooperation with India's neighbours, which was set on foot by the Delhi Conference and is now being continued by the Eastern Group Supply Council, India will do so on an ever-increasing scale as the war progresses.

"All these things constitute a real and indefensible advance in that progress towards true self-dependence and true quality which constitutional development can, and should, confirm but which they cannot of themselves create. Our desire in this House, shared (I think) by all parties, is that India should advance, and advance rapidly, all along the line in the indispensible prerequisites to the fullest conceivable measure of freedom. From that point of view, we welcome with pride her achievements in war as evidence of her growing capacity to meet her own defence. We welcome industrial progress, which will not only subserve the needs of that defence but contribute to her general economy strength. We welcome, perhaps even more, any measures that can raise the standard of nutrition and health of the vast agricultural majority of the population, which has, with staggering increase, risen from three hundred and fifty millions to four hundred millions of people in the last decide.

NO ENFORCED AGREEMENT WORTH WHILE

"Above all, we welcome every effort that Indians can make to come together and find a solution to India's complex and difficult problem, which will do justice alike to the claims of her diverse elements for the due recognition of their individuality and to the need of that wider unity, which is essential to her peace and prosperity. I have dwelt deliberately upon Indian responsibility in the matter, for unless Indians are prepared to face that responsibility now, they will fail to face it hereafter. Any agreement imposed by us from without cannot survive the withdrawal of our power to enforce it. Only a real agreement, freely reached can stand that test. It is for Indian statesmen to find that measure of agreement which is indispensable, if we on our side are to make our further contribution towards the completion of our own task in India, the task of joining with them in crowning the peace and unity already achieved with freedom" (Cheers).

MR. AMERY URGED TO VISIT INDIA

Mr. *Ammon* (Labour) said he felt some concern about Mr. Amery's opening statement. It suggested that there was practically no change in the situation now as compared with what it was when the subject was last before the House. It rather indicated that, strong as might be the hope of deriving assistance from India and achieving better understanding and closer relationship, we had made no further progress. The first thing that must impress us, he said, was that this was a vital subject for the British Empire and that, on India, the whole Empire might break down and break up. So far as our war effort was concerned, there was more man-power in India than in the rest of the British Commonwealth ; if only we could secure full and willing co-operation, it was difficult to estimate how much that would mean to our war effort. There was no better opportunity likely to occur or had ever occurred over a long period of years than existed while we had a government on such a line as we had now in power in this country, where everybody was concentrating on an endeavour to obtain the maximum unity effort, both in this country and in the rest of the Empire.

Mr. *Ammon* continued there was at least a very strong bond during the present struggle between India and this country and that was a common detestation of Nazidom and all that it represented. In that at any rate, we had India's full sympathy. He suggested to India that they would have been wise had they accepted the Viceroy's offer and endeavoured to have made the very best possible use of it and strengthened their position in that direction. It might have been hoped that they might have been content with Dominion Status but they had unfortunately not seen their way to do that, Mr. Ammon added. We were disappointed that the Viceroy's offer had received such small acceptance and welcome. Mr. Ammon urged Mr. Amery to go to India himself as a preliminary. There was a lot to be said for getting in the right atmosphere and for giving the people concerned the feeling that we were really concerned about them. He was not going to say that Mr. Amery's going there would solve all problems but it would do something to make a better atmosphere.

THE EXAMPLE OF THE PHILIPPINES

Mr. *Ammon* continued that it probably would be well if we gave consideration to introducing into Parliament, and getting embodied in an Act, that after a certain number of years—five, ten or twenty, perhaps—independence would be given to India. We should thus give a clear and definite objective to which they could strive. They would tend after a time to tone down the tendencies of the various sections there and they would make preparations for the position that was going to arise. Mr. Ammon emphasised that he was talking of independence, not of Dominion Status.

Mr. *Ammon* suggested we should make an approach to the problem from a new angle and set a certain number of years hence, when independence would be granted. A precedent, which must not be driven too far, was that set by the United States with regard to the Philippines, whereby in 1946 full independence would be given to that country as embodied in an Act of Congress, already passed. That would have the effect, he said, of turning the energies of agitators into making preparation for dealing with the conditions that would arise. It would give an opportunity for the British Government to take active steps to mould opinion there, to go on with education in a larger measure than it had done and to make it possible to arrive at some method whereby a greater measure of co-operation could be achieved between the people of both countries.

Don't be Bound by custom

Mr. *W. Roberts* (Liberal) said it was not enough for us and our Government to say to the Indian people in a negative way that they must settle their differences before we could do anything more. We had mistakes in the past but it was our duty now, and it was of vital importance, that we should make every effort to make some progress in associating Indians in the conduct of the war and in the control of India's contribution towards the war. Mr. Roberts pointed out that Mr. Amery should not be too particular and too punctilious about constitutional precedents which might be set up by any action that we now might take to carry out the vital principle that Indians should have very much greater control in the affairs of India during the war. If it would help the Secretary of State to go to India and meet Indians, custom should not stand in the way.

Mr. Roberts said he associated himself in deploring the attitude which the two big organisations had taken up in India. That the Congress leaders, whom one had met and who were associated before the war in supporting the democratic cause in many struggles, should now adopt the attitude that the people should not contribute towards the war effort was an attitude difficult to understand. At the same time, he continued, Muslims, while supporting the war, seemed, by accentuating their difference from the Hindus, to make it more difficult to attain Indian unity and self-government. Statesmanship must find a solution in which Indians faced and overcame their differences themselves.

Mr. *Godfrey Nicholson* (Conservative) said that we should concentrate on sending a definite message to India. He welcomed whole-heartedly Mr. *Amery's* speech. It must, he said, be firmly impressed on India that this was no longer a British but a purely Indian problem. The venue had left Westminster and was now in India. If India could agree on demanding any particular form of constitution she would receive sympathetic hearing. The problem facing civilisation was the simple one of survival. Was India aware of that ? The British Empire, whatever its faults, had guaranteed to India peace, law and order.

The time had come for very plain speaking to India if any constitutional progress were to be achieved. Mr. *Nicholson* continued. The people of this country and of India were indissolubly linked by a community of ideas as to what constituted decent living and decent behaviour. They were brothers in spirit.

British Government's "Dilemma"

Sir George Schuster (Liberal national) said that nothing could be more distressing than that at the present moment when all these decisions vitally affecting India's future were being taken, the Government should rest purely in official hands. But the British Government were in this dilemma. They wanted to transfer power. You could not ask representative Indians to share responsibility unless they had power. But you could not change the whole balance of constitutional power, and you could not transfer constitutional power, unless you fixed the whole structure of the new constitution. The conflict and disagreement which had already occurred over the 1935 Act as regards the Central Government proved the difficulties that lay in the way, but to men who trusted each other and wanted to co-operate, the answer was quite easy.

Let leading Indians come in as members of the Viceroy's Council in the same positions in which other Indians had gone into the Council in the past. They would have plenty of power but they must have courage too. They might have to share in unpopular decisions: perhaps they might lose political support for the future. He was sure that there were men in India who had that courage. That was what the Secretary of State offered, bnt all Indian political leaders, not only the Congress, would not have it. They wanted all sorts of guarantees of their constitutional position and some writers said quite openly that there must be real transfer of constitutional power now, that that was to be the acid test of whether the British Government ever meant anything. They said in effect, "We don't trust the British, but if we get the transfer of power now it will be something on which they cannot go back in future." That was just what could not be given short of the formation of a wholly new, properly balanced constitutional structure.

CONGRESS SEEKING PARTY DOMINATION

Sir George Schuster, continuing asked: Was it not possible that the Congress' order forcing the Ministers to resign was not merely a gesture of protest but also because Congress saw the danger of a provincial spirit of disunity growing up which might set up loyalties conflicting with the loyalty to the Congress ? He made no charges but these disquieting questions were being asked by many people and he must confess he was asking them himself. It was disquieting that the leading national party should be taking such a purely negative line seeking nothing but easy popularity which came to those who were against the Government, helping not at all in finding constructive solutions for the many problems of India. It was disquieting that the leading Indian party should not show a greater sense of reality, a truer appreciation of the emergency, but that it should recklessly seek to embarrass the British Government when Britain was fighting desperately not merely for her heroic existence but for the freedom of India as well. The most disquieting of all the suspicion that the real objective of the Congress was to establish party domination of the State in India parallel to the Nazi and Fascist party dominations in Germany and Italy. To the British mind there was an unpleasant familiarity in the course which the Congress Party seemed to be forcing Britain to go through. The British Government had made a gesture which they knew in their hearts to mean a real offer of transfer of power. Britain had found no response from the Congress, no effort at all to face the necessity of finding some balance among the parties in India and no recession from their demand to be the only party to speak for India. Thus the British Government began to feel that there lay behind all this a very sinister purpose that was being finally unmasked.

They felt these doubts, continued Sir George, but perhaps the final stage had not yet been reached. He made no charges. The doubts and questions he had raised might be wrong. He prayed that they might be. He appealed to Mr. Gandhi to prove them and if it were any help to him, Sir G. Schuster said, "Let me add that we are all to blame". The present leader of the Muslim League, Mr. Jinnah, was equally unpractical. Let us admit that we had been in the wrong. The British side might have been to blame. Its case might have been put badly and unimaginatively. The Government of India might have been very wooden. Sir George Schuster had always felt that there were very great difficulties in the handling of negotiations of this kind by the Viceroy. He had to consider his administrative position.

Sir George Schuster said he had always felt that if they admitted blame on the British side there was one person who was not to blame and that was the present Secretary of State. He succeeded to an extremely difficult position and since he had held it he had made repeated reasonable and most courageous efforts to solve the difficulties. Sir George Schuster said that the Commons and the British public were not to blame except possibly for a certain measure of indifference, but somehow or other they felt that they had been let down. They felt they had been so honest in their desire to find a constructive way to do what the Indians wanted and that if only the latter could have understood what was in British minds and what were their purposes, this situation could never have been allowed to arise.

ADVICE TO MR. AMERY

Sir George Schuster continued that he firmly believed also that the great body of Indian opinion did desire to have a free and fair democracy and not party domination and that they were willing to make a constructive effort to help in the solution. In these circumstances what were the British Government to do ? He wanted to say to the Secretary of State, "Go on with all possible steps to get representative Indians to join in the task of Government not only on the Viceroy's Council, but in the Provinces. Get men no matter what their political status is. Get some of the men who have shown their capacity as Dewans or in fields of commercial and business enterprise as well as well-known people in the political field. Appeal to them that there is a supreme chance of serving India, but do not say it is no use going on if representative parties do not support you." It was ridiculous to claim that there were no Indians capable of being Finance Members.

Sir George Schuster continued that he could not see why constitutional discussions in India should not go on during the war. There were immense preliminary problems to be discussed dealing with the essential difficulty of the mixture of communities which might be solved by some form of segregation of administrative units or by some different form of democracy from the form of parliamentary democracy that the British knew. All this required long study and should be tackled now. Could not they get the whole thing going in a different atmosphere? They had all got into the wrong atmosphere by approaching these questions through the leaders of the All-India political parties. These men had never shown their ability as practical statesmen. There were Provincial Ministers and men in the States who had proved themselves. Why should they not get together and try and start these constitutional discussions in a different atmosphere?

Indian Under-Secretary Suggested

Sir George Schuster said that he wanted to make one more suggestion. It seemed so important in these difficult times that we should get closer to India and we wanted India to get closer to us. Could nothing more be done in that direction? Would it not be possible to have an Indian Under-Secretary of State? Would it not be possible to bring over a man like Sir Tej Bahadur Sapru and put him in the House of Lords or we might even have a Congress leader, but anyhow let us have a genuine Indian like him here. Let him send back trusted words to India which would tell what the British people were fighting for now and banish the ridiculous idea that this was only another war for imperialistic purposes. Sir George Schuster believed that such a step might have a great effect. Finally he wanted again to record an appeal to all Indians, who had wisdom and the trust of their own people, to bring these gifts into the common task. "Let them", he said, "be courageous and strong, let them take their chances of their political future in both hands. Let them look back at the record of Congress and say 'let this be changed'. Congress in the past has always said, 'no'. You cannot save humanity or recreate a national India by saying 'no'" (Cheers).

The Most Democratic Party

Rev. Sorensen (Labour) said that whatever might be said about the alleged desire of the Congress in relation to Nazism, there was no party in the world more democratic than the Congress Party in India. The Congress required neither a dishonoured nor a blank cheque. What Congress had been doing was to secure from this country recognition that India had the right to her political independence. Although he appreciated the motive, he regretted the suggestion that great contribution would be made to an understanding between this country and India if we could persuade some Indian to come over here and be Under-Secretary. It would have been much better to have suggested that some Indian should come here as a member of the Cabinet. Why not Nehru or the leader of the Congress?

Sir *Sanley Reed* (Conservative) said that in all frankness and sincerity Mr. Amery's speech left him under a sense of depression. It did not take them anywhere, did not lead them any further on the road to a solution of the great problem of closer co-operation between India and the British Commonwealth at the present time. He could not quite reconcile the picture of India under the present regime with that which reached him from many other sources. India had been greatly moved, as the House had been greatly moved, at the position whereby men we knew and admired and with whom we had the closest friendship for many years were now in gaol. It was not a case that men were going to gaol for declining to co-operate with the Government. So far as these punitive measures were being exercised, they were being exercised against men who were deliberately obstructing the co-operation of others in the war effort.

Sir Stanley Reed continued: Active efforts to prevent others from co-operating was defiance of authority which no Government could pass by without allowing the whole foundation of the rule of law to collapse at a time of infinite peril not only to us but to India as well. When we saw on one side the Indian National Congress demanding complete independence, which must be fatal to India at the present time. and the Muslim League on the other hand demanding the splitting of India again into coteries of States, which would undo the work of the past one hundred and fifty years, we made the fatal mistake of running away with the idea that these two powerful organised bodies represented the whole of India. He believed that there were very large number of members of the Indian National Congress, who to-day would recoil from the idea of complete independence if faced with that issue and if equal and hon'ble partnership in the British Commonwealth were put before them they would regard that as entirely satisfying their ambitions and providing for Indians full scope for their full national development.

FAITH IN NON-POLITICAL INDIA

Sir *Stanley Reed*, continuing, said that not all Muslims wanted the plan advocated by the Muslim League. Was there nothing between the extreme view of the Congress on the one side and the extreme view of the Muslim League on the other to whom Mr. Amery could make his direct appeal and to whom he could direct his energies with a view to bringing them within the fabric of administration? There was a very great body in India not associated with either of these two political organisations. True, it had not the same efficient political propaganda and political machinery, but it represented a great body of the thought in India. He sometimes thought that there was a certain parallel in what we called Indian Liberals and the Liberals in England. Liberalism in England was a far more important force in this country than was represented by the Liberal Party in the Commons. So it was in India. There was a great body of Liberal thought bent on constructive work for its country within the Commonwealth.

"How were we to get rid of the suspicion that existed and convince India that we were determined to see India attain full status as a Dominion", asked Sir *S. Reed*. The only way this miasma could be swept away, he said, was by attempting to bring representatives of that school direct into the Government of India. He asked Mr. Amery to go back again and again and not to leave his task until he had found some means of harnessing this great body of broad liberal patriotism and constructive thought in the machinery of the Government of India, not to be deterred by constitutional niceties, not to be frightened away by the idea whether this was strictly correct. War was now approaching the borders of India. There was no one here who did not fully appreciate the value, strength and immensity of the Indian war effort. There was none who had not been profoundly moved by the gallantry and elan of Indian troops in Libya and East Africa. (Cheers). That was not enough. We had to mobilise the whole moral and political force and enthusiasm of as many people in India as could possibly be mobilised in that direction.

In conclusion, he asked Mr. Amery to consider again and again proposals which came from men of goodwill and patriotism with a view to seeing whether steps could now be taken whereby India might feel that not only her armed forces, munitions and her industries and interests were behind the war effort but the heart and soul of a great and generous people.

MR. GANDHI—A CHRISTIAN ANARCHIST

Mr. *Wedgwood* (Independent) said that to a large extent the difficult position we found ourselves in to-day was because both sides felt it essential that they should save their faces. Our real difficulty in India was not the Congress but Mr. Gandhi himself. Mr. Gandhi did not believe in Government. Mr. Wedgwood believed that the one thing that Mr. Gandhi regretted in his life was that he took part in the Round Table Conference. He was naturally a Christian anarchist and no amount of persuasion from Mr. Amery would shake his mind. It was extremely difficult with that frame of mind to believe in schemes of Government to which the Congress should agree.

Mr. *Vernon Bartlett* (Independent) said Mr. Amery had repeated the same old business that the only solution for the Indian problem depended on the Indians themselves. Mr. Amery might have given a warmer welcome to the discussions which had been taking place under the leadership of Sir Tej Bahadur Sapru. Surely something more could be done to encourage the middle movement in India. Mr. Bartlett could not believe that we could not increase the Viceroy's Executive Council without the danger of upsetting the present balance of Government.

EARL WINTERTON URGES GREATER WAR EFFORT

Earl Winterton (Conservative) agreed with Mr. Bartlett that no effort should be spared to find a way out, but he could not agree that there was any relationship at this moment between the political situation and what India was doing in the war effort. The great dominant fact overshadowing any discussion about the constitutional system for any part of the Empire, he said, is this—that we are going to defend against the enemy. (Cheers). There was the possible danger of a tidal wave of totalitarianism coming like a Ganges flood lapping up to the very frontier of India and for the first time in the strategical history of the relationship between Britain and India, there was danger from two sides and possibly a third. It was no use talking of constitutions when we wanted guns and tanks. We are not fighting this war with words. There was only one way to meet the Panzer divisions flooding through Greece. That was with more men trained and armed to the teeth and where could we find in the whole Empire better or more magnificent material to stand by our side and beside the troops of the Dominions in resisting that flood than in not one but the many races of India. He paid a whole-hearted tribute to the magnificent qualities and work of Indian troops to-day. One of his honourable friends had said that they were proving a major factor. They were not proving a major factor, he declared. That was his quarrel. They ought to be a major factor. It ought to be possible to raise two million men from India and equip them with tanks and guns. He did not blame the present Secretary of State nor the Viceroy, but the growth in India of munitions making was obviously required for modern troops.

Mr. Amery's Reply

Mr. *Amery* made a second speech in reply to the debate. He said : "I do not think there could have been a more satisfactory debate from my point of view not because honourable members have treated the Secretary of State with consideration and kindness but because of the real value which this debate will have in India when it is read and studied there. The House has shown itself with reference to India to be a truly liberal body. Speeches from all quarters of this House were true reflections of the spirit in which we are waging this war and the cause for which we are fighting. The debate illustrated to the full the fundamental universal goodwill of this House towards India and its aspirations. There were many admirable speeches. I would like to single out not only Earl Winterton but Sir George Schuster and Mr. Nicholson, who had exercised the privilege of goodwill, which is to speak frankly and straightly to one's friends and to those whom we do regard as our brothers in spirit.

"Universal goodwill towards India is not only characterisitc of honourable members of the House but underlies the policy and aims of His Majesty's Government. The policy of the Government announced last autumn offers India far more than ever before and the remarkable thing is that it is the policy not merely of Mr. Ammon's friends in the Cabinet or of the present Secretary of State but of the Prime Minister, who only a few years ago was the most stalwart and persistent opponent of the measure of self-government which fell far short of that pledge of complete Dominion Status as soon as Indians can agree after the war."

Pledges not Broken

Mr. *Amery* continued : "That is evidence surely that on our side there is unity and goodwill which is one of the pre-requisites of constitutional progress in India. It was suggested that we had broken our pledges to India at the end of the last war to confer independence upon her. I would remind the House of the actual pledges given. The Preamble to the Act of 1919 referred to the gradual development of self-governing institutions with a view to the progressive realisation of responsible government in India as an integral part of the British Empire. There was no mention of Dominion Status then. In 1929 Lord Halifax, the then Viceroy, declared—and truly—that it was implicit in the declarations of 1917 and the Preamble of 1919 that the eventual issue of India's constitutional progress would be the attainment of constitutional independence. But it had never been described as anything but gradual. The great Act of 1935 in no way fell short of the pledges given but even that fell a long way behind the clear declarations of policy made for a united country by a united government last summer. There is no essential difficulty so far as this country's intentions are concerned in India setting on the way to Dominion Status. The difficulty lies not so much in the devolution of authority as in making sure that there is an authority in India which can take over and will not break down or break up in the process. The difficulty does remain and it is no use pretending that it does not in India itself, in those divisions in India which have shown themselves with increasing acuteness as the prospect of free government comes nearer.

Mr Amery not Pessimistic

"It is very true that in that difficulty we are confronted by what has been described as a certain sense of frustration or depression. I see no reason why we should yield to that. After all let us remember that little more than a year ago war had been in progress for a good many months and we had not come to any understanding for a union of our political parties and there was in the House and country a considerable sense of frustration in the political situation. As the situation came home to us and the feeling of the ordinary man in the street

Sir *Nripendra Nath* did not want to belittle either the Congress or the League. But it was curious how at different times different views were taken by His Majety's Government of the magnitude of those two organisations. They had been repeating that India was with them in the war. But the Congress, everyone knew, was not in the war effort. The Congress, therefore, would become at least a not too serious factor, in the country. When it came to constitutional advance, the Congress was stated to wield considerable power. What about the Muslim League ? The League was saying that it was not hampering the war effort but at the same time, the League as such was unable to offer any help to Great Britain. The difference between the Congress and the League with regard to war was the same between Tweedledum and Tweedledee. "The Congress or the League is looked upon as a giant or a dwarf as it suits them."

When the demand for Pakistan was made, Mr. Amery sat on the fence. Without stating whether he wanted it or did not want it, Mr. Amery gave the slogan "India First". But as soon as this slogan was heard, a "thrill of horror" went through the frame of some politicians here and they cried that India consisted of two nations and it was a geographical blunder that it was made one. Mr. Amery hastly dropped his slogan and said instead, "We have got to consider the ninety million Muslims". Immediately, the Muslim League had become synonymous with the ninety million Muslims.

Seconding the resolution, Sir *Jagdish Prasad* said, "It is one of the main purposes of this conference to bring home to the British Government that a Government of India predominantly official and with a minority of Indians is illsuited to evoke that wilting effort, that sustained enthusiasm even when things are going none too well, that are essential if India is to play a decisive part in achieving victory. A rapid military expansion of her forces has been retarded by the regrettable state of our industrial development. Many gaps remain in her industrial equipment which must be filled even while the war lasts. The greatest care will have to be exercised to see that the economic structure of the country does not receive a shock on the termination of the war and therefore the immediate needs of the war should be coordinated with the long-term view of the industrial development of India. It is also of the utmost importance that a more active policy of industrialisation should form an essential part of a programme of post-war reconstruction which should be taken in hand now."

Turning to the "fundamental question" whether the Government of India as at present constituted can deal adequately and efficiently with a war of such tremendous proportions. Sir Jagadish Prasad said, "If the whole country is to be organised for war, if Indians are to be made to feel that this war is as much their concern as that of other parts of the Commonwealth, if they are to be exhorted to make the utmost sacrifices to save not only India but the Commonwealth from the horrors of Nazi domination, the Government of India must, speaking broadly, become a government of Indians."

Sir Jagadish Prasad warned Indians against giving the impression to the British people that any section of the people of India "stood aloof at a time of mortal peril". He added it was not the desire of the Indian people to stand unconcerned when the future of their own country was in the balance. They wished to exert themselves to the utmost to win the war. All that they asked was that they should be able to do this with the feeling that in the direction of the policy they had been placed in a position of genuine power.

Sir Jagdish Prasad next dealt with the demands contained in the resolution for the immediate expansion of the Viceroy's Executive Council and asked if the British Government were prepared in August last to have an Executive Council of twelve members of whom ten were to be Indians, whether it would be a grave danger if the entire Council consisted of only Indians. Even if there was a risk, he maintained it was worth taking because the psychological effect of such a step would be immense. Sir Jagdish Prasad wanted to know if the Government had realised sufficiently that one of the root causes of the present discontent in the country was a feeling of frustration and of helplessness that Indians of the greatest eminence and experience are unable to influence the Government's decisions affecting the future of the country for generations to come. If the Government were not careful, said Sir Jagdish Prasad, they would throw their staunchest supporters into utter despair.

The *Maharaja of Burdwan* said that this Conference had met to raise the status of India in the eyes of the world. India was not now an equal partner with the other Dominions. True, there were Indian troops abroad acquitting themselves wonderfully well. But it was also true that there was resentment in the country that India had not been allowed a voice in the matter of sending these troops overseas.

"I, with the Maharaja of Parlakimedi, am here with one object", continued the Maharaja of Burdwan. "We are here to say that we are one with you in the desire to raise the self-respect of this country. We want England to win. We also want to be able to participate in the victory and hence this resolution."

Continuing, the Maharaja of Burdwan desired the Conference to stress two points. Whatever the number in the Executive Council, the Conference should ask for complete Indianisation of the Executive Council. Another aspect he wanted to make clear was that every Indian was determined not to participate in any post-war Conference, except on a footing of equality. "We are not going there, as Sir Tej Bahadur Sapru went or as I went in 1926 to the Imperial Conference. At the end of the war, we should be equal partners in the Commonwealth."

Commenting on the resolution before the House, *Sir Chimanlal Sitalvad* declared that he was in perfect accord with the demands for the nationalisation of the Government of India and the Defence forces of the country. But the proposals to that end put forward in the resolution, he said, failed to take note of realities. It was suggested that the Governor-General's Executive Council should be immediately reconstructed by appointing all Indians on the Executive Council. "As the Congress and the Muslim League," Sir Chimanlal added, "the major political parties, refuse co-operation in this matter, the persons who can be appointed as Executive Councillors will be outside these bodies. I may not deny that there are eminent people outside these bodies, who do not yield in patriotism to any one and would make efficient Executive Councillors at the Centre. It must, however, be stated that these gentlemen will have no effective backing in the Legislature as well as in the country. It will, therefore, follow that the elected members in the Central Legislature belonging to the Congress and Muslim League will be able to throw out any measures that such Executive Councillors may bring before the Legislature. It will hence become necessary to enact these measures by certification of the Governor-General, against which procedure the country has protested so often. Moreover, those who agree to put themselves in such an unenviable position will be branded as unpatriotic. One fails to understand how such a reconstruction of the Executive Council of the Governor-General will, as stated in the resolution, enable the Government to get the utmost help from the people in men, money and material. Similarly the proposal to put the Defence Portfolio in charge of an Indian is very ideal. But there again, owing to the present attitude of the leading political parties, the position of the Indian Defence Member from outside such bodies and having no public support, will be untenable.

"This Conference has been avowedly called mainly for the removal of the present deadlock. The object can be achieved in one of two ways. The promoters of the present Conference should undertake, if they feel themselves equal to the task, to negotiate between the Congress, the Muslim League, the British Government and the Hindu Mahasabha, who have brought about the deadlock. In the alternative, they can inaugurate a powerful Centre Party and obtain for it the support of the people, so that they can get a sufficient number of their members elected to the Legislature and thus be able to carry on the Government of the country. Either of these two courses should be adopted and a mere expansion and complete Indianisation of the Executive Council of the Governor-General, by putting therein people without substantial following in the Legislature, will be of no avail."

Sir *Cowasji Jehangir* wanted to know if the resolution they were adopting applied only to those outside the Congress and the Muslim League. "How are we going to guarantee more war effort than is available to-day ?" He argued than unless there was a Coalition Government of the Congress and the Muslim League, there would be no mass support for the war effort. He advised the Conference to address themselves to the Congress and the Muslim League rather than to the Government.

Kunwar Sir Maharaj Singh deplored the fact that representatives of the Congress and the Muslim League were not present at the Conference. Replying to the criticism that the newly constructed Central Government would not be of a representative character, since the Muslim League and the Congress would be out of it, Sir Maharaj Singh wanted to know whom the present Home and Finance Members of the Government of India represented. He appealed to the Conference and to the public not to lose sight of the objective the Conference had in view.

Dr. *Shyama Prasad Mukherjee*, while supporting the resolution, criticised the provision leaving the responsibility for the administration of India during the war with the Crown. He could not agree with the view that there was any difference between Fascism and Nazism or British Imperialism. He agreed that so far as the present war was concerned, all Indians realised the need for Britain to win it, because a German victory would not be conducive to the cause of India. In his opinion, even if the Congress and the Muslim League did not join the new Executive Council, it would be wrong to assume that they would oppose the newly constituted Government.

Sardar Sir Jogendra Singh, after criticising the "flimsy gestures of the British Government to India", expressed the hope that better counsels would prevail among British statesmen and as a result of this India and Britain would be brought closer together.

Sardar Sant Singh criticised the policy of drift followed by the British Government in regard to the Indian constitutional issue and said that the resolution and the proposals contained therein were of a constructive nature. He wished that there was some sanction behind the resolution, so that Government could be forced to act.

Doctor Paranjpye declared that the resolution did not materially vary from those passed by the Liberal Party. If the scheme propounded in the resolution was accepted by the British Government, it was quite possible that the Congress might, as they did not in regard to Provincial Autonomy, agree to co-operate. And if the Congress and the Muslim League came together for the duration of the war, differences between the two parties would end.

Dr. Paranjpye concluding hoped that at this critical time both Mr. Gandhi and Mr. Jinnah would not insist upon their "pound of flesh."

Mr. *V. N. Chandavarkar* held that this resolution was not in any way different from the resolution passed by the Liberal Federation at its last meeting in Calcutta. While he did not expect any big things to happen as a result of this Conference, he felt satisfied that they had done their duty and the Government would not be in a position later on to say that no one outside the ranks of the Congress and the Muslim League was prepared to take the responsibility for Government.

Pandit Kunzru did not believe that the proposal to bring the Congress and the League together would succeed at the present moment, because both the parties, by their repeated declarations, had committed themselves to certain policies. It would not be wise to ask them to eat their own words and revise their opinion immediately. Pandit Kunzru added: "If the Conference failed, we will then have to completely withdraw from public life. But this should not deter us from making the effort, because there are occasions when we can serve our country better even by our failure."

Mr. *Fazal Ibrahim Rahimtoola* maintained that this Conference was not on a par with other ones, because it was not merely a Conference for the purpose of passing resolutions, but the Conference was out to make practical proposals, which would meet with the approval of Government and other parties in the country. In his opinion, it was wrong to presume that both the Congress and the Muslim League would not look at the proposals.

Sir Sultan Chinoy suggested that the Conference should address itself to bring about a communal agreement.

Dr. *B. S. Moonje* maintained that the communal bogey was the making of the British Government and, therefore, it was up to the British Government to lay the ghost of the communal question. He supported the resolution, becase it would create military-mindedness among the youth of the country.

Mr. *G. A. Natesan*, while deploring the attidude of the British Government, expressed the hope that the various parties in the country would take advantage of the opportunity provided by the Conference to unite and press for the demands contained in the resolution.

Mr. *T. T. Krishnamachari* held that the resolution in certain respects approximated to the Congress Resolution at Poona. He did not believe that there would be any opposition from the Congress if the British Government agreed to implement the suggestions contained in the resolution.

Mr. *V. D. Savarkar*, President of the Hindu Mahasabha, said that the Hindu Mahasabha stood for complete Independence, but it was prepared to join hands with any party, provided it worked for India's Independence. It might be that they might have to part company before they reached the goal, but it was a good thing to stand together in their onward march as long as possible. Personally, he did not believe that the British Government would accept their demands, as they were determined to keep all power iu their own hands.

Sir *Tej Bahadur Sapru*, winding up the debate and commending the resolution to the conference, paid a tribute to Sir Jagdish Prasad, without whose untiring zeal it would have been impossible to hold the Conference.

The resolution, Sir *Tej Bahadur* said, demanded a declaration from the British Government promising that India's situation after the war would be the same as that of other units of the Commonwealth. As a constitutional lawyer, he did not pin his faith on the Statute of Westminster. It was possible that the Statute might not survive the present war. It was also possible that the relations between Great Britain and her other constituents of the Commonwealth might undergo considerable readjustments. Hence, he wanted an assurance that whatever might be the status of these units, perfect equality for India with England as well as other constituents, in power and function, would be secured.

Regarding the question of time, Sir *Tej Bahadur* agreed that it was difficult to lay down a time-table in the matter of constitutional reforms. But that had been waiting since 1917, when the famous Montagu Declaration was made. He asserted that the pledges given by the British Government should be carried out before the patience of the people was tired out. He felt that it should not be difficult for Britain to carry out those pledges within a reasonable distance of time after the termination of the war. If the constitutional machinery was set up and the spade work was done, even now, it should be possible for the reforms to be completed within a year or a year and a half of the termination of the war.

If the British Government had made up their mind that India should attain that status at the end of the war, Sir Tej Bahadur Sapru asked why they should not begin to adjust the machinery even now, The machinery was already there in the Provinces, but the real seat of power was in the Centre, concentrated particularly in the hands of the Finance and Defence Members. If the country was to feel that its destiny was to reach the goal of free partnership, then the Government of India should be reformed and reconstructed. There might be some who might oppose the resolution, he added, because the Executive Council would remain responsible to the Crown during the period of the war, whereas the Congress Resolution was supposed to have said that it should be responsible to the Legislature. But the Conference was taking a more moderate view, because these proposals could be put into effect without any modification or amendment of the Government of India Act. He added that having regard to the present situation, it was, perhaps, better constitutionally to owe responsibility to the Crown than to the Legislature, which was of a mixed character, consisting of elected, non-elected and nominated elements.

Sir Tej Bahadur Sapru declared that the solution of the Indian problem required big imagination and big statesmanship which, he asserted, were conspicuous by their absence both in England and in India, It almost looked as though British statesmanship was totally bankrupt. If Mr. Amery wanted to know exactly what the situation was and the feeling in India, let him not address speeches across the seas, but let him come here and see things for himself. Let him bring, if necessary, half a dozen members of Parliament, meet members of the various parties and judge for himself. If Lord Willingdon could be sent on a mission to South America and other British statesmen could be sent from Britain to other parts of the Empire, it seemed to him absurd that questions affecting 400 million people should be settled by Radio broadcasts or speeches across the seas. He pleaded that the Indian question should be treated more seriously than had been done hitherto.

Sir Tej Bahadur Sapru made it clear that he for one, taking things as they were at present, did not believe that India should sever her connection with Britain.

Concluding, Sir Tej Bahadur said that a day would arrive when the combatants in Europe would sit at a Peace Conference. He did not wish that India should be represented at the Conference, except on her own rights, by representatives appointed by her National Government. He attached great importance to that.

The resolution was then put to vote and was carried unanimously.

The *Raja of Parlakimedi* proposed a vote of thanks, and the Conference concluded.

Mr. Amery on the Indian Deadlock

House of Commons—22nd April 1941

Mr. *L. S. Amery*, Secretary of State for India, moved a resolution in the House of Commons on the **22nd April 1941** to extend for another year the proclamations under which the Governors of Indian Provinces would assume the powers of Provincial Legislatures.

Mr. Amery said : "The purpose of the resolution which I am submiting to the House", he said, "is to extend for another twelve months the proclamations issued under the Provisions of Section 93 of the Government of India Act. Under the terms of that section, the Governor of a Province, if he is satisfied that a situation has arisen wherein parliamentary government cannot be carried on in accordance with the Act, can, by proclamation, assume all or any of the powers vested in provincial bodies and authorities. This situation arose in October, 1939, in consequence of the action of the Congress Party's so-called High Command in ordering Congress Ministries to resign. Proclamations under Section 23 were accordingly issued in seven Provinces and their continuance in force for a further twelve months was duly approved by the House on April 18 last yea . There has been no change in the situation since then and I regret we have no alternative to a further extension of these emergency provisions. These resolutions, however, are only concerned with seven out of the eleven Provinces of British India.

"In the four Provinces of Bengal, Assam, Sind and Punjab, with a population of something like one hundred million people—one-third of the whole population of British India—provincial self-government has continued to work uninterruptedly under composite governments, including Moslem and Hindu Ministers. On all questions which most nearly affect the ordinary life of the citizens—all questions, in fact, which occupy most of the attention of this House in times of peace—these hundr d million of Indians have now four years been enjoying the advantages of democratic self-government. Ministers and legislators have continued to gain experience and are making their contribution not only to the welfare of their constituents within the wide sphere of their direct authority but also to India's general war effort. We ought not to under-estimate the significance of this remarkable advance in self-government over so large a field. Nor can we afford to ignore the importance of the voice which these Provinces, through their Governments, are bound to exercise in any deliberations affecting the future constitution of India.

"From this point of view, it is a matter of deep regret that the two hundred million inhabitants of the other seven Provinces were, by an ukase of the Congress High Command, forbidden to continue to build up the practice and tradition of self-government. Their Governments, too, had made a satisfactory beginning and if they made mistakes—as even we have been known to do—the remedy lay with their electors.

Reaction To Suspension Of Parliamentary Govt.

"So far, indeed, as the provincial electorates are concerned, it must be admitted that they have nowhere shown any signs of distress at the suspension of parliamentary government—in this respect, no doubt, differing greatly from what would be the attitude of our own electors if deprived of the service of this Front Bench. The change to direct personal government by the Governors and permanent officials met with general acquiescence and, indeed, goodwill.

"Whatever political unrest there may be in India to-day has certainly not arisen in any way from the suspension of provincial self-government. There has been no discontinuity or abrupt reversal in either administrative or legislative policy. In a few instances, indeed, notably in connection with Prohibition, legislation has had to be modified in consequence of legal decisions. But, generally speaking, the work of beneficent social progress continues in full swing and with broad public approval. The House certainly need not fear that the continuance of direct government in these Provinces for another twelve months will of itself add to the difficulties of the political situation.

"What indeed, was really serious in the action of the Congress-controlled Ministries was not so much the direct and immediate result of their action in the Provinces themselves as the complete disregard displayed by the most powerful political organisation in India for the responsibilities of self-government and the indirect effect of this evidence of Congress methods upon the general political situation.

IMPLICATIONS OF RESPONSIBLE GOVERNMENT

"When we speak of responsible parliamentary government, we are apt to emphasise one aspect of that responsibility—namely, the responsibility of the government towards the party majority in the legislature. But responsible parliamentary government, if it is to work successfully, implies a three-fold responsibility. There is, first and foremost, the responsibility to the Crown, in other words, to the general welfare, the duty of maintaining the substantial continuity and efficiency of government—of seeing, in an old phrase, that 'the King's Government is carried on." There is, secondly, the responsibility to Parliament as an institution, founded, Mr. Speaker, upon your authority and upon the rights of the minorities, which, subject to the established procedure of Parliament, are in your keeping."

Mr. Amery continued, "It is only in the third place and subject to these dominating responsibilities that the Government is responsible to its supporters in Parliament for the promotion of particular policies in which they are interested. In the present case, the Ministers resigned not as the result of any difference with the Governors, not over any issue of Provincial policy, not at the instance of their own supporters. They resigned, prepared to bring about the complete break-down of administration and parliamentary life in their own Provinces at the orders of an outside executive, which wished in this imperious and irresponsible fashion to express its disapproval of the absence of a statement by the British Government of war aims framed to its liking.

"I can only say, whatever may have been the motives which inspired the conduct both of the Congress High Command and the Provincial Ministries, that there is no greater danger to democratic government in India as elsewhere than party totalitarianism. What has been even more immediately serious is the effect of this demonstration of Congress methods upon other important elements in India—non-Congress Provinces, the Moslem community generally and the Princes. It has confirmed to a point of fixed determination their already growing reluctance to take part in, or come under, any Central Government in India which is likely to be subject to the control of a majority in the Legislature, which, in its turn, would simply obey the words of the Congress Central Executive.

THE PAKISTAN DEMAND

"The Congress repudiates the Federal provisions of the Act of 1935 largely because they had weighted representation to some extent in the Legislature in favour of the minority element, in what the Congress regarded as an undemocratic sense. The Congress is, I fear, blind to the risk that no alternative constitution is now likely to emerge which could secure for it as great a measure of influence and control over India as a whole as it would have exercised under the present Act. The most significant symptom of the changed situation is the growing strength of the demand voiced by Mr. Jinnah, leader of the Moslem League, for complete severance from the rest of India of North-Western and North-Eastern zones, wherein the Moslems constitute a majority and their establishment as completely independent states, controlling their own foreign policy, defence, customs and finances. I am not concerned here to discuss the immense practical difficulties in the way of this so-called Pakistan project, stated in this, its extreme form, nor need I go back to the dismal record of India's history in the Eighteenth Century or to the disastrous experience of the Balkan countries before our eyes to-day in order to point out the terrible dangers inherent in any break-up of the essential unity of India (Cheers), at any rate, in its relation to the outside world. After all, there is no British achievement in India, of which we have better reason to be proud than the unity, internal peace and reign of law which we have given her (Cheers).

"It is enough for my purpose if I can impress upon the House, on the one hand, the underlying determination of Moslem India not to accept any constitution which does not give reasonable free play to the individual life of predominantly Moslem units and, on the other, the growing danger of preaching on both sides, Hindu and Moslem, of extreme and incompatible policies ("hear, hear"). It was a recognition of this danger as well as the hope that the gravity of the war situation might bring the parties together in a spirit of co-operation and responsibility that led His Majesty's Government to make a new statement of policy, which was made public by Lord Linlithgow in August last.

THE ESSENCE OF AUGUST STATEMENT

"What was the essence of that statement? It was that the frame-work of India's future constitution should be devised by Indians themselves and not by this House. That was a far-reaching and, indeed, revolutionary announcement, the full importance of which has not, I think, even yet been fully appreciated, either in this country or in India. It was, in fact, a recognition in advance of India's status as a dominion. That recognition was coupled with two conditions. One was that provision would have to be made, for the due fulfilment of those obligations which Great Britain's long connection with India had imposed on her.

"Some of these as for instance, the obligations towards the existing members of the Services are by their very nature terminable. But others, like those arising from India's present dependence upon this country for defence, will naturally be subject to modification with the growth of India's own capacity to defend herself unaided. Others, such as the treaty obligations of the Crown towards the Princes, are of a more enduring character. In any case, none of them stand in the way of shaping the structure of India's future constitution, which is to be essentially an Indian constitution, framed in accordance with Indian conceptions of Indian conditions and Indian needs.

"Even more important in this connection is the stipulation that the constitution itself, and also the body which is to frame it, must be the outcome of agreement between the principal elements in Indian national life. That is an essential pre-requisite to the success of the future constitution. For, if Indians cannot agree upon the kind of constitution they are prepared to work, how are they likely to agree upon the actual working of it? Our constitution here works because there is behind it an unwritten agreement, based upon centuries of tradition, as to the limits within which a majority can exercise its position of advantage. In all federal constitutions previous free agreement upon the nature of the constitution and of the limits within which majority rule can be exercised has been the condition upon which the various elements of a federation have been prepared to come together.

RECONSTRUCTION OF THE EXISTING ACT

"Anxious as we are to see the responsibility of the Indian Government resting upon Indian shoulders, we can only transfer that responsibility to somebody which can assume it without immediately breaking down or breaking up. Subject to that requisite of agreement, which is inherent in the circumstances of the Indian situation and not arbitrarily imposed by ourselves, the whole constitutional field is open for a modification or fundamental reconstruction of the existing Act. Indian statesmen need not be bound by the system of Government at the Centre contemplated in that Act or by the relations between that Centre and the Provinces and States. If they agree regarding the re-distribution of powers or the electoral system, that is a field open to them for settlement.

"If they come to the conclusion that our type of democracy, with an Executive dependent upon a Parliamentary majority, stands in the way of agreement and that India's needs would be better met by an Executive, deriving its authority more directly from the Federated units, like the American Executive, independent of the Legislature, that again is their responsibility. We who, in this House, wrestled for months with the intricacies of the existing Act—which I still look upon as a very remarkable piece of constructive legislation—should be the last to underrate the difficulty of the task which lies before Indian statesmanship.

"It is a task calling for sheer hard thinking in the working out of practical ways and means of solving an immediately complicated problem. It is a task which calls, above all, for that mediating and moderating spirit without which great things connot be achieved in human affairs. That is a task to which we have invited Indian statesmanship. While the decisive and final resolution of so fundamental an issue cannot take place in the midst of the life and death struggle in which we are engaged, there is nothing whatever to prevent Indian political leaders, Indian thinkers and Indian businessmen from engaging now in those preliminary discussions and studies which are so essential to success and which no more in India than elsewhere can be hastily disposed of. We are only too anxious to promote such study and discussion in every way possible. All the same, the main responsibility both for the initiation and the completion of this high inquiry rests with Indians themselves. We can only pledge ourselves to hasten to the utmost degree decision on all relevant issues that lies within our part. It is upon Indian statesmen and not upon us that the time-table of future constitutional progress depends.

Interim Proposals.

"So much for the major constitutional problem. There was a further question whether in the interval there was any practical step that the Government could take which, without prejudicing the major issue, could contribute towards its solution. There could, of course, be no question of changing over the whole basis of administrative and legislative power or placing India's war effort in the hands of an entirely new Executive. Nor could that have been done without at once raising those very issues of the division of power between conflicting elements in India, which are still unresolved. What we could do was to invite Indian leaders, representing the main political parties to join the Viceroy's Executive Council. The invitation to them was not only individually to take charge of important Departments of State but also to partake fully in the collective responsibility of the Council. Their inclusion would have brought Indian membership of the Council, official and unofficial, up to a substantial majority of the whole. But it would not have so altered the essential character of the Council as to deprive the Governor-General of his existing trusted advisers, or to commit the Indian leaders who joined it to any course, which would have deprived them of a free hand in dealing with the major problems of the constitutional future. We believed, and still believe, that it would give real power and valuable experience to men who have hitherto been in political opposition. We still believe that the creation of such a coalition Executive would have afforded an opportunity for Indian leaders in the atmosphere of a common effort for India's security to forget for a while their difference and begin to envisage their problems in the light of wider Indian patriotism.

The Satyagraha Movement.

"So far, our hopes have been disappointed. The Congress rejected out of hand both our major and interim proposals. Its attitude is, 'All or nothing', and by 'all' it means the immediate independence of an India, governed by a constitution which would ensure Congress control. It refused even to discuss the matter and proceeded to launch a curious campaign of Mr. Gandhi's devising. In pursuance of that campaign, Congress leaders, including ex-Premiers and ex-Ministers as well as selected members of the rank and file, have made speeches intended and calculated to interfere with the war effort. They have deliberately challenged fine or imprisonment with the same unquestioning obedience to the party whip as when they resigned office in the Provinces and, in many cases, I believe, with the same misgiving and reluctance. The situation thus created is naturally embarrassing as it was meant to be. But clearly the Government cannot punish ordinary offenders and overlook the same offences when committed by men whose position and whose course of action deliberately enhance their significance and their political effect.

"This campaign of civil disobedience by instalments has now been in progress for nearly six months. The first phase in which illegal action was confined to leading members of the Congress ended in January. The second phase, which included representatives of provincial and local committees, ended early this month and we are now in the rank and file phase. Magistrates, while vindicating the law, have treated the problem with commonsense, ignoring non-entities and in many cases, imposing a fine without the option of imprisonment. This latter procedure has been so discouraging to those whose chief inducement was the prospective electioneering value of a prison sentence that Mr. Gandhi has had to announce that payment of fine will count as an equally meritorious sacrifice in Congress hagiology (Laughter).

"On the whole, the movement has proceeded languidly and without evoking much popular interest, except in the United Provinces, which have in recent months contributed more than half the offences. By the middle of March, some 7,000 offenders had been convicted and some 5000 are still in prison. The whole business is as regrettable as it is irrational but the Government had and have no alternative to enforcing the law. Apart from the Congress, the Government's major policy for the constitutional future may be said to have relieved the anxieties of the various elements which compose India's national structure.

Extension of the Executive Council.

"As regards the more immediate policy of an extension of the Viceroy's Council, acceptance in principle unfortunately did not lead to actual agreement in detail. The Moslem League, in particular, asked for a measure of representation as against

War Situation a Peril to India

(1) The council of the National Liberal Federation of India views with grave concern the war situation as it has developed and is developing in Europe and recognizes that it is full of peril for India. The council is firmly of opinion that India's political progress is possible only if democracies emerge successful from the war. The council feels that India should cooperate whole-heartedly in the war effort but is deeply concerned to note that the Government have failed to create the psychological atmosphere necessary for mobilising to the maximum pitch the resources of India in men and material. In its opinion only a national government on the lines suggested by the Lib ral Federation at Calcutta and endorsed in material particulars by the Bombay Conference can enable India to organise her defences effectively and put forth her maximum effort for the war which is threatening to spread eastwards. It therefore earnestly urges the Government to create genuine and whole-hearted enthusiasm for the war by entrusting the direction and control of India's war effo t to an executive council composed of non-official Indians drawn from the main elements in India's public life. In its opinion it is imperative that his Majesty's Government should make it clear to the people of India that they propose to endow India with full control over her external and internal affairs after the war and make her a free and equal partner in the commonwealth of nations associated with England and that in the period of transition India will practically enjoy the same status in inter-imperial and international affairs as the dominions.

Mr. Amery's Speech Unsatisfactory

(2) The council of the National Liberal Federation has read with profound dismay the speech of Mr. *Amery* in the Commons debate on *April 22*. In its opinion, the spee h is not calcultated to promote communal harmony and unity which he has made a condition precedent to any political advance. The council cannot agree with the implication contained in Mr. Amery's speech that no useful purpose will be served by reconstructing the central Government on national lines unless at at least the Muslim League agreed to such reconstruction. It regrets to note that Mr. Amery has ruled out the formation of a central Government consisting ntirely of non-official Indians and that he is not in the present circumstances prepared to initiate any far-reaching measures of constitutional advance. In the opinion of the council, the speech of Mr. Amery is unsatisfactory not only in regard to the present but also in regard to the future as it refuses to indicate clearly the time within which India may expect to be endowed with full Dominion Status after the war. It also records its emphatic disapproval of Mr. Amery's statement that in the transitional period an Indianised government at the centre cannot be created in regard to international and interimperial matters as a full dominion. The council places on record its considered view that only a wise policy of bold and generous concession can enable India to pull her full weight in the war.

Pakistan Condemned

(3) The council of the National Liberal Federation of India records its unqualified condemnation of the scheme of partitioning India which is known as Pakistan as highly reactionary and anti-national and provides no solution of the minority problem. The council is sure that India will never reconcile herself to any proposal for partition, and it appeals to all Indians to resist the scheme to the utmost of their capacity. In the opinion of the council, the political situation has assumed a phase when it has become imperative for his Majesty's Government to make it clear beyond a shadow of doubt that they will not encourage any proposal for the partition of the country. The council affirms its firm faith in parliamentary democracy based on the principles of nationalism as the solution of India's constitution.

Indians Abroad

The council of the National Liberal Federation of India notes with appreciation the fact that the Feetham resolutions have been passed by the South African Parliament, thereby giving Indians in the Transvaal the right for the first time of owning land in the gold areas, which was hitherto prohibited to them, that an undertaking has been given that whatever be the findings of the Broom Commission on Indian penetration into predominantly European areas in Natal, no legislation would be undertaken during the currency of the war to force segregation on Indians, and that the Government of Field-Marshal Smuts has displayed a more liberal attidude towards Indians passing through South Africa and has incorporated the functions of the Indian Agent-General under the Capetown Agreement in the duties of the High Commissioner for India in South Africa.

At the same time the council considers that the areas thrown open to Indian ownership in the Transvaal under the Feetham resolutions are very inadequate and spell segregation, which is very repugnant to Indian self-respect, and that the danger of segregation in general of Indians in the South Africa has not been dissipated, and trusts that the participation of South African Indians and of India in the present war against racialism and in defence of democracy and human rights and of England and the Dominions including South Africa, will persuade the Government of South Africa to rise above racialism and promote genuine democracy in that country. The council is also of the opinion that unless and until racial equality is secured in South Africa, it will be prejudicial to Indians to countenance the proposal of Field-Marshal Smuts for a pan-African union and that therefore it must be strenuously opposed.

One resolution placed on record the council's appreciation of the work and achievements of Sir *B. Rama Rau,* the last Indian Agent-General and the first Indian High Commissioner in South Africa.

CEYLON

A resolution on Ceylon deplored the anti-Indian attitude of the Govt. of Ceylon which compelled the Government of India to prohibit the emigration of Indian labour, much to the detriment of Ceylon and which compelled the intervention of the Governor to protect the legitimate rights of Indians settled in Ceylon but still hoped that the Ceylonese Ministers would take up a more helpful and equitable attitude towards the Indian problem in Ceylon.

Crisis in Civilisation

Tagore's Birthday address at Santiniketan

Poet Rabindra Nath Tagore made a scathing condemnation of the British rule in India, in the course of his last message before his death on the occasion of his 80th. birthday celebrated at Santiniketan on Monday, the 14th. April 1941 by the Visva-Bharati. The following is an authorised English rendering of his address which was given in Bengali :

"With the advent of this year I have completed my eighty years of life. From the point I have now reached, I am enabled to see in clear perspective the vast stretch of time which I have already traversed. As I take a detached view of the beginning and development of my existence, I feel that in my own life as well as in the psychology of my country, a fundamental cleavage from the past has taken place. Believe me, this change has, within it, a profound cause of personal grief for myself.

"Our direct contact with the larger world of man was linked up with the contemporary history of the English people whom we came to know in those earlier days. It was mainly through their mighty literature that we formed our ideas with regard to these new-comers to our Indian shores. In those days the type of learning that was served out to us was neither plentiful nor diverse, nor was the spirit of scientific enquiry very much in evidence. Thus, our scope being strictly limited, it was the prevailing fashion among the elite of those days to fall back upon the language and literature of the English. Their days and nights were eloquent with the stately declamations of Burke, with Macaulay's long-rolling sentences ; discussions centred upon Shakespear's drama and Byron's poetry and above all, upon the large-hearted Liberalism of the nineteenth century English politics.

"Though tentative attempts were being made for gaining our national independence, at heart, we had not lost faith in the philanthropy and generosity of the English race. This belief was so firmly rooted in the sentiments of our leaders that they hoped that that the victor would of himself pave the path of freedom for the vanquished.

INFLUENCE OF ENGLISH LITERATURE

"This belief was based upon the fact that England at the time provided the persecuted all over the world with a home and shelter in her hospitable land. Any one who had striven for the integrity of his nation was sure to receive the most warm-hearted welcome at the hands of the English. Thus, in their character I had seen the purest ideal of philanthropy and I was led to set them on the pedestal of my highest respect. The generosity of their nature had not yet been vitiated by Imperialist pride. Their noble nature was to us a source of perpetual admiration. About this time I had the opportunity of listening to the speeches of John Bright, both in and outside Parliament. Even as a boy I was struck with his largeness of heart which overflowed all narrow national bounds and spread its influence far afield. That is why even in these days when England had fallen from her former grace, I remember and cherish my recollections of those other days.

"Certainly that spirit of abject dependence upon the innate goodness of our rulers was no matter for pride. What was remarkable, however, was the whole-hearted way in which we gave our recognition to human greatness even when it revealed itself in the foreigner.

"The best and the noblest gifts of humanity cannot be the monopoly of a particular race or country ; its scope may not be limited nor may it be regarded as the miser's board, buried underground. That is why the English literature which nourished our minds in the past, even now conveys its deep resonance to the recesses of our heart.

Civilisation East and West

"It is difficult to find a suitable Bengali equivalent for the English word 'civilisation'. That phase of civilization with which we were familiar in this country was known as 'good conduct', in other words, it was mainly a set of ethical codes. Narrow in themselves, these codes originated in a circumscribed geographical area. It was said that the rules of conduct which, for generations together, had held good in that strip of land, Brahmavarta by name, bound on either side by the rivers Saraswati and Drisadvati—were the rules to govern the society in general. In other words, conduct according to what our ancients said, was regulated by a number of traditions and conventions, however heartless or unjust they might have been. That is how a pharisaic formalism gradually got the upperhand of free thought and the ideal of 'good conduct' which Manu found established in Brahmavarta steadily degenerated into socialised tyranny.

"During my boyhood days the attitude of the cultured and educated section of Bengal, nurtured on English learning, was permeated with a feeling of revolt against those formal laws of conduct. A perusal of what Rajnarain Bose has written, describing the ways of the educated gentry of those days, will amply bear out what I have said just now. In place of the codes of conduct we accepted the ideal of civilisation as revealed in the character of the English people.

Parting of Ways

"In our own family this change of spirit was welcomed for the sake of its sheer rational force and its influence was felt in every sphere of our life. Born in that atmosphere and with my intuitive love of literature, I had naturally set the English on the throne of my heart. Such then was the state of affairs in the first chapters of my life. And then came the parting of ways, accompanied with a painful feeling of disillusion.

"I began increasingly to discover that those who accepted the best truths of civilisation disowned them with impunity, whenever questions of selfishness and greed were involved. There came a time when perforce I had to snatch myself away from mere appreciation of literature and contemplation of the great world of civilisation. As I emerged into the stark light of bare facts, the sight of dire poverty of the Indian masses rent my heart. Rudely shaken out of my dreams, I began to realise that perhaps in no other modern state had there been such hopeless dearth of the most elementary needs of existence.

"How could I help thinking that it was India that had kept replenishing the coffers of the British people ? Such travesty of the human ideal, such aberration in the mentality of the so-called civilised races, such criminal and contemptuous indifference to the crores of helpless Indian people I could never have imagined. I had associated the character of the English race which I had come to respect through their literature.

Benefits of Industrialisation Denied

"That mastery over machine through which the English had consolidated their sovereignty over their vast Empire, had been kept a sealed book away from the reach of this helpless country. And yet have we not seen with our own eyes what industrialisation did to Japan and how within a short time she achieved wonders ? I have also seen how Japan's civilised administration helped to distribute among her own people the fruits of her all-round progress. I have also been privileged to witness the unstinted energy with which Russia was trying to fight disease and illiteracy. Her industry and application has helped Russia in steadily liquidating ignorance and poverty and abject humiliation from the face of a vast continent. Her people have not observed distinction between one sect and another, one class and another. They have spread far and wide the influence of that human relationship which is above and beyond everything petty and selfish. Their astonishingly quick progress had made me happy and jealous at the same time.

"While in Moscow, I particularly liked one characteristic of Soviet administration and that was the pleasing fact that there was no conflict of interests on the score of Communal Award between Muslims and non-Muslims : a truly civilised administration impartially served their common interests.

"I have also seen Iran, newly awakened to a sense of national self-sufficiency, attempting to fulfil her own destiny, freed from the deadly grinding stones of the European Powers. It is significant that her good fortune dates from the day when she finally disentangled herself from the meshes of European diplomacy. With all my heart I wish well of Iran, may she deserve well at the hands of Fate.

"In the neighbouring kingdom of Afghanistan there is much to be desired so far as her education and society are concerned. But the fullest possibilities are there. And that is so, because up till now, she has not succumbed to the benumbing influence of any European Power, vaunting of its civilisation. Thus, these countries are now well on their way towards real progress.

Helpless under Dead Weight of Administration

"Under the dead weight of British administration India remained at the very bottom—static in her utter helplessness. So great and so ancient a civilisation as China, came to be corroded with the fatal addiction to opium into which her people were coerced. This insidious move was doubtless a part of the policy of exploitation of the weak. When we were about to forget the shameful history of how the British had seized a portion of China, we were painfully surprised by another event.

"While Japan was quietly devouring North China, her act of savage aggression was considered a minor incident by the insolent veterans of British diplomacy.

"We have witnessed from this distance how slyly the British statesmen took away the bottom out of the Republic of Spain, and we have also seen how a band of courageous Englishmen chivalrously laid down their lives for Spain. Even though the English had not aroused themselves sufficiently to their sense of responsibility towards China in the Far East, in their own immediate neighbourhood they have not hesitated to sacrifice themselves to the cause of individual freedom. Such acts of heroism reminded me over and again of the true English spirit to which in those early days I had given my whole faith. I do not even want remotely to think of the feeling of amity that then existed between England and Germany. What puzzles me is how within so short a period, its imperialist greed could bring about such tragic disintegration in the character of so great a race.

"One day I saw the English as a healthy nation, full of youthful vigour, ever ready to come to the help of those that needed it, and to-day I see them prematurely old, worn out by the plague of evil that has surreptitiously robbed the nation of its well-being.

Divide and Rule Policy

"I had to recount this tragic story of how gradually we came to lose faith in the civilisation of the West. Coming back to India, we feel that the blackest of evils that has come in the wake of British administration was much more than the rulers' shameful neglect and apathy to provide the minimum amenities of civilised existence.

"Their failure is nowhere more apparent than in the cruel way in which they have contrived to divide the Indians amongst themselves. The pity of it all lies in the fact that now perhaps they want to lay the blame at the door of our own society. This ugly and savage culmination of Indian history would never have been possible, if communalism and provincialism and lack of mutual faith were not sedulously encouraged to grow to their present vicious form, by some secret conclave holding the highest responsibilities in the system of administration.

"I can never believe that Indians are in any way inferior to the Japanese, either in intellect or in capacity. The fundamental difference between the two lies in the fact whereas India is not only overcome, but is also overwhelmed by the British, Japan had never allowed her interests to be clouded over by the benevolent protectorate of some European Power. Our rulers have established, what they call the government of 'law and order'—or, in other words, a policeman's administration.

"It is now no longer possible for us to retain any respect for that mockery of civilisation which believes in ruling by force and has no faith in freedom at all. By their miserly denial of all that is best in their civilisation, by withholding true human relationship from the Indians, the English have effectively closed for us all paths to progress.

"And yet my good fortune has often brought me into close contact with really large-hearted Englishmen. Without the slightest hesitation I may say that the nobility of their character was without parallel—in no country or community have I come across such greatness of soul. Such examples would not allow me to loss faith in the race, which produced them. I had the rare blessing of having Andrews —a Englishman, a real Christian and a true man—for a very close friend. To-day in the perspective of death his unselfish and courageous magnanimity shows all the brighter. The whole of India remains indebted to him for his various acts of charity which distinguished a life-time of dedicated service. But personally speaking, I am especially beholden to him, because he helped me to retain in my old age that feeling of respect for the English race with which in the past I was inspired by their literature and which I was about to lose completely. Along with his memory the innate greatness of his people will abide with me for ever. I count such Englishmen as Andrews not only as my personal and intimate friends, but as friends of the whole human race. To have known them has been to me a treasured privilege. They made me believe that English prestige will be saved from every shipwreck if there were more of such Englishmen. Had I not met them, not even the faintest hope would mitigate my despair with regard to the Western nations.

"Meanwhile, the demon of barbarity has given up all pretence and has emerged with unconcealed fangs and teeth, ready to tear up the world and spread devastation. From one end to another the poisonous fumes of hatred defile the atmosphere. This plague of persecution, which lay dormant in the civilisation of the West, has, at least, roused itself to create havoc and desecrate the spirit of Man. In our present luckless, helpless poverty have we not already seen this world-wide destruction at work ? A mortal combat has begun between one power and another, and no one knows what it will bring about in the end.

"The wheels of Fate will some day compel the English to give up their Indian empire. But what kind of India will they leave behind, what stark misery ? When the stream of their centuries' administration runs dry at last, what a waste of mud and filth will they leave behind them ! I had at one time believed that the springs of civilisation would issue out of the heart of Europe. And to-day when I am about to quit the world that stubborn faith has gone bankrupt altogether.

"To-day my one last hope is that the deliverer will be born in this poverty-stricken country and from the East his divine message will go forth to the world at large and fill the heart of man with boundless hope. As I proceed onward, I look behind to see the crumbling ruins of civilisation, strewn like a vast dung-heap of futility. And yet I shall not commit the grievous sin of losing faith in man. I would rather look forward to the opening of a new chapter in his history after the cataclysm is over and the atmosphere rendered clean with the spirit of service and sacrifice. Perhaps that dawn will come from this horizon, from the East where the sun rises. Another day will come when the unvanquished Man will retrace his path of glory, despite all barriers, to win back his lost human heritage. To believe in the final and irrevocable doom of humanity is certainly a crime, but I shall not be guilty of hugging illusion for reality.

"Finally, I shall proclaim that the day has come when it will no longer be safe for the mightiest of powers to give vent to proud complacence. We must realise the truth of what our sages said :

"By iniquity a man may thrive, may see many a good in life, may conquer his enemies, but iniquity, at last, is sure to overwhelm and destroy him."

The Chamber of Princes

Annual Session—New Delhi—17th to 18th March 1941

His Excellency the Viceroy, opening the session of the Princes' Chamber at New Delhi on the **17th March 1941**, stressed the importance of the Rulers of States "taking all possible measures to continue to deserve the reverence of the subjects and to strengthen and buttress the foundations upon which it rests."

"Union and co-operation," His Excellency continued, "are the foundation and the source of strength." Lord Linlithgow urged that the Princes should not allow themselves or their advisers to be diverted by any considerations of a personal character from ensuring that "where coperation is necessary, it shall take a form which no critic can assail on the ground that it is half-hearted. Such cooperation must, I recognise, involve sacrifices, as it must involve some surrender, or as I should prefer to say, some pooling of cherished sovereignty. But the need for such sacrifices is a stark reality, and I am wholly satisfied that those sacrifices, when they are made, will be amply repaid by results."

Nearly 45 Princes were present. The Maharaja of Bikaner, who had taken a leading part in the deliberations of the Chamber since its inception in 1921, was absent owing to the illness of the Dowager Maharani.

On arrival in the Chamber, His Excellency was received by the Chancellor, who introduced the Ruling Princes and Chiefs.

The Viceroy's Opening Address

The following is the text of His Excellency's address :—

"Your Highnesses, It is a great pleasure to me to meet you again this year and to preside over your deliberations, and I extend very cordial welcome to you all.

"I note with great satisfaction that the numbers attending this session of the Chamber are considerably higher than usual. That is, I have no doubt, the result partly of the natural desire of Your Highnesses to participate in discussions at the Imperial Capital during times so critical as those through which we are passing, and partly of the recent revision of the constitution of the Chamber, which has resulted in the addition of no fewer than 26 Rulers to those who enjoy the right of full membership. I would only say that it is a source of sincere gratification to me that of those new-members, so many should have been able to be present with us to-day ; and in taking the opportunity of welcoming them to the Chamber, I would express the hope that this reinforcement will prove a real source of fresh strength and vitality.

"It is a great satisfaction to me to know that the hopes which I voiced when I addressed Your Highnesses last year, in regard to the termination of the prolonged conditions of famine in Rajputana and Kathiwar have, thanks to a bounteous monsoon, been amply fulfilled, and that the anxieties which weighed upon so many of Your Highnesses and on your people as the result of the famine conditions which prevailed for so long, have been alleviated in so marked a degree.

Tribute to Late Ruler of Mysore

"Since the last meeting of the Chamber, death has taken a heavy toll. and the State of Limbdi in particular has suffered the loss of two of its Rulers. Those whose loss we mourn to-day include many close friends of all of us, and many who were outstanding figures in the Princely Order. We mourn the genial figure of His Highness the Maharana of Kolhapur. In the person of the late Maharao of Kotah, we have lost a Prince whose innate kindliness and solicitude for his subjects were well known. His late Highness the Maharaja of Mysore was a personality whose accomplishments would have won distinction in any walk of life As a Ruler, the manner in which he discharged the responsibilities of his great position, his close interest in the welfare of his subjects, his zeal for progress, for the advancement of justice, for the development of a higher sense of civic duty, and the simplicity of his mode of life, all of them impressed deeply those of us who had the privilege of his friendship and who had been able to see him in his own State and the example which he set enhanced the prestige of the Princely Order not only in this country but far beyond its borders.

"I am confident that it will be the wish of Your Highnesses to offer to the relatives of those Rulers who are no longer with us and to those who have succeeded to the responsibilities laid down by them, our sincere sympathy in their bereavement and our congratulations and good wishes in regard to the opportunities that lie before them.

"THE UNITY OF INDIA'S WAR EFFORT"

"When I last addressed Your Highnesses I remarked that, up to that time, no substantial call had been made on the manpower of India, but I added that, were conditions to alter, and were the war to take a different course, the offers of support of every kind so readily made by the Princes of India and so deeply appreciated, would be of the greatest value. Twelve months have indeed seen a vast alteration in the position, and the value of the cooperation of the States, and of the generous support which they have given in men, money and material has been proved in the most ample and signal way. The memorable words of appreciation spoken by His Imperial Majesty the King-Emperor in the message to India, which I have the honour to make public two days ago, will be fresh in the memory of all of us. Addressed as that message was alike to the Princes and the people of India, it brings out in a striking manner the unity of India's war effort, the great assistance she has given at a time of such critical importance to India and to the world, and the significance of the contribution made by the Princely Order and by British India alike.

"The contributions of the Indian States, under the inspiring leadership of Your Highnesses who are here to-day, and of other members of the Princely Order, have indeed been great. Their forces have been expanded, so that they could go forth to wherever the need was the greatest. By precept and by example they have encouraged their countrymen. They have been unstinting in their financial support, and their emblems are emblazoned to-day on countless weapons of war and on countless gifts of every kind designed to repair the injuries of war. The value of those generous contributions is enhanced by their spontaneity. If there is any complaint from Your Highnesses, I know only too well from my own conversations with so many members of the Princely Order, that it is, that the opportunities of service, and particularly of personal service in the face of the enemy, have fallen short of your own ardent desires.

"It is but natural, given the extent and the importance of the co-operation which the Indian States have given in the progress of the war, that you shoud have been concerned to play the utmost possible part in the various organisations which have been established to co-ordinate and to develop our war effort, and I have been at pains not only to keep in contact with His Highness the Chancellor and other leading Princes on this matter, but to do all in my power to keep the Indian States in close touch with current events of importance. The Technical Advisers from the Indian States rendered valuable service to India's representatives on that most important body, the Eastern Group Conference. The Indian States, in common with British India, will be represented on the Supply Council of the Eastern Group which has now been established, and on which the representatives of India sit side by side with the representatives of the Dominions of Australia, South Africa, New Zealand and of His Majesty's Government which will keep in touch with the Colonial Governments throughout the area. I would only observe in that connection that India's representative on that council, and my Supply Department shall be kept informed of the resources of the States, of their anxiety to assist by every means in their power, and of the contributions which they may be in a position to make towards the satisfaction of our ever-expanding needs.

"As Your Highnesses are no doubt aware, the States have obtained representation on the Export Advisory Committee, the Petrol Rationing Conference, the six Local Advisory War Supply Committees, and many other organisations established by the Central Government, and it is my sincere hope that steps which have been taken to bring about the closest co-operation between the Indian States and British India will be of mutual benefit, and will serve the best and truest interests of India as a whole.

PROBLEM OF INDIA'S DEFENCE

"His Majesty in his gracious messages touched on the military assistance given to the Empire's cause by the Princely Order and by the Indian States. I know that the many and varied problems which have inevitably arisen, and which will continue to arise from the close association of the Indian States forces with His Majesty's forces will be fully present to the minds of Your Highness. I know too, how fully you realise the relation of the test of active service to the present system. You will readily appreciate that in uniformity lies simplicity and efficiency. Much has already been done, in the process of assimilation, to diminish the differences that existed between types and conditions of military service in the Indian Army and in the States: and it is my confident hope and my belief that Your Highnesses will aproach, what problems of this nature yet remain for us, jointly to survey, in the determination that the eventual solution shall be that best fitted to serve the interests of India as a whole, and to secure her against external aggression.

"The mighty conflict in which we are now engaged must inevitably have reactions of profound importance on all countries and not the least on India herself. We are fighting for the cause of human freedom. We are fighting for ideals well known, readily accepted, commanding the full support of all. The magnificent example set by Their Imperial Majesties the King-Emperor and the Queen Empress, the way in which they have identified themselves with the feelings, the anxieties and the sufferings of their subjects throughout the empire, the extent to which they share the common danger, are known to us all. No example more inspiring could have been given. None could be more encouraging to all who are present here to-day.

"Subjects' Co-Operation—The Foundation of Strength"

"In India, Your Highnesses, representative of innumerable famous Ruling Houses, the inheritors of a great tradition of service, of an authority that has come down to you through long ages, need no reminder from me of the importance of taking all possible measures to safeguard that priceless heritage, to continue to deserve the reverence of your subjects, and to strengthen and buttress the foundations upon which it rests. For, this is a time of changing ideas and of new political conceptions, and the importance of taking such measures and taking them in time, needs no emphasis from me. In previous addresses to the Chamber of Princes, I had made certain suggestions on that subject. Those suggestions have been welcomed by many Princes, steps are being taken to adopt them in many parts of India with visible though not as yet spectacular results. I do not propose to repeat those suggestions to-day or to enlarge upon the subject, save to say, once more, that union and co-operation are the foundation and the source of strength. But to Your Highnesses and to the Princely Order I would make one earnest appeal, an appeal to which, I know, I can look with confidence for ready response. That appeal is that you should not allow yourselves or your advisers to be diverted by any considerations of a personal character from ensuring that, where co-operation is necessary, it shall take a form which no reasonable critic can assail, on the ground that it is half-hearted. Such co-operation must, I recognise, involve sacrifices as it must involve some surrender, or, as I should prefer to say, some pooling, of cherished sovereignty. But the need for such sacrifices is a stark reality, and I am wholly satisfied that those sacrifices, when they are made, will be amply repaid by results.

"Let me in conclusion remark that your agenda brings out most clearly not only that the normal function of the Chamber in such matters as the revision and the development of its constitution continues undisturbed by war-time conditions, it brings out also, and more important still, to what an extent it is your wish and your intention that this important and representative gathering, which I am so glad to see here to-day, shall be turned to wider account: and it shall demonstrate to the world, at this critical time, how whole-heartedly and unflinchingly the Princes of India share the common determination of all those who owe allegiance to His Imperial Majesty to see the present struggle pursued, with all the energies at their disposal, until victory has been achieved and the ideals for the preservation of which we are fighting, are secured beyond any question.

"I will not further keep Your Highnesses from your deliberations on the many important items that lie before you. There is much ground to be covered and I am confident that the results of this meeting of the Chamber will be of real and lasting value to your Highnesses and to your States."

Viceroy's Tribute to Departed Princes

On the occasion of the opening of Princes' Chamber, the Viceroy unveiled the marble bust of the late Rulers of Gwalior, Nawanagar and Patiala. His Excellency spoke as follows:

I am grateful to His Highness the Chancellor and the members and representative members of the Chamber for inviting me to preside over to-day's ceremony and unveil the busts of their late Highnesses the Maharajas of Gwalior, Nawanagar came home to the people in politics they realised that they had to sink political differences for the greater common cause.

"I see no reason why this process should not repeat itself in India also, though we must not forget how deep are the inherent divisions in India and how relatively remote even now war seems to many in India, above all among those whose whole career has been in political agitation and trouble and to whom political interest still seems the dominant one. We have to enable India to get out of that attitude, to get rid of the cocoon of old controversies into which elder Indian politicians spin themselves. It is from that point of view that I have welcomed the initiative of Sir Tej Bahadur Sapru and his friends. I am bound to point to the difficulties inherent in their first proposal because it is largely addressed to the wrong quarter and because it does not face these inherent Indian difficulties which are an obstacle. I certainly hope that these eminent and patriotic men will not cease their efforts, that in one way or another they will try to bring about unity in regard to the whole constitutional future of India. It is for them, far more than for us to judge the best way of achieving it.

"They will try, no doubt, to bring the leaders of two great organisations together. If they fail, it may well be that they could lay themselves out to get, through their personal eminence, greater measures of popular support from India itself—the building up of a party influential enough to get the attention of Indian parties and to enlist the support of those provincial governments to whose importance in the future constitutional scheme more than one speech has paid its tribute.

"There is no need for us to be despondent about the future even if the difficulties are great and even if it is not easy to discover one immediate remedy, above all a remedy devised from here. I assure the House that the Viceroy, to whose unwearied efforts tribute has been paid will not cease to try to find ways and means of implementing a policy which because it is ours we want to see succeed and carried out. I have no intention either so far as I am concerned or the Viceroy and Government of India are concerned, to look upon this matter with the idea that it should just drift along.

WAR EFFORT

"At the same time while there is an element of disappointment and discouragement in the purely political situation in India we should not overlook the fact that the political controversies in India are not the whole of India's life and outlook. Alongside all this deadlock and wrangles of leading Indian politicians and the more helpful efforts of Indian politicians to straighten out that particular aspect of things India is day by day feeling her feet. India is prosperous. There is more revenue for Central and Provincial Governments and not only under those Provincial Governments carrying on under democratic institutions but there is great deal of active social progress going on all the time. In the four Provinces conducting their own Governments they are very helpfully contributing to war effort. So is the whole public of India. Generous fund have flowed from every class of every purpose of war or for mitigation of suffering. One and a half millions for aeroplanes had been provided not only by Rajahs and wealthy industrialists but by the humblest peasants, policemen and soldiers. As to what India is doing in the actual field of war I agree that it will be desirable later to have a debate reviewing the broad field of India's war effort. The building up of an army of half a million in India and going beyond it with each increase of troops sent overseas is proceeding very actively and largely because good foundations were laid for it. Only the other day I received a letter from a distinguished soldier who had visited India after an absence of two years. He expresses his amazement at the progress made in the reshaping of India on the side of munitions.

MECHANISATION OF ARMIES

"I am bound to draw the attehtion of the House to the fact that the expansion of India's fighting strength is conditioned by the provision of modern war equipment and that is conditioned by machine tools and technical and skilled workers.

"India could produce two million fighting men. Unfortunately that is not enough. We have seen in the last few weeks a million of the bravest soldiers in the world, men I heard described in the last war as the finest infantry in Europe, equipped well according to the standards of the last war, scattered to the winds and broken in pieces by the armoured divisions which German foresight—and determination on war—provided while we in our self-delusion allowed locusts to eat the precious years we are now trying to retrieve for ourselves and India. In these matters India is dependent upon us and America also and can only slowly make good what ought to have been made good in previous years. Every effort is being made in that direction. The result of the Delhi Conference has been the setting up in India of the Eastern Group Supply Council with representatives from all governments of Dominions and Colonies east and south of Suez and of a central provision depot for all theatres of war in that part of the world. That is important now and it may be of immense consequence if the war develops in certain directions which we cannot yet foresee.

"In the same way every effort is being made to increase India's capacity to produce munitions. Young men are being trained by tens of thousands in India for technical and munition work and a smaller number are being sent for training to this country. Those who come here are trained at training centres and partly under carefully selected employers. They are not actually receiving pay but they receive an allowance for the purchase of suitable clothes and training allowances sufficient to cover the cost of upkeep and accommodation, with weekly pocket money. There are welfare officers specially attached to look after their well-being. I have every hope that the experiment will prove successful and it is widely welcomed in India itself. The training period is six months.

"India by the gallantry of her fighting men and the development of her industries is steadily establishing a real claim to equality with ourselves. The main constitutional task is inevitably for the moment far more in the hands of Indians themselves than in ours. We shall give them every help we can". The motions were agreed to.

Mahatma Gandhi's Statement on Amery's Speech

In this connection Mahatma Gandhi issued the following statement on Mr. Amery's speech which is charged with such emotion as he rarely puts into his public utterance. "Every line and every word of it breathes indignation—of a type somewhat unusual with the Mahatma", said the Rt. Hon'ble V. S. Srinivasa Sastri referring to it in his Ranade Hall speech at Madras on the 27th. April. The explanation must be sought in the fact that nothing repels Gandhiji so much as insincerity and Mr. Amery in his speech was so obviously concerned with making debating points that he had no use for sincerity. The following is the text of the statement :—

"I have read painfully the long report of the debate in the House of Commons on India. Distress has been known to have softened people's hearts and made them mindful of facts. But Britain's distress has evidently left Mr. Amery absolutely cool and untouched. This callousness makes me more than ever confirmed in my opinion that the Congress must abide by its policy of non-violence in spite of the heavy odds facing it.

"Mr. Amery has rendered no service to Great Britain by his contemptuous disregard of the situation as it exists in India and the facts that stare one in the face. He talks glibly of British rule having given peace to India. Did he not know what was happening in Dacca and Ahmedabad ? Who was responsible for keeping the peace in these two places ? I hope he will not throw in my face the fact that Bengal, at any rate, has self-government. He knows what a mockery that self-government is. He knows what little power for such emergencies toy Ministers have, whether they wear the Congress label, the League label or any other.

"I ask the very partinent question : Why has this long spell of British rule left the people so emasculated as to disable them from standing up against a few hundred goondas ? It is a humiliating spectacle, more for the British than for us, to see thousands of people running away from their homes through sheer fight, because a few goondas have found a favourable atmosphere for resorting to arson, murder and loot. The first act of any Government worth the name would be to teach its people the art of self-defence, but the foreign British Government had no concern about this fundamental welfare of India's citizens and so it deprived the people of the use of arms.

"All the handsome tribute that Mr. Amery pays to Indian troops falls flat on Indian soil, because, leaving aside Congress non-violence for the time being, if India had been equipped and trained for self-defence and if India had become a voluntary ally of Great Britain, I hold that all European Powers combined for destruction would not have touched Great Britain.

"Mr. Amery has insulted Indian intelligence by reiterating *ad nauseam* that Indian political parties have but to agree among themselves and Great Britain will register the will of a united India. I have repeatedly shown that it has been the traditional policy of Great Britain to prevent parties from uniting. 'Divide aud rule' has been Great Britain's proud and ill-conceived motto. It is the British statesmen who are responsible for the divisions in India's ranks and the divisions will continue so long as the British sword holds India under bondage.

"I admit that there is unfortunately an unbridgeable gulf between the Congress and the Muslim League. Why do not British statesmen admit that it is after all a domestic quarrel? Let them withdraw from India and I promise that the Congress and the League and all other parties will find it to their interest to come together and devise a home-made solution for the Government of India. It may not be scientific; it may not be after any western pattern; but it will be durable. It may be that before we come to that happy state of affairs, we may have to fight amongst ourselves. But if we agree not to invite the assistance of any outside Power, the trouble will last perhaps a fortnight and it will not mean even one day's destruction of human heads such as goes on in Europe to-day, for the simple reason that thanks to the British rule we are wholly unarmed.

"Mr Amery, in utter disregard of truth, misleads his ignorant audience that the Congress wants 'all or nothing'. Let me remind him that in order to placate British sentiment, the Congress descended to the Poona Resolution and when at Bombay it undid the Poona Resolution, I authoritatively stated that the British Government could not at the present moment grant or declare India's independence and that, therefore, for the time being, we should be satisfied with complete freedom of speech and pen. Was that 'All or nothing'? With Mr. Amery's state of mind, I suppose it is too much to expect him to have the elementary grace to acknowledge the studied moderation of the Congress in its desire not to embarrass the British Government whilst it is fighting for its very existence. Not having that grace, he turns the Congress moderation against it and claims that the Congress civil disobedience has fallen flat.

"It took my breath away when I read his statement about India's prosperity. I say from experience that it is a legendary thing. India's millions are becoming progressively pauperised. They are miserably clothed and underfed. Because there is one man's rule, he is able to produce a budget of millions. But I make bold to say that it is not only no proof of the prosperity of the famishing millions, but it is proof positive that India is being ground down under the Brish heel. It is the duty of every Indian, who knows anything about the distress of the peasantry, to rise in rebellion against this autocratic rule. Fortunately for humanity, India's rebellion is a peaceful revolt and I hope it will be through exclusively peaceful effort that India will realise her natural destiny.

"But I must not carry any further the painful dissection of Mr. Amery's performance. It hurts me to have to undertake even this very brief analysis of his speech. But it is so amazingly misleading that I felt I would be falling in my duty if I did not point out at least some of the most glaring discrepancies in that unfortunate utterance. Surely he could have rested content with the undisputed sway that he exercises over the destinies of over four hundred million people."

Standing Committee of the Bombay Conference

The following statement was issued by the Standing Committee of the Bombay Conference dated the 28th. April 1941:—

"The Standing Committee of the Bombay Conference have read Mr. Amery's speeches in the House of Commons with the care which they deserve. The Committee very much regret that the speeches should have betrayed such an amazing misunderstanding of the real political situation in India and displayed such an unsympathetic and unbending attitude towards the aspirations of India. The Committee feel that Mr. Amery has missed the opportunity of winning public confidence which was offered to the British Government, with the best intentions, by those who have a vivid appreciation of the dangers of the international situation They have, however, reason to apprehend that one certain effect of these speeches is going to be to strengthen the forces of disruption in the country and to create the impression that, in point of fact, the British Government have no desire to part with real power at this junction.

"The Committee regret very much that Mr. Amery should have adopted an attitude of self-complacency with regard to the position in India which was bound to create a wrong impression in Parliament, and probably on a large audience in America, that the present system of Government in India commands not only the acquiescence of the people of this country but also their goodwill. The Committee have no hesitation in saying that this is a complete travesty of the situation in India.

"The Committee, however, note with satisfaction that there were men in Parliament belonging to different parties some with considerable knowledge of India, such as Sir *Stanley Reed* and Sir *George Schuster*, who controverted Mr. Amery's assumptions then and there and warned him against the unwisdom and unfairness of his policy of drift at a time of such a grave peril. The Committee feel, however, that it would be unfair to Mr. Amery to hold him wholly responsible for creating this impression, as the original responsibility for giving a true estimate of the situation in India rests with the Government of India.

"No one in this country, and no one, particularly, connected with the Bombay Conference has ever minimised the desirability of reconciliation between the two important political bodies of India—the Congress and the Muslim League. The President of the Bombay Conference (who will issue a separate statement) was not unmindful of the desirability of removing misunderstanding at an early date, and he made endeavours before the Conference met at Bombay to explore the possibilities of bringing the contending parties together. The organisers of the Conference were, however, satisfied that, in view of the fundamental differences between the Congress and the Muslim League there was no prospect, within a reasonable distance of time, of those contending parties coming together. The Conference felt, at the same time, that it was intolerable that the progress of the country should be held up by His Majesty's Government merely because the two contending parties would not or could not compose their differences. In this connection, the Committee would refer to the statement made by His Excellency the Viceroy on the 8th August last : 'It is clear', said His Excellency, 'that the earlier differences which had prevented the achievement of national unity remain unbridged. Deeply as His Majesty's Government regret this, they do not feel that they should any longer, because of these differences, postpone the expansion of the Governor-General's Council'. For Mr. Amery now to insist upon agreement as a condition precedent to any change at the Centre, is really to go back on the declared policy of His Majesty's Government.

"The Committee would like the Secretary of State to consider whether the repetition of the advice that Indians should first settle their differences among themselves before expecting any constitutional change, could absolve him from the reproach, so pointedly made by Sir Chimanlal Setalvad in his recent statement on Mr. Amery's speech, namely, 'However profuse the assurances of the British Government may be as regards their intentions to make India a self-governing Dominion, no political party is convinced, because of past experience, of the British Government's sincerity, as regards parting with power."

"In view of the growing dangers to India from the war, those who assembled at Bombay put forward certain proposals which they were satisfied were practicable, and which, if accepted, would have had an excellent psychological effect on the country and stimulated genuine voluntary war effort to a much greater extent. The present policy of the Secretary of State is bound to have a deleterious effect on the minds of the people and on the situation in India, for which the entire responsibility must be his and of His Majesty's Government.

"According to the Secretary of State, the present position seems to be that until it pleases Mr. Jinnah to approve of any scheme, His Majesty's Government can do nothing to give effect even to their own intentions as announced in August last. Mr. Amery has referred to an unworthy insinuation made by Mr. Jinnah in his speech at Madras, to the effect, that the Bombay Conference was held in consultation with or at the instigation of some Congress leaders in the interests of the Congress. The Committee repudiate this categorically. The Committee would not have noticed such an aspersion, but for the fact that the Secretary of State referred to it in his speech in the House of Commons to the prejudice of the Conference and its organisers.

"It is not difficult to understand the working of the mind of the Secretary of State. He assumed that in seven provinces where the constitutional machinery of Government had been replaced by the personal rule of the Governors, the people were contened with the system of administration—an assumption which, if true, must bar out all proposals of advance even after the war. He apparently thought that the attitude of the Hindus did not require to be taken seriously into account, whereas he assumed that the Muslim League, in its present state of intransigeance represented the attitude of all the Muslims of India, or of an overwhelming majority of them, even though provinces like Sind and the North-West Frontier Province and considerable sections of Muslims in other provinces repudiate the authority and policy of the Muslim League and the leadership of Mr. Jinnah. These facts should, in fairnes, have been brought to the notice of the House of Commons.

"The Secretary of State has advised the Conference as to what it should do in future. Its members are according to him, to devote their energies to bringing about a settlement between the Congress and the League and, failing that, to attempt to form a Centre Party. Meanwhile, they are to remain satisfied with his promise of Dominion Status at an indefinite date, with an unrepresentative and un-influential Centre and personal rule in seven provinces. The Standing Committee are compelled, in view of their knowledge of the country, to reject this advice, for reasons of which Mr. Amery and his advisers in India cannot surely be ignorant. The Conference at Bombay was concerned with the immediate future during the war, not with long-range policies, which must bide their time. Even if a Centre Party were to emerge after a number of years, what guarantee is there that its proposals would receive any better treatment than have the united demands of Indian politicians in the past ? The burden of the Secretary of State's speech is that, before he can be prepared to consider any proposal, there must be the prior approval of Mr. Jinnah—a position which no self-respecting political party can accept or tolerate.

"The Committee desire to meet some of Mr. Amery's objections and raise some questions with regard to them. One of his objections is that the Conference proposal would mean not a modification of the present form of government, but its supersession by an entirely different form of Government. The present Government consists of four officials and two non-official Indians in addition to His Excellency the Commander-in-Chief. All the members of the Government are at present appointed by the Crown and are responsible to it. The Committee understand that, under the proposals made last August by the British Government, the number of official members was to be reduced to two and the total strength of the Executive Council increased to eleven. The Conference have proposed no change, either in respect of the appointing authority or in the responsibility of the Members of the Government to the Crown. All that it has suggested that not only two, but all the four official members should be replaced by non-officials. Does such a proposal amount to a supersession of the present system of Government ?

"The Secretary of State has chosen not to show his hand. The Committee are entitled to ask the British Government what their concrete proposals are. Does the Secretary of State object to the transfer of the important portfolios of Finance and Defence and, if so, why ? Sir George Schuster, himself the Finance Member of the Government of India from 1928 until 1934, expressed his belief, in the House of Commons, that competent Indians could be found for the Finance portfolio. The Committee have equally little doubt that a competent Indian can be found for the Defence portfolio. The Conference did not, as will appear from the resolution, want to affect the position and responsibility of the Commander-in-Chief ; and as both he and the Defence Member would be appointed by the Crown, it should not be difficult to adjust their mutual relations. The only construction that the Committee can put on the position taken by Mr. Amery is that key portfolios would not be tranferred to Indian hands. It is quite clear from this that, even if there had been a previous agreement between the main political parties, these portfolios would not have been entrusted to Indian members.

"Another point which has been raised by the Secretary of State is that the reconstructed Government would not get political support or even acquiescence from the legislature. This objection was fully dealt with in Sir N. N. Sircar's speech at the Bombay Conference, but the Committee would like briefly to refer to it here for the sake of completeness. The total strength of the Legislative Assembly is 143. Out of these, the Congress and the Muslim League combined total only about 60. They would be unable to defeat the Government without the help of other parties. In the absence of the Congress, the Congress Nationalist Party is the second largest party in the Assembly, and its leader, Mr. Aney has publicly supported the Bombay Conference proposals and is a member of this Committee. Considering that the proposal of the Bombay Conference was that the Executive should be responsible to the Crown and not to the legislature, the argument of a possible conflict between the Legislature and the Executive loses much of its force but even assuming that, at times, the Governor-General is compelled to resort to his power of certification, it is difficult to understand how his position would become worse if he were asked by the reconstituted Government to exercise that power than it is now, when he does so upon the recommendation of a mixed Council consisting partly of officials and partly of non-officials. All this fear of conflict between the Legislature and the Government reconstituted on national lines seems to be extremely hypothetical, as it assumes unreasonableness on the part of the Legislature and inability on the part of the Government to influence it.

"It has further been suggested that the reconstituted Council would create internal constitutional problems in relation to the provinces and the Princes. But even with the partial transfer suggested by the Secretary of State last year, there would have been a majority of non-officials in the Executive Council. There is not the remotest reason to assume that Indians in such positions would work in an unreasonable spirit, or would unnecessarily obstruct the Governor-General in the discharge of his responsibilities. Such technical objections presuppose a determination on the part of those who will be selected by the Viceroy to paralyse or to offer obstruction in the smooth running of the Government. On such a supposition, no constitutional advance can now or ever be made.

"The pertinent questions which the Committee would wish the Secretary of State to answer are (1) What is the interpretation to be placed on the following declaration which Mr. Amery made on behalf of His Majesty's Government on August 11, 1940:—"In spite of the discouraging attitude shown in Congress quarters, I still hope that they will be willing to take their part. If that should unfortunately not prove to be the case, Lord Linlithgow will, of course, go ahead, prepared to work, with those who will work with him and with each other". Is it the Secretary of State's latest view that unless Mr. Jinnah as the head of the Muslim League is willing to co-operate on his own terms, the co-operation of all other parties is of no political value whatever to the British Government? If that is not the intention, he should say so in explicit terms. (2) The other question which the Committee desire to ask is whether his advisers in India sincerely believe that it is impossible at the present moment for Mr. Jinnah to come to terms with the Congress or any other major party in India?"

"The Committee are utterly unable to follow the Secretary of State's reasoning that it would be very difficult to persuade Parliament to confer Dominion or quasi-Dominion powers on a reconstructed Executive Council. The resolution had suggested that, in regard to inter-imperial and international matters, the reconstructed Government should be treated on the same footing as the Dominion Governments. During and since the last war, the right of the Government of India to be represented at such conferences has been recognised invariably in practice. India has had, particularly since her admission to the League of Nations as one of its original members, direct representation, not only at the annual conferences of the League and its auxiliary at Geneva, but also at imperial and international conferences whenever they have been called. It seems unthinkable that, twenty years after such a principle has been in practice, the Secretary of State should refuse to concede the point that Indian delegations to such conferences should be appointed by the Government of India and receive their instructions from them.

"As regards the demand of the Conference that a time-limit should be prescribed for the inauguration of the Dominion Status after the termination of the war the Committee attach considerable importance to it, as without such a time limit the country cannot feel sure that India will get Dominion Status and Dominion powers within a responsible distance of time. It is surely not right to cast the whole burden on the shoulders of Indian statesmen; and the Committee feel that it is not possible to arive at a formula under which in certain given circumstances the time-limit fixed may be extended if necessary by another short period.

The Committee are not unmindful of the consideration that, at this grave moment, the thoughts of Englishmen are naturally concentrated on the war. They need increasing help—more men, more money, more material. The Committee and the people of this country at large are no less concerned in the outcome of the war, and are most anxious to help to the utmost in its prosecution, as it is seriously threatening the fate of India also. But they feel that such help will not come in abundance unless, at this critical juncture, the present policy of drift is abandoned, and Indians are placed in positions of real power and responsibility."

Sir Tej Bahadur Sapru's Statement

Sir Tej Bahadur Sapru, Chairman of the Bombay Non-Party Leaders' Conference, issued the following statement on the 29th. April 1941 :

The Standing Committee of the Bombay Conference has already issued a statement on Mr. Amery's speech in the House of Commons. There are, however, certain matters to which I should like to refer in my personal statement. I was most reluctant hitherto to say publicly that, for nearly two months before the Conference met at Bombay, I did all I could, in my individual capacity, to bring Mahatma Gandhi and Mr. Jinnah together. Even now, I should not like to disclose, without their permission, anything of the correspondence that passed between them and me. All that I can say is, that I have not been unmindful of the need for a communal settlement. Indeed, since December last, when I issued my first statement, and again in January, when I wrote an article in the *Twentieth Century*, I have been emphasising the need of these two leaders meeting each other. I gave this suggestion of mine the first place among the several suggestions that I made. I am surprised to note that Mr. Amery's speech shows that he is unaware of it, as I presumed that he would know something of it after conversations with the Viceroy.

This is not the time for me to apportion blame between the leaders. I regret to say that my efforts bore no fruit. As matters stand now, I am more than doubtful if the chances of a settlement between the two parties can be looked upon as at all bright. Mr. Jinnah's speech at Madras and Mahatma Gandhi's recent pronouncement show that, if anything, the gulf is wider than even before.

It was just when I was carrying on this correspondence that a European member of the Legislature, who has been criticising the Bombay Conference, wrote to me as follows, "I have been feeling for sometime that His Majesty's Government ought to take the initiative in the matter of a communal agreement. It is no use merely saying that such an agreement is a pre-requisite to any further constitutional discussions, and then leaving it at that." That was and still is my view. Those who talk of an agreement being a pre-requiste of further constitutional changes should not, in my opinion, content themselves with making repeated references to them, but should also take a hand in promoting such a settlement. I have seen no evidence of that either in England or in India. Long-range discussions and criticisms of the internal situation cannot help the people and do not redound to the credit of the Government.

Mr. Amery says in his speech that we have not been able to secure beforehand for our scheme any kind of agreement, if not between the Congress and the Muslim League, at any rate between the latter and other representatives of the Hindu majority. Surely, this new condition which is now solemnly put forward by the Government, could not have been absent from the minds of those who were responsible for making the declaration of August 8. And if it was present to their mind then, why did they not say that no kind of change in the constitution would be brought about except with agreement between the major contending parties ? During the Round Table Conference discussions when Mr. Ramsay MacDonald consulted me about the Communal Award, I told him point blank that if I were the British Prime Minister, I should not undertake that responsibility ; and yet, notwithstanding the fact that there was no agreement between the Hindus and the Muslims, Mr. Ramsay MacDonald's Government, which consisted also of Conservatives, went on with their scheme, gave first the Communal Award and then introduced the India Bill.

Bluntly put, Mr. Amery is mortgaging our future to certain intractable leaders. Expediencies of the hour are not always consistent with lasting policies seeking to achieve the permanent good of a vast country like India. Has Mr. Amery such a permanent policy ? If so, what steps is he taking to implement that policy ? What is his real contribution to the solution of the communal tangle ? Is he not, by his speeches, making the task of those who want a real settlement more and more difficult ? Is he strengthening the faith of Indians in British intentions ?

In ordinary circumstances, I should not have taken notice of what Mr. *Jinnah* said about me or the Conference over which I presided at Bombay, and I should certainly not have followed his example by lowering the level of public controversy by indulging in personalities. Let me, however, say that I am not aware of any kind of wire-pullers, Congress or non-Congress ; and during my long public life, I have never known anybody laying any kind of trap for me. These are clap-trap methods of controversy intended to create a prejudice against those from whom you differ ; and I am surprised that Mr. Amery, a seasoned politician and one accustomed to dealing with public controversies, should have even referred to what Mr. Jinnah said about the wire-pullers having laid a trap for me.

I can only assume that like several Europeans in India who have been publicly, in their speeches, saying that the Bombay Conference was really inspired by Congress, Mr. Amery is obsessed with the same idea. I can only say that not a word passed between Mr. Gandhi or any other Congress leader and myself at any time either in correspondence or in personal conversation with regard to the idea of holding the Bombay Conference or to the character of the resolution it should adopt. I may, however, say that when the Presidentship of the Conference was offered to me, I made it a condition precedent to my accepting it, that, at the Conference, no kind of communal issue should be raised. I was more than gratified that men like Mr. Savarkar and Dr. Moonje, who were present at the Conference, played the game and accepted the resolution. They are men with strong party convictions, and yet, for the sake of a settlement, they subordinated their party feelings to the common goal we had in view. I should have expected in fairness that Mr. Amery would have drawn the attention of the House to the fact. Let me say once again that I take the fullest responsibility for my judgment; it may be right or it may be wrong, but I have never in my life felt that anybody had laid a trap for me, neither a Secretary of State nor a political leader in India.

Mr. Amery has appealed to me and my friends not to cease from our efforts to concentrate, first and foremost, on bringing the contending elements together or on building up a strong Centre Party of men who are prepared to put India first. I shall be absolutely frank.

I believe Mr. Amery's indiscreet and unfortunate speeches on this subject have done the worst service to us, and he has no business to make that pious appeal to us when he himself has done nothing to promote unity among the contending elements in India. As regards our continuing these efforts, I shall be very glad if those in india who, parrot-like, repeat Mr. Amery's pious sentiments, will do something to show that they are in earnest about it. So far as I am concerned, I do not want any encouragement from any quarter, nor shall I feel discouraged in carrying out my convictors, merely because the Secretary of State, who is credited with having good intentions, has the unfortunate knack of expressing those good intentions in such language.

As regards the formation of a Centre Party, all that I wish to say is that I do not see any prospect of such a party coming into existence or functioning effectively so long as the present policy of Mr Amery and of the Government of India is maintained. At the same time, I should not like to stand in the way of those of my friends in Bombay and elsewhere who have a faith in the formation of such a party. I would wish them every success, but let them take steps and not merely repeat what Mr. Amery has been saying from a distance of six thousand miles. I am very doubtful that if a Centre Party was brought into existence, it would fare better at the hands of Mr. Amery or the Government of India. They could dispose of it easily, by saying that it did not contain an adequate number of Muslims or the Depressed Classes, that it had not yet developed a sufficient backing in the country and that it was bound to meet with opposition on the part of the Congress or the Muslim League——a fear which seems to have unnerved and indeed paralysed both Mr. Amery and the Government of India.

The National Liberal Federation

Council Meeting Resolutions—Poona—29th. June 1941

The council of the National Liberal Federation of India, which met at Poona on the **29th. June 1941** under the presidentship of Sir *Vithal Chandavarkar*, discussed the present political situation for over four hours.

Among those present were Dr. *R. P. Paranjpye*, the hon. Pandit Hridyanath Kunjru, Sir Cowasji Jehangir, the hon. Mr. P. N. Sapru, Dr. G. S. Mahajani, Mr. P. Kodandarao, Mr. G. K. Gadgil, Mr. N. R. Wadia and Pandit Hardat Sharma.

The following resolutions were passed :—

and I trust a similar principle would be laid down by the Utilisation Committee in the disposal of grants and rights to utilise the researches.

WAR AND PRIMARY PRODUCER'S PLIGHT

In the midst of the difficulties created by the accumulation of stocks of raw commodities, a relieving feature for the duration of the war, lessened the strain on the resources of this country, is the magnitude of the war orders placed on behalf of His Majesty's Government and other allied Governments for the purchase of arms, ammunition and other war supplies required for the prosecution of the war. These orders are of the value of about Rs. 83 crores and have b en responsible, to a large extent, for giving a fillip to some of indigenous industries which were experiencing serious difficulties in the pre-war period. While I recognise that these orders have come as a relief to the country in an otherwise depressing period, it does not compensate, as was contended by the Honourable the Finance Member in presenting the Budget Proposals, the Indian primary producer for the loss of his old Continental and traditional markets. It must be remembered that industry enterprise in India is responsible for the employment of scarcely 42 per cent of the Indian population, while more than 64 per cent is dependent, for its living upon the disposal of primary produce. As Indian economy is mainly based on the disposal of the country's primary produce the economic condition of the masses is dependent upon the prices which the country receives for its raw commodities. The placing of orders for the supply of raw materials has not materially improved the price level of the raw commodities and consequently. the financial standing of producer has practically remained at the level where it was in the pre-war period. The hon. the Finance Member himself admits that while, immediately after the war, the price level increased by 40 points, it has receded back, during the current year, to a level which is only 15 per cent higher than what it was at the beginning of the war. As I have indicated above, by a reference to the prices for India's main staple commodities, the primary producer has not gained as a result of the war orders placed by His Majesty's Government and other allied Governments. In fact, it must be remembered that the prices prevalent immediately before the war were themselves bordering on the depression level and do not constitute a proper criterion to judge the present prices. Moreover, it cannot be said that the rise in exports, which mainly represents manufactured articles, would compensate the country for the loss which it has suffered by the closure of the continental markets because, while the closure of these markets affected the price structure of the primary commodities, the depressing influence has not been counteracted by the increase of india's exports in manufactured articles. It would also be not fair for either the Honourable the Member for Communications or the Honourable the Finance Member to bring out, in support of their contention, the fact that there has been an increase in railway traffic and postal receipts and this can be taken as a sufficient indication to reflect an improvement in the general economic conditions in India over pre-war conditions. In normal times, these factors may be accepted as an indication to gauge the economic condition of a country but in times of war, they cannot be relied upon as a true pointer to the prosperity of a country. In is well-known that the increase in Railway receipts is mainly due to the increased war traffic and the enhancement of railway rates and fares which in itself is an indirect form of taxation on the people. As regards the postal receipts, the Honourable the Finance Member has himself admitted in his speech that the "larg revenue is almost wholly due to the effect of the increases in rates" and that the Government traffic has contributed substantially to the postal surpluses. There are a number of other circumstances such as, diminution in the motor transport facilities, necessity for resorting to telegraphic and cable communications for quick despatch of work, which have contributed to the greater yield of receipts under the Railways and the Postal Department and the e is no reason, I think, why these receipts should be pointed as an evidence of improvement in the economic conditions in the country.

As a result of the multifarious activities of the Supply Department of the Government of India, which has been responsible for the purchase of stores worth about Rs. 83 crores, the Government of India must have come in possession of very important information relating to the capacity, existing and potential, of the various indigenous industries to carter for war requirements. The Supply Department must have also come in possession of information, during the course of their investigations and enquiries, as to what articles could be manufactured in the country and what possibilities were there for the development of the existing industries and for the establishment of new ones, provided sufficient patronage by way of guaranteed orders was assured to such enterprises. I would, therefore, like to suggest that the Government of India should fully utilise all such information to the country's advantage. I am afraid this would not be possible with the existing machinery of the Government and for that purpose, a small Body composed of eminent Indian industrialists and Indian public men should be constituted into an Industrial Reconstruction Council to utilise all the material and information so far gathered by the Supply Department during the last 18 months of its existence, with a view to evolve an immediate plan for either suitably expanding the present situation which Indian industries will have to face after the termination of the present war would be serious enough to demand immediate consideration of this proposal in the interest not only of Indian industries but also of India's primary producers. The British Government have already appointed Sir Charles Innes, a former Commerce Member of the Government of India, to advise them and the British industries with regard to the industrial reconstruction in the United Kingdom after the war. I trust the Government of India would take immediate steps to bring into existence some such suitable machinery similar to the one recently provided for by the British Government to undertake investigations with regard to industrial reconstruction in the post-war period, and I am sure the Government would be doing something very helpful towards the solution of the problem of the utilisation of indigenous raw materials and towards diversifying India's industrial production after the war. Even with the best of wishes which the present Indian Commerce Member has towards the country's industrialisation, it would not be an easy task for an individual industrialist to take the necessary initiative in this direction. If India is to equip herself to face the post-war situation, then the establishment of a Council, as suggested above, would be an essential measure as our raw materials would not be required for some time to come, particularly, at a time when the resources of the masses of the country would be nearly exhausted. As new channels for trade and new markets would come into existence during the war, it is necessary that careful consideration should be paid to these problems from now.

India and Eastern Group Conference

The day-to-day urgencies of the war production and supplies felt by His Majesty's Government necessitated the holding of a conference of the countries of the Eastern Group, with a view to pool their resources for the prosecution of the war. The Government of India were instrumental in calling such a conference on behalf of His Majesty's Government in October last. India, no doubt, occupies a place of stragetic importance in the British Empire, but I am sorry to say that this position has not been fully utilised by His Majesty's Government in equipping themselves for the successful prosecution of the war. The holding of the Eastern Group Conference naturally, therefore, raised high expectations in India as regards possible expansion of her present industries and immediate establishment of Defence industries so very essential for a protracted war. The procedure which the Government of India adopted in associating commercial opinion by appointment of non-official advisers was not very happy and I am speaking from personal experience when I say that closer association was possible which would have engendered confidence in the public mind and which would have accelerated the pace of India's war effort. On the contrary, I feel there is a genuine feeling of apprehension, in the absence of any knowledge regarding the conclusions reached at the Conference as regards the likely repercussions of these decisions on the establishment and development of industries in India. The public is also in the dark as regards the functions and working of the newly established Eastern Group Council, and they would like to be enlightend whether the new Council is to direct the whole policy of the war purchases by His Majesty's Government in the Eastern part of the Empire, whether it would be competent for them to direct the placing of orders with a particular country so as to encourage the establishment of any Defence industries and whether it would be competent for the Council to advise the Governments of any of the Eastern Group countries to allow the use of foreign capital for the starting of such Defence indusuries. It is necessary therefore, for the Government of India to come forward and to remove all such apprehensions from the public mind on these questions. It will be still further helpful in removing public misgivings if the Government would come forward with an assurance that they would not allow any of the directions of the Eastern Group Council either to compromise or jeopardise India's economic interests and that it would not preclude India from establishing or developing any industries, particularly key and engineering industries in the country. I would further like to sound a note of warning that the Government of India should not agree to the creation of new vested interests under the control of non-Indians which are sure to be prejudicial to India's economic interests.

While on the question of the establishment of Defence industries, I welcome the recent establishment of the Aircraft Factory at Bangalore and I am sure the Indian commercial community will appreciate if I take this opportunity of paying their tribute to the perseverance and tenacity of purpose with which Mr. Walchand Hirachand carried on his endeavours in bringing this industry into existence. The efforts of the Government of India in identifying themselves with the country's aspirations to establish this important Defence industry and prevailing upon His Majesty's Government to allow these efforts to fructify, deserve felicitations from the commercial community. I only wish that their attitude had been similarly helpful towards the establishment of a shipbuilding Yard, at Calcutta. In the absence of any encouragement at the hands of the Calcutta Port Commissioners, the project pioneered by the Scindia Steam Navigation Company Limited for constructing a Shipbuilding Yard at Calcutta had to be given up and it had to be shifted to Vizagapatam. I hope both these ventures will be successful in due course and India will have a fully developed aircraft industry both for military and civil purposes as also a national shipbuilding industry on a scale large enough to meet the requirements of her large maritime trade and vast coastline. In fact the commercial community has felt that since a long time that had India possessed an adequate mercantile marine of her own, the acute difficulties about shortage of tonnage which has been one of the main causes for blocking up of large quantities of exportable goods even for the permissible markets could well have been avoided and the Indian primary producer would have been able to secure an appreciably higher price for his goods. A national mercantile marine apart from serving the needs of the large export trade of the country could have been extremely useful also as India's second line of defence. I trust the Government of India would realise the precarious position especially for the export trade of the country, created by the absence of a national mercantile fleet and take all measures necessary to encourage national shipping.

Plea for Greater Aid to Industries

The Government of India, as you must be aware, have already announced their policy of encouraging the establishment of such industries in the country as are helpful in furthering their war efforts. They have announced that these industries would not be left high and dry after the termination of the war. I would emphasise that this policy of protection and encouragement should be extended also to such other industries as have been established to meet the needs and requirements of the people of the country, particularly owing to the restricted imports from foreign countries. The Government can encourage these industries either through protective duties or grant of subsidies or purchases on behalf of Government departments or in other suitable manner. I need hardly point out the necessity of encouraging particularly capital industries like those for manufacture of machinery and machine tools, heavy chemicals, etc. But it would be essential, in pursuing a liberal policy of encouragement of industries, that the rigid criteria for grant of protection laid down by the Indian Fiscal Commission should be completely revised. It is recognised on all hands that the conditions prevalent when the Fiscal Commission reported 20 years ago have entirely changed and it is surprising that when the Governments of various countries are adopting new policies of encouraging their industries and making their countries self-sufficient in their vital needs, the Government of India should still adhere to the policy of discriminatory protection enunciated nearly twenty years ago. I would suggest therefore, that the Government should immediately set up suitable machinery which would deal expeditiously and sympathetically with claims of industries for protection. It is also necessary that such industries as are protected or encouraged by the Government or by the public as Swadeshi industries should in their turn realise their reciprocal obligations and encourage other Indian industries by purchasing their own requirements from them.

Although the Secretary of State for India has ranked this country amongst the highly industrialised countries of the world, we are all aware that large masses of the people in the country depend entirely upon agriculture for their living and the export of raw materials is the mainstay of the economy of the country.

The per-capita consumption of coal in India in the year 1936 was 1 metric ton as compared to 3.5 to 3.9 metric tons per person per year in Great Britain, the United States and Belgium, Germany and Canada from the next highest consumption group at a level just below 2.5 tons. It need hardly be pointed out that the differences in consumption are due mainly to differences in the extent of industrialisation. The very fact that a largely populated country like India has to face the problem of surplus coal shows the death of industrialisation in the country. While referring to the coal industry, I may point out that if industries are properly developed in India by laying down a well planned policy of industrialisation for the country, the coal resources of the country would play a vital role in supplying the needs of these industries. In the absence of such a policy we find the coal industry of the country experiencing practically a continuous slump and it cannot be foreseen what the position of the industry will be on the termination of the war. It is unfortunate that an imporant key industry like coal has been in such a precarious condition since a number of years. The problems of the industry are many and it is very essential that they should be properly investigated without delay.

Unemployment Problem

The question of industrialisation brings us to the serious problem of unemployment of middle class youngmen in the country which has been engaging the attention of the Provincial Governments, Universities and publicmen in the country since a long time. The proper remedy of the problem lies in pursuing a definite policy of industrialisation of the country. It is industrialisation alone which can absorb these thousands of qualified youngmen brought out by the Universities of the country. Some of the Universities have also technological institutions attached to them and the young men who receive this training would prove especially useful to the country in these days. The necessity of having a well qualified trained technical personnel for the industries of the country is obvious especially at the present time when we find some of the vital industries of the county so largely dependent on them.

India's war efforts in supplying the war requirements of His Majesty's Government have brought in their wake substantial sterling resources to the credit of India and in the hands of the Reserve Bank. I am glad the Government of India have taken a correct decision in terminating the present contracts of the three Company managed railways, viz., the B. B. & C. I., Assam Bengal and Tapti Valley Railways, and bringing them under the direct control of the Government of India. I would like, in this connection, to refer to the statement made by Sir Andrew Clow, the Communications Member, that the Government in purchasing these railways had not accepted the policy of substituting State management in place of the company management and they had taken the decision in respect of these railways on their own merits. While welcoming the Government's decision, to purchase these Railways which shows deference to public opinion I do not see why the Government of India should not follow this policy in all cases and determine the contracts of all the company-managed railways whenever they become due. It would facilitate laying down of a uniform policy and Government would be in a position to offer better and cheaper transport facilities if all the railway systems are controlled and co ordinated under one authority.

The reference to the control of these lines reminds me of another welcome decision taken by Government in purchasing the Bengal, Bombay and Madras Telephone Companies, licences of which expire in 1943, at a cost of Rs. 475 lakhs. It is a decision which, I am sure, would be welcomed by the public and I hope it would be possible for the Government of India to make available to the public still cheaper telephone services at these centres.

Commandeering of Dollars and Sterling Debt Repatriation

The recent decision taken by the Government of India in repatriating India's terminable Sterling Loan to the extent of Rs. 120 crores has decreased India's foreign liability to that extent and has been further helpful to His Majesty's Government in financing the persecution of the war in so far as a greater part of the sums so disbursed would be re-lent to His Majesty's Government, probably in the form of investment in the Defence Loans. It is a distinct service which India has rendered to His Majesty's Government in facilitating their wartime problems.

In this connection, I should like to point out that the total gold exports from India during the last year amounted to over Rs. 34 crores. It has been repeatedly urged on Government that they should seize every opportunity to purchase gold offered for export with a view to strengthen the currency gold reserves of the Reserve Bank.

The immediate need for His Majesty's Government for gold and dollar resources was so great that they had to ask the Government of India to commandeer all the dollar securities held by Indians both in British India and Indian States for their use. The country was surprised to see that His Majesty's Government should have gone to the extreme limit of commandeering India's dollar resources without giving any thought to the enormous loss which the holders of these securities would be put to by their disposal at the present juncture. These securities, the extent of which it is not possible for me or the commercial community to gauge, would have been a source of strength in our dealings with the United States of America in the postwar period of industrial reconstruction. I hope His Majesty's Government would consider it a moral obligation to make available to this country foreign resources whenever required during the currency of the war to the extent to which they have deprived the country of these resources. I am sure time will come when India will be in dire necessity of foreign exchange for establishing or expanding her industries in near future.

TAXATION POLICY

While criticising the Government of India's policy with regard to the disposal of the sterling resources, as also with regard to the commandeering of the dollar securities, I should like to offer some remarks on the Taxation policy of the Government of India. Since the outbreak of the war, during the past one year and a half, the Government of India have been finding out new avenues for taxing the country's resources without any regard for their repercussions on the taxable capacity of the general public and on the trade and industry of the country. In spite of our repeated protest, Government have increased Excise duties, Railway freight rates, introduced new measures of taxation such as, Excess Profits Tax and have increased the rates of taxes on income and postal and Trunk Telephone rates. In overhauling the Income-tax Act, they have introduced new methods under which less relief is granted to the industry in the assessment of its income. I apprehend the cumulative effect of all these measures would be to seriously affect the whole agricultural and industrial economy of India. As an illustration, I may point out that against a collection of Rs. 15 8 crores by the Government of India in 1938-39 from taxes on income, under the new rates they expect to collect more than Rs. 40 crores in the year 1941-42, normal taxation under this head practically being doubled during the period. The following figures would corroborate my statement.

Figures relating to Corporation tax and Taxes on Income for the last four years.

	Accounts. 1938-39	Accounts. 1939-40	Estimates. 1940-41	Estimates. 1941-42
Corporation Tax:	2,03	2,38	4,47	12,62
Income Tax Super Tax, E. P. T. other than Corporation Sax	13,74	16,99	20,50	27,46
	15,77	19,37	24,97	40.08

As nearly 90 percent of the income arising under this head is derived from trade and industry in the country. I would leave it to you to judge the extent of injury which is likely to result to the financial stamina of the indigenous industries. Nobody would dispute the fact that after the war, Indian industries would have to face severe competition from foreign countries. If these industries are not allowed to build up any reserves for such a contingency arising in the post-war period, the industrial development, to which the war orders have given an impetus, would receive a serious setback. I am sorry to say that the Honourable the Finance Member has not realised the enormity of the burden which he is asking the industries to bear during the war.

As the imposition of these taxes was necessitated by the huge expenditure which the Government of India were called upon to incur to mechanise and equip the Indian Land, Naval and Air Forces in accordance with modern requirements, the public is entitled to be assured that the substantial amounts that are being spent on this account are correctly debitable to this country and that no avoidable waste is incurred in the purchase of stores and equipment. In the absence of any popular control on military expenditure, there is an insistent demand that the Government of India should allay all public apprehensions in this regard by constituting a small Supervising Commission consisting of distinguished Indian public men with the necessary powers to advice Government with regard to their military expenditure and thus to check unauthorised expenditure or wrong debits to India and to see that the policy of the Government of India with regard to their military purchases reacts favourably on the expansion and development of Indian industries. I would like to point out further that when His Majesty's Government appointed the Chatfield Committee, in the terms of reference, they distinctly admitted that it would not be possible for India, with her limited resources for defence expenditure, to undertake increased cost of modern armaments and to equip and maintain the forces in India in accordance with modern requirements. According to the Chatfield Committee's recommendations, the total net capital cost for the purpose of modernising the Indian forces was estimated at Rs. 45 crores, and the Committee made it clear that "in their view, the funds required to meet this capital expenditure could not be found out of the resources available in India." In accepting this recommendation of the Committee, His Majesty's Government, in fact, admitted that India would not be in a position to bear such a heavy expenditure required for modernising her defence forces, and they, therefore, decided to seek the authority of the Parliament to provide three-fourths of this amount, that is, Rs. 34 crores, "as a free gift", while about Rs. 11 crores were to be advanced by way of a loan. Under the Chatfield Committee's programme, the whole of the amount of Rs. 45 crores was to be spread over a period of five years, while the necessities of the war forced the Government of India to decide to carry out the Chatfield Committee's recommendations within a period of three years, and the Indian taxpayer, who is admittedly poor compared to the taxpayer either in the United Kingdom. Canada, Australia or New Zealand, has been called upon to bear heavy burdens disproportionate to his income. In financing such huge capital expenditure, it is unfortunate that the Honourable the Finance Member should resort to measures of taxation which would directly affect the financial standing of the indigenous industries in years to come, instead of meeting such expenditure by programme of borrowing on a reasonable scale. I would not like to go into detailed analysis of the *per capita* income and the taxable capacity of the Indian Taxpayer, compared to the one in either the United Kingdom or the Dominion but would content myself with the reproduction of the following extract from a recent study on "The Conditions of Economic Progress" by Prof. Collins Clark, based on very instructive and informative data about comparative average real income per worker in some of the important countries in the world. According to his calculations—

"A standard of living of 1,000 International Units* per worker per year or more is found only in U. S. A., Canada, Australia, New Zealand, Argentine, Great Britain and Switzerland, containing between them 10 per cent of the world population, while about 53 per cent of the world's population including the whole population of India and China enjoys a real income per head of less than 200 'International Units'. Average real income per bread-earner in China and India is about 120 and 200 'International Units' respectively".

INDIA'S TAXABLE CAPACITY

Whatever formula or whatever process of analysis we may adopt, we come to the undisputed fact that India's taxable capacity, measured in terms of her *per capita* income, is far below the capacity of the taxpayer in the United Kingdom or in any of the Dominions, and those who are in day-to-day contact with trade and industrial interests have every ground to feel grave concern about the inevitable result of the present taxation programme of the Government of India on the competitive strength of the Indian industries in the post-war period. I trust that the Gov-

*An 'International Unit' is defined as the amount of goods and services which could be purchased for one Dollar in the United States over the average of the decade 1925-34, or an amount interchangeable with them.

ernment would seriously reconsider the whole situation and revise their taxation policy during the currency of the war and would not allow the economic structure of this country to be imperilled.

As a result of the situation developing on the Indian Frontiers owing to the extension of hostilities to Africa and their likely extension to the Balkan States, new liability was placed by the Government of India on the primary producers, their stock-holders and manufacturers in the form of a levy of War Risk Insurance chargeable at the rate of ½ anna per hundred rupees on the value on stocks held. It is rather premature at this stage of the war to forecast whether the country would be faced with any danger of risks arising out of hostile acts by the enemy, but in case such eventuality does not occur till the termination of the war, I would suggest to Government that the amounts received under this scheme which are at present credited to a separate fund, should, under no circumstances, be merged into the general revenues of the Central Government. It has been a charge which has to be paid and a premium against losses by the primary producers at great cost to themselve and no decision should be taken by Government in this regard until normal times prevail after the termination on the war. The Government should also consider whether it would be advisable to reduce the rate of premium in view of the remoteness of any risk arising on India's Frontiers during the present hostilities.

I would point out here that in the matter of legislation, the Government of India have taken a welcome step in the midst of their preoccupations, in putting on the statute book an Amending Bill revising the Indian Merchandise Marks Act in a manner helpful to India's manufacturing interests.

INDIANS OVERSEAS

I must refer here to another important step which the Government of India have taken in the administrative sphere and that is the raising of the staus of the present Agent of the Governor-General in South Africa to that of the High Commissioner. Under the new arrangement, the Government of India would be now in direct diplomatic communications with the Government of the Union of South Africa instead of through the Secretary of State for India in London. I would further suggest that it is necessary to have a similar representative of the Government of India with the Government of Burma, and the present post of the Government of of India's Agent should be converted into that of the High Commissioner for India in Burma. The magnitude of the trade and the complexities of the issues involved with regard to the status and safety of Indians and their property in Burma, as also with regard to emigration, require the creation of such a post. The commercial community is also glad to note the recent action of the Government of India in creating a Trade Commissioner's post in Australia, and appointing an Indian to it. Similar Trade Commissioners, as you must be aware, are also proposed to be appointed for Canada, South America and South Africa. I trust that Government would appoint more Trade Commissioners in important neighbouring countries such as, Iran, Afghanistan and New Zealand, where India's manufactured articles await development of further export markets. It has been recognised that the policy of appointing Indians on these posts has proved very successful as Indian Trade Commissioners have always performed their duties with dignity and understanding. I hope the Government would make it a policy of appointing Indians as the Trade Commissioners in various countries and that the choice would not be confined merely to members of the Civil Service or other officials as at present but non-officials having intimate knowledge of Indian trade and industrial conditions should also be appointed as Trade Commissioners.

The position of our countrymen overseas in the Dominions and in the British Colonial Empire did not improve during the year under review ; on the contrary, our relations with Ceylon were far from being happy. The Report, submitted by the Government of India to the Central Legislature regarding the Exploratory Conference between them and the Ministers from Ceylon, fully brings out the fundamental differences in the outlook of the two Governments towards this question. While the country fully supports the attitude adopted by the Government of India on such a vital question, it is deplorable that the Ceylonese Ministers could not agree to a very reasonable proposal put forward by the Government of India that full citizenship should be conferred on all Indians who could furnish proof (a) of five years' residence in Ceylon and (b) of a permanent interest in Ceylon. It is still more deplorable that the attitude of the Ministers towards Indians—who have been responsible for the economic prosperity of that Island—

should be constitutionally untenable and should call for intervention by the Governor of Ceylon.

Relations with the Government

As the Indo-Burma Trade Negotiations are proceeding, I do not wish to say anything about it at this stage. I would however, like to emphasise that even in the course of these negotiations the Government should safeguard to the fullest extent possible the legitimate rights and interests of Indians in Burma and their status as citizens. I hope the question of immigration of Indians into Burma will form a part of the general settlement of all questions outstanding betweeen the two countries. I would appeal to the Burma Government Delegation to adopt an attitude during these negotiations which would be helpful in arriving at an amicable settlement between our two neighbouring countries which have lived together for generations in peace and harmony and I would express the hope that the Trade Agreement would be in our mutual interest.

I may mention that whenever we have had occasions to come into contact with Members of the Council of His Excellency the Viceroy, we have marked their anxiety to understand the difficulties of trade and industry and appreciate their viewpoint as far as possible. As we have naturally more opportunities to meet the Honourable the Commerce Member in connection with various commercial and industrial matters, we are in a better position to know his desire to acquaint himself with our problems and assist us and remedy our grievances. This personal attitude of courtesy and helpfulness is, however, in sharp contrast with the attitude which certain departments of the Government have from time to time shown in regard to certain communications and representations submitted by the Federation of Indian Chambers. The Federation of Indian Chambers, I need hardly point out, as a representative body of Indian commercial opinion in the whole country, voices the demands and grievances of Indian trade, commerce and industries. Situated as we are *vis-a-vis* the Government of India and the British Government, it is an additional obligation on the Federation to give a lead in commercial and economic matters in the country and enlighten the public, especially the commercial community about their various problems. I hope, therefore, the Government on their part will fully appreciate the position and functions of the Federation and radically change their attitude in this respect.

Need for Political Peace

Before I conclude, I cannot help referring to the political stalemate in the country. It is really a tragedy that India and England are gradually drifting apart and even in an hour of life and death struggle against the Fascist States, British statesmanship is not prepared to change its policy and attitude towards India so as to recognise India's aspirations and clarify Britain's own war aims in their application to India. I am afraid the last August offer of His Excellency the Viceroy, instead of satisfying public opinion, has definitely antagonised it and subsequent declarations of the Secretary of State have done nothing to win over Indian public opinion. Leaving alone the question of extension of the Executive Council, the Government have done nothing to take the representatives of the Indian public and the commercial community into confidence in regard to their war efforts and defence policy. This policy, I am constrained to say, is also illustrated in respect of their conduct of administration with regard to important key departments such as Defence and Supply, their refusal to accelerate the policy of Indianisation of Defence and Civil Services, and their action in importing non-Indians for services even from the Colonies and the Dominions. This has created a feeling that while Britain wants India to help her in her hour of need, she is not herself prepared to reciprocate by any tangible action. That such a feeling is shared by even moderate political opinion in the country is evident from the following extract from the recent statement issued in reply to a message to India from members of the Parliament by certain prominent Indian Liberals :—

"How can India which is not assured of her future freedom, forget her humiliating position and work enthusiastically for the freedom of Enlgand and other nations?"

British statesmanship, I must candidly say, has failed to inspire any confidence in the minds of the Indian public about its intentions towards India and if genuine efforts are not made by His Majesty's Government to solve the Indian problem, it would lead to grave reactions on Indo-British relationship and prejudicially affect the interests of Britain and the British Commonwealth itself. If and Patiala. Your Chancellor has paid a moving tribute to the memory of these three Princes, all of whom had by varying and outstanding qualities and achievements, become familiar and popular figures in the India of their day. Nor were their fame and reputation confined to this country. The name of his late Highness of Nawanagar is still of household word in England by reason of his unique proficiency in England's national game. In that, as well as in other more serious spheres of public life, the late Maharaja of Patiala, too, won great distinction, while His Highness Maharaja Madho Rao Scindia's personality was such as to inspire confidence and affection in all with whom he came in contact—from the lowliest of his subjects to the King-Emperor himself. But we are to-day more concerned with the services they rendered to this Chamber with which all of them were so closely associated from those earliest days when, what was then known as the 'Conference of Ruling Princes and Chiefs' first began to meet here in Delhi. Of that aspect of their careers, His Highness the Chancellor has spoken in sincere and eloquent terms, and I gladly associate myself with all that he has said.

"In speaking of the late Maharaja Jam Saheb, His Highness' words were very naturally charged with family affection, and the thought will no doubt have occured to many of us, that nothing would have afforded greater pride and pleasure to His Late Highness than to have known that the great office of Chancellor on this unique Assembly, which he himself had held with such industry and distinction, would one day be so worthily filled by the successor on the *gadi* of Nawanagar.

"It will not be a conventional compliment or an undue straining of language, if I say that this ceremony, for which we have assembled to-day is, in respect of all the three Princes whose memory it is designed to perpetuate in this place, permeated by a certain filial sentiment, inasmuch as all of them had just claims to be described as fathers of the Chamber of Princes, for they had played no inconsiderable part in guiding the Chamber through its early days. For the vision which enabled them, as His Highness has reminded us, to appreciate its possibilities in the future, and to a great extent to carry them into actual effect, we may well be thankful. And it is for you, of the present generation, to see to it that the ideals and objects for which the Chamber was founded, and for which those whom we commemorate strove so loyally and well, are resolutely pursued, in the best interests of your Order as well as of India as a whole.

"I trust that the marble effigies which I am privileged now to unveil, will keep alive, for many generations te come, the great reputations which are so fresh in the memories of all of us present here to-day."

Resolutions—CONDOLENCE

After the Viceroy's Address, the Chamber of Princes adopted a resolution affirming loyalty to Their Majesties the King Emperor and the Queen and recordind abhorrence at the Nazi outrages.

On the motion of the Chancellor, the Chamber adopted a resolution of condolence on the demise of Their Highnesses the Maharajas of Mysore and Kolhapur, the Maharao of Kotah, the Maharaja of Bijawar, the Thakur Sahibs of Limbdi and Rajkot and the Chief of Nandgaon. The Maharajas of Dungarpur and Dewas (senior), the Raja of Sangli and the Raja of Dhenkanal associated themselves with the resolution.

Their Highnesses paid tributes to the departed rulers. The *Jam Sahib* made particular reference to the late Maharaja of Mysore, who, he said, was an embodiment of plain living and high thinking and "in his personality and achievements embodied a living argument in justification of the polity of Indian kingship.

The resolution was adopted, all members standing.

CONGRATULATION TO NEW RULERS

Ths *Jam Sahib* proposed and the *Raja of Sangli* seconded the resolution offering the congratulations of the Chamber to Their Highnesses the Maharaja of Mysore, the Maharao of Kotah and to the Thakur Sahibs of Rajkot and Limbdi on their accession to the gadi and to Their Highnesses the Maharajas of Dhar and Nabha on their investiture with ruling powers. Both the speakers extolled the interest these Rulers have already taken in the welfare of their subjects and expressed the hope that they would appreciate the utility of the Chamber of

Princes to the Order and would strengthen it by taking an active interest in its activities.

Tht resolution was unanimously adopted.

WELCOME TO NEW MEMBERS

The Chancellor next moved a resolution extending "cordial welcome to the Rulers recently admitted as members of the Chamber in their own right." The resolution was supported by the *Maharaja of Patiala*, the *Raja of Mandi* and the *Maharaja of Dewas* (senior).

In moving his resolution, the *Jam Sahib* traced the history of the enlargement of the Chamber of Princes. He said that as early as February 1932 the question was referred to a Special Committee consisting of Their Highnesses of Alwar, Bhopal, Bikaner, Nawanagar and Patiala and the Political Secretary to the Government of India. The opinions of the members of the Committee were sharply divided. The majority was in favour of a very limited addition to the membership of the Chamber, while the minority favoured a more liberal enlargement to make it as representative as possible.

The question was discussed by several other committees and ultimately in 1940, the Crown Representative admitted in their own right Rulers of twenty-six States, "whom" said the Chancellor, "we welcome to-day."

The *Jam Saheb* said that "the addition of these twenty-six members has further enhanced the representative character of the Chamber of Princes. There are a few others whose cases deserve special consideration and we share their disappointment that it has not been possible at present to include them as full members."

The Chancellor confidently hoped that the new members would prove a source of strength to the Chamber by taking active interest in its deliberations. "Moreover, they join us at a time when public opinion is critically focussed on the activities of our Order. As such, we expect our new colleagues that they will justify their Order by the ordered progress of their States and their solicitude for their people"

The resolution was adopted, after which the *Rajas of Seraikella*, *Bhor*, *Jamkhandi*, *Miraj* (Senior) and *Korea* thanked the Chamber on behalf of the newly admitted members.

NAZI OUTRAGES CONDEMNED

The last resolution unanimously adopted and moved by the *Maharaja Jam Saheb of Nawanagar*, ran as follows :

"The Chamber of Princes records its deep sense of the callous Nazi violation of all international law and morality culminating in the shameless bombing of Buckingham Palace. The Chamber offers its devout gratefulness to Providence for His protection of Their Majesties the King-Emperor and the Queen, and desires that this devoted expression of the personal attachment of the Indian Princes to Their Majesties and of the deep concern of the Princes for their welfare may be placed before Their Majesties."

The resolution was seconded by the *Maharaja of Patiala* and supported by the *Nawab of Bahawalpur*, the *Nawab of Rampur* and the *Raja of Sangli*.

The *Jam Saheb* declared : "No words of mine are needed to emphasise the unbroken record of the inalienable loyalty of the Princes to the person and throne of their beloved King-Emperor and the illustrious House of Windsor. This has over and over again been demonstrated in the normal activities of peacetime as well as in the fiery ordeals of the war during the past century and more of the Princes' relations with the Imperial Crown. Moreover, if anyone has truly deserved and won the love and loyalty of his people it is our beloved King-Emperor and also his gracious consort and we are aware how inspiringly Their Majesties are sharing the anxieties and privations of their devoted subjects during the present crisis."

Other Rulers who spoke asserted that the King was the symbol of the Common-wealh and embodied in his persons the best in the Empire. The Maharaja of Patiala said that the British Empire was the last refuge of civilisation and their King was the symbol of its unity. The Nawab of Bahawalpur said that any attack on the Buckingham Palace was an attack on the unity of the Empire and they must do their all to defeat the enemies of civilisation. The Nawab of Rampur said that the person of the King-Emperor was something sacred to the rulers of the States. The Raja of Sangli said that the enemy, by attacking the Buckingham Palace, wanted to strike terror in the hearts of the British people. In this he had totally failed.

The resolution was unanimously adopted, all members standing. The Chamber then adjourned.

Resolutions—2nd. Day—New Delhi—18th. March 1941

WAR ADVISORY COUNCIL

A resolution requesting the Crown Representative to revive the proposal for establishing a War Advisory Council was adopted by the Chamber of Princes, whice concluded its two-day session on the next day, the 18th. March.

The Chancellor, the *Jam Sahib*, moving the War Resolution said that the inspiring stand of England against the brutal Nazi air raids and the brilliant victories of the imperial and allied troops in Africa and Albania, in which the Indian troops had played such a magnificent part, had caused widespread gratification and he felt that they were entitled to share these rejoicings with the rest of the Empire. The Jam Sahib said that the Resolution reiterated the determination of the Indian Princes to continue to put forth their best efforts for the achievement of the final victory. "This declaration", he said, "has been already translated into action. The uptodate collections from the States in cash towards the various war purposes funds up to the end of January 1941 amounted to approximately Rs. 1,81,93,000 non-recurring and Rs. 41,71,000 recurring. In addition, our contributions to the interest-free Bonds amounted to Rs. 1.13 00,000 and to three per cent Defence Bonds to Rs. 66,00,000."

The *Jam Sahib* concluded, "To my mind it would be a denial of the best traditions of the States, and of the history of India if in the face of this clarion call of duty to suffering humanity, India faltered or hesitated. The present war will probably be a long one. We are prepared for it."

The *Ruler of Patiala*, who seconded the resolution, said that the courage of the British people was a living monument to the glory of great Britain. He said that the danger to India was clearly realised and people felt thas it was their war. "We must therefore do our utmost to assist His Majesty's Government to win the war."

The *Nawab of Bahawalpur* said that it was a matter of gratification that Indian troops had made so great a contribution, as a result of which their homes were made secure to-day.

The resolution was further supported by the Rulers of Dungarpur, Dewas (Junior) and Mandi and was passed unanimously.

STATES AND WAR EFFORT AT THE CENTRE

On the motion of the Chancellor, the *Jam Sahib*, who was supported by the *Raja of Bhor*, the Chamber adopted amendments in the first Regulations in the Appendix to the consideration of the Chamber.

The Chamber next considered the resolution relating to the demand of the Princes for closer association with the Centre in the war effort. The *Jam Sahib* moving the resolution, said that the exigencies of the situation demanded that the liaison of the States with the war effort at the Centre, particularly in the spheres of defence, supplies and industries, might be ensured on a regular basis and not through *Ad Hoc* committees set up for specific purposes. "It would further be appreciated", he added, "and I state this fact without implying any slur on the personal element involved, that the Government of India, as at present constituted, can only speak for British India. As such, while British India may be said to have a *liaison* with the war activities at the Centre through the Government of India, the States are out of the picture. We request that in the best interests of British India, the States and the Empire, such a state of affairs should not be allowed to continue any longer."

Proceeding, the Chancellor said, "Your Excellency, the Indian Princes genuinely share and wholeheartedly sympathise with your Excellency's difficulties at the present juncture. We have no share to add to them. We would not make the request embodied in this resolution but for our firm conviction that our request is not unreasonable and in fact, is likely to help in the progress of the war."

The resolution was supported by the *Nawab of Rampur* and the *Maharaja of Dewas* (Junior) and was adopted.

WORK OF THE CHAMBER DURING LAST YEAR

The Chamber of Princes heard a statement from its Chancellor on the work performed by the Chamber during the last year.

In the course of his statement, the Chancellor referred to the administrative reforms and "beneficent activities in the States" and said that the States with 87.4 per cent of the total population of the States, who were members of the Chamber of Princes, had got local bodies in their territories. States with 67.9 per cent of population had got legislative assemblies, out of which 35.3 per cent had a majority of elected members and 3.9 per cent had equality of elected and nominated members of the Assemblies. States representing 53.2 per cent of the total membership of the Chamber had recently appointed committees to examine the question of the further association of their subjects with the administration, 89.9 per cent of the population had already got the benefit of High Courts while the States representing 93.3 per cent of the total population had efficient police forces supervised by competent officers. The general incidence of taxation in the States had also been compared with and found lower than that of the adjoining British Indian provinces.

"We do not claim perfection for all the States' administrations", the Chancellor said. "At the same time the aforesaid statement of facts would show to all fair-minded persons that the Indian States are not anachronisms in the conception of a progressive State and that our administrations are based on a rule of law associated with growing beneficent actvities".

Referring to the other activities of the Chamber, the Jam Sahib said that the difficulties arising out of the Indian Income-Tax (Amendment) Act so far as it affects the States were under negotiations with the Government of India. The Standing Committee had taken up the question of maintaining the *status quo* with regard to the existing rights of States in such properties as had already been acquired in British India.

The Chancellor next referred to the question of the eligibility of Indian States' subjects for service in British India and said negotiations were in progress to secure a general declaration of eligibility for States' subjects for appointments under the Central Government and the Secretary of State. He added that the question of amending the Reserve Bank of India Act on a suitable occasion in future was uder consideration to secure eligibility of Rulers of Indian States to hold shares in the Bank.

On the motion of the *Ruler of Rampur*, who was supported by *their Highnesses of Dewas* (Junior), *Mandi* and *Sangli*, the Chamber adopted a resolution thanking the Chancellor for his work during the year.

Princes' Reply To Viceroy

The Princes, in their reply to the Viceroy's inaugural address, which was read by the Chancellor, said that they were not averse to the ordered progress of India. "On the other hand, the Princes are publicly associated with the desire to secure for India the fullest freedom and the highest status under the aegis of the British Crown. We wish, however, to avoid raising any big controversial matters during the present crisis and to concentrate all energies on the main purpose of the successful prosecution of the war. We have accordingly decided not to pass any formal resolution this year on the political situation in India so far as it affects the States. At the same time, we whole-heartedly welcome the declaration made by Your Excellency on August 8, 1940. and its elucidation in the House of Commons by the Secretary of State for India, which leave it to a body representative of the principal elements in India's national life, including the Indian States, to devise the frame-work of the new Constitution on the basis of a free and friendly agreement, subject to the due fulfilment of the treaty and other solemn obligations resting on His Majesty's Government. When the time comes, the Indian Princes shall not be found wanting in any reasonable contribution, which they may be called upon to make, for the discharge of their obligations to the Crown and towards the ordered progress of their States and their Motherland.

Co-ordination of States in Administrative Matters

"Your Excellency has also referred in your address to the suggestions made by you, in your previous addresses to the Chamber, that it is desirable for the smaller States with limited resources, to co-operate and combine in matters of administration so far as it may be necessary and practicable. This question has been receiving our careful and active consideration from all the view-points involved; and relying on Your Excellency's respect for the traditions of the Indian States and for the pledges given to the States, both big and small, in the successive authoritative pronouncements guaranteeing their internal autonomy and integrity, we take it as understood that Your Excellency's suggestions are intended to encourage co-operation, on a voluntary basis, having due regard to local conditions, in certain services of administration, without impairing the integrity and sovereignty of the States concerned. In order to encourage co-operative grouping on the aforesaid lines, we regard it essential that the proposed combination should proceed on the free consent and the voluntary co-operation of the Rulers themselves, and that it shall not rigidly be limited to the geographical boundaries of a group, in order that it may inspire mutual confidence and trust, which alone can ensure its smooth working. On this basis, Your Excellency may rely on it that, we and our advisers will not be diverted by any considerations of a personal character from ensuring that where co-operation is necessary it shall take a form which no reasonable critic can assail on the ground that it is half-hearted.

Question of Reasonable Alternative Schemes

"At the same time, there should be no fetish for any rigidily of pattern in a matter of such importance, and where the States concerned put up any reasonable alternative schemes of efficient administration or are prepared to co-operate with other important States, with adequate and efficient machinery in any branch of administration, such proposals may be sympathetically examined and, as far as possible, given a fair trial. We would also request that the promise made may be fully implemented so that the Chancellor may be taken into confidence, with regard to the various alternative schemes and suggestions under consideration, in order that the necessary modifications, if any, may be suggested in time, which may make it possible for the Chamber to lend its good offices towards a satisfactory solution of this delicate problem. Your Excellency has been pleased to state that your suggestions regarding joint services have been welcomed by many Princes, and steps are taken to adopt them in many parts of India with visible, though not as yet spectacular, results. Your Excellency would doubtless recognise that if the visible results have not been as spectacular as expected by Your Excellency, this has not been due to any deliberate indifference on the part of the Princes concerned. The pre-occupations of the States with war work perforce have resulted in some of these problems not receiving the attention which they would have received in normal peace time. Moreover, it will be recognised by all fair-minded persons that in the sphere of reform, prudence and farsight often enjoin, even on the most ardent reformer, the duty of paying due regard to local conditions and resources."

After this statement the Chamber of Princes adjourned *sine die.*

Federation of Indian Chambers of Commers

Fourteenth Session—New Delhi—22nd. to 24th. March 1941

The Presidential Address

The fourteenth session of the Federation of the Indian Chambers of Commerce commenced at New Delhi on the **22nd. March 1941**, under the presidency of Mr. *Amritalal Ojha.* The following is the text of Mr. Ojha's address :

I offer you a most cordial welcome to the Fourteenth Annual Session of the Federation of Indian Chambers of Commerce and Industry.

Since my predecessor addressed you in March last, a year of great anxiety and strain has passed with no prospects of the termination of the hostilities. On the contrary, during the later part of the year these have extended to Africa, and there is every indication of their further extension to the Balkan States and the Middle East. As I will have another occasion to address you on international matters, I do not propose to refer to these events beyond expressing my admiration for the traditional bravery of the Indian troops engaged in Africa, who have contributed to the decisive victory which the Imperial Forces have scored over the Italians ; the country can well be proud of the magnificent achievements of its sons on the field. My admiration, in no less degree, goes to those brave men, women and children of the United Kingdom, who are putting up a courageous and enduring fight for the survival of the British nation against the ruthless and barbarous onslaughts of the Luftwaffe. The morale of the civil population of the United Kingdom in face of the privations, misery and suffering which they are undergoing with faith and cheerfulness, is worthy of emulation by any country engaged in a life and death struggle, and to India, I am sure, it will be a source of inspiration in her present struggle.

War and Loss of Markets

The extension of the hostilities to the major part of the Continent of Europe and stricter application of the methods of economic warfare during the year adversely affected India's position as a country largely interested in the exports of her raw materials to foreign countries. The exports of primary products to continential markets suffered a heavy setback, resulting in unusual accumulations of raw commodities such as, cotton, groundnut, other oilseeds, wool, etc., in the country. The consequential result of such a situation was bound to be reflected in the downward trend of the prices for these commodities. According to Government's own figures, which I am reproducing below, it will be seen that the prices of all the exportable raw materials recorded a fall from the prices which prevailed in the first quarter of the war year. Although in some cases, these prices are higher than those which prevailed in August, 1939, it must be remembered that the pre-war prices were hardly economical so far as agricultural commodities were concerned. There is every likelihood of the present position as regards prices still deteriorating in future with the new crops coming into the markets.

Apart from closure of markets, the absence of shipping tonnage and the quota restrictions arising out of the methods of economic warfare, it must be said, with regret, that the attitude of His Majesty's Government has also not been very helpful in mitigating the rigours of these factors on the agricultural economy of India. The British Government have followed a policy in case of India's raw produce different from the one they have been following with regard to the primary produce of South Africa, Australia and New Zealand and even of a non-Empire country like Egypt. With a view to help Egypt's agricultural economy, an agreement was entered into with the Egyptian Government, under which the British Government contracted to purchase the entire Egyptian cotton crop during the war and one year thereafter at prices considerably higher than that of the crop bought during several recent years. If there is to be any loss on the transaction, it is to be borne by the British Government, while profits, if any, are to be equally shared between the two Governments, and the Egyptian share of the profits is to be utilised for the benefit of the Egyptian cotton cultivators. Similar agreements were entered into by the British Government with the Governments of South Africa, New Zealand and Australia in respect of the entire wool clips of these Dominions for the duration of the war and for one wool clip thereafter. The prices reported to have been offered, under these Agreements, are as high as 40 per cent over the pre-war prices. For example, for the 1939-40 South African wool clip, a price of 11.8d. per lb. was paid, compared to 8.3d. per lb. for the season preceding the war. Another important deal entered into by the British Government, in conjunction with the Governments of Canada and New Zealand, with some of the Dominions and Colonies, was with regard to the purchase of the entire exportable sugar crop of Australia, Union of South Africa, Mauritius, Fiji and the British West Indies. This agreement involved a total quantity of about 18 lakhs of tons of sugar, and these sugar producing countries would be able to dispose of about two lakhs tons more than was the case under the International Sugar Agreement.

The Dominions Example

All these agreements in respect of important primary produce of the Dominions and the Colonies, contributed largely in mitigating the rigours arising out of the closure of the markets and the economic warfare to these parts. In contrast to this generous attitude of His Majesty's Government towards the Dominions and the Colonies, the attitude of the Government of India, on behalf of His Majesty's Government, has been far from satisfactory. India's agricultural economy, on which depends the living of the millions of her primary producers, has not received due consideration at the hands of the British Government. On the other hand, the policy followed in India in respect of the purchase of raw materials required for the prosecution of the war has resulted in depressing the prices of these articles, as compared to the prices offered for similar goods by His Majesty's Government in other parts of the Empire. A pertinent example is afforded by the purchasing policy adopted by the British Government towards the purchase of Indian wool. At the beginning of the war, exports of Indian wool were allowed only to the Liverpool Auction Rooms and were not allowed even to U. S. A. The prices of Indian wool reached unfavourably to these restrictive measures, with the result that the British Government were able to purchase their requirements of wool in Indian market at appreciably lower prices. As a result of representations addressed by these interests concerned as well as by this Federation, exports to U. S. A. were subsequently allowed on quota basis in spite of increased demand from that country. Recently, exports to Liverpool market were also stopped. All these factors resulted in huge accumulations of stocks and in deterioration of the prices as compared to prices obtainable for similar quality wool in America. In spite of repeated submissions from the wool interests to the Government of India to prevail upon His Majesty's Government to enter into an agreement similar to the one with South Africa and Australia as regards purchase of the entire Indian wool clip, no action has been taken as yet, and the trade as also the primary producers have continued to suffer. Another example which I would like to refer to is with regard to the purchase of groundnut and oilseeds for the requirments of the British government. Groundnut, it must be remembered, is an important exportable crop and used to be exported in substantial quantities to the various countries in Europe. The groundnut trade, therefore, was one of the first victims of the closure of the continental markets. His Majesty's Government, instead of utilising the Government of India as their purchasing agents, appointed independent agents for their purchases in India. While the British Government paid their agents £10 per ton for the purchase of Indian groundnut, the Indian sellers scarcely received £7-10 to £8 per ton, and I understand that the whole of the margin was pocketed by the purchasing agents of the British Government. The growing disparity between the prices offered by His Majesty's Government and the prices at which Indian groundnut was sold was so apparent that the problem became very serious and would have resulted in a public scandal, had it not been for the commendable and prompt action taken by the Honourable the Commerce Member to the Government of India, and it must be said to his credit that under the new arrangement, the margin would be pooled into a fund for the benefit of the Indian cultivator. I am just giving these two examples to show how unsatisfactory has been the arrangement made by the British Government with regard to their purchases of raw materials in India and how it has not only resulted in depressing the prices of those commodities which are purchased but has also reacted on the whole price structure of raw commodities in this country.

Problem of Surplus Commodities

With a view to consider and find out a solution of the problem arising out of the surplus of raw commodities, the Honourable the Commerce Member accepted the suggestion made by my predecessor, from this platform, last year, for the establishment of an Export Advisory Council. I would like to take this opportunity to compliment publicly Sir Ramaswami Mudaliar for accepting our suggestion for machinery to be brought into existence for ascertaining the difficulties of the produce trade and export trade interests, thereby creating direct contact between the Government of India and the commercial community on question primarily affecting both the producers and the manufacturers. Although it is not possible to secure immediate solution of the intricate question of utilising the surplus stocks of raw commodities in the country, I have no doubt in course of time, the present unsatisfactory situation would be effectively remedied to the satisfaction of the primary producers in a manner which would give them some relief by way of greater return on their produce in the Indian market. I would like to make a suggestion towards the solution of this problem to the effect that the Government of India should first make up their mind as to the extent of the financial assistance to which they are prepared to go, before inviting the various interests concerned to offer suggestions with regard to either holding stocks of these commodities in reserve and releasing them in the market as and when necessary, or with regard to the utilisation of these commodities in the manufacture of new industrial products. The question of surplus commodities has really assumed serious proportions and failing a solution in the near future, the economic condition of the mass of people is bound to deteriorate and may even create some agrarian trouble. The question, therefore, demands immediate and serious consideration not only by the Government of India but also the commercial community and particularly, the manufacturing interests in the country.

Another solution suggested in this connection is the introduction of alternate crops. I would hesitate to offer any comments on this proposal but it must be remembered that agriculturists would not welcome any such suggestion unless alternate crops which they are asked to grow, would bring them similar or better financial results. It is, besides, very difficult to shift from one crop to another, as climatic and soil conditions sometimes may not be suitable for the proper cultivation of a particular alternate crop. It would, therefore, be advisable for the Government of India to investigate and ascertain the deficiency in the country of those food commodities which are utilised in their daily life by the people. It is essential, therefore, that the question of crop planning, should be actively pursued by Government before initiating any isolated action.

Apart from the proposals regarding alternate crops, I feel that one of the means of solution of this very serious question would lie in devising alternate uses of these raw materials for industrial purposes within the country. It has been suggested on more than one occasion in the past from various quarters that cotton, groundnut and oilseeds can be utilised for the manufacture of Rayon, Artificial silk, Margarine, Vegetable oils, Paints, Varnishes, etc. If proper efforts are made, both through governmental and private industrial enterprise, India would be in a position to manufacture the articles which used to be imported before the war from countries and in the process of the manufacture of which these very raw materials were utilised abroad.

Board of Industrial Research

For the purpose of investigating the alternate uses of these raw materials and bringing them within the industrial economy of India, the recent establishment of the Board of Industrial and Scientific Research by Government is a step in the right direction. It is fortunate that the Government of India were able to secure the services of Dr. Sir *Shanti Swaroop Bhatnagar*, a distinguished research scientist in India, as the director of the Board. I wish the decision to institute such a Board was taken by Government immediately after the last war. The importance of the problem of industrial and scientific research was fully realised by the British Government and the British industrialists, and, in the midst of the 1914-18 war, a permanent official organisation was started in July, 1915, under the name of the Department of Scientific and Industrial research, with a view to promote scientific and industrial research and the application of science to the solution of industrial problem and the development of new products as well as of new and improved processes of manufacture. His Majesty's Government placed at the disposal of this Department a fund of a million Sterling, with a view to bring into existence, with the help of Government aid and of the voluntary co-operative associations, a number of co-operative research associations for the purpose of carrying on researches on questions of vital importance to British industries. At present there are more than twenty-six research associations working in the United Kingdom and conducting very useful researches in consultation with the manufacturing interests. The lines on which these various associations are working are necessarily of a different character, and the inquiries undertaken relate to researches in highly developed industries which have to face intense competition in international markets. In India, our industries have not yet reached that stage where researches of highly technical character could be undertaken by the Board ; on the other hand, we require an entirely different policy to be followed by the newly created organisation to meet new problems arising such as the fuller utilisation of our raw materials and diversification of industrial production, with a view to secure self-sufficiency in some of the country's requirements of imported articles. I think it is necessary to put the existing Board on a permanent basis, with large finances made available to it for undertaking problems of both immediate and long range importance.

I am glad to find that, within the course of a year's existence, the Board has been able to achieve some results in their research investigations which they are now anxious to allow the industrial interests to utilise as commercial propositions. Although I approve of the recent establishment of the Industrial Research Utilisation Committee for this purpose, it seems to me to be rather an unwieldy body. I, for my part, would have much preferred to have a smaller group of eminent Indians interested in the industrial development of the country and representative of Indian commercial and industrial organisations, to advise Government as to the terms on which the results of the Scientific and Industrial Research Board should be made available to the public.

With regard to the work of the Utilisation Committee, I would like to sound a note of warning, that, in making these results available to the public, the nationals of the country should have the first right of refusal so as to realise the fundamental object of a policy of national industrial development. In fact a stipulation exists in the United Kingdom whereby the Department of Scientific and Industrial Research reserve to themselves "the right to veto the communication of the results of the research to a foreign person or foreign Corporation".

organization and promotion of industrial research throughout the country, and co-ordinate the immediate needs of the war with the long range policy of the industrial development of the country as a whole. While concentrating on what was immediately required to meet war needs, it must also be in a position to survey the long term industrial requirements of the country and to plan a programme of research to meet them. Perhaps after the urgent demands of the war were over, its composition could be enlarged and made more representative of the Universities, Government scientific services, the non-official scientific bodies and the industrialists of India so as to enable it to pursue its ultimate plan and policy.

Sir A. Dalal continued : "No institution, however well conceived and designed, can flourish except in suitable political atmosphere and conditions. It was the unfortunate experience of the last war that industries created under the stress of the war languished and died in the post-war period for want of encouragement and protection from Government. The activities of the Board will not lead to the creation of new industries unless industrialists are assured of reasonable protection from Government in the postwar period, when foreign competition will be keen."

Warning the Government against excessive control, the speaker said : "The progress hitherto made by the Board is not as rapid as we would have wished in war time. This is partly due to the constitution of the Board under which executive authority is concentrated in a central department of Government and partly to the inadequate staff provided for the very urgent and important work that has to be done. There is one other aspect on which I desire to touch and that is the financial. Even for a beginning, a grant of five lakhs of rupees is inadequate and shows to my mind an inadequate conception of the magnitude of the tasks involved. Associated with the Department of Scientific and Industrial Research in Great Britain are the great National Physical Laboratory at Teddington and important Boards, such as the Fuel Research Board, the Food Investigation Board, the Forest Products and Building Research Institutes and a number of similar bodies as well as Research Associations. While we must necessarily make a very modest beginning, the development of the Alipore Test House into a National Physical and Chemical Laboratory seems to be obviously and urgently required."

Sir A. Dalal then spoke on some developments in the steel industry in India during the last ten years. While the position regarding iron ore was highly satisfactory, he said, that regarding coal, particularly the coal required for the smelting of iron ore was far from satisfactory. The problem of cooking coals was one of conservation as well as safety and if proper attention was paid to conservation, the problem of safety would more or less automatically be solved. Legislation in the interest of safety which placed additional burdens on the industry without assisting it to dispose of its production in a more scientific manner was likely to worsen the situation by hastening the uneconomic exploitation of the good coals by the smaller colliery owners.

What was required, Sir A. Dalal said, was the rationalisation of production as well as consumption. In order to achieve the rationalisation of consumption, a thorough chemical and physical survey of the coalfields beginning with the Jheria coalfield, in conjunction with a scheme of coal utilization research was absolutely necessary. For that purpose it was necessary to create a Fuel Research Board as a branch of the Board of Scientific and Industrial Research with a proper personnel, adequate staff and funds. On the production side, the President said, the most important problem was that of the co-ordinated sequence of working the coal seams. On the consumption side, the chemical and physical survey into coal seams in India in conjunction with coal utilization research would, in the first place, enable them to determine the range and variety of coals suitable for cooking as well as boiler purposes. Research was necessary in order to ascertain whether with proper blending and mixing the demands of the metallurgical industry need be confined to the very limited Jheria field.

Similar research was also required in the case of power coals. The utilization of high ash coals for electrical generation at the source of production and the distribution of the energy thus supplied over large areas was another problem of the first magnitude. Low temperature carbonization tests with various classes of coal, particularly of high ash, which were unsuitable for metallurgical purposes and also unsuitable on account of high ash content for transport to distant areas for power purposes, should provide another field for the activities of the Board. A number of scientists from the platform of this Congress as well as outside have advocated the cheap production of domestic coke on a mass scale and the utilisation of the resultant tar for industrial purposes. The present very small production of soft coke was capable of very great extension if a market could be found for the coke as well as the resultant tar, even if the gases were ignored for the present. The Board should also investigate the question of the scientific preparation of coal for the market and buying and selling on specification. If his proposal for the establishment of a Fuel Research Board was approved, he would suggest that as the Jheria coalfield was practically the sole source of Indian coking coals and was also the centre of the Indian School of Mines, the headquarters of the Board should be situated at Dhanbad and the School of Mines and its laboratories which should be adequately equipped for the purpose, should be utilized for the investigations of the Board.

Sir A. Dalal then gave a survey of the progress made by the Tata Iron and Steel Company in the last decade. He described the improvements effected and additions made in coke ovens and blast furnaces with the resultant fuel economy ; a new gas cleaning plant had been erected as also a new power plant. He then described in detail a new steel making process for the rapid dephosphorisation of Indian pig iron, which, he said, was likely to have far-reaching effects on the establishment of several new industries in India. In the manufacture of rails, advance had been made in which there was a tendency to replace straight carbon rails with manganese rails. In the plate mill, the most interesting development was the installation of a modern normalizing furnace for plates.

Sir A. Dalal then described the researches conducted at Jamshedpur. Loy-alloy steels, chrome-manganese steel, bullet-proof armour plate, armour-piercing shot, telegraph wires and steel plates for aircraft manufacture were some of the many items mentioned by the President to illustrate the extent of researches conducted by the Company. He hoped that the facilities provided at Jamshedpur might in the near future become the centre of a National Metallurgical Laboratory and Research Institute and thus be enabled to play a greater and worthier part in the development of the metallurgical industry in India.

Concluding, *Sir Ardeshir Dalal* hoped that after the successful conclusion of the war India might emerge from it with the foundation of its industrial and political freedom well and truly laid so that she might be properly equipped to play her rightful part in peace and in war as a worthy member of the great Commonwealth of Nations.

The day's proceedings came to a close with a vote of thanks to His Excellency the Chancellor.

The National Institute of Science

Annual Session—Benares—2nd. January 1941

The Presidential Address

The suggestion that a Federal Ministry of Public Health should be established in India, was made by Sir *R. N. Chopra*, Director, School of Tropical Medicine, at the annual meeting of the National Institute of Science of India, held at Benares on the 2nd. January 1941. He also made an appeal for more funds and patronage for scientific and industrial research.

Sir R. N. Chopra, in the course of his address, at first traced the activities of the Council during the past year. It was unfortunate, he said, that nothing like a comprehensive scheme for the development and co-ordination of scientific resources and research in the country had been taken up so far. Owing to the stress of war conditions and the lack of funds for the necessary capital outlay, which such a scheme would involve, no comprehensive scheme had been evolved, but the establishment of a Board of Scientific and Industrial Research by the Central Government was a move in the right direction. It was to be hoped that the Government Test House at Alipore, which would carry on research would soon develop into the National Chemical and Physical Laboratories, each under its own Director, and be able to deal with the multifarious problems connected with industrial research in the country. Sir R. N. Chopra explained the provisions of the Drugs Act and hoped that after the framing of the necessary rules, by the Central Drug Technical Advisory Board and the Drugs Consultative

Committee, the Provincial Governments would set up Provincial Advisory Boards and testing laboratories in their respective provinces for the control of the drug trade in their areas. The steps which had been taken so far, he said, were undoubtedly far-reaching, but only a start had been made, and he hoped that before long the machinery would start working. As a result not only the drug manufacturers, but the public also would benefit from the proper standardization and control of this very important, but greatly neglected, industry.

Sir R. N. Chopra also welcomed the Bill, passed by the Central Legislature, for financing the work in connection with agricultural research in the country. He hoped that the Governments, both Central and Provincial, the scientists and the public would co-operate towards improving the present very backward condition of agriculture and livestock, which, with its undeveloped industries were mainly responsible for the impoverishment of this great land.

Sir R. N. Chopra also referred "to the labours of the National Planning Committee of the Indian National Congress which has been sitting at Bombay for the last two years under the distinguished Chairmanship of our national leader, Pandit Jawaharlal Nehru." "It was gratifying to learn", he said, "that the Committee was able to impress into its service more than three hundred of the country's foremost scientists, economists, industrialists and public men. We understand that about 21 of the 29 committees have already submitted their reports; these have been discussed by the National Planning Committee and resolutions have been taken on them. Let us hope that whatever be the outcome of the present struggle, the deliberations of these committees will act as guides for the administration in the future handling of the economic and social problems of the country."

Indian scientists' opportunities, Sir R. N. Chopra said, had been limited and their spheres of work greatly circumscribed; in most cases they had to work under serious handicaps which no amount of brilliance or hard work could surmount. Like European education, modern science in this country was an exotic planted very recently, rather hesitatingly and a little too reservedly, and though the young sapplings received a certain amount of protecting shelter, fostering care which was essential, was certainly not extended to them on a scale which alone would have made it possible for the tender plants to become acclimatized and flourish. As a result the growth of these tender sapplings had not only been greatly stunted but fortuitous. "Science is to play its proper part of the life of the country and the nation" he said, "it must receive more generous consideration not only at the hands of the Governments, both Central and Provincial, but also be supported generously by the public, the commercial and agricultural magnates and all those who have the means to help ; this alone will make it possible for India to assume its proper place in the scientific world and the comity of commercial nations."

Sir Chopra then read a paper on the "Organisation of Public Health and Medical Services in India".

After describing the landmarks in public health administration in India, such as the appointment of a Royal Commission to enquire into the health of the army in India in 1859, the report of the Plague Commission in 1904 following the outbreak of plague in 1896 and Reforms introduced by the Government of India Act of 1919 and the separation of preventive and curative departments, Sir R. N. Chopra said that the question at the present time was the lack of co-operation and consequently of co-ordination obtaining in many parts of India between the official Medical and Public Health Departments. The situation required to be met by a close *liason* between the two branches, such as, for exam le, obtained in the Government of India, where the Director-General of the Indian Medical Service, had the Public Health Commissioner working with him in his office as his principal staff colleague. Such an arrangement not only conduced to a close co-operation, but the distribution of work was facilitated. The urgent necessity for a friendly collaboration between the two departments, if the system was not to break down, was essential, and was recognised by experienced administrative officers of both departments. The Central Advisory Board of Health, establised in 1937, should prove a valuable agency in this direction.

Continuing, Sir R. N. Chopra said that the best solution of the problem appears to be the establishment of Ministries of Health in various Provinces modelled on the English System with suitable modifications in regard to the local conditions. He gave a historical review of the position of Public Health Service in Great Britain. In India, he said, a Federal Ministry of Health should be established at the centre to provide the necessary co-operation agency for the provincial local self-government departments, which were at present responsible for the supervision of local bodies and for public health administration in the provinces. This Ministry would also be responsible for the other health functions statutorily conferred on the Central Government by the Government of India Act of 1935. All problems in connection with curative and preventive medicine should be dealt with by one department divided into appropriate sections which, he suggested, might include:—Prison medical service; port sanitation and quarantine service; school medical service; public health including (a) medical intelligence, infectious diseases and international health, (b) nutrition, food and drugs administration including biological products, (c) environmental Hygiene including housing, water-supply, drainage, waste products and (d) industrial hygiene; Medical relief, including (a) maternity and child welfare, venereal diseases, tuberculosis, leprosy; (b) general practitioner services with special reference to rural dispensaries; (c) hospitals, (d) drug addiction, (e) health insurance; Lunacy; and Scientific Research.

For these purposes, Sir R. N. Chopra said, the Ministry should have a highly trained staff of expert advisers. The Director-General of Indian Medical Service, who as the Surgeon-General with the Government of India most nearly corresponded to the Chief Medical Officer of the Ministry of Health in England, had at present an insignificant number of specialists on his staff. The materials for the establishment of a Ministry of Health at the centre in India were all available. Thus, though many of the bureau were under private bodies, their directors acted as advisers to the Director-General, Indian Medical Service, who as a rule, was connected with such bodies as the Chairman of their Managing Committees.

The provision of a suitable staff of experts must devolve on the Federal Government and could not be relegated to the provinces. A carefully selected central staff would, to some extent, avoid the duplication of posts of highly specialised men in the component States of the Federation, while the position and prestige of the Federal Administration should enable it to attract the proper type of men. The selection of the Federal Chief Medical Officer should, however, be dependent on his having both Medical and Public Health experience, and his deputies must be given a chance to familiaries themselves with the wide range of the curative, preventive and constructive aspects of medicine in the country.

Speaking of public health organisation in the Provinces, Sir R. N. Chopra said that each province should have a Chief Medical Officer responsible to the Minister of Health of the province for the administration of the whole of the Medical subject with a number of deputies in charge of the various departments, e.g., prisons, schools, medical and public health problems. A provincial Board of Health under the Chairmanship of the Minister of Health should be constituted in each province. In the districts, District Health Committees should be formed for the same purpose. These should be presided over by the Collector of the district or the President of the District Board; the co-operation of both agencies was essential, and that alone would make it possible for these committees to work efficiently. So far as the rural population was concerned, medical men engaged in curative work should be able to undertake public health duties as well. Their education and training should be of such a nature as to enable them to do so without difficulty. The doctor engaged in combating epidemic diseases should be expected to undertake public health work when not dealing with outbreaks of infectious diseases. The rural doctor, who was the final link between the Health Services in this country and the people, should also be responsible for giving an elementary health education to the patients in connection with their immediate surroundings. Such instruction would be much more effective than general lectures and demonstrations to large audiences.

Concluding, Sir R. N. Chopra said that under the conditions prevailing in India at present, the State was essentially responsible for providing the necessary agencies for both preventive and curative medicine. Curative and preventive medicine must work as one single whole; to let them work separately in watertight compartments was sure to lead to confusion, while only an organisation of the nature detailed above would be able to deal successfully with the multifarious problems of public health in this vast country.

The Indian Statistical Conference

Fourth Session—Benares—2nd. January 1941

The Welcome Address

The fourth session of the Indian Statistical Conference was opened at Benares on the 2nd. January 1941, by His Excellency Sir *Maurice Hallett*, Governor of U. P., in the Sayaji Rao Gaekwar Library Hall.

Welcoming the President and the delegates. Sir *S. Radhakrishnan* pointed out that there were great dangers in the employment of the statistical method. They were all familiar with the slogan, "lies, damned lies and statistics." They had to understand that statistical investigations were quantitative, took note of the metrical aspect and omitted the qualitative side of life. When they talked about spending ten million pounds a day or of having lost a few thousands, they did not sufficiently realise how this was a squandering of human life and a waste of material treasure. Statistics tended to hide the sorrow of the human heart and tension of the human mind. They seemed to think that human beings were earth and water, and not flesh and blood. Subject to these limitations, statistical investigations were very useful. It was fortunate that they had as President of the Statistical Conference, one of their most illustrious countrymen, Sir Girja Shankar Bajpai, who was in charge of a great department of the State.

Governor's Opening Address

"The watchword of progress in this century is 'Planning'," said His Excellency *Sir Maurice Hallett*, in his opening address. His Excellency said that the State would inevitably take an increasing share of responsibility in the life of the ordinary citizen, and it was essential, in a world of ignorance and prejudice, that responsibility should be faced on facts, and not on wishful thinking. Science, he said, was no longer academic and must be applied to industrial development, to agriculture, to public health and perhaps most important of all to the development of the social structure.

"We are learning," he added, "that in order to plan we must first know what our resources are, what is the extent of the problem with which we have to deal, what are the forces against us, and since, we cannot foretell the future, we can guess at it successfully only from a scientific study of the past."

His Excellency wished the Conference would further the cause of Statistics more and more.

The Presidential Address

The collection of statistics would be attended with far greater usefulness if its purpose was proclaimed and its processes made intelligible to the ordinary citizen, declared Sir *G. S. Bajpai*, in his presidential address. He epitomised the science of Statistics as "the arithmetic of human welfare," and explained how in any given subject of social activity, the collection of statistics aimed at improving upon the results already achieved. In the industry of Agriculture, for example, statistics had a great function to perform, which would be of real value to the economy of a vast area. Putting forward a plea for more popular presentation of statistics, Sir G. S. Bajpai said : "A science which can only survive through popular recognition cannot afford to be esoteric. Readers of John Stuart Mill and Herbert Spencer will tell how lucid exposition can make the abstruse not only simple but attractive. You must mind your Spencer and Mill."

Sir Girija Shanker also dwelt on the value of the right use of propaganda methods to popularise the science of statistics.

The Convocation Addresses

The Calcutta University Convocation

The following is the text of the Address deliverd by the Right Hon'ble Sir Tej Bahadur Sapru, P.C., K.C.S.I., M.A., L.L.D., at the annual Covocation of the Calcutta University held on the 8th May 1941 :—

It is in no conventional sense but with a very genuine feeling that I thank you for inviting me to address a Convocation meeting of the premier University of our country. The request of your Vice-Chancellor that I should come here was irresistible Much as I should like to observe a discreet silence on some of the questions which are at present agitating the public mind, and thus refrain from adding to the volume of confusion and discord which unhappily is disfiguring our public life, I find myself at times compelled by circumstances to appear on the public platform which, I confess, has no attraction for me. I shall, therefore, appeal to your indulgence and forgiveness fo a little while when I shall be intruding myself upon your attention.

I have just said that the Calcutta University is the premier University of India and when in the next few pages I shall tell you what I have all my life felt about Calcutta and this University, I shall beg you to give me some credit for sincerity and not to assume that I am saying all this to flatter your vanity or to repay your hospitality. As a young man reading at Agra more than fifty years ago I came under the influence of that new school of thought in the social and political life of the country, the source and centre of which was Calcutta. Several of my professors and teachers were men from Bengal. Indeed, it is true to say that in those days the intellectual life of the United Provinces was not only moulded by Bengalis but was completely under the domination of Bengal. The youth of my province in those days derived their enthusiasm about social reform, in the limited sense in which that word is used in India, from Ram Mohun Roy and Keshub Chunder Sen, while their imagination in politics was fired by the never-to-be-forgotten oratory of Surendra Nath Banerjea, Lal Mohan Ghose, Ananda Mohan Bose and Kali Churn Banurji.

The period of formal separation commenced with the establishment of the Allahabad University in 1887. I say 'formal' because, although it was considered necessary for the growing needs of the United Provinces to establish a separate and independent University at Allahabad, yet it did not mean the termination of the influence of Calcutta, for it continued in full vigour for a considerable period after its establishment. Even to-day when the United Provinces can boast of five Universities, Bengal is fairly represented on the teaching staffs of several of them. The names of your distinguished Vice-Chancellors, professors, scientists, historians, doctors, Judges, lawyers, politicians and journalists are held in respect and esteem all over the United Provinces. If you are proud of Rabindra Nath Tagore, so are we, for, though it may be our misfortune to miss the grace and charm of his language in original, yet we are by no means unfamiliar with the depth of his feeling, the purity of his thought and the spirituality of his poetry. I do not wish to suggest or say that in the development of our intellectual and cultural life we had no heritage of our own to serve as a nucleus, for it is a fact that the indigenous culture of the United Provinces was already rich and varied—the result of a confluence of two streams, the source of one of which was at Benares and of the other at Delhi and Lucknow. I am, however, free to confess that the debt we owe to Bengal is by no means inconsiderable and it is certainly greater than that we owe to any other Province or any other University in India.

I am in no sense of the term an educationist. I should, therefore, be going beyond my depth if I were to undertake to advise you as to what changes and reforms you should bring about in the constitution of your University or in its internal working. I believe this task was entrusted more than once to two bodies of learned men, once in the time of Lord Curzon and again in the time of Lord Chelmsford. Much wisdom may lie buried in the tomes left to you by the Calcutta University Commission, which have, to a certain extent, influenced the decisions of other Universities. Among the 33 Vice-Chancellors whom you have had since 1857 when this University was established there are names of men like Henry Summer Maine, William Markby, William Hunter, Arthur Hob-house,

Gooroo Dass Banerjee, which would shed lustre on any University in the world, but there is one other name also which, while no less illustrious than any one of the names I have just mentioned, means to this University a great deal more than any other name in the list of your Vice-Chancellors and that name is Asutosh Mookerjee, for, so long as he was connected with this University, Sir Asutosh Mookerjee was Calcutta University and Calcutta University was Sir Asutosh Mookerjee. It was one of my rarest privileges in life to have come into contact with Sir Ashutosh Mookerjee, both at Calcutta and at Allahabad. There were so many sides to his life, so varied were his interests, so profound was his learning and so towering was his personality, that it is difficult for me to say which I admired most, but there is no doubt that the master-passion of his life was the Calcutta University. It is literally true, therefore, to say that in its period of adolescence the Calcutta University perceptibly bore the impress of his personality. In human affairs a great personality cannot escape controversy and it was inevitable that Sir Ashutosh's personality, translated in terms of his work at and for this University, should have raised some controversies. Controversies, however, arise and die; the spirit of the worker lives. That, I believe, is true of Sir Ashutosh's work in this University.

One of the remarkable features of this University, which distinguishes it from many others in India, is that from an early date it has worked for the establishment of a number of Professorships and has succeeded in a remarkable degree in getting them founded by generous donors. Among the founders of these Professorships the place of pride must be given to the honoured name of Prasunno Coomar Tagore, who, by his Will dated the 10th October, 1862, bequeathed to the University a monthly allowance of Rs. 1000 for the purpose of founding a Professorship of Law to be called the Tagore Law Professorship. A cursory glance at the list of Tagore Law Professors will disclose the names of some of the greatest jurists and lawyers not merely of Calcutta but also of other parts of India, and not merely of India but also of England and other countries, *e.g.*, Sir Frederic Pollock, Sir William Holdsworth, Dr. Garner and Professor Morgan; and if I may venture to refer to some Calcutta names without making any invidious distinction and without referring to those among them who are happily with us, at the head of them stand the names of Dr. (afterwards Sir) Rash Behary Ghose, Dr. (afterwards Sir) Gooroo Dass Banerjee, the Right Honourable Ameer Ali and Sir Asutosh Mookerjee himself. These are honoured names in the annals of Indian legal history and their contributions to legal science will stand out as monuments of learning wherever legal scholarship is valued and respected. The Minto Professorship of Economics was founded in 1909 and the first incumbent of the Chair was one who had already won distinction at Cambridge under Professor Marshall. I refer to Professor Manohar Lal—now Sir Manohar Lal, Minister of Finance in the Punjab. This Professorship, after a chequered career, is now designated as the University Professorship of Economics and it may sincerely be hoped that it will substantially enrich the economic literature of the country. You have also a Carmichael Professorship of Indian History and Culture, a subject which until recently was woefully neglected by our Universities, and I am glad to note that to perpetuate the memory of the late Sir Asutosh Mookerjee three Professorships—called the Asutosh Professorship of Sanskrit, the Asutosh professorship of Islamic Culture and the Asutosh Professorship of Medieval and Modern Indian History—have been established. The princely benefactions of Sir Tarak Nath Palit in 1912 and of Sir Rash Behary Ghose—both of them, I am happy to say, leaders of the legal profession in their days—have enabled the University to secure the services of some of the most distinguished scientists, such as Sir P. C. Ray, Sir C. V. Raman, Professor Meghnad Saha, Professor Ganesh Prasad, Professor Mitra, Dr. Guha and others. Your University, therefore, can, in my opinion, legitimately take pride that it has set an example to others in India in developing post-graduate studies and research; but here again we must acknowledge that the inspiration came from Sir Asutosh Mookerjee. The list of University publications at the end of your Calendar constitutes, in my humble opinion, a solid contribution to the advancement of learning, which should, above all others, be the primary function of a seat of learning.

Ideals of education change from generation to generation and what may be at a particular time a good ideal for a country need not necessarily be the same for another country. Into a discussion of the theory of education as imparted by our Universities I do not propose to enter, nor do I feel myself competent to do so. In his celebrated inaugural address delivered at the University of St. Andrews more than 70 years ago John Stuart Mill referred to and discussed the two kinds of education which the systems of schools and universities in his day were intended to promote. He says:

"Intellectual education, and moral education: knowledge and the training of the knowing faculty, conscience and that of the moral faculty—these are the two main ingredients of human culture; but they do not exhaust the whole of it. There is a third division which, if subordinate, and owing allegiance to the two others, is barely inferior to them, and not less needful to the completeness of the human being; I mean, the aesthetic branch; the culture which comes through poetry and art, and may be described as the education of the feelings, and the cultivation of the beautiful. This department of things deserves to be regarded in a far more serious light than is the custom of these countries."

It is not perhaps fashionable in these days to quote John Stuart Mill, but I have ventured to quote him because what he said in 1867 at the University of St. Andrews is to a very large extent true of the Universities in India today. Our Universities have been, ever since their establishment, promoting intellectual education and moral education, and I refuse to subscribe to the criticism that the result of the present system of education in British times has been to starve our intellectual or spiritual life. Most of our greatest thinkers, writers, poets and historians in our times have been either the direct products of our own Universities, or have come under their all-pervasive influence, or have been connected in some capacity or other with them. In the realm of Science I shall mention only two or three. Sir Jagadish Chandra Bose is an honoured name among you, so is Sir Prafulla Chandra Ray, who is happily with us. You may also claim credit for having furnished to Sir C. V. Raman opportunities for that great work which has brought him fame in the world of Science. In the realm of Literature the name of Dr. Tagore is held in reverence all over the civilised world. Outside Bengal another University can take credit for having produced Sir Mohammad Iqbal—a thinker and a poet in Persian and Urdu, to whom, I confess, I have felt irresistibly drawn ever since my youth. The Calcutta University may also take pride in having founded, under the leadership of Sir Jadunath Sarkar, a new school of Indian History. He has been the inspirer of many others in that field. It is the Madras University and your University which have given to the world an exponent of Hindu thought like Sir Radhakrishnan. In the spiritual field also you have produced in contemporary times a large number of thinkers and reformers, whose writings and speeches have profoundly influenced contemporary thought. It is, however, in what Mill called "the education of the feelings, and the cultivation of the beautiful" that Calcutta occupies a place of pre-eminence, for, if one Tagore has given us beautiful poetry, another Tagore will go down to history as the founder or promoter of a new school of painting. Let us, therefore, not succumb to political prejudices or bitterness and denounce the present system of education of our Universities as having been altogether barren of results, for while I strongly maintain that a whole nation cannot be educated in a foreign language— and I have always been a persistent advocate of the development of our own languages and culture—yet bare justice required that we must not deny that the Universities have played a great and noble part in enriching our national life and stimulating altruistic and patriotic feelings.

I have often asked myself the question as to what it is that the Universities may be expected to do at this time in our onward march, for while no one is more anxious than I that the academic serenity of our Universities should not be rudely disturbed by what are at times called the baser mundane pursuits, I also maintain that from a practical point of view no University in India can afford to live a sheltered life of isolation from the great stream of national life. It, therefore, seems to me that on two sides of their work the Universities can render lasting services to the country. On the scientific side I think our professors and post-graduate scholars can do a great deal to enrich the industrial and economic life of the country by the results of their researches. The field open to them is immense, the example of other countries whose economic and industrial prosperity is in no small measure due to the scientific work of their professors, teachers and graduates, should inspire them in this work, and in my opinion it should be the primary duty of every Provincial Government—and indeed of the Central Government—to help them in a generous measure with grants for the purpose of such useful pursuits. On the cultural side—and I use the word 'culture' in its largest sense as being

India has to bear the burden and obligations of a component unit of the British Commonwealth, she is surely entitled to demand and insist that the rights and powers enjoyed by the other Dominions should be vested in her. The demand for self-government amounts in the ultimate analysis to the demand for the right to control our own destiny and frame our own policy, social, economic and political in the interests of the country. The need for a transitional arrangement is denied by no responsible person but it is essential that this process should be speedy and automatic. In all earnestness I would, therefore, impress upon His Excellency the Viceroy the imperative necessity of taking immediate steps to end the present constitutional deadlock by responding to the demand for the establishment of national Government at the centre pending the final settlement of the wider constitutional problems. I am confident that such a declaration alone can solve the present deadlock, and I trust His Excellency will appreciate the gravity of the situation and take immediate steps to bring about a change of atmosphere.

Proceedings & Resolutions

PROTECTION TO INDUSTRIES

After the presidential address the first resolution was moved by Mr. *D. P. Khaitan* (Calcutta) which was as follows :

"While noting the statement made on behalf of the Government of India that industries needed for the prosecution of the war would be given assistance and protection after the period of the war, the Federation feels that more specific and definite lines of policy of protection and encouragement should be laid down not only in regard to industries which are essential for war purposes, but also in regard to such other industries as have been established to meet the needs and requirements of the people of the country, particularly owing to the diminution in foreign imports.

"The Federation is of opinion that such encouragement should be given as is found essential either through protective duties of grant of subsidies or purchases on behalf of Government Departments or in any other suitable manner. In giving such assistance, however, the Government should not be rigidly bound to the criteria for the grant of protection laid down by the Indian Fiscal Commission nearly twenty years ago, while the machinery for investigating and determining the claims for protection should not be so cumbersome or dilatory as hitherto."

Mr. *Khaitan*, criticising the Commerce Member's recent speech in the Assembly, said that he had not the slightest doubt that the Commerce Member was doing his best for the country from the difficult situation he was placed in, but there was no reason why he should find fault with the commercial community for putting forward their demands which were necessary for the development of industry. The commercial community knew what its interests were and what was needed for the development of industry. The Government must make a frank declaration about what they intended to do for creating confidence in the minds of the capitalists in order to enable to start new industries and develop the existing ones. Referring to the suggestion of the Commerce Member that industrialists should conserve their resources during the war, Mr. Khaitan said that before making such a suggestion, the Commerce Member should give advice to the Finance Member to leave their resources with them in order they might be conserved.

Sir Shri Ram wanted the House to tell the Commerce Member that it was his duty to see that the walls of protection were raised sufficiently high in order to ensure that the industries did not suffer after the war.

The resolution was supported by several other speakers, including *Lala Padampat Singhania* (Cawnpore), Mr. *J. C. Setalvad* (Bombay), and Sirdar *P. S. Sodhbans* (Lahore) and passed unanimously.

NEED FOR EXPORT ORGANISATION

Sir *Shri Ram* moved the second resolution :—"Having regard to the desirability and importance of developing an export market for Indian manufactured articles and having regard to the absence of first-hand information regarding the scope for such a development and with a view to study the conditions of the import trade in the British Dominions, Colonial Empire and neighbouring countries, the Federation suggests to the Government of India the organisation of trade missions, consisting of Indian businessmen, with the necessary technical staff, to visit those countries.

"The Federation further urges that a comprehensive export organisation be constituted by the Government of India to supervise and control, if necessary, the export of Indian goods in respect of their quality, strict adherence to samples and specifications, correct marking of goods as regards dimensions, etc., and that such an organisation should mainly consist of non-officials, representative of important indigenous manufacturing interests, and should be financed from the general revenues of the Central Government and, if necessary, by an imposition of a small cess levied on the production of exporting industries, just adequate to meet the maintenance of such an organisation. The export organisation should undertake such activities as the opening of commercial museums in India and abroad and the maintenance of technical staff at the offices of the Trade Commissioners, which would be conducive to the greater development of export trade in manufactured articles."

Sir Shri Ram said that such countries as Australia and East Africa, which before the war depended on Europe and Japan for textile goods, were finding it difficult during war-time to get their requirements. India, on the other hand, had huge surpluses of textile goods. Therefore, it was the best opportunity for Indian textiles to be exported to those countries. All such exports should be made through an organisation set up by the Government of India to ensure that goods according to samples and specifications only were sent out. This was necessary because they did not want the reputation of Indian goods to suffer in any way in the foreign markets, due to the desire on the part of some Indian exporters to have immediate gain.

The resolution was passed.

State Ownership of Railways

Sir *Abdul Halim Ghuznavi* moved:

"The Federation notes with satisfaction the decision of the Government of to terminate the contracts of the B. B. and C. I. and the Assam Bengal Railways and to take over the lines under State management from January '42.

"The Federation reiterates its considered opinion that the Government should take steps to acquire the remaining company managed railways as and when the termination of agreements with them becomes due, in order to achieve co-ordination and economy in the administration of railways.

"As the option for termination of the contracts with the Bengal and North Western Railway falls due on December 31, '42 for which previous notice has to be given before the end of the current year, the Federation strongly urges the Government of India to take steps accordingly for acquiring the B. and N. W. Railway."

Sir *Abdul* said that he had found from records that the Government had paid for the capital of the railways and passed them over to Britishers Such a position existed nowhere in the world. Having paid for the capital, it was the duty of the Government to see that no foreigner exploited the railways. But that was not done. This strange situation was brought predominantly before the public 25 years ago, as the result of which a Committee was appointed in 1920, presided over by Sir William Ackworth. That Committee came to the unanimous conclusion that the management of the railways by companies of English domicile should not be continued. After that report was out, the Government undertook to take over the management of the E. I. R. and G. I. P. When those railways were taken over, Sir Charles Innes, the then Railway Member, in the course of a speech in the Assembly, said that though the Government had taken over the management of those railways, the members should not bang the door on company-management of railways. He even hinted that Government wished to float British companies in India and make over the management of railways to them.

Sir *Abdul* said that the B. and N. W. Railway was not a State owned railway but even the Ackworth report was thirty years old. India to-day wanted Dominion Status—the Congress wanted independence; would she tolerate the exploitation of railways by British companies ?

After other speakers had supported it, the resolution was passed.

Indians Abroad

Kumararaja M. A. *Muthiah Chettiar* (Madras) moved: "The Federation deplores the failure of the Indo-Ceylon negotiations and appreciates the stand taken by the Government of India in this connection. The Federation regrets the measure to deal with the question of immigration and registration, unilaterally and independently of the Government of India. The Federation sincerely hopes that the Ceylon State Council will, even at this stage, reconsider their attitude and will desist from adopting any measures that would lead to further estrangement between the two countries, which are geographically, economically and culturally bound together.

"The Federation trusts that in the trade negotiations between India and Burma, which are now proceeding, adequate steps will be taken by the Government of India to safeguard the status, rights and interests of Indians in Burma.

"The Federation urges that India's Agents should be appointed in Fiji and British Guiana to look after the interests of the Indian population in those countries.

"The Federation earnestly hopes that the principal of equality of citizenship rights would be implemented in all parts of the British Commonwealth, irrespective of race or colour, and that the different Dominion and Colonial Governments would in practice, treat every section of the permanent population inhabiting their territories in a spirit of equality and fairness."

"One happy feature about this subject", said the *Kumararaja*, moving the resolution, "is that in India to-day there is unanimity of opinion about giving support to Indian nationals abroad."

He mainly dealt with the disabilities of Indians in Burma and Ceylon and emphasised the reasonable attitude taken up by them towards the rights of the native population. The Indians, he said, could not be accused of retarding the progress of the nationals of Burma and Ceylon. On the other hand, all Indians were willing to co operate with them in their endeavour to raise the Ceylonese-Burmese position, economically and politically.

In Burma, the speaker continued, one disability after another had been imposed on Indians. Rangoon was practically an Indian City but the Burmese now wanted to reduce the numbers of the Indian members of the Corporation. The Kumararaja did not know what more was in store there for the Indians. He was glad that the Government of India had dealt with this problem with a firm hand. He suggested that while considering the trade negotiations with Burma, it was absolutely necessary to come to an understanding with regard to the political status, rights and privileges of the Indians living there.

As regards Ceylon, the Kumararaja said that during the last five years, there had been a series of measures against Indians. He hoped that this resolution would go to the very heart of the Ceylonese people and that the statesmen of India and Ceylon would soon evolve a scheme acceptable to both the countries.

Rai Bahadur Lala Ramsarandas said that India did not wish to resort to retaliation. But if she decided to retaliate Ceylon would find herself in a very difficult position. He urged the Government of India to take strong measures at the end of the war; the Ceylonese should be dealt with in the same manner as they dealt with the Indians living in their land.

The resolution was passed and the meeting adjourned.

Resolutions—2nd. Day—New Delhi—23rd. March 1941

DEVELOPMENT OF KEY INDUSTRIES

Resolutions on the subject of the Eastern Group Council, taxation of incomes by Provincial Governments, export and import quotas and the surcharge in respect of freights on foodgrains and fodder were passed by the Federation of Indian Chambers of Commerce and Industry, which concluded its session to-day.

Mr. G. L. Mehta (Calcutta) moved the following resolution:

"In the absence of any knowledge regarding the conclusions reached at the Eastern Group Conference, the Federation wishes to give expression to the anxiety entertained by the Indian commercial community with regard to their likely repercussions on the establishment and development of Indian industries, and trusts that the programme laid down by the Conference would not, in any way, compromise or jeopardise India's economic interests.

"The Federation notes the establishment of the Eastern Group Council in India for co-ordinating arrangements for production and supply of munitions and stores in the various Empire countries east of Suez, and wishes to impress strongly upon the Government that such a programme of co-ordination should not preclude India from establishing or developing any industries, and, particularly, key and engineering industries in this country.

"The Federation has to stress that, in any programme of utilising India's resources and building up important industries, in pursuance of the programme laid down by the Eastern Group Council or the Roger Mission, the Government should see that the capital, control and management of such enterprises remain in the hands of Indians. The Federation suggests that the representative of the Government of India on the Eastern Group Council should remain in active contact with representative Indian commercial opinion and should consult it from time to time in regard to the practical measures to be adopted in pursuance of the policy laid down by the Council."

Mr. Mehta deprecated the tendency on the part of the Government to ignore the Federation in regard to important matters concerning the country's trade and industry. The Government convened the Eastern Group Conference without consulting the Federation or any representative commercial or industrial body. Even the so-called non-official Indian representatives were included in the conference, not on the initiative of the Government but on the suggestion of Sir Alexander Roger. But those non-officials did not represent any organisation. They were there in their individual capacity. The conference terminated four months ago, and yet the public of India had not been informed of its conclusions. The Government of England had held several secret sessions of Parliament to acquaint the public of their programme, but in India nothing had been done in that direction. The British Government wanted India's men, money and material, but did not want the co-operation of the Indian people. It was, therefore, not unnatural for Indians to entertain misgivings about the ulterior motive of the Government.

Thd speaker went on to state that Australia was receiving better treatment from the British Government. Some of the vital war industries were being located there. India was not being given a chance to develop her shipping industry, while Australia was to build ships even for the Royal Indian Navy. Australia was receiving better treatment in the manufacture of aeroplanes also. India, he said, was anxious to develop her industries, but not with foreign capital, as foreign capital meant foreign control. He hoped that India's representative on the Eastern Group Council would see that India's interests were not jeopardised.

Rai Bahadur Lala Ramsarandas said that in Great Britain all industries, which had taken birth during the war, were assured of a future after the war. They were being given a special margin of profit, so that they might be able to build up their reserves. In India, though the Commerce Member was trying to encourage industries, the Finance Member was imposing heavy taxation and defeating that object.

Mr. *D. N. Sen* (Calcutta), supporting the resolution, said that the general impression in the country was that, as the result of the creation of the Eastern Group Council, India would become a granary of raw material and Indians would be reduced to the position of hewers of wood and drawers of water.

The resolution was passed.

Income-Tax Collection

Mr. *J. J. Kapadia* (Bombay) moved : "The Federation draws the attention of the Government of India to the growing feeling of dissatisfaction at the administrative practices adopted by the various income-tax authorities, and urges the Government of India to issue necessary instructions in the matter so as to avoid hardship and harassment to the assessees."

Mr. Kapadia gave a series of instances of "hardship and harassment", and urged that member-bodies of the Federation should be asked to communicate to the Committee of the Federation the directions in which hardships had been caused, and that the Committee should, on its own initiative, invite a few income-tax experts to give first-hand information to the Committee, which should submit a comprehensive representation to the Government and, if necessary, wait in a deputation on the Member-in-charge.

Sir *Abdul Halim Ghaznavi* (Calcutta) accused the Congress Party in the Assembly and particularly its leader, Mr. Bhulabhai Desai, of responsibility for the passing of the Income-tax Amendment Act. The Muslim League and the Congress Nationalists opposed the measure, but the Congress Party helped the Government and Mr. Desai "made friendship with Sir James Grigg", with the result that the Government succeeded in putting it on the statute book. Sir Abdul Halim alleged that the income-tax authorities in Bombay and Calcutta, although they had other means of recovering penal assessments, choose to take away broken chairs, lotahs, drinking glasses and even clothes from the offices of assessees in order to humiliate them in the market. The resolution was passed unanimously.

PROVINCIAL AND CENTRAL SPHERES OF TAXATION

Mr. *Chunilal B. Mehta* (Bombay) moved the following resolution: "The Federation is of opinion that, as a consequence of the evolution of India's political structure on Federal lines, it has now become essential to demarcate clearly the limits of the Provincial and Central spheres of taxation, especially when both these authorities endeavour to levy taxation on the same income e.g., the tax on income from immovable property at a fairly substantial rate in the provinces of Bombay and the Punjab. While recognising that the British Parliament is alive to this matter as announced by the amendment recently enacted to the Government of India Act, 1935, the Federation submits that the least that can be done by the Government of India, pending suitable action in this behalf, is to take steps to see that the amount of the provincial tax is allowed as a deduction while computing the income for taxes imposed by the Central Government.

Mr. *V. K. Dhage* (Bombay), *Lal Gurusaran Lal* (Patna) and Mr. *Balkishan Munjal* (Amritsar) spoke in support of the resolution which was passed.

IMPORT AND EXPORT CONTROL

The meeting took up the next resolution reading:

(a) "In the opinion of the Federation, considerations of economic warfare have been unduly stressed in administering the existing restrictions on export. Such restrictions on the export and import trade with non-sterling countries are not conducive to the development of new export markets for the produce of this country and require to be modified for the purpose.

(b) "The Federation further invites the attention of the Government of India to the difficulties encountered by Indian merchants on account of the war-time restrictions on export trade and, in particular, wishes to point out complaints about:

(1) Difficulties arising out of lack of shipping tonnage:

"(2) inequitable allotment of shipping space;

"(3) administrative practice which prevents national interest in the trade getting its proper quota of the export business; and

"(4) appointment of non-national agencies for making purchases for, and on behalf of His Majesty's Government.

(c) "Having regard to the extension of import trade control to a variety of articles, the Federation urges the appointment of an Imports Advisory Council, with subsidiary bodies at different ports, with a view to facilitating the discussions and mitigation of practical difficulties arising out of the day-to-day application of the control.

(d) "The Federation strongly feels that, as a matter of general practice, contracts and commitments entered into before the institution of the control should be exempted from the provisions thereof, and that the goods covered by such previous contracts should be allowed to be imported."

Sir *Rahimtoola Chinoy*, criticising the working of the export control arrangements made by the Government particularly regarding oilseeds and wool, said with reference to wool, that if the Government both in Britain and India wanted to be fair to the Indian exporter, they could without any loss to themselves buy their requirements of wool in India and, the surplus might be allowed to be exported direct to the United States of America where Indian wool would fetch better prices to the ultimate benefit of the Indian wool producer.

Referring to the working of the import control, he said that Import Controllers had been given only limited powers, and red-tape delays had caused enormous loss and difficulty to many merchants. The Import Advisory Council, suggested in the resolution, he said, was intended to be on the lines of the Export Advisory Council now in existence. It would be advisable, he said, to appoint an Import Controller for adjustment of quotas of imports of steel.

Mr. *T. T. Krishnamachari* (Madras) seconding the resolution, dwelt on the "disastrous" results brought about by the present control established at only one stage of the transaction, and pointed out that a result of the present system of control in Madras has been that three non-Indian non-British firms had got almost the entire quota for groundnuts. He urged that the control should be continuous and extensive, and that a more rational distribution of quotas should be secured. He referred to the difficulties caused by the present "statistical black-out" consequent on the stoppage of publication of full figures of seaborne trade, and said that it was impossible to evaluate, with any degree of precision, the result of the control over imports, the quotas should be carefully examined before they were allotted to merchants, as otherwise they tended to be unfair.

Mr. *Haridas Lalji*, (Karachi) supported the resolution, which was passed unanimously.

IMPORTED RAW DRUGS

Moved by *Rajratna Seth, B. D. Amin* (Calcutta) and seconded by Dr. *H. Ghosh* (Calcutta), the meeting passed the following resolution :

"The Federation invites the attention of the Government of India to the fact that (a) the high freight charges levied by the railways on raw drugs and (b) the high duty levied by the Government on raw drugs imported into India, are proving greatly detrimental to the indigenous chemical and pharmaceutical industry in the country and tend to place it in an unfavourable position for competing with foreign products. The Federation, therefore, requests the Government of India (a) to reduce the freight charges on raw drugs by lowering their classification, as also by introducing a telescopic scale of rates and (b) to abolish entirely the import duty on raw drugs according to the recommendations of the Drugs Enquiry Committee."

OIL SEEDS INDUSTRY

The Federation passed the following resolutions moved from the chair :—

"Having regard to the growing importance of oilseeds as one of the chief cash crops of the country and the potentialities of the development of industries depending upon them, the Federation is of the opinion that an independent central organisation, on the lines of the Indian Central Cotton Committee, should be set up for oilseeds also, with a view to taking full advantage of such a valuable crop produced in the country.

"Further, the Federation earnestly requests that the Government should utilise the establishment of such a central organisation to investigate the various difficult problems that have arisen relating to the surplus stocks of oil-seeds during the present war conditions, and to adopt suitable measures with a view to giving the necessary relief to the primary producers.''

FREIGHTS ON FOOD-GRAINS

"The Federation views with apprehension the reference made by the Member for Railways to the possibility of the surcharge on railway freights being made applicable to food-grains and fodder, and impresses on the Railway Board that the condition of the masses in general would be adversely affected if these exemptions are withdrawn."

"The Federation raised its annual subscriptions from Rs. 150 to 200. The Federation also decided to charge an admission fee from new member-bodies of Rs. 500.

DEMAND FOR NATIONAL GOVERNMENT

A number of resolutions were next moved from the chair and passed. One of these urged the necessity for taking immediate steps to end the present constitutional deadlock by the establishment of a National Government at the Centre pending the final settlement of the wider constitutional problem.

DEFENCE INDUSTRIES

The Federation urged the Government to take immediate steps for the establishment of defence industries in India such as, the manufacture of motor vehicles, aircraft, merchantships and naval units, guns, and tanks and heavy chemicals, either under the direct control of the State or of the nationals of this country.

NATIONAL SHIPPING

"The Federation deplored that the Government had not only taken any effective steps to help National Shipping in securing substantial participation in India's maritime trade nor had they formulated any policy or plan for redeeming their oft-repeated assurances, but on the contrary had enforced measures, under the present emergency, that were practically operating as a set-back to the Indian shipping industry. The Federation strongly urged the Government to take all necessary steps to encourage efforts for the establishment of a ship-building industry in India, through the transfer of a shipyard from the United Kingdom, as well as by giving this industry the same priorities as were given to war industries in respect of steel, machinery, machine tools and technical personnel".

Educational Progress in India

JANUARY—JUNE 1941

The Indian Science Congress

28th. Session—Benares—2nd. January 1941

The Presidential Address

The 28th. Session of the Indian Science Congress was opened at Benares on the 2nd. January 1941 by H. E. *Sir Mau·ice Hallet*, Governor of the United Provinces, in the hall of the Sayaji Rao Gaekwar Library of the Benares Hindu University in the presence of a distinguished gathering of scientists of the country. Both at the commencement and close of the proceedings prayers were offered in Sanskrit, all standing. Sir *S. Radhakrishnan*, Chairman of the Reception Committee, in a speech, welcomed the delegates.

Welcoming the formation of the Board of Scientific and Industrial Research, Sir *Ardisher Dalal*, in his presidential address, said that the Board should co-ordinate the immediate needs of the war with the long-range policy of industrial development of the country as a whole.

Sir *Ardeshir*, in the course of his address, said; "A substantial part of the export trade of India has been lost since the war. Science can help in the utilization within the country itself of some of the raw materials which used to be exported. Researches are being conducted for instance on the use in India for lubrication purposes of some of the oil seeds of which the export has dwindled down and the surplus of which is likely to create serious economic trouble for the cultivator. Even a more acute problem is the stoppage of the import of many commodities essential for the economic life of the country, such as machinery, chemicals, etc."

"It is imperative", the President said, "that India should make herself self-sufficient with regard to such materials as are vital to the maintenance of her economic and industrial life so that the situation which had arisen during the last war and which has arisen once again may never recur. It is here that science can be of the greatest assistance to industry. Research has been described as the mother of industry and while some of the older and more traditional industries may have originated without the aid of science, it cannot be denied that all industries to-day depend upon science and research not only for their progress and improvement but also for their survival. Sad experience had proved to us beyond all doubt that, under modern conditions, no nation, however peacefully inclined, can expect even to live an independent existence unless it is highly industrialized. It is the industrial potential that is convertible into the war potential and the country that has the highest industrial potential and is prepared to convert it in the shortest time into war potential that stands the best chance in modern war-fare. As we have seen, it is not man power that counts in the highly mechanized warfare of the present day, but planes, tanks, guns, ships and the factories, plants and workshops behind them. The lesson for India is plain and she can only neglect it at her peril. It is no longer the question of a balanced economy or of mere material progress. It is necessary for India's very existence that she should be highly industrialized."

Continuing, Sir *A. Dalal* said, "There has been a tendency in the past in India for scientific and research work to be monopolized by Government Departments and although valuable results have been obtained, e.g., by the Survey of India, the Geological Survey, the Botanical Survey and in the investigation of tropical diseases, it is very necessary that organized industrial research should as far as possible be left to scientists and industrialists although of course Government has to see that the grants it makes are properly utilized."

Welcoming the appointment of the Board of Scientific and Industrial Research by the Government of India, Sir A. Dalal (who is a member of the Board) said, although the beginning of the Board might be small, its conception must be large and liberal. It must not, in its composition or working, bear the appearance of a mere 'ad hoc' body created to meet the immediate exigencies of the war. The demands of the war were no doubt urgent and must have priority over other demands, but the Board should function as a body charged with the undertake to accord a margin of preference of 15 per cent as compared with the preferential rate, whichever is greater.

8. The Government of India undertake to accord free entry to the following articles :—

Item No. In the Indian Customs Tariff	Description
13	Dyeing and tanning substances.
13(3)	Gums, resins and lac.
13(4)	Gums, Arabic, Benjamin (ras and cowrie) and Dammer (incuding unrefined batu) and resin.
40	Wood and timber.
40(2)	Furniture and cabinetware.
40(3)	Tea chests and parts and fittings thereof.
46(3)	Cotton, raw.
60	Lacquared-ware.
63	Iron or steel, old.
63 (1) to (28)	Iron or steel.
63(29)	Enamelled ironware.
64	Copper wrought and manufactures of copper.
64(1)	Copper, scrap.
65	German silver including nickel silver.
66	Aluminium.
66(1)	Unwrought ingots, blocks and bars of Aluminium.
67	Lead, wrought.
67(1)	Lead sheet for tea chests.
68	Zinc or spelter, wrought or manufactured, not otherwise specified.
69	Tin, block ;
70	Brass, bronze and similar alloys, wrought and manufactures thereof not otherwise specified.
70(1)	All sorts of metals other than iron and steel.

9. The Government of India undertake that the duty on the following goods shall not exceed the rate specified against each :—

Item No. in the Indian Customs Tariff	Description	Rate per cent
7	Potatoes and Onions	5
9	Coffee	10
9(3)	The following spices whether ground or unground, *viz.*, cardamoms, cassia, cinnamon, cloves, nutmegs and pepper . . .	10
9(5)	Betelnuts	20
13(2)	Cutch and gambier, all sorts	5
24(1)	Cigars	10
24(3)	Tobaco, unmanufactured	One anna per pound.

10. For the purpose of according margins of preference where an existing duty is not simply *ad valorem*, that is to say, when the duty is either specific or composite, a single *ad valorem* or specific duty may be fixed from time to time in consultation with the Government of Burma. Such duty shall be so calculated as to provide the prescribed margin having regard to the average value of goods of the like kind imported into India from Burma during the previous financial year.

PART II.—*Tariff treatment of Indian goods on import into Burma.*

1. *Free List.*—Goods of Indian origin of the kind which at present are duty free from whatever country imported will so long as no duty is imposed on those kinds when imported from countries other than India, continue to be duty free. If in Burma any duty is hereafter imposed on any such kind of goods a corresponding duty may, subject to Part III, be imposed on the like kind of goods of Indian origin.

2. *Cotton twist and yarn.*—The Government of Burma undertake to maintain

the existing margins of preference, except in the case of mercerized yarn on which the Government of Burma do not undertake to accord any margin of preference.

3. (*a*) In the case of articles (other than cotton twist and yarn) which under the Burma Customs Tariff are at present subject only to a standard rate and that rate does not exceed 15 per cent *ad valorem* the Government of Burma undertake to accord a margin of preference equal to the existing rate. (*b*) In the case of articles which under the Burma Customs Tariff are at present subject according to origin to either a standard or a preferential rate and those rates do not exceed 15 per cent and 10 per cent respectively the Government of Burma undertake to accord margins of preference equal to the existing standard and preferential rates.

4. *Cotton piecegoods.*—The Government of Burma undertake—

(1) to accord a margin of preference of 7½ per cent to Indian cotton piecegoods over corresponding goods of United Kingdom manufacture:

(2) not to levy a higher duty than 10 per cent on Indian cotton piecegoods; and

(3) not to increase the existing quota of Japanese cotton piecegoods which may be imported into Burma.

Explanation.—The expression "cotton piecegoods" means fabrics which at the date of the signature of the Agreement are assessable to duty on import into Burma under item 48 (3), item 48 (7) or item 48 (9) of the First Schedule to the Burma Tariff Act, 1934.

5. *Sugar.*—The Government of Burma undertake to carry out any measures which may be necessary to give effect to their declared intention of satisfying the demand for sugar in Burma (other than classes of sugar specifically excluded by agreement) in excess of local production, by means of imports from India.

6. *Salt.*—The Government of Burma undertake to accord a margin of preference equal to 50 per cent of the additional import duty leviable on salt imported from countries other than India or 8 annas per 100 Viss, whichever is the greater.

7. *Tea.*—The Government of Burma undertake to accord a specific margin of preference of one anna per pound against the preferential rate and of three annas per pound against the standard rate.

8. *Manufactured tobacco.*—The Government of Burma undertake that the duty on bidis shall not exceed 80 per cent of the lowest rate of duty leviable on cigarettes imported from India.

9. *Matches, motor spirit, silver and kerosene.*—The Government of Burma undertake that the duties on these goods shall not exceed the rates of excise duty for the time being leviable on similar goods produced or manufactured in Burma.

10. *Other articles subject to excise duty.*—Notwithstanding anything contained herein no article which in Burma is for the time being subject to a duty of excise shall be entitled on import from India to be subjected to a rate of duty less than the rate of excise duty for the time being in force.

11. (*a*) In the case of articles (other than cigarettes, iron and steel, and articles specified in paragraphs 1, 2 and 4 to 9) which under the Burma Customs Tariff are at present subject only to a standard rate and that rate exceeds 15 per cent *ad valorem* the Government of Burma undertake to accord a margin of preference of 15 per cent.

(*b*) In the articles which under the Burma Customs Tariff are at present subject according to origin to either a standard or a preferential rate and those rates exceed 15 per cent and 10 per cent respectively the Government of Burma undertake to accord a margin of preference of 15 per cent as compared with the standard rate or 10 per cent as compared with the preferential rate, whichever is greater.

12. The Government of Burma undertake to accord free entry in respect of the following articles :—

Item No. in the Burma Customs Tariff	Description
16(1)	Fish Canned
20(1)	Fruit juices
20(2)	Fruits and vegetables, canned or bottled
30(7)	Lead pencils
44	Paper

44(1)	Printing paper
44(2)	Printing paper
44(3)	Writing Paper
50(8)	Coir fibre, Coir yarn and Coir mats and matting
60	Glass and Glassware
60(1)	Glass Globes and chimneys for lamps and lanterns
60(3)	Glass bangles, glass beeds and false pearls
73(1)	Certain electrical instruments
73(2)	Certain electrical instruments
77	Instruments, apparatus and appliances other than electrical

13. The Government of Burma undertake that the duty on the following goods shall not exceed 5 per cent :—

Item No. in the Burma Customs Tariff	Description
7	Potatoes and Onions
8	Cocoanuts
28	Chemicals, Drugs and Medicines
28(5)	Magnesium Chloride
28(6) (*a*) & (*b*).	Certain Chemicals
28(7)	Certain Chemicals
28(8)	Certain Chemicals, Drugs and Medicines
28(14)	Toilet requisites
30 2) (*a*) (*b*), (*c*) & (*d*)	Paints
30(3) (*a*), (*b*), (*c*) & (*d*)	Paints
47(3)	Woollen Yarn
47(4)	Woollen Yarn
49(3)	Blankets and Rugs
51(1)	Woollen Hosiery

14. The Government of Burma undertake that the duty on the following goods shall not exceed 10 per cent :—

Item No. in the Burma Customs Tariff	Description
9	Coffee
9(3) (*a*) (*b*).	Certain spices
24(1)	Cigars
32(1)	Soap, toilet
49(4)	Woollen carpets
54	Boots and Shoes
54(1)	Boots and Shoes

15. The Government of Burma undertake that the duty on the following goods shall not exceed the rate specified against each :—

Item No. in the Burma Customs Tariff	Description	Rate
9(5)	Betel Nuts.	20 per cent.
22(1)	Ale and Beer	Rate of excise duty for the time being in force.
22(5)(*b*)	Drugs and Medicines containing spirit,	Double the rate of excise duty for the time being in force.
24(3)	Tobacco, Unmanufactured	1 anna per pound.
29(1)	Cinematographs films, exposed.	15 percent. (with separate tariff value for Indian films.)
48	Silk fabrics	15 per cent.
48(1)	Artificial silk fabrics,	15 per cent.
48(5)	Mixture fabrics	15 per cent.
51(3)	Cotton knitted fabrics.	15 per cent.
60(2)	Electric lighting, bulbs.	15 per cent.

16. Notwithstanding anything to the contrary in the foregoing paragraphs, the Government of Burma shall during the period of the war be at liberty to impose a surcharge of 5 per cent *ad valorem* on any class of goods imported from India, provided that a surcharge equal to, or greater than, this amount is also imposed on the same class of goods imported from all other countries.

17. For the purpose of according margins of preference where existing duty is not simply *ad valorem*, that is to say, when the duty is either specific or composite, a single *ad valorem* or specific duty may be fixed from time to time in consultation with the Government of India. Such duty shall be calculated as to provide the prescribed margin having regard to the average value of goods of the like kind into Burma from India during the previous financial year.

Part III—*General*.

1. Subject to the provisions of the two preceeding parts, the Contracting Parties undertake to accord each other Most Favoured Empire Nation Treatment.

2. Provision shall be made in the Agreement to the effect that in the event of circumstances arising which, in the judgment of the Government of India or of the Government of Burma, as the case may be, necessitate a variation in the terms of the Agreement, the proposal to vary its terms shall be the subject of consultation between the two Governments.

3. The margins of preference and other advantages referred to in Parts I and II apply only to goods of Burmese and Indian origin respectively. Definitions of what constitute goods of Burmese and Indian origin respectively and ancillary questions, (*e.g.*, certificates of origin) shall be determined by the parties in consultation.

4. The following matters to be covered by exchange of notes :

(*a*) The Government of Burma undertake not to impose an export duty on timber exported to India during the period of the war. and they take note of the declaration by the Government of India that if at any time after the expiry of the above-mentioned period the Government of Burma impose an export duty the Government of India will hold themselves free to withdraw the concession of guaranteed free entry.

(*b*) The Government of Burma undertake to accord to Indian goods in transit through Burma treatment not less favourable than that accorded to goods of any other part of the British Empire.

5. The Agreement is terminable at six months notice by either side.

The Agreement was signed on April 3, 1941, by Messrs. Ba Than, James Baxter and Tin Tut on behalf of the Government of Burma, while Sir A. Ramaswamy Mudaliar and Sir A. J. Raisman signed on behalf of the Government of India.

Indo-Burmese Relations in 1940

Agent's Survey of Legislation Affecting Indians

Relations between Indians and Burmans, legislation affecting Indians and the trend of immigration in 1940 are dealt with by the Agent of the Government of India in Burma in his Annual Report, published by the Education, Health and Lands De artment of the Government of India in April 1941.

The volume of sea passenger traffic from India to Burma exhibited no remarkable features. The seasonal trends were normal, but the maxima of incoming and outgoing flows were, on the whole, lower than the average of the past three years.

The Baxter Commission on Immigration completed its work during the year, but its Report was not made public. It devoted considerable attention to a factual examination of the recruitment and conditions of industrial labour, especially in the city of Rangoon. In addition to this. two Committees appointed by Government have been exploring in greater detail the same field. Neither Committee had submitted its report by the close of the year.

An interim report submitted by the Committee enquiring into conditions in Rangoon was, however, published, dealing with the limited field of dock labour in

Rangoon only. The report put forward proposals for a system of registration, designed to encourage decasualisation.

Legislative Measures

The most important legislative measures affecting Indians were the Tenancy Act, the Land Purchase Bill, the Land Alienation Act, and the City of Rangoon Municipal (Amendment) Bill. The Land Alienation Act occasioned no complaints. The administration of the Tenancy Act, which aimed at giving improved security of tenure to tenants, while adjusting rents to an equitable figure, was a feature of the period. Though intended by the original framers to be applied experimentally to limited areas where there was reason to think that rackrenting existed, the Act was introduced in such large areas, and at such a time of year, that it was impossible for the officers of the Government to comply with the law in making the enquiries prescribed before fixing fair rents and at the same time to pass the requisite number of orders before the harvest season.

As a result, methods were adopted which had the effect of a wholesale reduction of rents; in some cases to the level of the land revenue demand, and the further effect of depressing the value of agricultural land. The landlords, both Burman and Indian, were greatly perturbed, and endeavoured to get the executive instructions, which had been issued to rent Settlement Officers, reconsidered in the interests both of equity, as well as of compliance with the mandatory provisions of the Act. Failing in this, they applied to the Rangoon High Court for writs of *certiorari*.

A Full Bench, comprising the Chief Justice, the Hon'ble Justice Mya Bu, Kt., and the Hon'ble Mr. Justice Dunkley, gave judgment in favour of the landlords. In the course of the judgment, Their Lordships deemed fit to remark: "The proceedings of the respondents, as appear from their records, conformed in no respect whatever to the provisions of the Act. They held no enquiry in respect of each tenancy, they did not examine each landlord or each tenant, they paid no attention in respect of each tenancy separately to the considerations to which they were bound to have regard by the provisions of section 15 of the Tenancy Act."

Their Lordships held further "that their decisions constitute a grave injustice to the petitioners is manifest from the fact that the rents determined by them are in every case very much lower than the contractual rents, and in some cases are barely sufficient to cover the land revenue."

Enquiry Committee

Subsequently, as the result of a short notice resolution in the House of Representatives, a Committee was appointed consisting of Members of both Houses of the Legislature, and of experienced Settlement and Revenue Officers, to enquire into the working of the Act.

This Committee recommended the setting aside of the orders of Rent Settlement Officers, and the passing of an ordinance to achieve this purpose and to embody other provisions calculated to render possible the commencement of the peaceful cultivation of the next rice crop. Their recommendations were accepted by the Government of Burma, and an ordinance was promulgated on April 9, which set aside all the orders hitherto passed under the Act.

The immediate difficulties of the situation having been resolved, the Special Committee proceeded to go into the whole matter and revise the legislation, and a Bill based on their report was before a Select Committee of the House of Representatives at the close of the year.

In order to deal with outstanding rent settlement cases, or fresh cases arising in the intervening period, the Governor promulgated a second ordinance in terms of which fair rents were to be settled on the basis of arbitrarily fixed percentages of the normal gross outturn.

Land Purchase Bill

On the subject of the Land Purchase Bill, the Government of India took full advantage of the opportunity given them by the Government of Burma to comment on its provisions and the Government of India's views were considered by the Select Committee which had been appointed to deal with the Bill. The Select Committee incorporated amendments to the Bill in their Report, which went some way to meet the views expressed by the Government of India, and their Report came up for consideration during the Budget Session. In the autumn session, the Bill was passed by the Lower House.

A great deal of what had been suggested by Indian critics had been incorporated. There were still points, however, on which Indian opinion remained unsatisfied.

There was no provision for additional compensation in respect of the compulsory nature of the acquisition, and the Government of Burma had shown itself unwilling to provide any such compensation.

Secondly, there was no guarantee that the tenants in occupation of the land at the time when the land was purchased would receive preferential consideration, or indeed any consideration at all, when the time came to distribute the land to small cultivating owners.

The Government of Burma, in their tenancy legislation, laid great stres on the necessity for enhancing the security of tenure of the tenant. The Land Purchase Bill, if passed, would render a tenant liable to have his land purchased over his head any moment.

Indian Apprehension

Indians were apprehensive, because they felt that the tendency would be to purchase land owned and cultivated by Indians so as to redistribute it to Burmans, and because they felt that, in the co-operative societies proposed, Indians might not be welcome, and mixed societies of Indians and Burmans might not prove successful. This, among other matters in connection with the Bill, formed the subject of correspondence between the Government of India and the Government of Burma. At the close of the year, the Bill was before a Select Committee of the Senate.

The City of Rangoon Municipal (Amendment) Bill, which is designed to secure that at least half the members of the Rangon Corporation shall be elected Burmans, was passed by the Lower House in spite of Indian and European opposition, and was also under consideration by a Select Committee of the Senate at the close of the year. This Bill, too, was the subject of representations by the Government of India.

Registration of Foreigners

In January, 1940, an ordinance was made by the Governor of Burma called the Registration of Foreigners Ordinance, 1940. In this the definition of "foreigner" in the Foreigners Act was adopted, and the status of British Indian subjects was satisfactorily secured. This ordinance was in due course replaced by the Registration of Foreigners Act, 1940, which came into force at the end of March.

No complaints have been received by the Agent regarding either the working of the Ordinance or of the Act.

The Report states that a Manual has been prepared and issued by the Government of Burma for the instruction of officers in their powers and duties in the matter of the prevention and control of riots and that certain steps have been taken to strengthen the Police forces, while others remain under consideration. The cadre of the Rangoon City Police Force has been expanded, its equipment has been improved and a Volunteer Police Force, among whom are many Indians, has been enrolled.

Proposals for the strengthening of the Civil Police in the districts remain for the most part under consideration, but in many districts a Special Police Reserve Force, composed of Burmans and Karens, has been recruited for the purpose of assisting the regular Police Force in times of emergency.

Duty On Rice Exports

Except for difficulties owing to temporary curtailments in the volume of shipping available, trade was on the whole remarkably well-maintained. The price of rice remained at a high level. A feature of the rice market was the purchase of considerable quantities by Japan, which offset the loss of the normal Central European markets.

The closing week of the year saw an announcement by the Government of Burma of their intention to impose a duty on rice exports to India with effect from the new year.

On April 1. 1940, the Government of Burma gave notice to the Government of India under clause VII of the Indo-Burma Trade Regulation Order, 1937, of their intention to terminate the operation of the Order. Proposals for a new agreement were under consideration at the end of the year. (A Trade Agreement has since been signed.)

Hindu Moslem Affairs

Two periods of ill-feeling between the Hindu and Moslem communities in Rangoon city, accompanied by sporadic affrays and a regrettable loss of life, occurred during the earlier part of the year, the first at the end of January, and the second at the end of April. The methods adopted by the rioters were such as to render peculiarly difficult the task of protecting life and property, and of bringing the real offenders to justice. The strain on the Rangoon City Police was severe and prolonged, but the Commissioner and ranks stuck to their task with admirable patience. It is hoped that the strong measures which were adopted by the Government of Burma, and loyally accepted by Indians in Burma, will be found to have provided an opportunity for a genuine movement towards a permanent improvement in the relations between the two chief Indian communities.

Attempts to embroil Burmans with Indians in connection with the communal riots proved uniformly unsuccessful. An improvement in the tone of the Press is recorded, and overt acts against Indians progressively decreased. Although there was at one time some apprehension of trouble arising between landlords and tenants in connection with the working of the Tenancy Act, nothing serious occurred. Credit for this is given to the District Officers, whose efforts were, however, it is suggested, assisted by high paddy prices and by the good sense and forbearance of both landlords and tenants.

In conclusion, a tribute is paid by the Agent to the courtesy and consideration extended to him by the Government of Burma.

The Position of Indians in Burma

Indo-Burmese Immigration Agreement

"Since 1930 Burma has passed through two fundamental experiences which has focussed attention upon the foundations of her social life ; in the economic field, the collapse of prices during the prolonged period of the depression engendered a feeling of insecurity, a rapid growth in the indebtedness of her rural population and the serious agrarian problem of the largescale alienation of land, particularly in Lower Burma ; in the political field, the decade has been marked by the emergence of strong feelings of nationalism accompanied by the recognition of the country as a separate political entity with the extensive powers of its newly-created legislature. Against this background of awakened nationalism, there came to the fore the problems of the status and the employment of the Indians in Burma, marked by a progressive deterioration in the previously amicable relations between the two peoples which culminated in the very serious Indo-Burman riots of 1938," says the report of the Hon'ble Mr. *James Baxter*, Financial Adviser, who with two assessors (*U Tin Tut*, Bar-at-Law, I.C.S., and Mr. *Ratilal Desai*, M.A.) was appointed by the Government of Burma (by a Resolution of July 15, 1939) as a Commission of Inquiry to examine the question of Indian immigration into Burma.

The Commission was appointed on the suggestion of the Riot Inquiry Committee (under the Chairmanship of the Hon'ble Mr. Justice Braund) which, in two reports issued at the end of 1938 and early in 1939, drew attention to the existence of serious apprehensions in the minds of many Burmans that Indian immigration was largely responsible for unemployment or under-employment among Burmans.

Mr. Baxter presented his report to the Government of Burma in October, 1940. His recommendations were examined by both Governments and it was agreed, without commitment on either side, that these recommendations formed a suitable basis for negotiations. The Government of Burma, therefore, invited the Government of India to send a delegation to Burma.

The Government of India's delegation (which arrived in Rangoon on June 16, 1941) consisted of the Hon'ble Sir Girja Shankar Bajpai, K.B.E., C.I.E., I.C.S., with Mr. R. H. Hutchings, C.I.E., I.C.S., Agent of the Government of India in Burma, and Mr. G. S. Bozman, C.I.E., I.C.S., as Advisers, and Mr. V. Viswanathan, I.C.S., as Secretary.

The Burma delegation, led by the Hon'ble U Saw, Premier, included the Hon'ble U Ba Than, Commerce Minister, Hon'ble U Ba On, Labour Minister, and the Hon'ble U Htoon Aung Gyaw, Finance Minister. U Tin Tut, I.C.S., Commissioner on Special Duty, was Adviser and U Kyaw Min, I.C.S., Labour Secretary, was Secretary to the delegation.

On June 28, 1941, the draft Indo-Burmese Immigration Agreement was initialled in Rangoon and the Baxter Report, a joint statement by the two Governments and the terms of the Agreement were issued simultaneously in India and Burma on July 21, 1941.

Essential Points

Here are essential points of the Agreement, which comes into effect from October 1, 1941, and is valid for five years:

(1) Any Indian born in Burma who can produce evidence of permanent interest there can secure domicile.

(2) Any Indian now in Burma can acquire a Burma domicile under the Common law.

(3) Indians who can establish a total residence in Burma of seven calendar years between July 15, 1932 and July 15, 1941 will be termed "privileged immigrants" and, subject to a break clause, retain the full protection of Sub-Section 3 of Section 44 of the Government of Burma Act.

(4) Indians who do not wish to acquire a Burma domicile or who cannot establish seven years' residence in nine years, retain the protection of Sub-Section 3 of Section 44 of the Government of Burma Act so long as they remain in Burma.

(5) A Board of Immigration, composed of Indians, Burmans and Europeans, will examine and report upon quotas to be applied to new immigrants.

Joint Statement

Here is the full text of the joint statement by the Governments of India and of Burma, issued on July 21, 1941:—

"In two Reports issued at the end of 1938 and early in 1939, the Riot Inquiry Committee, under the Chairmanship of the Hon'ble Mr. Justice Braund, drew particular attention to the existence of a serious apprehension in the minds of many Burmans that Indian immigration was largely responsible for unemployment or under-employment among the indigenous population of Burma. The Committee recommended that, in the interests of both countries, some public examination of the grounds for the existing apprehension in Burman minds should be undertaken urgently.

"2. Accordingly the Government of Burma in a Resolution, dated the 15th July, 1939, after consultation with the Government of India, appointed the Hon'ble Mr. James Baxter to examine the question of Indian immigration into Burma, with the assistance of two Assessors U Tin Tut, I.C.S., and Mr. Ratilal Desai, M.A. Mr. Baxter presented his Report to the Government of Burma in October 1940. His recommendations were carefully examined by both Governments and it was agreed without commitment on either side that these recommendations formed a suitable basis for negotiation. The Government of Burma, therefore, invited the Government of India to send a delegation to Burma and the invitation was gladly accepted.

"3. As a result of the conversations the two Governments have agreed upon certain measures which in their view are calculated both to remove from Burman minds any reasonable apprehension that Burma may be subjected to undue economic competition by reason of Indian immigration and at the same time to secure for the Indian community settled and resident in Burma recognition of their legitimate rights.

Burma's Rights And India's Interests

"4. The text of the agreement is attached to this statement. The agreement is based upon two main principles, firstly, that Burma has, subject to the provisions of the Government of Burma Act, 1935, the right to determine the composition of her own population, and secondly, that Indians who have wholly identified themselves with the interests of Burma should enjoy the same rights as members of the permanent population.

"5. It is obvious that in the peculiar circumstances of the two countries, their geographical proximity, their cultural and economic ties and their long something larger than mere book lore—the Universities can be a focus and centre for the synthesis of different cultures and for the evolution of that common culture which should be the highest aim of Indian nationalism to achieve, if that phrase is not merely an empty phrase or a deceptive slogan. I have just spoken of different cultures and also of a common culture but I would like, with your permission, to be a little more explicit, for while in a sense it is true that we have certain types of different cultures in this country, yet it is no less true that the process of the evolution of a common culture, which is neither wholly Hindu nor wholly Muslim, has been ceaselessly at work during the last four or five centuries, if not longer, and was never more in evidence than in the Mughal times. That a common culture should have been the result of the impact of different communities, different religious ideals, and different outlooks on life, was inevitable. In the history of our country it was primarily the North of India which was the playground of different civilisations, different languages, different religions and different systems of morality. Bengal too did not altogether escape the operation of these forces and yet it is a fact which, in my opinion, cannot be legitimately contested that these differences led to an ever-increasing unity in thought, in language, in art, in music, in æsthetics, in architecture, in painting and in poetry. This process was not yet complete when new influences from the West began to make themselves felt. They have been in operation now certainly for over a century, if not longer, and we have been witnessing in our own times the growth of a culture—I use it again in its largest sense—which is neither wholly Hindu nor wholly Muslim nor wholly English. It is a mixture of all. I do not regret it. On the contrary I read in it the message and prophecy of a future in which, when the dust and din of the present-day controversies, which divide man from man and community from community, will have disappeared, each one of us will be able truthfully to say that India is neither my heritage nor yours, but a common heritage. The political problems which agitate our minds at the present moment are in all conscience very serious. It is not my purpose—and it would not be right for me on this occasion—to discuss them, but I venture to hope that whatever may be the noise in the market-place, the still small voice of reason may not be drowned altogether in Universities nor human feelings warped by mutual suspicions and hatreds. Do not let it, therefore, be said of our Universities in the words of Yeats that—

"Mere anarchy is loosed upon the world,
The blood-dimmed tide is loosed, and everywhere
The ceremony of innocence is drowned;
The best lack all conviction, while the worst
Are full of passionate intensity."

I, therefore, respectfully suggest to University men that it is their duty to think coolly and calmly and to direct their energies to the working out of a synthesis of the common ideas of a nationhood, although the siren voices of discord may be forcing themselves upon our ears to allure us to stagnation, if not ruin. I am not ignoring the differences that divide us. I do not consider it just or wise to ignore them, and yet taking together the things that divide us and the things that unite us I say it is by no means unfair to hold that those who live in India, whatever their religion or philosophy of life and from whatever part of the world their ancestors may have come in the past, do constitute a nation. When some 28 years ago Mr. (afterwards Lord) Asquith introduced the Irish Home Rule Bill in Parliament, he said that—

"In any relative sense Ireland is a nation. Not two nations but one nation. They say, What do you mean by a nation? I am not going to embarrass myself by any abstract definition, but these things are best argued by way of illustration, and I will take a most extreme and, I think, a most undeniable case... I mean Scotland. Will any one have the hardi-hood to deny that the Scots are a nation? They are not all, be it remembered, of one race. They are both Celts and Saxons and various other strains of blood among them. They are not all of one religion, and they are not by any means of one way of thinking about the problems of life, spiritual, intellectual, or material; and yet no one will deny that the Scots are a nation. Judged by any test that you can apply, the Irish is as definite and as separate a nationality as the Scotch."

I venture to present this passage from the speech of a great English statesman in the hope that it may have some effect on the placid minds of University men, if not on the contentious minds of the politicians. Is it, therefore, altogether a vain hope that our Universities may come to our rescue when our politicians have failed us, and that, out of the chaos of ideas and aspirations, it may be given to the Universities to evolve a cosmos of clear thinking and generous feeling ? Today the fundamental problem which we have to solve, is the freedom of India, that is to say, the achievement by her of a position and the attainment of powers which may enable her to mould her future according to her best judgment and give her a place of equality and honour in the comity of nations. It is easy enough to state this proposition, but difficult to rescue it from the chaos which surrounds it. It is somewhat significant that nearly all the doctrines, under the spell of which we find one section or another of the country at present, are of Western origin. and, if I may speak frankly, Europe at present should be a warning to us rather than an example to follow. This is not the time nor the occasion when I can discuss the specific issues raised in this country by the different schools of thought, but I venture to suggest that the Universities, instead of being the sound-boards of these conflicting ideas, should function as clearing-houses. They cannot, in my opinion, perform their legitimate functions and discharge their duty to the country in our peculiar circumstances, if their professors or their youngmen become partisans or advocates of one school or another. From them we are entitled to expect light and not darkness, and let them give us some of that kindly light.

In the affairs of men common calamities and common aims and common aspirations are a great uniting force. Today we are witnessing in England the spectacle of a common calamity having united men and women of all creeds and all political parties, working together and shedding their blood together against a common calamity. Two years ago who could have thought that men like Mr. Winston Churchill, Sir Archibald Sinclair, Mr. Ernest Bevin and Mr. Herbert Morrison would work together as members of a team against a common enemy—and yet this has happened. A nation which can so combine in the hour of common danger deserves to live and live with honour. Remember if June was the darkest hour in the life of England, today it can look forward with confidence to the dawn of a bright day, if it has not already opened. How has it come about ? Assuredly by that spirit of unity and singlemindedness which today characterise the people of England—from the King to the poorest of his subjects. Differences, social, political and economic, have yielded to the united will of the Nation. Is it, therefore, altogether impossible for us to combine and to unite for the achievement of common aims ? Let the Universities—I say in all sincerity –rise superior to the tyranny of slogans and let them take stock of the situation as it is and of the forces working round them and let them gaze upon the future steadily and advise the country accordingly. Let them be the seedbeds of a fertile unity and not the breeding places of a desolating disunity.

It is customary for the speaker on a occasion of this character to address the young graduates who are the recipients of degrees. I shall not waste much time in a long appeal to them. If they are leaving this University today, they are entering the bigger University of Life, and in that University the struggle is much keener and the disappointments perhaps more numerous. That struggle will make large calls on such reserves of knowledge as they have laid by here and above all on character which is far more necessary for real and lasting success than mere knowledge. The best wishes of every one will accompany them and I have no doubt that if the University can legitimately help them in setting them on their feet, it will do so—as indeed it seems to me to be its duty to do so. I know how the fear of unemployment—a problem in which I have been very much interested —eats into the minds of our youth and I also know how in their despondency some of them at any rate lose faith in the system of society in which they were born and how in their impatience with the inequalities and injustices of life they are tempted to curse that system and even to tear it by the roots. It is for this reason in particular that I have been most anxious that the Universities should definitely recognise their responsibility not for actually finding them jobs but for bringing them into touch with those who by reason of their situation in life may be in a position to help them. To the youngmen theselves I shall repeat the advice of John Stuart Mill given to the youngmen whom he was addressing in his speech at St. Andrews :—

"Nor let any one be discouraged by what may seem, in moments of despondency. the lack of time and of opportunity. Those who know how to employ opportunities will often find that they can create them : and what we achieve depends less on the amount of time we possess than on the use we make of our time. You and your like are the hopes and resources of your country in the coming generation. All great things which that generation is destined to do have to be done by some like you ; several will assuredly be done by persons for whom society has done much less, to whom it has given far less preparation, than those whom I am now addressing. I do not attempt to instigate you by the prospect of direct rewards, either earthly or heavenly ; the less we think about being rewarded in either way, the better for us. But there is one reward which will not fail you, and which may be called disinterested, because it is not a consequence, but is inherent in the very fact of deserving it ; the deeper and more varied interest you will feel in life ; which will give it tenfold its value, and a value which will last to the end. All merely porsonal objects grow less valuable as we advance in life : this not only endures but increases."

The Delhi University Convocation

The following is the text of the address delivered by the Hon'ble Sir Maurice Gwyer. K.C.B., K.C.S.I., L.L.D., Chief Justice of India at the nineteenth Convocation of the University of Delhi held on the 6th May 1941 :—

The Convocation which we are holding to-day had been a modest ceremony, as befits a period of transition. The University is, I hope, entering upon a period of greater usefulness and wider scope ; and you will have seen with your own eyes the physical changes which, in this building and elsewhere, it is now undergoing. To some of you, perhaps the majority, the University itself has been little more than a name ; and I dare say that only a few students, other than the scientists and lawyers, have ever entered its precincts, except possibly for the purposes of an examination. You may regret that your own University career has come to an end at a moment when, as I hope and believe, the University will be able to provide a more fruitful and stimulating career for all its children ; but I trust that you will not on that account lose your interest in it, and indeed that you will watch with growing appreciation and approval the efforts which are being made to transform it into a University worthy of the capital city of India. I hope that you yourselves have owed the University not a little ; and I hope that those who come after you will owe it even more.

I have said that the University is in a period of transition ; and by this I mean that it will become one day, not a University of the Province of Delhi alone, but a University drawing its students from all over India, as a metropolitan University ought to do. It is only on the threshold of this new career, and it has a long way to go before it can claim recognition for its new status. But I should like to tell you in a few words this afternoon what it is that we are trying to do in order to affect both the out-ward appearance of, and the spirit within, the University.

There can be few Universities in India which occupy a more attractive or a more historic site. A great deal can be made of it, if its future developments are carefully planned ; and when the further buildings which the University will require have been built in the positions which the experience of the University Architect may assign to them, when all the Colleges have moved up into this part of Delhi, and the whole area has been laid out with gardens and planted with trees and avenues, then I think that we shall have here a University city which will become a rival attraction to New Delhi itself. That of course is to look a long way ahead, but the great thing is to have a clear conception of what it is we want to do and to plan in advance. The first quadrangle for the new Science School is complete, and the second quadrangle will be finished before the end of the year. The building in which we now find ourselves is being renovated and redecorated, and I hope will be so much improved during the next twelve months that you will scarcely recognize it. A beginning is to be made with the reorganisation and replanning of the Library ; and perhaps—who knows ?—some kind benefactors, like the anonymous benefactor who has enabled the Library to be taken in hand this summer, will enable us to construct a Convocation Hall, examination rooms and other University buildings we require, to form a block facing and balancing the present University building, in accordance with the farsighed designs of our Architect. In his lay-out plans of the whole University site the Architect is also reserving space for new Colleges of the future, for those all-India scientific and academic institutions which even now are seeking a premanent home in the capital of India, for further developments, which at the present moment it is only possible dimly to perceive, like engineering, electrical and other technological departments.

But Universities are not composed exclusively of bricks and mortar, of Convocation tion Halls and examination rooms. These things are necessary and Universities must possess them ; but let them be put in their proper place. It is the spirit which lives in the buildings rather than the buildings themselves which is the essential thing. We want beautiful buildings in a beautiful setting, because, as I firmly believe, the surroundings in which students acquire the knowledge and intellectual discipline which a University ought to be able to give them at the most impressionable perid of their lives are a matter of the highest importance. Beauty exercises a profound influence on the growing mind, perhaps an unconscious influence, but a very real one ; and it is for that reason that I am very anxious to see our University city built and laid out in accordance with that vision of it which I have just described to you. But, if it is right that we should have a clear idea of the lay-out and design of our University and its buildings, it is equally essential that we should have a clear idea of the kind of life and atmosphere which we want the students to have who are going to come here. You will not expect me this afternoon to discourse to you on the purposes and objects of University education. That is much too vast a subject for a brief address on one of the hottest days of the year. But there are nevertheless one or two things which I should like to say to you.

In the first place, let us distinguish very clearly between school and University. A school is a place for those who are younger and whose minds are less mature. A University is a place for those who are on the threshold of manhood, who ought to have put away childish things. Boys go to a school to be taught by others, and they have to submit themselves to a discipline appropriate to their age. Young men go to a University to pursue knowledge and not so much to be taught by others as to learn how to teach themselves They too must submit themselves to discipline, which is a necessary thing whenever and wherever large bodies of men, young or old, are gathered together for special purposes. But it is discipline of another kind. A University student ought to be learning how to think for himself, and he will appreciate more than he did when he was a schoolboy what the reasons are for the mild discipline which is imposed upon him. In other words, he learns that he is being trusted, not compelled, to behave himself ; to discipline himself in his own interests as well as in the interests of the whole body of students to which he belongs ; to realize that self-control and toleration of the views of others is of the essence of intellectual freedom.

For a University student is not an isolated individual. He is one of a community and he will derive little benefit from his University career unless he appreciates that fact. Let me quote you three lines from a poet.

"What life have you if you have not life together ?
There is no life that is not in community.
And no community not lived in praise of God."

I fully recognize that at the present moment it is not easy for Delhi students to realize this life in community, scattered as they are in a number of Colleges, some of which are separated far from the others, and not yet looking to the University itself as the centre of their common life. But in spite of all these obstacles I hope that during the past few years you have all of you come to recognize your membership of something larger than the College to which you belong; and I believe that with the development of the University and the movement of the Colleges to this site that feeling of an identity of interest between all Delhi students will grow stronger and stronger. I hope by the autumn to have provided for the first time in the building in which we now are a Junior Common Room for the use of the students for whose instruction the University itself has assumed responsibility, and possibly for other students also, and I hope that in this Common Room they will begin to realize more than perhaps they have done hitherto what membership of the University means. When I speak of a Junior Common Room, I do not mean a playroom or a place for indoor sports. I mean a place for social intercourse and recreation. for reading or writing for the establishment of contacts and the creation of friendships. For the other aspects of a student's life it seems to me that an institution of another kind is required. I have already, on the Architect's advice, marked out a site in the

University grounds on which a Students' Union or Club might be built; and I hope that in the near future some one in whom the passage of years has not dimmed the remembrance of his own student days or his sympathy for youth will be willing to provide the University with the means of realizing this long cherished plan. I had also considered the possibility of some kind of University costume which might serve to indicate that common bond of which I have already spoken; but unhappy incidents last year caused me to lay the idea aside. One day perhaps I may take it up again.

I have said before, but it cannot be repeated too often, that the hallmark of a University education ought to be a sense of proportion and a sense of values. I think that in the University of Delhi it ought to be easier to achieve these two things than in many other places; for this University is situated in a city with a very great history, in a city which is now the capital of India, and in a city where, for good or ill, policies will always be discussed, plans made and decisions taken profoundly affecting the lives and interests of millions of mankind. I am not speaking now of any particular form of government; what I have just said must always be true of the capital city of a great country. And therefore students in Delhi, who will always be living, as it were, in the midst of great events, should be able more easily than most to realize what a sense of proportion and a sense of values really are, and to distinguish between the real thing and what is artificial or make-believe. I cannot conceive a student in any capital city taking no interest in the politics of his country, for he lives in the very centre of politics; and I should be sorry indeed to think that any aspect of Indian politics failed to arouse the interest of the students of this University. I hope that they will always study them and take the keenest interest in them, whether as an intellectual pursuit or with an ardent desire to play a part later on in the public life of their country; and their sense of proportion and of values will enable them to distinguish between that kind of interest or study and the more frivolous activities in which schoolboys and students of immature minds and uninstructed judgment at times indulge.

The sudden change from the stricter discipline of school to the easygoing life of a University sometimes goes to the head and produces strange consequences before the sense of proportion is a hieved. Youth is a time when everyone commits follies, and most of us can recall our own, sometimes with amusement and often no doubt with regret. But most of the follies of youth are harmless enough, so long as we do not take ourselves too seriously. Who has not laughed at the story of the three tailors of Tooley Street who gathered in a tavern to compose a petition to Parliament and began with these words :—"We, the people of England..."? It is when, like the three tailors, we lose our sense of proportion and take ourselves too seriously, imagining that we are the cynosure of every eye and that the world is hanging upon our lips, that we make that swift descent from the sublime to the ridiculous. I hope however that the students of Delhi, as befits the students of a metropolitan University, will everywhere be recognized by a happy combination of judgment and humour and by a dignity all their own.

You, the young men and young women who have taken your degrees to-day go out from the University to take your place among the leaders of the next generation of your country. I believe that you will be glad, when that time comes, to have learned, as I hope you have learned during your University career, that none can lead who have not first taught themselves to obey; to have become acquainted with the cleansing and antiseptic qualities of truth; to have realized how odious and ignoble a thing is faction and intrigue; to have grasped that self-respect is inconsistent with humility nor tolerance for the opinion of others with firmly held opinions of your own. If you take this knowledge away with you, you will have no reason to regret the years you have spent at this University.

I bid you all farewell and wish you all the success which you deserve and which I do not doubt you will achieve.

The Gurukul University Convocation

The following is the text of the address delivered by *Dr. Rabindranath Tagore* at the Convocation of the Gurukul University held in the year 1941—

I regret that my feeble body and a distressing malady do not allow me the pleasure of being present at this great gathering when the Snatakas of Gurukula University will bid farewell to their Alma Mater and go out boldly into the wide world fortified with the knowledge they have gathered at the feet of their masters. I wish them all success in their endeavours of the future and I bless them with all my heart.

That aspect of our education which has drawn my attention very considerably ever since I took to the arduous task of being a teacher I would like to emphasise once more before you. I am aware that I shall be repeating myself but that is inevitable for one at my age.

As a people, we must be fully conscious of what we are. It is a truism to say that the consciousness of the unity of a people implies the knowledge of its parts as well of its whole. But, most of us not only have no such knowledge of India, we do not even have an eager desire to cultivate it.

By aserting our national unity with vehemence in our political propaganda, we assure ourselves that we possess it and thus coutinue to live in a make-believe world of political day-dreams.

The fact is, we have a feeble human interest in our own country. We love to talk about politics and economics; we are ready to soar into the thin air of academic abstractions, or roam in the dusk of pedantic wildernesses, but we never care to cross our social boundaries and come to the door of our neighbouring communities, personally to enquire how they think and feel and express themselves, and how they fashion their lives.

The love of man has its own hunger for knowing. Even if we lack this concerning our fellowbeings in India, except in our political protestations, at least love of knowledge for its own sake could have brought us close to each other. But there also we have failed and suffered. For weakness of knowledge is the foundation of weakness of power. Until India becomes fully distinct in our mind, we can never gain her in truth, and where truth is imperfect, love can never have its full sway. The best function of our Education Centres is to help us to know ourselves; and then along with it, her other mission will be fulfilled which is to inspire us to give ourselves.

What has given such enormous intellectual power to Europe is her coordination of minds. She has evolved a means by which all countries of that continent can think together. Such a great concert of ideas, by its own pressure of movement naturally wears away all her individual aberrations of thought and extravagances of unreason. It keeps her flights of fancy close to the limits of reticence. All her different thought rays have been focussed in one common culture, which finds its complete expression in all the European universities.

The mind of India, on the other hand, is divided and scattered; there is no one common pathway along which we can reach it. We cannot but look with regret at the feebleness of stimulation in our academic training for the forming of our mind which in co-operation of knowledge and sympathy may comprehend the larger mind of the country. The most important object of our educational institutions is to help each student to realise his personality, as an individual representing his people in such a broad spirit, that he may know how it is the most important fact of his life for him to have been born to the great world of man.

We in India are unfortunate in not having the chance to give expression to the best in us in creating intimate relations with the powerful peoples of the world. The bond between the nations today is made of the links of mutual menace, its strength depending upon the forces of panic, and leading to an enormous waste of resources in a competition of browbeating and bluff. Some great voice is waiting to be heard which will usher in the sacred light of truth in the dark region of the nightmare of politics. But we in India have not yet had the chance. Yet we have our human voice which truth demands. Even in the region where we are not invited to act we have our right to judge and to guide the mind of man to a proper point of view, to the vision of ideality in the heart of the real.

Trade & Industry in India

JANUARY—JUNE 1941

Indo-Burma Trade Agreement

Heads of Agreement

The Delegates of the Governments of India and Burma, concerned with the Negotiation of a Trade Agreement to replace the India and Burma (Trade Regulation) Order, arrived at the following Agreement. The Agreement was signed on the 3rd April 1941 :—

PART I.—*Tariff Treatment of Burmese goods on import into India.*

1. *Free List.*—Goods of Burmese origin of the kinds which at present are duty free from whatever country imported will, so long as no duty is imposed on those kinds when imported from countries other than Burma continue to be duty free. If in British India any duty is hereafter imposed on any such kind of goods a corresponding duty may, subject to Part III, be imposed on the like kind of goods of Burmese origin; provided that in the case of broken rice (which was liable to duty on the 31st of March 1941, but became duty free on the 1st of April 1941) the Government of India undertake to accord a margin of preference of 10 per cent *ad valorem* or the amount of the duty, whichever is less.

2. (*a*) In the case of articles which under the Indian Customs Tariff are at present subject only to a standard rate and that rate does not exceed 15 per cent *ad valorem* the Government of India undertake to accord a margin of preference equal to the existing rate.

(*b*) In the case of articles which under the Indian Customs Tariff are at present subject according to origin to either a standard or a preferential rate and those rates do not exceed 15 per cent and 10 per cent respectively the Government of India undertake to accord margins of preference equal to the existing standard and preferential rates.

3. *Matches, motor spirit, salt, silver and sugar.*—The Government of India undertake that the duties on these goods shall not exceed the rates of excise duty for the time being leviable on similar goods produced or manufactured in British India.

4. *Other articles subject to Central Excise duty.*—Notwithstanding anything contained herein no article which in British India is for the time being subject to a duty of excise shall be entitled on import from Burma to be subjected to a rate of duty less than the rate of excise duty for the time being in force.

5. *Kerosene.*—The Government of India undertake (*i*) that the margin of preference as against foreign kerosene shall be 9 pies per Imperial gallon, and (*ii*) that the rate of customs duty shall not exceed the rate of excise duty for the time being in force in India on domestically produced kerosene; provided that during the period of the present war, the Government of India shall be at liberty to levy duties on kerosene from Burma equal to the duties applicable to kerosene imported from other countries.

(*Explanation.*—For the purposes of this paragraph and of other paragraphs in which the phrase "period of war" is referred to, the period of the war shall be interpreted as meaning the period elapsing between the date of signature of this document and the date of signature of definitive Treaty of Peace with Germany or one year after the conclusion of a formal Armistice with that country, whichever is earlier.)

6. *Tea.*- The Government of India undertake to accord a specific margin of preference of one anna per pound against th preferential rate and of three annas per pound against the standard rate.

7. (*a*) In the case of articles (other than cigarettes and tobacco, manufactured, and articles specified in paragraphs (1), (3) and (5) which under the Indian Customs Tariff are at present subject only to a standard rate and that rate exceeds 15 per cent *ad valorem* the Government of India undertake to accord a margin of preference of 15 per cent.

(*b*) In the case of articles which under the Indian Customs Tariff are at present subject according to origin either a standard or a preferential rate and those rates exceed 15 per cent and 10 per cent respectively the Government of India

Normally the seed is used for cattle, but when refined, the oil is edible and is mainly used in making margarine and as salad oil. As the seed is a by-product of India's great cotton crop, ample supplies are always available.

Southern India's immense production of cocoanuts has long made the country famous in the cocoanut oil market and in fact the description "Cochin Boiled White" represents a world standard of excellence in this particular product.

Of recent years India has figured as an importer of this oil, not because her own supplies are short, but because the lower priced oil from Ceylon has obtained an important part of the market in Central and Upper India, much to the detriment of growers in South India. India, however, has high quality oils to offer to the world.

Of the other oil crops which can be grown in this country, probably Tung or Chinese Wood Oil has one of the brightest futures. At present the Indian crop of seed is small—only about 20 tons (in 1937). However, now that it has been established that the Indian product is in every way comparable to the original Chinese oil, plantations are going ahead, particularly in Assam and Bihar. Attempts are also being made to grow the tree in the United Provinces and in the North West Frontier Province.

Tung oil has grown rapidly in popularity in recent years because as an ingredient of varnish it shows very high water-resisting properties, rapid drying and stands satisfactorily in climates of high humidity. It has become particularly popular with American varnish makers, who use it for making varnishes from resins and ester gums (it is not used with hard varnish resins because it solidifies on heating). Consequently, in view of disturbed state of China in recent years, supplies from other sources, including the U.S.A. itself, are being developed. North-eastern India appears to be eminently suitable as a growing area.

Another valuable paint ingredient is expressed from safflower seed, which is grown for its oil and also for its yellow dye, which should not be confused with saffron. Safflower, which has already been introduced as an oil seed crop in the U.S.A., yields an oil which is suitable for replacing linseed as it has the valuable property of preventing the yellowing of white or delicately tinted paints used in interior decoration.

Yet another useful paint oil, on account of its good drying qualities, is solanum oil which can be produced in commercial quantities from Solanum indicum—a very common undershrub in tropical India.

Hemp seed and niger seed oils, which are grown in commercial quantities in India, have in the past been sold to France and Germany as paint and soap oils respectively.

Among the non-drying vegetable oils, one of the most important to soap makers in India is mahua butter, a group of oils yielded by the seeds of the Russia species of trees common in many parts of the country and already commercially exploited, as their flowers are a leading source of alcohol. Apart from their soap making properties, these "butters" are edible and are used as a food locally in India.

Animal Products

The next large item on India's export list of raw materials is "Hides and Skins, raw and undressed." Since, however, this forms the subject of a separate discourse, we will only consider it briefly here in conjunction with bones and fats.

India's possession of one-third of the world's total cattle population, plus 26 million goats, 22 milion sheep and 14 million horses shows the hugeness of her resources of animal raw materials.

Under any western system of economics such a state of affairs should indicate a considerable dairying and butchering industry. But the exalted status which the cow occupies in the eyes of the vast majority of India's population and the woefully low standard of the cattle, definitely rule out such possibilities, though it will be agreed that so far as dairying goes, some progress is being made in improving India's cattle which are also the draught animals of the country.

India's huge cattle population does, however, provide the rest of the world with a very large proportion of its hides. India is estimated to produce 20 million cattle hides a year, while the U.S.A. comes second with 14½ million a year.. For goat and kid skins China normally comes first with India second, but owing to the virtual stoppage of Chinese supplies India occupies at present a unique place in world markets.

In 1939-40 India exported Rs. 4,12 lakhs worth of raw hides and skins, mainly to Europe and America and also to Australia. There is also a growing export of tanned hides and leather.

Arising out of this cattle industry is an export of over Rs. 30 lakhs worth of bones and bone-meal for manure, though this amount is obviously capable of great expansion if the demand justified it. Animal products also have a share in the Rs. 3 lakhs exports of tallow, stearine and wax.

Lac and Resins

Lac, which might with truth be termed an insect product, is the main part of the export item "gums, resins and lac" worth over Rs. 2,22 lakhs in 1939-40. Of this amount lac accounted for Rs. 1,90 lakhs. Indian production is between 40,000 and 50,000 tons of raw lac a year and most of this is sent abroad. The demand for lac has risen considerably since the outbreak of war, and research has shown that it is suitable for a large number of war purposes.

Lac is the resinous secretion of the insect coccus lacca, which also yields red dye, like its relative the cochineal insect. The lac insect feeds upon the twigs of certain trees and is cultivated especially in North India. In its refined form, in which it is usually packed for export, it is known as shellac. Research both to improve cultivation and to increase the number of uses of lac has been carried on energetically in India, and in spite of the competition of synthetic resins and lacquers Indian lac has contrived to hold its own and can take its place in the moulding industry, a field which has been greatly widened by the development of synthetic resins in recent years. At present between 30 and 40 per cent of the total world output of lac is used by the gramophone record industry, since synthetic lac cannot take the place of shellac for high class records.

Inquiries for possible new uses for shellac, especially for war-time needs, have been received by the London Lac Research Laboratory, which is financed by the Indian Lac Cess Committee, and it is reported that new uses of lac for road paints, anti-gas paints, luminous paints, shellac bitumen, spirit paints, quick setting cements and rapid-drying varnishes for mineral oil and petrol containers have been discovered. The uses of lac and modified lac as an adhesive binder in the electrical industries has been investigated with promising results. A black baking enamel of satisfactory quality has been prepared from refuse lac at low cost.

At present India supplies a very considerable proportion of the world's lac. According to the report of the Indian Government Trade Commissioner in New York for the last quarter of 1939, lac imports into the U. S. A. increased by about 172 per cent and India was the sole source of supply during this quarter. Similarly U. S. A.'s imports of unbleached shellac during the same quarter were practically all supplied by India.

Other forms of gums and resins which India can supply include turpentine and resin of the chir pine (*pinus longifolia*), one of the first forest products of which full utilisation has been made. Chir Pine resin production amounts to 88,484 cwt., yielding about 144,212 gallons of turpentine and 59,254 cwt. of resin. It is stated by Dr. S. Krishna of the Indian Forest Research Institute that the bulk of the oil after rectification, yields a turpentine which compares favourably with the American and French product.

The gum resin of the Salai tree (*Boswellia serrata*) is also stated by Dr. Krishna to be a possible source of turpentine substitute which has not yet been exploited on a commercial scale. The tree is common in Bihar, Orissa, Central Provinces, Rajputana, Central India and parts of the Deccan.

Mineral Resources

As a producer of minerals, India has a very long history indeed. Some of the earliest known steel has been found in Central India, and small deposits of iron ore have been worked from a very early age. Competition from modern industrial methods abroad severely set back such village smelters, but it was not until 1830 that attempts to exploit India's remarkable iron resources began on a large scale.

Since then Indian mining has progressed, often with violent fluctuations it is true, until the country to-day is the second biggest coal and iron ore producer in the Empire, the provider of a third of the world's output of manganese and three-quarters of the world's production of sheet and block mica. The list of minerals now in commercial exploitation in the country has lengthened considerably in recent years and in 40 years the production value has rocketed from less than £3½ millions in 1898 to £33 millions in 1938.

In considering the mineral raw materials noted below, we have to keep in mind these facts. That although the production of nearly all the minerals on India's list has shown very considerable increases, in many cases exploitation only affects a small proportion of the deposits known to exist; that many rich beds of coal and ores lie in corners of the country at present difficult of access; and that as the work of the Geological Survey of India proceeds, fresh mineral discoveries are liable to be made.

In 1938, the latest year for which full returns are available, the country's mineral production totalled nearly Rs. 34,14 lakhs, being a rise of 11·9 per cent over 1937.

Of this, coal accounted for Rs. 10,64 lakhs, representing 28,342,906 tons a peak figure.

In 1939-40 coal production had fallen to 25,056,000 tons, which, however, is above the average for the past decade.

These fluctuations have not prevented India's coal exports from increasing steadily year by year, the 1939-40 shipments of 2,009 790 tons being worth over Rs. 1,89 lakhs. India thus maintains her place as the second coal producing country of the Empire, the United Kingdom being first. Coal is at present mined in Bengal, Bihar (the main producer), the Central Provinces, Eastern States Agency and Hyderabad State, with smaller amounts from Assam, Baluchistan, Central India, Orissa, the Punjab and Rajputana.

Apart, however, from the Bengal-Bihar fields, where the finest quality coal is mined (the first Indian coal was cut at Raniganj in 1830), recent geological investigations have shown that India still has vast untapped reserves.

For example, in Assam the Langrin plateau between the Kashi and Garo Hills has form 60 million to 80 million tons of coal in one workable seam.

The Geological Survey Report points out that coal seams are exposed on the cliffs of the ravines cutting this plateau and that the ravine streams contain pebbles of coal.

Nearby in Nongstoin there is another seam containing about 70 milion tons of coal of strongly coking quality. In the Central Provinces and Berar, the Gondwana fields are esimated to contain about 17,000 milion tons, the reserves of workable coal being at least 5.150 million tons.

India's iron industry has grown so quickly that she is now the second largest producer of iron ore in the British Empire, yielding place only to the United Kingdom. But it is not generally realised that this industry is based on the greatest resources of high grade iron ore in the world. In the more accessible deposits in the Singhbhum district of Bihar and the adjoining Eastern States alone, there are 3,000 milion tons of ore averaging not less than 60 per cent of iron, according to the Geological Survey of India. In Bastar State, the reserves are estimated at 724 million tons of excellent quality ore. In the neighbouring Chanda and Drug districts of the Central Provinces, there are also important deposits, one of the most striking being in the Rajhana Hills where there are estimated to be 2½ milion tons of 67.5 per cent iron ore.

At present about three million tons of iron ore are raised each year in India, the major part of it at Singhbhum in Bihar and in the nearby Keonjhar States. Mysore State in south India, which has its own iron works, raised more than 35,000 tons in 1938.

In past years practically the whole of this ore went into Indian iron works for smelting but in '38 exports began to Japan at the rate of a million tons a year. She is also India's principal customer for pig iron, taking 323 000 tons out of a total production of 1,539.000 tons in '38. The United Kingdom came second, buying nearly 130,000 tons. In '39-40 pig iron production went still higher, to 1,837,600 tons.

Next on our list of minerals comes manganese ore, of which India accounts for about one-third of the world's output. An important adjunct of the iron and steel industry, manganese is inevitably vitally affected by world production of pig iron and steel and consequently during the industrial slump around 1932 Indian manganese was very seriously affected.

In 1933 production was a little over one-fifth of that of the peak year 1927 (1,129,353 tons) and the value less than one-twenty-second part of the 1927 value. Since then there has been a considerable recovery and all producing districts are now busy again. In 1938 production was 967,929 tons, worth more than Rs. 3,88 lakhs. Of this 518,342 tons were exported mainly to the United Kingdom, Japan and France. The Indian iron and steel industry consumes about 60.000 tons of manganese a year.

Main mining areas at the Balaghat, Bhandara and Nagpur districts of the Central Provinces ; Sandur, one of the Madras States ; Keonjhar and Bonai among the Eastern States : Singhbhum in Bihar, the North Kanara and Panch Mahals districts of Bombay, and Myore State.

The Central Provinces ores are usually a mixture of braunite and psilomelane. Their composition is very hard and thus the ore bodies tend to form small hills where quarrying is easy. According to Dr. A.M. Heron, former Director of the Geological Survey of India, the resources of ore in the Central Provinces are so large that the question of exhaustion has not arisen. He also states that though the known manganese deposits in Keonjhar and Sandur are not as large as those of the Central Provinces, "they are probably very numerous in country which has as yet not been fully explored."

Mica, as already mentioned, is one of India's mineral specialities since three-quarters of the world's supply of sheet and block mica is provided by this country. During 1938 Germany bought more than 30,000 cwt., being third, after Britain and the U.S.A., on the list of purchasers. There have been considerable increases in Indian production and export in the past few years, the 1938 production figure being 123,169 cwt. exclusive of waste and valued at Rs. 42 lakhs.

Mica deposits are widely distributed through the country, but it is reckoned that nearly 80 per cent comes from Bihar and most of the rest from the Nellore district of Madras. Other mica producing areas are Rajputana, Mysore, Gwalior and Travancore. Phlogopite is found in Travancore, the other deposits being muscovite.

Dr. Heron points out that though mining methods are primitive, the women workers of Bihar who are responsible for dressing and splitting the mica are so skilful that no doubt the excellence of their craft "contributes to the eminence of the Indian mica industry, for every year there is an import of some tons of foreign block mica into India for splitting, to be exported again in the form of fine splittings, 1/1000th inch being the usual thickness of the film."

An interesting by-product of the mica workings in Ajmer Merwara is beryl, a semi-precious stone in the same group as the emerald. The Ajmer-Merwara beryl is not gem quality and in normal times is shipped to Germany and America where it is used as ore from which the metal beryllium is extracted. Indian production has fluctuated in recent years between 324 tons in '33 and 17·4 tons in '38. There is no record of beryl production on such a large scale in the rest of the world.

As a petroleum producer India is, of course, overshadowed by her neighbour Burma, but nevertheless Indian production is incresing—from 75,657,857 gallons in '37 to 87,083,371 gallons in '38. Though this only represents 0.10 per cent of world production, it does mean an appreciable increase, especially from the Attock field in the Punjab where more than 21 million gallons were produced in '38. The Digboi field in Assam produced nearly 66 million gallons.

This internal production is, of course, only a fraction of India's own needs of kerosene, petrol and other mineral oils, but between 10,000 and 20,000 tons of paraffin wax are exported annually.

India's known deposits of base metals—tin, lead, zinc and copper—are poor. Tin occurs in the Bihar mica belt but is of no importance. Old lead and zinc workings are known to exist, but nowadays there is no production worth mentioning.

Copper has apparently been exploited in old workings scattered about the country but in only two places is there working on a commercial scale. The more important of the two is the Singhbhum copper belt in Bihar, where reserves of ore at the end of '38 amounted to 852 300 short tons, yielding 2·88 per cent copper. Production of refined copper is about 6,000 tons annually. A very small production of copper ore was reported in Mysore in '38.

A very large number of other minerals important to industry are shown in India's production list, though the quantity raised is often small and gives little indication of the country's potential supply. For example, bauxite, the material from which aluminium is produced ; according to the '38 returns only 4,634 tons were raised in that year. Practically all this was exported because as yet India has no factory to produce alumina.

It is known that India has vast deposits of good bauxite scattered all over the country. Typical examples are Tungar Hill, only 30 miles from Bombay City, where there are estimated to be 750,000 tons of bauxite of 49 per cent alumina content available. There are also vast qualities in the Balaghat, Jubbulpore, Mandala, Seoni and Nandgaon districts of the Central Provinces and in Bihar.

Ilmenite, the source of titanium dioxide, much in demand for tetanium paints, provides one of the most spectacular of Indian mineral developments in recent years. From a production of 400 tons in '22 output has rapidly risen to 181,047 tons in '38. Since '27 India has been the world's leading producer.

Ilmenite is recovered from the black sands near Cope Comorin, the southern tip of India in Travancore State, where it occurs in association with monazite, a source of thorium nitrate, and zircon, the production of both of which is increasing.

Zircon is used in the preparation of zirconia, a valuable refractory, and of metallic zirconium.

Of refactories India has a very considerable store. Kyanite, silimanite, quartzite and quartz-mica schist and corundum are all exploited, most of them in Singhbhum, the Eastern States and Ajmir-Merwara. Sillimanite occurs in Travancore and alone with corundum in Central India. Corundum is also found in the Salem district of Madras and in Mysore State.

Chromite, the oxide of chromium and iron used for furnace linings, is exploited in Baluchistan, where the main supplies appear to be, and in Bihar, the Eastern States, Bombay and Mysore.

Magnesite, another furnace liner, is found in almost unlimited quantities in the hills of the Salem district of Madras and also in Mysore State. More kilns are being erected in Salem and production is being raised from 1,200 to 1,600 tons a month.

Of the other minerals useful to industry, India is already producing in commercial quantities gypsum (Kashmir, Madras, Punjab, Rajputana, United Provinces), steatite (Guntur in Madras, Bihar, Central India, Central and United Provinces, Eastern States, Mysore and Rajputana), fuller's earth (Central Provinces, Punjab and Rajputana), barytes (Madras and Rajputana). ochres, of which very large quantities are readily available (Central India, Central Provinces, Eastern States, Madras, Orissa and Rajputana), graphite (Mysore, Central Provinces, Madras, Eastern States), tungsten, ore (wolfram) (Jodhpur State), asbestos (Eastern States, Mysore and Rajputana), felspar (Mysore and Rajputana), garnet sand (Madras), bentonite (Jodhpur), apatite (Bihar and Madras), tantalite (Monghyr in Bihar), and antimony ore (zinckenite) in Chitral State.

A great many of these resources have only been developed in recent years and production and export returns show considerable fluctuations. These are due not only to the variations in world prices affecting many minerals, but also to India's remoteness from the markets of Europe and America. Were a demand to grow up in the Eastern hemisphere, India could undoubtedly compete most successfully in such a market. In recent years this has been proved by Japan who is also remote from the Western mineral markets and has consequently purchased large quantities of her industrial minerals here.

Gold, (of which India has a large production in the Kolar area) and precious stones (diamonds in Central India and sapphires and aquamarines in Kashmir) have not been discussed here as they do not appear to come strictly within the scope of raw materials.

Mention should, however, be made of India's scrap metal. About 66,000 tons of non-ferrous scrap including brass, bronze, copper, white metal, etc., are normally available for export, in addition to large quantities of scrap iron and steel.

Raw materials, which though not providing very impressive export figures at present are capable of immense development, are to be found among India's timbers and fine woods.

When one considers the vast coniferous forest of the Himalayas, the teak and valuable furniture woods of the jungles of the Western Ghats and the availability of many and varied timbers in the jungles of the central parts of the country, it is obvious that the 1939-40 export of Rs. 17 lakhs worth of these materials is very small in relation to the vast potential. Of this amount teak alone accounted for nearly Rs. 4 lakhs. This figure does not of course include Burma teak, which nowadays enjoys a world market. It might however be pointed out that fine grades of teak have always been available in India itself and that the famous wooden East Indiamen, some of which were afloat for more than a century, were built at Bombay of teak obtained on the west coast.

Today it is reckoned that the annual yield of timber and fuel from India's forests amounts to about 290 million cubic feet a year. In British India 94,457 square miles, or over 11 per cent of the total area, is forest-covered and there are also extensive tracts in the States.

According to the timber price list issued by the Forest Research Institute, there are some 28 different Indian woods already in commerce and in some instances as many as a dozen different grades of one kind of timber are recognised.

They include Baing (*Tetrameles nudiflora*) from Assam (also well-known on the west coast), a white soft wood ; Benteak (*Lagerstroemia lanceolata*) from the west coast, a reddish brown moderately hard wood, in considerable demand and used for furniture, coffee cases, ship-building, etc. ; Bijasal (*Pterocarpus marsupium*), a very hard, close-grained durable wood which takes a high polish and is much used for door and window frames, furniture and agricultural implements ; obtainable in Bombay, Madras and Bihar.

Of the conifers, Blue Pine (*Pinus excelsa*) from the N. W. F. P. and the Punjab is much in demand, large quantities being floated down the rivers to the plains. The wood is moderately hard and is much used in constructional work. The trees are also tapped for their gum. Chir Pine (*Pinus longifolia*) which also comes from the N. W. F. P., the Punjab and the United Provinces, has moderately hard wood which though not quite as good as Blue Pine is cheaper and in considerable demand.

Deodar (*Cedrus deodara*), the Indian Cedar, is one of the most famous timbers of northern India and comes from the valleys of the Punjab and Kashmir. It is a moderately hard wood, strongly scented and oily ; much used for railway sleepers and in building.

Spruce and Fir (*Abies* and *Picea*), soft white wood similar to the European species, are available in the Punjab.

Dhupa (*Vateria indica*), the Indian Copal tree, found along the foot of the Western Ghats, besides giving the gum resin which makes an excellent varnish resembling copal, may be used for tea chests, packing cases, etc. Local boat makers use Dhupa for masts.

Civit (*Swintonia floribunda*) from Bengal is a greyish white, soft, even-grained wood and is said to last better than other woods in salt water. Another well-known timber which is found on the west coast and in the evergreen forests of Eastern Bengal and Burma is Gurjan (*Dipterocarpus species*). Available particularly in Bengal and Assam, it is a reddish brown hard wood with a well marked silver grain. Some of the species yield a wood oil which is much in demand in the areas where they grow. Timber is used for boat building and packing cases.

Gamari timber from the tree (*Gamelina arborea*) is yellowish or reddish white, with a glossy lustre. Even-grained, soft, light and strong, it does not warp or crack and is very durable under water. Boats, buoys and packing cases and much ornamental work are made from it and it is commonly employed wherever wood shrinkage is to be avoided. Found almost throughout India, Gamari is particularly available in Orissa and Eastern Bengal.

Haldu (*Adina cordifolia*) is another timber with almost an all-India availability, being obtainable in Assam, Bombay, Central Provinces, Madras, Bihar and Orissa. A yellow, moderately hard, even-grained wood, which is good for turning, furniture and cigar box making.

Hopea (*Hopea parviflora*) is a brown wood, hard and close-grained, from the damp forests of Malabar and South Kanara. It is a beautiful wood, much used in temple building in South Kanara ; it is not eaten by white ants.

Indian Rosewood or Blackwood (*Delbergia latefolia*) is of course world-famous, but not so well-known outside the country as its relative Sissoo, otherwise known as Shisham (*Dalbergia sissoo*).

Rosewood is found in many parts of India, reaching its best in the forests of the southern part of the Western Ghats, though it is also available in the Central Provinces and Orissa. Extremely hard and close-grained, this dark purple wood is very widely used for furniture making, and except for sandalwood, southern rosewood is about the highest priced timber in India. Shisham is the northern form of the species, being available in the United Provinces, the Punjab and Bengal. Less expensive than rosewood, the wood is very hard, close-grained and brown in colour. J. S. Gamble in his *Manual of Indian Timbers* describes it as "probably the finest wood in India" for furniture and carving and adds: "It is in regular demand for these purposes all over the North." It takes a high polish. Sissoo is also much used for carriage, cart and boat building, having lightness as well as strength and elasticity.

Irul wood (*Xylia xylocarpa*), one of the hardest woods in India, is available in Madras. Being very durable it makes excellent railway sleepers and can also be used as paving blocks, piles, telegraph posts, etc.

The Indian Laurel (*Terminalia tomentosa*) and its relative Kindal (*T. paniculata*) are both important timbers, the Laurel being found in many parts of the country (wood available in Bombay, Central Provinces, Bihar, Orissa and Madras) while the Kindal occurs in the south. Laurel wood is dark brown, very hard and beautifuly variegated with streaks of darker colour. Kindal, also hard, is grey.

A dark red, extremely hard and heavy wood is Mesua, sometimes known as Nahor (*Mesua ferrea*) used as railway sleepers and obtainable in Madras. It also grows extensively in Assam.

Next on the list is the Indian Mulberry (*Morus alba*) available in the Punjab. Like its relatives outside India, its fruit is eaten and its foliage used for silkworm culture. The wood is yellow or yellowish brown, has a pretty silver grain and is used for furniture, boats, agricultural implements, etc.

Perhaps the most decorative wood available in India is Padauk (*Ptercarpus dalbergoides*), a relative of Bijasal, already mentioned, found in the forests of the Andaman Islands. The heartwood, bright red and streaked with brown and black, is much in demand in Euro e and America for furniture, parquet floors, etc. The wood is durable and moderately hard.

Sal (*Shorea robusta*), available in Assam, Bengal, Bihar, Central Provinces, Orissa and the United Provinces, is one of the most extensively used wood in Northern India. The heartwood is brown, coarse-grained, hard and has a remarkably fibrous and cross-grained structure. It is much used in building for piles, beams, planking door and window posts and for railway sleepers.

Sandalwood (*Santalum album*), which may cost over Rs. 600 a ton, is available in the dry regions of South India and yields a hard, very close-grained yellowish brown wood, strongly scented by the oil characteristic of this tree. The wood is most commonly used for boxes and small articles, often beautifully carved, while India also possesses the important sandalwood oil industry.

Sandan, whose scientific name *Ougeinia dalbergoides*, is said to be taken from the city of Ujjain in Central India where the tree grows freely, is an excellent furniture timber, being hard, close-grained and mottled light brown in colour. Available in the Central Provinces, Bihar and Orissa.

Semul (*Bombax malabaricum*), the silk cotton tree with the spectacular flowers and masses of cotton, yields a very soft white timber useful for planking, packing cases, toys, etc. Available in Assam, Bihar and Madras.

Sundri (*Heriteira species*) is notable for its extreme toughness The timber is very hard and close-grained with dark red heartwood. Available in Bengal, it is extensively used for boat building, furniture, beams, planking and posts.

Finally, we have teak (*Tectonia grandis*), the chief export wood of India and Burma, and world-famous for its extraordinary durability probably due to the large amount of oil in the wood. As a ship-building wood and for good house carpentry it has long been known in many parts of the world. In India it is a general purpose timber for house and ship building, bridges, railway sleepers, furniture, etc. Teak has two main areas : Peninsular India (it is available in the Central Provinces, Madras and Bombay), and Burma. The timber is moderately hard and when freshly cut is a deep golden yellow, turning brown and finally nearly black with age.

Exports of Raw Materials from British India

	1937-38 Rs.	1938-39 Rs.	1939-40 Rs.
Coal	94,59,499	1,32,06,482	1,89,39,499
Other non-metallic Mining and quarry products	1,58,92,746	1,20,74,895	1,87,91,576
Fodder, bran and pollards	9,45,956	8,95,656	4,79,788
Gums, resins and lac (*i*)	1,88,74,582	1,50,09,855	2,22,39,714
Hides and skins, raw and undressed ...	5,04,10,063	3,84,66,560	4,12,33,731
Metallic ores and scrap iron and steel (*ii*) ...	2,74,43,500	1,67,22,516	2,28,21,620

	1937-38 Rs.	1938-39 Rs.	1939-40 Rs.
Oils, vegetable, mineral and animal (*iii*) ...	1,01,03,164	1,03,37,066	1,37,51,048
Oil cakes	2,42,57,726	3,01,19,532	2,02,90,118
Paper-making materials	5,15,802	5,42,536	5,24,465
Rubber, raw and crude	83,83,332	71,57,805	93,76,330
Seeds including oil nuts(*iv*)	14,18,64,637	15,09,21,693	11,89,74,049
Tallow, stearine and wax	3,61,309	3,27,311	3,21,808
Cotton, raw and waste ...	29,77,25,646	24,66,65,129	31,04,57,248
Jute	14,71,90,313	13,39,67,180	19,84,62,[illegible]99
Silk	3,11,445	2,37,752	4,50,039
Wool	2,64,55,835	2,98,68,271	3,23,34,414
Other textile materials ...	75,45,215	72,97,996	87,50,743
Wood and timber (*v*) ...	26,32,998	18,46,020	17,05,555
Miscellaneous (*vi*) ...	2,41,72,784	1,72,52,779	2,03,75,164
Total ...	81,45,46,552	73,29,17,034	86,02,76,208
Note.			
(*i*) Gums, resins and lacs include Lac ...	1,62,18,000	1,26,65,148	1,90,80,118
(*ii*) Metallic Ores, etc., include Manganese Ore	2,21,28,945	1,07,24,787	1,82,74,498
(*iii*) Oils include Cocoanut oil	1,31,469	1,13,169	90,260
(*iv*) Seeds include Castor ...	64,00,637	10,05,622	71,39,629
Ground-nut ...	8,93,29,631	9,92,72,141	7,19,01,488
Linseed ...	3,56,79,985	4,40,45,275	3,17,60,946
Rape ...	46,42,744	15,81,936	32,77,344
Sesamum (til) ...	19,18,289	14,80,551	7,48,739
(*v*) Wood and Timber include Teak ...	3,67,779	7,92,611	3,89,643
(*vi*) Miscellaneous include Bones and bonemeal (manur) ...	51,96,882	26,70,237	30,64,299

Tobacco

India's progress as a tobacco growing country has been little short of extraordinary. In fact production in this country is on such a scale that in 1936-37 India stood first of the world tobacco producers with 1,497,000 acres growing 1,375 milion lbs. while the U. S. A. came second with 1,437,000 acres and 1,153 million lbs.

The annual value of the Indian crop is about Rs. 18,00 lakhs and the chief areas for growing it are Bengal, Madras, Bombay, Bihar, the United Provinces and the Punjab.

Though a very considerable part of this tobacco is of course consumed inside the country, in 1937-38 42½ million lbs. of unmanufactured tobacco worth Rs. 1,18 lakhs was exported. The total yield of leaf in that year was 511,000 tons. Virginia tobacco is already in production in the Guntur area of Madras and has been introduced in Guzerat (Bombay).

A considerable amount of research is being undertaken to improve not only the crops of leaf, but also the curing and marketing. Export on the basis of the official Agmark grades is increasing and care is being taken to prevent marketing abuses such as have occurred in the past.

Though this enumeration of India's primary products may not seem brief, it is only the barest sketch in relation to the total potentialities of this subcontinent. These notes have been based in the main on the official classification of raw materials which have already found a market beyond India, while the others mentioned are those recommended by the exports attached to the Government of India. There has thus been no inclusion of materials future exports of which are speculative to say the least.

A considerable number of primary products, food grains and fruit for example, have hardly been touched upon, partly because India at present absorbs nearly all the output, or because since such materials do not go through manufacturing processes before reaching the consumer, they cannot really be classed as "raw."

political association, the problems arising from regulation of immigration are of special complexity and delicacy. Both Governments have approached these problems in a spirit of cordiality and mutual understanding and are agreed that in giving administrative effect to the measures now proposed the closest co-operation will be required in the same spirit of mutual adjustment and identity of purpose which characterised the negotiations. It is their earnest desire that the agreement now achieved will serve to remove any causes for misapprehension which may have arisen either between the two countries or between the two communities in Burma and may furnish a lasting foundation for the development in the future of the firmest ties of friendship and goodwill."

TEXT OF AGREEMENT

The following is the full text of the agreement initialled in Rangoon on June 28, 1941 :—

Definitions :

1. In this agreement, unless there is anything repugnant in the subject or context.—

(*a*) "dependant" means a person who is wholly and directly dependent for maintenance and support on a person who holds or is about to be granted a permit under the provisions of this Agreement and is related to such person as being—

(*i*) his wife, or

(*ii*) his or his wife's patent, or

(*iii*) his or his wife's daughter, or grand-daughter who is either unmarried or a widow or is divorced, or

(*iv*) his or his wife's son or grandson who is under the age of 18 years or, being over that age is permanently disabled and incapable of supporting himself ;

(*b*) "Indian" means a British subject domiciled in India or the subject of an Indian State ;

(*c*) "work," "skilled work" and "unskilled work" have the meanings assigned to them in Section 2 of the Indian Emigration Act, 1922.

Operation of Order in Council :

2. The Government of Burma agree that the notice given by them to terminate the operation of the Government of Burma (Immigration) Order, 1937, with effect from the 1st April, 1942, will be treated as withdrawn, and that notice to terminate the same will not be given before the 1st October, 1945.

Date of Operation :

3. Indian immigration into Burma will, with effect from the 1st October, 1941, be subject to regulations and restrictions, in the manner hereinafter explained.

Passports :

4. No Indian may enter Burma without a valid Indian passport containing his photograph and other particulars sufficient to establish his identity.

Passport Visas and Immigration Passports :

5. No Indian may enter Burma without a passport *visa* issued by or on behalf of the Government of Burma or an immigration permit issued by or under authority of the Government of Burma.

Passport Visas :

6. (1) The Government of India, or officers employed by them, may issue, on behalf of the Government of Burma and subject to terms and conditions imposed by the Government of Burma, *visas* on passports granted to Indians desiring to enter Burma as visitors or as students in educational institutions.

(2) A *visa* on an Indian visitor's passport will be valid for three months but this period may be extended by or under the authority of the Government of Burma up to a total stay in Burma of twelve months.

(3) A fee of Rs. 20. will be charged for visitors' *visas* but no fee will be charged for extensions.

(4) A student's *visa* will be valid for a stated period not exceeding five years.

(5) No fee will be charged for a student's *visa.*

Immigration Permits :

7. (1) Save as otherwise provided by the terms of this agreement, no Indian may enter Burma without one of the following classes of permits :—

(i) "A" permits, which will entitle the holder to remain in Burma for an indefinite period and to accept employment therein. No bar will be placed on the acquisition of a Burma domicile by holders of "A" permits :

(*ii*) "B" permits, which will entile the holder to reside in Burma for a specified period and to accept employment therein. "B" permits being for limited periods, will not allow the holders to acquire a Burma domicile. They will be issued for a maximum period of three years and may be extended at the discretion of the Government of Burma for further periods which, with the original period, may not exceed a total of nine years. The holder of a "B" permit may apply for an "A" permit on the same terms as an original applicant for an "A" permit.

(2) The issue of immigration permits will be subject to the terms and conditions set out in this Agreement and also to such other terms and conditions as the Government of Burma may prescribe after consulting the Government of India, provided that any other terms and conditions so prescribed shall not be inconsistent with the objects of this agreement. The acceptance of these terms and conditions shall be a condition for the entry of the immigrants into Burma.

Restrictions on the numbers of permits and visas :

8. (1) The number of "A" permits to be issued will be at the discretion of the Government of Burma and they will be issued only to persons whom the Government of Burma consider to be of sufficient financial standing or possessed of an assured income in Burma of sufficient amount and to be persons who are likely to be suitable for permanent residence in Burma.

(2) "B" permits will be issued within such limits as may be prescribed in any year or other period by the Government of Burma after considering the advice of an Immigration Board.

(3) The Government of Burma reserve power to impose limits on the number of students and visitors' *visas* to be issued by the Government of India on their behalf.

Dependants of immigrants with "A" permits or "B" permits :

9. (1) Applicants for "A" or "B" permits will be required to declare particulars of dependants whom they intend to bring to Burma either with them or at some future date.

Declared dependants :

(2) Should the applicant receive his permit, dependants declared under sub-clause (1) will be granted on application by the former the same class of permit as the applicant.

Undeclared dependants :

(3) Other dependants of the applicant may also, on application by him and at the discretion of the Government of Burma, be granted the same class of permit.

Limit of validity of dependants' permit :

(4) The period of validity of a permit granted to a dependant will not extend beyond the period of validity of the permit held by the person on whom they are dependant.

Land Frontier Migration :

10. The two Governments will co-operate in devising and effecting measures to deal with and to control immigration across the land frontier between the two countries. It is understood that this will require consultation by the Government of India with the Provincial Governments concerned.

Immigration Board :

11. The Government of Burma will institute at an early date an Immigration Board to examine the relevant date and to tender advice to the Government of Burma generally on matters of policy relating to Indian immigration into Burma and in particular on the fixing of quotas for the grant of permits. The Board will be of mixed racial composition and Burmans, Indians and Europeans will be represented on it.

Penalties for unlawful entry or unlawful residence in Burma :

12. The penalties imposable under Burma legislation shall not exceed imprisonment for six months or a fine of Rs. 1,000, or both on persons convicted before a Magistrate of an infringement of the immigration rules or of a breach of the conditions of a permit, or of making a false statement in order to obtain a permit or other privilege relating to entry to or residence in Burma or to secure registration as a privileged immigrant.

Literacy Test :

13. The Government of Burma may impose a literacy test on applicants for "A" permits :

Provided that such a test shall not be made in Burmese or in any other language indigenous to Burma.

Marriages or cohabitation between Indian male immigrants and women belonging to the indigenous races of Burma :

14. Marriage or cohabitation with a woman belonging to the indigenous races of Burma established to the satisfaction of the Government of Burma may be made a condition for the cancellation of permit or *visa* granted to a male Indian immigrant :

Provided that exceptions will be made of marriages entered into with the sanction of the Government of Burma and that such sanction will be given if the immigrant makes, before the proposed marriage, provision which is sufficient in the opinion of the Government of Burma for the permanent maintenance of the woman he desires to marry.

Fees for permits :

15. The following scale of fees will be charged for immigration permits :—

"A" permits.—Rs, 500.

"B" permits.—For unskilled labourers, an entrance fee or a *visa* fee, of Rs. 12 *plus* a residential fee of Rs. 5 for every year or part of a year for which the permit will be valid. For other "B" permits, an entrance fee or a *visa* fee, of Rs. 30 and a residential fee of Rs. 20 for every year or part of a year for which the permit is valid Arrangements will be made to enable immigrants to pay the residential fee in yearly instalments if they so desire.

Dependants—Half the rate per dependant of the fees payable by the immigrant himself.

Collection from Employers of visa *or entrance fees for "B" permits :*

16. The Government of Burma accept the principle that the incidence of entrance or visa fees and of the stamp duty charged in respect of "B" permit holders should fall on the employer and undertake to collect such fees from the employer or prospective employer in cases where a permit is issued at his instance.

Deposits :

17. Before entry into Burma a deposit of Rs. 20 will be made to the Government of Burma by person who are granted "B" permits and by their dependants to cover the cost of repatriating them. Repatriation will be, at the choice of the repatriated Indian, to the ports of (*a*) Calcutta, (*b*) Chittagong, (*c*) Madras, (*d*) Vizagapatam, and (*e*) Gopalpur. The deposit will be refunded if the person concerned leaves Burma of his own accord or obtains an "A" permit.

Stamp Duty :

18. Applications for all classes of permits under the immigration control arrangements shall be subject to stamp duty under the ordinary law of Burma.

Provision Relating To Indians Already In Burma

Indians who are born and bred in Burma and who have made Burma their permanent home :

19. The Government of Burma recognise that Indians who are born and bred in Burma, have made Burma their permanent home and regard their future and the future of their families as bound up with its interests are entitled to be regarded as having established a claim if they wish to make it, to a Burma domicile and therefore to the benefit of Section 144 of the Government of Burma Act, 1935.

Acquisition of Burma domicile by Indians in Burma :

20. No restriction will be placed on the acquistion of a Burma domicile under due process of law by Indians lawfully residing in Burma excepting those who by the terms and conditions of a permit which entitles them to reside in Burma are not given the right of residence beyond a specified period.

Privileged immigrants :

22. Indians who prove a total residence in Burma of seven calendar years between the 15th July, 1932 and the 15th July, 1941 will be termed "privileged immigrants."

Such privileged immigrants shall have the right to further residence and to the acceptance of further employment in Burma without limit of time but they will lose their status as privileged immigrants should they be absent from Burma for a continuous period exceeding one year after the 15th July, 1941.

A privileged immigrant, so long as he retains status, will be given the right of free re-entry into Burma on his return after an absence of less than twelve months.

Dependants of Privileged Immigrants ;

22. The following classes of dependants of a privileged immigrant will be given "A" permits free of charges for entry into Burma :—

(*i*) One wife if there is no other wife residing in Burma.

(*ii*) His sons below the age of 18 by the wife who is granted an "A" permit under this clause or by a wife residing with him in Burma,

(*iii*) His unmarried daughters by the wife who is granted an "A" permit under this clause or by a wife residing with him in Burma.

Indians who are already in Burma but have not qualified as privileged immigrants:

23. Other Indians who are in Burma on the 15th July '41, will be entitled to remain in Burma indefinitely and to accept work for an indefinite period and will retain their privileges under Section 44 of the Government of Burma Act, 1935.

Should an Indian of this class leave Burma for any period, his claim to re-entry will be dealt with in the same manner as an application for entry by a new Indian immigrant and if re-admitted into Burma, such person will be treated as new Indian immigrant with the exception that he will have a preferential claim to a "B" permit over new Indian immigrants.

Transitory Provisions:

24. During the transition period pending the constitution of an Immigration Board and the consideration by the Government of Burma of proposals to be made by the Board for the quotas for permits to be issued to Indian immigrants, the Government of India will prohibit the emigration to Burma of Indians for the purpose of unskilled work from the 21st July, '41 with the exception of seasonal labourers who may, at the instance of the Government of Burma, be granted passports up to numbers agreed upon between the two Governments.

Registration of Indians in Burma:

25. The Government of Burma will institute at an early date a system of registering Indians in Burma.

GENERAL

Power of Exemption:

26. The Government of Burma may exempt any person from any or all the conditions and restrictions that may be imposed under this Agreement.

Co-operation between the two Governments:

27. The two Governments will act in close co-operation to achieve the objects of the Agreement and will freely consult each other on points of difficulty that may arise.

In particular the Government of Burma will grant the Government of India an opportunity of commenting on proposals to fix quotas and on the recommendations of the Immigration Board on which such proposals are based.

* The Raw Materials of India

Even in the first century of the Christian era India was famed for her raw materials which found their way into the workshops of Egypt, Greece and Rome. That extremely experienced, though anonymous Greek merchant, who wrote the Periplus of the Erythrean Sea and so collected all the then known data on the Indian trade, remarked on the coloured lac, the ebony, the sesamum oil, the timber and the "honey from reeds" (we now know it as sugar) which India exported in those early days.

Much later, when the merchants of Western Europe established direct contact with Indian markets, they were chiefly interested in buying spices and manufactures such as the superb Indian fabrics.

So it was only in comparatively recent times that anyone realised the vast importance of India as a supplier of the type of raw materials which modern industry needs—the iron and coal and a score of other minerals; the vegetable oils for the maker of foods, soaps and paints; the fibres such as cotton, jute (a world monopoly here) and wool which modern textiles demand, the hides and skins, the timber, the raw drugs used by every community nowadays.

With the wide range of climate, from the rice and rubber growing lands of the far south to the wheat and the coniferous forests of the Punjab and the Himalayas, India is in a position to offer the world the widest possible selection of products which the soil can grow. Moreover, and this is especially the case since irrigation had made such headway, there is space to raise these crops on a very large scale indeed. It should not be forgotten that India is as big as Europe, excluding Russia.

Nineteen categories of raw materials are at present exported, according to the official classification. Of these "cotton, raw and waste" comes first (Rs. 31,04 lakhs), followed by jute (Rs. 19,81 lakhs), seeds including oilnuts (Rs. 11,89 lakhs), hides and skins (Rs. 4,12 lakhs), wool (Rs. 3,23 lakhs), metallic ores, scrap iron and steel (Rs. 2,78 lakhs), including manganese (Rs. 1,82 lakhs), gums, resin and lac (Rs. 2,22 lakhs), oil cakes (Rs. 2,02 lakhs), coal (Rs. 1,89 lakhs), "other non-metallic mining and quarry production" (Rs. 1,87 lakhs), oils, vegetable, mineral and animal (Rs. 1,37 lakhs), rubber (Rs. 93 lakhs) and smaller amounts of fodder, bran and pollards, paper-making material, tallow stearine and wax, silk and timber. These figures are for the year 1939-40.

The effect of the war on Indo-European trade has been to close markets for raw materials worth approximately Rs. 30,00 lakhs, consisting chiefly of raw jute, raw cotton, oil seeds and oil cake, hides and skins and smaller amounts of manganese ore, tea, oils, lac, manure, raw silk, raw hemp, coir and coffee. The European countries normally took about one-sixth of India's jute, one-sixth of her cotton, one-third of her oil cake, nearly half of her oil seeds and one-third of her hides and skins.

On the other hand, the trade returns for 1939-40 reveal that except for oil seeds and cake, which show an aggregate decline of Rs. 4,17 lakhs, nearly all India's major raw material exports marked impressive gains—raw jute and raw cotton leading with Rs. 6,44 and Rs, 6,37 lakhs respectively. True, these figures cover the first six months of war as well as six months' sales to the continent of Europe and they are therefore abnormal, but they do illustrate the elasticity of the Indian sources of supply. In the case of jute, for example, there has been a 50 per cent increase in exports, and the 1940 crop is forecast to show another 30 per cent rise!

Another example of India's potentiality as a provider of raw materials may be seen in the case of wheat. In years of poor prices India hardly enters the international market at all—400 tons exported in 1933—but when the prices are right the amount available is considerable—200,000 tons in 1936—a year when prices were about 75 per cent of normal average and 459,806 tons in 1937-38.

Cotton, Jute and Wool

If we examine India's raw materials on the existing basis shown by our exports, cotton is by far and away the most important—in fact it can be regarded as the outstanding money crop in the country. India is the world's second largest

* The following was published at the instance of the Government of India in the *Indian Information* dated the 15th September 1941.

producer. An average of about seven million 400-lb. bales are produced yearly and of this nearly half is available for export, being worth from Rs. 24,66 lakhs to Rs. 31,04 lakhs.

It is grown mainly in the great Black Earth region of the Deccan; the Oomras, which include parts of the Central Provinces and part of Bombay; in Kathiawar, in northern Mysore, in southern Madras, in Sind and in the Punjab. But, as Sir Chunilal V. Mehta, Bombay cotton magnate, has put it: "The bulk of the Indian crop still remains of the shortest and coarsest staple possible. The climatic characteristics of the Oomras tract are in a large measure responsible."

It is probably this main central block of cotton-producing country which has given India her reputation for a short staple product, mainly suitable for the cheap quality textiles woven in India and Japan who is India's biggest buyer of raw cotton.

On the other hand, it should be noted that in the past 20 years energetic measures have been taken to improve the quality of India's crop and in this respect the Indian Central Cotton Committee's work is most notable.

New breeds of cotton have been introduced; mixing cotton and transporting seed cotton from one region to another for mixing purposes have been made offences. While 25 years ago the amount of cotton of 15/16" staple grown in India was practically negligible the production of such cotton in 1937-38 was nearly half a million bales.

Cotton is the subject of another topic in this group so it is not necessary to go into details here. Let it be sufficient to point out that India's cotton is steadily improving and that supplies capable of spinning the hightest standard warp counts of 30's to 33's are obtainable. Crops of this cotton are now replacing varieties which would only spin 8's or 10's, in the Oomras tract of the Central Provinces and Berar.

Jute Second Most Important

Jute, the second most important Indian agricultural raw material, is of course a monopoly of the four provinces, Bengal, Assam, Bihar and Orissa, with Bengal growing about 90 per cent of the total. In the past seven years annual production has been about nine million bales of 400 lbs. each, of which about half is exported raw, the rest being manufactured into Hessian or gunny cloth in Indian mills.

During the past decade these mills have suffered severely through over-production and a critical stage had been reached late in 1938 when the Government of Bengal promulgated an ordinance restricting output. Further ordinances in 1939 fixed minimum prices for raw jute futures and Hessian futures.

The war, of course, immediately changed the situation, the mills having to work at high pressure to meet the rush orders for millions of sand-bags. Since then, the closure of the continental market (mostly for raw jute) worth Rs. 7,00 lakhs a year and the increase in the size of the crop, appear to have broken boom conditions.

Jute thus retains its place as the world's cheapest packing cloth. When first introduced into England it was used for ropes, door mats, carpets, etc., but since a method of spinning it was developed, this fibre has almost exclusively been used for making hessian or sacking cloth and in that form it is sold to nearly every manufacturing nation in the world.

Search For Substitutes

Such monopoly of the wrapping cloth industry has inevitably spurred others, and especially the totalitarian States, to seek substitutes. It was reported some time before the war that both Italy and Germany had produced "staple fibres," from 'esparto' grass and wood respectively, to replace jute.

Various other fibres have been reported in other parts of the world and the American tendency to use cotton or paper bags or to handle grain in bulk all seem liable to injure jute's hold on the world's sacking business. But the sudden upswing of business which followed the outbreak of war soon showed that jute hessian was still the most practical position of the lot.

It is possible, however, that the position may be stabilised as fresh uses for jute are developed. There is a large potential market for the fibre in making clothing materials, textiles for curtains, uppolstery, etc., and for finer types of canvas. At least one form of men's suiting, which contains a proportion of jute, has been successfully marketed in tropical countries.

Wool, Silk and Hemp

It is advisable to deal here briefly with the other fibres which India exports—they are wool, silk and hemp. Indian wool exports stood at over Rs. 3,00 lakhs during 1939-40, and much of it was bought for carpet making. While the war lasts, however, a good deal of the supply available in India is going into army blankets, thus giving the lie to the all-too-prevalent idea that wool from this country is too coarse for anything but carpets.

It is quite true of course that a great deal of rough wool is grown on the sheep around the villages in the hotter parts of the country, but on the other hand there can be no doubt about the extraordinary fineness of the product which comes from the animals raised along the edge of the desert and in the Himalayas.

The extremely fine quality of the fleeces which made Kashmir shawls famous is a case in point. That such quality is available in commercial quantities is proved by the woollen mills of Upper India, who buy supplies in the Himalayas and weave fine grades of cloth. Experiments are going forward in various parts of the country to improve wool yields, including crossing Indian breeds of sheep with Merino.

Silk exports are small, usually between Rs. 2 and Rs. 3 lakhs, though in the year war began they jumped to Rs. 4½ lakhs. India does not, however, appear ever to have been a raw silk exporting country on any considerable scale; in fact on balance she is an importer, manufacturing raw silk into valuable textiles on handlooms in such famous centres as Benares and Surat.

In the official classification of "other textile materials" exported raw hemp is the most important. Usually the total is between Rs. 70 and Rs. 80 lakhs—of which hemp takes the lion's share.

Vegetable Oils

The next great group of raw materials consists of oil seeds and nuts (Rs. 11,89¾ lakhs), oil cakes (Rs. 2,03 lakhs) and "oils, vegetable, mineral and animal" (Rs. 1,37½ lakhs). The major part of the oil is vegetable in origin.

The oil seed industry, as old as India itself, affects almost the whole of the country and since a very considerable proportion of the seeds grown are intended for domestic use—cooking, lighting, etc.—it is difficult to produce statistics of the amounts harvested each year. However, it may be assumed that the quantities actually exported are only a fraction of the total since Indian industry itself also consumes a considerable amount of the produce which comes on the market—particularly of castor seed.

In spite of this, however, India is reckoned the world's second largest supplier of oil seeds, the first in normal times being China. Owing to the present state of the latter country, however, it seems quite likely that as an exporter India probably holds the first place.

Loss of the continental markets, worth over Rs. 600 lakhs, has been partly made up by wartime demands elsewhere and during 1939-40 exports of raw seeds showed a drop of only Rs. 3,19 lakhs, partly offset by an increase of Rs. 84 lakhs in exports of oils.

Of the seeds exported, much the most important is ground-nut, Rs. 719 lakhs in 1939-40 (normal about Rs. 900 lakhs), linseed Rs. 3,17 lakhs, castor seed Rs. 71 lakhs (a big jump, apparently owing to war demand), rape seed Rs. 32 lakhs (an increase) and sesamum Rs. 7½ lakhs (a fall of 50 per cent). These, plus cocoanut oil (normal exports about a lakh a year), constitute the main export oil seeds out of a list of 131 different kinds shown in *Indian Vegetable Oils* (Bulletin No. 10 of the Indian Industrial Research Bureau).

The author of this Bulletin points out that exports of these seeds from British India average about a million tons yearly and that the chief use for vegetable oils both in India and in the West is for cooking, including margarine, soap making comes next, then paints and varnishes, lubricants (castor oil has an international reputation) and in medicine.

Nowadays, as export returns show, ground-nut is the main oil seed export. It is estimated that India grows from 2 to 3 million tons of this crop, mainly in Madras and Bombay Presidencies and Hyderabad State. About a million tons of this crop is exported, India being the leading exporting country of the world. In the West the oil is used for much the same purposes as olive oil and is frequently employed as an adulterant for the latter. It is a favourite oil for margarine making and is also used in soap. Ground-nut is usually exported in its shells as there is a considerable risk of the decorticated nuts heating and turning the oil rancid in transit.

Linseed, the next most important of the oil seeds, was the first to be commercially exported from India and for many years about half the world supply was grown here. In recent years Russia has headed the list of producers (though not of exporters), followed by Argentina who nowadays has taken India's place as an exporter. All the same, the Indian seed ranks next to the Baltic (North Russian) variety, which is reckoned the highest quality by international markets. The produce of Argentina and South Russia ranks lower than that of India.

The Indian export of seed has fluctuated widely in recent years, the value having been as high as Rs. 5,75 lakhs—in 1929-30. The main uses for the oil are of course in manufacturing paint and varnish, linoleum, oiled fabrics, printing inks, imitation leather and soft soap. The chief growing areas are the provinces of Bihar, Orissa, the Central Provinces, the United Provinces and Hyderabad State.

In spite of crops raised in Brazil and other countries, India still dominates the castor seed and castor oil markets of the world. For example, in 1937-38 seed worth Rs. 64 lakhs and nearly 2¼ million gallons of castor oil were exported. However, since in many parts of India castor oil is still in general use as a lubricant, only about one-third of the total crop normally reaches the export market.

Efforts are being made to improve the standard of the Indian crop, a series of experiments financed by the Imperial Council of Agricultural Research, having been started in Hyderabad State, the main growing area. Bombay, the Central Provinces, Bihar and Orissa also grow castor crops and much of the seed is locally crushed to provide a lubricant. The oil cake, being unsuitable as cattle food, provides a valuale manure. Castor oil's qualities as a lubricant have enabled it to stand comparison with mineral oil lubricants—even in such peculiar conditions of strain as racing cars and aeroplane engines. This oil, however, is stated to lack stability over a long period unless suitably treated, but recently the Indian Industrial Research Bureau reported that chemical investigations have resulted in the discovery of a dozen chemicals which are effective stabilisers when used in vegetable oils including castor, ground-nut and cotton seed oil. The Bureau regards oils as a potential source of good quality engine lubricants.

Apart from its well-known medical use as a purgative, castor oil is also valuable to industry as an ingredient of transparent soap.

Rape seed, the exports of which have shown violent fluctuations in recent years, and stood at Rs. 32 lakhs in 1939-40, constitutes a very large crop in India—about a million tons being grown each year, mainly in Bengal, Bihar, Orissa, the Punjab, Bombay, the United Provinces and the Central Provinces. Rape actually forms a group of seeds and not a single variety. The oil expressed from these seeds is generally known in India as mustard oil. In Europe the trade knows it as rape or colza oil. In India it is perhaps the most popular of all vegetable oils, being used for cooking, lighting and for personal use as a massage. In western industry, the oil is thickened by blowing air through it and it is then used in compounded lubricants.

Another oil seed which has a somewhat similar history to rape in the foreign market is sesamum, often known as gingelly or til in India. Although about 400,000 tons are grown each year in Bengal, Bihar, Bombay, the Central Provinces, Madras, the United Povinces and Hyderabad, only a comparatively small amount is exported ; Rs. 7½ lakhs worth in 1939-40 against Rs. 15 lakhs worth in 1938-39.

In India, however, sesamum oil has much the same uses as rape, except that it is considered superior to the latter, its more delicate flavour making it valuable for cooking. It is this quality of flavour which makes it possible to use sesamum as a substitute for olive oil. In western countries imports of the oils are used in making margarine.

Though the seeds and oils just discussed are the main items on India's list of exported vegetable oil materials, it is worth pointing out that there is a long list of other seeds of the same type, which according to the individual requirements of the foreign buyer might be well worth exporting.

For example, cotton seed, of which India is the world's second largest producer with eight million tons, being second only to the U.S.A. There has been a very marked decline in exports of Indian seed, despite a rise in the export of oil—over 368,000 gallons were exported in 1933-34.

The proved amount at Koh-i-Sultan is 85,000 tons of sulphur-bearing rock with an average sulphur content of about 60 per cent, although larger quantities of this high-grade material, say, 100,000 tons, may be anticipated. A further 300,000 to 400,000 tons of 35 per cent sulphur-bearing rock can be obtained by mining at another locality near Sanni which can be developed to yield more from the lower strata. Smaller deposits have also found in other places.

Dr. C. S. Fox of the Geological Survey of India, who reported the discovery, is of opinion that altogether some 500,000 tons of sulphur-bearing rock carrying roughly 35 per cent sulphur may be available, but this has yet to be established and even larger quantities may be available from these areas. The Geological Survey of India also have in hand investigations of several other sulphur occurrences.

The importance of these finds may be judged from the fact that sulphuric acid can be directly manufactured from rock sulphur with a content of 60 per cent, and pure sulphur can be extracted from this rock sulphur by a simple physical process.

Natural sulphur was first discovered in Baluchistan more than 40 years ago by the Geological Survey of India at Koh-i-Sultan and 30 years ago at Sanni. But one of the mines at Sanni caught fire and the prospecting operations had to be stopped and the mines closed. Since then it had come to be thought that there were no other sulphur deposits in the country.

Another method of obtaining sulphur has also been developed recently by the Board of Industrial and Scientific Research. It is by the burning of iron pyrites. Pilot plant experiments have shown that this process enables pure sulphur to be produced at a very reasonable price. In this process a by-product, iron oxide, is also obtained which can be used in the paint industry.

In fact, this process by itself would ensure a perennial supply of sulphur, as there is plenty of iron pyrites available in India. There are evidently fairly attractive supplies obtainable in Bihar, and deposits have also been located recently near Solon in the Simla Hills and others in the Tinnevelly district of Madras, but none of these deposits have fully proved yet.

India's Jute Industry

Considering that the exports of raw and manufactured jute constitute about one-quarter of the total value of the exports of Indian merchandise it comes as a surprise to most people to learn that, on the average, the jute crop is the product of only 1½ per cent of the total cropped area of British India. The cultivation of jute is confined almost entirely to the Provinces of Bengal, Bihar and Assam in North-east India and, of these, Bengal is the predominant producer, accounting for about 80 per cent of the total outturn of raw jute. Yet, even in Bengal, the area under jute is only a small percentage of the cultivated area, varying from about six to nine per cent. It may further be remarked that jute is probably the least known of the important commercial fibres though, in bulk, its annual production ranks second only to that of cotton. This is almost certainly due to the fact that its commercial history extends to only a little more than a century while that of wool, flax, hemp, silk and cotton goes back many centuries.

What is Jute ?

Jute is the fibre extracted from plants of the Genus *Corchorus*. The two species cultivated for the production of fibre are *Capsularis* which produces what is known to the trade as white jute and in the jute districts as *pat* or *koshta*, and *Olitorius* which gives us the fibres known as *daissee* (desi), *tossa* and *bogi*. Another fibre called *mesta* is also used in the jute trade but it is the fibre of a plant called *Hibiscus Cannabis* and is botanically distinct from *Corchorus*. The quantity produced is relatively small. The jute plant is an annual one and grows in a single stem without branches or twigs though these may begin to develop high up as the plant nears maturity. Premature branching stunts the growth and spoils the fibre and it is desirable that the plants should be ready for cutting before any twigs are developed. The plant consists of a central woody stick round which there is a bast layer in which the fibre is developed. It grows to an average height of eight to ten feet but much taller plants are frequent. The yield varies very considerably according to the district, the nature of the soil, river and weather conditions and the seed used. An average yield is about 16 maunds per acre but yields as high as 40 maunds have been recorded. The average yield appears, however, to have declined as cultivation has extended to areas which are possibly not quite suitable or where the *ryots* (cultivators) are insufficiently skilled in the cultivation of the plant. For instance, the Collector of Mymensingh reported in 1878 that the average yield of the crop in Mymensingh district as ascertained by the crop cutting experiments was 24 maunds per acre. The fibre consists on the average of about 6 per cent of the weight of the green plant.

The fibre obtained from *Capsularis*, the white jute of the trade, may vary in colour from white or cream colour to dark grey but the colour is largely determined by the water in which the plants are retted. The *Olitorius* fibre, tossa, bogi or daissee is of a finer texture, softer to the touch and stronger than white jute. In colour it varies from golden yellow to slaty brown and dark grey, the colour in this case also being influenced by the retting water.

Cultivation

Capsularis, white jute, is grown on both low and high lands. Low-land sowings commence in February and sowing may be done on the high lands as late as May. It is essential that low-land sowings should take place early because these lands are subject to innundation as a result of the seasonal rise in the rivers and it is desirable that sowing should be done in time to enable the plants to reach maturity before the rising rivers enforce cutting of the crop. In most seasons, however, much of the low-land crop has to be cut before maturity and, in consequence, the yield in these districts is low. The period for harvesting white jute varies from early June until September according to the district, the river levels and the times of sowing.

Olitorious is mainly a high-land crop and is sown later. It does not thrive in water-logged ground. The period of harvesting varies from August to October. About 6 seers of seed per acre are required for sowing *Capsularis* and 4 seers per acre for *Olitorius* though, of course, much depends on the quality of the seed.

There are, of course, various "qualities" known to the trade under different names but these are not botanically different and the variation in quality is usually attributable to the district in which they are grown or the method by which the fibre is extracted.

Expansion

Expansion was slow to begin with but twenty years later there were over four thousand five hundred looms at work on the banks of the Hooghly. Periods of prosperity were followed by rapid increases in the number of mills and the amount of machinery and it usually happened that the productive capacity outstripped the consumption and depression followed boom. It was these circumstances which led to the foundation of the body now known as the Indian Jute Mills' Association, one of whose chief objects was and is to endeavour to regulate production in accordance with demand. The following table will give an idea of how the industry has grown—

Year	No. of Looms.
1859	192
1879	4,572
1899	14,000
1909	30,700
1919	39,500
1929	51,000
1939	68,700

As the mill industry progressed the hand-loom industry declined but it was not until the eighties of last century that hand-loom jute fabrics disappeared from the annual statistics of the export trade. It is interesting also to note the wide distribution of these hand-loom products which were shipped to Great Britain, France, Germany, North and South America, Burma, Java, China, Australia and Africa. These hand-loom goods did not, of course, have the regularity of factory-made goods and, in the early days of the Calcutta mill industry, manufacturers' who had to compete only with hand-loom goods, paid little heed to consistency in sizes, weights and counts. Dundee, on the other hand, had established a reputation for a consistently high standard of production and when Calcutta manufactures began to reach consumers who were accustomed to handling Dundee goods, much troble followed until Calcutta mills realised that they had to give their customers goods which conformed consistently with the specifications.

Extraction

The plants are usually cut just after flowering as this time is considered to be the best for yield of fibre though earlier cutting may give finer fibre. Plants cut after the seed pods have formed give a coarser fibre.

After cutting the plants are tied in bundles and left for two or three days to allow the leaves to wither and drop off. The bundles are then submerged in water where they are allowed to remain for a period which may vary from ten days to three weeks. This is to some extent determined by the size of the plants but it also depends on whether the water has been previously used. If it has been used before, the time required for retting is shorter. The retting process consists in the fermentation of the soft pith of the plant which dissolves and leaves the fibre which can then be easily separated from the stick. The fibre is then washed, dried and made up into bundles ready for the market.

Early History

Jute has been grown in Bengal from time immemorial and the fibre wss used for the making of twine, ropes, matting and even clothing for the poorer people, spinning and weaving being done by hand with primitive apparatus made mainly of bamboos. Coarse cloth, called Chuttees, or gunny chuts, was made in lengths suitable for sacks and during the last quarter of the eighteenth century and the first half of the nineteeth century a large export trade in hand made gunny bags and cloth had developed. It is recorded that in 1850-51 over nine million pieces valued at over Rs. 21 lakhs were exported from Calcutta and the height of the hand-loom industry was reached in 1865-66 when over 41 million pieces valued at over Rs. 83 lakhs were exported.

The first recorded instance of jute fibre being sent out of India is the dispatch of a sample by the Board of Trade in Bengal in 1791. At this time the Directors of the East India Company instructed their officers to investigate the suitability of indigenous fibres for the manufacture of ropes for their ships and from 1792 onwards it is recorded that small consignments of jute along with Indian grown flax and hemp were sent to London. In 1796-97 65 tons of jute fibre were exported—19 tons to England, 6 to the United States and 40 to Hamburg. Various other consignments followed and were mostly used for the manufacture of ropes, twine and door-mats. In 1820, at Abingdon, in Oxfordshire, jute was, for the first time in England, spun into yarn and used in the manufacture of carpets. Two years later a consignment reached Dundee which was then the centre of the flax industry in Scotland but the flax spinners were unable to make satisfactory use of it and, after the failure of experiments extending over three or four years, the remainder of the consignment was used for making ropes. Dundee flax spinners were not, however, to be beaten and they continued to experiment with the mixing of jute with flax with the result that the stipulation "free from Indian jute" became quite common in contracts for flax yarns and cloth. In 1835 the flax crop was a failure and adulteration with jute became so common that notice of it was taken in the press. The demand for jute was such that prices in London and Liverpool rose to £17 per ton.

Establishment of the Industry in India

The first power-driven mill for spinning jute yarns in India was erected by a Mr. George Acland in 1855 at Rishra on the Hooghly about twelve miles from Calcutta. At first it consisted of only 48 spindles but was increased soon afterwards to give an output of 8 tons per day. Later on weaving machinery was added but the first power-loom factory was that established at Baranagore in 1859 by the Borneo Company. It consisted of 192 looms with the necessary preparing and spinning machinery and it is interesting to note that, even at that early date, this company obtained the services of an expert chemist to advise them on suitable batching mediums. This expert was David Waldie, the founder of D. Waldie & Co., Ltd., and the discoverer of Chloroform.

Establishment of the Industry in Dundee

One of the early complaints against jute was that it did not spin well because it was too dry, lacking natural moisture. By a coincidence, Dundee was then one of the chief centres of the whaling industry and, in 1832 it was discovered that, by the use of whale oil, jute could be rendered suitable for spinning into yarns of the desired weights on power-driven machinery. In 1835 Dundee spinners were turning out pure jute yarns, the yarns which were used for the "adulteration" of flax canvas. Modifications of weaving machinery followed and, in 1833, Dundee factories were producing jute cloth. In the same year the Dutch Government placed an order for jute bags to be used instead of flax bags for coffee from the Dutch East Indies and by this move firmly established the factory-made jute bag on a commercial basis. In 1840 Dundee received its first cargo—1,025 bales—of jute shipped there direct from Calcutta.

The spinning and weaving of jute in Dundee continued to expand in the years following but the next important event in the history of the industry was the outbreak of war with Russia in 1854. The Baltic countries were then, as now, the main source of flax supplies and the war put a stop to these supplies while at the same time increasing the demand for sacks and canvas. From 1854 to 1857 the jute industry in Dundee experinced its first boom, jute proving to be the most suitable substitute for flax. Then in 1861-65 came the American Civil War when supplies of cotton from the Confederate States were seriously curtailed by the Federal blockade and the Dundee jute industry again experienced a period of prosperity and expansion.

Consumption

In the days of the hand-loom industry and before jute manufacture was established abroad, the consumption of raw jute in India exceeded the exports of raw jute but, as the factory industry developed in Dundee, on the continent of Europe and in America, exports of raw jute increased rapidly and for many years the quantity of jute exported exceeded that consumed by the mills in India. The expansion of the mill industry in India gradually brought about a change and in 1909-10 Indian mills for the first time consumed a greater quantity than consumers abroad. This continued to be the case until 1927-28 when exports of raw jute again reached parity with those of jute manufactures. After two years exports of raw material declined but in 1934-35, owing to the voluntary restriction of manufacture, the exports of manufactures were again less than exports of raw material. This did not last long as Indian mills again increased their working hours and consumption. The following table compares the annual consumption of mills in India with the quantity of raw jute and jute manufactures exported in recent years :—

Year		Indian Mill's Consumption Tons	Exports of Raw Jute Tons	Exports of Manufactures Tons
1934-35	...	967,000	783,000	713,000
1935-36	...	1,048,000	739 000	783,000
1936-37	...	1,254,000	872,000	1,022,000
1937-38	...	1,340,000	666,000	999,000
1938-39	...	1,167,000	697,000	953,000

Factors Determining Size of Crop

As the demand for Jute Manufactures expanded so the crop increased. The extent of cultivation has, however, varied from year to year, the chief determining factors being weather conditions and prices. Given suitable weather conditions the main factor is the price prevailing during the sowing season. Another factor is the stock of old crop which cultivators are holding at sowing time but the cultivators' memories are short and they are more easily influenced by future prospects based on the prices obtainable at sowing time than on the prices they secured for the previous season's crop or the amount of it which is still unsold.

In the following table are given estimates of the outturn from 1920 to 1939 based on the actual arrivals of jute in Calcutta and the exports from Chittagong. It will be observed that there is a sudden increase in the crop in 1926-27 and that large crops were produced in the four years following and it may be pointed out that the season 1925-26 was one when prices touched record high levels. Prices continued relatively high till 1929-30 after which the accumulation of unconsumed stocks together with the depression in world trade brought about a slump in prices which was followed by a drastic curtailment of the crop. Since then efforts have been made by official and unofficial propaganda to regulate sowings in accordance with prospects of demand but not much success has been achieved. The Government of Bengal have now, however, obtained legislative sanction for compulsory regulation of sowings. A census was taken of the area under jute in 1940 and compulsory restriction of the acreage may be resorted to in respect of the 1941 crop :—

1st July to 30th June	Thousands of Bales (400 lbs. Net)
1920-21	75,92
1921-22	72,12
1922-23	57,90
1923-24	88,49
1924-25	87,18
1925-26	89,89
1926-27	122,48
1927-28	112,72
1928-29	104,42
1929-30	102,94
1930-31	100,75
1931-32	65,41
1932-33	86,63
1933-34	89,44
1934-35	97,91
1935-36	81,49
1936-37	106,97
1937-38	99,58
1938-39	80,12

In these statistics no account has been taken of village consumption which is estimated at 1½ to 2 lakhs of bales annually, of stocks remaining upcountry at the end of each season, or of arrivals by road. Stocks retained upcountry are often considerable and were believed to be very large in the years 1927 to 1929. Formerly statistics of road arrivals were available but they were discontinued some years ago. Since the advent of the motor lorry, road traffic has, however, increased and the 2 per cent usually added to cover this traffic may not be sufficient.

Development of Export Trade

In the early days of the jute industry in Dundee jute manufacturers concentrated mainly on sacking and coarse fabrics but, as the industry developed, they turned their attention to finer cloth. So in Calcutta for many years little attempt was made to produce anything but heavy sacking and coarse hessian. The superiority of Dundee goods was for long complacently accepted but, as Indian labour became more skilled and manufactures more enterprising Calcutta mills began to turn out a better class of goods. In the nineties of last century Calcutta goods established themselves in the North American burlap market where there had been up to then a strong prejudice in favour of Dundee goods. The proportion of machinery engaged in the manufacture of hessian cloth gradually increased but it was not until 1903 that the number of looms engaged in the manufacture of hessian cloth exceeded that of those employed on sacking and it was some years later still until the output of hessian cloth in tons surpassed that of sacking.

Statistics of the export trade in the early days are somewhat scanty as the official returns give the quantity only in yards of cloth and numbers of bags which form no real guide to the actual volume. Tonnage figures are available from 1918-19. The following table will give an idea ot the growth of the export trade in the last century.

Exports of Manufactured Jute Goods

	Quinquennial Average Thousands of Rupees.
1887-1892	2,42,88
1892-1897	4,17,04

	Quinquennial Average Thousands of Rupees.
1897-1902	6,91,39
1902-1907	11,81,84
1907-1912	16,82.62
1912-1917	31,31,95
1917-1922	46,99,.0
1922-1927	42,31,38

Annual Exports

	Tons.	Thousands of Rs.
1927-28	884,700	53,65,53
1928-29	911,500	56,90,49
1929-30	958,000	51,92,68
1930-31	766,600	31,85,80
1931-32	663,600	21,92,42
1932-33	679,700	21,71,18
1933-34	672,200	21,37,49
1934-35	684,700	21,46 83
1635-36	752,000	23,48.95
1936-37	971,600	27,94,38
1937-38	1,020,400	29,07.76
1938-39	965,200	26,21,97
1939-40	*Not available	48,76,17

The value of the jute goods exported reached its peak in 1928-29 when it was nearly fifty-seven crores of rupees and the greatest volume was in 1937-38 when it exceeded one million tons. The highest value per ton was, however, in 1918-19, when it was Rs. 772 and the lowest value coincided with the greatest volume in 1937-38 when the value per ton was only Rs.285.

As the Crimean War aud the American Civil war had brought prosperity to the Dundee industry so the war of 1914-18 gave a great impetus to the jute industry in Calcutta. Huge orders were received for sand-bags but these were not the only jute goods required for war purposes, sacks and bags of all kinds being required for the transport of foodstuffs and other materials to the Armies in the field and the Calcutta industry experienced a period of unparalleled prosperity. With various vicissitudes this prosperity continued on a smaller scale until the world-wide trade depression of the nineteen-thirties set in and a glance at the foregoing table of exports reveals how the industry fared. The slum was not, however, entirely due to the trade depression but in large measure to the expansion of productive capacity which, as was pointed out above, has in all periods of prosperity, tended to outstrip the demand.

Some months before the outbreak of the present war the Indian industry received large orders from the British Government for sand-bags and further orders were received after war was declared. Calcutta mills have also been engaged in the manufacture of other materials such as canvas and camouflage cloth and experiments are being carried on with a view to producing other goods to meet war requirements.

Crop Expansion

From being a comparatively crop producing fibre for a cottage industry jute-growing has expanded until it is the most important money crop of the peasantry of North-east India. In spite of that its cultivation has not been to any great extent more widely distributed than in its early days. There has, however, been some extension in recent years in Assam, where settlers from Bengal have been chiefly responsible for this development. Regular statistics of acreage and outturn of the jute crop in the early days are not available until the nineties and no estimates of the crop appear to have been made until the publication of Hem Chunder Kerr's report in which it was estimated that, in 1872, the area under jute in Bengal —which at that time included Bihar and Orissa—was 926,000 acres with an outturn of 1,35,68.000 maunds. In 1888 the outturn was estimated at 42 lakhs of bales (400 lbs. net). Annual Forecasts of the acreage and outturn began to be issued in 1892-93 and in that year the outturn was estimated at 57 lakhs of bales. This was regarded as inadequate for consumers' needs and Dundee Manufactures sent representations through the India Office suggesting that steps should be taken to increase the size of the crop. Propaganda was undertaken by the Government of Bengal and seed of approved varieties was distributed in following seasons. In the early years of the present century the Bengal Department of Agriculture commenced experiments with a view to discovering the varieties which gave the best outturn, those best suited to particular districts and the effect of manuring, etc. Investigation has been continuous since then and new varieties have been developed which give higher yields of fibre per acre though, at times, there have been complaints from the trade that has been achieved at the expense of quality.

Overseas Markets

In recent years overseas consumers of raw jute have taken, on an average, about forty per cent of the crop. As is natural from its early connection with the industry and its development, Great Britain is the largest overseas customer. taking between twenty and twenty-five per cent of the total exports of raw jute. Germany, the United States of America and France are also, in normal circumstances, large consumers. In recent years continental Europe has taken on an average more than fifty per cent of the total exports and, as these markets are now almost entirely shut off the seriousness of the present situation can be readily appreciated. The table given on this page shows the volume and value of exports in recent years to the principal consuming countries.

The United Kingdom demand is mainly for good qualities of jute and tossa, and Dundee is the chief destination of the exports of daissee fibre. Exports to Germany were largely of lower qualities. France was a customer for fine jute but most of the continental countries took lower qualities which is borne out in the difference in standard between Dundee grades and Outport grades. The U.S.A. are a good market for tossa for carpet yarns.

Volume & Value of Exports in Recent Years

	1936-37		1937-38		1938-39	
	Tons.	Lakhs of Rupees.	Tons.	Lakhs of Rupees.	Tons.	Lakhs of Rupees
United Kingdom ...	189,000	3,48	145,000	2,81	181,000	3,46
Germany ...	134,000	2,36	143,000	2,86	138,000	2,70
Belgium ...	70,000	1,24	55,000	1,05	48,000	74
France ...	86,000	1,58	65,000	1,35	76,000	1,50
Italy ...	76,000	1,40	73,090	1,51	46,000	91
U. S. A. ...	88,000	1,59	99,000	1,85	31,000	67
Japan ...	35,000	58	15,000	28	14,000	27

Development and Competition

For many years Indian mills were content to restrict their activities to the manufacture of standard sizes of hessian cloth and standard makes of bags. In recent years more attention has been paid to what are known as specialities and Indian mills are now turning out canvas, linoleum hessian, webbing, felting, etc. A development resulting from the war is the production of a union canvas made of cotton warp and jute weft. Other experiments are in progress and the Indian Jute Mills Association a few years ago set up a Research Department where problems connected with manufacture such as rot-proofing, waterproofing, etc., are receiving the attention of experts. Some years ago the Government of India set up a body known as the Indian Central Jute Committee and it has also established a Laboratory for Technological Research in Calcutta as well as an Agricultural Research Centre at Dacca. At present its activities are confined to the investigation of problems connected with raw jute as far as the spinning of the fibre but it is intended to undertake further experiments at an early date.

At the present time the industry is faced with many competitors. New fibres are being encouraged in many countries in the name of national self-sufficiency even if they cannot compete economically with jute. Mechanical harvesting of crops and bulk handling at ports and in transit are other threats to the industry. It is realised, therefore, that not only must efforts be made to meet this-competition but also new uses must be found for jute and jute goods and it is hoped that the researches and experiments now being carried out will achieve this object.

Exports of Raw Jute

The following statement gives a good idea of development of the export market for raw material and the importance of raw jute exports in India's foreign trade. The largest exports recorded in one year were 897,000 tons in 1923-24 but the highest value per ton was Rs. 586 in 1925-26.

Year.	Quinquennial Average Tons.	Thousands of Rupees.
1887-1892	509,700	7,40,56
1892-1897	559,400	9.51,76
1897-1902	617,900	9,56,16
1902-1907	702,000	15,75,49
1907-1912	756,000	18,18,85
1912-1917	658,000	20 54,35
1917-1922	442,000	14,85,67
1922-1927	656,000	27,26,96
	Annual	
1927-28	891,900	30,66,26
1928-29	897,900	32,34,92
1929-30	806,900	27,17,38
1930-31	620,000	12,88,47
1931-32	586,100	11,18,81
1932-33	563,000	9,73,03
1933-34	748,200	10,93,26
1934-35	752,300	10,87,11
1935-36	771,200	13,70,51
1936-37	820,600	14,77,10
1937 38	747,300	14,71,92
1938-39	690,400	13,39,67

(The above figures are for the Government year April to March).

Manufactures

The United States of America is at present India's best customer for manufactured jute goods. They take about sixty per cent in volume of the annual exports of hessian cloth, known in the States as burlap. In value they take about thirty per cent of the total exports of jute manufactures of all kinds. The Argentine Republic is the next largest customer for hessian cloth but its takings are only about one-third of those of the U. S. A. The United Kingdom takes about ten per cent of the exports of hessian cloth and Canada, Australia, the Philippines and the Straits Settlements are also good customers. The United Kingdom is also the principal customer for hessian bags and takes about thirty per cent of the exports. In the past two years this proportion has, of course, been considerably increased by the exports of sandbags to the British Government and to private customers. The United Kingdom also ranks as the biggest buyer of sacking cloth and it is also among the bigger buyers of gunny bags. In fact it takes, on an average, about ten per cent of the total exports of manufactured jute goods. Australia is the largest buyer of sacking bags, the exports being chiefly cornsacks and woolpacks. All the Indo-China and Malayan countries are good customers for heavy bags and there are also large exports of heavy goods to South and West Africa.

As mentioned above, Australia is the chief market for cornsacks and woolpacks but she also takes considerable quantities of bran bags and twill sacking. The market for twills includes Egypt and the Levant, South America and South and West Africa. The East Indies and the Far East are markets for heavy C's. South America (Chili) takes nitrate bags and there is a wide selection of markets for sugar salt and flour bags. Grain sacks are made chiefly for Egypt and the Levant. The cement bag trade with the United Kingdom was formerly important but was lost when the cement trade adopted paper bags. Some of this trade has been recovered as a result of the paper shortage due to the war. The effect of the war has not been so serious for the trade in manufactures as for the trade in the raw jute as the countries of Europe which are now cut off manufactured their own requirements from imported jute and took less than 5 per cent of the exports of manufactures.

However, if this outline serves to reveal only a few aspects of the amazing variety of supplies which Empire manufacture can obtain in India, it will have amply served its purpose.

Decorative Veneers

The development of modern techniques of furniture-making and the increased use of decorative veneers have opened a wide field for Indian timbers. In addition to rosewood, sissoo (with deep brown ring figuring), padauk, teak (often with a fine ripple figuring) and laurel (described as one of the world's most handsome woods with its ripple marked, and banded effects), the Forest Research Institute also suggest Kokko (*Albizzia lebbek*), a handsome golden brown wood streaked with lighter and darker bands, and having a golden sheen from the Andamans; White and Black Siris (*Albezzia procera* and *odoratissima*), similar to Kokko.

Poon (*Calophyllum tomentosum*), quietly ornamental, reddish brown with darker streaks and available at west coast ports; and Toon (*Cedrela toona*) light pink turning later to reddish brown and available in the United Provinces, Bengal, Assam and Madras.

Then there are the exceptionally handsome veneers of Chick rassy (*Chuckrasia tabularis*), handsomely figured with a satin-like sheen and golden brown. Comes from Kurseong, Bengal and Assam.

Mahogany is available in Madras, and Silver-grey Wood (*Terminalia bilata*) from the Andamans is a grey timber banded with darker streaks which is good for matched veneer work. Popular in Britain, Mundani (*Acrocarpus fraxinifolius* has light red heartwood with darker lines. The figuring is either a wavy grain or fiddle back; comes from Bengal, Madras, Coorg and Malabar Coast.

Silky Oak (*Grevillea robusta*) has a very ornamental silver grain and is obtainable from the Nilgiris.

Finally, Walnut (*Juglans regia*) from Hazara, Chamba and Bashahr (Punjab) and Kashmir, is considerably used in Europe and America as a veneer. The Indian form is rich greyish brown in colour, often with handsome figuring. Small quantities of walnut burs are obtainable.

(These woods are recommended by the Forest Research Institute for sliced veneers).

Minor Forest Products

A side-line of India's forestry is a large variety of papermaking materials. of which Rs. 5½ lakhs worth are exported annually. In addition to a number of timbers which might be used for such purposes there are also very large growths of bamboos and grasses such as Ramsar, Ulla and Sabai or Bhabar (the Indian equivalent of Esparto), Kraft, writing and printing papers can be produced. India already has a number of pulp and papers mills of her own and some 33,000 tons of bamboo pulp and 22,000 tons of Sabai grass pulp were produced annually before the war. About 70,000 tons of paper is made.

Since hostilities broke out work has increased considerably. Lac, gums, resins and oil-bearing tree seeds have already been described, but another valuable range of minor forest products are the raw materials for medical and perfumery purposes. Chief of these is, of course, sandalwood oil and also sandalwood which is exported for the oil to be distilled abroad.

Of several essential oils obtainable in India perhaps Palmarosa, from Rosha grass, is the most important. Containing 90 per cent Geraniol, it is the best source of this important ingredient for synthetic perfumes. Indian lemon grass oil contains 70-75 per cent citral and about 7,000 cwt, is exported annually.

There are a number of others including Linalol and Vetivert oil and it is believed that India could easily compete with Java in the essential oil trade since raw materials are available in abundance here.

Modern chemical developments provide many openings for forest raw materials. For example, a new type of detergent which has come into prominence has lauric acid as a basis. Dr. S. Krishna of the Forest Research Institute, has pointed out that the fats from the seeds of Actinodaphne Hookeri and several Litsea species, which belong to India's laurel family, yield as much as 90-96 per cent of trilaurin, whereas the present raw materials—cocoanut and palm kernel oil—only yield 45 per cent of lauryl glycerides.

Two tree seed oils which have recently taken their place in modern medicine are Hydnocarpus oil from Hydnocarpus Wightiana growing on the west coast, and

Chaulmoogra oil from the seeds of Taraktogenos Kurzii, found in Assam, Bengal and Burma Both oils are used in the treatment of leprosy.

Margosa (*nem*) oil from the seeds of Melia azardirachta which grows all over India and Burma, is regarded in Indian medicine as a specific for skin diseases and is used in medicinal soap in India.

Drug plants which grow wild in Indian forests include Atropa belladonna, Hyoscyamus, Podophyllum emodi, Artemisia brevifolia, Ephedra species and Strychnosum nux-vomica. There are many others, but these are the only ones which have been exploited on any large scale. Nux-vomica is the most important as an export, about 33,000 cwt. being sent abroad.

Artemisia and Ephedra have come into the export market in very recent years because of disturbed conditions in countries (notably China and Spain) which previously had a monopoly. There is a very considerable demand and in 1938 America bought 446,300 lbs. of Ephedra from India.

Other drugs indigenous to India include mentha, liquorice, aconite, juniper and valerian, and Col. Chopra, the famous Calcutta pharmacologist, claims that India possesses such a diversity of climate that it would be possible to cultivate in some parts of the country almost every drug of importance.

Another medical substance which can be produced in large quantities in India is papain, the dried milky juice of the rind of the papaya fruit (*Caurica papaya*). It is a digestive enzyme valued in medicine and can be employed in place of animal pepsin. It is also used in chewing gum. At present Ceylon is the chief exporter.

Two Indian vitamin sources are shark liver oil, stated by the Public Health Commissioner with the Government of India to be "an exceptionally potent source of vitamin A" and the Indian gooseberry (*Amla*), a very rich source of vitamin C. Both would provide very cheap raw materials for such purposes.

Exports of Raw Materials to Countries in the Eastern Group

	1938-39 Rs.	1939-40 Rs.
Aden and Dependencies	92,73,931	77,56,383
Ceylon	5,09,11,112	6,37,27,118
Burma	10,03,36,903	12,31,18,106
Straits Settlements	2,03,97,045	2,62,34,470
Hong Kong	78,26,998	94,73,745
Union of South Africa ...	1,49,21,824	2,83 96,799
Mauritius and Deps.	88,44 596	90,86,158
Zanzibar and Pemba	7,76,309	9,83,603
Kenya Colony	45,88,042	66,65,282
Australia	2,97,29,803	5,49,69,757
New Zealand	43,17,984	73,33,577
Other British Possessions (in which some of the Eastern Group territories are included)	2,29,50,119	3,34,69.638

(Statistics extracted from "Accounts Relating to the Sea-Borne Trade and Navigation of British India," for March 1940, Department of Commercial Intelligence and Statistics, India.)

India's Mineral Resources

One of the most striking features of India's economy during the last seven years has been the steady rise in her output of minerals. In 1938 the value of these was Rs. 34,21,87 929 or £ 25,536,412.

The principal of these, coal, iron and petroleum, are true measures of the industrial prosperity of a country, and to these may be added building materials and clays, which include stone, brick, cement, lime, pottery, tiles and road-metal.

Of the other mineral products of which the output figures have reached the million sterling mark in these seven years, manganese ore and mica are largely exported and the gold production is practically restricted to the four mines operating at Kolar in the Mysore State. Salt is in a position by itself. Its manufacture is a Government concern, and the value of the production, excluding the duty on it, varies between half a million to three-quarters of a million sterling. In addition India imports about half the value of her internal production, chiefly from Aden, Germany and Egypt, to supply the needs of Bengal and the adjoining country.

Spectacular percentage increases have taken place in the outputs of what may be termed the industrial minerals :—ilmenite, monazite, chromite, kyanite, magnesite and other refractories, gypsum, bauxite and graphite, though the individual amounts are not large. These are principally exported.

Building Materials

The building material for ordinary village uses in the Indian plains is essentially mud or silt, either used by itself or in the form of sun-dried or kiln-fired brick, set in mud mortar, or in lime made from *kankar*, the concentrations of carbonate of lime found in the alluvium of the plains, or from the deposits of excellent limestone in which Peninsular India is rich.

Of recent years numerous potteries run on up-to-date lines have arisen all over India, in and these tiles, ordinary bricks and fire-bricks, glazed earthenware pipes and sanitary fittings, telegraph insulators, domestic pottery and ornamental ware of excellent quality are made from ordinary clay, fire-clay and china-clay.

Every town has its associated brick-fields and there is a large internal trade in lime, burnt in localities favourably situated with regard to limestone and fuel.

The building-stones of India are justly famed through the magnificent Buddhist and Moslem architecture of Northern India and the ornate temples of the Peninsula.

In Northern India, the great expanse of the Vindhya system yields unsurpassable sandstones, in colours ranging from cream or buff to rich reddish-brown, from which gigantic blocks, thin slabs, and monoliths used for rafters and telegraph-poles, can be quarried. They are associated with limestones of excellent quality. The older marble of the Raialos is found in white, clouded grey and pink tints, and was used in the Taj Mahal at Agra and the Victoria Memorial in Calcutta, and there are many other varieties of white and coloured marble in Rajputana, one of which was used in the elaborately carved Jain temples of Dilwara.

The temple architecture of Southern India is largely carried out in granite and allied crystalline rocks, and in dolerite or epidiorite of so hard and tough a nature that the intricacy of the carving executed in it is well-nigh incredible.

Both the sandstones and the granites are admirably suited for public works of the strongest nature.

Amongst other well-known building-stones may be mentioned that from Porbandar, largely used in Bombay and Karachi, a soft foraminiferal limestone of sub-recent age, and the Karnul limestone of Shahabad in Hyderabad, which produces excellent flagstones and is also used for cement manufacture.

Slates are quarried near Dharmsala in the Kangra district, Punjab, and at Kund, near Rewari in the Gurgaon district, Punjab, and also near Monghyr in Bihar.

Bauxite

About 200,000 square miles of India are covered by the Deccan Trap, basalt which under suitable climatic conditions decomposes to form laterite. Laterite is a mixture of bauxite (aluminium hydroxide) and ferric hydroxide with some free silica and titania.

When the ferric hydroxide, silica and titania are low enough, the bauxite can be used commercially.

The production of Indian bauxite is chiefly from Katni in the Jubbulpore district, C. P., and Kaira district, Bombay, and for the last two years has been about 15,000 tons. Large deposits are known in Bilaspur and Mandala districts and Surguja and Jashpur States, C. P.. Kolhapur State, Bombay, Ranchi district, Bihar, and Jammu. Kashmir, and there are doubtless others still undiscovered, as bauxite is an ordinary-looking, clay-like rock, and is often covered by a layer of the ferruginous laterite.

It is believed that Indian bauxite is at present largely used as a filtering material in petroleum refineries, and for the manufacture of alum. Its utilisation for the preparation of aluminium, refractories and abrasives is now being undertaken.

Cement

The manufacture of cement started in India on a large scale in 1914, and since then the progress of the industry has been rapid. At present there are about 20 companies in operation, with a capacity of well over a million tons annually.

In most cases the limestone used belongs to the Vindhyans and can be so selected as to contain a considerable amount of the clay constituent required, the remainder if any, being made up from shales associated with the limestone, or from local surface silts. The small amount of gypsum necessary, 2 to 3 per cent, comes from Khewra in the Punjab, or from Jodhpur State.

Indian cement is made in several grades and is of such high quality that it has almost ousted imported cement. With the abundance of bauxite in India, there is likely to be an increasing production of aluminous rapid-hardening cement. India's great reserves of magnesite will also be invaluable in the manufacture of special cements.

Chromite

Chromite is mined in India at Hindubagh and Khanozai in Baluchistan, in the Shimoga, Hassan and Mysore districts of Mysore and west of Chaibasa, Singhbhum district, Bihar, and is known in several other localities.

The average production for the last three years (1936-37-38) has been 52,000 tons.

Most of the chromite is exported, but from the remainder chromite bricks of high quality are made for the steel industry.

Coal

The coalfields of India are of two ages, Lower Gondwana (Permian) and Tertiary which supply 98 and 2 per cent of the output respectively.

Coal-mining is India's most important mineral industry employing about 200,000 persons for an output of 28,342,906 tons in 1938, with an estimated value of Rs. 10,64,23,835 or £7,942,077. India comes ninth on the list of the world's coal-producing countries, with 2 per cent of the total.

The railways are the principal customers, taking about one-third of the output, followed by the iron and steel industry, which takes two and a half million tons annually, from which a recovery of about 71 per cent of hard coke is obtained. The remainder is distributed among factories, power-stations and smaller industrial concerns and the shipping industry. The domestic consumption of India has been estimated at about two million tons annually, which is negligible for a population of 330 million, but efforts are being made to popularise soft coke as a domestic fuel.

The last three years have seen a considerable increase in exports to foreign countries, chiefly Burma, Ceylon and the Far East, the figure for 1938 being 1,343,033 tons.

A Coal Grading Board, under Government, arranges for the classification and certification of the coal exported, so that buyers overseas may rely on the quality supplies. The following are the grades fixed by the Board :

Low Volatile Coals.

Selected Grade :—Up to 13 percent ash and over 7,000 calories or 12,600 B. T. Us.

High Volatile Coals.

Up to 11 per cent ash ; over 6,800 calories or 12,240 B. T. Us. and under 6 per cent moisture.

Grade No. 1—Up to 15 per cent ash and over 6,500 calories or 11,7000 B.T.Us	Up to 13 per cent ash ; over 6,300 calories or 11,340 B. T. Us. and under 9 per cent moisture.
Grade No. 2—Up to 18 per cent ash and over 6,000 calories or 10,800 B T.Us.	Up to 16 per cent ash ; over 6,000 calories or 10,800 B.T.Us and under 10 per cent moisture.

Grade No. 3—All coals inferior to the above.

Dr. *C. S. Fox* has estimated the total amount of coal in the Lower Gondwana Coalfields of India to be 60,000 million tons, of which 20,000 million tons may be considered workable, *i.e.*, it is in seams over four feet in thickness, averages 20 per cent ash (does not exceed 25 per cent on a mixture-free basis) and lies within 1,000 feet of surface.

Reserves of good quality coal, in seams of more than four feet in thickness, an ash content of 16 per cent on a moisture-free basis, and lying within 2,000 feet of the surface are now 4,850 million tons. Of this about 1,400 million tons are coking coal.

Coal was discovered in the Raniganj field, about 130 miles from Calcutta, in 1774, but mining did not really start until 1814. From that date until the railway reached Raniganj in 1855, coal was boated in Calcutta on the Damoder river. By the beginning of this century other fields, especially Jharia, had been opened out by railway connections and expansion of output was uninterrupted until 1919, with an all-India output of 22,628,039 tons in that year. In the following year it dropped to 18 million tons in round figures and since then it has fluctuated between 20 million tons and 24 millton tons, but a distinct improvement set in 1937 (25 million tons) and 1938 (28·3 million tons).

Pit's mouth values, which had kept between Rs. 2-8 and Rs. 3-8 a ton from the beginning of the century to the middle of the great War, stood above Rs. 7 during 1922-24 and then commenced a slump to between Rs. 2-14 and Rs. 2-12 in 1934-36, from which they are only now recovering.

The coalfields of Bihar and Bengal account for about nine-tenth of India's output ;—Jharia, Raniganj, Bokre, Giridih and Karanpura being the principal ones in order of output.

The Jharia field is the main source of coking coal of metallurgical quality. It contains 18 workable seams of a total thickness of 200 feet.

In the Raniganj field the coals of the lower measures (Barakar) are low volatile, high fixed carbon, the better of which form hard coke ; those of the upper measures (Raniganj) are mostly high volatile coals, and are non-coking with the exception of two seams. In the upper measures there are six seams aggregating 50 feet of coal, two of them 18 feet thick, and in the lower measures 12 workable seams, with not less than four feet of coal in each. All the Raniganj coals are good steam-raisers.

The Bokaro field is remarkable for the great thickness of its seams, up to a maximum of 126 feet of solid coal, which enables them to be won in vast open quarries. Two of the seams are of good coking quality.

The Giridih field, though small, produces the best metallurgical coke in India, made from the slack, while the lump coal is burnt in locomotives by the State Railways.

The large Karanpura field has recently been opened out. It also has remarkably thick seams up to a maximum of 90 feet, and some of its coal yields coke, if mixed with certain Jharia coals.

Outside Bihar and Orissa there are important coalfields in the Pench Valley of the Central Provinces, in the Korea and Talcher States of the Eastern States Agency and at Singareni and Tandur in Hyderabad State.

The remaining coalfields have each outputs of less than 300,000 tons annually.

Gypsum

Gypsum is the bedded variety of the mineral which in its crystalline form is known as selenite and when massive as alabaster. When calcined it is the well-known 'Plaster of Paris.'

It is a mineral characteristic of arid conditions, deposited in lagoons and salt lakes, and in India is widely developed in immense quantities, in the Cretaceous beds of Trichinopoly district, Madras, the Eocene of Baluchistan, Punjab, and the North-West Frontier Province, and associated with the Salt Marl in the Salt Range ; sub-recent deposits are those of Nagpur in Jodhpur and Jamsar in Bikaner.

The production of India has reached 70,000 tons, chiefly from Jhelum district, Punjab, Bikaner and Jodhpur States, and Trichinopoly district, Madras.

Gypsum is extensively used in cements and plasters, as paints and fillers, and as a 'top-dressing' in agriculture.

Ilmenite, Monazite and Zircon

It is convenient to treat these three minerals together, as they are all found (with rutile, garnet, &c.) concentrated by wave action, in the beach sands of Travancore for about a hundred miles along the coast on each side of Cape Comorin, in the extreme south of India. They are recovered by washing and magnetic separation.

The industry started in 1911, on monazite alone, which was then used as a source of thoria for gas mantles, and in 1918 the output reached 2,118 tons. It then practically died out, to one hundredweight in 1925, presumably owing to the supplanting of incandescent gas, lighting by electricity, but in 1922 the recovery of ilmenite and zircon had commenced and increased so remarkably that in 1938 the output of ilmenite attained 252,220 tons and of zircon 1,450 tons.

Ilmenite is the source of titania, a valuable white paint and used in certain alloys; zircon yields zirconia, a high-grade refractory, and also an alloy material.

Concurrently the output of monazite recovered, rising to 5,221 tons in 1938. This is no doubt partly due to cheaper costs, as monazite is now a by-product in the much larger scale production of ilmenite, but also to the discovery of uses for the Cerium in monazite, in such compounds as the spark-producing elements in pocket lighters, the tips of tracer bullets, and in searchlights and ultra-violet lamps. India is now the world's main source of these minerals.

Iron

In ancient times the people of India seem to have acquired a fame for metallurgical skill, and the reputation of the famous *wootz* steel, which was certainly made in India long before the Christian era and exported to the Mediterranean lands to be worked into the 'Damascus' blades, has probably contributed to the general impression that the country is rich in iron-ore of a high class. Its qualities, however, were not derived from any special virtues in the ore, but from the fuel, charcoal, and from the painstaking treatment of the iron, after the reduction of the ore, by repeated hammerings, re-heatings and carburisation in charcoal, anticipating the cementation process for crucible steel.

One of the finest examples of ancient Indian craftsmanship is the pillar at the Kutb Minar, south of Delhi; this is made of skilfully forged wrought iron, 23 feet inches in length, over a foot in diameter, and weighing six tons. It is believed to date from about 415 A.D.

It is true that throughout the Peninsula, which is largely occupied by ancient crystalline rocks, quartz-haematite and quartz magnetite schists are very common, but most of these occurrences consist of quartz and iron-ore so closely interbanded that only a highly siliceous ore of low grade (up to 40 per cent iron) can be obtained, and magnetic concentration has not been successful, owing to the intimate intermixture of the quartz, magnetite and haematite.

For a number of years, however, haematite ore-bodies of great size and richness have been recognised in a belt running through the Singhbhum district of Bihar, the Eastern States, and Orissa. and constituting what is one of the most important groups of iron-ore deposits of the world.

It has been calculated that there are 3,600,000,000 tons of this high-class haematite available, forming the upper portions of great ridges, rising 1,500 feet or more above the plain, along which for many miles the ore can be cheaply quarried in benches, by gangs of unskilled labour, and loaded straight into trucks, little or no selection being necessary.

At, for instance, Tata's Naomundi Mine, the average day's run of ore is 62 per cent iron, and they can arrange consignments to the works of anything up to 69 per cent iron, the latter containing only 1 per cent of impurities, theoretically pure haematite containing 70 per cent of iron and 30 per cent of oxygen. Ore containing less than 60 per cent iron is not used by the two large producing companies; the Mysore Iron and Steel Works use 55 per cent to 64 per cent ore.

Between 1830 and 1875 many attempts were made to produce iron on a commercial scale, using charcoal as a fuel, but all were failures, in spite of the genius of J. M. Heath, who first used manganese in the production of steel.

In 1875 trials were made of Indian coke at Kulti, on the Raniganj coalfield, at a plant which afterwards became that of the Bengal Iron Co., Ltd., and first succeeded in smelting iron on modern lines.

The first furnaces of the Tata Iron and Steel Co., Ltd., were blown in in 1911-12, followed ten years later by the Indian Iron and Steel Co., Ltd., and the charcoal-iron furnace of the Mysore Iron and Steel Works.

Since the beginning of the present century the annual production of iron-are in India has risen from 65,000 tons to 2,743,675 tons in 1938, representing 1,539,889 tons of iron smelted.

India is now the second largest producer of iron and steel in the Empire, excelled only by the United Kingdom.

Her reserves of ore are about three-quarters of those of the United States and are of better quality, than the bulk of the American deposits.

The ores are believed to have been originally banded haematite quartzites, the quartz of which has been leached and replaced to some extent by haematic.

Typically they run about 64 per cent of iron, sulphur is usually below 0·03 per cent, and phosphorus varies from 0·03 to 0.8 per cent. Titanium is low.

As these reserves are much larger than the available amount of coal suitable for making metallurgical coke, it would seem that India can, sooner or later, spare great quantities of ore for export.

In 1938, 264,151 tons of ore were exported to Japan. In that year, the total exports of pig-iron from India were 525,254 tons, of which 323,046 went to Japan, and 129,824 to the United Kingdom.

Kyanite and Sillimanite

Kyanite and sillimanite (and andalusite) are sillicates of alumina, all of which, when heated sufficiently highly, change to 'mullite.'

Mullite is a valuable refractory material for the construction of furnaces, especially for glass manufacture and in electrical work.

Nearly all the Indian kyanite at present on the market is quarried at Lapsa Buru, Kharsawan State, Bihar, and the average production for the last three years (1936-37-38) has been approximately 27,000 tons.

Sillimanite-corundum deposits are known in Nongstoin State in Assam, and at Pipra in Rewa, but transport difficulties have been against production ; there has also been a small output of sillimanite from Travancore.

Magnesite

Magnesite production commenced in India in 1902, from the "Chalk hills" in the Salem district, Madras, where the quantity of the mineral is practically inexhaustible ; it occurs in a network of veins over an area of 4½ square miles, standing up to a height of 140 feet in hillocks, from which it is quarried.

It is calcined to form either 'caustic' magnesia at a temperature of about 800° C or 'dead-burnt' at about 1,700° C. Caustic magnesia is the principal ingredient of 'Sorel' or 'oxy-chloride' cements and dead-burnt magnesia is a refractory used to line the furnaces in basic steel process, for which the bricks made in India are stated to be superior to the Australian bricks which they have supplanted.

The Indian production is about 26,000 tons annually, of which roughly 2,500 tons is from Mysore and the remainder from Salem.

Manganese-Ore

Deposits of manganese-ore are widely distributed in the ancient rocks of Peninsular India, and since the beginning of the century India has shared the position of the world's chief producer with Russia, sometimes one leading, sometimes the other.

As the demand for manganese is governed by its uses in the manufacture of steel, it is subject to great vicissitudes as the heavy industries rise and fall with the calls from trade and the manufacture of munitions.

This was particularly the case during the world trade slump in the years 1930-33, when India's production dropped to a little over a fifth of that of five years previous, with a value of less than one-nineteenth.

Recently, however, there has been a recovery, with the result that the production of India, for the first time in the history of the industry exceeded one million tons in 1937.

The United Kingdom, Japan, the United States and France, have been the principal customers.

The principal areas in which manganese-ore is mined are the Balaghat, Nagpur and Bhandara districts in the Central Provinces, Sandur State and Vizagapatam in Madras, the Panch Mahals district in Bombay, Singhbhum district in Bihar and the adjoining States of Keonjhar and Bonai.

The ores are mixtures psilomelane, braunite, and pyrolusite, and tend to form hills, so that quarrying is easily and cheaply carried out by gangs of unskilled labour. Many of the ore-bodies are of great size. The main disability under which the industry labours is the distance of the larger deposits from the nearest seaports.

Steatite

This mineral, also known as soapstone, potstone talc and agalmatolite, and in its powdered form as "French chalk" is one of the most variously used industrial minerals, in multitudinous minor ways, from idols and slate-pencils to switchboards and chemical tanks, and, powdered, from anti-adhesives, polishers and fillers to face-powders.

The annual production of India is reported as about 18,500 tons in 1938, the chief sources being Jaipur State, Guntur district in Madras, and Jubbulpore district in the Central Provinces, but there are numerous other minor deposits and probably a good deal of it does not come into the statistics.

Mica

India is the world's leading producer of sheet mica, which is mined mainly in Hazaribagh and Gaya districts in Bihar and Nellore in Madras, and to a minor extent in other districts in Madras and in Tonk State and Ajmer-Merwara in Rajputana, about 80 per cent coming from Bihar and most of the remainder from Nellore. This pre-eminence in the world's markets is due largely to the excellent quality of the so-called "Bengal ruby" mica of Bihar, but also to the great manual dexterity and cheapness of the aboriginals, mainly women and children, who trim and split the mica with crude soft-iron sickles (or shears in Nellore). So much is this the case that there is an appreciable import of block mica into India, to be re-exported in the form of splittings. Mica has been used in India for centuries for decorative and medicinal purposes.

The mica occurs as "books," giant crystals which have been found, exceptionally, as large as 10 feet in diameter, in great veins of pegmatite traversing mica schists. The mica, which is muscovite, occurs with felspar and quartz, and other minerals such as beryl, which from Ajmer is exported as an ore of beryllium.

The export of mica from India amounted to 297,343 cwts. in 1937, most of it going to the United Kingdom and the United States.

Petroleum

Petroleum has been successfully exploited in the Tertiary rocks at the extreme ends of the great plain of Indo-Gangetic alluvium, at Digboi in Assam and in the Attock district, Punjab, south-west of Rawalpindi at both of which places there are refineries.

The Digboi oil is particularly rich in wax. South of Digboi, in the Surma Valley of Cachar, are two other fields, Badarpur, which has proved disappointing, and Masipur, from which output has not yet been obtained.

In Attock petroleum is being produced from two fields, Khaur and Dhulian, 8 miles apart, the latter having recently been most successful, after great perseverance in the face of difficulties at Khaur.

In 1938 the production of Digboi was 66 million gallons and of Attock 21·1 million gallons in round figures.

Sulphur

Large deposits of high-grade rock sulphur have been discovered at Koh-i-Sultan in Baluchistan by the Geological Survey of India.

to some extent replacing bleached goods. In coloured goods, the largest individual line probably consists of "lungis and sarongs," but prints also form a substantial part of the trade. India's sendings have consisted chiefly of lungis and sarongs and woven coloured goods, but during the last two or three years, a fair quantity of prints have also been exported. The immediate prospects for India in the Ceylon markets have probably improved as a result of the war, and this improvement has already been reflected to some extent in the exports for the year 1939-40 which were more than three million yards in excess of the previous year. A great deal, however, depends on the intensity of Japanese competition.

Exports to Palestine

From the statistics available, it would appear that the normal pre-war market in cotton piece-goods amounted to about 40 million yards per year of which about half were coloured goods—chiefly prints—and the other half equally divided between grey and bleached varieties. Almost two-thirds of the trade seem to have been held by Japan, the next largest supplier being the United Kingdom with about 13 per cent of the trade and the next Italy with about 8 per cent. India hitherto has had only a very small share of the trade, but since the war and particularly since Italy's entry into the war and the closure of the Mediterranean many enquiries have been received from Palestine by mills and merchants, and goods are being despatched *via* Basra, Baghdad and the trans-desert route. The freight charges of the combined sea, river and land journey are naturally high, but despite this handicap exports from this country are likely to increase substantially during the period of the war and India can confidently hope to obtain some of the trade previously held by Italy and other European enemy countries.

Exports to Rhodesia

No information is available as to the recent sendings of Indian cotton piece-goods and yarns to Southern and Northern Rhodesia from the Indian Sea-borne Trade returns, but from other sources it has been ascertained that previous to the war, the total annual piece-goods imports into Southern Rhodesia amounted to something like 30 million yards and into Northern Rhodesia about 10 million yards. This trade was apparently divided between United Kingdom and India, but United Kingdom's share of the market was apparently about seven times as great as that of India. Japan had a small export trade amounting to 1 million yards per annum with Northern Rhodesia. It has not been possible to ascertain exactly how Indian piece-goods reach Rhodesia but apparently a fair proportion go by rail from Lorenzo Marques and Beria through Portuguese East Africa.

Exports to South Africa

Up-to-date figures of the total piece-goods trade of the Union of South Africa and its mandated territory of South West Africa are not available at the time of writing, but it would appear that in 1937, the total imports of piece-goods into the Union of South Africa proper amounted to 220 million yards of which United Kingdom's share was 174 million yards and Japan's 39 million yards. Belgium also had a fairly substantial trade (chiefly in cotton blankets) amounting to 3 million yards and Italy and United States of America also had small shares. India's share of the trade was exceptionally small owing to her inability to compete against the United Kingdom and Japan with the import tariffs at presen in force. The United Kingdom's predominant position is largely due to the preferential rates of duties accorded to her vis-a-vis all other countries. With the greater prosperity brought about by higher gold prices the total imports of piece-goods now probably greatly exceed the above mentioned figures. The trade statistics of the mandated territory of South West Africa are given in values only. The figure for 1937 for cotton piece-goods was £99,000, of which £35,000 represented the value of British piece-goods imports and £4,500 the value of German imports. Imports from South Africa were valued at £59,000, but this must have represented the value of cotton goods originally imported from other countries.

The imports of cotton yarn into the Union of Soth Africa are comparatively small, but India exported an appreciable quantity (£283,000) for the first time in 1939-40.

As already stated, India's share of the South African piece-goods trade previous to the outbreak of the war was negligible, never exceeding 300,000 yards, but in 1939-40 there was a sudden jump to 4·2 million yards of which half a million yards consisted of white goods and the remainder was almost equally divided between grey and coloured goods. The prospects for a greater export trade in cotton piece-goods and yarn to the Union of South Africa are favourable since the Union is now cut off from the supplies previously obtained from Germany, Italy, Belgium and Holland, and Japan may not be able to ship as much as formerly owing to exchange difficulties. India should be able to supply substitutes for the cotton blankets previously imported from Belgium and a large portion of cloths required for the making up trade and the cotton bag making trade. Many of the bleached cloths produced in India should also be readily saleable in the South African market.

Exports to British East Africa

The territories included are Kenya Colony, Uganda, Tanganyika Territory and Zanzibar. The total pre-war cotton piece-goods market was something like 130 to 140 million square yards per annum. Cotton yarn imports were negligible. About 30 per cent of piece-goods imports were grey, 10 per cent plain bleached and the rest coloured goods. In the coloured goods range, slightly more than a third consisted of piece dyed and slightly less than a third each were printed goods and woven coloured fabrics. In addition to piece-goods more than 3 million cotton blankets per annum are imported. The grey piece-goods trade before the war was very largely in the hands of Japan, but India had a small share amounting to something like 1½ million square yards. In the bleached goods also, the market was almost entirely monopolised by Japan, her share being 10 times as large as that of the United Kingdom, the second largest supplier. In printed khangas, a speciality trade, Holland had the largest share of the market in pre-war years, but the United Kingdom also had a substantial share and Japan appeared to be making rapid progress in competition against both countries. In printed goods, Japan held more than 90 per cent of the market, but India appeared to be making some progress and the United Kingdom still retained a small share of the trade. In dyed piecegoods, the position was very similar to that in printed goods and in woven coloured goods, the United Kingdom before the war held the second place to Japan, but her total trade was only 10 per cent of that of her Far Eastern competitor. Small quantities of woven coloured goods were also sent by United Kingdom, Belgium and Holland.

Cotton Blanket Trade

The European countries were considerable suppliers of cotton blankets, Germany, Czechoslovakia, Holland, Belgium, Italy and France in that order being the countries chiefly concerned in this trade. Japan was also a considerable supplier of cotton blankets, her share of the tolal markets being something like 5 per cent. India also participated in the blanket trade in East Africa in pre-war years, but her share of the market was very small.

The Indian trade statistics show that India's total sendings of cotton piece-goods to British East Africa amounted to 8·1 million, 5·9 million and 6·6 million yards in the years 1937-38, 1938-39 and 1939-40 respectively. The comparatively high exports in 1937-38 were due to Japan's temporary difficulties arising out of war with China. The beginning of the effects of the European war to be found in the year 1939-40, the figures of which show some improvement on those of 1938-39. In the current year (1940-41), the upward trend of India's exports have continued at an increased pace. In cotton blankets, which India is well adapted to produce, the immediate potentialities of the East Afrian markets are considerable since the chief previous suppliers, Germany, Holland, Belgium and Italy are cut off from the East African market by the British blockade. In piece-goods generally there are also distinct possibilities for India in lines such as printed khangas formerly imported from Holland, and it is also probable that India will obtain a greater share of the grey and bleached piece-goods trade hitherto monopolised by Japan owing to India's currency being linked to sterling.

Industry's Part in War Effort

India's exports of cotton piece-goods and yarn must be considered purely as a war phenomenon since in normal times the United Kingdom is able to supply the whole of her own requirements and in addition has a large surplus for export. The actual figures are, however, of very great interest indicating as they do the part which the Indian Cotton Mill Industry can play in the United Kingdom's war effort.

In this section, attention has been mainly devoted to those Empire countries actually represented at the Eastern Group Conference, and if it were desired to estimate the wartime prospects of India's overseas trade in cotton textiles, it would be necessary to take into consideration many Empire and non-Empire countries rather further afield than those to which reference has already been made. Some of the countries in this wider field are large consumers of piece-goods and are potentially large markets for India during the war, provided that freight and exchange difficulties can be overcome, since they have been cut off from previous sources of supply such as Holland, France, Germany, Belgium, Italy and Czechoslovakia.

The Millowners' Association, Bombay, would welcome enquiries and samples from overseas markets. It would be of considerable assistance to the Association in dealing with such enquiries, if individual requirements were set forth in detail. Particulars regarding the standing, etc., of the parties forwarding the enquiry, together with Bank references, if any, and the terms on which they are prepared to do business would facilitate matters considerably.

Paper making in India

Historical

Paper making in India is of some antiquity. At least one writer claims that a hand manufacture process had been known and practised from quite early times. But we are not now concerned with the evolution of craftsmanship so much as its establishment as a modern industry. This may be said to date from the year 1867 when the first Paper Mill, subsequently absorbed into a larger concern, was established on the Hooghly. During fifteen years of solitary existence this Mill made no very marked headway in either their technical or commercial departments. In 1879 a second Paper Mill in Upper India had come into production and in 1882 the third Mill was registered as a public limited company. These three, with a couple of smaller concerns in Gwalior and Poona, were the early pioneers in an industry which in its early days does not appear to have made a very strong appeal to the industrial *entrepreneur* of last century. By 1925, the year which the industry first made an organised appeal for protection by tariff, there were 9 mills in existence, whilst two more were projected. In the intervening years the number of mills in production has only been increased by two, bringing the total to 11 in '40. The relatively high capital outlay coupled with the admittedly difficult technical process has tended to keep down the number of paper-making concerns in India. For most of the time that paper has been made in India manufacturers have looked mainly to the domestic market for their sales, but the time has arrived when the paper making in India may be ranked amongst the country's potential exporting industries and reference is made to this aspect of the matter latter on this section.

Raw Materials

In its early days the Indian industry considered the manufacture of high class white paper rather beyond its capacity, and this was to some extent due to its dependence upon rags and waste paper for its raw material. But this crude practice was soon to change. Routledge in 1860 proved the virtues of Esparto—a semi-tropical grass—and in 1875 and 1879 reported upon the possibilities of Indian bamboo which served to draw attention to other Indian fibres. These are only incomplete records of the early experiments with Indian fibres, but it is known that two mills made use of Moonj (*Saccharum Moonja*) and Sabai (*Ischaemum Angustifolium*) in their first years. Moonj seems to have held the field in the beginning, for it made a very good paper. Sabai, however, presented less difficulty as regards treatment, and, therefore, soon came into universal favour among Indian mills. Having found in Moonj and Sabai ample resources of plant fibre it was perhaps natural that the Indian mills then in operation should at that time have made no effort to follow up Routledge's researches in bamboo—a much more difficult problem. But it is an interesting speculation to think of the possibilities had the technique of bamboo pulp manufacture received simultaneously the attention given in other countries to the technique of wood pulp manufacture. Possibly India might have come to the front as one of the world's most important producers of pulp and paper. What actually happened was that the industry based on Sabai grass, while relatively still in its infancy was almost put out of business by the competition of wood pulp. Nevertheless in bamboo it later found a new raw material of great value.

A few details about the homely indigenous fibre which provides the raw material for this great Indian industry may not be out of place at this point. Both the Tariff Board of 1925 and the Tariff Board of 1931 found that the supplies of bamboo in areas where the other conditions were favourable for exploitation were sufficient to meet the needs of all the paper mills in India and to leave a surplus from which an export trade in pulp could be developed. Apart from Assam and Chittagong, seven areas were specified as having been subjected to regular survey, one in Orissa, two in Madras and one in Bombay, from which the estimated yield of bamboo was 291,000 tons, and three in Burma from which the estimated yield was 16,61,000 tons. The quantity of bamboo available from surveyed areas of India now exceeds 6,00,000 tons against an estimate of 2,91,000 tons in 1930-31. Additional supplies are obtainable from unsurveyed areas for which no estimates are available. Assuming that 2·38 tons of bamboo on an average are required to make a ton of paper, the quantity of bamboo at present required by mills is about 40,000 tons. There is, therefore, an ample margin of reserve supply available for an extension of bamboo pulp manufacture. In Burma, where supplies of bamboo are even more abundant, no paper mills have as yet been established.

The advantage of bamboo as a raw material in comparison with wood is that the cutting rotation is on average 4 years as against 60 years for most species of wood. A disadvantage is that when bamboos seed, they die, and in any given area the supply may be curtailed for a period of 10 years. Bamboos seed 'gregariously' or 'sporadically' and the degree of sporadic seeding varies. Recent investigations indicate that the seeding of bamboos is more gradual than was at one time thought and does not extend to all species simultaneously. Further, the dead bamboo stems remain suitable for the manufacture of pulp for a considerable time, which tests have proved to be at least four years. The danger of a shortage of bamboo in any given area in consequence of seeding is not, therefore, considered serious.

After bamboo, grass is the second most indigenous material used in India. The species used for the making of pulp is "Sabai" grass which is grown mainly in the United Provinces, Bihar, Orissa and the Punjab. Whilst bamboo is the principal material on which the future of the paper industry mainly depends, grass as a constituent of paper has a recognised value and will continue to be used in conjunction with other materials as a necessary ingredient in the manufacture of certain classes of paper for which special bulk or tensile strength is required, just as Esparto grass is used by a particular class of mills in the United Kingdom. It is probable that, with improvement in the quality of bamboo pulp, mills which can obtain supplies of both bamboo and grass, will to some extent substitute bamboo pulp for grass pulp on account of its relative cheapness. But in the United Provinces and the Punjab, where adequate supplies of bamboo are not available, grass must continue to be the chief raw material. Waste paper and paper and cloth cuttings are also used as ingredients in the manufacture of cheaper classes of paper to a small extent by bamboo and grass mills and to a greater extent by other mills. The quantity used was 5,908 tons in 1936-37. Supplies are obtained by mills through contractors mainly from large towns where sufficient quantities are available for the collection of different qualities. White paper and paper cuttings are in most requirement. Coloured papers are sorted out from the white and used for the manufacture of inferior papers such as badami and brown packing. In most countries that make pulp, wood of the coniferous variety is the principal material used. In India, forests of coniferous trees—pine, spruce and fir—are available in the Himalays, but difficulty of extraction and lack of transport facilities, have hitherto stood in the way of the utilisation of wood for the manufacture of chemical pulp. It is doubtful if use can be made of spruce and fir on account of the inaccessibility of the areas in which they grow except in the Kashmir State. The possibilities of using pinewood are more promising. A number of auxiliary materials are used in the Indian industry. Some of them are indigenous; some have to be obtained from elsewhere. A limited quantity of wood pulp is imported either as bleached pulp ready for admixture with bleached indigenous pulp or as unbleached pulp which requires bleaching along with other material. The chief qualities imported are bleached sulphite pulp, and easy bleaching and unbleached strong sulphite. Small quantities of special kinds of pulp such as aspen and kraft pulp are imported for special lines of paper.

Manufacturing Indian Paper

As the manufacture of pulp from bamboo is exclusive to India, a brief description of the process should find a place in any survey of the industry, however brief. Imported pulp is no longer essential though for certain purposes it is sometimes added, but the best qualities of printing and writing papers can be made without its admixture. One of the main trends of research in recent years has been the increasing use of indigenous materials, which has in fact been an essential condition of the protection in certain categories of paper which the industry has enjoyed for some time past.

The initial stage in manufacture is the crushing or chipping of the raw bamboo into a form suitable for the subsequent processes. This mechanical treatment is necessary in order to disintegrate the fibre and render it accessible to the chemical reagents employed in the process of digestion. The experience of mills which manufacture pulp from bamboo, is that crushing in a series of rollers is more satisfactory than chipping the bamboo in chipping machines. The next process is the digestion or cooking of the disintegrated fibre, which is the chemical process by which the various substances other than cellulose are dissolved. These substances consist mainly of pectins and lignins in several forms. Two processes are in use, which may be described as the acid process and the alkali process. In the acid or sulphite process the chemicals used in the preparation of the acid liquor are sulphur and magnesia which in combination form magnesia-sulphite. The acid liquor is pumped into the digesters loaded with the bamboo chips by the direct overhead method and the temperature slowly raised by the admission of steam under pressure. The digesters consist of a mild steel shell lined with acid-resisting brick and are of different capacities. After cooking is completed, the contents of the digester are blown off into a 'blow pit' from which the spent liquor carrying the noncellulose material is drained leaving the bamboo pulp behind. The alkali process may be subdivided into two, the soda process in which the principal chemical used is caustic soda, and the sulphate process, and improvement on the soda process in which sodium sulphide is mixed with a small proportion of caustic soda. The application of the chemicals used can be made in more than one way. The 'fractional' and the 'cascade' methods are those at present in use in India. The average total period of cooking is 14 to 15 hours including washing of the pulp. Those mills using the alkali process have special plants for the recovery of chemicals. After the digestion or cooking process is completed and the pulp drawn off from the digesters, the next stage is washing and straining to remove impurities. The pulp is then pumped into a concentrator where the water is extracted and the concentrated pulp passed to a strong chest ready for the process of bleaching.

Where grass is used it is first dusted and then loaded into digesters. The process of digestion or cooking of grass is carried out in one operation at a constant pressure with sodium hydroxide either by the direct overhead or by the 'fractional' system. The pulp after digestion is broken up, strained, washed and bleached. After completion of the process of bleaching the bleached pulp is passed to the beating house. If imported bleached pulp is used, it is added at this stage. The process of bleaching is of great importance since the quality of the paper made depends largely on the attainment of the correct degree of consistency in the pulp. The length of time required for beating depends on the nature of the material from which the pulp is made. After beating the pulp is passed through the paper machine to emerge finally as paper.

In recent years a good deal of attention has been paid by Indian manufacturers to bringing their pulping and beating processes up to date, and the rapid improvement in the quality of Indian paper has undoubtedly been due to the replacement of obsolescent machinery by more up-to-date plant. There has been a fairly general introduction of sizing plants, calendering and super-calendering machines, new cutting and reeling machines and guillotines for trimming, whilst as a whole the tendency has been to introduce the electric drive for plant where it was not already present.

Markets For Indian Paper

For the sake of clarity we might very roughly classify those categories of paper which enjoy tariff protection and those which do not. Protected papers include all kinds of printing paper with the exception of chrome, marble, flint, poster and stereo containing no mechanical wood pulp, or in which the mechanical wood pulp amounts to less than 70% of the the fibre content. Writing paper is also protected. Unprotected papers include packing and wrapping paper, articles made of paper and *papier mache*, printing paper of all sorts which contain mechanical wood pulp and stationery. The report of the findings of last Indian Tariff Board to enquire into the paper industry made some interesting calculations as to the future of consumption and the capacity of the industry to meet it. During the period 1929 30 to 1936-37 consumption increased by 6,656 tons, an annual average increase of 951 tons. They calculated that consumption in future may fluctuate from year to year in accordance with the effect economic conditions may have on the purchasing power of the population, but over a period of years may be expected to increase with the spread of literacy and the growing demands of educational institutions. They thought it difficult to estimate the rate of increase, but it was likely to be higher than in the period 1929-30 to 1936-37 unless any abnormal circumstances intervene. They considered the average annual rate of increase during the next few years might be estimated at 1,500 tons per annum, distributed over the protected and unprotected classes of paper in the proportion of 62 and 38. On this calculation the demand for protected classes of paper might be expected to have risen to 57,000 tons by 1940-41 and of unprotected classes of paper to 35.000 tons, a total of 92.000 tons. By 1940-41 the capacity of established mills, they thought, would have increased to 63,900 tons. The capacity of new mills under construction or definitely projected was thus estimated at 95 600 tons, but it is unlikely that they will be in a position to manufacture to their designed capacities. Assuming an output of 80,000 tons, and allowing for the fact that three mills are designed to manufacture paper mainly of the unprotected classes, the production of protected classes of paper might exceed the demand by some 7,000 tons, but the total production would fall short of the total demand by 12,000 tons, taking protected and unprotected classes together.

These figures, which were compiled some two years ago before the situation had been so radically changed by the war, make an interesting comparison with a later calculation which appears in the last issue of *Indian Print and Paper*, which contains a detailed statement of imports of all kinds of paper into India for the twelve months ending March 1939 and which says that according to the latest information the present annual production of the Indian mills is 90,000 tons, a figure which excludes the output of one mill that has recently changed hands and has been temporarily out of production. During the immediate pre-war period, and since the commencement of hostilities there has been a sharp jump in output as the following table of imports and Indian mill production during 1938-39 reveals. It will be observed that, by comparison with the present estimated annual production of 90,000 tons, the Indian mills a little over eighteen months ago were producing at the rate of just under 60 000 tons per annum. The following are the main heads of imports into and production in India for the year 1938-39 :—

Imports

	Tons.
Paper containing substantial proportions of mechanical wood pulp	41,538
Old newspapers	47,384
Writing and printing paper substantially made from chemical pulp	37,654
Straw-boards, card, mill and pasteboards	27 057
Indian mill production	59,198
Total consumption ...	212,831

Excluding boards, it will be seen that imports into India are divided fairly evenly into paper made from mechanical wood pulp, old newspapers, and paper made from chemical wood pulp.

The *per capita* consumption of paper in India is as yet very small by comparison with the larger countries of America, with increasing literacy, an extension of primary education and an advancing standard of life amongst some 40 crores of people there is obviously great scope for enlarging paper consumption in this country, and it is in fact the possibilities of the long-term future that have led to the extention of the industry in our midst. The full effects of the war on Indian conditions and particularly on production have not yet been felt, because the outbreak of hostilities found most of the mills carrying large stocks which provided an alternative supply of paper to consumers who found themselves cut off from the sources from which they usually obtained their requirements. These stocks have, however, been worked off by now. Consumption has not only increased but it shows in addition a tendency to concentrate on more expensive kinds of paper, because those who formerly relied on cheap qualities of paper containing mechanical pulp, finding themselves unable to obtain supplies at a reasonable price, are using instead paper of the type manufactured by the Indian mills. A recent trade forecast says, there is thus likely to be a real shortage of paper in India, but the situation will not be so serious as in markets where mills for pulp and paper production do not exist.

The disabilities of the war are not entirely without their compensations however. The Indian paper-making industry has begun to think of the possibilities of the export trade, which now hold out opportunities that may not recur when peace returns. The chastening experiences of the past in the domestic market warn the industry against attempting an extravagant export programme which it will be beyond its capacity to sustain in more normal times; nevertheless, there is no reason why a footing should not be obtained in the markets of adjacent countries—particularly adjacent Empire countries. It is felt that an export trade developed on sound commercial principles will serve the industry in good stead long after the adventitious war-time aids to expansion have disappeared. In planning for the future the Indian paper-making industry is looking ahead to the days of peace rather than to the immediate advantages which have come to it as a result of the war. There are several cogent and severely practical reasons why it desires to begin building up its export business.

At any time on broad grounds the case for developing the export market is a strong one; in time of war it is enhanced by such factors as the desirability of preserving valuable foreign exchange. On this ground alone there are powerful arguments in favour of Empire countries buying such paper as they can from within the sterling bloc. In this respect India offers her neighbours considerable facilities for the position is that the Indian mills will have a surplus after meeting all the country's own requirements in the protected grades of paper and to a limited extent the demand for non-protected papers. It is the industry's considered opinion that Indian manufacturers are now in a position to export limited quantities of paper, which neighbouring Empire countries would probably prefer to take in preference to the American or Japanese products to which the war must force them in the absence of an alternative source of supply within the Commonwealth. Amongst India's immediate neighbours it may be mentioned that there are no paper mills in Burma, Ceylon, Malaya, and East Africa, and whilst there is some production in both Australia and South Africa, both are importing conntries.

India's Sugar Industry

India World's Largest Sugar Producer

It is of interest to know that there in conclusive evidence to show that India is the accredited birth-place of sugarcane, as also of cotton. Little attention was paid, however, to this industry until after the Great World War, when the desirability of utilising the sugar resources was examined without any tangible result by the Government of India. The sugar Committee, appointed in 1920, laid stress on the importance of sugar in the National Economy of India, and subsequently the Imperial Council of Agricultural Research, established in 1929, drew the attention of the Goverenment of India to the necessity of the establishment of this industry in India. This Council deserves great credit for the establishment of the modern sugar industry and its development to its present stage.

An important landmark in the history of the sugar industry was the year 1930-31, when a Tariff Board was appointed to consider the question of grant of protection to it. The development of this industry since the grant of adequate tariff protection to it, commencing from April, 1932, and the assurance by the Government of India to maintain it for a period of 15 years, has been magnificent.

From being a country which was mainly dependent on foreign sources for its requirements of sugar up to 1931-32, India has now become *the largest sugar-producing country in the world*, with an output far in excess of its present estimated annual requirements, and with a potential capacity (with its present equipment of factories) under normal conditions of working for production of about 1½ million tons of white sugar, *i.e.*, roughly 1½ times the quantity annually required for it for internal consumption at the present time.

As a result of the rapid development of this industry the import of sugar estimated at about 900,000 tons in 1929-30 and valued at about Rs. 150 millions has now practically disappeared and the country has been rendered absolutely independent of any foreign sources for the supply of sugar.* A glance at Table No. 1 will indicate the number of cane factories, from gur refineries, khandsari† and the net import of sugar in British India in Kathiawar ports during the last 9 years along with the estimates for the year '40-41.

It was in the year '36-37 that the total production of sugar in India exceeded for the first time its estimated consumption and there was a large carry-over of sugar estimated at over 200,000 tons to the subsequent season.

Since then as a result of the decline in the area under cane and the poor cane crop, the production of sugar fell considerably and about 300.000 tons of sugar had to be imported in 1938-39 to make up the deficit. During the year 1939-40, however. as a result of a large cane crop, the total production of sugar is estimated to be about 1,373,000 tons, and in view of the high prices of sugar, due to fixation of high minimum prices of sugarcane by the Governments of the United Provinces, and Bihar, approximating to about Re. 0-10-0 per maund of cane (about 11 maunds being required for making 1 maund of sugar). the total consumption of sugar, will according to general expectation. fall to about 950,000 tons only, in 1939-40. It is expected that there will be a large carry-over of about 400,000 tons of sugar at the commencement of the 1940-41 season.

The necessity for the export of sugar which was not realised acutely till the year 1939, has now arisen, and it is imperative for the country to find an outlet for the export of surplus production which is bound to be witnessed during the next season, in view of the bumper cane-crop which will be available, and also for subsequent seasons, unless the cultivation of cane, and manufacture of sugar are properly planned and carefully controlled.

International Sugar Agreement

India has been committed under the International Sugar Agreement concluded in 1937, not to export sugar to any country, other than Burma, by sea, for

* In August, 1940, the Government of India announced that imports of sugar from Java to India would be restricted to 35,000 tons in 1940-41.

† Khandsari is an off-white direct consumption sugar produced in small factories, chiefly in the United Provinces, the excise duty on which is considerably lower at Rs. -/8/0 per cwt. as compared with Rs. 3 per cwt. on factory sugar.

India's Cotton Mill Industry

There are 389 mills in India with about 10 million spindles and 200,000 looms. About 60 per cent of the spindles and 70 per cent of the looms are located in the Province of Bombay, the actual figures being six million spindles and 141.000 looms. About half of these, *i. e.*, 2.850,000 spindles and 67,000 looms are in the City and Island of Bombay. Ahmedabad, which is the other large centre of the Industry in the Province of Bombay, has nearly two million spindles and nearly 48,000 looms.

Bombay

The range of cotton materials produced in these two great industrial Cities extends over a very wide field, and it would be no exaggeration to say that they are capable of producing almost any grey, bleached, woven coloured or printed cotton fabric in general demand. Normally, however, when catering for the Indian market, the bulk of the cloths produced in Bombay City consists of light texture cloths made from medium count yarns, but a number of mills during recent years have specialised in fine count cloths, which compare in quality with the best exported from England, Grey and bleached plain weave cloths, such as longcloth, shirting, T. cloths, domestics and sheetings account for about 600 million yards of the City's total production, and the bulk of the remainder consists of dhoties—about 400 million yards—and coloured goods between 250 and 300 million yards. No detailed statistics are available as to total annual productions of bleached, piece dyed, woven coloured and printed goods which Bombay City mills turn out, but it can be stated that during the last few years the outturn of printed goods and the better qualities of bleached shirtings, cambrics, voiles and mulls has substantially increased.

Ahmedabad

Ahmedabad normally produces approximately 1,000 million yards of piece-goods per annum. Her production also covers a wide field, and the outturn of bleached goods, coloured goods and fine count cloth is somewhat greater than that of Bombay City. Ahmedabad also produces dhoties and saries on an extensive scale, and has made considerable progress in recent years in the production of cambrics and prints.

Madras

The Province of Madras has more than 50 mills, but many of them are purely spinning mills catering for the needs of the very important handloom weaving industry in that part of the country. Many of the mills are comparatively new and very well equipped. In the realm of cloth production, the main specialities of the Province are the famous Madras handkerchiefs—produced chiefly on handlooms—high class cotton coatings, bleached shirtings and drills, and Service Khaki.

Bengal

The Cotton Mill Industry in Bengal has made exceptional progress in the last ten years and this is not surprising in view of the fact that Calcutta is probably the largest single cotton piece-goods market in the the world. Up to the present, production has been almost wholly confined to grey and bleached goods with dhoties for home consumption predominating.

United Provinces

The United Provinces, with Cawnpore as the chief centre, produces more than 225 million yards of cloth per annum. Grey and bleached goods account for more than 95 per cent of the production, and the cloths produced are usually coarser in texture than those manufactured in Bombay and Ahmedabad since local cottons are almost invariably used. The main production is dhoties of the type used in Northern India. Other lines of manufactures for which the Cawnpore mills are famous are Tentage and dosuti fabrics.

Delhi and the Punjab

Delhi and the Punjab specialise mainly in coarse count cloths made from local short stapple cottons. Delhi produces considerable quantities of dhoties and tentage materials and excellent upholstery and tapestry fabrics, while the main line of production in the Punjab, where the mill industry is in its infancy, consists of longcloth and T. cloths.

Indian States

Production in Indian States has grown rapidly in recent years, and an extremely wide range of goods is being produced. Whilst most of the goods manufactured are made from coarse count yarns, there are a number of mills in Baroda State which specialise in fine count fabrics, and in centres like Indore, a large proportion of coloured goods are made. Appendices 2 (*a*) and 2 (*b*) give a rough idea of the nature and volume of production of cotton piece-goods and yarn in Indian mills.

The Home Market

According to the latest information available, mills in India during the last three years have turned out, on the average, about 4,000 million yards of cloth per annum. This enormous production with the exceptions of between 200 and 300 million yards exported by land and sea has been consumed in India itself. The production of cotton yarn has recently averaged slightly under 1,200 million lbs. per annum, of which about 40 million lbs. were exported, but this may be offset by a similar weight of yarn imported from overseas. Out of this 1,200 million lbs. of yarn, about 800 was utilised in the manufacture of cloth by the power loom industry and the great bulk of the remainer was consumed by the hand-loom industry which has recently been producing on the average about 2,000 million yards of cloth per annum. The figures are set forth in Table 1. Table 2 sets out the cloth position in detail.

At a first glance, it would seem that since India is still importing about 700 millon yards of cloth per annum, she would have difficulty in supplying the special wartime needs of European countries, but this is certainly not the case, since with markets readily available, the Cotton Mill Industry could readily increase its output by a more general resort to double shift working and more intensive day shift operation. The available information indicates that the present outturn of about 4,000 million yards represents the production obtainable by working India's total loomage for 300 days per annum and nine hours per day and a percentage of them working double shifts. If double shift working were more freely resorted to, production could be stepped up very considerably. If, for example, the equivalent of complete double shift working were resorted to, *i.e.*, 18 hours per day, the annual output of cloth could be raised to something like 6,000 million yards, provided, of course, that the types of cloth manufactured did not differ greatly from those being turned out at present and the necessary raw material and labour could be procured.

Table 1

Approximate poundage of Yarn available for consumption in India (In millions of lbs.).

	1936-37	1937-38	1938-39	Average
Total Indian Mill Production	1,054	1,159	1,303	1,172
Less—Exports by Sea ...	12	40	38	30
Exports by Land ...	7	5	7	6
Balance ...	1,035	1,114	1,258	1,136
Imports ...	29	22	36	29
Total ...	1,064	1,136	1,294	1,165
Less—Exports by Sea ...	..	..	1	..
Exports by Land ...	..	..	..	..
Quantity of Yarn available for consumption in India ...	1,064	1,136	1,293	1,165
Cloth produced in India in millions of pounds ...	782	864	920	855
Approximate equivalent in Yarn (taking 100 lbs. of yarn =112 lbs. of Yarn piece-goods)	698	771	821	763
Real balance of Yarn available for sale in India ...	366	365	472	402

Raw Material Supply

The problem of obtaining additional labour required would present no insuperable difficulties, but as regards raw material, taking the average of the three pre-war cotton years, the Indian Cotton Mill Industry consumed on the average about 3·4 million bales of cotton of which half a million bales were imported and 2·9 million bales were Indian grown. The average cotton crop in the same three years was round about 5·7 million bales. Allowing half a million bales of Indian cotton for extra factory consumption, this leaves an average exportable surplus of 2·3 million bales.

The exports of Indian cotton to those countries now cut off from Indian sources of supply were round about 800,000 bales in recent years. China and Japan may take slightly larger quantities of cotton during the war years, but even taking this factor into consideration and also assuming that imports of cotton into India from overseas will be reduced to bare necessities owing to shipping and exchange difficulties, it woud seem that India will have at least 500,000 bales of short and medium cotton,

Assuming an increased internal consumption of 300 million yards, a surplus of 250,000 bales of cotton is likely to be available in India during the war. This would be enough to produce another 353 million yards of cloth of coarse texture. The problem of the disposal of this additional cloth in India itself is largely dependent on the purchasing power of the agriculturist which is regulated by the prices he receives for the commodities he grows. Roughly speaking, his position cannot be said to have improved materially since the outbreak of war, but it has probably not gone worse judged by the criterion of commodity prices. Another factor which must be taken into consideration in regard to India's offtake of cloth is the probability of smaller imports of piece-goods from the United Kingdom than the immediate pre-war averages, but this can be set off for the next year or so against the reduction of the surplus output of Indian mills which has been building up bazaar and mill stocks in the last two years.

Table 2

Approximate yardage of piece-goods available for consumption in India (In millions of yards).

	1936-37	1937-38	1938-39	Average
Total Indian Mill Production	3,572	4,084	4,269	3,975
Less—Exports by Sea ...	102	241	177	173
Exports by Land ...	121	128	115	121
Balance ...	3,349	3,715	3,977	3,681
Imports ...	832	622	672	709
Total ...	4,181	4,337	4,649	4,390
Less—Export by Sea ...	11	10	13	11
Exports by Land ...	109	88	103	100
Total quantity of mill-made piece-goods available for consumption in India ...	4,061	4,239	4,533	4,279
Estimated production by hand-loom industry ...	1,751	1,746	2,259	1,821
Grand Total ...	5,812	5,985	6,792	6,200

Before dealing with the question as to the extent to which the Indian Industry can improve her position in overseas markets, it is perhaps desirable to give a bird's-eye view of the Indian Industry and the extent of India's overseas markets, particularly Empire markets, which might be interested in obtaining greater quantities of cotton piece-goods and yarns from India.

It must be remembered that one of the most important changes brough about by the war is that, for the time being and possibly for some years to come, many Western European countries have been cut off as suppliers of manufactured goods to what were formerly very substantial markets overseas, similarly these European countries can no longer obtain the commodities they formerly purchased from territories overseas. These two facts naturally have important repercussions on India's export trade. On the one hand, important markets for Indian cotton have been temporarily closed, raising a problem as to how India's cotton surplus can be utilised, whilst on the other hand, the Indian Cotton Textile Industry has been presented with an opportunity to supply a much larger proportion of the piece-goods requirements of territories in the African Continent, Malaya, the Dutch East Indies, Indo-China, Australia and New Zealand which formerly purchased large quantities of cotton manufactures from Japan, France, Italy, Belgium, Holland, Germany, Czechoslovakia and Polland. To the extent that Indian mills can obtain greater overseas markets in the territories cut off from their usual sources of supply, the problem of the disposal of the Indian cotton crop during the war is reduced.

Cotton Piece-Goods

The following tables sets out in round figures the sending of cotton piece-goods from India to her chief export markets in the two immediate pre-war years, and in the first year affected by the present conflict :—

Table 3

Export of Cotton piece-goods from British India. (In millions of yards).

	1937-38	1938-39	1939-40	4 months 1940-41 Apr./July.
Ceylon ...	27	19	24	10
Burma ...	94	87	110	39
Straits Settlements ...	24	17	23	9
Federated Malay States ...	4	3	6	2
Nigeria ...	13	8	5	9
Union of South Africa ...	·3	·3	4	4
Kenya and Uganda ...	3	3	3	2
Tanganyika Territory ...	5	3	3	2
Mauritius & Dependence ...	5	4	6	2
Australia ...	1	1	3	3
Portuguese East Africa ...	5	4	7	4
Egypt ...	24	3	2	4
Bahrein ...	3	2	2	·5
Iraq ...	5	2	3	1
Iran ...	7	4	..	..
	220	160	201	89
Other counrries ...	21	17	20	13
Total	241	177	221	102

Appendix 3 sets out India's cotton piece-goods exports in the last three years in greater detail. The year '37-38 was a year of comparatively heavy piece-goods exports, but figures returned to something like normal in the following year: the reason for the higher exports in '37-38 was Japan's pre-occupation in China which at the outset adverely affected her export trade. As the war went on, her difficulties were reduced and her anxiety to obtain foreign exchange made it essential to preserve her cotton cloth export trade at all costs. The rise in Indian cotton cloth exports in '39-40 was of course due to the European war, which stimulate the desire of Empire countries to trade within the Empire and thus overcome foreign exchange difficulties. The cutting off of German and Italian supplies of piece-goods to India's most important pre-war markets had probably very little effect on India's export trade in the first six months of the war since neither Germany nor Italy did a very large trade in cotton goods with Middle and Far Eastern countries.

The collapse of Holland, Belgium and France changed the outlook considerably, and new opportunities for an expansion of trade between India and the Free French, Belgian and Dutch Colonial possessions in Africa and the Far East had been opened up for India, provided that exchange and shipping difficulties could be overcome. It has also become evident that the British Dominions and Colonies east and south of Gibraltar are likely to become more interested than formerly in Indian cotton manufactures as a result of the war.

With such a very large home market, the Indian Cotton Mill Industry was until recently not vitally interested in overseas trade and until a few years ago her main efforts were directed towards capturing a greater share of the Indian piece-goods and yarn trade. While the ultimate limit has possibly not been reached as far as the home market is concerned, it would be true to say that for some time past, the Industry has been tending to produce in a number of lines, greater quantities than can conveniently be consumed in India itself, and this has caused a greater interest to be taken than ever before in overseas. This is particularly true of cotton mills in and near the City of Bombay, which have been experiencing difficulties in competing against up-country mills, making cloth from cotton grown in the immediate vicinity for purely local markets. The excellent shipping facilities available to many parts of the world from the port of Bombay have also stimulated Bombay's interest in overseas export markets. Up to the outbreak of war, interest was naturally centred on the fairly adjacent markets such as Ceylon, Burma, the Straits Settlements, Iraq and Iran, but in Iraq and Iran no progress whatever has been made owing to competition from Japan in the former market and Russian influence and competition in the latter. India's large pre-war export market was Burma followed by Ceylon and Malaya to which in 1939-40 India sent respectively 110 million, 24 million and 29 million yards of piece-goods. A substantial market which had been built up in Egypt by the year 1937-38 was almost cut off in the following year owing to the imposition of restrictive import tariffs for the benefit of the small and recently established cotton textile industry of Egypt.

In 1937-38, there was a spurt in the exports of cotton piece goods to Nigeria, but later on the trade to this country fell away considerably, the relative figures for 1937-38, 1938-39 and 1939-40 being 13 million, 8 million and 5 million yards respectively. It is possible that the figure for 1939-40 does not really represent the total Indian piece-goods exported to Nigeria, as it is understood that some of the goods destined for that country were sent in the first instance to the United Kingdom.

India has been sending cotton piece-goods to a large number of markets other than those just mentioned, but the quantities have been small except in the case of Portuguese East Africa through which territory trade has been carried on with the African hinterland. Portuguese East Africa has been regularly taking more than 5 million yards of cotton piece-goods per annum.

Cotton Yarn

The following table sets out in round figures the sendings of cotton yarn from India in the two immediate pre-war years and in the year 1939-40 :—

Table 4

Exports of Cotton yarn from British India. (In millions of pounds.).

	1937-38.	1938-39.	1939-40.	4 months 1940-41. Apr.-July.
United Kingdom ...	1·0	0·2	2·7	5·2
Aden and Dependencies ...	1·6	1·0	1·3	0·1
Burma	8·9	12·4	15·2	6·4
Straits Settlements	3·7	5·5	3·2	0·7
Hongkong	7·3	8·2	5·3	4·3
Turkey, European & Asiatic ...	6·4	0·3	1·0	...
Syria	3·0	3·4	2·2	0·1
Iraq	1·1	1·1	0·9	0·5
Thailand	1·7	1·0	0·4	0·2
Egypt	1·2	0·3	0·6	0·3
	35·9	33·4	32·8	17·8
Other countries ...	4·2	4·5	4·1	1·2
Total ...	40·1	37·9	36·9	19·0

The exports of cotton yarn from India in the last three financial years have averaged about 40 million pounds. As in the case of piece- goods, small quantities of yarn have been sent to a large number of markets, but the only real substantial market has been Burma to which 9 million, 12 million and 15 million pounds of yarn were sent in the years 1937-38, 1938-39 and 1939-40 respectively.

A good market for Indian yarn in the last four years has been Hongkong. Turkey and Syria took substantial quantities of yarn from India in 1937, but there was a great falling away in 1938-39 and 1939-40. The reasons for this fall are somewhat obscure, but there may be a revival in the future concurrently with the revival of the cotton piece-goods trade from India to that part of the world *via* Basra, Bagdad and the Trans-Jordanean route.

As far as the import trade in cotton yarn and piece-goods of the countries represented at the Eastern Group Conference is concerned, the position is somewhat as follows :—

Exports to New Zealand

The total market for cotton manufacture in New Zealand according to the New Zealand statistics, appears to be about £1,600,000 sterling per annum but of this trade India has hitherto held only an infinitesimal share. The Indian '39-40 trade statistics show that exports of cotton piece-goods to New Zealand amounted to only 67,000 yards, which would probably represent a value of about £1,600 or less than 1/10th of one per cent of the total New Zeland market. The types of goods sent from India were listed under the head "coloured, printed or dyed," but the bulk would probably appear to be khaki drill. To all intents and purposes, the New Zealand trade in cotton manufactures has in the past been in the hands of the United Kingdom and Japan, the proportions being roughly United Kingdom 13/16th, Japan 2/16th and other countries 1/16th. Taking all factors into consideration, India should be able to secure a greater share of this market during the war owing to the advantage which India possesses as a member of the Sterling Bloc countries. There should be no insuperable difficulty in regard to freight though the sailings from India are not now in pre-war years. There is a lack of information in regard to the types of goods required by the New Zealand market, and in these circumstances, all that can be said is that Indian manufactures are able to supply practically any goods which Japan has been manufacturing for the New Zealand market.

Exports to Australia

The total imports of cotton piece-goods into Australia appear to be round about 170 million square yards per annum ; in addition, Australia imports about 5 million pounds of cotton yarn. Here again, United Kingdom and Japan hold the major portion of the market, United Kingdom's share being slightly more than double that of Japan in the case of piece-goods and about six times that of Japan in the case of yarn. The share of all other countries immediately before the war amounted to 7 million yards only. The main lines of cotton piece-goods imported into the commonwealth appear to be of the coloured and bleached varieties with coloured goods predominating. There is also a substantial trade in greys including grey calico for bag making which hitherto has been monopolised by Japan. India for a number of years has had a small trade in cotton piece-goods with Australia and the Indian Sea-borne Trade returns show that she exported to the Commonwealth 700,000, 1 million and 3 million yards of cotton cloth respectively in the years '37-38, '38-39 and '39-40. The jump in '39-40 is particularly noteworthy and while the exact figures for current year are not yet available, it is known that the quantities so far exported exceed those of any previous year. A special difficulty which India has had in meeting this new demand from Australia is that the cloths most commonly required are very often of a width greater than the average mill in India can manufacture, and if Australia's full demands are to be met it will be necessary for her to substitute single width cloth for double width fabrics to some extent. A fair proportion of Australia's special wartime requirements are already being made by mills in India, but the potentialities in the matter of goods for civilian requirements have hardly been tapped.

Exports to Hongkong

Up-to-date data as to the total import trade in cotton manufactures of Hongkong is not available at present in India. Before the Sino-Japanese war a large quantity of piece-goods and yarn destined for the South China markets was distributed through Hongkong. In pre-war years, the total trade of Hongkong in cotton piece-goods averaged well over 100 million yards per annum. In addition to this, Hongkong imported more than 40 million pounds of cotton yarn. Two-thirds of the cotton piece-goods came from Japan and the bulk of the remainder from Northern China (Shanghai). United Kingdom trade had been falling away for many years, and in 1936 it dropped to the low figure of three million yards. Other countries among which India is included sent a total of 6 million yards of cotton piece-goods in 1936. The Northern China (Shanghai) mills used to be the chief suppliers of cotton yarn to Hongkong before the Sino-Japanese incident, and the shares of India and the United Kingdom were small in proportion In 1936 United Kingdom sent 1½ million pounds of yarn and Japan sent nearly 3 million pounds of yarn to Hongkong. Although in the first decade of the century Hongkong and China were great markets for Indian mill-made yarn, this trade practically disappeared after the last war owing primarily to the development of the cotton mill industry in Japan and secondarily to the growth of the cotton mill industry in and around Shanghai.

The sendings of piece-goods from India to Hongkong have never been large, but in the first two years of the Sino-Japanese conflict, the practical immobilisation of the Shanghai mills, combined with an antipathy to purchase from Japan, gave India opportunities of the temporary character, and in the years 1937-38 and 1938-39, India's sendings of piece-goods to Hongkong were half a million and one million yards respectively. These totals dwindled to 1,17,000 yards in 1939-40 owing to the re-opening of the mills in Shanghai and the over-running of more and more of China's territory by the Japanese.

The export trade in yarn from India also received a fillip in the first two years of the Sino-Japanese war, sendings rising from practically nothing to 7 million pounds in 1937-38 and 8 million pounds in 1938-39. There was a falling away to 5 million pounds in 1939-40 and since then India's sendings of yarn to Hongkong have been even less.

The yarn sent to Hongkong from India is chiefly for use in small hosiery works, whose products were afterwards exported to the United Kingdom under a preferential duty, provided that the raw material used was of Empire growth and manufacture. The future prospects of trade between India and Hongkong even if ample shipping space continues to be made available, are likely to remain small.

Exports to Shanghai

Shanghai is the most thickly populated city in China. It is also one of the most important sea-ports in Northern China and is the main distributing centre for the very wide area of land covered by the waters of 'Yang-tse' and 'Hoang-ho' rivers. No accurate estimate regarding the extent of Shanghai's import trade in piece-goods and yarn is available in the absence of separate data for Shanghai only. But whatever the statistical position, apart from the trend towards decentralisation noticed in recent years. Shanghai still remains the chief industrial centre in China. According to the statement published by the Chinese Import Customs in '36, there were in Shanghai 52 establishments manufacturing cotton piece-goods and other cotton manufactures, 61 making cotton clothing and 5 establishments making silk piece-goods and yarn, apart from several other concerns responsible for the manufacture of a variety of articles. The Sino-Japanese war resulted in the closure of several cotton mills in Shanghai and this was perhaps responsible for a slight increase in India's export cotton yarn and piece-goods to China in the years '38-39. Recent reports, however, indicate that industrial production has been restored in Shanghai and this is reflected in the drop in China's imports of cotton piece-goods and yarn from British India.

There has in recent years been a steady shrinkage in the import trade of China in cotton manufactures due mainly to increased production in China, and for this reason, even though the Sino-Japanese war were to contitue for some time there may not be any improvement in India's cotton piece-goods and yarn trade with Shanghai. The major portion of the textile trade was in the hands of Japan, but the United Kingdom held the lead in cotton yarn and threads.

Exports to Malaya

Malaya includes the colony of Settlements, the Federated Malay States and the Unfederated Malay States. The total trade of cotton piece-goods in pre-war years varied between 120 and 150 million yards. In '38 the total imports were 123 million yards. The whole of these imports are not actually consumed in the territories specified, the Straits Settlements in particular having a large entrepot trade with Siam and the Dutch East Indies. In view of the enormous consuming capacity of the Dutch East Indies and the fact that supplies have been cut off from Holland, it is almost certain that India's trade with the Straits Settlements will expand greatly during the period of the war and signs that this is the case have not been wanting during the last few months. India will, of course, have to compete against Japan for any new trade in the Dutch East Indies market, but the sentiment of the people and exchange facilities are likely to favour India in this competition. Another factor which operates in favour of India is that since 1934 imports into Malaya from foreign countires have been limited under a quota system ; India being a part of the Empire, is outside the scope of the quota arrangement, a fact of which she should be able to take advantage. Whilst two-thirds of the piece-goods, consumed in or distributed by Malaya consist of coloured goods, there is a substantial demand for bleached goods of various types similar to the finer quality of goods turned out by Indian mills. Piece dyed goods form about 25 per cent of the total trade, but in this line India's opportunities of increasing trade substantially will be affected to some extent by her difficulties in obtaining adequate supplies of dye-stuffs. The full extent of the Malayan market for cotton yarns has not been ascertained, but that this is a fairly important market may be judged from the fact that in the last three years India's exports to this territory have averaged 4 million pounds per annum. In the last three years India's total sendings of piece-goods to Malaya have averaged 26 million yards. In 1939-40 a record figure of 29 million yards was touched and the indications are that this record will be considerably exceeded in 1940-41 as a result of new demands created by the war situation. Hitherto the bulk of India's sending to Malaya have consisted of coloured goods, but the sendings of plain bleached and plain grey have been by no means insignificant.

Exports To Burma

Only just over three years ago, Burma was an integral part of British India, and the exports of cotton piece-goods and yarn from all countries to Burma were included in the all-India Sea-borne Trade Statistics. The total import of cotton piece-goods from all countries into Burma before the war averaged round about 170 million yards, of which about 100 million yards were supplied by Indian, whilst the remainder was shared between United Kingdom and Japan. In addition, Burma has regularly been importing substantial quantities of cotton yarn—chiefly coloured—the total import figures for 1937-38 and 1938-39 being 11·5 million and 16·5 million pounds respectively of which India supplied the bulk.

The pre-eminent position which India holds in the Burmese market is primarily due to long association and proximity, assisted by the quota system which came into force in 1937—which limits Japan's imports—and a system of preferential duties resulting from the Indo-Burma and Burma-Japanese Trade Agreements.

Exports to Ceylon

In the immediate pre-war years, Ceylon's total imports of cotton piece-goods were from 60 to 70 million yards per annum. The proportion of this trade held by different countries has varied considerably since 1934 when limitations on the imports of the various categories of piece-goods imported from 'foreign' countries were imposed. Immediately before 1934, Japan had obtained a stranglehold on the market at the expense of the United Kingdom, Holland and India, but in 1935 the total imports of all kinds of cotton cloth from Japan were limited to just under 12 million yards. The restrictions on Japanese imports have since been relaxed and Japan is now allowed to import grey cloth without limitation and the restrictions on imports of Japanese prints have been considerably relaxed with the result that in the immediate pre-war year Japan's share of Ceylon's piece-goods trade increased enormously. Since the imposition of the original quota in 1934, India's cotton piece-goods trade with Ceylon has considerably improved, but she has been unable to make headway in plain greys. The bulk of the cloths imported into Ceylon has hitherto been bleached and coloured goods with the latter preponderating. Greys form a small proportion of the market, but with the recent removal of the restrictions on Japanese greys, there are indications that they are moulding, oil-varnishes, spirit lacquers, adhesives, baking enamels, and new types of paints in connection with the war-time needs of the Defence Departments. In plastic moulding, considerable success has been attained in the large-scale production of electro-technical goods on the bakelite technique. Hitherto, the thermo-plastic nature of shellac made its ejection from hot moulds impossible, reducing thereby the speed of output. By combining shellac with formaldehyde and subsequently with urea, melamine, etc., it has been possible to increase the toughness of moulded goods, while hot, to such an extent that these could be ejected from the moulds at the same temperature without taking recourse to cooling. This marks an important feature in the future of shellac moulding in general. Combination of shellac with casein and vegetable proteins has opened a further line in plastic moulding to which considerable attention is being directed at the Institute. Laminated insulating boards of good performance have been prepared, the application of which in the production of electro-technical goods and articles of common domestic use is expected to increase the demand for shellac. It has also been possible to condense the phenolic fraction of coal-tar with shellac giving rise to plastic materials of promise both in the moulding and varnishing industries. The introduction of shellac in the injection moulding process is another promising line developed at the Institute. It has been possible to evolve shellac moulding powers, suitable for injection-moulding of electrical switches, bottle caps, buttons, etc., and the speed of production is so considerable and the operation so simple that a big market for shellac might be envisaged in this new field.

Shellac and its components have been made to yield excellent adhesives by combining them with glycerine and phthaleic anhydride, suitable for use in the manufacture of laminated fibre boards and safety glass.

Lacquer Industry in India

The development of lacquer industry in India is handicapped by the absence of solvents. As yet the hydrocarbon solvents, esters and higher alcohols are not produced in India, and hence a shellac lacquer, using alcohol as the main solvent, has been developed for spray-painting in general and motor-car finishing in particular. Such finishes could also be coated over thin metal or paper boards and gramophone records could be manufactured by stamping the sound grooves over these surfaces. Weather-resistant varnishes for spray-painting have also been developed by modifying shellac with various catalysts. An extremely resistant backing varnish has been produced from the distillation product of kiri (by-product in the manufacture of shellac) after vulcanisation and incorporation with linseed oil.

London Shellac Research Bureau

As a result of the researches conducted in London by the London Shellac Research Bureau (controlled by the Indian Lac Cess Committee), lac-oil varnishes have been developed. A new method of applying shellac-coatings by a dry process (hot-spraying) has been successfully completed and various paints and coatings for defence purposes have been developed.

To meet the specific needs of certain industries, the high melting, weather-resistant and quick-backing fraction of lac has been separated by extraction of total lac with organic solvents or weak alkalies. Already large quantities of this hard lac resin are being used in Great Britain in the electrical industry.

In America, Germany and England, lac is bleached by the use of sodium hypochlorite for various industrial uses. The Institute has investigated all the factors involved in the bleaching of lac with the result that it could be successfully commercially manufactured in this country with a possible export outlet.

Fundamental researches on the constitution of shellac specially that of soft lac resin, viscosity, solubility, and other physico-chemical properties including break-down voltage of shellac films and discs constitute an important activity of the Indian Lac Research Institute. These have yielded results of considerable importance to increase the commercial use of shellac.

Indian Hides & Skins Industry

India today can fairly claim to be the world's major supplier of hides and skins, both raw and half-tanned. It is reckoned that there are in India 225 million cattle and buffaloes, 46 million sheep and 58 million goats, which means that in this country are to be found one-third of all the cattle in the world—the largest cattle population of any single country.

From these vast numbers of animals it is estimated that 20 million cattle and 5¾ million buffalo hides are produced a year, puls 28 million goat and kid skins and 19 million sheep and lamb skins. It must be pointed out, however, that, particularly in the case of cattle, these figures are liable to fluctuation since it is calculated that from 70 to 80 per cent of the cattle hides are obtained from animals which have died natural deaths. Such a death roll inevitably is dependent on the incidence of famine, flood or epidemics of disease. Goat, kid and sheep skins which are usually obtained through slaughter of the animals for meat, remain more or less steady. Compared with other countries India stands first in the production of both, hides and skins.

About 75 per cent of the Indian production of raw hides and about 45 per cent of the goat and sheep skins are nowadays locally tanned, the remainder being exported raw. For many years Germany was a major buyer of these raw materials, and although after the Great War she recovered her position to some extent, the development of Indian tanning and increased purchases by the United Kingdom after the introduction of glace kid manufacture on a large scale in that country, have helped to spread India's market, although at the opening of the present war about a third of her hides and skins were still sold on the Continent of Europe.

During 1939-40 India exported raw and undressed hides and skins worth Rs. 412 lakhs while exports of half-tanned leather were worth Rs. 600 lakhs. Nearly all the latter were brought by the United Kingdom which nowadays takes more than half of India's exports of hides and skins.

In recent years, definite attempts are being made inside the country to improve the produce generally. For example, improvements in flaying methods are being introduced and this scheme is being backed by the tanners and shippers who have voluntarily contributed to a fund to pay a small premium direct to all flayers of A and B grade hides. This is tending to raise the standard of quality by obviating avoidable defects.

So far as the flat rate system of quotation goes, the evils inherent in it will hardly be reduced until buyers appreciate the value of the grading schemes which are now being officially encouraged. Systematic grading and marking of hides under the Agricultural Produce (Grading and marking) Act, by means of brass disks* is now in operation in a number of slaughter houses especially in North India. Four grades, A, B, C and Rejections, are prescribed in the rules under the Act. Nearly 4,65,800 kips and 2,50,700 buff-hides have been graded under the AGMARK scheme between January 1937 and December 1940. In kips, nearly 22 per cent were of A grade, 35 per cent of B, 37 per cent of C and 6 per cent Rejections. Amongst buff-hides, about 28 per cent were of A grade, 32 per cent of B, 35 per cent of C and 5 per cent Rejections.

With a view to grading cured hides also (slaughtered and dead) and to expand the scheme to handle a much larger number of hides, a re-organisation of hide grading is now proposed. The scheme, in the first instance, would be tried at important assembling markets, *e.g.*, *Calcutta* and *Cawnpore.* Details of the scheme are discussed in the Report on the marketing of Hides in India, which is being prepared by the Agricultural Marketing Adviser to the Government of India.

If buyers wish to ensure quality in their consignments they would be well advised to specify the standard Agmark grades in their contracts. Regarding the advantage of using the standard Agmark grades and quoting differential prices, an instance may be given of a mixed lot of 1,000 graded hides sent to Palestine. They fetched a farthing a lb. (2½ per cent) more than a similar lot of ungraded hides. It is reckoned, however, that the real extra value obtained by the buyer in this case was many times this small premium.

---

*The use of brass disks is now discontinued and instead the hides are suitably punched near the tail.

Goat, Kid, Sheep And Lamb Skins

Of the 47 million goat, kid, sheep and lamb skins produced each year about half of them are exported, usually in a raw, dry-salted, state. The U. S. A. takes about two-thirds of these raw skins while the United Kingdom takes more than three-quarters of the half-tanned, dressed skins most of which are exported through Madras.

The Indian goat, which normally is regarded by most agricultural and animal husbandry experts as little better than an unmitigated nuisance, does, however, come into its own in the skin business, for India supplies about one-sixth of the goat skins required by the world tanning industry. The effect of the almost total Japanese blockade on China has not yet become fully apparent in world statistics, but it seems possible that when full details are available they will show that India's share of the market has grown still greater.

High class glace kid is made from Indian goat skins and those from Bengal and Bihar are regarded as the best raw material for this purpose. Incidentally, glace kid is now being made in India and in addition to meeting local demand, exports worth Rs. 9·3 lakhs were made in 1938.

Reference had already been made to the fact that about half the hides and skins produced in India are tanned in the country. Exports of dressed hides are in varying degrees of finish from the half-tanned "East India tanned kips and calf skins" which are re-tanned and finished in the importing countries, to box and willow sides which are practically ready for the bootmaker.

Widespread Village Industry

Indian tanning, a very widespread village industry carried on by Chamars, a depressed class of Hindus, can be divided into two categories, indigenous and modern.

The indigenous types, in which the Chamars are supreme, covers four different forms of leather: the crude leather produced in the villages to meet local needs; buffalo sole leather which is bag tanned in the Punjab and in Bengal; Punjab tanned sheep skins, the Kabuli Bheris of the trade which are often used as cheap bookbinding leather, throughout India; and the half-tanned leather of Madras and Bombay. It is this fourth kind of leather which has found its way into international commerce, most of it first going to the United Kingdom when it is exported to other countries.

This indigenous tanning in the main uses avaram or turwar bark (cassia auriculata) which is obtained in southern and western India. Since the last war, however, great strides have been made in Indian tanning practice and in Madras cattle hides are nowadays tanned with wattle bark, large quantities of which are imported from South Africa. Goat and sheep skins are, however, still tanned with avaram, and the same medium is used in Bombay for cattle hides. The annual export of this half-tanned leather is worth about Rs. 600 lakhs.

Modern tanning, especially for producing leather for saddlery and military equipment, employs local tannins such as babul bark and myrobalans in dealing with buffalo and heavy cow hides. Such modern processes have been introduced in Cawnpore, one of India's biggest modern tanning centres, Agra, Calcutta and Madras, and buffalo hide is now being treated by modern methods to produce sole leather.

Chrome Tanning

Chrome tanning has also developed at a phenomenal rate in the country and tanneries in Cawnpore, Calcutta and Madras now produce leather for shoe uppers, such as box and willow sides from cow hide and box willow calf. Such leather has for some time been regularly exported to Africa, Burma, the Straits Settlements, Iran and Iraq, and since the operation of the Ottawa trade pact the United Kingdom has taken a growing amount of these leathers exports to the U. K. rising to over Rs. 54 lakhs in 1937.

In recent months the capacity of the Indian hides and skin industry and the tanneries in the country has been proved by the order for army boots, worth Rs. 100 lakhs, placed by the British Government in India. This order is being filled at the rate of 125,000 pairs of boots a month. Such work does not by any means represent the total capacity of the industry since apart from other and smaller orders, the rapidly increasing Indian Army also has to be shod and the normal internal demand is being met without any dislocation being caused.

Finally, an interesting development in the hide and skin business in recent years has been the growth in exports of lamb and kid fur skins. These are particularly attractive goods (some of the North Indian varieties of sheep belonging to the same species as that producing the well-known "Persian Lamb") and 5,000 pieces were exported in 1928. That was a humble beginning and the demand was so brisk that by 1936 exports exceeded 2,000,000 skins. It is quite possible that with the demand for warm equipment during the war, India's fur skins can play a very useful part.

Coffee Industry in India

It is a fascinating story that lies behind the introduction of coffee into India. In about 1600 A. D., Bababudan Sahib, of beloved memory, rallied the faithful, in front of a holy cave high up on the Chandragiri Hills in Mysore State, to give battle to a murderous bandit chieftain, who had entrenched himself on the Hills and, with his hordes, was devastating the country. The *Poligar* and his men perished. Bababudan Sahib who had sailed forth in the spirit of a crusader announced to his followers that he had decided to go on a pilgrimmage to the Holy City of Mecca and disappeared into the cave. All through the long weary months his faithful followers, both Hindu and Muslim, watched and waited at the mouth of the cave till the holy man reappeared, and communicated to them the glad news that he had brought from the Holy Land as gift for them seven seeds of a wondrous plant which would serve as "food and drink" to them. These seeds were planted on the Chandragiri Hills which from that day came to be known as the Bababudan Hills. The foundation of the coffee industry in India was thus and truly laid by Bababudan Sahib.

History records that the tiny plants from the Bababudan stock carried across the seas started the big plantations in Dutch East Indies and Brazil. Dutch East Indies got its first coffee plants from Cannanore in Malabar in 1696. These having been destroyed by floods, a second consignment from India followed three years later and became the forerunner of the *arabica* coffee plantation of the Dutch East Indies. In 1760 coffee plants taken from Goa in Portuguese India to Rio de Janeiro introduced coffee cultivation in Brazil.

Development of Coffee Growing in India

In India, for well-nigh two centuries the light of coffee appears to have been hidden under the bushel. It was only in 1799 that the possibilities of coffee as a commercial crop attracted the attention of the East India Company. An experimental plantation was opened in Tellicherry in the same year and in its wake regular plantations sprang up all over the slopes of the Ghats in South India.

The grim determination and the dogged perseverance of the pioneers of the coffee industry wrought a miracle. In less than a century thousands of acres of wild jungle on the almost inaccessible heights of the mountain ranges were cleared and converted into smiling coffee gardens. And by 1872, India was able to export as much as 25,000 tons of coffee.

And its Fall

A series of reverses then followed. The fungus leaf-disease, *Hemeleia vastratrix* and the coffee steam-borer made it increasingly difficult for estates situated in certain areas to pay their way. Also keen competition in the world markets from foreign coffees contributed to the decline of the Indian coffee industry with the result that from about 300,000 acres the area under coffee shrank to its present level of about 200,000 acres.

Location and Extent of Present Cultivation

There are few hills in the world so well-suited to the growing of high quality coffee as the hills of South India. High altitude, sunny slopes, a tropical sun, plentiful rains, a good forest soil rich in humus content and a well-drained sub-soil are some of the ideal conditions under which coffee grows on these hills and yields the product reputed for its excellent characteristics in the cup.

The more important of these hills are the Bababudan, Koppa and Mudigre Ranges in the Mysore State; the Nilgiris, Nedubattam, Shervaroys, Anamallais and Pulneys in the Madras Presidency; Kannan Devan in the Travancore State; Billigiris situated partly in the Mysore State and partly in the Madras Presidency and Nelliampathies part of which lies in the Cochin State and the rest in the Malabar district of the Madras Presidency. Besides these, wholly hilly regions like North and South Coorg and Wynaad also grow coffee. About half the total area under coffee in South India is in the Mysore State, a quarter in the Madras Presidency, a fifth in Coorg and the remainder distributed between Travancore and Cochin States.

Varities Grown and Types

All the three important varieties of coffee known to the world, *viz.*, *Coffea arabica*, *Coffea robusta* and *Coffea liberica*, are grown in South India. The *Coffea arabica* of South India claims its descent, as already stated, from the finest of this variety grown in its home country of Arabia and brought to India by Bababudan Sahib. More than 90 per cent of the coffee area in India is planted to *Coffea arabica*.

Coffea robusta was introduced from Java in 1910. It occupies less than 10 per cent of the total area under coffee.

Many types of *arabica* appear to have been tried from time to time. 'Chik' was one of the first in the field and flourished till it succumbed to the attacks of the coffee stem-borer and the leaf-disease. 'Coorg,' a new type found resistant to the leaf-disease, then became popular. The 'Kent' type well-known for its vigour, robustness and bean quality is now the most popular.

The Coffee Tree and its Produce

The coffee tree begins to yield from its third year, though it attains full maturity only in its fifth year of life. The useful life of a coffee tree is reckoned to be about 50 years, provided of course, year in and year out, the costly cultural operations are attended to and the delicate trees are fed with proper manures and protected against pests and diseases, and the shade under which they are grown is regulated from time to time.

The coffee tree yields only one crop in a year in India. It blossoms in March-April with the first showers received after the preceding dry period. The berries mature and ripen in the course of the next nine to ten months, those on higher elevations taking a longer time to mature than others. In some areas, the crop is ready to be harvested as early as September, while in others it is as late as January. For the same reason, harvesting which is generally done in three rounds to ensure that only fully ripe berries (cherries) are picked in each round lasts till May, in certain areas.

Preparation of the Produce for the Market

Like any other fruit crop, the cherry picked off the coffee tree is perishable in its raw state and cannot therefore be marked as such. It has to undergo further treatment before the final product, the coffee bean may be taken out of it in a state conducive to its keeping quality.

This is achieved in either of the two ways described below.

Plantation (Parchment) Coffee

The first of these known as the "wet" or "washing" method is an elaborate process in which the outer skin of the cherry and the sticky matter beneath are gently removed by pulping and washing. This leaves the coffee beans inside the cherry each encased in a soft parchment covering. Coffee in this form is known as 'parchment coffee.'

The next stage in the preparation is the drying of parchment coffee in the sun so carefully and so well that all but a very small percentage of moisture is left in it and the parchment-covering turns brittle. The further processes of peeling off the parchment-covering, the grading of beans according to their shape and size, and the careful garbling of each grade by picking out by hand all blemished and out-of size beans, complete the preparation of coffee for the market by the 'wet' method. The final product of this process goes under the trade name "Plantation Coffee," with or without the additional qualifying word "Parchment" to ensure that no misunderstanding is caused as to the superiority in quality of the coffee in question, owing to the special preparatory treatment it has received.

Native (Cherry) Coffee

The other method of preparation of coffee for the market is a simpler one. Cherries as they are harvested are dried in the sun till the outer skin of the cherry, the soft parchment-covering of the beans inside, and the sticky matter in between dry up forming a husk and leaving the beans loose inside the husk. Such cherry-dried coffee is then decorticated by pounding it in a mortar or by passing it through a huller. The beans thus separated from the husk are then graded, if necessary. The final product of this process is called "Native Coffee" or "Cherry-dried Coffee" and sometimes "Native (Cherry) Coffee."

Uncured and Cured Coffees

To the final products of either of the two methods of preparation described in the foregoing paragraphs, the general term "cured coffee" is applied. It means that coffee fruits as harvested have been subjected to certain preservative processes, and the beans obtained from these processes are ready for the market. Conversely, "uncured coffee" means coffee in any of its various forms before it is cured. This term is, however, generally applied only to dry coffee in the parchment or in the husk.

Curing

"Curing" is the collective term applied to all the processes to which uncured coffee is subjected before it is turned into cured coffee. A "curer" is a person who undertakes the curing of coffee. There are a number of such curers, large and small, firms and individuals, in South India employing large numbers of labourers during the season in their "curing yards" or curing establishments."

It is gratifying to note that the curing of coffee in India is acknowledged to be the best in the world in all its principal markets. The intense heat of the sun during the curing season is a natural advantage enjoyed by South India. Added to this is the great care bestowed by curers on every process of curing, which, as they have learned from their long experience, enhances the cup qualities of Indian coffee and ensures for it the first rank among the coffees of the world.

The grading of coffee beans according to their shape and size is as important to the consumer as the cup qualities. Uneven size and shape lead to irregularities in roasting and consequent inferior liquor. In the process of grading, the pea-shaped beans or "pea-berries" are separated from the flat-shaped beans or "flats." The flats are again graded into first, second and third sizes according to certain fixed standards based on the width and thickness of the beans adopted by each curer who also exercises his own discretion in naming his grades and using grade marks such as "O," "A," "B," "C," etc. The beans that are not fit to go into any of the above groups form a separate grade called "Triage."

Monsooned Coffee

In the days of sailing ships, Native (cherry) coffee sent to Europe used to take some six months for the voyage, with the result that in the damp hold of the ship coffee lost its original colour and became white. With the opening of the Suez and speedy transport on steam-ships, complaints were received from Europe that the coffee had not the flavour it had before. Merchants in Mangalore rose to the occasion and devised and perfected the process known as "monsooning coffee," in which the coffee acquired the special flavour preferred by many consumers in Norway, France and Switzerland.

Monsooning of coffee is an art. With the break of the South West Monsoon late in May or early in June, Native (cherry) coffee is evenly spread, about 4 to 6 inches thick, in airy godowns open on all sides and raked from time to time for about 4 or 5 days. It is then packed loose in gunny bags and stacked in piles with sufficient space between rows for the monsoon winds to blow continuously on each bag. The beans are bulked and re-packed once a week or poured from one bag to another to avoid their getting mouldy and for even "monsooning." In about a month and a half the coffee assumes a silvery white colour when it is considered to be fully matured and ready for shipment.

Characteristics of Various Growths

Coffees are valued on their quality, substance or body, flavour or aroma and point or hardness in the cup. It is on these very desirable characteristics that the various growths of Indian coffees have earned for them a reputation in the most fastidious market of the world, namely, London. Mysores are noted for their full soft liquor with velvetty flavour and richness. Billigiris, Nilgiris and Naidubatum fall in the same class with good quality, distinctive flavour, soft and thickish liquor. Shervaroys are distinguished by their fine aroma, while Coorgs yield a strong liquor. Nellampathies yield a soft liquor while Anamallais, Kannan Devan and Palnis are preferred for their sound liquor. It is seldom that Indian coffees fail to satisfy the requirements of a fastidious blender.

The market valuation of coffees is also partly dependent on their external characteristics. A few of the salient features of the various growths of Indian coffee are the following :—

BABABUDANS	...	Medium Bold, Round and Thick, Greenish-Greyish.
MYSORES	...	Bold to Medium Bold, Greenish-Greyish to Greyish, Coated.
COORG	...	Medium Bold, Greenish, slightly Coated.
NILGIRIS	...	Bold, Longish, Bluish-Greyish, not Coated.
NAIDUBATUM	...	Medium Bold, Greenish to Greenish-Greyish, not Coated.
BILLIGIRIS	...	Fairly Bold, Greenish, slightly Coated.
SHERVAROYS	...	Medium Bold, Roundish, Greenish not Coated.
ANAMALLAIS	...	Bold, Greenish, fairly Coated.
NELLIAMPATHIES	...	Bold, Roundish, Greenish, Coated.
KANNAN DEVAN	...	Medium Bold, Greenish, slightly Coated.
HALNIS	...	Small to medium Bold, Greenish, slightly Coated.

India's Position in the World Production of, and Trade in, Coffee

The annual world production of coffee is estimated at about 2½ million tons. Brazil accounts for 60 per cent of this, Colombia takes the next place with 11 per cent and Dutch East Indies follows with 5 per cent. India's share is less than 1 per cent. About 50 per cent of the world trade in coffee is monopolised by Brazil while Colombia accounts for about 15 per cent. and Dutch East Indies about 6 per cent. India's share is low and only about 0·5 per cent.

Production, Home Consumption and Exports

The normal commercial crop is estimated at 18,000 tons. In a lean year it may be as low as 16,000 tons and in a bumper year as high as 24,000 tons.

Though coffee has been grown in India for several centuries, the popularity of the beverage is still confined to the southern parts of India. The total consumption of coffee in India is only about 10,000 tons as against a consumption of 18,000 tons in Canada, over 16,000 tons in the Unions of South Africa, 15,000 tons in the United Kingdom and 750,000 tons in the United States of America. The *per capita* consumption of coffee in India is extremely low being only a small fraction of a pound, whereas in the United States of America it is about 15 lb. and in Sweden 16 lb.

The annual exportable surplus of Indian coffee is over 8,000 tons. The buyers of Indian coffee in the recent past have been France, the United Kingdom, Norway, Belgium, Australia (including New Zealand), Germany, Iraq, Netherlands, Arabia, Burma, Bahrein Islands, Asiatic Turkey, Czechoslovakia, Canada, United States of America and Ceylon, in their order of importance.

Future of the Indian Coffee Industry

After a series of ups and down in the past, the industry has now shrunk to about 200,000 acres under cultivation with an estimated commercial crop of about 18,000 tons of cured coffee, of which the home consumption is only about 10,000 tons, the balance being the exportable surplus. And while the world's makets continue to be flooded with comparatively inferior coffees, the large exportable surplus of Indian coffee is a serious problem to the industry.

The Indian Coffee Cess Committee, constituted by the Central Government in 1935 under the provisions of the Indian Coffee Cess Act XIV of 1935 has set out on the long and difficult journey of expanding the market for Indian coffee in India and overseas, but, for various reasons, of which the chief are finance and the present war, the goal is not yet within sight.

Glass Industry in India

Recent archaeological discoveries and excavations have now established that glass vessels and ornaments were in use in India in the early Christian era. Enamelled glass is known to have been manufactured in India in the 17th century. Belgaum, Mysore and United Provinces were also reputed to possess glass factories in the 17th and 18th centuries though such factories were not of the modern type.

Manufacture of glass in India on modern lines dates from the nineties of the last century when some pioneer efforts were made in this direction, and to a certain extent, credit is due to a factory at Talegaon in Poona District which had done a great deal of pioneer work in training men for glass factories and popularising the industry. Between the years 1892 and 1908 many factories on modern lines were started but most of them were not successful. The Indian Industrial Commision attributed the failures to the inadequate technical skill, ignorance about the qualities of the raw materials, and the peculiaiities of Indian labour and local conditions.

In spite of these failures 16 new factories were established during the period of 1908 to 1913 but in 1914 when the war broke out, not more than half of them were in working condion. During the war period of 1914 to 1918 the Indian Munitions Board encouraged the manufacture of glassware in India, and as a result new factories were established, and it was estimated that about Rs. 15,00,000 were invested in the industry. During the period of 1918 to 1932 the duty on imported glass was increased from 15 per cent to 30 per cent, and this gave a further stimulus to the industry with the result that 22 new factories were established during the period.

In the year 1932 there was an enquiry by the Tariff Board into the prospects of the glass industry, and the requirements thereof in respect of protection. The Tariff Board took a survey of the then known factories and the table below gives a list of the factories existing to the information then available.

Province or State.	Glass Manufactures' Association.	Glass Bangles Industrial Association, Ferozabad Bangle factories.	Directors of Industries				Dr. Drane	All sources
			Bangle factories.	Others.	Bangles.	Others.	Bangles and fales pearls.	Others.
Punjab ...	1	..	..	1	..	1	..	1
United Provinces	8	20	8	7	25	4	23	11
Bengal ...	6	..	..	7	..	4	1	10
Bombay ...	4	..	2	4	..	5	3	6
Central Provinces	2	..	..	2	..	2	..	2
Bikaner ...	1	..	..	..	..	..	..	1
Nizam Dmn. ...	..	..	..	1	..	..	..	1
Total ...	22	20	10	22	25	16	27	32

Larger Number of Factories

After the Tariff Board enquiry the stimulus to the establishment of glass factories was on the increase and to-day we have a still larger number of factories :

Bengal	...	...	28
Bombay	...	...	19
Delhi	..	...	1
Indian States	...	...	11
Madras	...	...	1
Punjab	...	...	3
United Provinces	...	...	33
			101

The Tariff Board made further recommendations to the Government of India for an increase in duty on various kinds of glass manufactured.

These recommendations by the Tariff Board were not, however, accepted by the Government for various reasons, and there was no increase in the duty imposed a period of 5 years ending in 1942. While the question of the export of sugar was of academical interest till 1939, till when India's production of sugar was not in excess of her requirements (and that explains why the industry did not seriously interest itself in the removal of the ban), the question has now assumed considerable importance, and it is agitating the minds of the commercial community, the public, and indeed, also, of the Government of India.

The outbreak of the European War in 1939 has made the International Sugar Agreement inoperative due to various reasons, amongst which are the restriction of imports and exports of sugar to and from belligerent countries, alterations in the map of Europe as a result of several countries being treated as part of Germany, and consequently the disturbance in the Export quotas assigned to various countries, and violation of the terms of Agreement by them.

India's Surplus Sugar

The virtual suspension of the International Sugar Agreement as a result of the dislocation caused by the devastating war in Europe, and the availability of a large surplus of sugar in India which must be exported have, thus, created within the last few months an entirely new state of conditions which the Government of India may examine, if necessary, in consultation with Empire Countries and the Government of the United Kingdom, with a view to lifting the ban on export of sugar from India, by sea route immediately.

Table No. 1

Total number, and prodnction of sugar fram cane factories, gur refineries, khandsari, net import of sugar in British India and imports in Kathiawar ports during the last 9 years, and estimates for 1940-41.

(November-October Statistics)

Year (Nov.-Oct.)		No. of Cane factories working in India	Cane Factory Production (Nov.-Oct.)	Sugar Refined from Gur (January-December)	Khandsari (Conjectural estimates) (Nov.-Oct.)	Total Production of Sugar in India	Net Import (Excluding Re-exports) of Sugar in British India (Nov.-Oct.)	Import of Sugar in Khathiawar Ports (Nov.-Oct.)
			(Tons)	(Tons)	(Tons)	(Tons)	(Tons)	(Tons)
1931-32*	...	32	158,581	69,539	250,000	478,120	438,797	92.678
1932-33	...	57	290,177	80,106	275,090	645,383	321,081	68,649
1933-34	...	112	453,965	61,094	200,000	715,059	233,366	87,094
1934-35	...	130	578,115	39,103	150,000	767,218	197,775	113 364
1935-36	...	137	932,100	50.067	125,000	1,107,167	86,962	45 218
1936-37†	...	137	1,111,400	19,500	100.000	1.230,900	11,960§	12,870
1937-38	...	136	930,700	16,600	125,000	1,072,300	9,410	12,284
1938-39	...	139	650,800	14,200	100,000	765,000	254,430 (10 months)	76,700 (8 months)
1939-40	...	143	1,241,700	31,700	100,000	1,373,400	34,700	32,200
1940-41‡	...	145	950,000	50,000	200,000	1,200,000	...	...

*Figures of Gur production for calendar year 1932 are added to figures for 1931-32 and so on.

†Factories in Burma, and production of sugar in Burma are excluded from 1936-37 season.

‡Our estimates.

§Imports in Burma excluded from, April 1937, onwards.

Table No. 2

Acreage under sugarcane, under improved varieties, production of cane per acre, gross production of gur, and calculated production of cane-crop from 1930-31 to 1940-41 :

Year		Total acreage under sugarcane in thousand acres	Acreage under improved varieties in thousand acres	Average cane production per acre (in tons)	Gross production expressed as gur (in thousand tons)	Calculated production of sugar-cane (10-11 factors) (in thousand tons)
1930-31	...	2,905	817	12·3	3,359	35,780
1931-32	...	3,076	1,170	14·1	4,116	43,316
1932-33	...	3,425	1,845	14·9	4,859	51,129
1933-34	...	3,422	2,295	15·3	5,055	52,455
1934-35	...	3,602	2,433	15·1	5,293	54,346
1935-36	...	4,154	3,056	15·3	6,102	61,202
1936-37	...	4,582	3,452	15·6	6,932	67,322
1937-38	...	3,869	2,968	15·5	5,579	55,637
1938-39	...	3,130	2,673	15·0	4,375	43,100
1939-40	...	3,705	...	15·0	4,547	...
1940-41	...	4,215	...	...	...	...

Table No. 3

Per Capita Consumption of Sugar

U. S.	...	...	...	...	103 lbs.
U. K.	...	...	...	...	112 „
Java	...	...	...	...	11 „
Denmark	...	...	...	...	128 „
Egypt	...	...	...	...	28 „
Japan	...	...	...	...	20 „
Australia	...	...	...	...	114 „
New Zealand	...	...	...	...	115 „
India ...	...	...	...	...	24 „ (including *Gur*).

Table No. 4

Comparative Growth rf the Sugar Industry in the Verious Provinces Since 1931-32.

(No. of came-factories working)

Province	1931-32	1932-33	1933-34	1934-35	1935-36	1936-37	1937-38	1038-39	1939-40 (Est)
U. P. ...	14	33	59	65	67	68	68	69	72
Bihar ...	12	19	33	34	35	33	33	32	33
Punjab & Sind	1	1	5	6	4	5	3	3	3
Madras ...	2	2	4	8	8	11	8	7	7
Bombay ...	2	1	4	5	6	6	7	7	7
Bengal ...	...	...	2	5	6	6	6	8	9
Orissa ...	...	...	...	...	...	...	2	2	2
Indian States	...	...	4	5	9	8	9	11	11
Burma* ...	1	1	1	2	2	3	2	2	2
Total for India	32	57	112	130	137	137	136	139	143

*Burma excluded from 1936-37 onwards from the total for India.

A serious effort was made during the year 1940, by the industry which approached the Government of India for being permitted to export sugar to the U. K. by releasing the country from the ban on export. The industry also expressed its preparedness to sell sugar at a heavy sacrifice in price as compared with the internal price of sugar in the country, (the offer was made for sale at about Rs. 4 per maund ex-port delivery at any port in India, as compared with the internal price of Rs. 12 including the excise duty, which would be refunded in the case of export sugar) with a view to removing the dead-weight of the huge surplus.

It is well-known that as result of the dislocation caused by the war, the failure of the West Indies sugar crop and the restriction on sugar imports in the United Kingdom for a variety of reasons, the U. K. has had to go on ration in regard to sugar during 1940. At such a juncture, the Indian industry is in a position to render valuable assistance to the U. K. as also other Empire countries by providing sugar at a reasonable rate for this season and also perhaps the next and thus make it possible for these countries to avoid inconvenience to its public in the matter of an important article of diet, and, incidentally, can also render suitable help to itsef by removing this surplus production.

It is a pity, however, that although the Government of India arranged for the offtake of Indian sugar (of quality D 24 and above) approximating to about 100,009 tons for export to the U. K., which was negotiating for the purchase of exportable surplus sugar from Empire sources (Australia, Union of South Africa, Mauritius, Fiji, and British West Indies), the effort proved abortive inasmuch as the industry could not arrange to export the same due to there being insuperable financial difficulties in the removal of the sugar from the possession of Banks at the considerably low rate at which the U. K. offered to buy the same. As a consequence, negotiations for sale of sugar to the U. K. were dropped for the time being. The industry hopes, however, that the Government of India will devote their most earnest attention to this problem and save the industry from the impending crisis by enabling it to remove a substantial portion of its surplus production of about 300,000 tons in new markets.

It would be of interest to note here that the United Kingdom ranks, next to the United States, as the largest sugar importing country of the world. Of the 1938-39 imports in U. K., 54 per cent came, from Empire sources, and the balance from Cuba, Dominican Republic, Peru, and Java. The normal annual consumption of sugar in U. K. is about 2,300,000 tons. Due to rationing, the consumption in 1939-40 in U. K. will be of the order of 1,900,000 tons of which about 1,400,000 tons will have to be imported, internal production being estimated at 510,000 tons in 1939-40.

The quantity of sugar available in 1930-40, for the United Kingdom, according to the latest information. from Empire sources, stated in a preceding paragraph, are as follows ;—

Australia	...	...	564,000 tons
Union of South Africa	...	...	215,000 tons
Mauritius	...	...	262,000 tons
Fiji	...	...	127,000 tons
British West Indies	...	...	518,000 tons
Total	...	...	1,686,000 tons

It was estimated that India could supply about 300,000 *tons in* 1939-40, *and in* 1940-41.

In this connection it must be observed *that India now produces a superior quality and higher grades of sugar, equal to Java. which are suitable for export, and with a proper planning, can ensure the supply of the stipulated quantity from year to year, which can be safely depended upon by any country with which arrangements are made.*

It is not generally realised that at the present time India has about the largest area under cane cultivation in the world. From a total area of about 3 million acres under cane cultivation, in 1930-31, there has been a considerable expansion in acreage, the maximum being in 1936-37 when it exceeded 4½ million acres. and the estimated area for 1940-41 is 4,215,000 acres as compared with 3,705.000 acres in 1939-40. Concurrently, with the expansion of cultivation, there has been witnessed an equally marked improvement in the quality of the cane. The acreage under improved varieties of cane improved from 817,000 acres in 1930-

31 to about 3,452,000 acres in 1936-37. The average cane production per acre has also increased from 12·3 to 15·6 tons, but yet it is remarkably small as compared with other countries like Java, and admits of considerable improvement by comprehensive research work. A glance at Table No. 2 shows the total area under sugarcane, the area under improved varieties, the gross production of *gur*, and the calculated production of sugarcane from 1930-31 to 1940-41 :

No picture of the sugar industry in India would be complete without a reference to the importance of the cottage industry of *Gur*-manufacture which consumes about 4 times the quantity of cane consumed by white sugar factories annually, approximating to about 65 per cent of the annual cane-crop. The calculated net production of *Gur** which is an article of direct consumption, has been varying between 2,728,000 tons and 4,268,000 tons during the last few years, as compared with the production of sugar varying between 800,000 tons and 1,300,000 tons. The *per capita* consumption of *Gur* is roughly about 24 lbs. while that of sugar varies between 6 and 7·5 lbs. *Gur* is not only used as a sweetening ingredient in food and drink but is a wholesome article of diet. Almost all the *Gur* produced in one year passes into consumption in the same year and there is neither any export nor any carry over for the next season.

With an improvement in the general standard of living and the gradual industrialisation of the country, there has been some increase in the consumption of sugar but it cannot be said that it has been at the expense of *Gur*.

It would be of interest to compare the figures of the *per capita* sugar consumption for the crop year September 1, 1938 to August 31, 1939, in the various important countries of the world from the Table No. 3.

It will thus be seen that there is a great room for improvement in the sugar consumption in the country but it depends to a large extent upon the price at which sugar and *gur* are made available to the masses, and the increase in the purchasing power of the people, as a result of prosperous economic conditions.

It is interesting to note that the most important sugar-producting regions in India are sub-tropical, comprising the United Provinces, and Bihar,† where the industry is chiefly concentrated and which are responsible for the growth of about 64 per cent of the total acreage under cane, and for the production of about 75 per cent of the total sugar produced in the country.

Table No. 4 will show the comparative growth of the sugar industry in the various Provinces, as also in the whole of India since 1931-32.

There has been an improvement in the efficiency of extraction of Indian factories since the Sugar Committee reported in 1920. At that time the average recovery was 6·25 per cent which has now improved to about 9·5 per cent in the Indian factories. The Indian Industry is thus improving its efficiency, and with a progressive improvement in the quality of cane, which largely influences the recovery of sugar, the rate of recovery will show a further improvement. The maximum recovery obtained in any factory in India has been 12·25, which compares very favourably with the recovery in Java.

One or two interesting features of the industry in India which may well be commented upon here are that the industry in India is a seasonal industry, the cane factories working for about 4 to 5 months in the year, between the months of November and April. It is only in one part of the country, *viz*., Mysore, in Southern India, that the industry is working for a period of 9 months during the year. Besides, unlike Java, where factories cultivate cane on their own land, or land under their control, the cane-cultivation in India is almost entirely outside the control of factories, which purchase their cane from ryots having small holdings of land, and are there-fore not in a position to arrange for harvesting when cane has reached maturity and is in the optimum condition. This is a serious handicap all over India, except in the Bombay Presidency where factories grow their own cane. But with adequate research, and co-operation with cultivators, this handicap should be minimised, as the ultimate prosperity of the industry hinges on the availability of cheap, disease-free cane, of the requisite quality and high sucrose contents.

The United Provinces Government have enacted legislation this year for permitting manufacture of power-alcohol, for compulsory admixture with petrol. with a

---

*Gur, which may most nearly be described as hard-boiled massecuite contains 50 to 80 per cent of sucrose, 8 to 20 per cent inverted sugar, and small quantities of mineral salts.

† The number of sugar mills in U. P. and Bihar is 105 out of the total number of 143 operating in India in 1939-40.

view to utilising the surplus molasses of factories, and to enable the development of a new industry.

The development of the sugar industry during the last decade has been romantic, but it would not do to rest on past laurels. Efforts must be continued to improve its efficiency further by reduction of price of cane which would be possible if the total tonnage per acre is increased, and quality of the cane improved, and by decreasing the cost of manufacture, by increasing the length of the cane-crushing season by the growth of early and late ripening varieties, by the utilisation of by-products like molasses and bagasse, and by increase in recovery of sucrose. It is absolutely essential to decrease the price of sugar with a view to increasing the consumption of sugar in this country, and to enable the industry to export the surplus production to neighbouring countries like Afghanistan, Tibet, Nepal, Burma, Ceylon and also to the United, Kingdom, and other foreign countries, even to any extent that is possible.

Lac Cultivation in India

What Lac is

The name 'Lac' originated from the Sanskrit word "Lakh" meaning hundred thousand, no doubt referring to the innumerable insects that take part in secreting the resin. It is the only resin of animal origin secreted by an insect *Laccifer lacca*, which feeds on the sap of certain trees, exuding the resin during its life-cycle.

In the epic of the Mahabharatha, we read that the Kauravas built a palace of lac (Jatugriha) and invited their rival cousin, the Pandavas, to live in it with the ulterior object of destroying them by setting fire to the palace. In the Periplus, written about 80 A.D., lac-dye is mentioned as being conveyed to Aduli on the African coast of the Red Sea; and in the Ain-i-Akbari (about 1590) it is recorded that Akbar the Great made use of the resin mixed with pigments to prepare varnishes for the screens of public buildings. The first recorded export of lac to Europe took place in about 1607. At the present time, the consuming countries in the order of importance are the United States of America, England, Germany (till September '39) and Japan.

Lac yields two distinct products, a dye similar to cochineal, which is also an insect product, and a resin. In the early days, it was the dye which made up the bulk of the trade, but with the discovery of the aniline dyes, both cochineal and lac dye trades came to an end. Fortunately, about this time the importance of the lac resin and the method of utilizing it had been discovered in Europe, and it is now *the resin* which makes up the lac trade.

The industries into which shellac enters are many and varied. The most important is the gramophone records industry which consumes 30 to 40 per cent of the annual output; the electrical and paint and varnish industries utilise about 35 per and the hatting trade a further 10 per cent. Other industries using lac include such diverse trades as sealing-wax manufacture, photographic materials, the confectionery trade, munitions and fire-works, anti-fouling compositions for ships' bottoms, grinding-stones, micanite, shoe dressings, bangles, toys, etc.

From the manifold uses to which shellac is put, it might be supposed that it holds a safe place in the world's markets. This is not, however, generally the case, Only the shellac record still stands supreme in the gramophone industry, though attempts have been made by synthetics to oust it. Although shellac has not yet been synthesized and no product has yet been produced in the laboratory capable of fulfilling its manifold uses, synthetic substitutes have been produced which are extremely satisfactory for some of the applications in which lac is used. Among these, Bakelite, a phenolformaldehyde condensation product, is now largely used in the electrical trade. In the varnish trade, cellulose preparations are firmly established, partly owing to the ease with which they can be applied. The synthetic resin industry is extremely well-organised and has progressed very rapidly in spite of the trade depression during 1929-33. In this respect, great advantage to the shellac industry would accrue, if shellac were standardised like the artificial resins.

The synthetics owe their position both to their intrinsic performance and also to the efforts of the consuming countries to be self-sufficient and independent of external sources of supply in times of emergency. The prospect of finding new uses for a combination of this natural resin with the artificial resins should be good ground for co-operation between the two industries for their mutual benefit.

One of the difficulties in the shellac trade has been the fluctuations which occur in its price. The production is also subject to considerable variation from year to year. A number of factors may result in short crops, the most important being unfavourable climate, faulty methods of cultivation, insect pests, and neglect of cultivation at times of low prices. Owing to these facts and to the possibility of competition from synthetics, the Government of India instituted an inquiry which was carried out by Mr. (now Sir) H. A. F. Lindsay, I.C.S., and Mr. C. M. Harlow, I.F.S., with the object of placing the industry on a sound economic basis. Their report, which was published in 1921, recommended research into the subject. For this purpose the Indian Lac Research Institute was started in August 1925, at Namkum, five miles from Ranchi, in the very heart of the principal lac-growing area. The Institute had originally laboratories for biochemical and entomological research to which in subsequent years, physico-chemical, applied chemical and electrical research laboratories have been added. An experimental lac factory was completed in 1930, and there is a plantation in which as many of the important lac hosts as possible are represented. The plantation also contains a number of probable hosts undergoing tests. The Institute is financed by a cess on exported lac shellac and lac refuse which was between 2 annas and 4 annas per maund during 1922-1936, and 5-7 annas since August 1936; the increase in the cess was to provide funds for the widening scope of research which was felt so necessary in view of the competition from synthetic resins.

The primary object of research was to devise improved methods of cultivation, to improve the quality of lac produced by growing healthy strains, and to minimize the effect of insect enemies. Later, the scope of research was extended to find new uses for shellac in the industries which were rapidly being developed by the synthetic resin trade, and to organise research in consuming countries in co-operation with the industries using lac; a marketing survey was carried out in India to improve the existing marketing methods.

Lac is practically an Indian monopoly and is grown over a very wide area including Assam and Burma. The chief areas of cultivation are, however, Chota Nagpur, the Feudatory States of Orissa, and the Central Provinces. This principal area produces about 85 per cent of the lac of commerce, Chota Nagpur alone being responsible for 50 per cent of India's annual output of lac. Ceylon, Java, the Federated Malay States, Indo-China and Siam produce small amounts of lac, and even of this, the greater part finds its way to India, *viz* Calcutta, to be manufactured into shellac. The annual production of crude lac in India varies between 600,000 and 1,200,000 cwt., and the exports of lac of all kinds (including seedlac) vary from 400,000 to 800,000 cwt. with a present value of about 20 millions of rupees, the maximum having been as high as 100 millions of rupees. On page 444 are given export figures (volume and value) for the last 20 years.

Lac Producing Insect

The insect which produces lac is one of the scale insects and is known as *Laccifer lacca.* It lives as a parasite feeding on the sap-juices of certain trees, which are therefore known as lac-hosts. Among the more important of these are *Schleichera trijuga* (Kusum), *Butea frondosa*, (Palas), *Zizyphus jujuva* (Ber), *Acacia Catechu* (Khair), *Zizyphus Xylopyra* (Ghont) and *Cajanus indicus* (Arhar). The insect starts life as a tiny red-coloured larva just over half-a-millimetre in length. These larvae, which emerge (or swarm) in large numbers from the bodies of the mature female insects, are active and capable of crawling a considerable distance.

In order to ensure the maximum crop, the host trees are pruced some time prior to utilization as hosts, so that they may provide as great a number as possible of long green succulent shoots on which the larvae may settle.

Brood Lac

The lac from which swarming is about to occur is known as brood lac. The larvae are introduced to the host tree on which it is proposed to raise a lac crop by tying a number of sticks of brood lac to it: this is known as inoculation or artificial infection as distinct from natural infection which occurs on trees without any human intervention. The larvae settle on the young shoots, insert their mouth parts, which are in the form of sucking tubes (the proboscis), through the bark into the sap-carrying tissues of the tree, and start seeding by suction.

The larvae, consisting of approximately 30 per cent males and 70 per cent females, begin to grow and secrete round their bodies a coating of resin which forms a cell in which they live; and by the coalescence of one cell with another, as resin secretion continues, a continuous or semi-continuous encrustation of lac is formed round the twigs.

A few weeks after settlement of the larvae the male insects emerge out of their small cells, fertilize the females and die. The females never leave their cells but continue to secrete lac; within their ovaries the eggs which will produce the young of the next generation develop; thus the female is almost entirely responsible for the production of lac.

The female insect lays her eggs within the lac cell in a space known as the incubating chamber, which is formed by a contraction of her body; within this chamber the eggs hatch, and the larvæ emerge out through a hole known as the Anal Tubercular Pore. When mature, the lac is cut from the tree for use as brood or for sale. This cycle occurs twice a year but there are two series which overlap. Lac grown on trees other than Kusum swarms in June-July and October-November giving two* crops termed the Baisakhi and the Katki. Lac grown on Kusum, or on other trees using Kusum brood, swarms in June-July and February March, giving two crops known as the Jethwi and Aghani at approximately equal intervals.

Three Stages of Manufacture

After being cut from the tree, the lac may be sold for manufacture before the larvae have emerged, in which case it is known as *ari*, or it may be sold after swarming when it is called *phunki*. The process of manufacture consists of three stages; the lac is first scraped away from the stick by hand (or in the case of Kusum lac it is crushed in a roller crusher and any pieces of stick removed by picking and winnowing) and then crushed into small grains. The next process is that of washing, to remove the impurities and the red-coloured lac-dye, the resulting product being called seedlac. Seedlac is converted into shellac by melting it in long sausage-shaped cloth bags about two inches in diameter, before a charcoal fire. During the heating process the bag is twisted, and this pressure, combined with heat, squeezes the melted resin material out through the cloth. The plastic mass is well basted by means of an iron spoon in order to mix its constituents, resin and wax. Then, if button lac is being made, small quantities of the molten material are dropped on a zinc sheet, where they spread out into circular buttons about three inches in diameter and ¼ inch thick. If shellac is being made, a portion of the molten material is spread out into a thin sheet on the surface of a glazed earthenware cylinder containing hot water. The sheet, so formed, is about 2 feet long and 1½ feet broad, which being still plastic can be removed from the hot cylinder by the dexterous finger manipulation of the worker. This is then held in front of the fire and stretched as much as possible into a large thin sheet which is broken up when cold, the resulting flakes being the shellac of commerce.

Various By-Products

This process, while fairly efficient, results in a number of by-products which sell at low prices and yet contain quite high percentages of shellac. Of these by-products the more important are molamma, separated as dust from the seedlac; kiri, the dirt and refuse which remain in the bag after the melting process and which is removed by splitting open the bag and lifting it out; and finally passewa, which is obtained from the cloth of the bags by boiling them, after use in dilute soda solution.

Below is given a short resume of the activities of the Indian Lac Research Institute to improve the condition of the lac industry.

Cultivation Of Lac

A thorough survey has been made of the life-cycle of the lac insect and other insects associated with it. As a result, it has been possible to devise simple natural and artificial control methods for the efficient production of lac. A systematic study of the various host trees with reference to the methods and seasons of pruning them has led to definite improvements. All improvements in the methods of cultivation which have arisen out of the researches conducted at the Institute are being made available to the raiyats through demonstrators trained

Export Figures (Volume & Value) Of Lac

Year.			Weight. Cwt.	Value (Rupees in thousands).
1920-21	...	...	308,937	75,826
1921-22	...	...	434.934	79,158
1922-23	...	...	476,011	1,02,652
1923-24	...	...	485,671	90,627
1924-25	...	...	427,017	75,506
1925-26	...	...	539,924	69,010
1926-27	...	...	592,030	54,724
1927-28	...	...	543,584	69,886
1928-29	...	...	743,403	86,426
1929-30	...	...	668,914	69,672
1930-31	...	...	547,151	31,374
1931-32	...	...	463,724	18,394
1932-33	...	...	418 300	12,424
1933:34	...	...	730,988	24,644
1934-35	...	...	586,002	32,996
1935-36	...	...	487,581	15,836
1936-37	...	...	833,964	23,421
1937-38	...	...	664,671	16,218
1938-39	...	...	643,848	12,665
1939-40 (10 months)	...	...	667,893	15,466

at the Institute. For exam·le, the demonstrators teach the cultivators how to forecast the emergence of the lac larvae by observing the changing colour of the lac cells approaching maturity so that brood for infection may be cut in time and the final crop harvested. They also demonstrate how and when to prune their trees, and how to destroy inimical insects by soaking the lac crops in water, etc.

Improving Manufacture of Shellac

Although it is impossible radically to change the method of manufacture of shellac under existing economic conditions, various simple but important factors, for the better manufacture of lac even according to the present small-scale process have been formulated and brought home to the manufacturers. One aspect of this problem which has received considerable attention is the recovery of lac from by-products through a not very costly solvent-extraction process so that some, at least, of the more go-ahead manufacturers may adopt this process.

At present most of the lac produced in India (about 97 per cent) is exported to foreign countries to be used there in a large number of industries. America is by far the largest consumer taking more than 50 per cent of the total production with England and, till lately, Germany taking about 20 per cent each. Recent reports from America show that 25,089,234 lbs. of shellac were imported during the first 11 months of 1939, a large part of which was employed for moulding gramophone records the production of which has greatly increased in recent years. Extensive broadcasting by radio of music was expected to have a detrimental effect upon the volume of gramophone record production but the reverse of this has resulted. Having become more familiar with music of all kinds, the public enjoys arranging its own home programmes and has bought combination radio phonographs in great numbers thus increasing the demand for gramophone records. Apart from the gramophone record industry, and the floor polish and furniture finishing industries which up to date utilize most of the lac, there are literally hundreds of small applications in practically every industry.

Work Of Lac Research Institute

Recent work of the Institute covers investigations to improve the performance value of shellac products in their existing uses and also to find new uses for lac. There have been several improvements in the methods of applications of shellac in the varnishing and polishing industries through the addition of various materials which could be classified as accelerators, hardeners and plasticisers.

Of the new uses, mention should be made of its application for plastic upon foreign imports. The Indian Industry, however, has made further progress in the number of factories and the total value of local manufactures. The Government of India has however, given special concessions to the glass industry in the matter of the duty on soda ash which forms a substantial percentage of the cost of raw materials in glass, as will be seen from the table given below.

Table showing the percentage cost of raw materials in glass

	Indian.	English.	Belgian.	German.
Sand ...	23	27	9	19
Soda Ash ...	67	61	87	79
Lime or Limestone	10	12	4	2
	100	100	100	100

The Government reduced the duty for all imported Soda Ash consumed in the glass factories and the glass manufacturers have thus obtained substantial help from Government.

The Tariff Board also recommended the establishment of a technical research institute for glass, and the United Provinces established a glass technology section in Benares with a view to developing this Industry. Steps have been taken for the installation of modern equipment in some of the factories, and modern furnaces and new machines have been introduced with the result that the cost of the production in the local factories has been considerably reduced. With the introduction of modern methods and with the help of the Technical Institute, new lines of glass products are now manufactured by the local factories such as glass, beads, false pearls, ornamental glass plates, tubes, pipes and a number of other articles which were hitherto not manufactured by the local industry.

Recently, as a result of the encouragement, advice and technical direction provided for by the Government, the local industry has now developed a new product known as the windolite, which is a substitute for glass to be used for building purposes. Similarly, the local industry has now extended its scope in the matter of glass tubes and surgical and laboratory requirements of glass products. In addition to the lines indicated above, the local industry is now manufacturing and supplying the Defence Deparments of the Government of India with many of their requirements in various types of glass.

In its present stage the industry is divided into two well defined categories.

(1) THE INDIGENOUS COTTAGE INDUSTRY.—The artisans in villages purchased the glass blocks or cakes manufactured by the modern types of glass factories and made out of them bangles in small furnaces in their homes. Such cottage industry is to be found particularly located in the District of Ferozabad in the United Provinces and in the District of Belgaum in the South of Bombay Presidency. Similar types of cottage industry is also to be found to a certain extent in the Indian State of Mysore. This cottage industry, however, had to face severe competition from the factory industry which started manufacturing the rough type of bangles in competition. For some time there was keen competition also from Japanese manufacturers who introduced the silken type of bangles as also certain ornamental types. The cottage industry was unable to face the competition by the factory industry in Japan and in India, but the Indian factory has now established itself in spite of the competition from Japan and more than one-third of the total requirements of India in respect of bangles are now supplied by the local factories. As a result of the competition from Japan the cottage industry has given place to the factory industry in this respect also, and the cottage industry is now more or less restricted to the rough products only and on a smaller scale.

(2) MODERN FACTORY INDUSTRY AND CLASSIFICATION OF FACTORIES.—As stated above the modern factory industry is still restricted to the production of the following classes of glass goods :—

(1) Glass cakes for bangles.
(2) Beads, bottles, lampware, phials, tableware, etc.
(3) Factories, which are run on extensive scale, produce the sheet and plate glass.
(4) The factories which have recently started manufacture of surgical and laboratory requirements in glass.

Only two factories are equipped with the machinery for the production of sheet and plate glass, plain as well as ornamental.

Glass Imports

The value of the imports in India of all kinds of glassware came to about Rs. 2,53,00,000 in 1926-27 and it decreased to Rs. 1,65,00,000 in 1931. The latest figures of imports, however, show a further fall and in 1938-39 the value of the total imports was only Rs. 1,25,00,000.

Indian Production Of Glass

The total value of glass manufactures in India was estimated to be about Rs. 80,00,000 prior to the Great War in 1914 and the Tariff Board estimated the value of the total annual production in 1931 at Rs. 1,40,00,000. According to a very conservative estimate the yearly production of glass and glassware is today estimated to be in the vicinity of Rs. 2,00,00,000. Thus the Indian Industry which was supplying about one-fourth of the total requirements of India prior to the War of 1914 is now able to meet the local requirements to the extent of over 50 per cent of the annual consumption. Fifteen years before, the value of imports stood at Rs. 2,50,00,000. It has now been reduced to one-half of that figure while the value of local manufacture has increased to about 250 per cent of what it was in 1911.

A very important feature of the Indian Glass Industry is the capacity of the modern factories to export glass and glassware from India to foreign countries. In the year 1935-36 the total value of exports of Indian glassware amounted to Rs. 29, 600. It steadily rose to Rs. 49,000 in 1936-37, and leaped up to Rs. 1,29,590 in the year 1937-38. The figure for 1938-39 stood in the vicinity of Rs. 1.16,000 but in the ten months period from April 1, 1939 to January 31, 1940, India has exported glass and glassware of the value of Rs. 1,15,672 as against Rs. 88,000 in the ten months of the previous year.

The table below shows the countries and the value of the export trade in Glass products from India.

It may be mentioned here that the Indian Munitions Board were able to secure a good deal of their requirements from the Indian factories during the period of the last War, and in this War also the Supply Department is reported to have placed substantial orders with the local glass factories and the industry is reported to be rendering highly useful service to the defence of India and the British Empire.

The Indian Industry is passing through a period of transition and hopes to attain its full growth in every direction. The requirements of the Defence Department and the sister territories of the Empire will, it is hoped, provide the inspiration to the industry to manufacture such articles as may be in demand in territories concerned.

Glass and Glasswares exported from India to various countries in '33-34—'37-38.

GLASS AND GLASSWARE,	1933-34	1934-35	1935-36	1936-37	1937-38
Aden and Dependencies ...	2,702	1.800	2,306	5,136	4,999
Bahrein Islands	6,701	1,541	1 010	7,999	16,625
Ceylon (excluding Maldives) ...	6,330	9,045	7,302	8,274	16,185
Burma	...	...	...	...	54,115
Federated Malay States ...	1,575	3,649	1,950	513	7,465
Other British Possessions ...	8,084	11,102	6,688	7,050	11,022
Total British Empire ...	25,452	27,137	19,266	28,972	1,10,411
Native States in Arabia other than Maskat Territory and Trucial Oman	3,390	3,143	2,356	14,880	4,550
Iran	380	4,625	3,468	2,103	6,922
Japan	8,903	50	5	...	32
Other foreign countries ...	7,767	7,862	4,475	3.262	7.675
Total Foreign countries ...	20,440	15,683	10,284	20,244	19,179

Table showing the shares of the provinces in the Export Trade.

	1933-34	1934-35	1935-36	1936-37	1937-38
Share of Bengal ...	11,274	4,012	3,448	5,432	61,760
" Orissa ...	...	...	...	...	50
" Bombay ...	25,636	25,123	18,030	37,363	51,567
" Sind ...	1,257	936	565	1,161	1,133
" Madras ...	7,640	12,729	7,549	5,115	14,080
" Burma ...	85	20	8	145	...
Total ...	45,892	42,820	29,600	49,216	1,28,590